The Protestant Ethic
and the Spirit of Capitalism
with
Other Writings on the Rise of the West

MAX WEBER

The Protestant Ethic and the Spirit of Capitalism with Other Writings on the Rise of the West

FOURTH EDITION

Translated and Introduced by
Stephen Kalberg
Boston University

New York　　Oxford
OXFORD UNIVERSITY PRESS
2009

Oxford University Press, Inc., publishes works that further Oxford University's
objective of excellence in research, scholarship, and education.

Oxford   New York
Auckland   Cape Town   Dar es Salaam   Hong Kong   Karachi
Kuala Lumpur   Madrid   Melbourne   Mexico City   Nairobi
New Delhi   Shanghai   Taipei   Toronto

With offices in
Argentina   Austria   Brazil   Chile   Czech Republic   France   Greece
Guatemala   Hungary   Italy   Japan   Poland   Portugal   Singapore
South Korea   Switzerland   Thailand   Turkey   Ukraine   Vietnam

Published by Oxford University Press, Inc.
198 Madison Avenue, New York, New York 10016
http://www.oup.com

Oxford is a registered trademark of Oxford University Press

Library of Congress Cataloging-in-Publication Data

Weber, Max, 1864–1920.
  [Protestantische Ethik und der Geist des Kapitalismus. English]
  The Protestant ethic and the spirit of capitalism with other writings on the rise of the West/Max
  Weber; translated by Stephen Kalberg.—4th ed.
      p. cm.
  Includes bibliographical references and indexes.
  ISBN 978-0-19-533253-7 (alk. paper)
  1. Capitalism—Religious aspects—Protestant churches. 2. Protestant work ethic. I. Kalberg,
  Stephen.
  II. Title.
    BR115.C3W413 2009
    306.6—dc21

                                                                                2008027674

Printing number: 9 8 7 6 5 4 3 2 1

Printed in the United States of America
on acid-free paper

CONTENTS

GENERAL INTRODUCTION: MAX WEBER AND THE MODERN WEST

Max Weber's famous study, *The Protestant Ethic and the Spirit of Capitalism* (*PE*), continues to be one of the most daring and widely read treatises in the social sciences across the globe. First published in a journal in German in 1904–1905, expanded in 1919 and printed in book form in 1920, and translated into English in 1930, its influence upon a broad range of research can scarcely be overestimated. Students and scholars across an array of disciplines have grappled with the relative merits of "the Weber thesis" for generations. According to the intellectual historian H. Stuart Hughes, *PE* is "one of the great works of the social thought of our time—an almost unique combination of imaginative boldness in its central hypothesis and meticulous scholarship in its documentation" (1974, p. 319). The intense controversy that surrounded its provocative argument at the outset has, remarkably, continued almost unabated to this day.

In *PE*, Weber claimed that one important source of the modern work ethic and orientation to material success must be located *outside* the arena of market interests, business astuteness, and technological innovation. To a significant extent, a *spirit* of capitalism — an ethos — originated from the realm of religion, he contends, namely, from a "Protestant ethic" formulated in sixteenth- and seventeenth-century Calvinist, Methodist, Baptist, Pietist, and Quaker churches and sects in England, Holland, and the American Colonies. These "Puritans" placed systematic work and a striving for profit in the middle of their lives. Little else appeared to matter greatly to them, not even family, friendship, leisure, or hobbies.

Weber maintains that any discussion of the origins of the spirit of capitalism must acknowledge this central *religious* source. And this spirit in turn significantly pushed the expansion of a range of factors in the modernizing West otherwise unfolding into a constellation that favored the development of modern, or *industrial*,[1] capitalism.[2] *PE*'s insistence — culture must not be neglected, however modest its role — set the parameters for numerous debates on the origin of modern capitalism. It stands tall as a genuine classic of the twentieth century.

Interpreters of Weber, as well as a large audience of scholars concerned with economic modernization in general, have largely failed to recognize the place of this "essay on cultural history" (Marianne Weber, 1975, p. 356)

---

1. Weber distinguishes sharply between capitalism (which existed, he argues, universally) and modern capitalism (which he sees as developing in the eighteenth and nineteenth centuries in the West). See pp. 72, 82–87, 211–15.

2. *PE* has generally been viewed as articulating a far more ambitious goal: to locate *the* source of modern capitalism in the Protestant ethic. Its aim was actually far more modest. See pp. 74, 95–97.

in his large corpus of sociological writings; it must be viewed as *one* major investigation in a series of related studies. Shortly after completing *PE*, Weber began to explore two massive themes. He first turned to the question of the *uniqueness* of the modern West. What were its specific features vis-à-vis China, India, the Western ancient and medieval worlds, and the civilizations of the Middle East? Second, in astonishing detail and utilizing comparative cases and rigorous procedures, Weber examined many of the *causes* behind the particular historical pathway taken in the West.

Scrutinizing these themes from a variety of perspectives in approximately nine volumes, the theorist of the "spirit of capitalism" created a sweeping sociological analysis of the West's uniqueness and development. His scholarship came to be dominated by this theme and, in particular, by an historical development at the center of the West's pathway: the origin and unfolding of modern capitalism. This theme constitutes the major focus of this volume. To him, the rise of the West pivotally involved the rise of modern capitalism (pp. 211–215).

Hence, situated in the context of Weber's entire oeuvre, *PE* must be understood as the initial case study in an ambitious project. Its central themes — the Protestant ethic thesis, the uniqueness of the West, and the multiple causes behind the rise of modern capitalism — are addressed throughout this collection. The introduction to Section 1 focuses on *PE* and summarizes its aims and contours (see pp. 7–58). Weber's overarching agenda concerns us now.

Interpretations of Weber's works have far more frequently focussed on *PE* and a series of his concepts rather than his broad-ranging writings on the rise of the West. Even today his careful definitions — or "ideal types" (see Glossary) — of, for example, charisma, power, authority, the status group, and the bureaucracy are studied and utilized throughout the social sciences. Unfortunately, these orientations among scholars — toward *PE* and specific ideal types — have legitimated a widespread perception: the full yield of Weber's sociology can be found in his study on the spirit of capitalism and in the precision of his concepts. This interpretation, however, neglects the overarching themes that unify his works.

This volume takes a different tack. Weber's massive opus, it is maintained, articulates an overriding theme: the uniqueness of the West and the rise of modern capitalism in the West. Both *PE* and Weber's familiar ideal types can be located "within" the parameters of this large project. Its major features will soon capture our attention. A brief sketch of Weber's life and central concerns will facilitate illumination of its boundaries.

MAX WEBER: THE MAN AND HIS CENTRAL CONCERNS

Shortly after his birth in Erfurt in 1864, Max Weber's family moved to Berlin. His ambitious father, soon elected to seats in the Prussian state government and the Reichstag, became a key figure in the Berlin city government. The social conscience of Max's well-educated mother, who descended from a long line of distinguished scholars and successful businessmen, was highly influenced by mid-century American Unitarian and English Progressive theology. After raising seven children, she became an activist in liberal religious circles. While the father's active engagement in the political issues of the time followed an ethos of pragmatism and realism, the mother's example conveyed to young Max a heightened sensitivity to moral questions, an appreciation of the ways in which a life of dignity must be guided by ethical standards, and a respect for the worth and uniqueness of every person.

A precocious child, Weber early on developed a strong love of learning. His rigorous schooling in Berlin emphasized a classical curriculum — history, philosophy, literature, and languages — and the regular writing of interpretive essays. Upon graduation he studied law and economic history in Heidelberg, Berlin, and Göttingen. At the unusually young age of 30, Weber was appointed in 1894 to a full professorship at the University of Freiburg. He moved to the University of Heidelberg two years later to accept a chair in Economics. He died in Munich in 1920.

A significant incident occurred during a visit by his mother to his home in Heidelberg in the summer of 1897. Unexpectedly, Weber's father appeared and commenced a heated argument with his mother. The young Weber, who had passively witnessed his mother's mistreatment for years, then evicted his father—who died seven weeks later. This configuration of events seems to have served as the catalyst for the paralyzing mental illness that afflicted Weber for more than five years. He had regained much of his strength by 1903, and a three-month journey with his wife in the fall of 1904 throughout the American East, Midwest,[3] and South further raised his spirits (see Marianne Weber, 1975, pp. 279–304; Scaff, 2005; Riesebrodt, 2005, pp. 42–46; Roth, 2001). Nonetheless, he did not teach again until the last two years of his life.

Standing between two worlds, Weber's generation experienced the past as starkly delineated from the present. The German agrarian countryside of feudal manors and small, self-contained villages had remained basically unchanged for centuries, while industrialization proceeded rapidly in Europe's cities throughout the latter half of the nineteenth century. Fully uncharted waters seemed ahead, and the pulsating pace of change left Weber and many of his colleagues with a deep sense of foreboding. Urbanization,[4] bureaucratization, secularization, and a breathtaking expansion of capitalism took place on a vast scale. All continuity between past and present appeared to have vanished forever.

Seeing vividly before them a new era in opposition to familiar traditions and values extending back over 2,000 years of Western history, Weber's contemporaries began to pose a series of fundamental questions. How can we live under modern capitalism, which gives priority to the laws of the

---

3.   Weber journeyed as far west as Guthrie, Oklahoma. For an account of his very brief visit there, see Scaff, 2005, pp. 88–91. See also Marianne Weber's report (1988, pp. 291–94).

4.   Fritz Lang's classic film on the modern city, *Metropolis*, although made in 1926, vividly depicts the bleak vision of the future in turn-of-the-century Germany.

market over longstanding traditions, ethical values, and personal relationships? Does the new order rest upon a stable foundation? What will be left to guide our lives in this new epoch? The philosopher Wilhelm Dilthey queried: "Where are to be found the instruments for surmounting the spiritual chaos that threatens to engulf us?"

Among scholars, these urgent concerns led naturally to questions regarding the *origin* of this "new cosmos." What were its sources? What *causal forces* drove the making and unfolding of the industrialized world? If these queries could be answered, the nature of this new universe would be better understood. The parameters would be charted within which possible change could realistically take place.

Weber never shared the bleak "cultural pessimism" of many of his contemporaries, especially Georg Simmel and Friedrich Nietzsche (Kalberg, 1987, 2001b). And he refused to lend support to the many Romantic movements of his time, all of which sought a "simpler" society similar to the world now past. Indeed, Weber welcomed emphatically the freedoms and rights the modern world bestowed upon the individual, arguing that "it is a gross deception to believe that without the achievements of the [Enlightenment] Age of the Rights of Man any one of us, including the most conservative, can go on living his life" (1968, p. 1403). He spoke and wrote tirelessly on behalf of strong and contending political parties, and advocated an "ethic of responsibility" for politicians, constitutional guarantees for civil liberties, an extension of suffrage, and strong parliaments. In addition, he sought to erect social mechanisms that would sustain pluralistic, competing interest groupings in order to check the growth of large bureaucracies—a development, he believed, that would effectively disenfranchise citizens and curtail democratic governance.

Nevertheless, and despite indefatigable political activism, skepticism and ambivalence pervades Weber's view of the twentieth century. His scholarship arose out of questions similar to those asked by his more fatalistic colleagues. What "type of person" (*Menschentyp*) will inhabit this new universe? Amid the overwhelming pressures of everyday life in industrialized societies, how will persons be able to avoid becoming narrow specialists and, moreover, manage to orient their lives to ethical values? Will not the sheer instrumental-rational calculations typical of the modern capitalist economy push aside *all* values? In modern industrial societies dominated by large-scale organizations, scientific worldviews, and the strategic calculation of advantage in economic exchanges, what are the realistic *parameters* for social change in the direction of an intensification of value-oriented action? "We 'individualists' and supporters of 'democratic' institutions," he warned, "are swimming 'against the stream' of material developments" (1978b, p. 282).

Weber feared the looming onset of the "practical rational" life marked by unreflective reactions to the random flux and flow of external occurrences. Juxtaposed with a rigidly structured workplace and the expansion of bureaucracies, this "way of life" would eventually call forth a stagnant society populated by highly conforming persons lacking high ideals, individualism, and a "devotion to a cause." Ethical values and a sense of ethical responsibility for one's actions would then gradually fade, he maintained. How then could compassion, charity, and the ethos of universal brotherhood survive and actively organize, guide, and direct life? Values alone, he held, offer dignity and a sense of self-worth (see 1946b, pp. 117–25; Kalberg, 2003a, pp. 171–79). Did the values-based spirit of capitalism, which assisted the birth of the new economic order, also call forth, two centuries later, a "steel-hard casing" devoid of compassion (pp. 157–58)?[5]

Living amid accelerated social, cultural, economic, and political transformations that indicated to him the conclusion to a millennia-long journey, Weber's research pursued these sweeping questions and dilemmas. They stand behind his sociology and capture his overarching concerns, ones he will explore throughout an expansive body of works. They remain pivotal in the writings assembled in this volume.

PE can be seen as Weber's earliest attempt to define the modern West's specific features and to identify major causes behind its development. How do his post-*PE* investigations in this regard diverge significantly from this classic study? His expanded view of causation, his linkage of the long-term past with the present, and his rigorous comparative procedures should be introduced at the outset.

MAJOR FEATURES OF WEBER'S ANALYSIS

Ideas and Interests

As noted, *PE*'s focus upon ideas, beliefs, and values has been widely understood as anchoring Weber's entire sociology. He has frequently been labeled an idealist. However, *PE* must be comprehended as "one side" of his overall project (pp. 125, 159, 215–216). The selections below bring *PE* together with a wide range of Weber's later writings on religion, law, the economy, types of rulership (*Herrschaft*), and types of cities. They demonstrate the centrality of "ideas *and* interests" — "religion *and* world" — throughout his sociology and, in particular, in his analysis of the uniqueness of the West and the origins and development of modern capitalism.[6]

---

5.   As these remarks convey, Weber's ambivalence regarding the modern West is apparent throughout his works. "Western rationalism" and "modern Western rationalism" are used in a purely descriptive manner; an advance of the human species, Western superiority, or "progress" is not implied. Weber remains quite critical of the modern West even while noting its accomplishments (see Kalberg, 2001b, 2003a).

6.   Ideas, in Weber's phrase "ideas and interests," will be understood here to include beliefs and values. This conforms to Weber's usages of this phrase with one prominent exception: "ideas" also refers to the cognitive processes of religious thinkers attempting to solve the problem of theodicy. (This usage is reconstructed at Kalberg, 2001a; see also 1990.)

Weber's studies on the "economic ethics" of Confucianism, Daoism, Hinduism, and Buddhism[7] have often been perceived by commentators as placing, as does *PE*, the emphasis on the ideas side of the causal equation. Religious beliefs and their influence on the conduct of the devout come to the forefront in these volumes, it is insisted, and the "other" side — "interests" — is neglected.[8] These interpreters have then asserted that modern capitalism failed to unfold first in China and India, according to Weber, because of the omission in their religions of a "functional equivalent" of the Protestant ethic. On the basis of this reading, several generations of scholars sought, through empirical studies, to disprove (or prove) "the Weber thesis" by discovering (or failing to discover) equivalents in Asia. If to develop at all, they maintained, modern capitalism required a counterpart to Puritanism. Conversely, to these commentators the absence of an equivalent explained "economic backwardness."

This unilinear approach fundamentally distorts Weber's position—in both *PE* and Economic Ethics of the World Religions (EEWR). *PE*'s unforgettable concluding passage, which stresses the incompleteness of this investigation, rejects all idealist versions of historical change (see p. 159). And this disavowal thoroughly penetrates the EEWR volumes, as well as *General Economic History (GEH), The Agrarian Sociology of Ancient Civilizations (AG)*, and Weber's analytic treatise, *Economy and Society (E&S)*.[9] Although he continued after *PE* to investigate the influence of religious beliefs upon economic activity, Weber added the "other side" of the causal equation in *E&S*, EEWR, *GEH*, and *AG*: the impact of interests ("external forces") upon ideas ("internal forces") remains as important in these writings as the influence of ideas upon interests. Economic, rulership, legal, and other groups must be regularly addressed and their causal weight assessed, he contends. The necessity for a mode of procedure that *intertwines* ideas and interests is repeatedly stressed. For example: "Every . . . attempt at explanation, recognizing the fundamental significance of economic factors, must above all take account of these factors. However, the opposite line of causation should not be neglected . . . " (p. 216; see 1968, p. 341).

The EEWR studies, *E&S*, *GEH*, and *AG* fundamentally broaden *PE*. Weber contests all research oriented exclusively toward functional equivalents of Puritanism and criticizes, as monocausal and one-sided, all explanations for economic development that refer only to ideas, beliefs, and values. His

---

7. These volumes (*The Religion of China* [1951] and *The Religion of India* [1958]), in addition to *Ancient Judaism* 1952, are the major studies in his series titled Economic Ethics of the World Religions. For details on this series, see pp. 183–184, 313–19.

8. The terms here in quotation marks, and those in the last paragraph, are Weber's. They are pivotal throughout his texts below.

9. For example: "Religion nowhere creates certain economic conditions unless there are also present in the existing relationships and constellations of interests certain possibilities of, or even powerful drives toward, such an economic transformation" (p. 243; see pp. 215–16). Nonetheless, to this day nearly every introductory textbook in sociology contrasts Weber as an "idealist" to the historical materialism of Marx.

post-*PE* investigations offer complex, multidimensional — "world *and* religion" — causal arguments. This will be our theme, particularly in Section 4.

The Interlocking of the Long-Term Past with the Immediate Present

In one sense, Weber's approach to the study of modern capitalism's ascent in the West is infrequently practiced in the social sciences today and deserves explicit mention. He is convinced that the *long-term* past must be thoroughly scrutinized. Many social groupings in the present possess long-range roots, he insists.

Weber's post-*PE* analysis of modern capitalism's rise begins in the distant past—with Antiquity and the Middle Ages. Ancient Judaism's monotheism greatly influenced early Christianity's Deity, which in turn shaped the contours of Puritanism. The medieval city called forth Roman law and citizenship, both of which laid down significant antecedents on the pathway toward modern law, the modern state, and modern capitalism. And feudalism's "contract" between lord and vassal, which formalized reciprocal responsibilities, formed a clear precedent for the modern constitutional state's division of powers. Furthermore, in the Middle Ages the Catholic church, in developing Canon law, introduced the notion of "office charisma"—an early precursor, according to Weber, of the modern bureaucracy's specialization of tasks, demarcation of offices, and location of authority "impersonally" in the office rather than in the person as such.

Ideas, beliefs, values, traditions, and interests endure, Weber insists, *if* politically and economically powerful "social carriers" — coherent organizations, strata, and classes — coalesce behind them and support them. They then may survive through centuries and even millennia. Other groups that crystallized in the distant past live on in altered form. The secularized version of the Protestant ethic — the spirit of capitalism, as carried especially by a great variety of large and small business organizations — constitutes Weber's most famous example. Indeed, our own era, he emphasizes, is pervaded by the legacies from groups originating in the distant past. Today's society can be understood only if the social scientist comprehends its varied historical sources.[10]

Weber also recognizes that groups influential in past centuries often seem to possess quite implausible features to us. "We moderns" rarely explain economic activity by reference to religious belief (p. 159). Dominated by a worldview anchored in the empiricism of the social and natural sci-

---

10.   This paragraph contains the major terms that comprise the conceptual armament Weber repeatedly utilizes to convey the intimate interlocking he sees of past and present: antecedent, precedent, precursor, legacy, and carrier groups (see Glossary). As will become evident, his sociology stands alike against organic holism and all schools that focus exclusively upon cross-cultural *structural* similarities. Innumerable groups, as cohesive and powerful carriers of varieties of ideas, beliefs, values, traditions, and interests, remain at the foundation of Weber's sociology.

ences, our epoch seldom views the supernatural as a causal force. Instead, generally awarded priority are structural factors (such as social class and level of education), economic and political interests, unencumbered rational choices, the psychological and biological make-up of persons, and the exercise of power. Weber contends that, in times past, religious belief often had a greater influence on daily life than today.

Social scientists must seek to *understand* (*verstehen*) the activities of others contextually, he maintains—in terms of the universe of subjective meanings (see Glossary) in which *they* live and the nature of *their* motives for acting. Researchers oriented to groups in distant periods and foreign lands must especially do so, however difficult it may be to perform the indispensable leap of imagination into an unfamiliar and even "unbelievable" milieu. According to Weber, a comprehension of the present remains impossible without an understanding of its formative influences in the long-range past—even though an empirical impact is only infrequently direct. This cornerstone of his sociology must be kept in mind if his difficult texts are to become accessible.

The Comparative Experiment and Weber's Contextual Causality

Weber's later investigations diverge from *PE* in a further pivotal way. The uniqueness of the West and the rise of modern capitalism can be explained adequately, he holds, only through rigorous cross-civilization comparisons that seek, first, to isolate the West's specific features and, second, to facilitate causal explanations of this particularity. Weber utilizes the methodology of the comparative experiment on behalf of these goals and focuses on multiple groups. As practiced in EEWR, *E&S*, *GEH*, and *AG*, this procedure will become apparent in the readings in Section 4. Its use can be briefly illustrated.

Population growth, technological innovations, and the presence of raw materials are all rejected as powerful causes for the advance of modern capitalism: they were not exclusively present in the West and absent elsewhere. Weber also eliminates, through case-by-case comparisons, geographical factors.

When offering comparisons in order to isolate uniqueness and viable causes, he moves away from monocausal procedures. Instead, Weber asserts that *constellations* of groups must be scrutinized and compared rather than groups in isolation. Crucial also are their conjunctural interactions in delineated *contexts* and the ways in which, as a result, unique configurations are formed. He identifies, in EEWR, *E&S*, *GEH*, and *AG*, vast arrays of types of law, rulership, salvation paths, economies, and cities in a variety of civilizations (see Kalberg, 1994b, pp. 149–50). The many clusters of groups conducive to the unfolding of modern capitalism in China, India, and the ancient West were, he found through comparisons, in the end outweighed by a series of opposing constellations of groups.[11]

---

11.   Unfortunately, a thorough discussion of Weber's contextual-conjunctural mode of causation cannot be offered in this volume. See Kalberg, 1994b.

For example, Weber notes a variety of nonreligious obstacles to economic development in China, such as an absence of a "formally guaranteed law and a rational administration and judiciary" (see p. 215; see also 1951, pp. 85, 91, 99–100). In India he sees constraints placed upon migration, the recruitment of labor, and credit by the caste system (see pp. 361–69; see also 1958, pp. 52–53, 102–06, 111–17). Weber discovers as well, however, an entire host of facilitating forces that nonetheless failed to bring about modern capitalism, such as, in China, freedom of trade, population growth, occupational mobility, an increase in precious metals, and the presence of a money economy (see pp. 349–61; see also 1951, pp. 12, 54–55, 99–100, 243).[12]

Weber's comparative experiments and emphasis upon configurations of groups, rather than single groups, also isolated the particularity of the West at a general level: he discovered a unique degree of "structural heterogeneity." A higher degree of pluralistic tension between relatively independently developing spheres (the economy, religion, law, and rulership realms) distinguished the Western developmental path from China, India, the Middle East, and the ancient West. The resulting conflicts in the modernizing West called forth a comparative openness—and hence a societal flexibility that facilitated further cross-sphere conflict and competition. Indeed, competing spheres introduced a dynamism that Weber sees as both specific to the West and conducive to modern capitalism's rise. These themes are addressed directly in Section 4.

AN OVERVIEW

Weber's enormous research project speaks to the large questions of his day—and ours. Taken together, his writings define the uniqueness of the West and establish the major parameters for capitalism's specific historical journey to modern capitalism. They also offer a multicausal, comparative, and configurational analysis of its origin and development.

Section 1 turns to the "case study" that initiated Weber's agenda. *The Protestant Ethic and the Spirit of Capitalism* must be understood as his earliest attempt to comprehend, however indirectly, modern capitalism's uniqueness and origins. His investigation commenced with a delimited hypothesis: could religious values have played a role in calling forth the spirit of capitalism? However, we recognize today that the "full Weber thesis" moved beyond the analysis offered in *PE*. Reprinted and partially retranslated in Section 2, his two short essays on the American Protestant sects play an indispensable supplementary role. They describe how Puritan beliefs and values intensely influenced the activity of the devout as a consequence of a social-psychological dynamic specific to the sect.

---

12. Weber was quite convinced that modern capitalism could be *adopted* by — and would flourish in — a number of Eastern civilizations. Indeed, he identified the forces that would allow this to occur in Japan (see 1958, p. 275 and pp. 270–82). Yet adoption, he insisted, involved different processes than his concern: the *origin*, in a specific region and epoch, of *modern* capitalism.

Section 2 concludes with "Prefatory Remarks" ("PR"), one of Weber's seminal essays. It takes the reader away from the spirit of capitalism to a far more encompassing theme: the "special *characteristic features* of Western rationalism and, within this particular type of rationalism, the characteristic features of modern Western rationalism" (p. 216; emph. in original). Although written much later, "PR" directly poses Weber's major post-1910 questions: how did particular configurations of multiple groups in the West— "Western rationalism" and "modern Western rationalism" — arise and form facilitating *deep contexts* for capitalism's origin and expansion? And how did further constellations of groups assist its transformation into modern capitalism? Moreover, "PR" conveys clearly Weber's shift away from a focus upon a single life-sphere — religion — to a multicausal methodology: his sociology now charts the interaction of this arena with a series of other major realms, especially the law, economy, and rulership spheres. Configurations of "world and religion" groups are now his concern. This *tour de force* serves to introduce Weber's conceptually and thematically more complex *E&S*, EEWR, and *GEH* texts. They are presented in Sections 3 and 4.

Section 3 focuses on the "religion side" of the equation. It places *PE* in the context of Weber's expansive comparative investigations on the "economic ethics of the world religions." In order to assess the extent to which Puritanism's *world mastery* orientation can be said to be singular, Weber offers comparisons to Confucianism, Hinduism, Buddhism, ancient Judaism, Islam, and ancient Christianity. Did a connection exist, he queries in a manner parallel to his exploration in *PE*, between the conduct each great religion expected of devout believers and *economic* activity? Did activity in a particular "direction" — *toward* the world or, as for the mysticism salvation path, *away* from the world — imply consequences for the redemption of the faithful? Did religions outside the West articulate an economic ethic similar to Puritanism? The extent to which these great religions weaken magic is also pivotal to Weber, for sorcery has always presented a powerful obstacle to systematic economic activity, he maintains. Finally, he wishes explicitly to explore the degree to which religious ethics in China, India, and the Middle East extended beyond elite strata of believers and into the general population, as occurred in the West.

The subjective meaning component of Weber's sociology again becomes starkly manifest in these readings. As in *PE*, he seeks to reconstruct a particular religious universe and then to *understand*, by reference to it, which activities became meaningful to believers. He wishes throughout to ascertain the consequences for daily life and, especially, for economic activity.

Moving to the "other side," Section 4's readings define and explore the broad array of *world* groups that constituted Western rationalism and modern Western rationalism. They attend mainly to "interests" rather than "ideas." Different economies, types of rulership and law, types of cities, and social carriers are his focus. However, Section 4 seeks also to convey how configurations of world groups interacted with Christianity and, in particular, with Puritanism. *Both sides* come to the forefront in these selections—*and* their ubiquitous interplay. In the West, constellations of groups indigenous to the world's religions formulated deep contexts that sustained capitalism and assisted its transformation into modern capitalism. It unfolded, Weber emphasizes, within "tracks" formed in part in Antiquity and comprehensively by the Middle Ages.

Hence, Section 4's readings take Weber's expanded methodological and thematic frameworks as their foundation. Multicausal and comparative procedures dominate his post-*PE* sociological works, and groups are now "located" in configurations of world and religion groups. A shift away from the religious origins of the spirit of capitalism is apparent; the development of capitalism — and its metamorphosis into modern capitalism — is now explicitly investigated. Weber's project becomes apparent as one of massive proportions.

This volume's boundaries and limitations must be emphasized. It makes no attempt to offer Weber's *complete* writings on the rise of the West. Such a collection would require many more selections on the development of democracy, modern law, modern bureaucracy, and the state, as well as further readings on the rise of modern capitalism. According to Weber, the roots of each development extend back, as for modern capitalism, to the Middle Ages and, in part, to Antiquity. And their origins and expansion are likewise anchored in multicausal, world *and* religion constellations of groups.

In addition, selections on the "dynamic autonomy" course of religious rationalization from ancient Judaism to Puritanism, rooted in the problem of theodicy, would have to be included, as well as readings on the many *world* groups that sustained this development.[13] Furthermore, many texts on China, India, and the Middle East would have to be included in order to isolate the West's uniqueness and to demarcate major causes in respect to its significant historical developments. Finally, the rigor of Weber's mode of causal analysis would have to be explained (see Kalberg, 1994b) and applied. Hence, his full "rise of the West" analysis cross-cuts his entire oeuvre; its relevant passages are too numerous to be encompassed in one volume. Indeed, any collection of his writings claiming comprehensiveness on this theme would have to include almost all of his sociological writings.

The volume presented here intentionally focuses upon *one* major line of development within Weber's massive "rise of the West" sociology: the unfolding of modern capitalism. This theme commands far more attention throughout his works than any of the others. Nonetheless, the selections here cannot claim to be exhaustive. Because of space limitations, many passages have had to be omitted. The editor has sought to select Weber's *most important* texts on the long-range development of modern capitalism.[14]

---

13.   This "de-magnification" process has been reconstructed at Kalberg, 2001a.

14.   Remarkably, only one book-length reconstruction and interpretation exists of Weber's analysis of the rise of the West: Schluchter's *The Rise of Western Rationalism* (1981; see also 1989; 1996, pp. 105–244). However, even his ambitious effort remains quite incomplete; moreover, it is burdened by a series of Parsonsian presuppositions.

A detailed commentary by the editor introduces each section. These introductions offer summaries of complex dynamics and relate them to this volume's central themes. Weber never lost sight of his burning questions. Repeatedly, whenever the "civilizational rationalisms" indigenous to China, India, and the West appeared to acquire cohesion, he reformulated a pivotal query: how do persons in different social contexts, whether small in scale or encompassing entire civilizations, create meaning in their lives? In his terminology, what divergent patterns of regular action, as found in groups, became meaningful in Asian, Middle Eastern, and Western civilizations? And in the ancient, medieval, and modern eras? Which configurations of life-spheres and carrier groups, for example, became juxtaposed in ways that endowed methodical work with an intense meaningfulness, indeed even for a believer's salvation? Answers to these queries became especially urgent to Weber. Ethical action, a reflective individualism, and an ideal of universal compassion had arisen in the West, he was convinced, out of rulership, legal, economic, and religious contexts now in danger of disappearing. Surely this concern in part served to call forth Weber's wide-ranging interest in comparative questions.

Three appendixes conclude this volume. The first comprises two further texts on the Protestant ethic thesis. They render *PE*'s main points in an especially clear manner.

The second appendix turns first to the abundant *PE* endnotes (which are longer than the text itself). Many gems are buried here. Some notes clarify, and offer support for, important aspects of Weber's argument; others convey his unusual sociological insight into a variety of related subjects. In this section, one-sentence summaries by the editor of particular endnotes aim to provide a further guide to *PE*.

The third appendix offers brief bibliographies on the major commentary on *PE* and on Weber's "life and work." A Glossary of key terms and a chronology of his life conclude this volume.

Stephen Kalberg

1

The Protestant Ethic and the Spirit of Capitalism

INTRODUCTION TO THE TRANSLATION

Stephen Kalberg

Every sentence of Weber's seems a precarious victory over the complexity of facts.

Reinhard Bendix

This translation of *The Protestant Ethic and the Spirit of Capitalism* (PE) has been guided by two goals. First, I have sought to render Weber's text more accessible to the many audiences it has now acquired: scholars, students, undergraduate instructors, and, not least, the general reader. Second, I have attempted to retain the integrity of Weber's study by offering a close-to-the-text translation. The full substance of his thought must be conveyed, and his nuanced, complex reasoning must be captured accurately. Indeed, I have sought to provide a translation that offers the reliability of meaning and precision of intention, especially in respect to Weber's fine-grained causal lines of argument, indispensable to scholars of his works. In sum, I have placed a premium upon *both* readability and accuracy. For many texts, fulfillment of both of these goals would not present a large challenge to a translator. Unfortunately, in this respect, *PE* deviates from the norm and strays far afield from the "user-friendly" ideal.

Published originally in two parts in a social science journal *Archiv für Sozialwissenschaft und Sozialpolitik*, in 1904-05 (vol. 20, pp. 1–54 and vol. 21, pp. 1–110),[1] Weber knew that his audience of scholars would be conversant with the entire landscape of Western history. As difficult as it may be for us to imagine today, his readers were quite capable of tracing the ebb and flow of Western civilization's unfolding since the ancient Greeks. All had attended elite schools (*Gymnasien*) that emphasized philosophy, literature, and languages, and all had benefited from three cycles of instruction over a nine-year period on the entire history of the West. Weber was well aware that his shorthand references—whether to ancient Greek mythology, medieval monastic orders, or civil wars in England—would be readily understood.[2] Moreover, in keeping with the format of scholarly writing in Germany at

---

1. Weber reviewed and expanded the text in 1920. This translation, as the earlier translation by Talcott Parsons, used the 1920 version. This is the only *PE* that Weber authorized for publication in book form. See *Gesammelte Aufsätze zur Religionssoziologie*, vol. 1, pp. 17–206 (Tübingen: Mohr, 1920). The original *PE* in *Archiv* was published for the first time in English only recently (see Weber, 2002a). Despite urging from his publisher soon after the journal publication to expand and complete his essays for publication in book form, Weber repeatedly postponed doing so (see Fischoff, 1944, p. 69; Lehmann, 2005, p. 10). He emphasized their incompleteness in his first reply to his critic Rachfahl; see Weber, 2001, pp. 83 (note 30), 85 (notes 34 and 36)
2. Approximately 1% of youth attended these elite schools. Graduation from this type of school alone allowed admission to a university. Ringer (1969) refers to this closed, highly educated circle as "German mandarins."

the time, he knew that "matters of presentation" required little attention. Unfortunately, publishers in Weber's time in Germany did not employ copyeditors.[3]

Weber's study not only lapses occasionally into abbreviated formulations and fails to provide identifying cues to obscure persons and places, it also confronts the reader frequently with sentences one-half page in length and paragraphs two or three pages long. Multiple clauses reside within each sentence, as Weber continuously struggles to lay out his theme in all its complexity. Yet even when he succeeds in doing so in a nuanced fashion, he frequently calls attention to qualifications and emphasizes the milieu-specific contingency of his statements.

Any attempt by a translator to render Weber's text in a manner that exactly captures his own writing style will stand opposed to the first goal mentioned above: readability and accessibility. This aim has required conformity to a practice frequently followed in German-English translations, namely, the radical shortening of sentences and paragraphs. In addition, in order to designate more clearly major and minor emphases, I have occasionally inserted parentheses into long sentences that proved impossible to shorten.

However, it soon became apparent that my goal of readability and accessibility would not be adequately achieved through these measures alone. Hence, several propaedeutic aids became indispensable:

a) Persons, places, groups, and documents have been identified in short bracketed phrases inserted into the text.

b) Some persons, places, groups, and documents have been further identified in new endnotes; [sk] follows these endnotes.

c) Occasional endnotes that clarify Weber's argument have been added; [sk] follows these endnotes.

d) Short, supplementary phrases have been added to the text, in brackets, on those occasions where Weber's shorthand formulations require clarification.[4]

e) Translations, in brackets, of all foreign language passages have been added. *All passages in brackets in the text and endnotes are mine.*

f) Terms that are key to Weber's argument — "technical terms" — have been defined in the Glossary.

---

3. In any case, owing to the extremely high social prestige of professors in Weber's Germany, editing of manuscripts by publishers, as is common today, would have been impossible. One consequence of this situation was that bibliographical entries were often not given in complete form. This holds for *PE* as well. Numerous fragmented entries were completed in the German paperback edition of 1979, edited by Johannes Winckelmann (Gütersloh: Gütersloher Verlagshaus). I have consulted this volume in this regard; these additions have been evaluated and, when appropriate, included here. I am grateful to the late Professor Winckelmann and to his assistants: Professor Constans Seyfarth, Professor Walter M. Sprondel, and Professor Gert Schmidt.

4. Explanatory passages have been added in particular whenever Weber uses phrases such as "of interest to us *here*" and "for *our* theme" without identifying clearly his point of reference.

g) With only a few exceptions as required by context, the translation of all technical terms has been standardized throughout. In this manner, Weber's forceful call for terminological precision in the social sciences has been respected and the major threads of his argument can more easily be followed.[5]

h) Innumerable partial bibliographical entries have been adjusted and completed.

i) An extra space has been added (****) on the occasion of a thematic shift in the *PE* text.

In two important ways, Weber *did* assist his audience: first, through regular italicization. Although italicization at the level he practiced is generally not permitted today in English publications, Weber's frequent italicization is retained. He regularly orients and guides his reader to concepts, themes, and distinctions central to his argument through this mode of emphasis. Second, Weber inserts nuance through regular use of inverted commas ("national character"). This practice has also been retained, as it indicates his unwillingness to accept fully a number of commonly used concepts and his awareness of their problematic and controversial character.

Finally, this translation designates the paragraphs and endnotes that Weber added in 1920 when he prepared *PE* for publication in his three-volume series, Collected Essays in the Sociology of Religion (see pp. 183–84).[6] All such paragraphs and endnotes are followed by [1920].[7] These additions mainly involved (a) responses to criticism of *PE* published in journals and newspapers from 1907–1910; [8] (b) responses to books by his colleagues Sombart and Brentano; (c) independent clarifications of his argument; [9] (d) comparisons of ascetic Protestantism to Islam, Hinduism, Buddhism, and Confucianism; (e) reference to an overarching process in the developmental history of Western religions according to which magic became eliminated (*Entzauberung*) as a viable mechanism to assist the search for salvation; (f) reference to an overarching "rationalization process" (see pp. 313–19); and (g) extensions of bibliographical sources.

This translation was first published seven years ago. The new edition offers several improvements: typographical errors have been adjusted, awkward sentences have been smoothed out, and translation errors have been corrected. The text and endnotes have undergone further annotation. The editor's introduction to *PE* has been thoroughly revised; discussions have been added on the enduring controversies surrounding *PE* and its broad impact upon the social sciences. Appendix I, which offers two of Weber's

---

5. This was one of the weaknesses of the Parsons translation. For a general commentary, see Kalberg, 2001c.

6. Single sentences and words altered or added in 1920 are *not* designated. However, Weber's major additions were in full paragraph form.

7. A recent German edition has distinguished the '04–05 and 1920 versions. See Weber, 1993.

8. Weber's answers, to his critics have been collected now in two separate volumes. See Weber, 2001, 2002a.

9. These are fairly rare (for example, the contrast between asceticism and mysticism).

further writings on "the Protestant ethic thesis," is new; Appendix II expands the earlier list that summarized *PE* endnotes of particular interest; and Appendix III extends the earlier bibliography of commentary on this classic volume.

Generous friends, colleagues, and students have assisted my work on this new translation. A number of persons offered specialized assistance at various points along my journey: David Chalcraft, Mark Childerhose, Lutz Kaelber, Adam Kissel, Julia Michaels, Donald Nielsen, Guenther Roth, Ilana Silber, and Eduardo Weisz. Their helpfulness has been a source of inspiration to me.

Robert J. Antonio, Ira J. Cohen, Lyn Macgregor, and Michael Moody read an entire early draft of the text and offered comments that altered the direction of my work. My bi-cultural assistant, Jessica Sturgis-Horst, tirelessly tracked down dozens of obscure references. The imprint of Lyn Macgregor, an exceptional writer, is apparent on nearly every page. Ulrich Nanko, a theologian in Stuttgart, located innumerable obscure persons and documents in the best German encyclopedias. John Drysdale, a native speaker of English, closely evaluated the entire translation. Barbara Mathieu of Oxford University Press, offered a careful eye for detail and worked tirelessly—and with great patience—on this volume. Sherith Pankratz, Senior Sociology Editor at Oxford University Press, accompanied this complex project with great skill and judgment. Finally, I owe my greatest debt to Michael Kaern, a native speaker of German who checked the translation line by line. He unfailingly answered my many questions, large and small, and counseled on a daily basis with patience, insight, and high generosity of spirit. I am far more grateful to all than can be put into words.

INTRODUCTION TO
THE PROTESTANT ETHIC

Stephen Kalberg

[Asceticism] viewed the acquisition of wealth, when it was the fruit of work in a vocational calling, as God's blessing. (pp. 151–52*)

By no means can the content of religious ideas be deduced from "economic" forces. These ideas are, and nothing can change this, actually, for their part, the most powerful elements shaping "national character"; they carry purely within themselves an autonomous momentum. (p. 543, note 96)

One should not overlook that I sought to demonstrate how, despite doctrines opposed to mammonism, the spirit of this ascetic religious devotion gave birth, just as in the businesses run by cloisters, to economic rationalism. This religious devotion did so because it placed a psychological reward upon what was crucial: rational motivations conditioned by asceticism. This alone mattered, and this is precisely the point of my entire essay. (p. 527, note 8)

For sure, even with the best will, the modern person seems generally unable to imagine how large a significance those components of our consciousness rooted in religious beliefs have actually had upon culture . . . and the organization of life. (p. 159)

Max Weber argued in *The Protestant Ethic and the Spirit of Capitalism* (*PE*) that a question grounded in religious concerns ultimately directed the seventeenth century Puritan faithful toward systematic work habits and a methodical pursuit of material success: Am I among the few who are saved? This query appears no longer to be of burning urgency in the nation most influenced by Puritanism, the United States.

However, the dedication of Americans today to work and success, Weber would argue, can be in part explained as a long-term legacy of the Puritan tradition.** In 1999, the United States replaced Japan as the worldwide leader in number of hours worked per person per year; Europeans, in contrast, work approximately two-thirds as many hours per year as Americans. Americans read daily on the one hand of people who are exhausted and deprived of sleep and others who "love their work." Expressions that reflect the centrality of work in our lives are pervasive: we arrange "working lunches," we "work out" daily, we "work" on love, our relationships, our personalities, and our tans. We praise the work ethic of our peers and "hard workers" are generally assumed to be people of good character. A salary in-

---

*   Otherwise unidentified page numbers in parentheses refer to the text that follows.
**   The endnotes to this Introduction are found at pp. 49–54. The reference list is also at the conclusion to this chapter (pp. 54–58).

crease is awarded often to the "most dedicated" employee—a person who works, with pride, not only days but also nights and weekends. If we take naps, they must be "power naps." "Workaholics" take "working vacations." Many people define self-worth according to their success in a profession.[2] A steady orientation to career goals and the disciplined organization of one's life to that end are praised.[3]

Were Weber alive today, he would see these pivotal features of American society as secularized legacies of ascetic Protestantism. However, fascinated by the enduring impact of the Puritan heritage in the United States,[4] his quest in *PE* was primarily that of a historical sociologist: (1) to discover the *religious sources* in the past of the idea that life should be organized around systematic work and material success, and (2) to argue that this manner of organizing life played a significant part in calling forth the spirit of capitalism. To him, this particular focusing of life appeared originally in a specific historical epoch and in identifiable groups. These were religious groups, and they introduced the Protestant ethic, Weber maintains. As first manifest in the spirit of capitalism and visible even today, the legacies of this ethic have proved long-lasting. In the end, as we shall see, both the Protestant ethic and the spirit of capitalism placed into motion significant thrusts that facilitated the rise of modern capitalism.

Written in Heidelberg in the summer of 1904, the first part of *PE* (pp. 61–97) was printed a few months later in the *Archiv für Sozialwissenschaft und Sozialpolitik* (Volume 20) when Weber and his wife were traveling in the United States. Finished in March, 1905, upon his return to Germany, the second part (pp. 101–59) appeared in June, 1905, in the same journal (Volume 21). Although Weber noted that the libraries at Colgate and Columbia Universities, as well as the libraries of small colleges "scattered all over the country," would be of use for his "cultural history" study, he managed to conduct very little research during his visit. As he reported in a letter, "I did not see much more than where the things are that I ought to see" (Marianne Weber, 1988, p. 304; see also p. 253).

PE is a difficult text. An understanding of its complex analysis can be facilitated by a brief overview of its central organizational axes, the intellectual context within which Weber wrote, and *PE*'s general aims. The next section turns to these themes. The subsequent two sections summarize and comment upon *PE*'s frequently misunderstood argument. On the one hand, Weber's multidimensional analysis of the Protestant ethic's origins is examined (Section II); on the other hand, the development from this ethic to, first, the spirit of capitalism and then, second, to modern capitalism is investigated (Section III). Although lengthy, these discussions offer only highlights of Weber's analysis and fail to capture its extreme subtlety; they cannot substitute for a reading of the text. *PE* is then located within the methodological and research frameworks that define Weber's sociology as a whole (Section IV). Finally, Sections V and VI summarize major themes in the longstanding "Weber thesis" controversy and the wide-ranging impact of this classic study upon the social sciences of the twentieth century.

I. *THE PROTESTANT ETHIC AND THE SPIRIT OF CAPITALISM*: ORGANIZATIONAL AXES, THE INTELLECTUAL CONTEXT, AND OVERALL AIM

Organizational Axes

The distinction between "capitalism" and "modern capitalism" stands at the foundation of Weber's entire analysis in *PE*. Capitalism, as involving the exchange of goods and calculations of profit and loss balances in terms of money, has existed in civilizations in all corners of the globe from ancient times to the present. The assessment of balances has been more efficient in some epochs and societies than in others, where it remained "primitive" and approximated guesswork. However, a calculation of income and expenses, or "capital accounting," has been found universally, as has "the expectation of profit based upon the utilization of opportunities for exchange" (p. 208). Moneylenders, merchants engaged in trade, entrepreneurs investing in slaves, and promoters and speculators of every sort have calculated profits and losses in every epoch (pp. 75–76, 208–12; 1927, p. 334; 1968, p. 91).[5]

Weber turns quickly away from such "adventure capitalism" and "political capitalism" to a discussion of the distinguishing features of *modern* capitalism: a relatively free exchange of goods in markets, the separation of business activity from household activity, sophisticated bookkeeping methods, and the rational, or systematic, organization of work and the workplace in general.[6] Workers are legally free in modern capitalism rather than enslaved. Profit is pursued in a regular and continuous fashion, as is its maximization, in organized businesses (see pp. 208–13; 1927, pp. 275–351; 1968, pp. 164–66; Kalberg, 1983, pp. 269–276).

Nevertheless, because it refers to formal aspects only (the "**economic form**"), Weber insists that this definition of modern capitalism is incomplete; modern capitalism involves *also* the organization of economic activity in terms of an "economic *ethic.*" This *ethos* legitimates and provides the motivation for the rigorous organization of work, the methodical approach to labor, and the systematic pursuit of profit typical of modern capitalism. It implies the following: "the idea of the *duty* of the individual to increase his [or her] wealth, which is assumed to be a self-defined interest in itself" (p. 71; emph. in original); the notion that "labor [is] an absolute end in itself" (p. 78); the desirability of "the acquisition of money, and more and more money, [combined with] the strictest avoidance of all spontaneous enjoyment of it" (p. 72); the view that the "acquisition of money . . . is . . . the result and manifestation of competence and proficiency in a vocational calling" (p. 73); and a "particular *frame of mind* that . . . strives systematically and rationally *in a calling* for legitimate profit" (p. 80; emph. in original).[7]

This "modern economic ethic" Weber designates the "spirit of capitalism."[8] Its violation, he asserts, involves not merely foolishness but "forgetfulness of *duty*" (p. 71; emph. orig.). The eighteenth-century American printer, inventor, entrepreneur, businessman, and statesman Benjamin Franklin embodied this *ethos,* according to Weber, as apparent from his attitudes toward work, profit, and life in general (pp. 70–71). As Weber notes in his "Prefatory Remarks" essay:

> The origin of economic rationalism [of the type which, since the sixteenth and seventeenth centuries, has come to dominate the West] depends not only on an advanced development of technology and law but also on the capacity and disposition of persons to *organize their lives* in a practical-rational manner. (p. 216; emphasis in original; see pp. 250–51)

Typically, Weber isolates the distinctive qualities of the spirit of capitalism through comparisons, above all to the ***traditional economic ethic.*** He does so mainly along two axes: attitudes toward work and the business practices of employers.

Work was perceived as a noble and virtuous endeavor wherever the spirit of capitalism reigned. Throughout their communities, persons engaged in labor were accorded respect and believed to be of good character. Work played a central role in the formulation even of a person's sense of dignity and self-worth. This "elevation" of work to a special position in one's life resulted, Weber contends, from an array of modern historical conditions.

However, adherents to the traditional economic ethic regarded work as involving drudgery and exertion. A necessary evil, it must be avoided as soon as customary and constant economic needs had been met. Labor here was approached in an unfocused and lackadaisical manner. Moreover, people understood work as only one arena of life, deserving of no more attention, concentration, or time than activities oriented, for example, to families, hobbies, friendship, and leisure in general. Those who comprehended work in this way could not be induced to increase productivity even if employers introduced a piece-rate system that provided monetary incentives for faster and more efficient work. On the contrary, because work was viewed negatively and other activities positively, a higher piece-rate led to less labor: Employees could earn in a shorter period of time the amount of money necessary to fulfill their accustomed needs. More time to pursue leisure activities would then become available. As Weber notes:

> The opportunity of earning more appealed to [them] less than the idea of working less. . . . People do not wish 'by nature' to earn more and more money. Instead, they wish simply to live, and to live as they have been accustomed and to earn as much as is required to do so. (p. 77; see pp. 76–79, 433)

Until relatively recently, the traditional economic "spirit" also held sway over persons engaged in business. Whereas employers imbued with the spirit of capitalism sought profit systematically, organized their entire workforce according to the rules of productive and efficient management, reinvested profits in their companies, and saw themselves as engaged in harsh, competitive struggles, economic traditionalism implied a more comfortable and slow-paced manner of conducting business. Set by longstanding custom rather than by the laws of the market, prices and profits generally remained constant. The circle of customers remained unchanged, and relations between workers and owners were regulated largely by tradition. Because the workday lasted generally only from five to six hours, there was always time for friends and long meals. Although capitalist in terms of the use of capital and the calculation of income and expense, a leisurely ethos characterized the entire approach to moneymaking and to business (pp. 77–82).

Weber is proposing that these differences between the traditional and modern orientations toward work and business management are not insignificant. Moreover, although economic forms and economic ethics "exist generally in . . . a relationship . . . of 'adequacy' to each other," there is no " 'lawful' dependency," and they may exist separately (pp. 80–81; see pp. 238–39). On the one hand, even though the spirit of capitalism strongly infused Benjamin Franklin's habits and general way of life, the operations of his printing business followed those typical in handicraft enterprises (p. 80). On the other hand, the traditional economic ethic might combine with a highly developed capitalist economy (such as Italian capitalism before the Reformation). After comparing the widespread capitalism in Florence in the fourteenth and fifteen centuries (where activity directed toward profit for its own sake was viewed as ethically unjustifiable) with the economic backwardness of eighteenth-century Pennsylvania (where a spirit of capitalism was "understood as the essence of a morally acceptable, even praiseworthy way of organizing and directing life"), Weber concludes that capitalism itself did not produce the spirit of capitalism (pp. 85–88).[9]

* * *

How did the "revolution" (p. 80) that brought economic traditionalism to an end take place? What are the sources of this monumental shift to a modern economic ethic? And how did it happen that work moved to the center of life? To Weber, the approach to work "as if [it] were an absolute end in itself . . . is not inherently given in the nature of the species. Nor can it be directly called forth by high or low wages. Rather, it is the product of a long and continuous process of education and socialization" (p. 78; see p. 468, note 17). He is convinced, in light of the extreme immutability and endurance of the traditional economic ethic, that it could only be banished by persons of unusually strong character (p. 82). Yet such an orientation of activity toward hard work appears fully "irrational" and unnatural viewed from the perspective of the spontaneous enjoyment of life (pp. 78, 83–85, 88).

This is Weber's concern. Rather than investigating the origins of modern capitalism, the rise of the West, or capitalism as such, this case study seeks to discover the specific religious "ancestry" of the *spirit* of capitalism (see note 18). It explores the origins of a "modern economic ethos" and the vocational specialist: "My discussion above all *explicitly and intentionally limited* itself to this theme; namely, to the dvelopment of the vocational specialist person (*Berufsmenschentums*) as concerns his significance as a component of the capitalist 'spirit' " (2001, p. 76 [transl. altered; emph. in original]).

In defining this task, Weber was responding critically to a heated discussion in German scholarship. The unorthodox focus of "the Weber thesis" on the importance of a spirit of capitalism separated *PE* clearly from the major orientation of this debate—namely, toward capitalism as an economic form. In fact, the explorations by his colleagues into the origins of modern capitalism denied the independence of an economic ethic. By explicitly seeking to broaden the boundaries of this controversy in an unwelcome direction, *PE* immediately set off a furor. A glance at the main contours of this debate is indispensable before turning to Weber's analysis. Doing so will situate *PE* within the intellectual currents of its time and demarcate its uniqueness.

The Intellectual Context: The Controversy Over the Origins of Capitalism and Industrialism

Nearly all participants in the debate on the origins of modern capitalism and industrialism 100 years ago in Germany offered analyses that neglected the role of culture. The dominant explanations can be mentioned only briefly.

The Intensification of Avarice. A number of German scholars argued that, in earlier times, the "acquisitive instinct" (p. 75) was less developed or even nonexistent. In the eighteenth and nineteenth centuries, however, they saw avarice and greed as becoming stronger. Modern capitalism resulted from an intensification of the "pursuit of gain," they held (p. 208).

This characterization of more recent centuries as ones in which the "striving for . . . the greatest profit" (p. 208) has become more widespread, Weber contends, does not bear up once experimental comparisons are undertaken. The "greed for gain" can be found among "all sorts and conditions of men at all times and in all countries of the earth, wherever the objective possibility of it is or has been given" (p. 208). To him, the "*greed* of mandarins in China, of the aristocrats in ancient Rome, or the modern peasant is second to none" (p. 74–75; emph. in original). Because such an *auri sacra fames* (greed for gold) has existed universally and is "as old as the history of man," it fails to offer a causal explanation for *his specific* problem: the rise of a spirit of capitalism in the eighteenth century in the West. Finally, Weber will argue that the rise of modern capitalism involves a "tempering" of all acquisitive desires; indeed, such a "restraining" of avarice—and its channeling into a *methodical* orientation toward work—is indispensable, he will hold, for the systematic organization of work and production in permanent businesses (pp. 74–75, 208, 433–34).

The Adventure and Political Capitalism of Charismatic Entrepreneurs. Other scholars in Germany were convinced that the desire of great charismatic entrepreneurs for riches pushed economic development past the agrarian and feudal stages to mercantilism and modern capitalism. Typically engaged in gigantic commercial ventures often involving the continent-spanning trade of luxury items, these unscrupulous and egocentric promoters, financiers, bankers, merchants, and speculators ushered in the modern epoch simply on the basis of their extraordinary energy (pp. 71–72, 75–76).

Again, however, Weber discovers this adventure and political capitalism universally. Yet these types of capitalism never called forth *modern* capitalism. Furthermore, he refuses to view the exceptional commercial daring of these sporadically appearing "economic supermen" as implying the continuity of disciplined action requisite for shattering the traditional economic ethic. Isolated individuals alone could never call forth this monumental transformation; rather, an organizing of life common to whole "*groups* of persons" (emph. in original), all *intensively* oriented toward profit and the rational organization of labor and capital, would be necessary (pp. 74–76).

Evolution and Progress. In *Der moderne Kapitalismus* (1902), Werner Sombart, Weber's colleague and friend, holds that the expansion of production, trade, banking, and commerce can best be understood as clear manifestations of a society-wide unfolding of "rationalism" and progress in general. In this view, the spirit of capitalism constituted simply further, and not unusual, evidence of a general evolution. To Sombart, societal progress as a whole deserves explanation rather than the separate component elements in this broad-ranging evolutionary process.

Weber opposes Sombart vehemently. "Society" is too global a level of analysis, he claims. Instead, the separate societal "realms" (*Lebensbereiche*), "orders" (*Lebensordnungen*), or "spheres" (*Lebenssphären*), which together comprise a "society," must be examined. If one proceeds in this manner, a *nonparallel* development in the various realms becomes evident rather than a general evolutionary process, Weber insists. For example, a systematization, or "*rationalization*," in the sphere of law (in the sense of increasing conceptual clarity and the refinement of the content of the law based upon a fundamental written source, such as a constitution) reached its highest point in the Roman law of the Middle Ages. On the one hand, however, this type of law remained far less developed in a number of countries where a rationalization of the *economy* advanced farthest. In England, for example, a less rationalized form of law—Common law—prevailed. On the other hand, Roman law remained strong throughout southern Europe, an area where modern capitalism developed quite late (pp. 86–88). In neither region did the law and economy realms develop in a parallel fashion.

These and similar observations persuaded Weber to reject the notion of "general evolutionary progress" and to focus his attention on a variety of societal orders rather than "society" as an organic whole. He investigated the realm of religion in *PE* and, later, in his three-volume analytic treatise, *Economy and Society* (1968), the domains of law, rulership (*Herrschaft*), status groups, "universal organizations" (the family, the clan), and the economy (see Kalberg, 1994b, pp. 53–54, 103–117; 1996, pp. 50–51; 1998, pp. 221–25).

The Jews as the Carriers of Modern Capitalism. Sombart's book, *The Jews and Modern Capitalism* (1913), argues that the Jews as a group are the major social carriers of modern capitalism. He views the putatively typical business dealings of Jews as decisive: the loaning of money for interest, continuous speculation, and the financing of wars, construction projects, and political activities. In addition, Sombart argues that an "abstract rationalism," which allegedly characterizes Jewish thinking, is identical with the "spirit of capitalism" of English Puritans. The wish to make money dominates in both groups.

Weber disagrees forcefully on all points both in *PE* and in later writings (see pp. 147–48, 290–99; 536–37, notes 68 and 69; 1927, pp. 358–59; 1968, pp. 1202–04).[10] He views the innovation-averse economic ethos of the Jews as "traditional" and notes their absence among the heroic entrepreneurs in the early stages of Western European capitalism. Furthermore, he sees the capitalism of the Jews as a form of the speculative capitalism that has existed universally rather than as involving a systematic organization of production, labor, and the workplace in general (pp. 146–48). Finally, Weber argues, the outcaste position of the Jews kept them outside the pivotal craft and guild organizations of the critical medieval period, and their double ethical standard, which followed from this outcaste position (strong ethical obligations to other Jews, yet less stringent obligations at times in economic relationships with non-Jews), hindered the unfolding of measures of economic efficiency across the economy.

Historical Materialism, Economic Interests, and the Power of the Dominant Class. Although the "internal contradictions" of capitalism constituted the major concern of Karl Marx, his writings clearly yield an analysis of its origin. For him, the rise of modern capitalism can be equated with the overthrow of the feudal aristocracy and the hegemonic rule of a new class: the bourgeoisie. Ownership of the means of production (property, factories, technology, tools, etc.) by this class, as well as its economic interests and sheer greed, were believed to be crucial; they stood as foundational ingredients in the quest of capitalists to acquire more and more wealth. As the bourgeoisie became larger and more powerful, trade, banking, production, and commerce expanded. Eventually, factory-based capitalism came into being.

A "spirit of capitalism" could play little part in the historical materialism of Marx. Had he been alive to address Weber's thesis, Marx would have viewed this ethos as arising directly out of the economic interests of the bourgeoisie; the set of values it implied would be understood as nothing more than an expression, in abstract form, of the economic interests of this class. Such an "ideology" served, Marx argued frequently, to justify the hegemony of the dominant class and to sedate workers into accepting their misery and exploitation.

PE rejects this analysis completely. The economic interests of this class, Weber insists, did not give birth to the spirit of capitalism. Franklin himself offers evidence against this position: his economic ethos far preceded the formation of a bourgeoisie (pp. 74, 84–85). Moreover, Weber rejects a pivotal Marxian assumption:

> The assumption is . . . by no means justified *a priori* . . . that, on the one hand, the technique of the capitalist enterprise and, on the other, the spirit of 'work as a vocational calling,' which endows capitalism with its expansive energy, must have had their *original* sustaining roots in the same social groupings. (p. 469, note 24; emph. in original; see, e.g., pp. 239–40, 249)

As noted, even those members of the bourgeoisie who proved to be economic supermen were incapable, Weber maintains, of the sustained and group-based thrust necessary for a rupturing of economic traditionalism. Finally, he found that the spirit of capitalism was formulated and cultivated above all by self-made parvenus from the modest circumstances of the middle classes rather than by the entrepreneurs of a commercial elite (the "patrician merchants") (pp. 79–80, 214–17). To him, the "youth of these ideas—the capitalist spirit—is altogether more thorny than was assumed by the 'superstructure' theorists" (p. 74).[11]

Miscellaneous Forces.   Many historians and economists emphasize the importance for economic development of technological innovations, geographical forces, the influx of precious metals from the New World, population increases (see pp. 431–33; 1927, pp. 258–59), and the growth of cities and science. Weber examines all of these arguments. Through scrutiny of comparative cases, he deduces that favorable technological and scientific inventions, population and climatological changes, urban expansion, and other factors had existed in the Middle Ages in the West, in the ancient world, and in a number of epochs in China and India—yet modern capitalism had failed to appear first in these civilizations.[12]

* * *

In these ways,[13] *PE* seeks fundamentally to recast the ongoing debate toward an exploration of the spirit of capitalism (pp. 74–88). Weber laments the exclusion of such a discussion and the dominant orientation to an "economic form." By insisting that any explanation of modern capitalism's early development must acknowledge a rational economic ethic as a sociologically significant causal force, and that an investigation of its sources must take place, he seeks (1) to bring values unequivocally into the debate and (2) to legitimize an investigation of their causal origins.

He is attempting, in other words, to persuade his readers that "cultural values" must no longer be neglected. However complicated it may be to investigate their sources and to assess their influence, values should not be regarded, Weber holds, as passive forces generally subordinate to social structures, power, classes, evolution and progress, and economic and political interests. The spirit of capitalism had significant noneconomic and nonpolitical roots, he contends.

Empirical Observations, the Turn Toward Religion, and the Aim of The Protestant Ethic

A trial-and-error pathway never characterizes Weber's search for the religious sources of the spirit of capitalism. Rather, at the outset he upholds a view not uncommon in the Germany of his time: *Religious belief* influences work habits and approaches to business, as well as life in general. Hence, queries regarding differences between Protestants and Catholics appear to him a quite plausible and natural orientation for his research (see Nipperdey, 1993). Indeed, since his teenage years, Weber had been reading theological literature, including the American Unitarians William Ellery Channing and Theodore Parker (see Roth, 1997).

Although relationships between occupational status, educational attainment, Catholicism, and Protestantism were acknowledged among journalists and the educated public in Germany in the 1890s, as well as earlier,[14] very little social science research had addressed this theme. As he pondered English and American Puritanism in the mid-1890s, Weber read the massive study by the economic historian Eberhard Gothein, *Wirtschaftsgeschichte des Schwarzwalds* (1892) (Economic History of the Black Forest), which called attention to Calvinism's strong role in spreading capitalism. Although greatly impressed by Gothein (pp. 9–10), Georg Jellinek's *The Declaration of the Rights of Man and Citizens* (1979 [1895]) inspired Weber "to take up the study of Puritanism once again."[15] The centrality of devout Dissenters in seventeenth-century England for the emergence of fundamental political rights and liberties had been documented by Jellinek: " [His] proof of religious traces in the genesis of the Rights of Man . . . gave me a crucial stimulus . . . to investigate the impact of religion in areas where one might not look at first" (cited in Marianne Weber, 1975, p. 476).

In the late 1890s, Weber encouraged a student to examine the influence of religion on social stratification in the southwest German state of Baden. Martin Offenbacher's statistical investigation concluded that distinct differences existed between Protestants and Catholics in regard to occupational choices and levels of education: Protestants dominated as owners of industrial concerns, while Catholics were more often farmers and owners of businesses utilizing skilled labor. Protestants' generally higher levels of education accounted for their disproportionately high employment as state civil servants and their unusually high earnings if they remained in the working class (1900, pp. 63–64).[16]

The publication in 1902 of Sombart's two-volume work, *Der moderne Kapitalismus*, appears to have motivated Weber to intensify his own research (see Lehmann, 1987, 2005). In his chapter on the origin of the capitalist spirit, Sombart had dismissed the role of Protestantism, especially Calvinism and Quakerism, as "too well-known to require further explanation." Instead, he discovered "empirical proof" of capitalism's origins in the high esteem accorded to the possession of money, indeed to the addiction to "sparkling gold" that appeared in the European Middle Ages. To Sombart, "the Protestant religion was not the cause but the result of modern capitalist thinking." He provoked his readers to discover "empirical proof of *concrete-historical contexts* to the contrary" (1902, vol. 1, pp. 380–81; emph. in original; see vom Brocke, 1987; Lehmann, 1993, pp. 196–98; Marshall, 1982, pp. 36–40).[17]

Weber took up the challenge, and he most likely completed his research for *PE* in 1903. Against Sombart he responds vigorously. Even external social structures of extreme rigidity, such as those typical of religious sects, Weber asserts, should not be viewed as themselves calling forth homogeneous patterns of action (see pp. 239–40, 249). How then could capitalism do so? The studies he had read in the 1890s pointed in a different direction. As well, Weber notes the unusually methodical and conscientious work habits of young women from Pietistic families in Baden (pp. 78–79). Even this:

> Analysis derived from [early twentieth-century] capitalism has indicated to us yet again that it would be worthwhile simply to *ask* how these connections between people's capacity to adapt to [modern] capitalism, on the one hand, and their religious beliefs, on the other, could have been formulated during the youth of [modern] capitalism. (p. 79; emph. in original)

He then explicitly states his aim in *PE*:

> It should here be ascertained only whether, and to what extent, religious influences *co*-participated in the qualitative formation and quantitative expansion of this "spirit" [of capitalism] across the globe. (p. 97; emph. in original)

Whether religious beliefs constitute the "specific ancestry" of the spirit of capitalism must be investigated.[18]

Weber's description of his step-by-step procedure responds to Sombart's provocation even more directly. He will first investigate whether an "elective affinity" (*Wahlverwandtschaft*) exists between certain religious beliefs of the Reformation and a vocational ethic (*Berufsethik*). If this "meaningful connection" (*sinnhafter Zusammenhang*) can be established, he will then be able to clarify the "way" and "general direction" in which religious movements, as a result of this elective affinity, influenced the development of *material culture*, or practical, workaday life.[19] Only then will it be possible to assess "to what degree the historical origin of central features of our modern life ... can be attributed to religious forces stemming from the Reformation, and to what degree to other forces" (p. 97).

Weber's complex and multilayered analysis in *PE* can be broken down into two major stages: (1) his investigation of the origins of the Protestant ethic and (2) his linkage of the Protestant ethic to the spirit of capitalism.

II. THE ORIGINS OF *THE PROTESTANT ETHIC*: WEBER'S ANALYSIS

In searching for the spirit of capitalism's religious ancestry, Weber scrutinizes medieval Catholicism, Lutheranism, and the ascetic Protestant churches and sects from two perspectives: the extent to which religious belief calls forth motivations that give rise to a *methodical-rational organization of life*, and the degree to which religious belief places *psychological rewards* directly upon systematic economic activity. He is convinced, as discussed, that only methodical activity of extreme rigor and continuity in large *groups* of people possesses the capacity to call forth a "revolution" against the traditional economic ethic (pp. 80–83, 118). The intense sustaining power indispensable to do so could not be mustered by means-end action (*zweckrationales Handeln*) on behalf of the accumulation of wealth.

The lay Catholicism of the Middle Ages never linked the important question—am I among the saved?—to economic activity. On the contrary, the faithful believed themselves to be saved if they regularly prayed, confessed their sins, sought to uphold the commandments, and engaged in "good works." Moreover, Weber emphasizes, the church acknowledged human imperfection and provided a mechanism to ameliorate the sinner's anxiety: the Confession. By unburdening their conscience to a priest and performing the penance he imposed, the devout were enabled to conduct their lives in an "accounting" fashion: sinful behavior, however reprehensible, could be balanced out over the long run by repentance and the more frequent practice of charitable good works. A cycle of sin, atonement, and forgiveness—a "series of *isolated* actions" (p. 114)—characterized lay Catholicism rather than the placing of uninterrupted psychological rewards upon a systemized and rigorously directed way of life. Only the "religious virtuosi"—monks and nuns—organized their lives in a methodical-rational manner, yet they remained in monasteries "outside the world" (pp. 114–15).

Finally, medieval Catholicism maintained a highly negative image of merchants and businessmen in general. Their perceived lust for gain placed riches above the kingdom of God and thereby endangered the soul, and their exploitation of persons on behalf of economic gain opposed the Christian ethic of brotherhood and group solidarity. An unequivocal axiom prevailed: *homo mercator vix aut numquam potest Deo placere* (the merchant may conduct himself without sin but cannot be pleasing to God) (p. 85; 1927, pp. 357c–58; 1946b, pp. 331–32; 1968, pp. 583–87, 1189–91). To Weber, among Catholics a traditional economic ethic prevailed.

In banishing the confessional and the parallel salvation paths for lay and virtuoso believers, Lutheranism distanced itself from medieval Catholicism. In doing so, and in introducing the idea of salvation through faith—penitant humility, an inward-oriented mood of piety, and trust in God—as its doctrinal fulcrum, Lutheranism placed qualitatively different psychological rewards on the believer's action (pp. 105, 112). Moreover, and salient to Weber, Luther introduced the idea that work in a "calling" (*Beruf*) was given by God. In essence, believers had been *called* by God into a vocation, or specific line of coherent work, and hence were duty-bound to it.

Nevertheless, Weber fails to discover the religious origins of the spirit of capitalism here (pp. 89–94). Psychological rewards were not attached to occupational mobility because all callings for Luther were of equal value (p. 90). In addition, Luther never extolled "success" in a vocation or an intensification of labor beyond the standards set by each calling. Instead, one's religious duty involved a reliable, punctual, and efficient performance of the tasks and obligations required by the vocation itself. Indeed, a "moral legitimation of vocational life" now appeared (p. 90), and the mundane work-life of all believers became penetrated by a religious dimension.

Thus a dramatic step away from Catholicism had been taken. However, a systematization of life as a whole did not occur in Lutheranism. Furthermore, because God firmly defines the boundaries for each vocation and station in life (*Stand*), Luther saw the acquisition of goods beyond this level as morally suspect and sinful (pp. 91–92). In the end, Weber concludes that the economic ethic of Lutheranism remained basically traditional—all the more because it retained the Catholic ethic of brotherhood and thus opposed the impersonal exchange characteristic of relationships in the marketplace (pp. 92–94; see 1968, pp. 514, 570, 600, 1198).

Weber then turns to *ascetic* Protestantism: the sects and churches of the seventeenth century, most prominently Calvinism, Pietism, Methodism, and the adult baptizing groups (the Baptists and the Quakers). How did a *Protestant ethic* originate with these groupings? Only a sketch of Weber's argument can be offered here.

John Calvin of the Sixteenth Century and Puritanism of the Seventeenth Century

In the sixteenth century, John Calvin formulated a religious doctrine built on three pillars. First, in opposition to Catholicism and Lutheranism, he accepted the Old Testament's view of God as an all-powerful and omniscient deity far superior to all previous gods and separated from earthly mortals by an unbridgeable chasm. Also a wrathful and vindictive deity, this "fully transcendent," majestic God was prepared at any moment to strike against sinful human beings. Because He was a distant and mighty being, His motives remained beyond human comprehension; they were understood only by Him (pp. 105–06; see pp. 489–90, n. 19).

Second, this inscrutable God had, Calvin argued, unalterably "predestined" for all time only a tiny minority to be saved; everyone else was condemned to eternal damnation. The activities of believers, whether they confessed sins, performed good works, or donated to charity, would not change this "double decree": A few were saved; most were damned. One's "salvation status" was preordained. Moreover, Calvin's abolition of the confession brought the priest's absolution of the sinner to an end (pp. 106–08).

These two pivotal components of Calvin's thought became variously intertwined with a further crucial and "entirely central" idea from him: "[T]he cosmos of the 'world' serves the majesty of God and His self-glorification." This is its purpose—namely, terrestrial life exclusively exists to extol His honor and glory. Hence, the faithful constitute simply the "tools" of His will and His commandments (see pp. 105–06, 109; 532, note 39). With this turn, the Catholic and Lutheran salvation paths—isolated good works and faith—became increasingly viewed as incapable of calling forth action adequately intense and internally unified (pp. 111–112, 144; 507–08, note 122).

These major tenets formed the core of Calvin's teachings and established the outer parameters within which subsequent revisions would have to occur. It was important to Weber that, however grandiose they appeared, these fundamental axioms failed to provide believers with an acceptable set of enduring beliefs: Salvation remained uncertain for even the most devout among the faithful (p. 110). Moreover, because neither a church nor ministers possessed a special connection to God, profound spiritual guidance remained absent. Indeed, the doctrine of predestination, especially when combined with a notion of God as omnipotent, vengeful, and unknowable, led logically to fatalism, loneliness, and extreme anxiety among believers. In an epoch in which an overriding question—Am I among the saved?"—dominated to a degree scarcely comprehensible today, the despair of the devout became unbearable (pp. 105–10, 122; pp. 500–01, note 76). Despite John Calvin's advice—"steadfast faith" and a call for the faithful simply to consider themselves among the saved (pp. 110–11)—an impasse had been reached.[20]

This despair and uncertainty could not long be tolerated, Weber emphasized (see p. 110; pp. 495–96; p. 198, note 46). Ministers and theologians alike saw the necessity for adjustments; revisions had to occur—especially if competing congregations were to retain their memberships. To varying degrees, the predestination axiom and Calvin's harsh God underwent amelioration throughout the sixteenth and seventeenth centuries, Weber maintains.[21] As innovations congealed, and although one's status among the chosen few was never completely secure, believers increasingly found cause to convince themselves of their place among the elect. Dilemmas could be mitigated and anxiety assuaged, the faithful concluded, if certain avenues of action were successfully pursued. A focus upon them, Weber contends, became important by the early seventeenth century in the daily lives of the lay devout. He states his theme succinctly: ". . .we wish to ascertain which psychological motivations gave direction to the organization of the believer's life and held the individual firmly to it" (p. 102).[22] *What* religious sources stood at the foundation of the Protestant ethic?

Often misunderstood by commentators, *PE's multidimensional* causal analysis must be briefly adumbrated. It will be first addressed by reference to two fundamental themes: (a) the many ways in which the Protestant ethic "sanctified," or rendered "providential," methodical work, the acquisition and possession of wealth, and virtuous conduct and (b) the multiple ways in which the faithful attempted to answer the *certitudo salutis* question—am I among the saved—by discovering *signs* perceived to indicate God's favoring grace. The central features of this ethos, which "co-participated" in the formation of the spirit of capitalism, can then be addressed: (a) the believer's "rationalization," or systemization, of action to a "this-worldly asceticism" that tightly controlled and organized life in a "methodical-rational" manner (*methodisch-rationale Lebensführung*), and (b) the value-based, internally coherent Puritan "style of life."[23] This "Protestant ethic" confronted on the one hand, and directly revolutionalized, the traditional economic ethic, Weber insists, and on the other hand served as the major religious source for the spirit of capitalism.

The Protestant Ethic I: Sanctification, the Certainty of Salvation, and the Search for Signs

The Sanctification of Methodical Work, Wealth, and Virtuous Conduct. Puritanism called methodical work, the pursuit of wealth, and virtuous conduct to the forefront. Rather than involving purely "utilitarian" activities, all now became *providential*. Labor, which became sanctified for a number of reasons, first captures our attention.

A group of seventeeth-century theologians and ministers argued that the purpose of life itself involved work. With the revisions undertaken by these "Puritan Divines," St. Paul's maxim regarding an "ethical duty to work"—"if anyone will not work, let him not eat"—became "hardened." Now, for example, even those in possession of great wealth could not refrain from labor, as the prominent Puritan minister Richard Baxter stressed, for it is God's commandment. Work was simply ordained by God; He "willed" and desired the faithful to labor (pp. 142–44).

In addition, rather than intermittent work, *methodical* labor in a *vocational calling* (*Beruf*) is "commanded to all" by God, Baxter maintained. Suffering believers benefit from this sustained activity in a variety of ways. By facilitating an orientation to the "impersonal societal usefulness" that promises God's glory, regular work keeps in check all egocentric wishes. Labor in a calling also provides stability to the believer's life by offering continuity and combatting confusion. And God is gratified by the active execution of His will by believers in a rigorous manner—that is, in vocational callings (see pp. 109, 142–45, 155–56). In turn, systematic labor is seen as a way of working for God's glory (1968, p. 1200).

Even further advantages are offered, according to Baxter, by a vocational calling, which "God's providence reserves for everyone" (p. 143). The stress upon continuous and systematic work, which enables a focussing of the energies of the devout upon God and His plan, serves to tame creaturely desires. In doing so, and as a mechanism opposing the "unclean life" and all sexual temptation, labor in a vocation provides moderation to life—thereby further assisting the concentration upon God and the soul's "uplifting." "Intense worldly activity," not least, dispels the overwhelming doubt, anxiety, and sense of moral unworthiness that accompanies the doctrine of predestination. Unceasing work in a calling also enables the faithful simply *to consider* themselves among the chosen (pp. 105–06, 110–11, 142–43; p. 495–96, note 46).

In these various ways, labor in a vocational calling acquired a *religious* significance. It became sublimated away from all utilitarian purposes and sanctified—thereby undergoing an alteration of its subjective meangingfulness.[24] To Weber, believers' *exclusive* striving for the kingdom of God, . . . through fulfillment of the duty to work in a vocational calling . . ., must have promoted the 'productivity' of work" (p. 156; emph. in original). A parallel transformation took place in respect to *wealth*: Its exclusively mundane meaning faded and it became providential.

Ascetic Protestants, as noted, sought to contribute to the creation of God's kingdom. His goodness and justice would surely be served if His earthly cosmos became one of wealth and abundance. A kingdom of poverty and destitution would only dishonor this omniscient deity, and hence the exemplary "city on the hill" must be built by believers *in majorem Dei gloriam,* or for God's glory. Indeed, because wealth enhances His majesty, this omnipotent deity *wants* His kingdom to be one of abundance. Riches became sanctified and methodical work, as a crucial means of creating His prosperous kingdom, acquired a further special dignity. Both served as mechanisms to increase God's glory (pp. 109, 142–43).

Finally, Puritanism strongly sanctified virtuous conduct. Although His motives were unknowable, a vain deity obviously demanded that His will be executed and His standards upheld. Righteous conduct in strict conformity with His commandments must be undertaken, and an overcoming of undirected and spontaneous instincts must be achieved. The purpose given to the human species—to honor and glorify God—required believers, despite the double decree, to consider themselves among the chosen and to conduct their lives according to divine commandments. Now sanctified, "good behavior" became activity rewarded by this mighty deity. A greater taming of the *status naturae* and a more consistent focus upon God's wishes resulted. A further element of order, stability, and continuity was introduced into the believer's life.

* * *

In sum, the ascetic Protestant devout bestowed clear psychological rewards upon constant labor, the search for riches, and virtuous conduct. A providential halo now encompassed their subjective meaningfulness. Nonetheless, *this* sanctification of an array of activities must be comprehended as *one* component only in Weber's many-sided analysis of the Protestant ethic's origins. Although helpful to the faithful worried about the *certitudo salutis* question, it addresses only incompletely—and in too linear a manner—their most urgent concern: Am I among the saved? Moreover, and even though a sanctification of activities owing to God's wants and commandments laid a firm cornerstone for the Protestant ethic, this line of argument fails to explain the origins of two of its critical elements: this-worldly asceticism and the methodical-rational organization of life. Their sources are located elsewhere—namely, in the apparent resolution to this all-important query offered by additional revisions by the Puritan Divines to Calvin's thought.

Weber's further analysis of the Protestant ethic's origins addresses the "certainty of salvation" theme forcefully. It seeks (a) to explain how Puritans, unable to bear continuing uncertainty, wrestled unceasingly with the salvation dilemma, and (b) to comprehend how certain new activities came to be viewed as satisfactory responses to the conundrum confronted by the devout. Anxious and lonely, the faithful concluded in the latter sixteenth and early seventeenth centuries that *signs* of their salvation existed, Weber perceives. Once sought and discovered, this "evidence" from God convinced believers of their membership among the predestined few in a far more effective manner than the sanctification of activities discussed above. Crucial to Weber is a *psychological* dynamic that results from (a) an interweaving of strong rewards placed upon industrious work, riches, and virtuous conduct, (b) a search by the faithful for signs of their favorable salvation, and (c) an acknowledgment by the devout that God's energy is "operating within."

The *juxtaposition* of these themes *and* the ways in which the certainty of salvation dilemma now became at least partly resolved despite the predestination decree, had the effect, Weber maintains, of placing far more intense psychological rewards upon *this-worldly asceticism* and a *methodical-rational* organization of life. Because now vigorously sanctified, both contributed in a sustained manner to the formation of a Protestant ethic sufficiently powerful to suppress comprehensively the *status naturae*, direct the focus of the faithful in an even more manifold manner toward God, banish the traditional economic ethic, and form significant thrusts toward the spirit of capitalism. Resting upon this dynamic rooted in the pivotal *certitudo salutis* question, the realm of religion now places psychological rewards upon this-worldly activity to such a degree that regular economic exchange can no longer be adequately comprehended as exclusively involving utilitarian calculations and astute business procedures, Weber insists.[25] The Protestant ethic now assumes an independent profile capable of influencing political and economic developments, he contends. His analysis must be briefly explored.

The "Certainty of Salvation" Question and the Search for Signs of One's Salvation.

The ascetic Protestant faithful in the sixteenth and seventeenth centuries felt compelled to identify signs of God's blessing in order to alleviate unbearable anxiety and insecurity. Despite His incomprehensible and unalterable predestination decree, their search continued—for the devout reasoned that this omnipotent and omniscient deity would in the end offer assistance to those He had predestined. The idea that evidence of His grace could be discovered contained a mighty power, Weber holds, to motivate anxious believers to undertake new activities.

Rather than linear or monocausal, his analysis rests upon a variety of interacting developments. Signs of God's favor took various forms: the *capacity* of the faithful to undertake the systematic work required by a vocational calling, to *remain* focused upon the goals of acquiring great wealth and upholding His commandments (even while engaged in daily activities and exposed to the world's "temptations"), and to *sustain* the "feeling" of being penetrated by Him. Indeed, the devout concluded that the ability to execute certain activities pleasing to Him, and to experience particular emotions, demonstrated the presence of His strength "operating within"—and hence His grace. Both Puritanism's this-worldly asceticism and its methodical-rational ordering of life according to ethical values found here their major source and enduring thrust. These various *signs* must be addressed separately.

Methodical Work as a Sign of One's Salvation. For all the reasons mentioned above, the general prominence of labor for Puritans insured its centrality in all discussions regarding the burning question of whether indications of one's chosen status existed. The idea that a capacity for systematic work might constitute a sign of one's salvation arose mainly out of the practical problems confronted by pastors seeking to offer guidance to distraught believers.

The continuous orientation to labor in a vocation required unusual and extreme effort, discipline, and wakefulness. In a cosmos dominated by an omnipotent and omniscient Deity who wished His faithful to labor in a vocation, ministers, theologians, and laity alike came to conclude that the intense energy necessary to maintain righteous conduct *must* have originated from Him. Divine powers were present and acting within them, sincere believers were convinced. Moreover, a capacity to perform continuous labor derived ultimately from intense belief—and this devoutness *could* originate only from the favoring hand of an all-powerful divinity, the faithful knew. Hence, rigorous work became viewed as *testifying* to an internal relationship with Him. In other words, anyone capable of adopting a systematic orientation to labor, as God willed, could do so only *because* of His blessing: *evidence* of God "operating within" accompanied the capacity to so.[26] And this omniscient being, the faithful reasoned, would surely choose to assist in this way only those He had predestined for salvation (p. 110, 118, 151–52; 1968, p. 572).

To Weber, the source of this idea's power to organize the believer's entire life around disciplined work was apparent. Its capacity to answer *the* burning question favorably—Am I among the saved?—*convinced* the faithful of their membership among the predestined few. They concluded that a sign of God's favor had been given to all who sought to labor methodically and discovered an ability to do so. A distinct and massive psychological reward now became placed upon systematic work. As Weber notes:

> . . . the religious value set on tireless, continuous, and systematic work in a vocational calling was defined as absolutely the highest of all ascetic means for believers to testify to their elect status, as well as simultaneously the most certain and visible means of doing so. (p. 152; see pp. 155–56)

The intensity of Puritanism's focussed orientation toward methodical labor could be explained only in this manner, Weber holds. A further step away from the traditional economic cosmos, where the orientation of work in a utilitarian manner on the one hand and toward traditions on the other hand dominated, had been taken with this development—for both entrepreneurs and workers. An additional sign of their favorable salvation status could be discovered by business-oriented persons: the accumulation of wealth and the successful acquisition of profit.

Wealth and Profit as Signs of One's Salvation. A further particular adjustment of Calvin's theology by Baxter and the Puritan Divines proved significant for an understanding of the manner in which a systematic striving for wealth and profit tended to resolve the all-important question of one's salvation. Although the devout could never know their state of grace with certainty, they could logically conclude—in light of God's desire for an earthly kingdom of abundance to serve His glory—that a believer's actual production of great wealth constituted a favorable sign from this omnipotent and omniscient deity. The condemned would never be allowed to praise His glory, Baxter reasoned. Surely "the acquisition of wealth, when it was the *fruit* of work in a vocational calling, [was viewed as] God's blessing" (p. 152). Again, God's hand must be operating within the devout. Indeed, business-oriented believers could now seek *to produce* the evidence—literally, material success—that would convince them of their status as among the chosen.

Because now directly salient to the overarching dilemma of salvation, riches acquired a more comprehensive *religious* significance and psychological reward. This more thorough sanctification of wealth implies to Weber an even more methodical striving by believers to attain riches, and the criticism of the wealthy since antiquity—their riches must have been acquired through dishonest means—now faded. Similarly, the opportunity to compete with others in search of a profit never appeared randomly, the Puritan knew; rather, an all-powerful God had offered a chance to acquire wealth—and thus a favorable sign had been given (see pp. 145–46, 151–52); 1951, p. 245).

> In no other religion was the pride of the predestined aristocracy of the saved so closely associated with the man of a vocation and with the idea that success in *rationalized* activity demonstrates God's blessing as in Puritanism. (1968, p. 575; emph. in original; see also p. 556)

> And since the success of work is the surest symptom that it pleases God, capitalist profit is one of the most important criteria for establishing that God's blessing rests on the enterprise. (1968, p. 1200; see below, p. 199)

Two further indications assisted believers subjectively to view themselves as among the predestined few, according to Weber: virtuous conduct and the feeling of being "possessed" by God.

Becoming Holy as a Sign of One's Salvation: Virtuous Conduct. Virtuous conduct proved difficult in light of the proclivity among mortal creatures to sin. Taming the impulses of the flesh and orienting life in a consistent fashion to God's decrees required heroic discipline. Of course, even if the actions of mere mortals pleased this vindictive deity, the predestination decree could never be altered.

However, various revisions of Calvin's doctrines by Baxter and other Puritan Divines communicated to the faithful the idea that, *if* they proved capable of mastering base desires and leading dignified lives oriented systematically to the commandments, *then* the heroic capacity to do so had been in fact bestowed upon them by their God. After all, He was omniscient and all-powerful. Moreover, as noted, the devout knew that their energy derived from the very strength of their belief, and they were further convinced that unusually intense faith emanated from God. His will was operating within them (pp. 112–13)—and this majestic divinity would naturally convey powerful belief and energy *only* to those He had predestined. Thus, the systematic organization of life to accord with the deity's commandments itself served as evidence to believers of their favorable salvation status.

This component of Weber's argument can be restated in a slightly different terminology. The faithful knew that an answer to the crucial "certainty of salvation" query required a *striving* to live the sanctified, or holy, life. Indeed, an inability to muster the requisite self-confidence to do so, or to combat doubts, was believed to indicate "insufficient faith—a condition that surely would not characterize the saved (pp. 110–11). Conduct must become and remain consistent with God's laws, for such devoutness could be comprehended as a sign of one's salvation status: God's hand, acting within the predestined by bestowing intense belief, had rendered the faithful capable, as His "tool" on earth, of obeying His laws. Obedience itself constituted a psychological reward (pp. 110–13, 120–21, 127, 146–47; see 1968, p. 572).

In this manner, conduct in conformity with Christian ideals created evidence for believers of their salvation; it *testified* to their capacity to serve as God's tool and hence to their status among the elect. Their integrity and upright demeanor was recognized by others as a sign of membership among the chosen few.

> The calling to salvation could be recognized by the believer . . . through the consciousness of a central and unified relationship between this—his short—life and the transcendental God and His will: namely, through the consciousness of a "sanctification." In turn, . . . sanctification could testify to itself only through activities desired by God—that is, through activities to which He gives His blessing, namely, ethical action. Hence, ethical action itself—for this action gives to the believer certainty that he is God's tool—provides certainty of salvation. In this manner a rational-ethical methodicalness to life acquired the strongest conceivable psychological premium. Only the life emanating from a unified core and oriented to firm and ordered foundational principles could be considered a life pleasing to God (pp. 282–83; see below pps. 113, 127).

This achievement affirmatively answered the crucial *certitudo salutis* question, as did systematic work in a vocation and the acquisition of wealth. It further tamed the *status naturae* and held in check residual anxiety and fatalism deriving from enduring predestination concerns.

"Feeling" as a Sign of One's Salvation.   As significant signs, methodical work, the possession of wealth, and virtuous conduct in accord with God's commandments all testified to the likelihood of salvation. Methodists, Pietists, Baptists, and Quakers, even while acknowledging these all-important indications, emphasized a further means to address anxiety and to attain some certainty of membership among the chosen: the acquisition of a *feeling* of being possessed by God.

This emotion at times penetrated the devout thoroughly. An "awareness" of the deity and an "awakening" became intense, and the faithful experienced a oneness with God that transported them to an extraordinary holy realm. A supernatural force was believed to be at work within. And of course this magnificent Deity, the devout were convinced, would possess only those He had deemed among the saved.

Weber emphasizes that the faithful, in search of this possession by God, upheld the basic tenets of ascetic Protestantism noted above. They acknowledged that labor in a vocation pleased God, that He desired the building of a kingdom of abundance to serve His majesty, and that He wished His commandments to be strictly upheld. Although less entrepreneurial and in general less exclusively focused upon work and the attainment of wealth than occurred among Calvinists, the orientation toward a vocational calling of Pietists, Methodists, Quakers, and the Baptists nonetheless possessed a providential halo.[27]

These brief remarks have summarized the several ways in which, according to Weber, the *certitudo salutis* question motivated the devout to search for signs of their salvation. They indicate that his exploration of the Protestant ethic's origins moves far beyond a linear analysis of how work in a calling, wealth, and virtuoso conduct become sanctified. Rather, multiple moving elements characterize his explanation. Furthermore, as the notion became more widespread in the seventeenth century that signs of one's grace could be discovered, believers moved away from a focus upon the predestination doctrine's severe consequences—massive fatalism, despair, and anxiety—and Calvin's harsh Old Testament God. Instead, as demarcated by the Puritan Divines, an orientation to these signs moved increasingly to the forefront. More and more the depressed and bleak Puritan became the "can do" tool of God's will.

Weber's analysis of the Protestant ethic's origins now addresses two final components: the methodical-rational organization of life at its foundation and Puritanism's value-based, internally unified "style of life." The Protestant ethic's great empowerment will now come into focus, according to Weber: namely, the capacity of the particular subjective meaning it called forth among believers both to shatter the traditional economic ethic and to serve as a religious source for the spirit of capitalism.

The Protestant Ethic II: This-Worldly Asceticism and the Puritan Style of Life

The Puritan's this-worldly asceticism called forth a methodical-rational organization of life that tamed the *status naturae* and comprehensively sanctified heretofore mundane, utilitarian activities. According to Weber's analysis this *asceticism* proves a critical component at the foundation of the Protestant ethic. It also plays a crucial role in the formation of the Puritan style of life. A new "type of person" will now embark upon the stage of Western history, he maintains.

This-Worldly Asceticism: The Methodical-Rational Organization of Life and "World Mastery." As carried mainly by groups of seventeenth-century Puritans, a methodical-rational organization of life characterized the Protestant ethic, Weber contends. An unusual and manifold "rationalization"—or systematization—of energies circumscribed the impulsive and spontaneous *status naturae* and calls forth a tempered, focussed, and dispassionate frame of mind. Hence, a "reversal" of the "natural life" occurs, Weber holds, one grounded in a comprehensive orientation by sincere believers to the supernatural realm—and without which such an implausible overturning of the *status naturae* would have been meaningless (see pp. 72–73, 83, 120–21).

Religious values now radically penetrated devout believers. A "meaningful total relationship of the organization of life to the goal of religious salvation" became foremost (1968, p. 478), and labor in a calling more and more existed only as an expression of a conscious striving for other-worldly salvation. As tools of God's will and His commandments, the faithful became alert, "ascetic saints."

> Puritan asceticism . . . worked to render the devout capable of calling forth, and then acting upon . . . those motives that . . . , through the practice of asceticism itself, [could be] "trained" against the "emotions.". . . The goal was to be able to lead an alert, conscious, and self-aware life. Hence, the destruction of the spontaneity of the instinct-driven enjoyment of life constituted the most urgent task. (pp. 116–17; see also 1968, pp. 572–73)

A qualitative distinction must be made, Weber maintains repeatedly, between this methodical-rational organization of life on the one hand and the frame of mind of the lay Catholic rooted in a "series of isolated actions," the Lutheran's penitent humility and inward-oriented mood of piety, and the common "affirmation of the world" typical of all utilitarian, means-end rational activity on the other hand (pp. 72–73, 78–80, 112–14, 121–23).

Although work had also been elevated in an earlier epoch to the center of life and had become empowered comprehensively to rationalize action, these developments in the seventeenth century took place in a qualitatively new fashion. A wide-ranging organization of life had characterized medieval monks; however, these *other-worldly* ascetics lived in monasteries "outside the world" unlike the Puritans who, engaged in earning a livelihood in commerce, trade, and other endeavors, lived "in the world." Nevertheless, owing to their ultimate focus on God's laws and salvation in the next life, their values belonged "beyond" the workaday world—namely, to the religious realm. They acted *in* the world in a methodical and ethical manner, yet their lives neither emanated from terrestrial concerns nor were they lived *for* them, Weber insists (pp. 115, 139–40; 1968, p. 549). The workaday life was devalued in comparison to the next life .[28]

Still, because "this world" constituted the arena both for impersonal service to God's glory and for activity capable of testifying to the believer's elect salvation status, routine conduct in general acquired a far greater focus and intensity than sheer utilitarian action.[29] It became enveloped in a religious halo (pp. 77–78; see 1968, p. 543).

> The special life of the saint—fully separate from the "natural" life of the flesh—could no longer play itself out in monastic communities set apart from the world. Rather, the devoutly religious must now live saintly lives *in* the world and amidst its mundane affairs. This *rationalization* of the organized and directed life—now in the world yet still oriented to the supernatural—was the effect of ascetic Protestantism's *concept of the calling.* (p. 140; emph. in orig.; see also pp. 116–17, 249; 1968, pp. 546, 578)

In this context Weber cites a maxim from the sixteenth-century German mystic, Sebastian Frank: "*Every* Christian must now be a monk for an entire lifetime" (p. 118).

Indeed, because the devout could acquire a psychological certainty of salvation only in an ethical *surpassing* of the utilitarian calculations of everyday routines, Weber holds that there has "perhaps . . . never been a more intense form of religious valuation of moral *action*" (p. 114; see p. 296; 1968, p. 498). A great "activism" characterized this asceticism, he argues: As instruments of an ethical and commanding Deity, believers were obligated consistently to carry God's laws *into* the practical activities of everyday life; they must transform—even revolutionize—its haphazard events to conform with His commandments. God's glory deserved nothing less than this "mastery of the world" (*Weltbeherrschung*) on behalf of His sacred aims: "The genuine Christian . . . wished to be nothing other than a tool of his God; for here he exclusively sought his dignity. And because this is what he wished to be, he was a useful instrument to transform and master the world rationally" (see p. 289).

Firmly grounded in this-worldly asceticism, the methodical-rational organization of life—"the Protestant ethic"—contributed in these ways to the initiation and completion of two tasks Weber believes of utmost historical centrality: the banishment of the traditional economic ethic and a "co-participation" in the formation and expansion of the spirit of capitalism. These themes capture our attention after a brief summary of Puritan asceticism's "style of life."

The Puritan Style of Life: This-Worldly Asceticism.   PE's last chapter clarifies how wealth, profit, competition, upward mobility, and methodical work all acquired a further providential meaning with the expansion of the Protestant ethic. Weber also outlines here a distinctly Puritan frame of mind and style of life.

People engaged in business and oriented to profit were now, as the Protestant ethic spread across several nations, no longer scorned as calculating, greedy, and self-interested actors; rather, they became perceived by others as honest employers engaged in a task given by God. A good conscience was bestowed upon them, even those engaged in hard competition (pp. 146, 154). Similarly, the reinvestment of profit and surplus income signified loyalty to God's grand design and an acknowledgment that all riches emanated from the hand of this omnipotent Deity. Because believers viewed themselves as merely the earthly trustees of goods awarded by their Divinity, all wealth had to be utilized on behalf of *His* purposes only—that is, to build the affluent kingdom that would praise His glory (pp. 150–52).

Hence, the devout practiced frugality, restricted consumption (especially of luxury goods), and saved in large quantities. A preference to live modestly characterized the Puritan outlook, for to indulge desires would weaken the required focus upon God's will, the faithful knew. Although wealth was now created on a large scale, its enjoyment became "morally reprehensible," and the pursuit of an ostentatious mode of living became perceived as obstructing the goal of creating in His honor the righteous kingdom on earth. The search for riches as an end in itself, and all avarice and covetousness, became strictly prohibited (pp. 142, 150–52).

Furthermore, the appropriate demeanor must accompany these modest living habits: reserve, self-control, respectability, and dignity. All deep affectual ties to others, which would only compete with the more important allegiance to God, must be avoided. After all, the emotions were of no relevance to the all-important "certainty of salvation" question, the Puritans knew. On the contrary, indispensable was an alert and cerebral monitoring and directing of action. Continuous activity—not leisure and enjoyment—increased the majesty of God. And an unwillingness to work, or a lapse into begging, assumed now a providential meaning,[30] as did the believer's use of time—for "every hour not spent at work is an hour lost in service to God's greater glory" (p. 142–43). "Time is money" and it must not be "wasted." The "responsible" person of "good moral character" now appeared (pp. 142–44, 150).

Finally, owing to the Puritan perception of the feudal aristocracy as lacking an orientation to God and hence as decadent, the purchase of noble titles and an imitation of the manorial lifestyle, as common among the nouveaux riches in sixteenth and seventeenth century Europe, could not appeal to these sincere believers. This "feudalization of wealth" precluded the reinvestment of profits in a business and further pulled persons away from an orientation to God. Property, the Puritans knew, must be used alone for purposes of production and to increase wealth (pp. 146, 152–53; 1968, p. 1200).

Taken together, these features constitute the Puritan "life outlook" and "style of life" of the seventeenth century:

> Rejected are all vain glorification of the self and of all other things of the flesh, feudal pride, the spontaneous enjoyment of art and life, "levity," all waste of money and time, eroticism, or any other activity that detracts from the rational work in one's private vocation and within the God-willed social order. The curtailment of all feudal ostentation and of all irrational consumption facilitates capital accumulation and the ever-renewed utilization of property for productive purpose. . . . (1968, p. 1200)

When combined with the methodical-rational organization of life rooted in this-worldly asceticism, this style of life comprised the Protestant ethic's uniqueness, Weber maintains. A new "type of person" now appeared forcefully on the stage of Western history: temperate, dispassionate, restrained. This "modern ethos" both uprooted economic traditionalism and stood at the source of the spirit of capitalism, he contends (see pp. 142–46, 447).

III. FROM *THE PROTESTANT ETHIC* TO THE SPIRIT OF CAPITALISM AND MODERN CAPITALISM: WEBER'S ANALYSIS

The Opposition to the Traditional Economic Ethos

As noted, age-old, obdurate economic traditionalism could be banished, according to Weber, only by patterns of action qualitatively more systematic and intense than utilitarian action oriented exclusively to economic interests and profit-making. After all, trade, commerce, and the pursuit of wealth have existed universally, he reasons. Entrepreneurial astuteness and "business savvy," as well as all intelligent modes of making one's way in the world (*Lebensklugheit*), can be found in every epoch and civilization. All of these endeavors were rooted in pragmatic and sustained goal-oriented activities. Nonetheless, the traditional economic ethic was uprooted only rarely. And even charismatic adventure capitalists, who can be found universally also, failed to cause its weakening (pp. 71–72, 75–76, 208).

Weber insists that the Puritan anchoring of methodical orientations toward work, wealth, competition, and profit in the *certitudo salutis* question proved significant. The concerted bestowing of religion-based psychological rewards upon vocational labor was alone endowed with the capacity to uproot the traditional economic ethic. The tenacity and "lasting resilience" (p. 82) of this *coherent group* of persons—Puritan employers and workers—must be acknowledged, he argues. The "internally binding" set of religious values that motivated work "from within," and the search for material success, introduced the "life organized around ethical principles."

This cohesive patterning of action confronted directly, and then replaced, economic traditionalism (p. 120, 120–23; see 76–80).

To Weber, the manifold ethical dimension that penetrated the Puritan's economic activity constituted a "revolutionary" force against economic traditionalism. It also forcefully called forth a spirit of capitalism.

From the Protestant Ethic to the Spirit of Capitalism

Carried by churches and sects, the Protestant ethic spread throughout many New England, Dutch, and English communities in the seventeenth century. Disciplined, hard labor in a calling marked a person as among the chosen, as did the wealth that followed from a steadfast adherence to Puritan values. This ethos was cultivated in entire regions in Benjamin Franklin's era one century later. However, its religion-based ethical component had become weaker with this expansion and transformed—namely, into an "ethos with a utilitarian accent" (pp. 71–72, 154–55, 157–58).

Weber refers to this ethos as the spirit of capitalism: a configuration of values that implied the individual's duty to view work as an end in itself, to labor systematically in a calling, to increase capital, to earn money perpetually (while avoiding enjoyment of it), and to comprehend material wealth as a manifestation of "competence and proficiency in a vocational calling" (p. 73). Adherents to this mode of organizing life, rather than perceived by others as among the saved, were believed to be community-oriented citizens of good moral character. Immediately recognizable, their stalwart demeanor no longer served to testify to firm belief and membership among the elect; it indicated instead respectability, dignity, honesty, and self-confidence.[31]

Franklin represented this spirit in *PE*. Business astuteness, utilitarian calculations, or greed fails to account for the *origin* of his disciplined life, Weber contends; legacies of ascetic Protestantism contributed substantially. Indeed, such an interpretation is confirmed by the presence of an ethical element in Franklin's manner of organizing and directing his life, Weber holds (pp. 71–73). Yet a conundrum here appears. How had the ethical dimension in the Protestant ethic, now shorn of its foundational salvation quest and "in but not of" the world components, survived into Franklin's era?

Long before the religious roots of ethical action had become weakened, the Puritan's ethical values had expanded beyond their original social carriers—ascetic Protestant churches and sects—to another carrier grouping: Protestant families. For this reason, these values remained central in childhood socialization *even* as Colonial America experienced a gradual loosening of the all-encompassing influence of these congregations. Parents taught children to set goals and organize their lives methodically, to be self-reliant and shape their own destinies as individuals, to behave in accord with ethical standards, and to work diligently. They encouraged children to pursue careers in business and see virtue in capitalism's open markets, to seek material success, to become upwardly mobile, to live modestly and frugally, to reinvest their wealth, to look toward the future and the "opportunities" it offers, and to budget their time wisely—just as Franklin had admonished in his writings (pp. 70–71). Families also stressed ascetic personal habits, hard competition, and the importance of honesty and fair play in business transactions. Through intimate, personal relationships,[32] children were socialized to conduct themselves in a restrained, dispassionate manner and to do so by reference to a configuration of guiding values.

In this way, action oriented toward values originally carried by ascetic Protestant sects and churches endured long after the weakening of these religious organizations. An orientation toward ethical action became cultivated also in community organizations, including schools. Protestantism's "sect spirit," now routinized into maxims, community norms, a particular demeanor, and familiar customs and traditions, continued to influence new generations; they remained integral in Franklin's America (see pp. 185–204; Nelson, 1973, pp. 98–99, 106-08). Yet the ancestry of this spirit of capitalism was not "this-worldly" but "other-worldly," Weber contends. The Protestant ethic constituted its heritage: ". . . the Puritan's sincerity of belief must have been the most powerful lever conceivable working to expand the view of life that we are here designating as the spirit of capitalism" (p. 152):

> One of the constitutive components of the modern capitalist spirit, and, moreover, generally of modern civilization, was the rational organization of life on the basis of the *idea of the calling*. It was born out of the spirit of *Christian asceticism*. (p. 157; emph. in original)

Having illustrated "the way in which 'ideas' become generally effective in history" (p. 96), *PE* now reaches its conclusion. Weber has traced the lineage of the spirit of capitalism and discovered significant nonutilitarian, nonpolitical, and noneconomic roots. A Protestant ethic had, *PE* affirms, "*co*-participated" in the formation of the spirit of capitalism (p. 97).[33] The realm of values had played a prominent causal role.

Modern Capitalism: The Decline Today of the Methodical-Rational Organization of Life and the Hegemony of Means-End Rational Action

Although Weber holds that his concern remains the spirit of capitalism's religious origins, a further theme unavoidably looms throughout *PE*: the sources of modern capitalism. Indeed, he addresses this theme directly in several passages in *PE*. Weber's articles in response to his critics do so even more (see pp. 435–48; 2001).

Ascetic Protestantism called forth the organized, directed life at the very root of today's "economic man," he contends (p. 153). As the "only consistent carrier" of a methodical-rational life *in* the world, the Puritans "created the suitable 'soul' for capitalism, the soul of the 'specialist in a vocation' " (2001, p. 73; see pp. 116–17, 157–58). The spirit of capitalism provided the "ethical style of life 'adequate' to the new capitalism" (2001, p. 95) and the "economic culture" that served as a legitimating foundation for modern capitalism. More generally, *an elective affinity* exists between the ethically rigorous devoutness of ascetic Protestants on the one hand and the "modern culture of capitalism" and "economic rationalism" on the other hand, he insists (p. 67; see 1968, pp. 479–80):

> [The] spirit of (modern) *capitalism* . . . finds its most adequate form in the modern capitalist company and, on the other hand, . . . the capitalist company discovers in this frame of mind the motivating force—or spirit—most adequate to it. (p. 80)

To Weber, the rational work ethic of Puritans, and their style of life generally, gave a strong boost to the development of modern capitalism:

> It is clear that this style of life is very closely related to the self-justification that is customary for bourgeois acquisition: profit and property appear not as ends in themselves but as indications of personal ability. Here has been attained the union of religious postulate and bourgeois style of life that promotes capitalism. (1968, p. 1200)

Indeed, the "significance [of the Protestant ethic] for the development of [modern] capitalism is obvious" (p. 151; see 1968, pp. 1200, 1206).[34] Puritanism had revealed the "psychological aspect of modern economic development" (2001, p. 72).

PE's last pages leap across the centuries in order briefly to survey a new theme: the "cosmos" of modern capitalism. In broad strokes and unforgettable passages, Weber briefly explores the fate today of "this-worldly" directed action and the life organized methodically by reference to a constellation of ethical values. The question of how we *can* live under modern capitalism preoccupied him for his entire life.

Firmly entrenched after the massive industrialization of the nineteenth century, "victorious capitalism" now sustains itself on the basis of *means-end rational* action alone, he argues. In this urban, secular, and bureaucratic milieu, neither Franklin's spirit nor the Protestant ethic's asceticism endow methodical work with subjective meaning. As these value configurations so significant at the birth of modern capitalism collapse and fade, sheer utilitarian calculations move to the forefront. Today, modern capitalism unfolds on the basis of an inescapable network of pragmatic necessities.

Whether employees or entrepreneurs, people born into this "powerful cosmos" are coerced to adapt to its market-based, functional exchanges in order to survive. The motivation to work in this "steel-hard casing" involves a mixture of constraint and means-end rational calculations. A "mechanical foundation" anchors the modern era, and "the idea of an 'obligation to search for and then accept a vocational calling' now wanders around in our lives as the ghost of beliefs no longer anchored in the substance of religion" (p. 124). In one of his most famous passages, Weber tersely captures the significant transformation at the level of subjective meaning and motives: "The

Puritan *wanted* to be a person with a vocational calling; we *must* be" (p. 157; emph. in original; see pp. 57–58, 447–48).

This new epoch ushers in a further *type of person*, he maintains. Intimately linked to capitalism's internal workings, the frame of mind of *the specialist* varies distinctly from that of the "cultivated man" of the eighteenth and early nineteenth centuries (see 1968, pp. 998–1002). Now lost, this era of the multitalented Wolfgang von Goethe (1749–1832) is longed for by many. Capitalism will not vanish, however, Weber maintains, and he mocks the many nostalgic thinkers of his day in Germany who expected a return to the past (p. 157), Moreover, material products today, owing to modern capitalism's oft-praised capacity to create high standards of living, acquire "an increasing and, in the end, inescapable power over people—as never before in history" (p. 158).

This theme connects directly to a theme familiar to us, one underlying the entire expanse of *PE*. Methodical-rational lives organized rigorously on the basis of internalized value configurations appeared with Puritanism's "ascetic saints." The devout tamed the *status naturae* and, owing to intense *belief*, severed their action from the firm grip of tradition on the one hand and all sheer utilitarian, "practical rational" orientations to given tasks on the other hand. The *directed* life replaced the life flowing to the beat of a random succession of events. The sincere faith of the devout—who lived *in* but not *of* the world—enabled these unusual and complex achievements, for their rigid focus upon God's decrees implied a firm guiding of activities by *ethical* values.

However, to Weber the more dignified life—the life directed comprehensively "from within" (1949, p. 18)—now appears endangered. Amid the dependency today of most persons upon a modern economy characterized by sweeping coercion, practical rationalism, impersonal exchange relationships, and narrow specialization, a cultivation on a broad societal scale of the life organized by reference to ethical values seems utopian. The person unified internally by core values—"the personality"—would soon disappear, Weber fears. Moreover, modern capitalism—this "grinding mechanism"—will "[determine] the way of ordering life ... with overwhelming force..., perhaps ... until the last ton of fossil fuel has burnt to ashes" (p. 157–58).[35]

This acknowledgment of his brief commentary upon capitalist societies today reveals Weber's analysis in *PE* as characterized by four discrete stages (see chart on the following page).

IV. *THE PROTESTANT ETHIC* AS AN EXAMPLE OF WEBER'S SOCIOLOGY

PE was written during sociology's infancy. Trained as an economic and legal historian, Weber began to call his research "sociological" only in the last third of his career. *Sociology* is never used in *PE*. He refers to this volume at

The Protestant Ethic and the Spirit of Capitalism: Stages of Weber's Analysis

	Period	Organization	Types of Action	Religious Belief
I. **Calvin**: Fatalism as result of doctrine of predestination	16th cen.	small sects	value-rational	yes
II. **Baxter**: The Protestant ethic (Puritanism)	17th cen.	churches and sects	value-rational (methodical this-worldly activity)	yes
III. **Franklin**: The spirit of capitalism	18th cen.	communities	value-rational[36] (methodical this-worldly activity)	no
IV. The **"specialist"**: capitalism as a "cosmos"	20th cen.	industrial society	means-end rational	no

"Powerful Lever" "Affinity" "Adequacy"

Adapted from Kalberg, "On the Neglect of Weber's *Protestant Ethic* as a Theoretical Treatise" (*Sociological Theory*; 1996, p. 63), with permission from the American Sociological Association.

times as an "essay in cultural history" and at other times as a "sketch" on the relationship between religious belief and conduct.

Nevertheless, central ingredients of his sociology of *interpretive understanding (Verstehen)* are apparent throughout *PE*. Among Weber's many works, *PE* offers perhaps the best and most vivid example of how he combines his major methodological tool, the *ideal type*, with his methodology of interpretive understanding designed to grasp subjective meaning (see 1949, pp. 42–45, 85–110; 1968, pp. 3–26). His research is driven by a wish to understand how social action, often viewed by observers as irrational, foolish, and strange, becomes plausible, "rational," and "meaningful" once its social context is understood (see Kalberg, 1998, 2003).

Several procedures in *PE* illustrate Weber's mode of conducting sociological research. Their brief examination now will assist comprehension of this classic volume and his sociology of interpretive understanding in general. His critics have frequently gone astray owing to their neglect, and misunderstanding, of his basic presuppositions and procedures.[37] Having reviewed his mode of research, we are prepared to examine "the Protestant Ethic debate."

* * *

Frame of Mind.   From vantage points of interest to him, Weber demarcates "frames of mind" (*Gesinnungen*) throughout *PE* as well as his sociology generally. As they relate to economic activity, he discusses the frames of mind of adventure capitalists, medieval entrepreneurs, feudal aristocrats, Puritan employers and workers, workers and employers immersed within economic traditionalism, and the patrician capitalists of the seventeenth century. The frames of mind of the Catholic, Lutheran, Pietist, and Puritan (Reformed Calvinists, Methodists, Baptists, and Quakers) faithful capture his main attention.

Weber articulates major components of each group's subjective meaning; how it occurs, for example, that Puritans view methodical work seriously and orient their entire lives accordingly. He attempts to understand the *meaningfulness* of systematic work to this group of people rather than to evaluate or judge it; he seeks to do so by investigating the motivations that underlie the rigorous work patterns of the faithful. Instead of referring to the unconscious, however, as a disciple of Freud would do, Weber attempts to comprehend how work becomes meaningful by analyzing the beliefs, and the psychological rewards they imply for specific conduct, of an ideal type—an unusually representative figure—of Puritanism, such as Baxter.

For this reason, he studies the historical-cultural context within which Puritan devotion crystallized: the sermons the devout heard, the Bible passages and doctrinal statements they read, and the character of their religious community. Indeed, in seeking to convey to his reader the frame of mind of these believers through this method of interpretive understanding, Weber avoids the domain of psychology proper. He also rejects, as explanatory concepts, national character, genetic makeup, innate disposition (greed and lust for gain), and developmental-historical laws. Economic and political interests must be considered, according to Weber, but they alone fail to offer adequate explanations for the Puritan's conduct and frame of mind. He attends repeatedly to the extent to which a particular frame of mind implies an uprooting of persons from the *status naturae* on the one hand and purely this-worldly, utilitarian calculations on the other—and an organization of life around ethical values.

Owing to its focus on arrays of specific groups and the motives of their members, this procedure avoids reference to the global concepts utilized in organic holism theorizing (society, community, tradition, modernity, particularism, universalism, evolution, or progress), all of which Weber finds too diffuse. His methodology also forcefully rejects an exclusive orientation to charismatic figures. Instead, he chooses an "intermediary" level of analysis between global concepts and "great men" theories of historical change: the varying subjective meaning of persons *in groups* as captured by ideal types and explored through interpretive understanding.

Case Studies. The task of sociology involves the causal explanation of specific cases, according to Weber, rather than the discovery of history's developmental tendencies or the formulation of general laws that predict future events. Even Weber's systematic treatise, *Economy and Society,* abjures any quest to discover general laws. Instead, it charts out empirically-based ideal types that, as heuristic tools, assist researchers to undertake causal analyses of specific cases of their choice (see 1949, pp. 56–57, 72–84; 1968, p. 10; Kalberg, 1994b, pp. 81–142; 2003a, pp. 145–47).

Weber offers a causal explanation for the rise of a particular case in *PE*: the spirit of capitalism. He attempts to identify its religious sources and persuade his readers, through both empirical documentation and logical argument, that these sources are plausible causes. In his terms, he seeks to demonstrate that the Protestant ethic constitutes an "adequate cause" for the spirit of capitalism.

Weber's orientation to causal explanations of specific phenomena is often neglected, not least because of the massive scale of the cases he chooses to investigate. For example, in his Economic Ethics of the World Religions volumes, he studies the origins of the caste system in India (1958; Kalberg, 1994b, pp. 177–92), the rise of monotheism in ancient Israel (1952; Kalberg, 1994a), and the rise of Confucianism in China (1951; Kalberg, 1994b, 1999).

The Influence of Culture. *PE* emphatically addresses one aspect of culture—religious belief—and its impact on economic activity. Even "purely" means-end rational action in reference to the laws of the market, Weber insists, possesses a cultural aspect. Market-oriented activity is played out not merely according to economic interests but also in reference to an economic culture, and work today in a vocation "carries with it an *ascetic* imprint" (p. 157; emph. in original). Yet this demarcation in *PE* of the cultural orientations of action that underlie and legitimate everyday activity occurs throughout Weber's sociology. He explores, for example, in addition to a broad array of economic cultures, a variety of political cultures "behind" the exercise of power (see, for example, pp. 412–15; 1968, pp. 980–94, 1381–1462; 2005, pp. 277–89; Kalberg, 1997, 2003a, 2003b) and an array of legal cultures that legitimate the orientations of persons to laws (see 1968, pp. 809–92).

Weber's cognizance of the causal capacity of culture is apparent as early as *PE*'s first chapter. The assumption that the *origins* of an economic ethic, whether traditional or modern, can be explained by reference to social structures—an "economic form"—is rejected. To him, as noted above, even identical external structures of extreme rigidity, such as those typical of religious and political sects, let alone those of the factory and the bureaucracy, fail to call forth homogeneous patterns of action. The Calvinist, Methodist, Pietist, Quaker, and Baptist sects and churches all advocated distinct doctrines, as did sects in India (see 1946e, p. 292) and believers oriented their lives accordingly. The same must be said, Weber is convinced, of strata and classes (pp. 86, 238–40, 469, note 24). Similarly, although he acknowledges the influence of institutions (such as schools, families, the state, the military) on action, he notes repeatedly how cultural contexts, often rooted in regional religious traditions, have an impact upon institutions (pp. 63–68, 84–85). This impact is so prevalent that, viewed comparatively, quite different patterns of action exercise heterogeneous influences even when they appear in institutions possessing similar structures.

Weber's articulation of the capacity of culture to shape social contexts also places his sociology in direct opposition to rational choice, neo-Marxist, and "economic man" theories. *PE*, as well as an array of his other writings, argues that sustained economic development, for example, whether occurring today in Asia, Latin America, or central Europe, is a complex process not moved along only by economic interests, market calculations, and wage incentives.

PE contends that a sociology oriented exclusively to economic and political interests, social structures, classes, power, organizations, or institutions is theoretically inadequate. The diverse ways in which cultural values form important contexts for conduct, albeit often obscure and scarcely visible, runs as a major thread throughout Weber's works.

The Interpenetration of Past and Present. He refuses in *PE* to take the immediate present as his point of reference. Indeed, his analysis rejects the idea of a disjunction between past and present and offers a host of examples that demonstrate their interwovenness. Weber emphasizes in *PE*, as well as in his sociological writings generally, that recognition of history's impact remains indispensable for an understanding of the present. Although possible, radical change, he concludes, is rare—despite his acknowledgment that heroic charismatic leaders may, given facilitating contexts, sever past and present abruptly (see 1968, pp. 1111–19). The past lives on into the present as an influential force even when massive transformations—urbanization, industrialization, secularization—occur: "That which has been handed down from the past becomes everywhere the immediate precursor of that taken in the present as valid" (1968, p. 29; transl. altered) In particular, the orientation of action to values often survives great structural metamorphoses, thereby linking past and present.

In general, Weber's "open" theoretical framework grounded in multitudes of specific groups, as captured by ideal types, and his position that the domains of religion, law, rulership, and the economy develop at uneven rates (pp. 86–88; see 1968), place his "view of society"—an array of multiple, dynamically interacting spheres, each potentially endowed with an autonomous causal thrust and unfolding along its own pathway—in opposition to other approaches. First, perspectives that elevate a single variable (such as class or the state) to a position of general causal priority are opposed, as are, second, all schools of thought that conceptualize social life by reference to sets of encompassing dichotomies (such as tradition-modernity, particularism-universalism, and *Gemeinschaft-Gesellschaft*). To Weber, these exclusive concepts exaggerate cross-epochal disjunctions and downplay the deep interlocking of past and present. Moreover, because to him very few significant developments from the past ever die out fully, he argues that a charting in the immediate present of economic and political interests on the one hand, or "system needs" and "functional prerequisites" on the other hand, can serve sociological analysis only in a preliminary, trial-and-error fashion (1968, pp. 14–18).[38] The past always permeates deeply into the present, even molding its core contours, according to Weber. His concepts "social carrier" and "legacy" illustrate how this penetration takes place.

The Linking of Past and Present: Social Carriers and Legacies. Weber's analysis of how the Protestant ethic survives—in secularized guise as a spirit of capitalism carried by families, schools, and communities—offers a vivid illustration of the way in which values and ideas from the past for him endure as legacies and influence the present. The crystallization of a new status group, organization, or class to cultivate and carry values and ideas is crucial if these values and ideas are to remain viable. Thus, rather than focussing on ideas and values alone, *PE* explores ideas and values *in reference to* the churches, sects, organizations, and strata that bear them. This theme also is found throughout Weber's sociology.

He especially emphasizes in *PE* how values and ideas either resonate with pastoral care practices in churches or else become transformed by pastors attentive to the "religious needs" of lay believers. A back-and-forth movement characterizes his analysis. Although they retain an autonomous capacity, values and ideas must become located in strong carrier groups to become effective. At times, just the sheer logical rigor and persuasiveness of ideas regarding salvation may *themselves* call forth values and a carrier group (see pp. 104, 118–19; Kalberg, 2001a). However, if they are to endure, even in these cases values and ideas must eventually stand in a relationship of elective affinity with the religious needs of members of a carrier group (see pp. 238–42).

In general, Weber is convinced that patterned action of every imaginable variety has arisen in every epoch and civilization. Nonetheless, he stresses that, if specific conduct is to become prominent in a particular milieu, cohesive and powerful social carriers for it must crystallize. Only then might its influence range across decades and centuries. As Weber notes: "Unless the concept 'autonomy' is to lack all precision, its definition presupposes the existence of a bounded group of persons which, though membership may fluctuate, is determinable" (1968, p. 699; transl. altered).

He defines a wide variety of carrier groups in *Economy and Society*. Regularities of action in some groupings can be recognized as firm, and carriers can become powerful in some cases; others fail to carry conduct forcefully and prove fleeting. Patterned action may fade and then, owing to an alteration of *contextual* patterns of action, acquire carriers and become reinvigorated, influential, and long-lasting. At times coalitions of carriers are formed; at other times carriers stand clearly in a relationship of antagonism to one another. The view of society that flows out of *Economy and Society*—as constructed from numerous competing and reciprocally interacting patterns of social action "located" in carrier groups—readily takes cognizance of the survival of certain conduct originating in the past and its significant influence, as a legacy, upon action in the present.

Weber often charts such legacies in the religion domain. He does so not only in regard to work in a vocation. In the United States, innumerable values, customs, and practices deriving from Protestant asceticism remain integral even today (see below, pp. 185–204). For example, the "direct democratic administration" by the congregation practiced in Protestant sects left a legacy crucial for the establishment of democratic forms of government, as did the unwillingness of sect members to bestow a halo of reverence upon secular authority (see p. 204).[39] The Pietists and baptizing sects in particular paved the way for political tolerance (see pp. 412–15, 510–11, note 129).

The Routinization and Sublimation of Motives, the Maxim of Unforeseen Consequences, and the Aim of Interpretive Understanding. Weber depicts the transformation from Franklin's spirit of capitalism to today's "victorious capitalism" as involving a *routinization* of the motives behind economic activity from value-rational to means-end rational. The alteration of motives in *PE* moves in the diametrically opposite direction when Weber emphasizes that great variation exists across Catholicism, Lutheranism, and ascetic Protestantism in the extent to which they *sublimated* the *status naturae*. Did religious doctrines call forth the methodical-rational organization of life among the faithful that tamed impulsive and spontaneous human nature?

Both the routinization and sublimation of motives prove pivotal in *PE*. However, a focus on the way in which motives for action vary across a spectrum, and the significance of this variation for the continuity of action and even for the *ethical* organization of life, as well for economic activity, stands at the foundation of Weber's entire sociology. Sociologists who wish to practice his method of interpretive understanding, he asserts, must be attuned to these distinctions.

Weber stresses in *PE*, as well as elsewhere in his works, that such shifts at the level of motivation are frequently unforeseen; they are often blatantly antagonistic to the intentions of persons at the beginning of the process. Surely Weber's Puritans, who worked methodically as a consequence of *other-worldly* considerations, would be appalled to see that their systematic labor and profit-seeking eventually led to levels of wealth threatening to their frugal and modest style of life oriented to God (pp. 153–54; 1968, p. 1200). Moreover, their great riches created a highly advanced technological universe anchored ultimately by laws of science based on empirical observation rather than by the laws of God and methodical-*ethical* conduct oriented to Him. A scientific world view, cultivated and developed by the modern capitalism that ascetic Protestantism helped to call into existence, opposes in principle—for it refuses to provide legitimacy to a "leap of faith"—all world views rooted in religion (see 2005, pp. 330–35, 337–38).

Finally, Weber emphasizes in *PE*, as well as throughout his sociology, that those born into today's "powerful cosmos," where pragmatic necessities and sheer means-end calculations reign, can scarcely imagine the actual contours of the religion-saturated world of the past. Even with the best of wills, "the modern person" can barely conceive of work in a vocation as motivated by that crucial query in the lives of the seventeenth-century devout: Am I among the saved (see p. 159; 2005, pp. 325–27)? The dominance today of radically different assumptions regarding typical motives for action obscures our capacity, Weber believes, to comprehend how conduct was differently motivated in the past. Indeed, to the detriment of their research, sociologists often unknowingly impose present-day assumptions on action in the past. An accurate understanding of subjective meaning is thereby precluded.

For this reason also, Weber calls for a sociology of interpretive understanding that seeks to comprehend "from within" the subjective meaning of persons through detailed investigation of *their* milieux of values, traditions, emotions, and interests. This procedure will extend the sociologist's capacity to grasp the meaning of action, he is convinced. Determined to comprehend human beings as "meaning-seeking creatures" (see Salomon, 1962, p. 393) and to understand how people in various epochs and civilizations endow their actions with meaning, Weber hopes that his method of interpretive understanding will be used in this expansive manner. Furthermore, he hopes that, through comparisons, the unique features and parameters of eras, civilizations, and distinct groupings will be isolated. Important insight will be gained in the process (see 2005, pp. 332–34).

As noted above, *PE* has often been misunderstood. The major contours of the durable "Protestant Ethic controversy" can be addressed only briefly.

V. THE PROTESTANT ETHIC DEBATE

Controversy surrounded *PE* immediately after its publication. While at time quiescent, generations of critics and defenders have debated vehemently "the Weber thesis" up to the present.[40] Arguably, no other volume in the social sciences in the English-speaking world has generated a more intense and long-term discussion.[41] As will become apparent, most of Weber's critics never mastered his complex argument.

Some commentators failed to see either the centrality of the *certitudo salutis* question or its powerful capacity—grounded in the doctrine of predestination, an Old Testament view of God, and pastoral care concerns—to give an impetus to religious development from Calvin to seventeenth-century Puritans. Others never acknowledged that conduct oriented to God's laws and disciplined work, despite the logical consequences of the doctrine of predestination, was understood by the Puritans as *testifying* (*sich bewähren*) to intense belief, which was believed to emanate originally from God. Many interpreters neglected Weber's analysis of how believers seek to serve God as His "tool"—and then to systematize to unusual degrees their entire lives around work, material contributions to His community, and His laws. Still others were unaware of the several ways the devout discovered signs of God's favoring hand, and the manner in which these signs motivated the organization and direction of their activity. Weber's early critics, as well as many later commentators, refused to take cognizance of his pivotal distinction between action guided by *values* and oriented to the supernatural, and other, basically utilitarian, action. Furthermore, Weber's analysis of how motivations for action, and even an unintended ethos, may arise through religious beliefs and practices, and how belief may further call forth psychological rewards that direct action, was often omitted from the commentary. Unfortunately, attention to a concern of no relevance to Weber was often emphasized: a salvation religion's official teachings and formal doctrines. The major themes of the controversy are adumbrated here in succinct form.[42]

"Weber Is an Idealist." Many commentators have argued that *PE* exaggerates the causal influence of religion. Some have seen an "idealistic determinism" (Tawney, 1930); others contend that the Protestant ethic arose out of capitalism and must be seen as an epiphenomenon of economic transformation. These critics have ignored Weber's own direct statement regarding the limitations of *PE*: ". . . it can not be, of course, the intention here to set a one-sided spirtualistic analysis of the causes of culture and history in place of an equally one-sided 'materialistic' analysis. *Both* are *equally possible*" (p. 159; emph. in original; see pp. 550–51, notes 142, 143). Commentators have also neglected his massive comparative studies on the uniqueness of the West (1927, 1968, 1951, 1952, 1958; see pp. 183–84), all of which attend *both* to "ideas" and "interests." This theme is addressed throughout Sections 2–4 of this volume.

"The Rise of Modern Capitalism Is Not Explained." A vast array of critics have misunderstood the aim of *PE*. They have comprehended this volume as designed to offer an analysis of the rise of modern capitalism—and then dismissed it as sorely incomplete. At this point the commentators divide into two groups. Some discover Puritanism (for example, in France or Hungary) yet conclude that its presence failed to introduce capitalism—thereby misunderstanding Weber's "more modest" aim. Other critics fault Weber for omitting the role of, for example, population changes, technological innovations, the discovery of the New World, the circulation of precious metals in a world economy, and the growth of the modern state and modern law. The Kiel historian of Germany and Holland, Felix Rachfahl (1867–1925), was the earliest critic to argue that *PE* had not explained the consequences of either the Protestant ethic or the spirit of capitalism for economic development. However, Weber states his more modest aim repeatedly:[43] as noted, he sought to examine the extent of religious influences upon the formation and expansion of the *spirit* of capitalism (p. 97; see also pp. 158–59).[44]

"Weber Misinterprets Doctrines." Church historians in particular have been critical of Weber's discussions of Catholic, Lutheran, and ascetic Protestant doctrines. Others have dissected John Calvin's teachings and failed to discover an emphasis upon work in a vocation. These latter scholars have failed to note Weber's distinction between Calvin's doctrines and the ascetic Protestantism of the sixteenth and seventeenth centuries. He locates the source of the Protestant ethic in the Puritanism of this latter period

rather than in Calvin's teachings, and he emphasizes the many revisions of Calvin's thought faith introduced by Baxter and the Puritan Divines. Moreover, Weber holds that Calvin recommended "steadfast " to believers rather than methodical work in a vocation (see pp. 110–11).[45]

"Capitalism Is Universal." Commentators frequently insisted that capitalism pre-dated Puritanism. They discovered it to be significantly widespread in the ancient and medieval worlds in the West, as well as in China and India. Although Weber maintaines that his main concern in *PE* involved the origins of a Protestant ethic and the extent of its influence upon the spirit of capitalism, capitalism's general origins, as discussed, are also of interest to him. His discussion of this theme, however, as noted, distinguishes sharply between modern capitalism on the one hand and political and adventure capitalism on the other hand. While the former arose only in the early modern West, the latter two types of capitalism appeared universally, he argues.

"Elongating and Relativizing the Weber Thesis." Many critics have expanded and relativized the Protestant ethic thesis: They have located the origin of the major groupings Weber attended to in much earlier epochs. Some discovered "Protestant asceticism: in medieval Catholicism—hence they argued that it predated Puritanism and constituted its foundation. At this point, however, the critics neglected Weber's distinction between Puritanism's "this-wordly" asceticism and the medieval monk's "other-worldly" asceticism. Others located a "capitalist spirit" much earlier than did *PE* and emphasized its capacity to mold the evolution of Puritanism. Weber contends that these critics equated his definition of the spirit of capitalism with the charisma of great "adventure" and "political" capitalists (see next paragraph). Against this school of "relativizing critics" he also maintains that a weakening of economic traditionalism did not itself imply the birth of either a Protestant ethic or a spirit of capitalism.

"Fugger and Alberti Carried a Spirit of Capitalism." A long list of critics have maintained that the great medieval entrepreneur Jacob Fugger and the Renaissance thinker Leon Battista Alberti possessed a spirit of capitalism essentially similar to Benjamin Franklin's. These commentators further held that the spirit of capitalism blossomed forth exclusively out of practical interests and utilitarian business astuteness. A religious source must be seen as both superfluous and historically inaccurate, they insisted.

In endnotes added in 1919 to *PE*, Weber counters this attack by repeating and elaborating upon his defense against the "relativizing" critics. While noting that Alberti and Fugger had accommodated to, rather than changed, the economic conditions of their time, Weber insists that the central issue here involves a distinction—pivotal for him yet unacknowledged by the critics—between means-end rational action on the one hand and value-rational action oriented to a testifying to belief on the other hand. Motives vary, he emphasizes, and the "practical-rational" approach to life is not dominant in all groupings in all historical epochs (see p. 216).

The ways in which values may motivate action was neglected by this commentary, he maintains. Indeed, a *methodical* aspect—an element indispensable for the birth of the spirit of capitalism—was *alone* introduced by action oriented to values, Weber holds. He discovers its source in the Protestant ethic. Moreover, this constellation of values proved central in a further, also unacknowledged, manner: At the foundation of this-worldly asceticism and a methodical-rational organization of life, it alone manifested the systematic intensity requisite for a shattering of the traditional economic ethic. Finally, through the spirit of capitalism, it placed into motion a significant push toward modern capitalism.

These critics neglected, in other words, *PE*'s emphasis upon the ways in which—owing to certain circumstances related to religious belief, the certainty of salvation question, and the necessity among the devout to testify to their own salvation in their vocational callings—motives became fundamentally altered and, in reference to values held dear, *intensified*. Sanctified activities must be distinguished from utilitarian endeavors just for this reason, Weber argues: They are oriented beyond the realm of pragmatic considerations to large and crucial questions that concern one's destiny in the next life and relationship to the supernatural arena. The *PE* analysis, and its particular *psychological* dimension, cannot be fully comprehended without an acknowledgement that motives, in this manner, are sociologically significant. This response by Weber relates directly to a further frequent criticism of *PE*.

"Anxiety Is Too Thin a Thread." Further critics have summarized the Protestant Ethic thesis in a manner that reduced drastically its subtlety and complexity. The most frequent commentary in this regard understood Weber's answer to his query—the religious origins of the motivation to work methodically in a vocational calling—as one that focussed exclusively upon the overwhelming anxiety and uncertainty caused by the Predestination doctrine. Work, it was held, constitutes a mechanism to address this severe anxiety (p. 111); it effectively focusses energy upon tasks given by God and hence away from anxiety regarding one's personal salvation. Commentators then asked Weber *how work* became elevated to the forefront. His putative main answer—work alleviates anxiety—has been criticized as obscure, doubtful, and incomplete. Anxiety must be seen as too thin a thread, they then insisted, to explain the Protestant ethic's origin.

However, this manner of summarizing *PE*'s argument left out too much. It omitted one of Weber's crucial points: He sought to provide an explanation for the origins of *an ethos*, that is, a "Puritan style of life." Moreover, the critics neglected the ways in which a *variety* of motives stand at the center of his analysis and the context that as, Weber stresses, sanctified work: an omnipotent, omniscient, and wrathful God possessed an array of specific wants and wishes. They omitted also his crucial distinction between these wishes and the essential revisions undertaken by Baxter and other Puritan Divines, all of which enable believers in search of the *certitudo salutis* to move beyond their anxiety and to engage in the sanctified action that constituted to them a *sign* of membership among the elect.

Furthermore, the critics omitted discussion of the entire psychological dynamic that first pulled the devout away from the *status naturae* on the one hand and utilitarian activities on the other hand. This dynamic awarded premiums to work, profit, wealth, virtuous conduct, and the conviction by the faithful—God is "operating within"—that called forth this-worldly asceticism, the methodical-rational organization of life, and the Puritan style of life. Finally, the critics ignored that which, according to Weber, distinguishes ascetic Protestant believers: They live *in* but not *of* the world. For this reason, as noted, a "natural" mode of living is reversed, indeed to such an extent that a trajectory toward this-worldly asceticism is then placed into motion. The anxiety of the faithful plays only a limited part in Weber's multifaceted argument.

In sum, a dynamic and multidimensional tapestry characterizes the *PE* analysis. Anxiety must be understood as comprising a single link on the complex pathway that elevated work in a vocation and the search for wealth to the center of believers' lives.

"Historians Versus Sociologists." PE has been discussed in depth, and and for generations, by historians and sociologists alike. From this commentary, clear disciplinary patterns have emerged.

A preference for the empirically-testable statement, and a dislike for the sociologist's typical attention to patterns within and across large groups, has been manifest among historians. In generally focussing upon *PE*'s discrete points, they have faulted Weber either for inappropriately selecting his sources or failing to offer adequate empirical evidence. His use of a construct—the ideal type—to investigate a single case has been met with massive criticism. The generalizations Weber formed on the basis of this heuristic tool have been uniformly greeted with suspicion; exceptions to his "broad strokes" have been frequently discovered. His "errors" have then been utilized as evidence to refute his general position. In addition, many historians have failed to appreciate that Weber's study addressed the question of the origins of *modern* capitalism rather than of capitalism as such.

Sociologists, denigrated by historians as unqualified to assess Weber's research, fall at the other end of the spectrum. They have often avoided serious evaluation of Weber's specific points and focused instead upon *PE* as a treatise that provides a provocative "modernization theory."[46] Moreover, sociologists have too frequently addressed criticisms by historians regarding particular aspects of Weber's research by noting, first, their unawareness of his related comparative project on the economic ethics of world religions, and second, their misunderstanding—or rejection—of his ideal type-based methodology and interpretive sociology of subjective meaning. Weber's classic investigation starkly deomonstrates that these two camps lack a common ground. Marshall saw at this point a clear message: ". . . sociology and history must move forward together—or not at all" (1982, pp. 10–12, 133–40, 170–73).

In sum, Weber's many critics have often misunderstood and simplified his analysis.[47] Despite regular indictments, "the Weber thesis" survives to this day and must be confronted by scholars seeking to understand the rise of modern capitalism in the West. "[*PE*] has lost nothing of its power to fascinate" (Lichtblau and Weiss, 1993a, p. vii). Indeed, its reception has expanded over the last forty years beyond Germany, the United States, England, France, and Italy and now extends throughout Asia. Arguably, it remains "the most famous and widely read [text] in the classical canon of sociological writing" (Chalcraft, 2001, p. 1). The influence of *PE* has been manifest both through its generation of studies that seek directly to test the Weber thesis and its capacity to stimulate a wide variety of research.[48]

VI. THE INFLUENCE OF *THE PROTESTANT ETHIC*

Of the empirical investigations that have sought directly to test Weber's conclusions, Gordon Marshall's study of seventeenth-century Scotland has been by far the most ambitious and impressive. *Presbyteries and Profits* (1980) examined on the one hand the exhortations of Scottish "pastoral theologians." They advocated, he discovered, a mode of organizing life that placed at the center this-worldly asceticism, a monitoring of one's use of time, and systematic work in a calling. On the other hand, Marshall investigated the "economic practices and beliefs" of a variety of capitalists in Scotland. An ethos "of at least sections of the Scottish business community" identical to Weber's "spirit of capitalism" was apparent (1980, p. 221). On the basis of massive archival data, Marshall concluded: ". . . we have demonstrated an 'elective affinity' between the ethic of Scottish Calvinism and that of Scottish capitalist enterprise during [the seventeenth century] (1980, p. 222).[49]

Three recent empirical studies also confirm Weber's thesis (see Kaelber, 2005). In his investigation of Colonial America, James Henretta identified a "Protestant ethic" and then, several generations later, a "spirit of capitalism." The biographies of merchants, he contends, provide evidence for the existence of a religion-based calling, indeed one that introduced a methodical orientation toward business and profit (Henretta, 1993, pp. 327ff). Similarly, in her investigation of Welsh immigrants in Ohio, Anne Kelly Knowles documented widespread entrepreneurial activities rooted in ascetic Protestantism. She discovered as well substantive constraints in this community that dictated frugal, modest, and unostentatious behavior (Knowles, 1997). Finally, in their study of Joseph Ryder, a successful merchant capitalist in Leeds in the eighteenth century, Margaret Jacob and Matthew Kadane found Weber's "three key features of ascetic Protestantism—diligence in a spiritual and vocational calling, making use of one's time, and material asceticism" (2003, p. 24). Ryder's extreme monitoring of his behavior on behalf of an avoidance of sin was combined with a methodical orientation toward economic opportunities. However, his accumulation of worldly goods remained subordinate to, and never threatened, his spiritual concerns (2003, pp. 25–28, 42–44).

PE, however, has been widely influential in a further manner; it has stimulated a broad array of investigations across the social sciences throughout the twentieth century. A daunting task will confront the scholar who attempts to chart out its far-reaching impact. Indeed, it may be "virtually im-

possible to catalogue the entire range of 'Protestant ethic' scholarship"
(Swatos and Kivisto, 2005, p. 113). Chalcraft affirms this point: "Every year
sees new contributions in various fields and it would undoubtedly take a
lifetime to become fully conversant with all the literature germane to *PE*"
(2001, p. 2; see Eisenstadt, 1968, p. 3).[50]

PE's influence upon the "development and modernization" literature
can scarcely be underestimated. As Bryan Turner has noted, "Weber's classic study . . . to a large extent has defined the nature of the historical sociology of capitalism."[51] Of course, the "dialogue" on the "rise of modern
capitalism" occurred for the most part in reference to Marxism and
neo-Marxism (see Antonio and Glassman, 1985). *PE*'s opposition to such
schools was supported by American structural-functionalists of the 1940s
and 1950s, all of whom understood their emphasis upon the role played by
values in "modernization processes" as deriving directly from Weber's research (see Parsons, 1966, 1971; Bellah 1985). Many insisted that the absence
of "functional equivalents" of the Protestant ethic in Asian and Latin American nations accounted for slow economic development in these regions.[52]
Later Marxist-oriented, "world systems" sociologists, many of whom focused upon questions of economic development in Latin America (see
Frank, 1967; Wallerstein, 1989), continued the critical dialogue with *PE*.
"Globalization" theorists, whether leaning more toward a neo-Marxist approach or focusing more upon the influence of new technologies, also have
carried on a dialogue with *PE*'s emphasis upon values and ideas. The
sweeping analyses by David Landes (1998) and Claudio Veliz (1980) have
defended a Weberian position.

However, *PE* has generated research far beyond immutable questions involving the strength of economies and the direction of their development.
In a classic study, Robert Merton discovered that Puritan groupings in the
seventeenth century offered a milieu particularly conducive to the development of science and new technologies (Merton, 2001; see Borkenau,
1934). Catholic-Protestant differences have been investigated in a vast array of studies, including ones on voting behavior, levels of education, and
rates of occupational mobility. In all cases, *PE* has stood explicitly or implicitly in the background (see Yinger, 1957; Lenski, 1963). Benjamin Nelson, a
distinguished polymath and scholar of Weber's work, called attention to
the Protestant background of American entrepreneurs:

> He who would write the history of the "Protestant ethic" in the United States
> would be obliged to devote many sections to such notable figures as John D.
> Rockefeller, Sr., Henry Ford, Frederick Taylor,. . . and many others. . . . The
> underlying motif in the life and work of these men was to drive toward the
> fullest rationalization of conduct and organization so as to generate the
> greatest possible outputs of incomes over losses and costs. The men above
> named are paradigms of the Protestant ethic in action. (Nelson, 1973, pp.
> 107–08; see also p. 110).[53]

A less orthodox view of American society—its development in more recent years toward mass consumption and a generalized "McDonaldization"—flows directly out of *PE*'s last chapter (see Ritzer, 1998, pp. 4, 77–78, 164).

PE, described by Daniel Bell as "probably the most important sociological work of the twentieth century" (1996, p. 287), must be understood as Weber's earliest attempt to understand the multiple origins of the modern world. The acknowledged complexity of this research project required him to utilize, at the beginning of his investigations, a delimited framework only. A single theme captured his attention: the possible causal role played by religious values. Hence, from the outset, Weber recognized *PE* as incomplete (p. 159). Nonetheless, he insisted that "this side" of his project must be given its due. Attention to interests—the "other side" of his broadranging endeavor—captures our attention in Section 4. Before addressing this large theme, we turn to Weber's analysis of American ascetic Protestantism in Section 2 and his discussion of the economic ethics of "the world religions East and West" in Section 4.

Endnotes

I would like to thank Lutz Kaelber and Robert J. Antonio for helpful comments on this introduction.

1. Weber uses *Puritan, ascetic Protestantism,* and the *Protestant Ethic* in a fundamentally equivalent manner. See, for example, 1968, p. 1198. He clarifies his broad use of *Puritan* on several occasions. It includes, on the one hand, even the seventeenth-century poet John Milton, for he also "[rationally oriented his] practical life to God's will" (see p. 489, n. 15), and on the other hand, "the religious movements oriented toward asceticism in Holland and England, and without distinctions regarding a church's organizational agenda and dogma" (p. 486, n. 5). Germany's "ascetic Pietists" are also included (see pp. 125–30). *PE*'s concluding chapter (pp. 141–59) constructs Puritanism as an amalgam of the Calvinist (Presbyterian), Methodist, Baptist, and Quaker churches and sects.

2. Thus, as a matter of course, newly introduced persons in the United States quickly query one another regarding the type of work each does. Elsewhere, in contrast, it is generally considered rude to turn the topic of conversation to work immediately after an introduction.

3. Juliet Schor's book (1992) illustrates the endurance of the ascetic Protestant heritage in dozens of ways. See also Hochschild (1990) and Kalberg (1992).

4. See p. 535 (note 54); see also the Protestant sects essays below, pp. 200–20.

5. Weber fairly frequently returns in later writings to arguments formulated originally in *PE*. At times his points are more clearly rendered in the later texts. When this occurs, reference to the later relevant passage is provided.

6. Weber uses "rational" in many ways. This usage—indicating a systematic, or methodical, aspect—is frequent. The term does not imply "better" or "superior" (see Kalberg, 1980).

7. The commentary upon *PE* has frequently insisted that capitalism pre-dated seventeenth century Puritanism. On this point, argued originally by his critic

Rachfahl in 1909, Weber acknowledged his failure in *PE*'s 1904–05 version to emphasize clearly his interest in the origins of *modern* capitalism. See Weber's response to Rachfahl (2001, pp. 55–61, 85 [notes 34 and 36]). His 1919 revisions frequently add "modern" in front of "capitalism." However, he is not thorough in doing so; when appropriate "modern" has been added in brackets.

8. Following Weber, the terms *modern economic ethic, rational economic ethic,* and *spirit of capitalism* will be used as synonyms. *Ethos* and *ethic* are also synonymous terms.

9. Weber's critics past and present have attacked this position repeatedly. See pp. 44–45.

10. In order to strengthen his argument against Sombart, Weber significantly expanded the endnotes on this theme in his 1920 revisions. These endnotes are marked. In a letter to Sombart in 1913, Weber states: "... *perhaps not a word* is correct [in your book] concerning Jewish religion" (see Scaff, 1989, p. 203n.). On Sombart and Weber generally, see Lehmann (1987, 1993), Riesebrodt (2005, pp. 37–38), and Chalcraft (2005).

11. See also, for example, 1968, pp. 70, 341, 480, 630; 2001, pp. 35, 75; Otsuka (1976). Sombart supported also this Marxian analysis. Weber's rejection in *PE* of "developmental laws" (or "laws of economic development") as explanations for historical change is directed against Marx, though also against an array of German and English scholars.

12. These themes are rarely dicussed in *PE*. They appear in numerous passages throughout Weber's other writings (see, for example, 1927, pp. 352–54; 1968, p. 1180; 1972, pp. 118–21, 131 [note 26]; see Otsuka 1976, pp. 86–90; Kalberg 1994b, pp. 153–54). His rejection of such causal forces as alone adequate constitutes a foundational point of departure also for his Economic Ethics of the World Religions series (see pp. 183–84).

13. These positions were central in the debate on the origin of modern capitalism during Weber's time. In *PE* he also argued against minor streams in this ongoing controversy (especially in the endnotes added in 1920), such as Karl Lamprecht's biology-based evolutionary determinism (p. 512, note 133), all proponents of "national character" (p. 95), the many theorists who understood social change as resulting from changes in laws, and, finally, Hegelians who viewed ideas as causal forces. The crucial questions are neglected, Weber insists, by Hegelians. Did *social carriers* crystallize to bear the ideas? Did they exist as cognitive forces only? Or did ideas also place "psychological rewards" upon action? See note 25 below; pp. 102, 238–97; Kalberg, 2001a.

14. A pamphlet written in 1887 by Weber's uncle, the Reformation and Counter-Reformation historian Hermann Baumgarten, who was very close to his nephew, notes this theme in a vivid passage: "Where Protestants and Catholics live together, the former occupy predominantly the higher, the latter the lower rungs of society. . . . Where the Catholic population flees higher education or cannot attain it, the Protestants must inevitably gain a considerable lead in public administration, justice, commerce, industry, and science" (Marcks 1894, p. 16).

15. Weber deleted this remark when he revised *PE* in 1919. It appeared originally in the second installment (1905) of *PE* (see Weber, 2002, p. 155).

16. Chapter 1 of *PE* borrows its title, "Religious Affiliation and Social Stratification," from Offenbacher's book.

17. On the background to the writing of *PE*, see Poggi (1983); Roth (1992); Nipperdey (1993); Lichtblau and Weiss (1993a); Lehmann and Roth (1993); Schluchter and Graf (2005); Lehmann (2005, pp. 1–7, 21–22). Weber's interest in this theme extends at least back to a lecture course offered in 1898.

18. Weber resists quantification of this influence (see pp. 152, 448; see note 34 below). For his restatement of this aim at the end of *PE*, see pp. 122–23. See also pp. 159, 71–72, 74, 86–88, 102. See further the numerous statements in the essays in response to his early critics where he restates his goal in *PE* (2001, pp. 70, 74, 76, 95; see below, pp. 436–38). Many of these passages illustrate Weber's awareness of the multiplicity of causes for historical developments, as well as of the necessity to view single factors contextually (see Kalberg, 1994b, pp. 39–45, 98–102, 168–76). Fischoff's formulation on Weber's aim is succinct: "Weber's limited thesis was merely that in the formation of this pattern of rationally ordered life, . . . the religious component must be considered an important factor" (1944, p. 63).

19. This is nearly a literal rendering of Weber's passage below at p. 97.

20. A problem with the predestination double decree did not exist for Calvin, who considered himself among the elect (pp. 110–11).

21. Hence, Weber emphasizes that his concern is Calvin*ism* and not Calvin's personal views (see p. 489, note 11). Legions of theologian critics have misunderstood Weber on this point.

22. Although Weber's analysis does seek to establish the psychological presuppositions that led to the formation of the Protestant ethic, it never intends to unveil general psychological postulates or rules, as will become apparent. Moreover, his psychology abjures a Freudian foundation of any sort (see 1978, pp. 383–388). Rather, it is always grounded in *historical* changes—in this case transformations unique to the European sixteenth and seventeenth centuries.

23. As will be noted later, these themes are intertwined.

24. Zaret offers examples from the writings of several Divines. See 1993, pp. 252–53.

25. Weber is firm on this point. (See the Glossary entry "psychological motivations.") He maintains, especially against his critics Sombart and Brentano, that his argument does not revolve around "what was theoretically or officially *taught* in the ethical manuals of the time" or the codifications of rules for appropriate conduct" by writers on ethics (p. 102). Weber wishes to identify which rules, because infused with *salvation* rewards, become "psychologically effective" (p. 486, note 7; see p. 500, note 63). In other words, his interests lie not in the admonitions contained in the theological doctrines and texts or their "correct" exegetical interpretation; rather, Weber's focus remains upon the ways in which doctrines place psychological rewards on certain conduct and even, in some cases, upon a comprehensive organization of life. The commentary upon *PE* by theologicans in particular has seldom grasped this focus.

26. We "moderns" must here avoid superimposing our views upon the sixteenth century. Methodical work today is viewed as part and parcel of our daily lives; that is, as "normal." Weber would argue, however, that this habitus is itself in part a residual of the Protestant ethic (pp. 102, 159).

27. These differences of intensity and degree vis-à-vis Calvinist "world mastery" are extremely diverse, Weber emphasizes, and cannot be explored here. Owing to its emphasis upon feelings, Pietism (although clearly cultivating asceticism) stands for him as the most divergent case. See pp. 124, 128. On Methodism on feelings, and comparisons to Calvinism, see p. 131.

28. Weber here refers to inner-worldly asceticism as "Janus-faced" (*Doppelgesicht*): to focus on God and the question of salvation, a turning *away* from the world and even rejection of this random, "meaningless, natural vessel of sin" (see, e.g., 1968, p. 542) was indispensable. On the other hand, on behalf of ethical values and the creation on earth of God's kingdom, a turning *toward* the world and its mastery was necessary (see 1946a, p. 327). This Janus-faced character of action itself bestowed a methodicalness that separated this sanctified action from action motivated by sheer economic interests, as well as practical concerns generally. See below.

29. "Only in the Protestant ethic of vocation does the world, despite all its creaturely imperfections, possess unique and religious significance as the object through which one fulfills his duties by rational behavior according to the will of an absolutely transcendental God" (1968, p. 556).

30. The devout understood an "unwillingness to work [as] a sign that one is not among the saved" (p. 143). Those living in poverty could not possibly be among the saved (pp. 146; 546; note 117). Being poor now indicated not laziness alone but also a poor *moral* character. In this context, Weber notes, "charity becomes an impersonal operation of poor-relief for the greater glory of God" (1968, p. 1200).

31. The origins of the American emphasis on honesty and candor toward all as a central aspect of "good character," to be manifested both in personal conduct and even in the political realm (as an ideal), must be sought here. For the Puritan, righteous conduct that testified to one's elect status emanated ultimately from God's strength *within* the believer (see p. 112)—and He could not be other than honest. For the same reason, persons speaking to Puritans would not dare speak dishonestly.

32. Weber argues that the teaching of *ethical* values, if it is to occur, necessarily involves a strong personal bond. See, for example, pp. 426–30; 1927, pp. 357–58; 1946a, p. 331; 1968, pp. 346, 585, 600.

33. That Weber acknowledges the existence of other origins of this spirit is apparent. See pp. 97, 550, notes 138, 142; 2001, pp. 32, 95–96.

34. "[The effect of] the stricture against consumption with this unchaining of the striving for wealth [led to] *the formation of capital* . . . which became used as *investment* capital. . . . Of course, the strength of this effect cannot be determined exactly in quantitative terms" (p. 152; emph. in original; see also p. 543, note 97).

35. This theme will be re-visited at various points throughout this volume.

36. Significantly, the value-rational action—the spirit of capitalism—of Franklin is oriented, as the Protestant ethic, *both* to individuals *and* to a community, while the means-end rational action of the individual entrapped within the "powerful cosmos" of industrial capitalism is oriented merely to the individual's survival. For recent discussions of this significant shift, see Bellah (1985), Etzioni (1996), Hall and Lindholm (1999), Putnam (2000), and Kalberg (1997, 2001b).

37. Fischoff notes that commentators on Weber's *PE* "almost universally disregarded" the "massive later work on the general theme of the sociology of religion, which in many respects constitutes a supplement and correction of the earlier work" (1944, p. 59).

38. The interweaving of past and present is a complex and important theme throughout Weber's writings. Unfortunately, it cannot be addressed in detail here. See Kalberg, 1994b, pp. 158–67; 1996, pp. 57–64; 2003a, pp. 164–68; 2008.

39. As did Lutheranism, Weber points out, in Germany (pp. 111–12; see 1968, p. 1198).

40. See the listing below of studies dedicated to this debate (pp. 455–56). Marshall's (1982) volume is by far the most ambitious.

41. Zaret calls this debate "the longest-running in modern social science" (see 1993, p. 245).

42. Themes will be our focus here rather than a discussion organized either chronologically or in terms of major players. The criticisms against Weber have been ordered differently by Sprinzak (1972) and Nelson (1973, p. 84).

43. Hence, Weber's response to Rachfahl: "this is not my theme" (see 2001, p. 100; see Chalcraft, 2005).

44. Weber stressed that the spirit of capitalism has *many* origins; *PE* constitutes simply its major *religious* source (see p. 97). Further, modern capitalism's rise does not unequivocally require, he argues, either the presence of a Protestant ethic or its "functional equivalent" (as many interpreters believed in the 1950s and 1960s). His goal in the post-*PE* series on the economic ethics of Hinduism, Buddhism, and Jainism in India, and Confucianism and Daoism in China, is to understand the reasons behind the development of *modern* capitalism *earlier* in the West than in India or China. See pp. 183–84.

45. Nelson notes that "the many criticism of Weber by unsympathetic American church historians can readily be shown to go far beyond the evidence" (1973, p. 97).

46. Some sociologists have been engaged in historical-sociological work that follows a pathway "between" the two groupings. See, for example, the classical studies by Bendix (1956, 1964); more recently see Silber (1995), Kaelber (1998), and Gorski (2003).

47. Writing more than sixty years ago, Fischoff came to the same conclusion (1944, pp. 57–59, 71–73). More recently, Nelson (1973, pp. 77–85), Marshall (1982, pp. 9–12, 168–73), and Ray (1987, p. 97) agree. After his wide-ranging review of the controversy, Marshall holds that the entire debate has "been dogged from the outset by the grinding of particular religious, political, or theoretical axes; by a widespread tendency to oversimplify Weber's argument through increasing reliance on inaccurate secondary expositions of it and by the routine employment of certain rhetorical devices . . . in order to disguise intellectual and empirical weaknesses. . . ." (1982, p. 169). He sees both sociologists and historians as emerging from this controversy with little credibility intact (p. 171).

48. Only a very brief indication of the vast literature on these themes can be offered here. See Eisenstadt (1968), Nelson (1973, pp. 87–106), Marshall (1982), and Ray (1987).

49. However, Marshall makes no claims regarding the "activities of labouring people." On this group, he argues, the data available do not allow a "firm substan-

tive conclusion" (1980, p. 261). In respect to capitalist entrepreneurs, Marshall's argument in favor of the Weberian over the Marxian thesis (their ethos arose from their economic activity as such) is cautious, yet decisive (see pp. 254–62).

50. Chalcraft notes literature in the sociology of religion, development, work, and organizations as significantly influenced by *PE*. He lists as well *PE*'s impact upon works by historians, theologians, and literary critics (2001, p. 2).

51. This remark appeared on the jacket cover to the prior edition of this volume (Roxbury Publishing, 2002).

52. Weber, as noted, owing to the *multi*causal foundation of his post-*PE* writings, would have viewed this research as misguided. See pp. 183–84, 313–19.

53. Nelson argues more generally: "Preliminary evidence indicates that wherever, with rare exceptions, Protestantism has taken hold, institutions having the character of the Protestant emphasis on transformation have taken hold" (1973, p. 110; see Eisenstadt, 1968).

References

Antonio, Robert J. and Ronald M. Glassman. 1985. *A Marx-Weber Dialogue*. Lawrence, KS: University Press of Kansas.

Bell, Daniel. 1996. *The Cultural Contradictions of Capitalism: Twentieth Anniversary Edition*. New York: Basic.

Bellah, Robert. 1985 [1957]. *Tokugawa Religion: The Cultural Roots of Modern Japan* (New York: The Free Press).

Bendix, Reinhard. 1956. *Work and Authority in Industry*. Berkeley: The University of California Press.

———. 1977 (1964). *Nation-Building and Citizenship*. Berkeley: The University of California Press.

Borkenau, Franz. 1934. *Der Übergang vom feudalen zum bürgerlichen Weltbild*. Paris: Felix Alcan.

Brocke, Bernhard vom, ed. 1987. *Sombarts 'Moderne Kapitalism.'* Munich: Piper.

Chalcraft, David. 2001. "Introduction." Pp. 1–20 in *The Protestant Ethic Debate: Max Weber's Replies to his Critics, 1907–1910*. Translated by A. Harrington and Mary Shields. Liverpool: Liverpool University Press.

———. 2005. "Reading Weber's Patterns of Response to Critics of *The Protestant Ethic*: Some 'Affinities' in and Between Replies to Felix Rachfahl and Werner Sombart." *Journal of Classical Sociology* 5 (1): 31–52.

Davis, Wallace M. 1978. "Introduction." *American Journal of Sociology* 83 (5): 1105–10.

Eisenstadt, S.N., 1968. "The Protestant Ethic Thesis in an Analytical and Comparative Framework." Pp. 3–45 in *The Protestant Ethic and Modernization: A Comparative View*, edited by Eisenstadt. New York: Basic Books.

Etzioni, Amitai. 1996. *The New Golden Rule*. New York: Basic Books.

Fischoff, Ephraim. 1944. *The Protestant Ethic and the Spirit of Capitalism: The History of a Controversy*. Social Research II; 53–77.

Frank, Gunder. 1967. *Capitalism and Underdevelopment in Latin America*. New York: Monthly Review Press, 1967.

Gorski, Phillip. 2003. *The Disciplinary Revolution: Calvinism and the Rise of the State in Early Modern Europe*. Chicago: The University of Chicago Press.

Gothein, Eberhard. 1892. *Wirtschaftsgeschichte des Schwarzwalds*. Strasbourg: Treubner.

Hall, John and Charles Lindholm. 1999. *Is America Breaking Apart?* Princeton: University Press.

Henretta, James. 1993. "Protestant Ethic and the Reality of Capitalism in Colonial America." Pp. 327–46 in *Weber's Protestant Ethic*, edited by Hartmut Lehmann and Guenther Roth. New York: Cambridge.

Hochschild, Arlie. 1990. *The Second Shift: Working Parents and the Revolution at Home.* London: Piatkus.

Hughes, H. Stuart. 1974. *Consciousness and Society.* London: Paladin.

Jacob, Margaret C. and Matthew Kadane. 2003. "Missing, Now Found in the Eighteenth Century: Weber's Protestant Capitalist." *American Historical Review* 108: 20–49.

Jellinek, Georg. 1979 (1895). *The Declaration of the Rights of Man and of Citizens.* Westport, CT: Hyperion Press.

Kaelber, Lutz. 1998. *Schools of Asceticism: Ideology and Organization in Medieval Religious Communities.* University Park: Pennsylvania State University Press.

———. 2005. "Rational Capitalism, Traditionalism, and Adventure Capitalism: New Research on the Weber Thesis." Pp. 139–64 in *The Protestant Ethic Turns 100*, edited by William H. Swatos and Kaelber. Boulder: Paradigm Publishers.

Kalberg, Stephen. 1980. "Max Weber's Types of Rationality: Cornerstones for the Analysis of Rationalization Processes in History." *American Journal of Sociology* 85, 3: 1145–79.

———. 1983. "Max Weber's Universal-Historical Architectonic of Economically-Oriented Action: A Preliminary Reconstruction." Pp. 253–88 in *Current Perspectives in Social Theory*, edited by Scott G. McNall. Greenwood, CT: JAI Press.

———. 1987. "The Origin and Expansion of *Kulturpessimismus*: The Relationship Between Public and Private Spheres in Early Twentieth Century Germany." *Sociological Theory* 5 (Fall): 150–64.

———. 1992. "Culture and the Locus of Work in Contemporary Western Germany: A Weberian Configurational Analysis." Pp. 324–65 in *Theory of Culture*, edited by Neil J. Smelser and Richard Münch. Berkeley: University of California Press.

———. 1994a. "Max Weber's Analysis of the Rise of Monotheism." *The British Journal of Sociology* 45, 4: 563–84.

———. 1994b. *Max Weber's Comparative Historical Sociology.* Chicago: The University of Chicago Press.

———. 1996. "On the Neglect of Weber's *Protestant Ethic* as a Theoretical Treatise: Demarcating the Parameters of Post-War American Sociological Theory." *Sociological Theory* 14 (March): 49–70.

———. 1997. "Tocqueville and Weber on the Sociological Origins of Citizenship: The Political Culture of American Democracy." *Citizenship Studies* 1 (July): 199–222.

———. 1998. "Max Weber's Sociology: Research Strategies and Modes of Analysis." Pp. 208–41 in *Reclaiming the Argument of the Founders*, edited by Charles Camic. Cambridge, MA: Blackwell.

———. 2001. "The Modern World as a Monolithic Iron Cage?" *Max Weber Studies* 1 (May): 178–95.

———. 2003. "Max Weber." Pp. 132–92 in *The Blackwell Companion to Major Social Theorists*, edited by George Ritzer. Oxford: Blackwell Publishers.

———. 2008. "The Perpetual and Tight Interweaving of Past and Present in Max Weber's Sociology." Forthcoming in *History Matters*, edited by David Chalcraft, John Howell, Lopez Menendez, and Hector Vera Martinez. (Aldershot, UK: Ashgate Publishers).

Knowles, Anne Kelly. 1997. *Calvinists Incorporated: Welsh Immigrants on Ohio's Industrial Frontier.* Chicago: The University of Chicago Press.

Landes, David S. 1999. *The Wealth and Poverty of Nation.* New York: Norton,

Lehmann, Hartmut. 1987. "Ascetic Protestantism and Economic Rationalism: Max Weber Revisited After Two Generations." *Harvard Theological Review* 80 (3): 307–20.

———. 1993. "The Rise of Capitalism: Weber versus Sombart." Pp. 195–209 in *Weber's Protestant Ethic: Origins, Evidence, Contexts*, edited by Lehmann and Guenther Roth. New York: Cambridge University Press.

———. 2005, "Friends and Foes: The Formation and Consolidation of the *Protestant Ethic* Thesis." Pp. 23–52 in *The Protestant Ethic Turns 100*, edited by William H. Swatos and Lutz Kaelber. Boulder: Paradigm Publishers.

Lenski, Gerhard. 1974. *The Religious Factor.* New York: Doubleday.

Lichtblau, Klaus and Johannes Weiss. 1993a. "Einleitung der Herausgeber." Pp. vii–xxxv in *Max Weber: Die protestantische Ethik und der 'Geist' des Kapitalismus*, edited by Lichtblau and Weiss. Bodenheim: Athenäum Hain Hanstein.

———, eds. 1993b. *Max Weber: Die protestantische Ethik und der 'Geist' des Kapitalismus.* Bodenheim: Athenäum Hain Hanstein.

Little, David. 1984 (1969). "Bibliographical Essays." Pp. 226–259 in Little, *Religion, Order and Law: A Study in Pre-Revolutionary England.* Chicago: The University of Chicago Press.

Mackinnon, Malcolm H. 1993. "The Longevity of the Thesis: A Critique of the Critics." Pp. 211–44 in *Weber's Protestant Ethic: Origins, Evidence, Contexts*, edited by Hartmut Lehmann and Guenther Roth. New York: Cambridge University Press.

Marcks, Erich. 1894. "Einleitung." Pp. 3–25 in Hermann Baumgarten, *Historische und politische Aufsätze und Reden.* Strasbourg: Truebner.

Marshall, Gordon. 1980. *Presbyteries and Profits.* Oxford: Clarendon Press.

———. 1982. *In Search of the Spirit of Capitalism.* London: Hutchinson.

Merton, Robert K. 2001 (1938). *Science, Technology, and Society in Seventeenth Century England.* New York: Howard Fertig.

Nelson, Benjamin. 1973. "Weber's Protestant Ethic: Its Origins, Wanderings, and Foreseeable Futures." Pp. 71–130 in *Beyond the Classics?* Edited by Charles Y. Glock and Phillip E. Hammond. New York: Harper and Row.

Nipperdey, Thomas. 1993. "Max Weber, Protestantism, and the Debate around 1900. Pp. 73–82 in *Weber's Protestant Ethic: Origins, Evidence, Contexts*, edited by Hartmut Lehmann and Guenther Roth. New York: Cambridge University Press.

Offenbacher, Martin. 1900. *Konfession und soziale Schichtung.* Tübingen: Mohr.

Otsuka, Hisao. 1976. *Max Weber on the Spirit of Capitalism.* Translated by Kondo Masaomi. Tokyo: Institute of Developing Economies.

Parsons, Talcott. 1928. " 'Capitalism' in Recent German Literature: Sombart and Weber." *Journal of Political Economy* 36: 641–61; vol. 37 (1929): 31–51.

———. 1966. *Societies: Evolutionary and Comparative Perspectives.* Englewood Cliffs, NJ: Prentice-Hall.

———. 1971. *The Evolution of Societies*, ed. and with an introduction by Jackson Toby. Englewood Cliffs, NJ: Prentice Hall.

Putnam, Robert D. 2000. *Bowling Alone.* New York: Simon and Schuster.

Rachfahl, Felix. 1909. "Kalvinismus und Kapitalismus." *Internationale Wochenschrift für Wissenschaft, Kunst und Technik* 3 (39–43): Columns 1217–38, 1249–68, 1287–1300, 1319–34, 1347–66.

———. 1910. "Nochmals Kalvinismus und Kapitalismus." *Internationale Wochenschrift für Wissenschaft, Kunst und Technik* 4 (689–702): Columns 717–34, 753–68, 775–94.

Ray, Larry. 1987. "The Protestant Ethic Debate." Pp. 97–125 in *Classic Disputes in Sociology*, edited by J. Anderson, J. A. Hughes, and W. W. Sharrock. London: Allen & Unwin.

Riesebrodt, Martin. 2005. "Dimensions of the *Protestant Ethic*." Pp. 23–52 in *The Protestant Ethic Turns 100*, edited by William H. Swatos and Lutz Kaelber. Boulder: Paradigm Publishers.

Ritzer, George. 1998. *The McDonaldization Thesis: Explorations and Extensions*. London: Sage.

Rollman, Hans. 1993. " 'Meet Me in St. Louis': Troeltsch and Weber in America." Pp. 357–82 in *Weber's Protestant Ethic: Origins, Evidence, Contexts*, edited by Hartmut Lehmann and Guenther Roth. New York: Cambridge University Press.

Roth, Guenther. 1985. "Marx and Weber on the United States—Today." Pp. 215–33 in *A Weber-Marx Dialogue*, edited by Robert J. Antonio and Ronald M. Glassman. Lawrence, KS: University Press of Kansas.

———. 1992. "Zür Entstehungs- und Wirkungsgeschichte von Max Webers 'Protestantische Ethik.' " Pp. 43–68 in Karl Heinrich Kaufhold, Guenther Roth, and Yuichi Shinoya, *Max Weber und seine "Protestantische Ethik."* Düsseldorf: Verlag Wirtschaft und Finanzen.

———. 1992. "The Young Max Weber: Anglo-American Religious Influences and Protestant Social Reform in Germany." *International Journal of Politics, Culture, and Society* 10, 4: 659–71.

Salomon, Albert. 1962. *In Praise of Enlightenment*. Cleveland: World Publ. Co.

Scaff, Lawrence. 1989. *Fleeing the Iron Cage*. Berkeley: The University of California Press.

———. 1998. "The 'Cool Objectivity of Sociation': Max Weber and Marianne Weber in America." *History of the Human Sciences* 11, 2: 61–82.

Schluchter, Wolfgang. 1989. *Rationalism, Religion, and Domination: A Weberian Perspective*. Berkeley: The University of California Press.

———. 1996. *Paradoxes of Modernity*. Stanford, CA: Stanford University Press.

———. and Friedrich Wilhelm Graf, eds. 2005. *Asketischer Protestantismus und der "Geist" des modernen Kapitalismus*. Tübingen: Mohr.

Schor, Juliet. 1991. *The Overworked American*. New York: Basic Books.

Silber, Ilana. 1995. *Virtuosity, Charisma, and Social Order*. Cambridge, UK: Cambridge.

Sombart, Werner. 1902. *Der moderne Kapitalismus*. Leipzig: Duncker & Humblot.

———. 1969 (1913). *The Jews and Modern Capitalism*. New York: Burt Franklin.

Sprinzak, Eduard. 1972. "Weber's Thesis as an Historical Explanation." *History and Theory* 11: 294–320.

Swatos, William and Lutz Kaelber, eds. *The Protestant Ethic Turns 100*. Boulder: Paradigm Publishers.

——— and Peter Kivisto. 2005. "The Contexts of the Publication and Reception of the *Protestant Ethic*." Pp. 111–38 in *The Protestant Ethic Turns 100*, edited by William H. Swatos and Lutz Kaelber. Boulder: Paradigm Publishers.

Tawney, R. H. "Foreword." Pp. 1–11 in *Max Weber: the Protestant Ethic and the Spirit of Capitalism*. Translated by Talcott Parsons. New York: Charles Scribner's Sons.

Troeltsch, Ernst. 1931. *The Social Teachings of the Christian Churches* (2 vols.). Translated by Olive Wyon. New York: Harper Torchbook.

Veliz, Claudio. 1980. The Centralist Tradition in Latin America. Princeton: Princeton University Press.

Wallerstein, Immanuel. 1989. *The Modern World System III*. New York: Academic Press.

Weber, Marianne. 1975 (1926). *Max Weber.* Translated by Harry Zohn. New York: John Wiley and Sons.

Weber, Max. 1927. *General Economic History.* Translated by Frank H. Knight. Glencoe, IL: Free Press. Originally: 1923. *Wirtschaftsgeschichte.* Edited by S. Hellman and M. Palyi. Munich: Duncker & Humblot.

——. 1946a. "Religious Rejections of the World." Pp. 323–59 in *From Max Weber: Essays in Sociology (FMW)*, edited and translated by H. H. Gerth and C. Wright Mills. New York: Oxford. Originally: (1920) 1972. "Zwischenbetrachtung." Pp. 537–73 in *Gesammelte Aufsätze zur Religionssoziologie* (hereafter *GARS*), vol. 1, edited by Johannes Winckelmann. Tübingen: Mohr.

——. 1946b. "The Social Psychology of the World Religions." Pp. 267–301 in *FMW*. Originally: (1920) 1972. Pp. 237–68 in *GARS*, vol. 1.

——. 1949. *The Methodology of the Social Sciences.* Edited and translated by Edward A. Shils and Henry A. Finch. New York: Free Press. Originally: (1922) 1973. Pp. 489–540, 146–214, 215–290 in *Gesammelte Aufsätze zur Wissenschaftslehre*, edited by Johannes Winckelmann. Tübingen: Mohr.

——. 1951. *The Religion of China.* Edited and translated by Hans H. Gerth. New York: The Free Press. Originally: (1920) 1972. "Konfuzianismus und Taoismus." Pp. 276–536 in *GARS*, vol. 1.

——. 1952. *Ancient Judaism.* Edited and translated by Hans H. Gerth and Don Martindale. New York: Free Press. Originally: (1920) 1971. *Das antike Judentum. GARS*, vol. 3, edited by Johannes Winckelmann.

——. 1958. *The Religion of India.* Edited and translated by Hans H. Gerth and Don Martindale. New York: Free Press. Originally: (1920) 1972. *Hinduismus und Buddhismus. GARS*, vol. 2, edited by Johannes Winckelmann.

——. 1968. *Economy and Society.* Edited by Guenther Roth and Claus Wittich. New York: Bedminster Press. Originally: (1921) 1976. *Wirtschaft und Gesellschaft.* Edited by Johannes Winckelmann. Tübingen: Mohr.

——. 1978. "Freudianism." Pp. 383–88 in *Weber: Selections in Translation*, edited by W. G. Runciman and translated by Eric Matthews. Cambridge, UK: University Press. Originally: (unabridged) 1990. *Briefe 1906–1908, Max Weber Gesamtausgabe II, vol. 5*, edited by Rainer Lepsius and Wolfgang J. Mommsen. Tübingen: Mohr.

——. 2001 (1907–10; 1972). *The Protestant Ethic Debate: Max Weber's Replies to his Critics, 1907–1910.* Edited by David Chalcraft and Austin Harrington and translated by Harrington and Mary Shields. Liverpool: Liverpool University Press. Originally: *Archiv für Sozialwissenschaft und Sozialpolitik* 25 (1907): 243–49; vol. 26 (1908): 275–83; vol. 30 (1910): 176–202; vol. 31 (1910): 554–99.

——. 2002 (1904–1905 and 1907–10). *The Protestant Ethic and the "Spirit" of Capitalism and Other Writings.* Edited, translated, and with an introduction by Peter Baehr and Gordon C. Wells. London: Penguin Books. *PE* originally: *Archiv für Sozialwissenschaft und Sozialpolitik* 20 (1904): 1–54 and 21 (1905): 1–110.

——. 2005. *Max Weber: Readings and Commentrary on Modernity*, edited by Stephen Kalberg. Oxford, UK: Blackwell Publishers.

Yinger, Milton. 1957. *Religion, Society, and the Individual.* New York: Macmillan.

Zaret, David. 1993. "The Use and Abuse of Textual Data." Pp. 245–72 in *Weber's Protestant Ethic: Origins, Evidence, Contexts*, edited by Hartmut Lehmann and Guenther Roth. New York: Cambridge University Press.

PART I

THE PROBLEM

Modern capitalism has as little use for liberum arbitrium [easygoing] persons as laborers as it has for the businessman fully without scruples in the running of his company.

(p. 75)

The question of the motivating forces behind the expansion of modern capitalism is not primarily one of the source of money reserves that can be used by capitalist firms, but above all a question of the development of the spirit of capitalism. Wherever this spirit becomes active and is able to have an effect, it acquires *the money reserves to be used as fuel for modern capitalism's activity—not the other way around.*

(p. 82)

This transformation [in ethical qualities] has been scarcely visible to all who investigate external changes only (such as a massive influx of new money), alterations in the forms of organizations, or changes in the organization of the economy. Nevertheless, these ethical qualities have been decisive for the infusion of economic life with this new spirit of capitalism.

(p. 83)

[sk]

RELIGIOUS AFFILIATION AND SOCIAL STRATIFICATION[1]

A glance at the occupational statistics for any country in which several religions coexist is revealing. They indicate that people who own capital, employers, more highly educated skilled workers, and more highly trained technical or business personnel in modern companies tend to be, with striking frequency,[2] overwhelmingly *Protestant*.[3] The variation in this regard between Catholics and Protestants has often been discussed, in a lively fashion, in Catholic newspapers and journals in Germany,[4] as well as at congresses of the Catholic Church.

According to the statistics, this variation between Catholics and Protestants is prominent where differences in religious belief and in nationality—and hence differences in the extent of cultural development—are found in the same region. Germans and Poles in eastern Germany come to mind.[5] Yet the numbers demonstrate as well that differences are equally apparent in nearly all areas where capitalism, in the period of its great expansion [in the eighteenth and nineteenth centuries], possessed a free hand to reorganize, according to its requirements, a population socially and to order it by occupations. Differences according to religious belief became all the more striking to the extent that these changes occurred.

Of course the disproportionately high percentage of Protestants among the owners of capital,[6] the more highly educated skilled workers, and those employed in large industrial and commercial companies[7] can in part be traced back to historical forces[8] from the distant past. Moreover, religious affiliation may not appear to be the *cause* of economic activity; rather, differences in religious belief may seem, to a certain extent, to be the *result* of economic factors. After all, participation in certain economic activities assumes in part some ownership of capital to begin with, in part a costly education, and in part—most frequently—both. Today this participation is tied to ownership of inherited wealth or at least to a certain material affluence. It must also be noted that, in the old German Empire, a large number of the richest and most economically developed areas—favored by nature or a geographical location that facilitated trade and commerce—turned Protestant in the sixteenth century. This held especially for the majority of the wealthy cities. The effects of this wealth benefit Protestants in the economic struggle for existence even today.

The historical question then arises, however: What reasons explain the particularly strong predilection in the most economically developed regions toward a revolution in the Catholic Church [in the sixteenth century]? The answer is by no means as simple as one might at first believe.

Certainly the shedding of the old **economic traditionalism** would seem essentially to support both the tendency to doubt, even religious belief, and the resistance to traditional authorities. Nevertheless, that which is today so often forgotten must be noted here: the Reformation of the sixteenth century not only involved the *elimination* of the Catholic Church's domination (*Herrschaft*)[9] over the believer's life in its entirety, but also the substitution of one form of control by *another*. A highly agreeable domination that had become a mere formality, one that was scarcely felt in a practical manner, was replaced by an infinitely burdensome and severe regimentation of the entire **organization of the believer's life** (*Lebensführung*). Religion now penetrated all private and public spheres in the most comprehensive sense imaginable.

A classic adage succinctly characterizes the Catholic Church's domination as it was earlier even more than today: "The heretic must be punished, but the sinner must be treated leniently." This view was upheld at the beginning of the fifteenth century in the richest, most economically developed regions on earth, and it is upheld even now by groups of people with thoroughly modern orientations to economic activity. In contrast, the domination of Calvinism as it existed in the sixteenth century in Geneva and Scotland, at the end of the sixteenth and beginning of the seventeenth centuries in large parts of Holland, in the seventeenth century in New England, and even in England from time to time, would constitute for us today the most absolutely unbearable form of control by the church over the individual. Large segments of the old commercial aristocracy at that time experienced Calvinism in just this way. Yet the religious activists of the Reformation period, who arose in the most economically developed nations, complained that religion and the church exercised too little domination over life rather than too much.

How then did it happen that precisely the most economically developed nations of that period, and (as will become apparent) specifically their upwardly mobile **middle classes** (*"bürgerlichen" Mittelklassen*), not only allowed this heretofore unknown Puritan tyranny to encompass them; rather they even developed a heroic defense of it? *Middle* classes *as such* had only rarely submitted to religious tyranny of this degree prior to the sixteenth and seventeenth centuries, and they have never done so since then. Not without reason, [the Scottish writer and historian Thomas] Carlyle [1795–1881] referred to this defense as "the last of our heroisms." [English in original.]

* * *

But let us proceed. Could it be, as noted, that the greater ownership of capital by Protestants and their more frequent participation at the top levels of the modern economy are to be understood today in part as a consequence of their historical possession of substantial wealth and their success in passing it on to succeeding generations? Further observations, only a few of

---

Terms defined in the Glossary appear in boldface type upon first use in each chapter in Sections 1 and 2.

which can be mentioned here, indicate that the causal relationship surely *cannot* be formulated in this manner.

First, as is clearly demonstrable, Catholic parents in [the German states of] Baden and Bavaria, as well as in Hungary, for example, enroll their children in different *types* of programs and curricula from those chosen by Protestant parents. The percentage of Catholic students enrolled in the "accelerated" tracks and schools, and then graduating, remains significantly below the percentage of Catholics in the population as a whole.[10] Of course, one is inclined to explain this difference largely by reference to the greater transfer of wealth by Protestants across generations.

This line of reasoning, however, fails to offer an adequate explanation for a second observation. *Within* the group of Catholic graduates enrolled in the accelerated tracks and schools, the percentage of students who decided to take courses in preparation for university study in technical fields or for careers in commerce and industry (or other middle-class ways of making a living in business) lagged *far* behind the percentage of Protestant graduates who decided to do so.[11] Catholics preferred courses of instruction that emphasized languages, philosophy, and history (*humanistische Gymnasien*). Reference to varying levels of inherited wealth will not account for these differences in respect to schooling. Indeed, they must be acknowledged in any explanation for the lower rates of entry into business by Catholics.

Third, an even more remarkable observation helps us to understand the lesser representation of Catholics among skilled *workers* in modern, large industrial concerns. It is well-known that the factory takes its skilled laborers to a large degree from the younger generation of handicraft workers. Thus, the factory leaves the training of its labor force to the crafts. Once skills have been acquired, the factory pulls workers—or "journeymen"—away from the crafts. This situation holds much more for Protestant than for Catholic journeymen. That is, Catholic journeymen demonstrate a much stronger inclination to remain in their crafts and thus more often become master craftsmen. In contrast, Protestants stream into the factory at a comparatively higher rate and then acquire positions as high-level skilled workers and industrial managers.[12] In these cases the causal relationship is undoubtedly one in which a *learned inner quality* decides a person's choice of occupation and further course of occupational development. And this inner quality is influenced by the direction of one's upbringing, which in turn is influenced by the religious climate in one's native town and one's parental home.

The less frequent participation of Catholics in modern business life in Germany is indeed all the more striking because it opposes an age-old[13] (as well as present-day) empirical rule of thumb: ethnic or religious minorities, as "dominated" groups standing opposite a "dominant" group, and *as a consequence of* their voluntary or involuntary exclusion from influential political positions, have been driven to an especially strong degree into the arena of business. Hence, in Germany the most talented among the minority, who might, if not oppressed, hope for the highly sought-after positions at the top levels of the state civil service, instead seek to satisfy their ambitions in the realm of business. Unmistakably, this situation holds for the undoubtedly economically advancing Poles in Russia and eastern Prussia, where, as Catholics, they were a minority (in contrast to their situation in the province of Galicia in Poland, where they were the majority population). It also holds for earlier groupings: the Huguenots in France under Louis XIV, the Nonconformists and Quakers in England, and, last but not least, the Jews for two thousand years. Catholics in Germany, however, do not today follow this pattern. There seems to be no evidence (or at least no clear evidence) of a movement of this minority into large-scale industry, commerce, and business in general. In the past as well, in Holland and England and in both periods of toleration as well as those of persecution of Catholics, in contrast to Protestants, evidence for any particular *economic* development among Catholics cannot be found.

A different situation existed for Protestants. *Both* as ruling *and* ruled strata and *both* as majority *and* minority, Protestants (especially the denominations to be discussed later [in this study]) have demonstrated a specific tendency toward *economic rationalism*. This tendency has not been observed in the same way in the present or the past among Catholics, regardless of whether they were the dominant or dominated stratum *or* constituted a majority or minority.[14] Therefore, the cause of the different behavior must be mainly sought in the enduring inner quality of these religions and *not* only in their respective historical-political, external situations.[15] Our first task will be to investigate which of the elements in the characteristic features of each religion had, and to some extent still have, the effects described above. [1920]

* * *

On the basis of a superficial consideration of the matter and from the vantage point of certain modern impressions, one could attempt to formulate the contrast as one in which Catholicism's greater "estrangement from the world" (*Weltfremdheit*)—the ascetic features proclaimed by its highest ideals—had to socialize believers to be more indifferent to material and consumer goods. In fact, this explanation corresponds to the familiar mode of evaluating these differences popular in Germany in both religions [at the turn into the twentieth century]. German Protestants employ this view in order to criticize every (real or presumed) ascetic ideal in the Catholic way of organizing life. Catholics answer by reproaching Protestants for the "materialism" that has arisen from a secularization of the very meaning of life, holding Protestantism responsible for this development. A modern writer has attempted to capture the contrasting behavior of German Protestants and Catholics in regard to ways of making a living:

> The Catholic . . . is more calm and endowed with a weaker motivation to become engaged in business, retains as cautious and risk-averse an approach to life's journey as possible, and prefers to get by on a smaller income rather than to become engaged in more dangerous and challenging activities—even if they

may lead to greater honor and wealth. It is evident, in light of a popular and humorous maxim in Germany—'one can either eat well or sleep peacefully'—that the Lutheran gladly eats well. On the other hand, the Catholic prefers to sleep undisturbed.[16]

This "wish to eat well" may indeed correctly sum up the motivation of those Protestants in *Germany today* who remain rather indifferent believers—at least in part and even though it remains incomplete as an explanation. Matters were quite different in the past, however. As was commonly acknowledged, precisely the opposite of a natural and uncomplicated "enjoyment of life's pleasures" (*Weltfreude*) characterized the English, Dutch, and American **Puritans**. And, as will become evident, this approach to life is one of their traits of most importance to us. Moreover, French Protestantism,[17] for example, for centuries and to a certain extent even today, has retained the stamp imposed upon the Calvinist churches generally—although chiefly upon those "under the cross"[18] in the epoch of the religious struggles—namely, a certain severity rather than a natural enjoyment of life. Yet Protestantism was one of the most important carriers of industrial and capitalist development in France, as is well-known. This has remained so even if, owing to persecution, only on a small scale. Was this severity related to Protestantism's important role in capitalist development? This will be our query later.

One might be inclined to call this Protestant severity and the strong penetration of the believer's organization of life by religious interests "estrangement from the world." If one wished to do so, however, *then* the French *Calvinists* of the present, as well as of the past, must be viewed as at least as estranged from the world as, for example, the *Catholics* of northern Germany, whose Catholicism is undoubtedly more heartfelt than that of any other group of people. Moreover, *both* groupings are distinguished in parallel ways from the dominant religious groupings in their respective nations [Catholicism in France and Lutheran Protestantism in Germany]. Unlike French Calvinists, an immediate enjoyment of life is typical of lower-status Catholics in France, while an actual antagonism to religion characterizes French Catholics of higher status. And unlike Catholics of northern Germany, lower-status Protestants in Germany today have become immersed in mundane business activities and higher-status Protestants manifest a dominant indifference to religion.[19]

* * *

Hardly any examples could demonstrate more vividly than these parallels that vague ideas, such as Catholicism's (alleged!) "estrangement from the world" and Protestantism's (alleged!) materialistic "enjoyment of life's pleasures," remain at too high a level of generality to be helpful. This holds for the analysis of the present, despite the fact that exceptions can be found, but it is especially the case for the past. If one nonetheless wished to use such diffuse concepts, *then* further observations would at once become salient and unavoidable. These would lead to a question: Could not the entire contrast between estrangement from the world, asceticism, and church-based piety on the one hand, and the earning of one's living under capitalism on the other, be understood as actually implying an inner **affinity** (*innere Verwandtschaft*)?

A striking relationship, to begin with only an external observation, has already become apparent to us: an unusually high number of persons affiliated with precisely the most spiritual forms of Christian piety came from business-oriented social circles. This origin was common in particular for a remarkably large number of Pietism's most devout believers. One might speculate here that the explanation involves a type of extreme reaction—by more spiritually inclined people less well adapted to vocations in commerce and sales—against the view that money and wealth have a vulgar, evil, and debasing influence ("mammonism"). Many of these Pietists, like St. Francis of Assisi [1181–1226, founder of the Franciscan mendicant order], have often actually depicted the course of their own "conversions" in just this manner.[20] Similarly, the conspicuous occurrence that unusually successful capitalist entrepreneurs were frequently the sons of ministers, including even Cecil Rhodes [1853–1902, the rich adventure capitalist and defender of British colonialism in Africa], could be explained as a reaction against an ascetic upbringing.

This mode of analysis, however, proves powerless to explain those cases in which a capitalist's virtuoso business sense *combines* in the same person, and groups of persons, with the most intense forms of piety that penetrate and order the believer's entire life. In fact, far from rare, this combination constitutes precisely the distinguishing aspect for whole groups of the historically most important Protestant **sects** and churches.

Wherever it has appeared, Calvinism in particular[21] demonstrated just this combination. Although Calvinism cannot be said to have been linked to a particular single class in the period of the expansion of the Reformation into various territories (as little as were the other Protestant faiths), it is nonetheless characteristic, and in a certain way "typical," that monks and industrialists (both retailers and craftsmen) were particularly highly represented among those, for example, proselytized into the Huguenot churches in France.[22] Indeed, groupings oriented to commerce remained in disproportionately high numbers in these churches even during the periods of persecution.[23] The Spaniards as well knew that "heresy" (that is, Calvinism from the Netherlands) "promoted the spirit of commerce." This conclusion corresponds fully to the views articulated by [the British statistician and political economist] Sir William Petty [1623–87] in his discussion of the causes for capitalism's growth in the Netherlands. [The economic historian W. Eberhard] Gothein, [1863–1923] appropriately,[24] depicts the Calvinist diaspora as the "capitalist economy's seed-bed."[25]

Of course it could be argued that the superiority itself of the French and Dutch economic cultures, out of which the Calvinist diaspora primarily arose, constituted the decisive factor. Or central significance might be attributed to the powerful effect of the exile experience and the uprooting it entailed from all of life's customary and traditional relationships.[26] This combination of a business orientation with intense piety was the situation in France in the seventeenth century, as we know from the struggles of [Jean Baptiste] Colbert [1619–83, diplomat, reformist finance minister under Louis XIV, and proponent of mercantilism and colonialism]. Even Austria, not to mention other nations, directly imported Protestant manufacturers occasionally.

Nevertheless, it should be noted that not all Protestant denominations exhibited an equally strong effect on capitalism's growth. Calvinism[27] exercised an apparently strong effect also in Germany, in the *Wuppertal* region as well as elsewhere, and the **"reformed"** faiths seem to have promoted the development of the capitalist spirit, as became especially clear in comparison to other faiths. Lutheranism, for example, in the *Wuppertal* region proved less powerful in this respect. Comparisons of both large-scale situations and individual cases lead to this conclusion.[28] [The British historian Henry Thomas] Buckle [1821–62] and a number of English poets, especially [John] Keats [1795–1821], have documented similar relationships in Scotland.[29] [1920]

Even more striking is the connection (as we need only to be briefly reminded) between a religious regimentation of life and the most intensive development of a sense for business. This connection is apparent in the large number of precisely those sects whose "estrangement from life" (*Lebensfremdheit*) has become as familiar as their wealth. The *Quakers* in England and North America and the *Mennonites* in Germany and the Netherlands particularly come to mind. Even the absolute refusal of the Mennonites in East Prussia to perform military service did not prevent Frederick William I [1688–1740, king of Prussia] from declaring their indispensability as **social carriers** of industry. This example is just one, although one of the most clear in light of the particular qualities of this monarch, of the many well-known illustrations of this situation. Finally, a combination of intense piety with an equally intensely developed business sense, as well as success, likewise exists among the German *Pietists*, as is well-known in Germany. One need only think over the history of Calv, [a major center of Pietism], in southwest Germany in comparison to that of Catholicism in the Rhineland.[30]

* * *

An accumulation of further examples in this purely preliminary discussion is unnecessary. The few illustrations already noted all lead to the same conclusion: the "spirit of work" or "progress" (or whatever else it may be called), whose awakening one is inclined to attribute to Protestantism, should not be understood as implying a natural and uncomplicated "enjoyment of life's pleasures." Furthermore, this "spirit of work" should not be comprehended as otherwise somehow involving "enlightenment," as many today now believe. The old Protestantism of [Martin] Luther

[1483–1546], [John] Calvin [1509–64], [John] Knox [1505–72], and [Gisbert] Voët [1589–1676][31] had very little to do with what is today called progress. Indeed, their Protestantism stood directly antagonistic to a number of central elements of modern life that even the most fundamentalist believer today would not wish to banish.

Hence, if an inner affinity is to be discovered at all between certain streams of the old Protestant spirit and the modern culture of capitalism, our investigation—for better or worse—must *not* attempt to find this affinity in this Protestant spirit's (allegedly) more or less materialistic, or even anti-ascetic, "enjoyment of life's pleasures." It should focus instead on Protestantism's purely *religious* features. [Charles de Secondat, baron de] Montesquieu [1689–1755, the French social philosopher, writer, and opponent of absolutism], described the English as having advanced "farther than other peoples in three important ways: in respect to piety, commerce, and freedom" (see *Spirit of the Laws*, bk. 20, ch. 7). Could it be that the superiority of the English in regard to commerce, as well as their aptitude for free political institutions (the discussion of which belongs in another context), is perhaps connected to the unusual piety Montesquieu attributes to them?

A whole multitude of possible relationships immediately, if only dimly, appear before us if we frame the question in this manner. Thus, we must take as our task to *formulate*, as clearly as possible and despite full cognizance of the inexhaustible diversity that lies within every historical case, that which now appears to us diffusely. To do so, however, we must necessarily abandon the arena of vague and general depictions heretofore our plane of reference. Instead, we must attempt to penetrate the characteristic qualities and distinctiveness of the great religious worlds of thought given to us historically in the diverse forms of Christianity.

Nevertheless, a few remarks are indispensable before proceeding in this direction. The particular features of the phenomenon for which we intend to offer an historical explanation must first be discussed. A commentary on the meaning (*Sinn*) that such an explanation can possibly have within the framework of these investigations will then follow.

CHAPTER 11

THE SPIRIT OF CAPITALISM

The title of this study uses a concept that sounds rather intimidating: the *"spirit* of capitalism."[1] What should be understood by it? An attempt to provide even an approximate "definition" immediately unveils certain difficulties that are embedded in the essence of this investigation's purpose. [1920]

If one can discover at all an object for which the phrase *spirit of capitalism* is meaningful, then it can only be a specific *historical case*. Such a singular entity is nothing more than a complex of relationships in historical reality. We join them together, from the vantage point of their *cultural significance*, into a conceptual unity.

Such a historical concept, however, cannot be defined according to how it is "demarcated" vis-à-vis other concepts (*genus proximum, differentia specifica*). This holds if only because the concept denotes a phenomenon that is of qualitative importance as a consequence of its individual *uniqueness*. Moreover, this concept must be gradually *put together* from its single component parts, each of which is taken out of historical reality. Therefore, the final formation of the concept cannot appear at the beginning of the investigation; rather, it must stand at its *conclusion*. In other words, how our understanding of a spirit of capitalism is to be best defined will have to unfold only in the course of our discussion and only as its main outcome. Only a definition formulated in this manner will be adequate to the particular vantage points of interest to us here.

In turn, it must be recognized that these vantage points (which are still to be discussed) by no means constitute the only ones possible in reference to which the historical cases under consideration can be analyzed. Other vantage points would identify other features of our historical cases as "essential," as is true with every historical case. From this premise it follows unequivocally that whatever one understands by a spirit of capitalism by no means necessarily can or must correspond to *that which we* will note as essential in our exegesis here. This must be acknowledged, namely, the central role played by the researcher's particular vantage point in identifying what is essential to each case, as it belongs to the very essence of the formation of historical concepts—an endeavor that does not aim, in terms of its methodological goals, to trap reality in abstract, general concepts (*Gattungsbegriffe*). Rather, when forming historical concepts, we strive to achieve something different: to order reality into tangible, causal connections that are stable and, unavoidably, of a *unique* character.[2]

That being said, and even if we succeed in demarcating the case we are attempting here to analyze and explain historically, our concern now cannot be to offer a conceptual definition. Instead, our focus at the beginning should be only to provide a provisional *illustration* of the activity implied here by the term *spirit of capitalism*. Indeed, such an illustration is indispensable in order to attain our aim now of simply understanding the object of our investigation. On behalf of this purpose we turn to a document that contains the spirit of concern to us in near classical purity, and simultaneously offers the advantage of being detached from *all* direct connection to religious belief—hence, for our theme, of being "free of presuppositions."

Remember, that *time* is *money*. He that can earn ten shillings a day by his labour, and goes abroad, or sits idle one half of that day, though he spends but sixpence during his diversion or idleness, ought not to reckon that the only expense; he has really spent or rather thrown away five shillings besides.

Remember, that *credit* is *money*. If a man lets his money lie in my hands after it is due, he gives me the interest, or so much as I can make of it during that time. This amounts to a considerable sum where a man has good and large credit, and makes good use of it.

Remember, that money is of the *prolific, generating nature*. Money can beget money, and its offspring can beget more, and so on. Five shillings turned is six, turned again it is seven and threepence, and so on, till it becomes a hundred pounds. The more there is of it, the more it produces every turning, so that the profits rise quicker and quicker. He that kills a breeding-sow, destroys all her offspring to the thousandth generation. He that murders a crown, *destroys* all that it might have produced, even scores of pounds. . . .

Remember this saying: The good *paymaster* is lord of another man's purse. He that is known to pay punctually and exactly to the time he promises, may at any time, and on any occasion, raise all the money his friends can spare.

This is sometimes of great use. After industry and frugality, nothing contributes more to the *raising* of a young man in the world than punctuality and justice in all his dealings; therefore never keep borrowed money an hour beyond the time you promised, lest a disappointment shut up your friend's purse for ever.

The most trifling actions that affect a man's *credit* are to be regarded. The sound of your hammer at five in the morning, or nine at night, heard by a creditor, makes him easy six months longer; but if he sees you at a billiard-table, or hears your voice at a tavern, when you should be at work, he sends for his money the next day; . . . [he] demands it before you are able to pay.

It shows, besides, that you are mindful of what you owe; it makes you *appear* a careful as well as an *honest man,* and that still increases your *credit*.

Beware of thinking that you own all that you possess, and of living accordingly. It is a mistake that many people who have credit fall into. To prevent this, keep an exact account both of your expenses and your income. If you make an effort to attend to particular expenses, it will have this good effect: you will discover how wonderfully small, trifling expenses mount up to large sums, and will discern what might have been, and may for the future be saved, without occasioning any great inconvenience.

For six pounds a year you may have the use of one hundred pounds if you are a man of known prudence and honesty.

He that spends a groat a day idly, spends idly above six pounds a year, which is the price of using one hundred pounds.

He that wastes idly a groat's worth of his time per day, one day with another, wastes the privilege of using one hundred pounds each year.

He that idly loses five shillings' worth of time, loses five shillings and might as prudently throw five shillings into the sea.

He that loses five shillings not only loses that sum, but all the advantage that might be made by turning it in dealing, which by the time that a young man becomes old, amounts to a comfortable bag of money.

It is *Benjamin Franklin*[3] [1706–90] who preaches to us in these sentences. As the supposed catechism of a Yankee, Ferdinand Kürnberger satirizes these axioms in his brilliantly clever and venomous *Picture of American Culture.*[4] That the spirit of capitalism is here manifest in Franklin's words, even in a characteristic manner, no one will doubt. It will not be argued here, however, that *all aspects* of what can be understood by this spirit are contained in them.

Let us dwell a moment upon a passage, the worldly wisdom of which is summarized thusly by Kürnberger: "They make tallow for candles out of cattle and money out of men." Remarkably, the real peculiarity in the "philosophy of avarice" contained in this maxim is the ideal of the *credit-worthy* man of honor and, above all, the idea of the *duty* of the individual to increase his wealth, which is assumed to be a self-defined interest in itself. Indeed, rather than simply a common-sense approach to life, a peculiar "ethic" is preached here: its violation is treated not simply as foolishness but as a sort of forgetfulness of *duty*. Above all, this distinction stands at the center of the matter. "Business savvy," which is found commonly enough, is here not *alone* taught; rather, an *ethos* is expressed in this maxim. Just *this* quality is of interest to us in this investigation.

A retired business partner of Jakob Fugger, [1459–1525, an extremely wealthy German financier, export merchant, and philanthropist], once sought to convince him to retire. Yet his colleague's argument—that he had accumulated enough wealth and should allow others their chance—was rebuked by Fugger as "contemptible timidity." He "viewed matters differently," Fugger answered, and "wanted simply to make money as long as he could."[5]

Obviously, the spirit of this statement must be *distinguished* from Franklin's. Fugger's entrepreneurial daring and personal, morally indifferent proclivities[6] now take on the character, in Franklin, of an *ethically*-oriented maxim for the **organization of life**. The expression *spirit of capitalism* will be used here in just this specific manner[7]—naturally the spirit of *modern* **capitalism**. That is, in light of the formulation of our theme, it must be evident that the Western European and American capitalism of the last few centuries constitutes our concern rather than the "capitalism" that has appeared in China, India, Babylon, the ancient world, and the Middle Ages. As we will see, *just that peculiar ethic was missing in all these cases.*

Nevertheless, all of Franklin's moral admonishments are applied in a utilitarian fashion: Honesty is *useful* because it leads to the availability of credit. Punctuality, industry, and frugality are also useful, and are *therefore* virtues. It would follow from this that, for example, the *appearance* of honesty, wherever it accomplishes the same end, would suffice. Moreover, in Franklin's eyes an unnecessary surplus of this virtue must be seen as unproductive wastefulness. Indeed, whoever reads in his autobiography the story of his "conversion" to these virtues,[8] or the complete discussions on the usefulness of a strict preservation of the *appearance* of modesty and the intentional minimizing of one's own accomplishments in order to attain a general approval,[9] will necessarily come to the conclusion that all virtues, according to Franklin, become virtues *only to the extent* that they are useful to the individual. The surrogate of virtue—namely, its appearance only—is fully adequate wherever the same purpose is achieved. Indeed, this inseparability of motive and appearance is the inescapable consequence of all strict utilitarianism. The common German tendency to perceive the American virtues as "hypocrisy" appears here confirmed beyond a doubt.

* * *

In truth, however, matters are not so simple. Benjamin Franklin's own character demonstrates that the issue is more complex: his character appears clearly, however seldom, in his autobiography as one of candor and truthfulness. It is also evident in Franklin's tracing of his realization—virtues can be "useful"—back to a revelation from God that was designed, he believed, to guide him onto the path of righteousness. Something more is involved here than simply an embellishing of purely self-interested, egocentric maxims.

The complexity of this issue is above all apparent in the *summum bonum* ["supreme good"] of this "ethic": namely, the acquisition of money, and more and more money, takes place here simultaneously with the strictest avoidance of all spontaneous enjoyment of it. The pursuit of riches is fully stripped of all pleasurable (*eudämonistischen*), and surely all hedonistic, aspects. Accordingly, this striving becomes understood completely as an end in itself—to such an extent that it appears as fully outside the normal course of affairs and simply irrational, at least when viewed from the perspective of the "happiness" or "utility" of the single individual.[10] Here, people are oriented to acquisition as the purpose of life; acquisition is no longer viewed as a means to the end of satisfying the substantive needs of life. Those people in possession of spontaneous, fun-loving dispositions experience this situation as an absolutely meaningless reversal of a "natural" condition (as we would say today). Yet this reversal constitutes just as surely a guiding principle of [modern] capitalism as incomprehension of this new situation characterizes all who remain untouched by [modern] capitalism's tentacles.

This reversal implies an internal line of development that comes into close contact with certain religious ideas. One can ask why then "money ought to be made out of persons." In his autobiography, and although he is himself a bland Deist, Franklin answers with a maxim from the Bible that, as he says, his strict Calvinist father again and again drilled into him in his youth: "Seest thou a man vigorous in his **vocational calling** (*Beruf*)? He shall stand before kings" (Prov. 22:29). As long as it is carried out in a legal manner, the acquisition of money in the modern economic order is the result and manifestation of competence and proficiency in a *vocational calling. This competence and proficiency* is the actual alpha and omega of Franklin's morality, as now can be easily recognized. It presents itself to us both in the passages cited above and, without exception, in all his writings.[11]

In fact, this peculiar idea of a *duty to have a vocational calling*, so familiar to us today but actually not at all self-evident, is the idea that is characteristic of the "social ethic" of modern capitalist culture. In a certain sense, it is even of constitutive significance for it. It implies a notion of duty that individuals ought to experience, and do, vis-à-vis the content of their "vocational" activity. This notion appears regardless of the particular nature of the activity and regardless, especially, of whether this activity seems to involve (as it does for people with a spontaneous, fun-loving disposition) nothing more than a simple utilization of their capacity for labor or their treatment of it as only a material possession (as "capital").

Nevertheless, it is surely not the case that the idea of a duty in one's vocational calling could grow *only* on the soil of [modern] capitalism. Rather, our attempt later to trace its roots will take us to a period prior to [modern] capitalism. Naturally it will be argued here even less that, under *today's* capitalism, the subjective acquisition of these ethical maxims by capitalism's particular social carriers (such as businesspersons or workers in modern capitalist companies) constitutes a condition for capitalism's further existence. Rather, the capitalist economic order of today is a vast cosmos into which a person is born. It simply exists, to each person, as a factually unalterable casing (*unabänderliches Gehäuse*) in which he or she must live. To the extent that people are interwoven into the context of capitalism's market forces, the norms of its economic action are forced onto them. Every factory owner who operates in the long term against these norms will inevitably be eliminated from the economy. With the same degree of inevitability, every worker who cannot or will not adapt to the norms of the marketplace will become unemployed.

Thus, through a process of economic *selection*, the capitalism that today dominates economic life socializes and creates the economic functionaries that it needs, both owners of businesses and workers. Nevertheless, the limitations of the notion of "selection" as a means to explain historical phenomena can be grasped here vividly. In order for a particular type of organized life and a particular conception of a vocational calling adapted to the uniqueness of modern capitalism to be "selected" (that is, more than others), obviously they must first have originated among—and as a mode of thinking be **carried** by—*groups* of persons rather than simply by isolated individuals. Hence, it is the origin of this mode of thinking, and its carrier groups, that actually needs to be explained.

* * *

We can address the idea of naive historical materialism—that such "ideas" arise as a "reflection" or "superstructure" of economic situations—in more detail only later. It must suffice adequately for our purpose at this point to call attention to the fact that the capitalist spirit (according to our definition here) without a doubt existed *before* "capitalist development" in the colony (Massachusetts) where Benjamin Franklin was born. (In contrast to other regions in America, one complained in New England as early as 1632 about specific appearances of a particularly calculating type of profit seeking.) Moreover, for example, in the neighboring colonies that were later to become the southern states of the union, this capitalist spirit remained distinctly less developed despite the fact that the southern states were called into being by large-scale capitalists for *business* purposes. In contrast, the New England colonies were called into existence for *religious* reasons by ministers and seminary graduates, together with small-scale merchants, craftsmen, and farmers. Thus, in *this* case at any rate, the causal relationship between ideas and economic situations lies in the direction opposite from that which would be postulated by the "materialist" argument.

But the youth of these ideas—the capitalist spirit—is altogether more thorny than was assumed by the "superstructure" theorists, and its unfolding does not proceed in the manner of the blossoming of a flower. The capitalist spirit, according to the meaning of this concept thus far acquired, became prominent only after a difficult struggle against a world of hostile powers. The **frame of mind** (*Gesinnung*) apparent in the cited passages from Benjamin Franklin that met with the approval of an entire people would have been proscribed in the ancient world, as well as in the Middle Ages,[12] for it would have been viewed as an expression of filthy greed and a completely undignified character. Indeed, antagonism to this frame of mind is found even today, particularly (and on a regular basis) in those social groups least integrated into or adapted to the modern capitalist economy. This was the case not because "the acquisitive instinct" in precapitalist epochs was perhaps less well-known or developed, as is so often said, or because the *auri sacra fames* [craving for gold] was then, or is even today, *smaller* outside modern, **middle-class** capitalism, as is depicted in the illusions of modern-day romantic thinkers. Such arguments will not isolate the distinction between the capitalist and precapitalist spirit: the *greed* of the mandarins in China, of the aristocrats in ancient Rome, and of the modern peasant is second to none. And as anyone can experience for himself, the *auri sacra fames* of the Naples cab driver, or *barcajuolo* [Venetian gondolier], representatives in Asia of similar trades, and craftsmen in southern Europe and Asia is even unusually *more intense*, and especially more unscrupulous, than that of, for example, an Englishman in the same situation.[13]

The universal sway of *absolute* unscrupulousness in establishing one's own self-interest as the legitimate operating assumption for the pursuit of money has been specifically characteristic of precisely those countries where the development of a middle-class capitalism—measured against the standards of modern Western capitalist development—has remained "backward." The absence of *coscienziosità* [conscientiousness] among [wage] workers[14] in such nations (such as Italy in comparison to Germany) has been, and to a certain extent still is, the major obstacle to the unfolding of modern capitalism, as every factory employer knows. Modern capitalism has as little use for *liberum arbitrium* [easygoing] persons as laborers as it has for the businessman fully without scruples in the running of his company, as we already have learned from Franklin. Hence, because its strength has varied, an "instinct" to pursue money cannot be the decisive issue.

The *auri sacra fames* is as old as the history of humanity known to us. We shall see that those who without reservation surrendered themselves to it as an *instinct*—the Dutch captain, for example, who "would sail through hell for profit, even if he burned his sails"—were *in no way* representatives of that frame of mind from which the specifically modern capitalist spirit burst forth as *a mass phenomenon*. That is what matters here. Acquisition unrestrained by internally binding norms has existed in all periods of history; indeed, it has existed wherever its expression was not circumscribed. In relationships across tribes and among peoples fundamentally unknown to each other, as well as in warfare and piracy, trade unbounded by norms has been the rule. A double standard prevailed in such situations: practices considered taboo "among brothers" were permitted with "outsiders."

As an "adventure," capitalist acquisition has found a place in all those economies that have known valuable objects as quasi-money forms of exchange and offered the chance to utilize them for profit. These economies have been based on, for example, *commenda*,[15] tax farming,[16] state-guaranteed loans, and the financing of wars, state functionaries, and the courts of princes. Coexisting everywhere with these external modes of economic organization were persons with an adventurous frame of mind—who mocked all ethical restrictions on action. An absolute and willfully ruthless striving for profit often stood hard and fast alongside a strict adherence to age-old traditions. Then, as these traditions began to disintegrate, a more or less broad-ranging expansion of an unrestrained quest for gain took place. In some situations, it intruded even into the core of social groups. [1920]

Hence, adventure capitalism did not imply an ethical affirmation and shaping of this new situation. Rather, the intrusion of an unrestrained quest for gain was only *tolerated* as a new reality; it was treated with ethical indifference or as a disagreeable but unavoidable presence. This was the normal position taken by all ethical teachings. Moreover, and of more essential importance, this view characterized the practical behavior of the average person in the epoch prior to modern capitalism, namely, before a rational use of capital in a managed manner and a systematic capitalist organization *of work* became the dominant forces determining the orientation of economic activity. This toleration of the unrestrained quest for gain, however, constituted everywhere one of the strongest inner barriers against the adaptation of persons to the preconditions of an organized, middle-class capitalist economy. [1920]

In the sense of a certain norm-bound style of life that has crystallized in the guise of an "ethic," the spirit of capitalism has had to struggle primarily against a specific opponent: that type of experiencing, perceiving, and ordering of the world that we can denote [*economic*] **traditionalism**. Every attempt to offer a final "definition," however, must be postponed. Instead, and of course only in a provisional manner, we will attempt a clear rendering of this term by reference to a few special cases. The workers first capture our attention.

* * *

One of the technical means used by the modern employer to achieve the highest possible productivity from "his" workers, and to increase the intensity of work, is the *piece-rate* method of payment. People are paid according to the fruits of their labor. In agriculture, for example, the harvesting of the crops requires the highest possible intensity of labor field by field. This requirement is common not least because, owing to the unpredictability of the weather, extraordinarily large profits and losses depend upon the greatest conceivable acceleration of the harvesting. Accordingly, the piece-rate method is customarily employed. Wherever the size of the harvest and the intensity of the company's work rhythms increase, so does the employer's interest in accelerated harvesting. Thus, employers have repeatedly attempted to interest workers in increasing their productivity by increasing the piece rate. Indeed, in doing so employers believed they were offering workers an opportunity to earn, in very short periods of time, what appeared to them an extraordinary wage.

Just at this point, however, peculiar difficulties became apparent. Remarkably, increasing the piece rate often led to less productivity in the same period of time rather than more. This decline occurred because workers responded to the increase by decreasing their daily productivity. For example, a man has been accustomed to harvesting 2 ½ acres per day and to receiving one German mark for every acre of grain harvested. He thus earns 2 ½ marks every day. If the piece rate is raised to 1 ¼ marks per acre, he needs to harvest only 2 acres per day in order to earn the same amount as before, and this, according to the biblical passage, "allows enough for him." Yet the employer's hope of increasing productivity by increasing the piece-rate has been disappointed (if the worker had harvested 3 acres, he would have earned 3 ¾ marks).

The opportunity of earning more appealed to him less than the idea of working less. He did not ask: "If I produce as much as possible, how much money will I earn each day?" Rather, he formulated the question differently: "How long must I work in order to earn the amount of money—2 ½ marks—I have earned until now and that has fulfilled my *traditional* economic needs?"

This example illustrates the type of behavior that should be called economic "traditionalism." People do not wish "by nature" to earn more and more money. Instead, they wish simply to live, and to live as they have been accustomed and to earn as much as is required to do so. Wherever modern capitalism began its task of increasing the "productivity" of human work by increasing its intensity, it confronted, in the precapitalist economy, an infinitely obdurate barrier in the form of this definition of work. Even today modern capitalism everywhere encounters economic traditionalism the more "backward" (from the perspective of modern capitalism) are the very laborers it depends on.

But let us again return to our illustration. Owing to the incapacity of the higher piece-rate to appeal to the "acquisitive sense," it would appear altogether plausible to attempt to do so by utilizing the opposite strategy: by *decreasing* piece-rates, to force workers to produce *more* in order to maintain their accustomed earnings. Moreover, two simple observations seem to have held true in the past, as they do today: a lower wage and higher profit are directly related, and all that is paid out in higher wages must imply a corresponding reduction of profits. Capitalism has been guided by this axiom repeatedly, and even from its beginning, and it has been an article of faith for centuries that lower wages are "productive." In other words, lower wages were believed to enhance worker productivity. As Pieter de la Court, [1618–85, Dutch textile manufacturer and strong proponent of fully unregulated trade and competition], contended (completely in accord in this respect with the old Calvinism, as we will see), people work only because, and only so long as, they are poor.

Nevertheless, the effectiveness of this presumably tried and proven strategy has limitations.[17] Capitalism surely required, for its development, the presence of population surpluses that kept the market costs of labor low. Indeed, under certain circumstances an overly large "reserve army" of workers facilitates capitalism's quantitative expansion. It slows down, however, its qualitative development, especially with respect to the transition to work in organizations that require intensive labor. A lower wage is in no way identical with cheaper labor. Even when scrutinized in reference to purely quantitative considerations, the productivity of work can be seen to sink, under all circumstances, when wages are too low to sustain good health. If retained in the long run, such a wage often leads plainly to a "selection of the least fit." The average farmer from Silesia harvests today, when he exerts himself fully, little more than two-thirds of the land in the same amount of time as the better paid and better nourished farmer from Pomerania or Mecklenburg. Compared to the Germans, the Poles' capacity for physical work declines more and more the farther to the east their homeland.

Even considered purely from the business point of view, lower wages fail, as a pillar of modern capitalist development, in all those situations where goods are produced that require any type of skilled labor, where expensive and easily damaged machines are used, and in general where a significant degree of focused concentration and initiative is demanded. In these circumstances the lower wage does not prove economically feasible, and its effects lead to the opposite of all that was originally intended. This holds in these situations for the simple reason that a developed sense of responsibility is absolutely indispensable. In addition, it is necessary to have a *frame of mind* that emancipates the worker, at least *during* the workday, from a constant question: With a maximum of ease and comfort and a minimum of productivity, how is the accustomed wage nonetheless to be maintained? This frame of mind, if it manages to uproot the worker from this concern, motivates labor as if labor were an absolute end in itself, or a "calling."

Yet such a frame of mind is not inherently given in the nature of the species. Nor can it be directly called forth by high or low wages. Rather, it is the product of a long and continuous process of socialization. Today, sitting triumphantly dominant, modern capitalism is able to recruit its workers in all industrial nations and in all the branches of industry in these nations relatively easily. Yet in the past recruitment was everywhere an extremely difficult problem.[18] Even today, without the assistance of a powerful ally, modern capitalism does not always reach the goals that, as we will further note below, accompanied it in the period of its early development.

$* * *$

An illustration will again offer clarity. A portrait of the older traditional approach to work is very frequently provided [in the early twentieth century] by *female* workers, above all by those who are unmarried.

An almost universal complaint among employers concerns the absolute incapacity and unwillingness of women workers to give up customary and once-mastered modes of work in favor of other, more practical work techniques, and their inability to adapt to new forms of labor, to learn, and to focus the mind's reasoning capacities, or even to use it. This view holds in particular for German young women. Efforts to organize work in a simpler and, especially, more productive manner come up against complete incomprehension. Increases in the piece-rate [designed to raise production] strike against the wall of habit without the least effect.

The situation is often different only with young women from a specific religious background, namely for women from Pietist homes (not an unimportant point for our reflections). One hears often, and it is confirmed by occasional statistical studies,[19] that by far the most favorable prospects for socialization into the rhythms of the workplace exist among young women in this category. The capacity to focus one's thoughts in addition to an absolutely central element—the capacity to feel an "internal dedication to the

work"—are found here unusually frequently. Indeed, these qualities combine with an organized approach to economic activity that, on the one
hand, *calculates* earnings and their maximum potential and, on the other
hand, is characterized by a **dispassionate** self-control and moderation—all
of which increase productive capacities to an unusual degree.

The foundation for perceiving work as an end in itself, or a "calling," as
modern capitalism requires, is here developed in a most propitious manner. And the prospect for shattering the leisurely rhythm of economic traditionalism as a *consequence* of a religious socialization is at its highest.

* * *

This analysis derived from [early twentieth century] capitalism[20] has indicated to us yet again that it would be worthwhile simply to *ask* how these
connections between people's capacity to adapt to [modern] capitalism, on
the one hand, and their religious beliefs, on the other, could have been formulated during the youth of [modern] capitalism. That these connections
existed in a similar manner earlier can be concluded from many fragmented observations. For example, the ostracism and persecution that
Methodist workers in the eighteenth century encountered from their fellow
workers, as implied in the frequent reports of the destruction of their tools,
can in no way be understood exclusively or predominantly in terms of their
religious eccentricities (of these England had seen quite enough, and of an
even more striking character). Rather, their unambivalent "readiness to
work hard," as one would say today, was the issue here.

Nonetheless, let us turn again to the present and specifically to employers. We must do so in order further to clarify the meaning of "economic traditionalism."

* * *

In his discussions of the genesis of capitalism,[21] [the German economic
historian Werner] Sombart [1863–1941] distinguishes two great principles
according to which economic history has unfolded: the "satisfaction of
needs" and "acquisition." The development of economies tended toward
one or the other depending, on the one hand, upon the extent to which personal *needs* were decisive or, on the other hand, the degree to which barriers
were placed upon acquisition, an independent striving for *profit*, and the
possibility of striving for profit. The type and direction of economic activity
varied accordingly.

At first glance, Sombart's "satisfaction of needs" seems to correspond to
what has here been called economic traditionalism. This is indeed the case *if*
the concept of need is equated with *traditional need*. However, if it is not,
then large numbers of businesses that must be considered "capitalist"—according to the form of their organization and even in the sense of Sombart's
definition of "capital"[22]—fall out of the category of "acquisition" economy
and move into the category of "satisfaction of needs" economy. For example, even businesses operated by private employers on the basis of the

transformation of capital (that is, money or goods with a monetary value) into profit through the purchase of the means of production and the sale of products—that is, businesses undoubtedly capable of being organized as "capitalist"—can retain the character of economic traditionalism. This situation, even in the course of the modern development of the economy, has not been simply the exception. Instead, it has been the rule, despite continuously reappearing interruptions and intrusions from a spirit of capitalism that has been repeatedly rejuvenated and become ever more powerful.

Rather than being in "lawful" dependency, the capitalist form of an economy and the spirit in which it is operated in fact exist generally in a less determinant relationship, namely, one of "adequacy" to each other. Nonetheless, if we provisionally employ the phrase "spirit *of* (modern) *capitalism*"[23] to refer to the particular frame of mind that, as in our example of Benjamin Franklin, strives systematically and rationally *in a calling* for legitimate profit, then we are doing so for historical reasons. We do so on the one hand because this frame of mind finds its most adequate form in the modern capitalist company and, on the other, because the capitalist company discovers in this frame of mind the motivating force—or spirit—most adequate to it.

Of course, it may happen that "spirit" and "form" do not come together at all. The "capitalist spirit" permeated Benjamin Franklin at a time when the organization of his publishing business did not vary from the older, traditional form typical in a handicraft shop. We shall also see that, on the threshold of the modern epoch, the capitalist entrepreneurs of the commercial aristocracy were by no means exclusively or predominantly the social carriers of that frame of mind here designated as the spirit of capitalism.[24] On the contrary, the upwardly mobile strata of the industrial middle classes were far more so. Similarly, in the nineteenth century, the classical representatives of this spirit were the Manchester or Rhineland-Westphalia upstart newcomers to wealth from modest circumstances, rather than the aristocratic gentlemen from Liverpool and Hamburg whose commercial fortunes were inherited from the distant past. Matters were not different even as early as the sixteenth century. The founders of the new *industries* of this period were predominantly upstart newcomers.[25]

For example, surely a bank, a wholesale export company, a large retail concern, or, finally, a large cottage industry that produces goods in homes can be operated only in the form of a capitalist business. Nevertheless, all of these businesses could be managed according to a spirit of strict economic traditionalism. In fact, it is *impossible* to carry out the operations of a large bank of issue[26] in a different manner, and the foreign trade of entire epochs has been based upon monopolies and regulations rooted strictly in economic traditionalism. The revolution that brought the ancient economic traditionalism to an end is still in full motion in retail trade—and we are not referring to the type of small-scale businesses that are today calling out for state subsidies. It is just this transformation that destroyed the old forms of the cottage-industry system (to which modern forms of work in the home are related only in form). The course and significance of this revolution, even though these matters are well known, can be again illustrated by reference to a specific case.

* * *

Until the middle of the nineteenth century, the life of a cottage-industry putter-out in many branches of the textile industry in Europe[27] was altogether easygoing, at least compared to today. One can imagine the typical routine. Peasants arrived in the city home office with their woven fabric (often, as in the case of linens, mainly or entirely produced by hand out of raw materials). They then received for it, after a thorough—often certified—evaluation of the quality, the standard price. In those situations where markets were long distances away, the putter-out's customers were middlemen who also traveled to the city. In search of traditional quality rather than specific patterns, they either purchased from the home-office warehouse or picked up orders placed long in advance. They in turn placed further orders with the peasants for the particular cloth in demand.

The exchange of letters normally sufficed and travel to visit customers occurred infrequently and at long intervals, if at all. Slowly and increasingly, the sending of samples became more common. Business hours were typically moderate—perhaps five to six hours a day and occasionally considerably less, but sometimes more if a busy season existed. Earnings, although small, were adequate to maintain a respectable standard of living and, in good times, to permit the saving of small sums. In general, rooted in a strong consensus regarding basic business practices, among competitors a relatively high compatibility and existed. There was time for long daily visits to a social club and, occasionally, also early evening drinks and long talks with a circle of friends. A comfortable pace of life was the order of the day.

If one looked simply at the business character of the employer, at the indispensability of the movement of capital and its turnover within the business, and finally at the objective side of the economic process or the type of accounting, this was a "capitalist" form of organization in every respect. However, scrutiny of the *spirit* that inspired the employer also indicates that it was a "traditionalist" business; a traditional approach to life, rate of profit, amount of work, management of the business, and relationship to workers is apparent. The circle of customers remained constant as well. The manner of acquiring customers and markets was also traditional. All these factors dominated the operation of this business. Fundamental to this circle of employers, one can clearly state, was an "ethos."

At some point this ease and comfort were suddenly upset. Indeed, change occurred often even in the absence of an accompanying qualitative change of the organizational *form*, such as a changeover to a closed shop or the power loom. What happened frequently was simply that some young man from a family that ran a cottage industry moved out of the city and into the countryside, carefully selected weavers for his particular needs, and increasingly tightened their dependence and his supervision over them. In the process he transformed peasants into workers. At the same time he began to increase markets by directly catering to the final consumer: he took the retailing completely into his own hands, personally sought out customers, visited them regularly every year, and attempted above all to adapt the quality of his goods exclusively to the customers' needs and wishes. In these ways, he knew how to do justice to his customers, and simultaneously he began to institute a basic principle: "low prices, large sales."

Again and again, that which is always and universally the result of such a "rationalization" process occurred: whoever did not follow suit had to suffer loss and destruction as the consequences. The comfortable old ideal collapsed and crumbled in the face of a bitter competitive struggle. Considerable fortunes were won, yet they were not simply taken to the bank to earn interest. Rather, they were continuously reinvested in the business. And the old leisurely, easygoing approach to life yielded to a disciplined temperateness. Those who consumed little and *wanted* instead to acquire and earn rose to the top, and those who remained stuck in the old ways *had* to learn to do with less.[28]

Several cases are known to me in which small loans from one's relatives placed this entire revolutionary process into motion. As a rule, however, and important here, this transformation was *not* called forth by, for example, a massive influx of new *money*. Rather, a new *spirit* came into play: the spirit of modern capitalism. The question of the motivating forces behind the expansion of modern capitalism is not primarily one of the source of money reserves that can be used by capitalist firms, but above all a question of the development of the spirit of capitalism. Wherever this spirit becomes active and is able to have an effect, it *acquires* the money reserves to be used as fuel for modern capitalism's activity—not the other way around.[29]

* * *

But the entrance of the spirit of capitalism did not foster peace. The earliest of its innovators regularly confronted a flood of mistrust, occasionally hatred, and above all moral indignation. Frequently outright legends were created about secret and dark skeletons in the early lives of proponents of this spirit (several cases of this sort are known to me). It is not very easy for anyone to be so naive as not to recognize that only an unusually firm character could protect such a "new style" employer from a loss of his calm self-control and from economic as well as moral catastrophe. In addition, clarity of vision and strength to act decisively were required. Furthermore and above all, under these new circumstances only very specific and highly developed "ethical" qualities would be capable of winning over the absolutely indispensable trust of customers and workers. Finally, only such qualities could make possible the lasting resilience necessary to overcome innumerable obstacles and, most important, to undertake the infinitely more intensive workplace tasks now required of the employer. Because these ethical qualities were of a specifically different *type* from those adequate to the economic traditionalism of the past, they could not be reconciled with the comfortable enjoyment of life.

As a rule, the bold and unscrupulous speculators or the adventurous persons in pursuit of riches, such as are encountered in all epochs of economic development, have not created this transformation. It has been scarcely visible to all who investigate external changes only (such as a massive influx of new money), alterations in the forms of organizations, or changes in the organization of the economy. Nevertheless, these ethical qualities have been decisive for the infusion of economic life with this new spirit of capitalism. Nor were the "great financiers" pivotal. Rather, a different group proved central: men raised in the school of hard knocks, simultaneously calculating and daring but above all *dispassionate, steady*, shrewd, devoted fully to their cause, and in possession of strict, middle-class views and "principles."

One might be inclined to believe that not the slightest connection exists between these *personal* moral qualities and any ethical maxims, let alone any religious ideas as such. One might be further inclined to see here an essentially negative relationship: one could contend that leading an organized life oriented to business assumes a capacity to *withdraw* oneself from long-standing religious tradition. Hence, according to this line of reasoning, liberal "Enlightenment" views would constitute the adequate foundation for the life organized on behalf of business activity. In fact this argument is in general correct *today*. As a rule, a religious undergirding of the life oriented to business is absent.

Furthermore, wherever a relationship between business activity and religious belief exists, it turns out to be a negative one, at least in Germany. People who are saturated by the capitalist spirit *today* tend to be indifferent, if not openly hostile, to religion. The thought of pious boredom in paradise has little appeal for their activity-oriented natures, and religion appears to this group as a mechanism that pulls people away from the very foundation of existence—their work. If one were to question these people regarding the "meaning" of their restless hunt, which is never happy with possessions already owned—and for this reason alone must appear meaningless from the point of view of a completely this-worldly orientation of life—they would at times answer (if able to answer at all): "to care for the children and grandchildren." Nevertheless, because this motivation is apparently far from unique to them, and influences in the same manner all those with the approach to business of "economic traditionalism," they would more frequently offer the simple and more correct answer: With its stable work, the business is "indispensable to life." This answer is indeed the single actual motivation, and it immediately renders obvious the *irrationality*, from the point of view of one's personal happiness, of this organization of life: people live for their business rather than the reverse.

Obviously the inclination to seek power and esteem, which is gratified by the simple fact of ownership, plays a role here. When an entire people becomes fascinated with all things quantitatively large, as in the United States, then this romantic obsession with great size has an impact, with irresistible charm, upon the "poets" among businesspersons. This remains so even though the actual leaders among them, and especially the perpetually successful, are by and large not seduced by this fascination. Moreover, the behavior typical now of upwardly mobile capitalist families in Germany—the harried attempts to acquire landed estates and the patent of nobility for sons who, at the university and in the army officer corps, had behaved in a manner designed to banish all memories of their social origins—must be seen for what it is: a product of the decadence of status-climbing latecomers.[30]

The **ideal type** of the capitalist employer,[31] as appeared in Germany in a number of distinguished examples, has had nothing to do with this kind of more crass or more fine snobbery and social climbing. Such employers shy away from ostentatious display and all unnecessary expenditures, as well as the conscious enjoyment of their power. Moreover, the reception of the many awards they receive, as evidence of the general societal respect for them, is discomfiting to them. In other words, their organized life often carries a certain ascetic aspect, just as was apparent in the "sermon" by Franklin quoted above (and an exploration of the historical significance of just this important point will soon be our task). It is actually in no way unusual, but highly common to find in Franklin a degree of detached modesty, indeed a modesty essentially more candid than that reserve he recommends in such a prudent manner to others. He "has nothing" from his wealth for himself personally, except that irrational sense of having "fulfilled his calling" (*Berufserfüllung*) well.

Just this, however, is exactly that which appears to the precapitalist person so incomprehensible and puzzling, so vulgar and repulsive. That anyone could conceive of the idea of defining the exclusive goal of his life-long work as sinking into his grave weighed down with a heavy load of money and goods—this seems comprehensible to the precapitalist person only as the product of perverse drives: the *auri sacra fames*.

* * *

At the present time, in light of our political, legal, and economic institutions, and the forms of business and the structures that are unique to our economy, Franklin's spirit of capitalism could be understood as a pure product of adaptation, as noted. The capitalist economic order, it could be argued, needs this devotion to a "calling" of moneymaking. This devotion could then be seen as a type of behavior, in respect to external consumer goods, closely tied to this economic structure and the conditions of the capitalist order's victory in the earlier economic struggle of existence—indeed to such an extent that any necessary connection between this "acquisitive" manner of organizing life and a unified "worldview" (*Weltanschauung*) of any sort must be entirely rejected *today*.

It could be argued, in other words, that it is no longer necessary for this organization of life to be supported by the approval of any religious authority figures. Moreover, the influence of the norms of a church upon economic life, to the extent that they are still perceptible at all, could be viewed as an unjustifiable interference. The same could be said of all regulation of the economy by the state. Commercial-political and social-political interests then determine a person's "worldview." And those who do not adapt their organization of life to the conditions that make for success in capitalism's open market either fail or, at least, never move up.

This entire mode of argument, however, must itself be seen as a manifestation of our own time, a period in which modern capitalism has succeeded in emancipating itself from its old supporting framework. Capitalism, it will be remembered, managed to burst asunder in the late Middle Ages the old [feudal] forms of economic regulation only in alliance with the developing power of the modern state. We wish here to argue, in a preliminary fashion, that capitalism's relationship to the religious powers could have been exactly parallel—namely, a coalition between capitalism and religious belief tended to burst asunder the old economic traditionalism. It should be investigated here whether, and in what way, just this *was* the situation.

Surely it scarcely needs to be proven that the spirit of capitalism's comprehension of the acquisition of money as a "calling"—as an end in itself that persons were obligated to pursue—stood in opposition to the moral sensitivities of entire epochs in the past. The doctrine of *deo placere vix potest* [the merchant cannot be pleasing to God] was taken as genuine in medieval times (just as was the position of the Gospels against the taking of interest),[32] and was incorporated into Canon law and applied to the activity of the businessman. This was also evident in the view of St. Thomas Aquinas [1224–74, the most significant philosopher and theologian of the Middle Ages], who characterized the striving for profit as moral turpitude (including even unavoidable and thus ethically permitted profit).

Nonetheless, these positions held by the church stood in contrast to the radical opposition to the accumulation of wealth apparent in fairly broad circles; that is, these doctrinal positions already marked significant *accommodation* by Catholic doctrine to the interests of financial powers in the Italian cities, which were politically allied very closely with the church.[33] Yet even where Catholic doctrine accommodated still more, as for example happened with [the Dominican friar and bishop] Anthony of Florence [1389–1459], the perception never entirely disappeared that activity oriented to acquisition as an end in itself involved a fundamentally disgraceful situation, albeit one that existing realities made it necessary to tolerate.

A few ethical thinkers of the period, particularly adherents of the Nominalist school,[34] accepted as given the business practices of capitalism that had developed by that time. They then sought to demonstrate the legitimacy of those practices and, above all, to prove that commerce was necessary. Finally, they viewed the industriousness that arose out of trade as a legitimate source of profit and as ethically acceptable (though not without criticism). In general, however, the dominant teaching rejected the spirit of capitalist acquisition as moral turpitude, or at a minimum refused to value it as ethically positive. [1920]

"Moral" views, such as those of Benjamin Franklin, would have been simply inconceivable. Indeed, this was the position above all among capitalists themselves. Even when their life work followed religious traditions, they knew that their activities were at best ethically indifferent and only tolerated. Owing to the constant danger of a collision with the church's prohibition of usury, their activity remained suspect, indeed precisely with respect to the status of the believer's soul. As the sources indicate, on the occasion of the death of wealthy people quite considerable sums of money flowed from their pockets to religious institutions as "conscience money." In some cases this money even moved back to former debtors as compensation for sums unjustly taken as "usury."

The situation was different (aside from heretics and those viewed as possessing suspicious beliefs) only for those in patrician circles, for the nobility had already internally emancipated itself from religious traditions. Nevertheless, even skeptics and nonchurchgoers also believed it appropriate to make amends to the church through a lump sum donation to cover all eventualities. It seemed better to do so as insurance against the uncertainties of one's condition after death. At any rate (at least according to the more lax conception, which was very widespread), an external sign of submission to the commandments of the church was believed to be adequate to ensure salvation.[35] At precisely this point, either the *amoral* or even *immoral* nature of the activity of capitalists, skeptics, and nonchurchgoers, according to their *own* understanding of this activity, becomes evident.

* * *

How then does it come about that activity which, in the most favorable case, is barely morally tolerable becomes a "calling" in the manner practiced by Benjamin Franklin? How is it to be explained historically that in Florence, the center of capitalist development in the fourteenth and fifteenth centuries and the marketplace for money and capital for all of the great political powers, striving for profit was viewed as either morally questionable or at best tolerated? Yet in the business relationships found in small companies in rural Pennsylvania, where scarcely a trace of large-scale commerce could be found, where only the beginning stages of a banking system were evident, and where the economy was continuously threatened with collapse into sheer barter (as a result of a simple lack of money), the same striving for profit became viewed as legitimate. Indeed, it became understood as the essence of a morally acceptable, even praiseworthy, way of organizing and directing life.

To speak *here* of a "reflection" of "material" conditions in the "ideal superstructure" would be complete nonsense. Hence, our question: What set of ideas gave birth to the ordering of activity oriented purely to profit under the category of a "calling," to which the person felt an *obligation*? Just this set of ideas provided the ethical substructure and backbone for the "new style" employer's organized life.

Some have depicted **economic rationalism** as the basic characteristic of the modern economy in general. Sombart in particular, often in successful and effective discussions, has done so. Surely he has done so correctly if "economic rationalism" refers to the increase in productivity that results from the organization of the production process according to *scientific* vantage points—hence the banishing of the situation in which gains were restricted owing to the naturally given "organic" limitations of people. This rationalization process in the arenas of technology and the economy undoubtedly also conditions an important part of the "ideals of life" in the modern, middle-class society in general.

Work in the service of a rational production of material goods for the provision of humanity has without question always been hovering over the representatives of the capitalist spirit as a directing purpose of their life's labors. For example, one needs only to read about Franklin's efforts in Philadelphia in the service of community improvement to understand immediately this completely self-evident truth. Moreover, the joy and pride one feels in giving "work" to numerous people and in assisting the economic "flowering" (in the manner in which this term is associated, under capitalism, with population and trade figures) of one's hometown belongs obviously to the unique, and undoubtedly "idealistically" driven, satisfactions of the modern business establishment. And, likewise, the capitalist economy rationalizes on the basis of strictly *quantitative* calculations and is oriented to the sought-after economic success in a systematic and dispassionate manner.

These operating principles are inherent in and fundamental to capitalism. They contrast directly with the situation of the peasant who lives from hand to mouth, to the guild craftsmen in the medieval epoch who maintained market advantages rooted in old customs, and to the "adventure capitalist" who was oriented to political opportunities and irrational speculation. Thus it appears that the development of the "capitalist spirit" can be most easily understood as one component part in a larger and overarching development of rationalism as a whole. It appears further that this spirit should best be comprehended as derived from rationalism's basic position in respect to the ultimate problems of life. Hence, according to this interpretation, Protestantism would come into consideration historically only to the extent that it played a role as a "harbinger" of purely rationalistic views of life.

However, as soon as one seriously attempts to formulate the problem of the development of the spirit of capitalism in this way, it becomes clear that such a simple approach to this theme is inadequate. The reason is that the history of rationalism *by no means* charts out a progressive unfolding, according to which all the separate realms of life follow a *parallel* developmental line. The rationalization of private law, for example, if understood as the conceptual simplification and organization of the subject matter of the law, attained its heretofore highest form in the Roman law of later antiquity. It remained least rationalized, however, in some nations with the most highly rationalized economies. England offers an example. During the period of the development of [modern] capitalism in this nation, the power of large guilds of lawyers prevented the rebirth of Roman law. In contrast, rationalized Roman law has consistently remained dominant in the Catholic areas of southern Europe [where modern capitalism, compared to England, remained underdeveloped].

[Two more examples for the nonparallel development of the separate realms of life must suffice.] First, the purely secularized philosophy of the eighteenth century [the Enlightenment] surely was not based alone, or even primarily, in the highly developed capitalist nations. This philosophy of Voltaire [1694–1778] is even today the broad common inheritance of the upper and (what is more important practically) middle strata, especially in the Roman Catholic nations. Second, if one understands by the phrase *practical rationalism* that way of organizing life according to which the world's activities are consciously referred back to the practical interests of the *particular person*, and are judged from his or her specific vantage point,[36] then this style of life was typically unique primarily to *liberum arbitrium* [easygoing] peoples. Even today practical rationalism permeates the flesh and blood of the Italians and the French. And we have already convinced ourselves this is not the soil that primarily nourishes persons who relate to their "calling" as a task, as [modern] capitalism needs.

A simple sentence should stand at the center of every study that delves into "rationalism." It must not be forgotten that one can in fact "rationalize" life from a vast variety of ultimate vantage points. Moreover, one can do so in very different directions. "Rationalism" is a historical concept that contains within itself a world of contradictions.

Our task now is to investigate from whose spiritual child this matter-of-fact form of "rational" thinking and living grew. The idea of a "calling," and of the giving over of one's self to *work* in a calling, originated here. As noted, the entire notion of a "calling" must appear fully irrational from the vantage point of the person's pure self-interest in happiness. Yet the dedication to work in the manner of a "calling" has in the past constituted one of the characteristic components of our capitalist economic culture. It remains so even today. What interests *us* here is precisely the ancestral lineage of that *irrational* element which lies in this, as in every, conception of a "calling."[37]

CHAPTER III

LUTHER'S CONCEPTION OF THE CALLING

An audible echo from the religious realm unmistakably resonates in the German word *Beruf*. Perhaps even more apparent is this connotation in the equivalent English term **calling**: one's *task* is given by God. The more vigorously we place the accent on this term in actual usage, the more perceptible becomes the religious echo.

If we now trace this word historically and across the languages of the great civilizations, it quickly becomes apparent that an expression denoting a *calling* (in the sense of endowing work, as a demarcated arena, with a position in one's life) is just as little known among the predominantly Catholic peoples as it was among the peoples of classical antiquity.[1] Such an expression, however, does exist among *all* predominantly Protestant peoples. It is further apparent that a diffuse, unique ethnic character of the languages in question (such as the expression *spirit of the German people* implies) is not the issue here. On the contrary, the present-day meaning of the term *the calling* derives from *Bible translations*—indeed not from the spirit of the original but from the spirit of the translators.[2]

In the translation into German by Luther, *Beruf* appears to be used earliest in our present-day meaning in a passage from the Old Testament in Jesus Sirach (11:20–21).[3] It then quickly acquired its present significance in the everyday language of all Protestant peoples. There had been *no* trace of this expression earlier, either in secularized literature or in sermons. As near as I can tell, it appears instead only in the writings of one German mystic, and his influence upon Luther is well-known.[4]

Moreover, just as the meaning of the word is new, so is (and this should be well-known) the *idea* new. The concept of the calling is a product of the Reformation. This is not to say that certain early signs of an appreciation of daily work, as found in the notion of a calling, were not already visible in the Middle Ages and even in (*late* Hellenistic) Antiquity, as will be addressed later. At any rate, one aspect was unequivocally *new*: the fulfillment of duty in vocational callings became viewed as the highest expression that moral activity could assume. Precisely this new notion of the moral worth of devoting oneself to a calling was the unavoidable result of the idea of attaching religious significance to daily work. The earliest conception of a calling in this sense was produced in this manner.

Hence, the concept of *calling* expresses the central dogma of all Protestant denominations, a dogma that rejects Catholicism's division of the ethical commandments into *praecepta* [that which is commanded] and *consilia* [that which is advised]. The single means of living in a manner pleasing to God changes accordingly: an ascetic withdrawal from the world, as practiced by monks, and the clear **surpassing** of the world's routine morality of daily life that such asceticism implied, is now replaced by *this-worldly work*. This work involves the fulfillment of duties, all of which derive from the [social and occupational] positions of each person. The "calling" for each person is defined through these positions.

Luther[5] developed these ideas in the course of the first decades of his reform activities. At the beginning, quite in keeping with the dominant medieval tradition, (as exemplified, for example, by Thomas Aquinas),[6] Luther viewed this-worldly work as belonging to the realm of the flesh. Although said to be desired by God and the indispensable natural foundation of the devout life, work had no moral salience, any more than eating and drinking.[7] However, with the more clear implementation of his notion of "salvation through the single believer's faith" (*sola fide*) in all its consistency, which resulted in an increasingly acute contrast to the Catholic evangelical councils of monks and friars (which Luther saw as "commanded by the devil"), the meaning of the calling became steadily more important to him.

To Luther, a monastic *organization of life*, and the monk's perception of it as legitimate in the eyes of God, is now obviously of no value whatsoever. Moreover, Luther understands monasticism as a product of an egoistic lovelessness that withdraws from one's duties in the world. By contrast, this-worldly work in a vocation appears to him to be a visible expression of brotherly love, a notion he anchors in a highly unrealistic manner indeed and in contrast (almost grotesquely) to the well-known passages of [the founder of modern economics], Adam Smith [1723–90].[8] Luther does so mainly by indicating that the division of labor forces every person to work for *others*. Owing, however, to the essentially scholastic[9] nature of this justification, this argument is soon abandoned. Luther emphasizes instead, and with increasing vigor, that the fulfillment of one's duties in the world constitutes, under all circumstances, the only way to please God. This fulfillment, and only this, is God's will. Therefore, every permissible calling is of absolutely equal validity before God.[10]

* * *

That this moral legitimation of vocational life was one of the Reformation's most influential achievements, and in particular the achievement of Luther, is truly beyond doubt. It may even rightly be understood as self-evident.[11] It stands worlds away from the deep hatred with which the contemplative voice of [the French mathematician and philosopher Blaise] Pascal [1623–62][12] repudiates all favorable evaluation of activity in the world. Such activity can be explained only by reference to vanity or slyness, according to Pascal's deepest conviction.[13] The broad-ranging **utilitarian *adaptation* to the world** practiced by Jesuit Probabilism[14] stands even further away from Reformation views. Yet how the practical significance of this achievement of Protestantism is to be presented in a detailed manner seems a conundrum. This achievement is more often dimly perceived than clearly recognized.

First of all, it is scarcely necessary to establish that Luther's writings, for example, cannot be spoken of as having an inner affinity with the capitalist spirit in the way in which we have until now defined this phrase (or by the way, in any manner whatsoever). Even those church circles that most eagerly praise every "achievement" of the Reformation are not today allied with capitalism in any of its forms. Even Luther himself would undoubtedly have harshly repudiated any relationship with the **frame of mind** that came to the fore with Franklin.

Of course, one should not take his complaints against the great adventure merchants, such as Fugger[15] and others like him, as evidence of his opposition to this frame of mind. Surely the struggle of Luther and others in the sixteenth and seventeenth centuries against the *privileged* position, either legal or factual, of certain large commercial companies can best be compared to the modern campaign against the privileges of trust companies, rather than be understood as a manifestation of the *economic traditionalist* frame of mind. The Huguenots and the **Puritans**, both supporters of the spirit of capitalism, were (alongside the Lutherans) also engaged in the bitter struggles against the large commercial companies, against the House of Lombardy bankers, and against the *Trapeziten*.[16] They also opposed the monopolists, bankers, and large-scale speculators favored by the Anglican Church and the kings and parliaments of England and France.[17] After the battle of Dunbar (September 1650), [Oliver] Cromwell [1599-1658][18] wrote to the Long Parliament: "Be pleased to reform the abuses of all professions, and if there be any one that makes many poor to make a few rich, that suits not a Commonwealth." Yet it is apparent from other passages that Cromwell is completely infused with a specifically "capitalist" mode of thinking.[19]

In contrast, and even compared to the writings of late Scholasticism, Luther's numerous statements against usury and against interest in general reveal an altogether "backward" understanding of the essence of capitalist acquisition (viewed from the perspective of modern capitalism).[20] Of particular prominence was his support for the argument (already discredited by Anthony of Florence) that monetary measures remained incapable of enhancing productivity.

We need not, however, be more specific here regarding this point. The idea of a calling in the *religious* sense was capable of taking, when viewed from the vantage point of its consequences for the organization of life in the everyday world of work, a variety of forms. The achievement of the Reformation, in contrast to the Catholic position, was primarily to increase drastically the infusion of work (organized by a calling) with a moral accent and to place a **religious** value, or **reward**, on it. How the idea of a "calling," which gave expression to just this achievement, further unfolded depended on the particular formation of the notions of piety in the different Reformation churches.

* * *

The authority of the Bible, from which Luther believed he took the idea of the calling, actually generally favored economic traditionalism. In particular, the Old Testament never expresses an idea of surpassing the routine morality of daily life. This notion is not found in the Old Testament's classical prophecy and is otherwise visible only in scattered and incomplete passages. A religious idea extremely similar to that of the calling is formulated strictly only in one sense: Every believer must stay at his "livelihood" and leave the godless to strive for gain. This is the meaning of all those passages that directly address occupations. The Talmud makes the first break from this idea, but it is only a partial break and not a fundamental one. Jesus' position is characterized, in classical clarity, in the typical entreaty of the ancient Near East: "Give us this *day* our daily bread." Moreover, the presence of a radical element in Jesus' teachings that rejects the world as it is, as manifest in the μαμωνᾶς τῆς ἀδικίας [the sinfulness of ownership], excluded any *direct* linking of the modern idea of the calling with Jesus personally.[21]

In the era of the Christian apostles, as it is expressed in the New Testament and especially in St. Paul, the notion of a calling in one's worldly vocation was viewed either with indifference or, as in the Old Testament, essentially in the manner of economic traditionalism. The eschatological expectations that filled the first generations of Christians account for this indifference and traditionalism: because all changes awaited the coming of the Lord, the devout wished only to remain in the status and occupation in which God's "call" had found them—and to continue to labor as before. In this way, the faithful would not become impoverished and burdensome to fellow believers. And, in the end, the period of waiting would last only a short time.

Luther upheld economic traditionalism, and increasingly so, throughout the course of his development from approximately 1518 to approximately 1530. He read the Bible through the lens of his mood at the given time.[22] In the first years of his reform activity and as a consequence of his understanding of the calling essentially in terms of the basic survival of the person, Luther's thinking about the appropriate *type* of this-worldly activity was dominated by views having an inner affinity with the eschatological indifference of St. Paul (expressed in 1 Cor. 7:20–24).[23] Luther was convinced that people of every status can become saved; to lend importance to the *type* of calling in this short pilgrimage of life would be meaningless. Therefore, the striving for material gain that goes beyond one's own needs, Luther argues, must be a symptom of one's lack of grace. Indeed, because striving for gain appears to be possible only at the expense of others, this pursuit must be viewed as an unequivocal abomination.[24]

An increasing estimation of the significance of work in a calling develops for Luther parallel to his own increasing engagement in the affairs of the world. As this occurs, he simultaneously comes to see each person's particular calling as, more and more, a special command of God to that person: the tasks incumbent upon a particular position must be fulfilled because Divine Providence has placed the believer in *this* position. After the peasant uprisings [1524–25] and the struggles against the *Schwarmgeister*,[25] Luther increasingly comes to see the objective historical order—into which God places the individual—as a direct manifestation of Divine Will.[26] The increasingly strong emphasis on the role of providential forces, even in life's disjointed happenings, now leads him more and more to emphasize the importance of Divine Will as "fate," an idea that proved compatible with economic traditionalism: the individual should basically *stay* in the calling and status in which God has first placed him. His striving in this life should remain within the boundaries of his existing life situation.

Hence, whereas Luther's economic traditionalism at the beginning was anchored in Pauline indifference to the world, his economic traditionalism later flowed out of an increasingly more intense belief in Divine Providence[27] that identified an unconditional obedience to God[28] with an unconditional submission to one's given lot. This way of thinking could not at all carry Luther to a fundamentally new way of linking work in a calling with *religious* principles, or in general to the formulation of a substantive foundation for such a linkage.[29] The purity of *doctrine*, as the single infallible criterion of Luther's church, had itself inhibited the development of new views in the realm of ethics. To Luther this doctrine stood as increasingly irrevocable after the [peasant] uprisings of the 1520s.

* * *

Thus, Luther's conception of the calling remained tied to economic traditionalism.[30] As a divine decree, the calling is something that must be *submitted to*: persons must "resign" themselves to it. This accent in Luther's writings outweighs the other idea also present in his thought: that work in a calling is one, or actually *the*, task given to people by God.[31] The development of orthodox Lutheranism stressed even further the idea of a resignation to one's calling.

With respect to ethical action, Lutheranism did not involve an ascetic notion of duty. Hence any possibility for a surpassing of the routine morality of daily life was eliminated. The negative consequences for ethical action become apparent once an acknowledgment of this aspect of Lutheranism is combined with its central features: the preaching of obedience to secular authority and believers' resignation to their life-situation as it is given to them. These admonitions for obedience and resignation constituted, in its earliest stage, Lutheranism's only ethical contribution.[32]

As will be explained when we turn to a discussion of medieval religious ethics, the idea of the calling in this formulation of Lutheranism had already been worked through for the most part by the German mystics. [Johannes] Tauler [1300–1361] established the principle of the equal value of clerical and this-worldly callings and the *lesser* value of the monastic forms of ascetic works and service.[33] These positions both resulted from the

decisive significance he accorded to the ecstatic-contemplative incorporation of the divine spirit through the soul. Thus, compared to the mystics,
Lutheranism implied, in a certain way, actually a step backwards. This occurred to the extent that (for Luther and more so for his church) the psychological underpinning for a rational vocational ethic became rather
unstable, compared to the views of the mystics (which often remind one
partly of the Pietist and partly of the Quaker psychologies of faith).[34] As has
yet to be demonstrated, this instability developed precisely *because* Luther
remained suspicious of mysticism's inclination toward ascetic self-discipline; he saw such self-discipline as a form of salvation through good
works. For this reason, mysticism in Luther's church had to fade more and
more into the background.

Hence, as can be ascertained so far, the idea of the calling for Luther had
only an uncertain impact on that which *we* are here seeking to understand:
[the emergence of the spirit of capitalism]. At this point we have not sought
to determine more.[35] This conclusion, it must be noted, does not in the least
imply that the Lutheran alterations of religious life may not have had a
practical significance for the development of the spirit of capitalism. Indeed the contrary holds. Nonetheless, we can now see that Lutheranism's significance for the unfolding of this spirit is not to be *directly* derived from the
position of *Luther* and his church in regard to a this-worldly vocational calling.
Other Protestant denominations may more clearly establish a connection
between the calling and the spirit of capitalism. It makes sense now for us to
turn to those denominations that establish a connection between *practical*
life and religious belief in a more direct manner than Lutheranism did.

* * *

The striking role of *Calvinism* and the Protestant *sects* in the history of
capitalism's development has already been noted. Luther found in [the
Swiss Reformation theologian Ulrich] Zwingli [1484–1531][36] a "spirit quite
different" from his own, as did Luther's spiritual descendents, especially
Calvinists. With a vengeance, Catholicism considered Calvinism to be its
real opponent, from its early stages and to the present.

These enmities can be viewed first by reference to purely political causes.
As the Reformation was inconceivable without Luther's personal religious
development and was spiritually determined in a lasting manner by his personality, an enduring practical impact of Luther's works would have been,
without Calvinism, equally inconceivable. But the cause of the shared Catholic and Lutheran antipathy to Calvinism clearly lies in Calvinism's uniqueness. Even a superficial glance at Calvinism reveals a formulation of the
relationship between the religious life and earthly *action* completely different
from those found in both Catholicism and Lutheranism.

This difference is evident even in literature that exclusively uses explicit
religious motives. One need only compare, for example, the ending of *The
Divine Comedy* [by Dante Alighieri, 1265–1321], where the poet in Paradise
stands passive and speechless before the mystery of the Divine, to the con-

clusion of that poem we are accustomed to call the "Divine Comedy of Puritanism." After the description of the *expulsion* from Paradise, [the English poet John] Milton [1608–1674] concludes the last song of *Paradise Lost* as follows:

> They, looking back, all the eastern side beheld
> Of paradise, so late their happy seat,
> Waved over by that flaming brand; the gate
> With dreadful faces thronged and fiery arms.
> Some natural tears they dropped, but wiped them soon:
> *The world was all before them, where to choose*
> *Their place of rest, and Providence their guide.*
> They hand in hand with wandering steps and slow,
> Through *Eden* took their solitary way.[37]

And a little earlier Michael had said to Adam:

> . . . Only add
> Deeds to thy knowledge answerable; add faith;
> Add virtue, patience, temperance; add love,
> By name to come called Charity, the soul
> Of all the rest: then wilt thou not be loth
> *To leave this Paradise, but shall possess*
> *A Paradise within thee, happier far.*[38]

Every person immediately feels that this powerful expression of the grave Puritan turning-to-the-world—that is, the valuing of life's matter-of-fact activities as a *task*—would never have been expressed by a medieval writer. Yet this turning-to-the-world is just as incompatible with Lutheranism, as is apparent, for example, in the hymns of Luther and [the poet and composer of confessional hymns] Paul Gerhardt [1607–76].

We must be more specific at this point. This vague sense that significant differences exist here must now be replaced by a somewhat more precise conceptual *formulation* of these differences. Moreover, the inner causes of these differences [between Catholicism, Lutheranism, and Calvinism] must be investigated.

The Task of the Investigation[39]

The appeal to "national character" (*Volkscharakter*) [as the source of these differences] is not only generally a confession of *ignorance*; it is, in this instance, entirely invalid as well. On the one hand, it would be historically incorrect to ascribe a unified "national character" to the English of the seventeenth century. "Cavaliers" [supporters of Charles I] and "Roundheads" [Puritans and supporters of Parliament] perceived themselves not simply as two groups but as radically different human species—and whoever studies them attentively must agree with them on this point.[40] On the other hand, a contrast in national character between the English merchant adventurers and the old Hanseatic merchants in Hamburg is as little to be found as any significant distinction between the English and Germans at the end of the Middle Ages. Furthermore, those differences that did exist can be clearly explained by reference to varying political constellations.[41] The power of the religious movements, not alone but above all other factors, created the differences noted here. These differences are familiar to us even today.[42]

This investigation of the relationships between the old Protestant ethic and the development of the capitalist spirit begins with Calvin's innovations, with Calvinism, and with the other puritanical sects. Nevertheless, the selection of this point of departure should not be understood as implying an expectation to discover the capitalist spirit in one of the founders or representatives of these religious groups (the awakening of which would then be viewed, in some way, as the *goal* of his life work). We surely will not be able to believe that any one of them considered the striving after the world's consumer goods as an end in itself; that is, as an ethical value.

Moreover, one point in particular should be kept in mind above all: Programs of ethical change were not the central issue for any of the religious reformers who must be examined for this investigation, such as Menno [Simons, 1469–1561, founder of the Mennonites], George Fox [1624–91, founder of the Quakers], and [John] Wesley [1703–91, co-founder of the Methodists]. These men were not the founders of societies for "ethical culture" or representatives of a humanitarian striving for social reform or cultural ideals. The salvation of the soul stood at the center of their lives and deeds—and that alone. Their ethical goals and the practical effects of their teachings were all anchored in the salvation theme and must be seen entirely as the *consequences* of purely religious motives. Furthermore, we must therefore be prepared to note that the cultural influences of the Reformation were to a great extent (and perhaps even predominantly from our particular vantage point) the unforeseen and even *unwanted* results of the [theological] labor of the Reformation figures. Indeed, the cultural influences stood often quite distant from, or precisely in opposition to, all that the religious reformers had in mind.

Hence, in its modest manner, the following study might perhaps constitute a contribution to the illumination of the way in which "ideas" become generally effective in history. In order, however, to prevent misunderstandings at the outset in regard to the manner in which we are here asserting that purely ideal motives may become effective forces, a few further small clarifications on this theme may be permitted. These clarifications can serve as concluding comments to the introductory discussion [presented immediately above and in chapters 1 and 2].

* * *

It should be directly stated that studies such as this one are in no way concerned with the attempt to *evaluate* the substantive ideas of the Reformation by reference to either social-political or religious vantage points. Instead our goals concern aspects of the Reformation that must appear to persons with a religious consciousness as peripheral and related to superficial matters only. After all, it is our task to investigate and to clarify the impact that religious motives had on that web of development in the direction of our modern, specifically "this-worldly"-oriented life and culture generally—a development that grew out of innumerable, fragmented historical forces. Thus, we are in the end asking a question: Which characteristic features of our modern life and culture should be *attributed* to the influence of the Reformation? In other words, to what extent did the Reformation serve as a historical cause of these characteristic features?

On the one hand, in asking this question, we must of course emancipate ourselves from the point of view that the Reformation can be "deduced" from economic transformations as a "developmental-historical necessity." Constellations of innumerable historical forces had to interact if the newly created churches were to endure. By no means can reference to a "law of economic development" or, more generally, to economic points of view of whatever sort, do justice to the complexity of these developments. Rather, political processes, in particular, had to interact with economic forces.

On the other hand, we shall not defend here two foolish and doctrinaire theses[43] in any form: (1) that the capitalist spirit (in the still provisional use of this term utilized here) *could* have originated *only* as an expression of certain influences of the Reformation, and (2) that capitalism as an *economic system* was a creation of the Reformation. The latter position is rendered once and for all untenable by the simple fact that certain important *forms* of capitalist business companies are drastically older than the Reformation.[44] Instead, it should here be ascertained only whether, and to what extent, religious influences *co*-participated in the qualitative formation and quantitative expansion of this spirit across the globe. We wish further to assess which practical *aspects* of the *culture* upon which [modern] capitalism rests can be traced back to these religious influences.

In light of the immense confusion of the reciprocal influences among the material foundation, the forms of social and political organizations, and the various spiritual streams of the Reformation epoch, we can only proceed in the following manner. *First*, we will investigate whether (and in what ways) specific "**elective affinities**" (*Wahlverwandtschaften*) between certain forms of religious belief and a vocational ethic (*Berufsethik*) are discernible. Doing so will allow us, whenever possible, to illuminate the type of influence that the religious movement, as a consequence of these elective affinities, had upon the development of economic culture. In addition, the general *direction* of this influence upon economic culture, as a consequence of these elective affinities, can be clarified. Second, *only after* this influence has been satisfactorily established can an attempt be made to estimate to what degree the historical origin of the values and ideas of our modern life can be attributed to religious forces stemming from the Reformation, and to what degree to other forces.

PART II

THE VOCATIONAL ETHIC

OF

ASCETIC PROTESTANTISM

Above all, . . . fundamental for our discussion is the investigation of the idea of a testifying to one's belief as the psychological point of origin for methodical ethics.

(p. 121)

Finally, and of central importance, the special life of the saint—fully separate from the "natural" life of wants and desires—could no longer play itself out in monastic communities set apart from the world. Rather, the devoutly religious must now live saintly lives in the world and amidst its mundane affairs. This rationalization of the organized and directed life—now in the world yet still oriented to the supernatural—was the effect of ascetic Protestantism's concept of the calling.

(p. 140)

As far as its power extended, the Puritan life outlook benefited under all circumstances the on-going trend toward a middle-class, economically rational organization of life. This outlook was, of course, far more important than the mere facilitating of the formation of capital. Indeed, it was the most substantial and, above all, single consistent social carrier of this middle-class mode of organizing life. Just this rational organization of life stood at the cradle of modern "economic man."

(p. 153)

A religion of predestination obliterates the goodness of God, for He becomes a hard, majestic king. Yet it shares with religions of fate the capacity for inducing nobility and rigor in its devotees.

(1968, p. 572)

[sk]

CHAPTER IV

THE RELIGIOUS FOUNDATIONS OF THIS-WORLDLY ASCETICISM

There have been four major historical **carriers** of **ascetic Protestantism** (in the manner in which "ascetic Protestanism" is used here): (1) Calvinism *in the form* it took in the major regions it dominated in Western Europe, especially during the seventeenth century; (2) Pietism; (3) Methodism; and (4) the **sects** that grew out of the baptizing movement (the Baptists, Mennonites, and Quakers).[1] None of these carriers of ascetic Protestantism were absolutely separate from any of the others, and the distinction vis-à-vis the non-ascetic churches of the Reformation cannot be strictly maintained.

Methodism originated in the middle of the eighteenth century within the Church of England. Rather than aiming to create a new church, the founders of Methodism were more intent on awakening an ascetic spirit inside this state church. Indeed, Methodism became separate from the Anglican Church only later in the course of its development, and mainly after its transplantation to America.

Pietism grew out of the soil of English, and especially, Dutch Calvinism. Through barely perceivable linkages it remained tied to Calvinism until the end of the seventeenth century. Under the effective influence of [the German theologian Phillipp Jacob] Spener [1635–1705],[2] it then became, in a manner only partly grounded in dogma, incorporated into Lutheranism. It remained a movement inside the Lutheran church. Only the followers of [Count Nicolaus von] Zinzendorf [1700-1760],[3] who had been influenced in part by the Hussite and Calvinist echoes in the Moravian Brethren (*Herrnhuter*) sect,[4] were, like Methodists, pushed against their will to form a peculiar sort of sect outside the Lutheran Church.

Calvinism and the baptizing movement were sharply divided and hostile toward one another at the beginning of their development. The Baptists of the later seventeenth century, however, became closely associated with Calvinism.

At the beginning of this century the boundaries of these groups were permeable, as was even the case among the Independent sects in England and Holland. And as the history of Pietism demonstrates, the transition to Lutheranism was also gradual, as was that from Calvinism to the Anglican Church, despite the fact that Anglicanism was related to Catholicism through its external features as well as through the spiritual inclinations of its most devout adherents. Indeed, although the broad following of the ascetic movement (which will be referred to, in the most general sense of this amorphous term, as *Puritanism*),[5] and especially its most ardent proponents, attacked the very foundation of Anglicanism, the differences between them became sharp only in the midst of conflicts and even then only gradually. Moreover, the relationship between these groups remains unchanged even if we completely leave aside the questions of governance and organizational structure. For the moment these questions do not interest us.

Even the most important dogmatic differences, such as those concerning the doctrines of **predestination** and justification, merged into one another in a wide variety of combinations. Hence, the preservation of distinct church communities was quite often hindered, even at the beginning of the seventeenth century. Above all, and this is most important for us here, identical manifestations of the *moral* **organization of life** are found, regardless of whether we turn to the four carriers of ascetic Protestantism noted above or to any of the many denominations that arose out of them. We shall see that similar ethical maxims can be attached to various dogmatic foundations. Moreover, the highly influential literary devices employed in the organized care of the soul influenced one another in the course of time. This holds mainly with respect to the casuistic manuals[6] of the various faiths. Great similarities are found among them despite the notoriously different ways in which they organized practical life.

* * *

Thus, it might almost seem that we would do best to ignore the dogmatic foundations and ethical theories of these churches and sects. Instead we could focus our efforts purely on their moral practices (to the extent that they can be ascertained). To do so, however, would not be wise. Of course it is true that the dogmatic roots of ascetic morality, which varied across different denominations, died off after terrible struggles. Nonetheless, the original anchoring of ascetic morality to these dogmas not only left strong legacies in the "undogmatic" subsequent ethics; in addition, *only* knowledge of the content of the foundational ideas teaches us to understand how this ascetic morality was connected with the thought about the *next life*. Indeed, the next life absolutely dominated people's religious thinking at that time. The moral awakening, which considerably influenced the *practical* life of believers, would *not* have been set in motion without the overarching power held by the next life over the believer.

Obviously the issue for us does not involve what was theoretically and officially *taught* in the ethical manuals of the time. This is not to deny that such teachings certainly had a practical significance through their influence on church discipline, pastoral care, and preaching.[7] Our interest, however, is altogether otherwise: we wish to ascertain which *psychological motivations* gave direction to the organization of the believer's life and held the individual firmly to it. Although these motivations were created both through religious belief and the practice of the religious life, to a great degree particular religious beliefs stood at their origin. People at that time brooded over seemingly abstract dogmas to an extent that becomes understandable to us today only if we comprehend the connection of these dogmas with practical-religious interests.

Now an exploration of a few dogmatic considerations[8] becomes indispensable. This remains so even though they must appear just as tedious to nontheologians as they will seem hurried and superficial to those well-versed in theology. We can only proceed by examining the religious ideas as **ideal types**, namely, as constructed concepts endowed with a degree of consistency seldom found in actual history. Precisely *because* of the impossibility of drawing sharp boundaries in historical reality, our only hope of identifying the particular effects of these religious ideas must come through an investigation of their *most consistent* [or "ideal"] forms.

A. CALVINISM

Now the set of beliefs[9] around which the great political and cultural conflicts in the most highly developed capitalist nations in the sixteenth and seventeenth centuries—the Netherlands, England, and France—were fought was Calvinism.[10] Hence, we first turn to these beliefs.[11]

The doctrine of *predestination* was seen at that time as Calvinism's most characteristic dogma, and this view remains generally true even today. To be sure, debates have been fought over the question of whether this doctrine constituted "the most essential" dogma of the **Reformed Church** or whether it was simply an "appendage."

Judgments about the extent to which a historical force is essential are of one of two types: they may be judgments rooted in values and faith. Here the essential in regard to the historical force is understood as the single factor "of interest" or of lasting "value." On the other hand they may be judgments regarding the *causal* significance of the historical force in relation to other historical forces. Here the concern is one of historical judgments regarding the attribution of causality.

Our question concerns the extent to which cultural-historical *effects* are to be attributed to the doctrine of predestination. These effects appear quite strong. The doctrine of predestination shattered [Johan von] Oldenbarneveldt's [1547–1619] struggle [against the Dutch state],[12] and the schism in the Anglican Church became irrevocable under [the anti-Puritan monarch] James I [1566–1625] owing to dogmatic differences over this doctrine between the Crown and Puritanism. Indeed, the *doctrine of predestination* came to be perceived as the primary danger posed by Calvinism to the state, and the state struggled against it.[13]

The great synods of the seventeenth century—the **Dordrecht** and **Westminster** above all—but also countless smaller ones, placed the elevation of this doctrine to canonical validity at the center of their work. It served as the fixed point of reference for innumerable heroes of the *ecclesia militans* [battling sects and churches]. In the eighteenth and nineteenth centuries it called forth divisions in the churches and became the battle cry of the Great Awakening movements. Hence, the doctrine of predestination cannot be overlooked. Yet it may no longer be familiar to every educated person today. For now, let us become acquainted with its major features through several passages from its authoritative source: the Westminster Confession of 1647. The Independent and Baptist believers took their positions on predestination from this document.

> Chapter 9 (of Free Will), No. 3. Man, by his fall into a state of sin, hath wholly lost all ability of will to any spiritual good accompanying salvation; so, a natural man, being altogether averse from that Good, and dead in sin, is not able, by his own strength, to convert himself, or to prepare himself thereunto.

> Chapter 3 (of God's Eternal Decree), No. 3. By the decree of God, for the manifestation of His glory, some men are predestinated unto everlasting life, and others foreordained to everlasting death.

> No. 5. Those of mankind that are predestinated unto life, God, before the foundation of the world was laid, according to His eternal and immutable purpose, and the secret counsel and good pleasure of His will, hath chosen in Christ unto everlasting glory, out of His mere free grace and love, without any foresight of faith or good works, or perseverance in either of them, or any other thing in the creature as conditions, or causes moving Him thereunto, and all to the praise of His glorious grace.

> No. 7. The rest of mankind God was pleased, according to the unsearchable counsel of His own will, whereby He extendeth, or with-holdeth mercy, as He pleaseth, for the glory of His sovereign power over His creatures, to pass by, and to ordain them to dishonor and wrath for their sin, to the praise of His glorious justice.

> Chapter 10 (of Effectual Calling), No. 1. All those whom God hath predestinated unto life, and those only, He is pleased, in His appointed and accepted time, effectually to call, by His word and spirit (out of that state of sin and death, in which they are by nature) ... taking away their heart of stone, and giving unto them an heart of flesh; renewing their wills, and by His almighty power determining them to that which is good. . . .

> Chapter 5 (of Providence), No. 6. As for those wicked and ungodly men, whom God as a righteous judge, for former sins, doth blind and harden, from them He not only with-holdeth His grace, whereby they might have been enlightened in their understandings, and wrought upon in their hearts, but sometimes also withdraweth the gifts which they had; and exposeth them to such objects as their corruption makes occasion of sin; and withal, gives them over to their own lusts, the temptations of the world, and the power of Satan: whereby it comes to pass that they harden themselves, even under those means which God useth for the softening of others.[14]

Milton's judgment on this doctrine was well-known: "Even if I land in Hell, this God will never command my respect."[15] Our concern, however, is not to evaluate this doctrine of predestination. Rather, we wish to assess its historical significance. We can only cast a glance at the question of this doctrine's origin and the contexts of ideas with which it merged in Calvinist theology.

Two possible paths led to the doctrine of predestination. The phenomenon of the religious feeling of salvation goes together with the feeling of certainty that the salvation destiny of every person must be exclusively attributed to the hand of an objective power—and one's own influence has not the slightest effect. The combination of these two pathways held especially for the most passionate and active believers, whom we see repeatedly in the history of Christianity since St. Augustine [354–430 C.E.].[16] The powerful mood of happy certainty, which releases the tremendous tension caused by the feeling of sinfulness, seemingly breaks over the faithful with great suddenness. As it does so, any possibility of the idea that this unimaginable gift of salvation could be attributed, in any way, to the helpful effects of one's own actions is destroyed. The idea that one's state of grace may be connected to achievements or qualities of one's own belief and will is likewise banished.

At the peaks of his highest genius, when Luther was capable of writing his *On the Freedom of the Christian* [1521], this "secret decree" of God also constituted for him the most firm and absolutely singular and ungrounded source of his religious state of grace.[17] Luther never formally abandoned the notion of predestination. However, it never acquired a central position in his theological thought; indeed it moved more and more into the background. The significance of the idea of predestination diminished to the same extent that Luther, as a responsible political actor in the church, was forced to become more of a "political realist." [Luther's ally Philipp] Melanchthon [1497–1560] quite intentionally avoided incorporating this "dangerous and gloomy" doctrine into the Augsburg Confession [1530].[18] Moreover, the church fathers of Lutheranism took a firm stand on this doctrine: salvation can be lost (*amissibilis*), but it can be won back through penitent humility and faithful trust in the word of God and the sacraments.

* * *

Precisely the opposite development occurred with Calvin: the significance of the doctrine of predestination noticeably increased in the course of his polemical debates over dogma with his opponents.[19] It was fully developed only in the third edition of Calvin's *Institutes* [1543], and it acquired its central position only after his death in the great conflicts that the Dordrecht and Westminster synods attempted to bring to a close. For Calvin, unlike for Luther, this "horrible decree" (*decretum horribile*) is *not lived* but *thought*. Therefore, the significance of predestination increases with every further growth in the consistency of Calvin's thought in the direction of his religious interests: toward God alone and not individuals. God does not exist for people; rather, people exist to serve the Will of God.[20] Everything that takes place, including the fact that only a small part of humanity will be called to be saved (an idea Calvin never doubted), becomes meaningful only in light of their service to a single goal: the glorification of God's majesty. To apply the standards of earthly "justice" to His sovereign commands is nonsensical and an infringement upon His majesty.[21] *Free* and obedient to no law, God and God alone can make His decrees comprehensible and known to us. He does so only insofar as He finds it good to do so.

We can be certain regarding these fragments of the eternal truth, and only these fragments. All else, including the *meaning* of our individual destiny, is surrounded in dark mysteries that are impossible to fathom and to gauge. A complaint from the damned, for example, that their destinies were undeserved would be similar to animals grumbling about not having been born as human beings. Separated from God by an unbridgeable gulf, all creatures deserve from Him—to the extent that He does not choose another way for the glorification of His majesty—only eternal death.

We know only that a part of humanity will be saved and the rest damned. To assume that service to God or faults of people could play a part in co-deciding this destiny would be to understand God's absolutely free decisions, which have existed as absolutes from eternity, as capable of being changed by human influence. This idea is unthinkable. Out of the New Testament's image of the "father in heaven," who acts according to motives understandable by humans and who delights in the return of every sinner to the fold as a woman rejoices in finding lost coins [Luke 15, 8–10], there develops here a transcendental Being totally inaccessible to human understanding. From eternity, and entirely according to God's inaccessible decisions, every person's destiny has been decided. Even the smallest detail in the universe is controlled.[22] Because His decrees are firm and unalterable, His grace cannot be lost once granted and cannot be attained once denied.

For the mood of a generation that devoted itself to the grandiose consistency of the doctrine of predestination, its melancholy inhumanity must have had one result above all: a feeling of unimaginable inner *loneliness of the solitary individual*.[23] The question of eternal salvation constituted people's primary life concern during the Reformation epoch, yet they were directed to pursue their life's journey in solitude. Moreover, the destiny they would encounter at journey's end had been unalterably set for them since eternity. And no one could help them.

Because only the "elect" can understand the divine word spiritually, no priests could assist believers. And performance of the sacraments would not be helpful: although commanded by God to increase His glory and therefore to be scrupulously observed, the sacraments did not constitute means to acquire divine grace. Rather, they existed only as subjective *externa subsidia* [external supplements] to one's faith. Indeed, no church existed to assist believers. Although the axiom *extra ecclesiam nulla salus* [there can be no salvation outside the Church] remained in place, in the sense that whoever stayed apart from the true church could not belong among the elect,[24] the damned also belonged to the (external) church. Moreover, the condemned *should* belong to the church and comply with its discipline. Membership was necessary for them not in order to acquire salvation (for this is impossible), but because they also, to serve God's glory, must be coerced to uphold His commandments. Finally, even God could not help the faithful. Christ died only for the predestined few,[25] and God had decided that his martyrdom would benefit them for all eternity.

* * *

This absolute disappearance of all aids to salvation through the church and the *sacraments* constituted an absolutely decisive contrast to Catholicism. And in Lutheranism this development had not been carried out in a fully consistent manner. That overarching process in the history of religion—the *elimination of magic* from the world's occurrences (*Entzauberung der Welt*)[26]—found here, with the doctrine of predestination, its final stage. This development, which began with the prophecy of ancient Judaism in the Old Testament, rejected, in conjunction with Greek scientific thought, all *magical* means for the salvation quest as superstition and sacrilege. Even at funerals the genuine Puritan scorned every trace of magical ceremony and buried his loved ones without song and ceremony. He did so in order to prevent the appearance of "superstition" in any form; that is, any trust in the efficacy for salvation of forces of a magical-sacramental type.[27] [1920]

There were not only no magical means that would turn God's grace toward believers He had decided to condemn, but no means of any kind. The resulting spiritual isolation of believers, when combined with the harsh teaching that the body was separated absolutely from God and worthless, provided the basis for Puritanism's absolutely negative position toward all aspects of culture and religion oriented to the sensuous and to **feelings**: they were useless for salvation and they promoted sentimental illusions and idolatrous superstition. Hence Puritanism fundamentally turned away from all culture that appeals to the senses.[28] Furthermore, the spiritual isolation of believers formed one of the roots for that individualism, which tends to be pessimistic and without illusions,[29] found in the "national character" and institutions of peoples with a Puritan past—the effects of which are influential even today. The contrast is striking between this pessimistic individualism and the entirely different way in which the "Enlightenment" later viewed persons.[30]

* * *

We find traces of the doctrine of predestination's influence in basic manifestations of the life organization and life outlook in the historical epoch of concern to us [the sixteenth and seventeenth centuries]. Even in later times this influence is still visible, namely, in those periods when this doctrine's validity as religious dogma was in the midst of disappearing. Predestination can actually be understood as only the *most extreme* form of the *exclusive* trust in *God*, the analysis of which constitutes our theme here. It is visible, for example, in the remarkably frequent repetition in the English Puritan literature of the warning against all trust in the helpfulness of others and in friendship.[31] Even the mild-mannered [English minister Richard] Baxter [1615–91; see below pp. 141–48] advised his flock to be deeply mistrustful, even of best friends. [The English theologian Lewis] Bayly [1565–1631] explicitly recommends that no one be trusted and that compromising information should not be communicated to anyone. God alone should be your confidant.[32]

In connection with this orientation of life in those regions of fully developed Calvinism, and in striking contrast to Lutheranism, the practice of the sacrament of private confession silently vanished, although the reservations of even Calvin himself related only to the possibility for sacramental misinterpretation. This change proved enormously significant, first of all for the nature of Calvin's influence upon the devout, and second, as a psychological stimulus for the development of the believer's ethical posture of sacramental confession. The mechanism of sacramental confession that had provided a regular "release" of an emotion-laden consciousness of guilt was now eliminated.[33]

The consequences of the abolition of confession for practical, everyday morality will be discussed later. The results for the general religious situation of believers are obvious. Despite the necessity of membership in the true church for one's salvation,[34] the interaction of the Calvinist with his God took place in a deep spiritual isolation. Whoever wishes to experience the unique effects[35] of this peculiar mood can turn to the book most widely read in all of Puritan literature: [John] Bunyan's [1628–1688] *Pilgrim's Progress* [1678].[36] The passages on [the hero] Christian's behavior are central. Once he recognizes that he has been living in the "city of the damned," Christian hastens to follow the call to commence his pilgrimage to the Heavenly City. Wife and children clinging to him, he staggers forth across the fields, sticking his fingers into his ears and crying "life, eternal life."

No refinement could better capture the mood of the devout Puritan, who is basically concerned only with himself and thinking only of his own salvation, than the naive disposition of this tinker, writing in his cell and receiving the applause of the entire world. In a manner somewhat reminiscent of [the Swiss writer] Gottfried Keller's [1819–90] play, "[Die drei] gerechten Kammacher" [The Three Righteous Comb-makers], this mood is expressed in the smug and ingratiating conversations Christian has along the way with others equally possessed. The thought that it would be pleasant to have his family by his side occurs to him only after he himself is safe.

Christian's tormenting fear of death and of the next life is the same as we experience so urgently and comprehensively with [the Catholic moral theologian] Alphonsus of Liguori [d. 1787], as [the church historian Johann von] Döllinger [1799–1890] describes him to us.[37] Just this [obsession with one's salvation] remains far distant from the spirit of prideful orientation to the existing world as expressed by Machiavelli in his depictions of the glory of the citizens of Florence [*History of Florence*, Bk. III, ch. 7]. In their struggles against the pope and his prohibitions, these citizens place "the love of their native city above their fear for the salvation of their souls." Moreover, of course, the fears of Christian and Liguori remain even farther away from the sensibility that Richard Wagner [1813–83] bestows upon Siegmund before his fatal battle: "Then greet for me Wotan, greet for me Valhalla. . . . But truly [Brünnhilde], do not speak to me of Valhalla's cold delights."[38] Nevertheless, it must be noted that, in regard to the *effects* of their fears, Bunyan and Liguori characteristically diverge: the same fear that drives Bunyan's Christian to all forms of self-humiliation motivates Liguori to a hectic and systematic struggle with life. What is the origin of this distinction?

* * *

It seems at first to be puzzling. How can that tendency toward a spiritual loosening of the individual from the tightest ties that encircle him and hold him in the world be connected to Calvinism's undoubted superiority in respect to social organization?[39] As odd as it at first appears, precisely this superiority follows from the specific orientation that the Christian notion of "brotherly love" was now forced to acquire: Calvinist beliefs, which emphasized the spiritual isolation of each person, pushed this ideal away from its accustomed meaning.

This orientation derived first of all from dogma.[40] The world exists, and only exists, to serve the glorification of God. The predestined Christian exists, and only exists, in order to do his part to increase God's glory in the world through the implementation of His commandments. Indeed, God wants the Christian to engage in community activity *because* He wants the social organization of life to be arranged according to His commandments, and thus according to the goal of serving His greater glory. The social[41] work of the Calvinist is in the end work *in majorem gloriam dei* [for the greater glory of *God* (Weber's emphasis)]. It follows that work in a *calling* is also affected by this aim, and hence this-worldly work stands in service to the community as a whole.

Already with Luther we found that work in a calling, within an economy with a division of labor, was derived from the ideal of "brotherly love." But what remained for Luther an unstable, purely conceptual construction became, for the Calvinists, a central component of their ethical system. "Brotherly love," because it can only be in service to *God's* glory[42] and not to fulfill *physical desires*,[43] is expressed *primarily* in the fulfillment of the tasks of a calling—tasks that are given by *lex naturae* [natural law]. In the process work in a calling becomes endowed with a peculiarly objective, *im*personal character, one in the service of the rational formation of the societal cosmos surrounding us. For just the marvelously purposeful construction and furnishing of this cosmos, which is apparently—according to the revelation of the Bible as well as natural insight—designed to serve the *usefulness* of the human species, in fact allows work in the service of all impersonal, societal usefulness to promote the glory of God—and hence to be recognized as desired by Him.

In this manner the complete elimination of the problem of theodicy,[44] as well as all those questions concerning the "meaning" of the world and of life which have caused so much anguish to other believers, was comprehended by the Puritans in a completely unproblematic way. This was the case for the Jews as well, although for entirely different reasons. In a certain sense this elimination of the problem of theodicy held for the nonmystical strains of Christianity generally. In addition to this succinct rendering of the theodicy dilemma, a further force appeared with Calvinism, indeed one that cast its influence in the same direction: even though, in regard to religious matters, Calvinism placed the particular person fully on his own, a division between the "person" and the "ethic" (in Sören Kierkegaard's sense [in which a moral compass is lost]) did not exist for this version of ascetic Protestantism. [1920]

The significance of this argument for Calvinism's political and **economic rationalism** cannot be analyzed at this point. The source of the *utilitarian* orientation of the Calvinist ethic can be found here, as well as important peculiarities of the Calvinist conception of the calling.[45] We must now return once again to a consideration specifically of the doctrine of predestination.

* * *

The key problem for us, first, is clear: How was this doctrine *tolerated*[46] in an epoch in which the next life was not only more important than all of life's mundane and practical interests, but also, in many respects, more certain?[47] A particular question must arise immediately for every single believer. It forces all such **this-worldly** interests into the background: Am *I* among the predestined who have been saved? How can *I* become certain of my status as one of the chosen?[48]

The question of salvation was not a problem for Calvin himself. He felt himself to be a "tool" of God's will and was certain of his state of grace. Accordingly, to the question—"How could persons become certain of their own election?"—Calvin basically offered only this answer: We should be content with the knowledge that God has chosen, and content with the steadfast faith in Christ that comes from true belief. Furthermore, he fundamentally rejected the assumption that people could discern from others' behavior whether they were chosen or condemned. According to Calvin, such a belief constituted a presumptuous attempt to intrude into God's secrets. The elect, he believed, in this life distinguish themselves in no external way from the condemned.[49] With the single exception of that *finaliter* [ultimate], steadfast, believing trust, all subjective experiences of the chosen few, as *ludibria spiritus sancti* [puppets of the Holy Spirit], are also possible among the damned. Thus the chosen are, and remain, God's *invisible* church.

As normally occurs, the situation for Calvin's epigone followers was different. This becomes apparent as early as [the French reformist theologian and direct ally of Calvin Theodor] Beza [1519–1605], and above all for the broad stratum of ordinary believers. The *certitudo salutis* [certainty of salvation] question must have become for them, in the sense of the *recognition* of one's state of grace, intensified to the point of absolutely overriding significance.[50] Wherever the doctrine of predestination was adhered to, the question could not be avoided of whether infallible signs (*Merkmale*) existed that allowed recognition of one's membership among the *electi* [chosen]. For the development of Pietism, which arose first from the soil of the Reformed Church, this question was of central significance. Indeed, in certain ways it remained, at times, even constitutive for Pietism. This was also true, how-

ever, outside Pietism. When we consider below the very broad-ranging political and social significance of the Reformed doctrine and practice on
communion; we will have to discuss the role played by the ascertainment of
the individual's state of grace in regard to, for example, the question of admission to communion; that is, in regard to the religious ceremony that
proved decisive for defining the social position of participants throughout
the entire seventeenth century.

However, it was impossible to retain Calvin's approach, at least to the extent that the question of one's *own* state of grace arose.[51] His answer to the
question, which never formally abandoned orthodox [Lutheran] doctrine
in principle, referred to his own testimony: steadfast faith would produce
salvation.[52] Above all, at the practical level of providing pastoral care for
the devout, where the suffering caused by the doctrine of predestination
was experienced at every turn, Calvin's response proved inadequate.
These difficulties were addressed in various ways.[53] Insofar as the notion of
"predestination" was not reinterpreted, rendered milder, or basically abandoned,[54] two interwoven types of advice for pastoral care emerged.

On the one hand, it became a matter of duty pure and simple for believers to *consider* themselves among the elect few and to repel every doubt
about their state of grace as nothing more than the temptations of the
devil.[55] This type of advice seemed plausible because a lack of self-confidence in one's status as chosen was believed to result from insufficient
faith; and insufficient faith results only from the insufficient effects of God's
grace. Thus, the admonition of the apostle—for the believer to "make firm"
his or her own calling—is interpreted as a duty to acquire, in the course of
one's daily struggle, the subjective certainty of predestination and justification. In place of humble sinners, to whom Luther promises grace if they
trust themselves to God in penitent faith, Calvinism now bred self-confi-
dent "saints."[56] They were found often in those steel-hard (*stahlharten*) Puritan merchants of capitalism's heroic epoch. Indeed these "saints" are
occasionally found even today.

On the other hand, a further type of advice was offered by those engaged
in pastoral care to address the suffering caused by the uncertainty of one's
salvation status. *Work without rest in a vocational calling* was recommended
as the best possible means to *acquire* the self-confidence that one belonged
among the elect.[57] Work, and work alone, banishes religious doubt and
gives certainty of one's status among the saved.

The reasons that this-worldly work in a calling could be understood as capable of *this* achievement (that it could be viewed, so to speak, as the suitable
mechanism for the release of emotion-based religious anxiety) must be sought
in deeply rooted peculiarities of the religious sensibility cultivated in the Reformed Churches. These unique aspects come to the fore most clearly when
contrasted to Luther's doctrine: a justification of a certainty of salvation derives from faith alone. Schneckenburger's excellent lectures[58] analyze these
differences in a subtle and objective manner and without value judgments. For
the most part, the following brief observations simply tie into his discussion.

*　*　*

As Lutheran theology developed in the course of the seventeenth century, the ultimate religious experience for Lutheran piety was the *unio mystica* [sacred, mystical union] with the Divine.[59] As indicated by this expression, which is unknown in Reformist doctrines in this form, of importance is a substantial feeling of God (*Gottesgefühl*), namely, the sensation of an actual penetration of the Divine into the soul of the devout. This penetration must be understood as having the same qualitative effects that contemplation had upon the German mystics. It is characterized by its *passive* character, which is oriented to fulfillment of a desire for *rest* in God, and by its purely devotional looking inward (*Innerlichkeit*).

As is well-known from the history of philosophy, a religious devotion oriented to mysticism can become closely allied with a decidedly down-to-earth sense of reality in respect to the empirically given. Indeed, as a consequence of mysticism's rejection of dialectical doctrines, this kind of religious devotion may often directly underpin this practical sense of reality. Moreover, in a similar manner mysticism can also indirectly support the rational organization of life. Nevertheless, mysticism's relationship to the world's everyday tasks and occupations naturally displays an incapacity to bestow a positive evaluation upon external activity. Lutheranism, however, added a further element [the effect of which was to move this religion even more in this direction]: The *unio mystica* in Lutheranism combined, because of original sin [which stains all humans], with a deep feeling of personal unworthiness. This feeling should carefully maintain the *poenitentia quotidiana* [daily penitence] of the Lutheran believer; its goal was to preserve humility and candor, both of which were indispensable for the forgiveness of sins.

In contrast, from the beginning Reformist religious devotion stood in opposition to Pascal's quietistic flight from the world and to Lutheranism's purely inwardly-oriented, devotional mood of piety. The Reformed Church precluded, as a consequence of God's absolute transcendence vis-à-vis the human species and hence His incomprehensibility, the real penetration of the Divine into the human soul. According to Calvin, *finitum non est capax infiniti* [the finite is not capable of understanding the infinite]. Instead, the coming together of God with His chosen elect could only occur and enter the consciousness of believers in a different manner: God *operated* (*operatur*) in the devout and they were conscious of His powers. Hence, believers were aware that their *action* arose out of the belief that was caused by God's grace. This belief in turn, the faithful also knew, legitimized itself through the quality of this action caused by God.

*　*　*

Highly significant differences in regard to the crucial conditions for the believer's salvation status[60] are now becoming articulated, as are distinctions pivotal for the classification of all practical religious devotion in general. Namely, it is now apparent that the religious virtuoso can convince himself of his own state of grace insofar as he feels himself to be *either* a vessel *or* a tool of divine power. In the case of the former, his religious life tends toward a mystical culture of feelings; in the latter, it tends toward ascetic *action*. While Luther stood closer to the former case, Calvinism belonged to the latter. The Reformed devout wanted, as did Lutherans, to be saved *sola fide:* on the basis of faith alone. However, because to Calvin all sheer feelings and moods remained suspect, even though they might appear lofty,[61] a **testifying** to belief, as given by its objective *effects* upon action, had to be offered. Only then could belief provide a secure foundation for the *certitudo salutis*. The call to salvation must be *fides efficax*,[62] or an "effectual calling" (as stated in the **Savoy Declaration** [1658]).

One may now pose the next question: By *what* signs were the Reformed devout able, beyond a doubt, to recognize the right belief? By leading an organized Christian life that served to increase *God's glory*. Exactly what fulfills this goal is to be derived from His will. And this will is revealed directly in the Bible or indirectly out of the purposeful orders of the world (*lex naturae*)[63] created by Him. One's own state of grace can be determined largely through a comparison of the state of one's own soul to the soul of the elect (the patriarchs of the Old Testament come to mind).[64] Only the chosen actually *have* the *fides efficax*;[65] only they are capable, on the basis of a *regeneratio* [regeneration] and the sense of holiness (*sanctificatio*) that thereby follows, of dedicating their entire lives to increasing God's glory through actual (and not simply apparent) good works. To the extent that believers are aware of their transformation —at least in terms of its fundamental character and enduring intention (*propositum oboedientiae*)—*as resting upon a power living in them*[66] that seeks to increase His glory (hence a power not only willed by God but above all *caused* [67] by God), they acquire the highest reward Calvinism **strives** for: the certainty of grace.[68]

That this certainty is to be attained is confirmed by 2 Cor. 13:5 ["Examine yourselves, to see whether you are holding to your faith. Test yourselves. Do you not realize that Jesus Christ is in you?—unless you fail to meet the test."].[69] Yet good works are absolutely unsuitable to serve as means for the acquisition of this certainty: because even the saved are still mere humans determined by human wants and desires, all that even they do falls infinitely short of God's demands. Nevertheless, good works are indispensable as *signs* of election.[70] They are technical means, but not ones that can be used to purchase salvation. Rather, good works serve to banish the anxiety surrounding the question of one's salvation.[71] In this sense they are occasionally openly described as "indispensable for salvation" or directly linked to the *possessio salutis* [possession of salvation].[72]

At a practical level, this doctrine basically means that God helps those who help themselves.[73] Thus, as it is also noted on occasion, the Calvinist *himself creates*[74] his salvation. More correctly: the Calvinist creates for himself the *certainty* of his salvation. *Unlike* in Catholicism, however, the creation of this certainty *cannot* be built from a gradual accumulation of single, service-oriented good works. It is comprised instead of the *systematic self-control* necessary, in *every moment*, when the believer stands before the alternatives: Am I among the saved or among the damned? With this point we arrive at a very important stage in our discussion.

* * *

It is frequently noted that this development of ideas in the Reformed churches and sects, which has been worked out with increasing clarity,[75] has been subject to criticism from the Lutheran side. "Salvation through good works" (*Werkheiligkeit*),[76] it is argued, is actually the issue here. Now although Calvinism has correctly defended itself by rejecting any identification of its *dogmatic* position with the Catholic doctrine of good works, this criticism from Lutheranism holds as soon as the point of reference becomes the *practical* consequences for daily life of the average Reformed believer.[77] For there has never been perhaps a more intense form of religious valuation of moral *action* than that which Calvinism produced in its followers. Key, however, for the practical significance of this type of "salvation through good works," is first of all the recognition of the *qualities* that characterize the corresponding organization of one's life, and the qualities that distinguish it from the everyday life of the average medieval Catholic.

One can attempt to formulate the distinction [between the Catholic and Calvinist orientations to daily action] roughly in this way. The normal lay Catholic[78] in the medieval period, in regard to ethical matters, lived in a sort of "hand to mouth" fashion. First of all he conscientiously fulfilled his traditional duties. Above and beyond these duties, however, his "good works" normally were not necessarily connected. At any rate, the Catholic's good works and duties were surely not of necessity **rationalized** into a life-*system*. Rather, they remained a series of *isolated* actions that the faithful could carry out as the situation required: whether to atone for specific sins, to follow more closely the advice of one's priest, or to acquire in a certain manner at the end of the believer's life insurance credits.

Of course it is true that this Catholic ethic was an "ethic of conviction" (*Gesinnungsethik*), yet the concrete *intentio* of the *isolated* actions decided their value. Moreover, the *isolated* actions—good or bad—were credited to the believer and influenced his life on earth as well as his eternal destiny. Entirely realistically, the Catholic Church concluded that the human species was *not* an absolutely and clearly determined unity to be valued as such. Rather, people's moral lives were viewed as (normally) influenced by conflicting motives and often by contradictory modes of behavior. Of course, the church demanded, as an ideal also of believers a *principled* transformation of life to conform to God's commandments. Even this demand, however, was in turn weakened (for the average believer) by one of the church's most important mechanisms of power and socialization: confession. Its function was deeply interwoven with the internal uniqueness of Catholic religious devotion.

The "elimination of magic" from the world—namely, the exclusion of the use of magic as a means to salvation[79]—was not followed through with the same degree of consistency in Catholicism as in Puritanism (and before it only in Judaism). To the Catholic,[80] *salvation through the sacraments* was available as a mechanism that compensated for his own short-comings, and the priest was a magician who carried out the miracle of transubstantiation in the mass. The pivotal power had been bestowed upon the priest. The faithful could turn to him for assistance in contrition and penitence. Because the priest provided the means of atonement and bestowed hope for salvation and certainty of forgiveness, he granted the believer a *relief* from tremendous *tension*. By contrast, the Calvinist's destiny was to live inseperable from this tension, one that could not be lessened. [1920]

A friendly and humane comforting did not exist for these believers. Moreover, they could not hope that hours of weakness and frivolity could be compensated for with intensified good will during other hours, as could Catholics and Lutherans. The Calvinist God did not demand isolated "good works" from His faithful; rather, if salvation were to occur, He required an intensification of good works into a *system*.[81] There was here no mention of that genuinely humane cycle, followed by the Catholic, of sin, repentance, penitence, relief, and then further sin. Nor was there any discussion in Calvinism of devices or mechanisms (such as a defined period of punishment) that would balance one's entire life account and then provide, through the means of grace offered by the church, atonement for sins. [1920]

In Calvinism, the practical-ethical action of the average believer lost its planless and unsystematic character and was molded into a consistent, *methodical* organization of his life as a whole. It is surely no accident that the name *Methodists* remained attached to the carriers of the last great reawakening of Puritan ideas in the eighteenth century, just as the term *Precisians* (which is substantively fully synonymous with Methodism) was used to refer to their [Dutch] seventeenth-century spiritual ancestors.[82] For only through a fundamental transformation of the meaning of one's entire life—in every hour and every action[83]—could the effect of grace, namely a raising of believers out of the *status naturae* [natural state] and into the *status gratiae* [state of grace], be testified to through action.

The life of this "saint" was exclusively oriented to a transcendent goal: salvation. Precisely *for this reason*, however, its this-worldly, practical course was thoroughly *rationalized* and exclusively dominated by a single point of view: to increase God's glory on earth. Nowhere has this vantage point—*omnia in majorem dei gloriam* [all for the greater glory of God]—been taken with such complete seriousness.[84] However, only a life guided by constant reflection could constitute a life empowered to overcome the *status naturae*. Indeed, with this alteration of meaning in the direction of an ethical organization of life, Descartes' *cogito ergo sum* was taken over by the early Puritans.[85] This rationalization now provided Reform piety with its uniquely *ascetic* character. Moreover, in this manner it established its inner affinity[86] with, as well as its unique contrast to, Catholicism. Similar developments, of course, were not foreign to Catholicism.

* * *

Christian asceticism undoubtedly contains within itself highly diverging features in regard to external appearance as well as meaning. In its highest forms in the West, however, asceticism bore a thoroughly *rational* character as early as the Middle Ages. Some forms of asceticism were rational even in Antiquity. The world-historical significance of the way that monks in the West led their lives in an organized manner rests precisely upon Western monasticism's asceticism, as does the contrast of Western monasticism to the monasticism of the East (in terms of its general classification rather than in its entirety).

The organization of life in Western monasticism was emancipated from all random flight from this world and all heroic self-torture. This liberation held, in principle, even as early as St. Benedict [480–547], more so for the [French Benedictine] monks of Cluny [910], yet more so for the [French] Cistercians [1098] and, finally, most decisively, for the Jesuits [1534].[87] This organized life, which was systematized, thoroughly shaped, and methodical-rational, had the goal of overcoming the *status naturae*. Thus, it enabled believers to escape the power of irrational drives and all dependence upon the world and nature as given, to subordinate life to the supremacy of the organized will,[88] and to subject their actions to a permanent self-*control* and a *reflection* upon their ethical implications. Hence, this methodical-rational organization of life sought to train the monk objectively—to become a worker in service to God's kingdom—and, in this manner, subjectively: to guarantee the salvation of his soul.

Just as it constituted the goal of the *exercitia* [religious exercises] of St. Ignatius [of Loyola, 1491–1556] and the highest forms of rational monastic virtues in general,[89] this *active* self-control constituted also Puritanism's defining practical ideal of life.[90] Even in the reports on the trials of its martyrs one can see that the reserved calm of the Puritan faithful stood opposed to the confused rambunctiousness of noble prelates and state officials, whom the devout held in the deepest contempt.[91] Indeed, just this high esteem for a reserved self-control comes to the fore even now in the best representatives of the English and American "gentleman."[92] As can be said for every "rational" asceticism, Puritan asceticism (in the everyday language of today)[93] worked to render the devout capable of calling forth and then acting upon their "constant motives," especially those motives that the believer, through the practice of asceticism itself, "trained" against the "emotions."

In this manner, and in *this* formal-psychological meaning of the term, Puritan asceticism socialized the believer to become a "personality." In contrast to a number of popular ideas, the Puritan goal was to be able to lead an alert, conscious, and self-aware life. Hence the destruction of the spontaneity of the instinct-driven enjoyment of life (*triebhaften Lebensgenusses*) constituted the most urgent task. The aim was to bring *order* into the believer's way of leading his or her life, and asceticism was the most important *mechanism* for doing so.

On the one hand, all these decisive themes are found as fully developed[94] in the rules of Catholic monasticism as in the basic tenets of the Calvinist organized life.[95] The tremendous power of these religious groups to overcome the *status naturae* rests upon this methodical taking hold of the entire person. As evident, in particular if compared to Lutheranism, precisely this feature of Calvinism undergirded its capacity as an *ecclesia militans* to insure the success of the cause of Protestantism. On the other hand, the basis for the *contrast* between Calvinist and Catholic asceticism is obvious: the privilege of advice from the *consilia evangelica* [Catholic Church hierarchy] disappeared in Calvinism. The restructuring of Christian asceticism followed from this development; it now became purely *this*-worldly.

* * *

This is not to say that the "methodical" life in medieval Catholicism remained confined to the cells of the monastery; that was by no means the case either in theory or in practice. Rather, as has already been pointed out, despite the greater moral moderation of Catholicism, an ethically unsystematic life did *not* fulfill, even for the this-worldly life, its highest ideals.[96] For example, a powerful attempt to achieve the full penetration of everyday life by asceticism was undertaken in the Third Order of St. Francis. It was not the only such attempt, as is well-known. Indeed, works such as *Nachfolge Christi* [*Imitatio Christi*; The Disciples of Christ][97] clearly demonstrate—precisely *through* the manner of their strong effect—that the mode of organizing life they preached was perceived as morally *higher* than that morality viewed as simply fulfilling the minimum basic requirement, namely, the customary morality of everyday life. This morality was actually *not* evaluated according to standards, as Puritanism had already begun to do. Furthermore, the *practice* of certain Catholic religious institutions, above all the granting of indulgences, was repeatedly contested by the beginnings of a systematic, this-worldly asceticism. For this reason the granting of indulgences during the period of the Reformation was perceived as the church's fundamental weakness rather than as a peripheral abuse.

The decisive difference involved another issue, however. In medieval Catholicism, the person who lived methodically in the religious sense par excellence was *actually only the monk*. He remained the only figure to do so. Hence, the more intensively asceticism took hold of the individual, the *more* it drove him *out of* everyday life and into the monastery—precisely because the uniquely holy life was to be found only in a **surpassing** of everyday morality.[98] Luther first abolished this mode of leading the religious life, and Calvinism here simply followed Luther.[99] It must be emphasized that Luther abolished the monasteries not as an actor fulfilling some "developmental historical trend" (*Entwicklungstendenz*), but entirely because of his personal experiences. They were, by the way, at the beginning quite unclear in regard to the direction in which they would lead; later, however, they were pushed further by the *political* situation.

The essence of the type of religious devotion that now came to the fore was captured by [the German mystic and popular author] Sebastian Franck [1499–1542].[100] The significance of the Reformation could be found, Frank argued, in this new situation: now *every* Christian must be a monk for an entire lifetime. A dam was now erected that prevented asceticism from flowing away from everyday life, and those persons of passionate and serious spiritual nature—the best representatives of which had heretofore been delivered into monasticism—were now instructed to pursue their ascetic ideals *inside* a this-worldly, vocational calling.

Calvinism, however, in the course of its development, added a positive element: the idea of the necessity of *testifying to one's belief* in a this-worldly vocational calling.[101] In adding this element, Calvinism bestowed a *positive motivation* toward asceticism upon broader strata of persons endowed with religiously oriented natures. In place of the spiritual aristocracy of the monk outside of and above the world there now appeared, once its ethic was anchored in the doctrine of predestination, a spiritual aristocracy of saints predestined from eternity *in* the world.[102] With its *character indelebilis* [unchangeable character], this aristocracy was eternally separate from the other part of humanity: the damned. In principle unbridgeable and, because of its invisibility, more mysterious[103] than the division that visibly separated the medieval monk from the world, this gulf between the saved and the damned invaded *all* social sentiments with a piercing harshness. Hence, in light of his sinfulness, an attitude of compassionate helpfulness towards one's neighbor—coming from an awareness of one's own weakness—could not be the appropriate response of the elect who, because chosen by the grace of God, were saints. More suitable instead was a hatred and contempt for the sinner as an enemy of God, one who carried with him the marks of the eternally condemned.[104]

This mode of perceiving the social world was capable of such an intensification that, under certain conditions, it could flow into the formation of *sects*. As happened with the "Independents" of the seventeenth century,[105] such a development occurred when genuine Calvinist belief—divine glory requires that the damned, through the church, be brought to submit to His commandments—was outweighed by the conviction that God would be disgraced if the condemned were found among His devout flock, if the damned participated in the sacraments, or if they (as pastors) administered them.[106] In a word, a movement toward the formation of sects was set into motion wherever the Donatist view of the church appeared as a consequence of the idea that a testifying to one's belief is necessary, as happened in the case of the Calvinist Baptists.[107] In those situations where the demand for a "pure" church as a community of the elect was not followed fully to its logical end, and thus did not lead to the formation of a new sect, various new arrangements for church governance arose out of the attempt to separate the chosen from the damned. A special position, it was believed, must be retained for the elect. Church administrators and the minister, for example, must be among the saved.[108]

* * *

Of course, the ascetic organization of life received its firm norms from the Bible. The action of the faithful could be continuously oriented to these norms and believers clearly needed them as guidelines. For us, the most important aspect of the Calvinists' often-noted "mastery of the Bible" is their view that the *Old* Testament, because its moral rules were just as inspiring as those of the New Testament, must be accorded dignity at a level of complete *equality* with the New Testament—at least to the extent that they perceived these moral rules as not exclusively addressing the historical situation of Judaism and as not explicitly abrogated by Christ. The law of God was given as an ideal for *believers* in particular and it stood as a valid norm, even if it was never fully to be reached.[109] For Luther, in contrast, the exact opposite held, at least at the beginning: he extolled the *freedom* from subordination to the Old Testament laws as a divine privilege bestowed upon the faithful.[110] Yet in the entire orientation of life of the Puritans one feels the effect of Hebrew wisdom, as found in the passages they read most (Proverbs and certain psalms). The sense of a closeness to God but also of a fully **dispassionate** dimension is clear. The *rational* character of this Hebrew wisdom is particularly apparent: the suppression of the mystical and, in general, of the *feeling* aspect of religion. Sanford[111] correctly traced this aspect to the influence of the Old Testament.

Nevertheless, Old Testament rationalism was essentially of a petty-bourgeois and traditional character. The powerful pathos of the great prophets and many of the psalms was a component of it, as were elements that later provided points of linkage to the development of a religious devotion specifically based on feelings.[112] This connection took place as early as the Middle Ages. Thus, it was Calvinism's *own* components—namely, its foundational ascetic character—that in the end again led it to select out and assimilate the congenial elements of Old Testament piety.

Now the systematization of a life organized around ethical principles, as common to both Calvinist Protestant asceticism and the rational forms of life within the Catholic monastic orders, becomes manifest purely externally in the way in which the "precise" Puritan Christian perpetually *monitored* his state of grace.[113] Indeed, even the devout believers' diaries—in which sins, temptations, and acts that indicated progress toward grace were perpetually recorded, even in tables—were shared alike by modern Catholic piety, which was mainly a Jesuit creation (namely in France), and the most zealously church-oriented Calvinist circles.[114] However, whereas the keeping of a diary in Catholicism served to insure the completeness of the believer's confession or to offer to the *directeur de l'ame* [director of the soul] the documents necessary for authoritarian guidance of the (mostly female) faithful, the Reformed Christian *himself*, with the help of these diaries, "felt his own" pulse. Significant moral theologians all note the importance of these diaries, and Benjamin Franklin's daily accounting offers a classical example; his tabular-statistical entries marked his progress in cultivating particular virtues.[115] In contrast, the old medieval conception of God's accounting (found even in the ancient world), as depicted by Bunyan, reaches such a point of characteristic tastelessness that the relationship of the sinner to God is compared to the relationship between a customer and a shopkeeper: whoever once falls into debt may at best pay off the cumulative interest, using the yield of all his acts of service, but never the debt itself.[116]

As he monitored his own behavior, the later Puritan monitored also the behavior of God and discovered His finger in every single detail of life. Moreover, and in opposition to the teachings of Calvin himself, the Puritan knew why God had decided in this or that way. Hence the striving to make life holy and sanctified could almost assume the character of a business.[117] A penetrating Christianization of the entire being was the consequence of this *methodicalness* now required for the leading of a life organized around ethical principles. In contrast to Lutheranism, Calvinism forced this methodical organization of life upon the believer.

If one wishes to acquire a correct understanding of the particular effect Calvinism had on believers, one must keep continuously in mind that this *methodicalness* was decisive. It follows, on the one hand, that just *this* Calvinist version of Christianity could first have had this influence upon believers. It also follows, on the other hand, that other Protestant denominations must have had an effect in the same direction if their ethical motivations were the same in regard to the decisive point: the idea of testifying to belief through one's action. [1920]

* * *

Until now we have been concerned with Calvinist religious devotion. Accordingly, we have assumed that the doctrine of predestination forms the dogmatic framework for Puritan morality in the sense of a methodical-rational and ethical organization of life. We have done so because this doctrine in fact extended far beyond the circle of the religious grouping that in every way remained strict adherents of Calvin, the "Presbyterians." It was contained not only in the Savoy Declaration of the Independents of 1658, but also in the Baptist-influenced confessions of Hanserd Knollys [1599–1691] of 1689.[118] Although the greatest community-organizing and administrative genius of Methodism, John Wesley, believed in the universality of grace, the great agitator of the first Methodist generation and its most consistent thinker [and co-founder], George Whitefield [1714–70], adhered to the doctrine of predestination. So also did the occasionally highly influential circle around Lady [Selina Countess of] Huntingdon [1707–91, Whitefield's disciple, who organized his followers into a cohesive body of Calvinist-Methodists in Wales].

In the fateful epoch of the seventeenth century, according to the magnificent consistency of this doctrine, believers were considered to be the tools of God and the executors of His providential decrees. Precisely this idea was cultivated and maintained in England by the warring representatives of the "holy life."[119] The doctrine of predestination, in conveying this notion of believers as God's tools, forestalled a premature collapse of religion-oriented action into a purely utilitarian ethos of good works. The concerns of this world would have been the focus of such an ethos and this utilitarian posture would never have been capable of bringing the faithful to make unheard of sacrifices on behalf of irrational and ideal goals. Moreover, in an ingenious manner, the doctrine of predestination linked absolute determinism, the complete transcendence of the supernatural realm, and the belief in unconditionally valid norms.[120] Simultaneously, this linkage was in principle much more *modern* than the milder doctrines that addressed more the feelings of the devout and subjected even God to moral laws. Above all, as will be repeatedly apparent in the sections below, fundamental for our discussion is the investigation of the idea of a *testifying* to one's belief as the psychological point of origin for methodical ethics.

$$* * *$$

We proceeded above by examining the doctrine of predestination and its significance for everyday life. In addition, because the idea of testifying through action to belief recurs on a regular basis among the denominations still to be considered, it proved feasible to study this idea first, with Calvinism, in its "pure form." In other words, we constructed a model of the way in which belief and ethics are connected; this model can now be "applied" to the further denominations. In this exercise, because the consequences of the doctrine of predestination were the most broad-ranging, it was necessary to begin with this doctrine.[121]

Within Protestantism, the *doctrine of predestination* had great consequences among its earliest followers, in particular with respect to the ascetic formation of an organized life. Lutheranism, however, most thoroughly blocked its impact. Indeed, Lutheranism formed the *most principled* antithesis to Calvinism. A (relative) lack of moral awareness (*sittlichen Ohnmacht*) arose from Lutheranism rather than an ascetic organization of life. Apparently, the Lutheran *gratia amissibilis* [loss of grace], which could always be won back again through penitent contrition, contained *as such* no motivational push toward a systematic, rational formation of the believer's ethical life (which is important for us as a product of ascetic Protestantism).[122] Rather, Lutheran piety left largely unaltered the spontaneous vitality of instinctive action and the untempered life based on feelings. It lacked this motivational push toward an uninterrupted self-control and hence toward a *planned* regulation of one's own life in any sense. Here Lutheranism stood in contrast to the motivational impulse contained in the mighty teachings of Calvinism.

A religious genius, such as Luther, could live spontaneously in this atmosphere of uninhibited openness to the world and without danger of sinking back into the *status naturalis*—as long as the strength of his enthusiasm lasted! Also the simple, delicate, and peculiarly devotional form of piety that adorns some of the most distinguished representatives of Lutheranism is rarely found on the soil of genuine Puritanism. Lutheranism's morality unbounded by firm rules is likewise also not discovered in this Puritanism. Rather, parallels to Lutheranism are far more likely to be found, for example, in the mild Anglican religious devotion of [the prominent theologians Richard] Hooker [*ca.* 1554–1600] and [William] Chillingsworth [1602–44], among others. For average Lutheran believers (and even for the more sincere), nothing was more certain than that they would be pulled out of the *status naturalis* only temporarily—that is, so long as the influence upon them of a particular confession or sermon lasted.

The striking difference between the ethical standards of the courts of Reformist and Lutheran princes was well-known in the Reformation period. The Lutheran courts had sunk into drunkenness and raw behavior.[123] In comparison to the asceticism of the baptizing movement, the helplessness of the Lutheran clergy, with its sermons based upon pure faith alone, was similarly common knowledge. What one perceives today in the Germans as the behavior of easy-going congeniality (*Gemütlichkeit*) and a "lack of affected mannerisms"[124] contrasts to the behavior of the Anglo-Saxons. A more thorough destruction of the spontaneity of the *status naturalis*, as apparent even in physiognomy, occurred in England and the United States. Upon meeting Americans and English, Germans are normally inclined to perceive precisely this destruction of spontaneity as strange, namely, as a certain internal constraint, a narrowness of manifest emotional range, and a general inhibitedness.

These are all contrasts in the organization and direction of life that fundamentally result from the *lesser* penetration of asceticism into the life of the Lutheran believer as compared to that of the Calvinist. The aversion of every spontaneous "child of the world" to asceticism is evident in this child's every sensation. As a result of its doctrinal teachings on the acquisition of salvation, Lutheranism lacks the psychological motivation capable of endowing the organization of life with a systematic element. If present, this element would have compelled a methodical rationalization of the Lutheran's life.

* * *

This motivation toward a methodical rationalization of life, which conditions the ascetic character of piety, *could* undoubtedly be produced through a variety of religious ideas, as we will soon see. Calvinism's doctrine of predestination offered only *one* among diverse possibilities. Nevertheless, we have become convinced that this doctrine not only possessed an entirely unique consistency; in addition, it stood out because of a great psychological effectiveness.[125] If considered exclusively from the vantage point of the religious motivation provided by their asceticism, the *non*-Calvinist ascetic movements must be seen as involving a *weakening* of Calvinism's internal consistency.

Although not always the case in the empirical-historical course of development, the Reformist form of asceticism was, for the most part, either imitated by the other ascetic movements or taken as a comparative and complementary point of reference. The latter view arose when its basic principles were diverged from or expanded upon. At times, an asceticism appeared which was no different from Calvinism in terms of its consistency, despite its anchoring in different beliefs. This development, wherever it occurred, generally resulted from church *government*. This theme, however, must be discussed in a different context.[126]

B. PIETISM

Viewed *historically*, the idea of predestination is also the point of departure for the ascetic movement normally referred to as *Pietism*. As long as it remained inside the Reformist Church, a drawing of firm boundaries between Pietist Calvinists and non-Pietist Calvinists is nearly impossible.[127] Almost all of the major representatives of Puritanism have at times been considered to be Pietists. Moreover, it is fully legitimate to view all of the interconnections between the doctrine of predestination and the idea that the devout must testify to their belief as Pietist expansions upon Calvin's original doctrine. As noted, all of these interconnections are grounded in the interest in acquiring a state of subjective certainty regarding one's salvation (*certitudo salutis*).

The origin of asceticism's revival within Reformed communities has been, especially in Holland, very often associated with a rejuvenation of the doctrine of predestination, which had from time to time been forgotten or had become less viable. For this reason, in the case of England, one tends normally not to use the term "Pietism" at all.[128] But even Reformed Pietism on the Continent (in Holland and along the lower Rhine River [in southwestern Germany]) was, at first, primarily simply an intensification of Reformed asceticism, just as was the religious devoutness of Bayly, for example. The defining emphasis was so thoroughly shifted to the *praxis pietatis* [practice of piety in daily life] that dogmatic orthodoxy fell into the background and occasionally seemed merely a matter of indifference. Along with other sins, dogmatic errors at times might also occur among the predestined. And experience indicated that, for numerous Christians, the effects of their faith became manifest over time, despite their unfamiliarity with the basic theological issues. On the other hand, it became evident that mere theological knowledge would not at all introduce the sense of certainty regarding salvation that followed from a testifying to belief through conduct.[129]

Hence, membership among the elect could not be testified to through theological knowledge.[130] For this reason, amidst a mistrust of theology[131] and despite Pietism's continued official affiliation with the scholars and theologians (which belongs among its characteristic features), it began to gather the followers of the *praxis pietatis* into **conventicles** set apart from the world's mundane activities.[132] In doing so, Pietism wished to bring the invisible church of saints back to earth and to render it visible. The Pietists hoped to accomplish this, however, without following through in a fully consistent manner, that is, by supporting the formation of sects. Instead, protected in the conventicle community and separate from the world's influences, the Pietists attempted to lead lives oriented in all details to the will of God. In doing so, also in the visible aspects of their daily lives, they sought to remain certain of their own elect status. Through an intensified asceticism, the *ecclesiola* [assembly] of true converts wished already in this life to enjoy (as did all Pietist groups) the blissfulness of community with God.

This latter effort contained an element internally related to the Lutheran *unio mystica*. It very often led to a stronger cultivation of the element of *feeling* in religion than would be acceptable to the average Reformed Christian. To the extent that *our* vantage points come into consideration, *this* was the decisive feature to be addressed regarding the "Pietism" that developed upon the soil of the Reformed Church. For those specific forms of medieval religious devotion possessing an inner affinity to feelings (which were fully foreign to Calvinist piety) channeled practical religious devotion in the direction of a this-worldly enjoyment of salvation, instead of in the direction of an ascetic struggle to acquire a certainty of salvation in the next life. Moreover, along the way, feelings *could* become subject to such an intensification that religious devotion acquired a clearly hysterical character.

* * *

As is familiar to us from innumerable examples, through a neuropathically grounded alternation between half-conscious conditions of religious ecstasy and periods of nervous exhaustion (which are perceived as "distant from God"), Pietists in *effect* aimed for the direct opposite of the dispassionate and strict discipline that took hold of all people adhering to the Puritan's systematized holy life. That is, Pietists aimed for a weakening of those "inhibitions" that bolstered the Calvinist's rational personality against the "affects."[133] Similarly, in the process the Calvinist idea of the depravity of all physical desires, if understood by Pietists in terms of *feelings* (for example, in the form of regret, shame, and guilt), *could* lead to a deadening of vitality in one's vocational calling.[134] Even the idea of predestination *could*, in contrast to the genuine tendencies of rational Calvinist religious devotion, lead to fatalism if it became the object of a conversion based on mood and *feelings*.[135] Finally, the need to separate the chosen from the world *could*, if a powerful intensification of *feeling* occurred, lead to a kind of quasi-communistic, cloister-like community. This occurred repeatedly in Pietism and even in the Reformed church.[136]

As long, however, as Reformed Pietism did not strive for this extreme effect, which was produced by a cultivation of *feelings*, and sought instead to acquire certainty of salvation through a this-worldly *vocational* calling, Pietist principles had in the end two practical effects. They led to a *still* stricter ascetic control of the organized life in one's calling, and they anchored in religion the ethical significance of the calling even more firmly than did normal Reformed Christians (who were viewed by the "fine" Pietists as second-class believers practicing merely a worldly "respectability"). In Pietism, the religious aristocracy of the elect, who strove all the more to the forefront to the same extent that the development of Reformist asceticism was taken seriously, were henceforth organized voluntarily in the form of conventicles inside the church, as occurred in Holland. By contrast, in English Puritanism the religious aristocracy pushed in part for a formal distinction between active and passive believers in the *governing* of the church and (corresponding to the above analysis) in part for the formation of separate sects.

* * *

German Pietism, which is associated with the names of Spener, [the German theologian August Hermann] Francke [1663–1727], and Zinzendorf,[137] was founded on the soil of Lutheranism. It leads away from the doctrine of predestination. Nevertheless, this development does not necessarily take us away from the train of thought from which this doctrine had logically arisen. This proximity is visible in particular in the influence exercised by English-Dutch Pietism upon Spener, as he himself noted. It is apparent as well, for example, in the readings undertaken by Bayly in his first conventicles.[138]

At any rate, from *our* particular vantage point, in the end Pietism implies the penetration, into those geographical regions untouched by Calvinism, of the methodically cultivated and monitored life, that is, an *ascetic organization of life*.[139] Lutheranism, however, must have experienced this rational asceticism as a foreign element, and the lack of consistency in German Pietist doctrine was a result of the problems that grew out of the difficulties Lutheranism experienced with asceticism. In order to ground dogmatically the systematic-religious organization of life, Spener combines Lutheran trains of thought with distinctly Reformist elements: the notion that good works as such are undertaken with the intention of *honoring* God[140] and the Lutheran belief (which also resonated with the Reformed Church) in the possibility for the elect to arrive at a relative degree of Christian perfection.[141]

Yet precisely the element of logical consistency is lacking in Spener's theorizing. Although the organized Christian life-conduct was also essential for the Pietism of Spener (who was strongly influenced by mysticism),[142] he weakened its systematic character. In a somewhat unclear, but essentially Lutheran, way of describing more than grounding, Spener never attempted to derive the *certitudo salutis* [certainty of salvation] from a striving by the believer toward elect status. Instead of the idea of a testifying through conduct to one's belief, he selected the less strict Lutheran notion of faith (as discussed earlier) as the mechanism through which the believer could feel certain of his salvation.[143]

As long, however, as the rational-ascetic component in Pietism retained the upper hand over the element of feeling, the ideas decisive for our vantage point again and again came forcefully to the fore. First, the methodical development of the believer's own holiness in the direction of ever higher degrees of consolidation and perfection, as monitored by conformity to *God's laws,* constitutes in Pietism a *sign* of one's state of grace.[144] Second, it is God's providence *at work* in just this improvement by the faithful; after patient waiting and *methodical reflection,* He is giving a favoring sign to believers.[145] Work in a calling was also for Francke the ascetic means *par excellence.*[146] He was firmly convinced (as were the Puritans, as we shall see) that God himself, through the success of the believer's work, was blessing His chosen.

Moreover, as a surrogate (*surrogat*) for the "double decree" [according to which a few were saved and most were condemned], Pietism created ideas that were essentially the same, although less vibrant, than those following from the idea of predestination (for example, the idea that God's special grace had established an aristocracy of the elect).[147] The same psychological consequences of this idea followed for both Pietists and Calvinists (as described above). Included among them, for example, was so-called *Terminism,*[148] which had been generally imputed to Pietism by its opponents (doubtless incorrectly). Although it was universal, this teaching assumed that salvation would be offered either only once in a lifetime (and then at a specific moment) or at some moment for the last time.[149] Those who miss this particular moment can no longer be helped by the axiom of universal grace. Thus, Terminists found themselves in the same situation as those under Calvinism who had been neglected by God.

* * *

In effect, this Terminist theory came quite close, for example, to Francke's position. Abstracted from his personal experiences and widely dispersed throughout Pietism (and perhaps even dominant within it), his theory assumed that grace could be acquired only under unique circumstances. It would appear once and in a particular manner, namely, after "penitence" had led to a "breakthrough."[150] Yet not everyone, according to the Pietists' own views, was predisposed to have such an experience. On the one hand, those unable to induce it, in spite of instructions by the Pietists in the use of ascetic methods to this end, were viewed by the chosen as belonging to a type of passive Christian. On the other hand, through the creation of a *method* for bringing about "penitence," the attainment of God's grace also became, in effect, for the Pietists the goal of a *rational* human program. And the many reservations regarding private confession (which were shared broadly among Pietists, although not by Francke, for example), as indicated by the repeated questions addressed to Spener, especially by Pietist *pastors,* arose out of this idea of grace as reserved for a few only. These reservations, as also occurred in Lutheranism, contributed to a weakening of the foundations of the confessional. It was now more and more believed that the *effect* of grace, as acquired through repentance and as visible in devout patterns of conduct, must be decisive for viable absolution. Mere "contrition" would never suffice.[151]

Zinzendorf's idea of a religious *self*-judgment repeatedly merged into the idea of the believer as a "tool" in God's hands. This merging occurred even though, as a result of orthodox attacks, this idea vacillated. Admittedly, the conceptual framework of Zinzendorf—this remarkable "religious dilettante," as [the distinguished German Protestant theologian Albrecht] Ritschl [1822–89] called him—can scarcely be clearly comprehended in respect to the themes important for us.[152] Zinzendorf described himself repeatedly as a representative of "Pauline-Lutheran interpretation" and as *against* the "Pietist-Jacobeans,"[153] who remained fixated upon the *commandments*. However, and despite his own Lutheranism,[154] which he continuously emphasized, Zinzendorf permitted the practices of the Brethren Congregation.[155] As is evident in their notarized protocol of August 12, 1729, he even supported them in spite of positions that clearly corresponded in many respects to the Calvinist idea of an aristocracy of the elect.[156] The much discussed assignment of the office of elder to Jesus Christ, in the protocols of November 12, 1741, expressed a somewhat similar notion (also externally). Moreover, of the three "branches" within the Brethren Congregation, the more Calvinist branch and the more Moravian branch were from the beginning essentially oriented to the vocational ethic of the Reformed Church. Finally, fully in accordance with the Puritan position, Zinzendorf expressed the view (in his talks with John Wesley) that, even though the chosen may not always be aware of their elect status, *others* could *recognize*, from the manner of their conduct, their status as among the saved.[157]

* * *

By contrast, however, the element of feeling became very prominent in the particular piety of the Herrnhuter branch of the Brethren movement.[158] These believers repeatedly sought out Zinzendorf, in particular, in order to thwart directly the tendency in his community toward the striving, in the Puritan sense, to elect status through asceticism.[159] Instead, they wished to bend the notion of good works in a Lutheran direction.[160] Moreover, there developed in Zinzendorf's Pietism, influenced by those who rejected the conventicles and wished to maintain Confession, an essentially Lutheran-influenced tendency to bind the mediation of salvation to the sacraments. Finally, certain aspects of Zinzendorf's own positions had the effect of strongly counteracting the rationalism of the organized and directed life; for example, his view that the *childlike nature* of the religious experience is best understood as a sign of its genuineness (a basic principle particular to him), and that the drawing of *lots* constitutes a device to reveal God's will.

Indeed, such views standing against the rational organization of the believer's life became so prominent that, as far as Zinzendorf's impact is concerned,[161] on the whole anti-rational, *feeling*-based elements played the greater role (as apparent in the piety of the Herrnhuter much more than in other branches of Pietism).[162] The connection between moral conduct and the forgiveness of sins in [the Pietist Bishop August Gottlieb] Spangenberg's [1704–92][163] volume, *Idea Fidei Fratrum* [Idea of Brotherly Trust], is likewise weak,[164] as in Lutheranism in general. Zinzendorf's rejection of the Methodist striving for perfection corresponds, here as well as elsewhere, to his basically eudaemonistical ideal. He wished, namely, to allow believers, even in the *present*,[165] to experience salvation (or "blessedness") through *feelings*. Moreover, Zinzendorf opposed advising the faithful to follow the Calvinist route; that is, he opposed the effort to acquire certainty of salvation for the *next life* through rational work and an organization of their present lives.[166]

Nonetheless, [other elements in Zinzendorf's teachings had the effect of introducing the organized and directed life among believers]. An idea unique to the Brethren Congregation remained viable in Zinzendorf's theology: the idea that the decisive value in the activity of the Christian life lies in missionary work and (as thereby brought into association with it) in work in a calling.[167] In addition, the practical rationalization of life from the standpoint of *utility* was an essential component of Zinzendorf's view of life.[168] Similar to other representatives of Pietism, this rationalization followed for him, on the one hand, from his firm dislike of philosophical speculation (which, he believed, endangered religious belief) and his corresponding favoring of isolated empirical information,[169] and on the other hand from the professional missionary's shrewd knowledge of the world. As the fulcrum of missionary activity, the Brethren Congregation was also a business organization, one that directed its members into paths of inner-worldly asceticism. Exactly in the manner of a business, Pietist asceticism first sought "tasks" to undertake and then, in a dispassionate and planned manner, to organize life in reference to them.

However, the ideal of the Christian apostles' missionary life, from which arose the glorification of the charisma of apostolic *propertylessness* among the "disciples" (chosen by God through "predestination"),[170] opposed Pietism's further development in this direction. Indeed, this apostolic ideal constituted an obstacle that effectively meant a partial rejuvenation of the privilege of receiving advice from the *consilia evangelica* [Catholic Church hierarchy]. This development certainly inhibited in Pietism the creation of a rational ethic, in the manner of Calvinism, for the believer's vocational calling, even though it was not precluded (as the example of the baptizing movement's transformation will shortly demonstrate). An idea of work as occurring *solely* "for the sake of a calling" [as in Calvinism] strongly prepared the pathway—far more effectively and on the basis of an internal relationship—toward such a vocational ethic.

* * *

In summary, if we consider German Pietism from the vantage point that *for us* is here central, we must confirm, all in all, a vacillation and instability in regard to the religious anchoring of its asceticism. The anchoring of Pietism in asceticism is considerably weaker than the iron-clad consistency of Calvinism's grounding in asceticism. In part Lutheran influences and in part the *feeling* character of Pietist religious devotion account for the weakening of asceticism in Pietism.

To depict this feeling component as, compared to *Lutheranism*, something unique to Pietism is surely a great simplification.[171] In any event, however, in comparison to *Calvinism*, the intensity of the rationalization of life in Pietism must necessarily be less. The reason is that the inner motive, deriving from the thought of having to testify over and over again from the beginning to a state of grace that gives security for an eternal *future*, has in Pietism been re-directed onto the *present* as a result of its orientation to the believer's feelings. In place of the certainty that the predestined ever strove to attain anew through unceasing and successful work in a calling, there came humility, timidity, exhaustion, and insecurity.[172] In part, these qualities were a consequence of an awakening of feelings in Pietism oriented exclusively to spiritual experiences, and in part they resulted from the Lutheran form of confession. Although indeed viewed in many ways with deep skepticism, Pietism still tolerated this form of confession for the most part.[173]

Precisely that uniquely Lutheran way of seeking salvation is manifest in all this. Rather than a practical "striving toward holiness"the "forgiveness of sins" is crucial here. The need to *feel* a (this-worldly) reconciliation and community with God now takes the place of the systematic and rational searching to acquire and maintain certain *knowledge* of one's future (next-worldly) salvation. As in economic life, where the inclination to enjoy the present conflicts with the rational organization of the "economy" (which is rooted of course in a provision for the future), so it is, in a certain sense, in the arena of religious life.

Hence, on the one hand the orientation of religious need toward a spiritual *feeling*-emotion (*Gefühlsaffektion*) in the present evidently implies, in contrast to the need of the Reformed elect to testify to their belief (which is oriented exclusively to the next world), a *hindrance* upon any formation of motivations toward the rationalization of this-worldly *action*. On the other hand, the Pietist's orientation to the present and feelings was nonetheless clearly capable of developing a more *methodical* penetration by religion into the entire organization of life than the orientation to faith of the orthodox Lutheran, which remained bound to scripture and the sacraments. From Francke and Spener to Zinzendorf, Pietism as a whole developed an *increasing* emphasis on the feeling aspect of belief. This emphasis, however, was not the result of some "developmental tendency" inherent to Pietism that expressed itself in this manner. Rather, these differences vis-à-vis Lutheranism and Calvinism followed from contrasts in the religious (and social) contexts out of which their leading representatives arose. This point cannot be explored now, nor can a further theme: how the uniqueness of

German Pietism became manifest in its social and geographical *distribution* in Germany.[174]

* * *

At this point we should once again remind ourselves that Pietism's emphasis on the believer's feelings, in contrast to the Puritan elect's religious organization of life, is of course a distinction that shades off into a series of gradual transitions. Nevertheless, if a reference to one practical consequence of this difference may be permitted here (at least in a provisional way), one could note that the virtues cultivated in Pietism tended more often to be those developed on the one hand by the civil servant, middle-management employee, worker, and craftsman "dedicated and devoted to their occupations,"[175] and on the other hand by the employer who adopts a predominantly patriarchal and *condescending* stance toward his workers that is pleasing to God (in the manner of Zinzendorf). In comparison, the virtues cultivated by Calvinism appear to stand in a relationship of greater **elective affinity** to the restrained, strict, and active posture of capitalist employers of the middle class.[176] Finally, as Ritschl[177] has already emphasized, the *purely* feeling-based variety of Pietism is a religious pastime for "leisure classes" [English in original].

This discussion has in no way offered an exhaustive characterization of Pietism. Nevertheless, the conclusions arrived at here correspond to certain differences in the unique economic orientations of peoples under the influence of the Pietist or the Calvinist forms of asceticism. These differences are visible even today.

C. METHODISM

The linking of a feeling-based, yet also ascetic, religious devotion with an increasing indifference to, or rejection of, the dogmatic foundations of Calvinist asceticism also characterizes *Methodism*, the English-American counterpart to continental Pietism.[178] The name already indicates what struck contemporaries as unique to its followers: the "methodical" and systematic organization of life with the aim of attaining the *certitudo salutis*. *This* was the concern of the faithful from the beginning in this church also, and the question of certainty regarding salvation remained at the center of all religious seeking.

Despite all the differences between them, the undoubted affinity of Methodism with certain branches of German Pietism[179] is visible above all in the carrying over of this methodicalness, in particular, into the inducement of the *feeling-based* act of "conversion." Moreover, owing to Methodism's orientation from the beginning to missionary work among the common people, the feeling component (awakened in John Wesley through Herrnhuter-Lutheran influences) took on a very strongly *emotional* character, especially on American soil. Belief in God's undeserved grace (and with it, simultaneously, the direct awareness of exculpation and forgiveness) resulted under certain circumstances from an intensification of the penitence struggle to the point of the most alarming states of ecstasy. Indeed, Methodists in America preferred to seek this ecstasy on the "anxious bench."[180]

This emotional religious devotion entered into a peculiar coalition, despite significant internal difficulties, with an ascetic ethic that had been stamped, once and for all, with an element of Puritan *rationality*. In contrast to Calvinism, which held all orientation to feelings to be a delusion and therefore suspect, Methodism, in principle, at first viewed the purely *felt* absolute certainty of forgiveness as the single, undoubted foundation for the *certitudo salutis*. Believers were convinced that this state of feeling flowed from the unmediated presence of the Holy Spirit, the appearance of which could be normally specified by day and hour. According to Wesley's teachings, which present a consistent intensification of Calvinist doctrine on the striving of the devout toward salvation (though they were also a decisive departure from this orthodoxy), one who is saved in this manner can acquire "salvation" even in this life. By virtue of the effect of divine grace within the believer, such "salvation" occurs through a second (normally separate and likewise often sudden) spiritual process: a striving toward salvation that leads to the acquisition of a consciousness—in the sense of being without sin—of *perfection*.

However difficult it may be to reach this goal (which is acquired for most only near the end of life), a striving to reach it is absolutely necessary. It guarantees definitely the *certitudo salutis* and substitutes a happy certainty for the "moody" brooding of the Calvinists.[181] Moreover, striving to attain this consciousness of perfection marks the true convert, to himself and to others, as a person over whom sin, at least, "no longer has any power." Therefore, despite the decisive significance to Methodists of *feelings*, which offer evidence to believers themselves of their salvation, an orientation to *God's laws*, because it indicates holy conduct, must also be maintained.

* * *

[Wesley further clarified the nature of this conduct.] Wherever he struggled against those who, in his time, advocated the performance of good works as the means toward salvation, his efforts ultimately had the effect of rejuvenating again an old Puritan idea: good works are not the actual cause of salvation, but only the means to recognize whether one is among the saved. Moreover, this recognition can occur only if the good works are carried out exclusively for God's glory. To Wesley, the correct conduct did not *alone* suffice, as he had learned from his own experience; rather, the *feeling* of being among the saved must also be present. (Wesley himself occasionally described good works as a "condition" for salvation, and he emphasized, in the Declaration of August 9, 1771,[182] that those who fail to perform good works are not among the truly devout.) In this manner, the Methodists have continuously stressed that they are distinguished from the Anglican Church, namely, by the type of their piety rather than by their doctrine. For Methodists, the significance of the "fruit" of belief was normally grounded in 1 John 3:9 ["No one born of God commits sin; for God's nature abides in him, and he cannot sin because he is born of God"], and conduct was understood as a clear *sign* of membership among the saved.

Nevertheless, and in spite of all this, difficulties remained for Methodists.[183] For those who held to the doctrine of predestination, a shift of the *certitudo salutis* took place; namely, away from a consciousness of being among the saved as resulting from the ascetic organization of life and a continuously renewed testifying to one's belief through conduct, and toward the unmediated *feeling* of grace and perfection.[184] This displacement occurred because the believer's certainty—*perseverantia*—now became connected to the penitance struggle, which took place only *once*. One of two conclusions was signified by this shift. First, among believers endowed with weak constitutions, an antinomian interpretation—[not adherence to scripture, but faith alone is necessary]—of "Christian Freedom" followed, and hence a collapse of the methodical organization of life. However, whenever this outcome was rejected, a second conclusion presented itself: a certainty among the saved[185] of their salvation that climaxed in dizzying heights. Here a *feeling-based* intensification of the Puritan model is apparent.

In light of attacks by opponents, Methodists sought to address these two outcomes. On the one hand, they did so through an increased emphasis on the normative validity of the Bible and the indispensability of a testifying to belief.[186] On the other hand, and as a consequence of this increased emphasis, they did so by strengthening anti-Calvinist doctrines within Methodism, namely, Wesley's teaching that grace can be lost. His vulnerability[187] to strong Lutheran influences, as mediated by the Brethren Congregation, strengthened this development and increased the *indeterminateness* of the religious orientation of Methodist morality.[188]

As a consequence, essentially only the concept of "regeneration" [English in original] was in the end consistently maintained: a manifest feeling-based certainty of salvation resulted directly from the believer's *faith*. Regeneration served as the indispensable foundation for the believer's state of grace and it implied a striving toward salvation. To the extent this process of making the believer holy followed, this implied a freedom (at least fictitious) from the power of sin, and as well a corresponding devaluation of the significance of the external means of grace, especially the sacraments. In any event, an intensification of the doctrine of predestined grace and Election characterized the "Great Awakening" [English in original] that everywhere followed Methodism (for example, in New England).[189]

* * *

Thus for *our* investigation, in terms of its ethic, Methodism appears to be a formation as precariously grounded as Pietism. The striving for the "higher life" [English in original], however, also served Methodism, as it did Pietism, as a "second blessing," namely, as a type of surrogate doctrine of predestination. Moreover, growing from the soil of England, Methodism oriented its ethical practice fully toward England's Reformed Christianity, wishing to be its "revival." Accordingly, the emotional act of conversion was *methodically* induced. Once attained, a pious enjoyment of a sense of community with God did not exist in Methodism, unlike in Zinzendorf's Pietism based on feeling. Rather, awakened feeling in Methodism was immediately guided into the pathway of a rational striving for perfection.

Hence, the emotional character of Methodist religious devotion never led to a spiritual Christianity based on feeling in the manner of German Pietism. That this distinction was connected to a theology in Methodism that placed less emphasis on a development of the feeling of *sinfulness* (in part precisely owing to the emotional pathway followed in the conversion process) has already been demonstrated by Schneckenburger, and his argument has remained unchallenged in subsequent scholarship. Rather, the *Reformist* foundation of Methodism's religious sensibility remained central. The arousal of feelings took the form of an occasional, boisterous [*korybantenartig*] but then restrained, enthusiasm. As such, it failed to detract from the rational character of the Methodist organization of life.[190]

In this way, Methodism's "regeneration" produced in the end only a *complementary* component to the pure idea of salvation through good works: a religious anchoring of the ascetic organization of life after the abandonment of the idea of predestination. The sign offered by conduct, which was indispensable as an indication of the believer's true conversion (its "precondition," as Wesley occasionally noted), was substantively the same as in Calvinism. In the following discussion of the idea of the calling,[191] we will see that Methodism, as a later theology,[192] contributed nothing new to its development.[193] Hence it can be essentially left aside.

D. THE BAPTIZING SECTS AND CHURCHES[194]

The Pietism of the European Continent and the Methodism of the Anglo-Saxon peoples are secondary developments both in respect to their ideas and their historical unfolding.[195] On the other hand, the second, next to Calvinism, *independent* carrier of Protestant asceticism was the *baptizing* movement. The sects[196] that arose from it in the course of the sixteenth and seventeenth centuries, either directly or through the assimilation of its forms of religious thinking, were the *Baptists*, *Mennonites*, and, above all, the *Quakers*.[197] With these sects, we arrive at religious communities that possess ethics resting in principle upon a foundation opposed to Reformist doctrines.

The following brief overview, which of course calls attention only to that which is important to *us* here, will not do justice to the diversity of this movement. Once again, the primary emphasis will be placed on developments in the older capitalist countries.

We have already become acquainted with the rudiments of the idea that is historically, and in principle, most important in all of these communities (although its scope for cultural development can become fully clear to us only in a different context): the "believers' church" [English in original].[198] According to this notion, the religious community (the "visible church" in the terminology of the churches of the Reformation)[199] was no longer viewed as a sort of repository of trust established to serve supernatural aims; that is, as an *institution* (*Anstalt*) that necessarily included both the saved and the unsaved, whether in order to increase the glory of God (Calvinism) or to mediate salvation to persons (Catholicism and Lutheranism). Rather, the religious community now became viewed as a community of *sincere believers and the elect*—and only these persons. In other words, it existed as a "sect"[200] rather than as a "church" (see pp. 169–97). The manifest principle of the sect—exclusively those adults who have innerly acquired and then overtly declared sincere belief are to be baptized—should symbolize this understanding of the religious community.[201]

For the baptizing sects, "justification" of a person's devoutness *through* this belief, which was confirmed repeatedly and insistently in all discussions among the faithful, was radically different from the idea of a "juridicial" *attribution* of service to Christ, as prevailed in the orthodox dogma of the old Protestantism [Lutheranism].[202] Rather, in the sects this justification involved more of a *spiritual conversion to belief* in Christ's sacrifice and gift of salvation. It occurred through an individual *revelation*; that is, through the effect of the Holy Spirit inside the believer—and *only* in this manner. This revelation was offered to everyone. The devout must simply wait for the Holy Spirit and avoid resisting His arrival through their sinful attachment to the mundane world.

As a consequence, the significance of faith—in the sense of the knowledge of church doctrine, though also in the sense of a penitent focusing on God's grace—moved now into the background. Instead, a renaissance of the spiritual-religious (*pneumatisch-religioser*) ideas of early Christianity (though naturally with strong modifications) occurred.[203] The sects, for example those for which Menno Simons created in his *Book of Fundamentals* [*Fundamentboek*] (1539) an acceptably unified doctrine, wanted to be *the* true, blameless Church of Christ, as did the other baptizing sects. Like the original community of apostles, they wished to be constituted exclusively from believers *personally* awakened and called by God. The elect, and only the elect, are brothers in Christ—for they, like Christ, have been created spiritually directly from God.[204]

The consequence of these ideas was apparent to the first baptizing communities: faith did not suffice. Instead, members should practice a strict *avoidance* of "the world." Only absolutely necessary interactions with nonmembers were permitted. Moreover, following the exemplary life of the first generations of Christians, sect members must engage in the strictest study of the Bible. Indeed, as long as the old spirit of these sects remained alive, this principle of avoidance of the world never fully disappeared.[205]

* * *

These motives dominated the baptizing sects' early period. They retained from this era a principle that we have already become acquainted with from Calvinism (even though somewhat differently grounded): the absolute *condemnation of all deification of human wants and desires*, for their cultivation rendered worthless the reverence owed exclusively to God.[206] The fundamental importance of this principle will repeatedly come to the fore. The organization of life according to the Bible was viewed by the first generation in the baptizing communities from Switzerland and southwest Germany in a radical manner similar to that found originally in St. Francis: a sharp rejection of all worldly pleasures and a strict conformity with the lives of the apostles should prevail. In fact the lives of many of the first adherents of these sects remind one of the life of St. Aegidus [that is, of St. Giles, the eighth century monk and "helper in need" in France and Switzerland].

This exceptionally strict adherence to the authority[207] of the Bible, however, stood somewhat weakly against the spiritual character of religious devoutness. What God had revealed to the prophets and the apostles was not all that He could, or wanted, to reveal. On the contrary, according to the testimony of the early Christian community, as the German mystic [Kaspar von] Schwenckfeld [1489–1581][208] taught against Luther, and [the Quaker] Fox later taught against the Presbyterians, the long-term endurance of scripture as manifest in the daily lives of the faithful as the effective power of the Holy Spirit who speaks directly to those individuals who want to hear Him, rather than simply as a written document, constitutes the single identifying mark of the true church. A well-known doctrine arose from this idea of continuing revelation, which was later developed by the Quakers in a consistent fashion: the inner manifestation, according to it, of the Holy Spirit as reason and *conscience* is of ultimate importance. The exclusive authority of the Bible was pushed aside with this teaching, though not its validity. Simultaneously, a further development was introduced that ultimately resulted in the radical removal of all remnants of the Catholic Church's doctrine of salvation.

Together with all churches that upheld predestination (and above all the strict Calvinists), all denominations with adult baptism practiced the most radical devaluation of all sacraments as means to salvation. In the case of the Quakers, this removal included the abandonment of even the sacraments of christening and communion.[209] Hence, a process that "eliminated magic" from the world was placed into motion by these denominations and carried through to its final conclusion [1920].

Only that "inner light" of continuing revelation now enabled believers to acquire true understanding, even of the biblical revelations of God.[210] On the other hand, at least according to Quaker teachings, which here drew matters out to their full conclusion, the effect of this inner light could be extended to persons who had never known the biblical form of revelation. The dictum *extra ecclesiam nulla salus* [no salvation outside of the Church] was valid only for this *in*visible church of those illuminated by the Holy Spirit. *Without* the inner light, human beings, and even persons guided by natural reason, remained pure creatures of desires and wants.[211] All baptizing congregations, including the Quakers, felt the Godlessness of such persons to be reprehensible, indeed almost as much as did the Calvinists. Nevertheless, the rebirth that the Holy Spirit brings, if we *wait for Him* and inwardly give ourselves over to Him, *can* lead to a condition—because caused by God—in which the power of sin is completely overcome.[212] This condition can be so intense that relapses, or even the loss of the state of grace, factually become impossible. However, the attainment of this condition does not invariably occur; instead, as is the case later in Methodism, the individual's degree of perfection is subject to an unfolding development.

All baptizing communities, however, wanted *pure* congregations in the sense of members of blameless conduct. The inner disengagement from the world and its mundane interests, and the unconditional submission to the domination of God who speaks to believers through their conscience, were also themselves unerring signs of one's saved status. Corresponding conduct was thus a necessity for salvation. As a gift from God, salvation could not be earned. Nevertheless, those who lived according to their conscience—and only these devout believers—were permitted to view themselves as among the saved. In this sense "good works" were *causa sine qua non* [indispensable] if believers were to see themselves as among the saved.

* * *

It is apparent that this series of ideas, which we have summarized from the writings of [the Scottish Quaker Robert] Barclay [1648–1686], is the same as the Reformed doctrine for all practical purposes. Surely it was developed under the influence of Calvinist asceticism, which existed before the rise of the baptizing sects in England and Holland. During the entire first period of his missionary activity, George Fox preached on behalf of a serious and spiritual conversion to this asceticism. Because the baptizing sects rejected the notion of predestination, however, the specifically *methodical* character of their morality rested psychologically primarily on the idea of *waiting* for the effect of the Holy Spirit. Even today this idea provides the defining characteristic of the "Quaker Meeting." It has been aptly analyzed by Barclay.

The overcoming of the instinctive and the irrational, as well as the passions and the prejudices—that is, of the "natural" human being—is the aim of this silent waiting. People must be silent in order to create the deep stillness in the soul that alone allows God to speak to them. Of course, the effect of this "waiting" *could* be to lead to conditions of anxiety or to prophecies regarding the future. Moreover, under certain conditions, and as long as eschatological hopes continued to exist, waiting might flow into an outburst of chiliastic[213] enthusiasm, as is possible in all similarly grounded types of piety and as actually occurred in the sects that imploded in Münster.[214]

"Waiting" was somewhat altered, however, as members of the baptizing congregations began to stream into this-worldly vocational callings. The original idea—God speaks only when human wants and desires are silent—was changed. The devout were now apparently taught to *deliberate* calmly before acting and to orient their action only after a careful investigation of the individual *conscience*.[215] This calm, dispassionate, and supremely *conscience*-bound disposition of character then became manifest in the practical life of the later baptizing communities (as occurred also, and to an unusual degree, among the Quakers).

The radical elimination of magic from the world's occurrences did not allow internally a pathway of development other than one leading to this-worldly asceticism. However, these baptizing groups were pushed in the direction of work in a vocation not only by this development; an external factor was also important: their unwillingness to have anything to do with the political powers-that-be, and their machinations, also pushed them in this direction [1920].

In the first generation, of course, things had been different. The leaders of the baptizing movement's oldest congregations were irredeemably radical in turning away from the mundane world. *Not all* believers, however, even in this period viewed the strict organization of life, in accord with the ideals of poverty of the apostles, as unconditionally required for proof of one's saved status.[216] Even wealthy persons were found in this generation. Indeed, even before Menno, who stood squarely on the soil of the this-worldly vocational virtues and in support of private property, the serious and strict morality of the baptizing groups had in practice turned in this direction. The facilitating groundwork for this turn had already been laid by Reformist ethics,[217] and the pathway in the direction of an *other*-worldly, monastic form of asceticism had been, since Luther, precluded. He had condemned monasticism as not in conformity with the Bible's teachings and as involving an ethos of good works. The baptizing congregations, as had others, followed Luther on these points.

Despite these developments toward the notion of a this-worldly vocational calling, the baptizing sects did not yet move unequivocally in this direction. Even leaving aside the quasi-communistic communities of the early period (which cannot be discussed here), residuals remained of the radical turning away from the mundane world evident in the movement's oldest congregations. One baptizing sect, the so-called Dunckers (*Dompelaers*) [in Germany, founded in 1708],[218] has continued to condemn higher forms of education up to our own time, as well as every possession that goes beyond life's basic necessities. Moreover, for Barclay, for example, the notion of "being true to one's vocational calling" is not conceptualized in the manner of the Calvinists or even the Lutherans. Instead, following St. Thomas of Aquinas, Barclay comprehended it as *naturali ratione* [naturally rational], namely, as an unavoidable *result* of the entanglement of the faithful in the world's activities.[219]

* * *

Nevertheless, and even though we can see in these views a weakening of the Calvinist notion of the calling similar to that found in many of Spener's statements and in German Pietism, the intensity of interest in a this-worldly vocational calling among the baptizing sects essentially *increased*. There were various reasons. First, the increase resulted from a rejection of employment in all state offices, a rejection that was originally understood as stemming from a religious duty to withdraw from the world. This view endured, at least in practice, for the Mennonites and Quakers (even after it had been abandoned in principle) as a consequence of their strict refusal to use weapons and to swear oaths (refusals that disqualified persons from civil service positions). Second, together with this disqualification there developed an insurmountable opposition in all of the baptizing denominations to every sign of an aristocratic style of life (*Lebensstil*). This opposition arose in part as a consequence of the prohibition against all deification of human wants and desires (as it did for the Calvinists) and in part as a result of the apolitical (or even anti-political) principles just mentioned.

In these ways the entire dispassionate and conscientious, methodical organization of life in the baptizing communities was pushed down the pathway of the *un*political vocational life. In the process, the immense significance awarded by their salvation doctrine to the monitoring of action by the conscience (the very capacity to do so was viewed as an individualized revelation from God) now gave a particular orientation to conduct in vocational life. In turn, this conduct had great significance for the development of important aspects of the capitalist spirit.

This theme of this-worldly asceticism will become more familiar to us in the following chapter. However, it can be addressed only to the extent that it appears possible to do so without entering into a consideration of the entire political and social ethics of Protestant asceticism. We will then note (if a single point may now be alluded to) that the specific form taken by this-worldly asceticism among the baptizing congregations, especially the Quakers,[220] was expressed, according to the judgment of the seventeenth century, in the practical testifying of believers to that important principle of the capitalist "ethic" previously cited in the treatise by Benjamin Franklin: "honesty is the best policy" [English in original].[221] In contrast, we will surmise that the effects of Calvinism are more to be seen in the direction of unchaining the private economy's energy to expand. For Goethe's maxim, despite the formal legality of the business activity of the Calvinist "saints," remained in the end often valid also for these devout believers: "Those who act are always without a conscience; only those who observe have a conscience."[222]

The full significance of a third important reason that contributed to the intensity of the baptizing denominations' this-worldly asceticism can be addressed only in another context. Nevertheless, a few observations on this subject may be made now, if only to justify the procedure chosen here for our presentation.

* * *

We have intentionally decided here *not* to commence our discussion with a consideration of the objective social institutions of the old Protestant churches and their ethical influence. We have especially decided not to begin with a discussion of *church discipline*, even though it is very important. Instead, we will first examine the effects on *each believer's* organization of life that are possible when *individuals* convert to a religious devoutness anchored in asceticism. We will proceed in this manner for two reasons: this side of our theme has until now received far less attention, and the effect of church discipline cannot be viewed as always leading in the same direction.

In those regions where a Calvinist state church held sway, the authoritarian monitoring of the believer's life was practiced to a degree that rivaled an inquisition. This supervision *could* work even *against* that emancipation of individual energies originating out of the believer's ascetic striving to methodically acquire a sense of certainty as belonging among the saved. It did so under certain circumstances. Just as mercantilist regimentation by the state could indeed give birth to industries but not (at least not alone) to the capitalist "spirit" (which this regimentation crippled in various ways, wherever it assumed a despotic-authoritarian character), the church's regimentation of asceticism could have the same effect. Wherever the church developed too far in a harshly authoritarian direction, it coerced believers into adhering to specific forms of external behavior. In doing so, however, under certain circumstances the church then crippled the individual's motivation to organize life in a methodical manner.

Every explanation of this point[223] must note the great difference between the effects of the despotic-authoritarianism of state *churches* and the effects of the despotism of *sects*. The latter rests upon voluntary subjection. The creation by the baptizing movement, in all its denominations, of "sects" rather than "churches" contributed to the intensity of its asceticism. Such intensity occurred as well, to varying degrees, in the Calvinist, Pietist, and Methodist communities. In *practice*, all were pushed in the direction of forming voluntary communities.[224]

* * *

It is now our task to follow out the effect of the Puritan idea of a vocational calling on how people *acquire goods and **earn a living***. We are now prepared to do so, having attempted to offer in this chapter a sketch of the way in which the religious anchoring of the calling idea developed. Although differences in details and variations in emphasis exist in the diverse communities of religious asceticism, the vantage points decisive for us have been present and manifest, in effective ways, in all of these groups.[225]

To recapitulate, decisive again and again for our investigation was the conception of the religious "state of grace." Reappearing in all the denominations as a particular status [English in original], this state of grace separated people from the depravity of physical desires and from "this-world."[226] Although attained in a variety of ways depending upon the dogma of the particular denomination, possession of the state of grace could *not* be guaranteed through magical-sacramental means of any kind, through the relief found in confession, or through particular good works. Rather, it could be acquired only through a *testifying to belief*. Sincere belief became apparent in specifically formed conduct unmistakably different from the style of life of the "natural" human being. For the person testifying to belief there followed a *motivation* to *methodically supervise* his or her state of grace. An organizing and directing of life ensued and, in the process, its penetration by *asceticism*.

As we noted, this ascetic style of life implied a *rational* formation of the entire being (*Dasein*) and the complete orientation of this being toward God's Will. Moreover, this asceticism was *no longer opus supererogationis* [an achievement within the capability of only a few], but one expected of all who wished to become certain of their salvation. Finally, and of central importance, the special life of the saint—fully separate from the "natural" life of the wants and desires—could no longer play itself out in monastic communities set apart from the world. Rather, the devoutly religious must now live saintly lives *in* the world and amidst its mundane affairs. This *rationalization* of the organized and directed life—now in the world yet still oriented to the supernatural—was the effect of ascetic Protestantism's *concept of the calling*.

At its beginning, Christian asceticism had fled from the world into the realm of solitude in the cloister. In renouncing the world, however, this asceticism had assisted religion, through the church, to dominate the world. Yet, in retreating to the cloister, asceticism left the course of daily life in the world by and large in its natural and untamed state. But now Christian asceticism slammed the gates of the cloister, entered into the hustle and bustle of life, and undertook a new task: to saturate mundane, *everyday* life with its methodicalness. In the process, it sought to reorganize practical life into a rational life *in* the world rather than, as earlier, in the monastery. Yet this rational life in the world was *not of* this world or *for* this world. In our further exposition we will attempt to convey the results of this dramatic turn.

CHAPTER V

ASCETICISM AND THE SPIRIT OF CAPITALISM

In order to comprehend the connections between the basic religious ideas of *ascetic Protestantism* and the maxims of everyday economic life, it is necessary above all to draw upon those theological texts that can be recognized as having crystallized out of the practice of pastoral care. In this [sixteenth- and seventeenth-century] epoch, everything depended upon one's relationship to the next life, and one's social position depended upon admission to the sacrament of communion.[1] Moreover, through pastoral care, church discipline, and preaching, the clergy's influence grew to such an extent (as any glance in the collected *consilia, casus conscientiae*, and other documents will indicate)[2] that we today are *simply no longer* capable of comprehending its broad scope. Religious forces, as they became transmitted to populations through *these regular practices* and became legitimate and accepted, were decisive for the formation of "national character."[3]

In contrast to later discussions in this chapter, we can *here* treat *ascetic Protestantism* as *a* unity. Because, however, English **Puritanism,** which grew out of Calvinism, provides the most consistent foundation for the *idea of a vocational calling,* we are placing one of its representatives at the center of our analysis (in accord with our previous procedures). *Richard Baxter* [1615–1691] is distinguished from many other literary representatives of the Puritan ethic on the one hand by his eminently practical and conciliatory posture, and on the other by the universal acknowledgment accorded his works. They have been repeatedly reprinted and translated.

Baxter was a Presbyterian and apologist for the **Westminster Synod**, although in terms of dogma he moved gradually away from an orthodox Calvinism (like so many of the best ministers of his time). Because he was hostile to every revolution, to all sectarianism, and especially to the fanatical zeal of the "saints," he opposed Cromwell's usurpation. Yet Baxter remained unusually tolerant of all extreme positions and impartial toward his opponents. His own projects were essentially oriented toward a practical advancement of the religious-moral life. On behalf of these endeavors he offered his services, as one of the most successful practitioners of pastoral care known to history, equally to Parliament, to Cromwell, and to the Restoration.[4] He continued to do so until he departed from his pulpit, which took place before St. Bartholomew's Day.[5]

Baxter's *Christian Directory* [1673] is the most comprehensive compendium of Puritan moral theology. Moreover, it is oriented throughout to the practical issues he dealt with in his pastoral care. In order to offer appropriate comparisons, Spener's *Theological Considerations* [1712], as representative of German Pietism, Barclay's *Apology* [1701], as representative of the Quakers, and occasionally other representatives of the ascetic ethic[6] will be referred to (generally in the endnotes, however, owing to space restrictions).[7]

* * *

If we examine Baxter's *Saints' Everlasting Rest* [1651] or his *Christian Directory* or even related works by others,[8] we are struck at first glance by his judgments regarding wealth[9] and its acquisition, and by his emphasis on the New Testament ebionitic[10] proclamations [which scorned wealth and idealized the poor].[11] Wealth as such is a serious danger and its temptations are constant. Moreover, in light of the overriding significance of God's kingdom, the pursuit[12] of wealth is seen as both senseless and morally suspect. Indeed, to Baxter, asceticism appeared oriented *against* every striving to acquire the products of this world in a far more pointed manner than to Calvin, who never saw wealth among the ministry as a barrier to its effectiveness. On the contrary, wealth led to a thoroughly desirable increase of clerical prestige, according to Calvin, and he allowed the ministry to acquire profit from their fortunes wherever it could be invested without causing difficulties. Yet in Puritan writings examples that condemn the pursuit of money and material goods can be accumulated without end. They can be contrasted with the ethical literature of the late medieval period, which was far less strict on this point. Moreover, the Puritan literature's suspicion of wealth was thoroughly serious. Its decisively ethical meaning and context, however, can be articulated only after somewhat closer scrutiny.

What is actually morally reprehensible is, namely, the *resting* upon one's possessions[13] and the *enjoyment* of wealth. To do so results in idleness and indulging desires of the flesh, and above all in the distraction of believers from their pursuit of the "saintly" life. Furthermore, the possession of goods is suspect *only because* it carries with it the danger of this resting. The "saint's everlasting rest" comes in the next world. On earth, in this life, in order to become certain of one's state of grace, a person must "work the works of Him who sent him, while it is day" [John 9:4]. According to the will of God, which has been clearly revealed, *only activity*, not idleness and enjoyment, serves to increase His glory.[14]

Hence, of all the sins, *the wasting of time* constitutes the first and, in principle, the most serious. A single life offers an infinitely short and precious space of time to "make firm" one's own election. The loss of time through sociability, "idle talk,"[15] sumptuousness,[16] and even through more sleep than is necessary for good health[17] (six to eight hours at most) is absolutely morally reprehensible.[18] Franklin's maxim —"time is money"—is not yet expressed by Baxter, yet this axiom holds in a certain spiritual sense. Because every hour not spent at work is an hour lost in service to God's greater glory, according to Baxter, time is infinitely valuable.[19] Thus, inactive contemplation is without value and in the end explicitly condemned, at least if it occurs at the expense of work in a calling,[20] for it pleases God *less* than the active implementation of His will in a calling.[21] At any rate, Sundays exist for contemplation. For Baxter, it is always those who are idle in their vocational callings who have no time for God, even on the day of rest.[22]

Accordingly, a sermon on the virtues of hard and continuous physical or mental *work* is continuously repeated, occasionally almost with passion, throughout Baxter's major treatise.[23] Two themes come together here.[24]

* * *

First, work is the tried and proven *mechanism* for the practice of *asceticism*. For this reason, work has been held in high esteem in the Catholic Church from the beginning,[25] in sharp contrast not only to the Middle East but also to almost all the regulations followed by non-Christian monks throughout the world.[26] Indeed, work constitutes a particular defense mechanism against all those temptations summarized by the Puritan notion of the "unclean life." The part played by these temptations is by no means a small one. Sexual asceticism in Puritanism is different only in degree, and not in principle, from that in monastic practice. As a result of the Puritan conception of marriage, sexual asceticism is more comprehensive simply because, even in marriage, sexual intercourse is permitted *only* as a means, desired by God, to increase His glory through the fulfillment of His commandment: "be fruitful and multiply."[27] Just as it is a bulwark against all religious doubt and unrestrained torment, the admonition "work hard in your calling" constitutes a prescription against all sexual temptations (as do a temperate diet, vegetarianism, and cold baths).[28]

Second, in addition and above all, as ordained by God, the purpose of life *itself* involves work.[29] [The Apostle] Paul's maxim applies to everyone without qualification: "if anyone will not work, let him not eat."[30] An unwillingness to work is a sign that one is not among the saved.[31]

The divergence of Puritanism from medieval Catholicism becomes clearly evident here. Thomas Aquinas also interpreted Paul's maxim. Work is simply a *naturali ratione* [naturally rational] necessity, according to him,[32] in order to maintain the life of the individual and that of the community. Paul's maxim, however, ceases to hold wherever this aim is not relevant, for it offers simply a general prescription for all and fails to address each person's situation. That is, it does not pertain to those people who can, without working, live from their possessions. Similarly, contemplation as a spiritual form of activity in God's kingdom naturally takes priority over this maxim in its literal sense. In addition, according to popular theology, the highest form of monastic "productivity" was to be found in the increase of the *thesaurus ecclesiae* [the church's spiritual treasures] through prayer and choir service.

These violations of the ethical duty to work were, of course, abandoned by Baxter. In addition, and with great emphasis, he hardened his basic principle that even wealth does not free people from Paul's unconditional maxim.[33] For Baxter even those with many possessions shall not eat without working. As God's commandment, this maxim remains in effect even if it is not necessary for people to work in order to fulfill their needs. The wealthy, just like the poor, must be obedient to this principle.[34] Besides,

God's providence reserves a calling for everyone without distinction. It is to be recognized by each person, and each person should work within his calling, according to Baxter. Moreover, this calling is not, as in Lutheranism,[35] a fate to which believers must submit and reconcile themselves. Rather, it is God's command to each person to act on behalf of His honor.

This seemingly inconsequential nuance had broad-ranging psychological consequences. It went together with the Puritan understanding of the **providential** interpretation of the economic cosmos familiar to us from the Scholastics.[36] Yet the Puritan outlook (*Anschauung*) constituted a further development of Scholasticism's ideas. Here we can once again, and most conveniently, make a connection to the thinking of Aquinas.

* * *

The idea of society's division of labor and occupational stratification has been conceptualized, by Aquinas (to whom we can again most conveniently refer) as well as others, as a direct outcome of God's divine plan for the world. The placement of people into this cosmos, however, follows *ex causis naturalibus* [from natural causes] and is random (or, in the terminology of the Scholastics, "contingent").

Luther, as we noted, viewed the placement of people in given status groups and occupations—which followed out of the objective historical order—as a direct emanation of God's will. Thus, a person's abiding *persistence* in the position and circumscribed situation assigned to him by God constituted a religious duty.[37] It was all the more so because the ways in which Lutheran piety connected the devout to the mundane "world" as given were, in general, from the beginning uncertain, and remained so. Ethical principles, in reference to which the world could be transformed, were not to be extracted from Luther's constellation of ideas (which never became fully severed from Paul's notions of indifference to the world). Hence, Lutherans had to take the world simply as it was. In Lutheranism *this acceptance*, and only this acceptance, could become once again, endowed with a notion of religious duty.

The Puritan view, once again, nuanced the providential character of the interplay of private economic interests in yet a different way. Here the providential purpose of occupational stratification can be recognized from its *fruits*. This view is consistent with the Puritan proclivity toward a pragmatic interpretation, and Baxter offers statements on this theme that remind one (on more than one occasion) immediately of Adam Smith's familiar deification of the division of labor.[38]

The specialization of occupations makes it possible for workers to develop skills. For this reason it leads, Baxter argues, to a quantitative and qualitative increase in worker productivity and thus serves the "common best" [common good], which is identical with the prosperity of the greatest possible number. So far, the motivation remains purely utilitarian and closely related to points of view already common in the secular literature of the period.[39] But just at this point the characteristic Puritan element comes to the fore. Baxter places a discussion of the motivation involved at the center of his analysis:

> Outside of a firm calling, the workplace achievements of a person are only irregular and temporary. This person spends more time being lazy than actually working.

Moreover, Baxter's manner of concluding this discussion also reveals the Puritan dimension:

> And he (the worker with a vocational calling) will perform his work *in an orderly fashion* while others are stuck in situations of constant confusion; their businesses fail to operate according to time or place[40]... Therefore a 'certain calling' (or 'stated calling' at other passages) is best for everyone.[41]

Intermittent work, into which the common day laborer is forced, is often unavoidable, but it is always an unwanted, transitional condition. The systematic-methodical character required by this-worldly asceticism is simply lacking in the life "without a calling" (*Beruflosen*).

Also, according to the ethic of the Quakers, a person's vocational calling should involve a consistent, ascetic exercise of virtues. One's state of grace is *testified to* through the *conscientiousness* with which the believer, with care[42] and methodicalness, pursues his calling. Rational work in a calling is demanded by God rather than work as such.

The Puritan idea of a calling continually emphasizes this methodical character of vocational asceticism rather than, as with Luther, the resignation to one's lot as irredeemably assigned by God.[43] Hence, for Puritanism the question of whether one may combine multiple callings is unequivocally answered affirmatively—if doing so proves beneficial to the common prosperity or to the individual[44] and is not injurious to anyone, and if it does not lead to a situation in which one becomes "unfaithful" to one of the combined callings. Indeed, even the *change* of vocational callings is not at all viewed as reprehensible, if carried out in a responsible manner. On the contrary, when made for the purpose of securing a vocation more pleasing to God[45] (that is, corresponding to the general rule here, to a more useful calling), then the initiative should be taken.

Most important, the usefulness of a vocational calling is assessed mainly in moral terms, as is its corresponding capacity to please God. A further criterion is closely bound to this moral dimension, namely, according to the degree of importance of the goods produced in the calling for the "community." A third criterion, one clearly the most important at the practical level, is also central in assessing a calling's usefulness: its economic *profitability* for the individual.[46] For if his God, whom the Puritan sees as acting in all arenas of life, reveals a chance for turning a profit to one of His faithful, He must do so with clear intentions in mind. Accordingly, the believer must follow this opportunity and exploit it:[47]

If God show you a way in which you may, in accordance with His laws, acquire more profit than in another way, without wrong to your soul or to any other and if you refuse this, choosing the less profitable course, you then cross one of the purposes of your calling. You are refusing to be God's steward, and to accept His gifts, in order to be able to use them for Him when He requireth it. You may labour, for God, to become rich, though not for the flesh and sin [Weber's emphasis].[48]

* * *

Hence, wealth is only suspect when it tempts the devout in the direction of lazy restfulness and a sinful enjoyment of life. The striving for riches becomes suspect only if carried out with the end in mind of leading a carefree and merry life once wealth is acquired. If, however, riches are attained within the dutiful performance of one's vocational calling, striving for them is not only morally permitted but expected.[49] This idea is explicitly expressed in the parable of the servant who was sentenced to hell because he failed to make the most of the opportunities entrusted to him.[50] *Wishing* to be poor, it was frequently argued, signifies the same as wishing to be sick.[51] Indeed, it would be abominable for it would be seen as a searching for salvation through good works and hence as detrimental to God's glory. Furthermore, begging by those capable of working is not only sinful (as indolence) but also, according to the apostles, opposed to brotherly love.[52]

Just as the endowment of the stable vocational calling with ascetic significance sheds an ethical glorification around the modern *specialized expert*, the providential interpretation of one's chances for profit glorifies the *businessperson*.[53] Asceticism on the one hand despises equally the refined nonchalance of the feudal noble and the parvenu-like ostentation of boasters. On the other hand, it shines a full beam of ethical approval upon the **dispassionate**, "self-made man" of the **middle class**.[54] A common remark—"God blesseth his trade"[55]—refers to these saints[56] who have followed God's every decree with success. Moreover, the entire force of the *Old Testament God*,[57] which required His disciples to become pious in *this* life,[58] must have influenced the Puritans in the same direction. According to Baxter's advice, the devout must monitor and supervise their own state of grace through comparisons to the spiritual condition of biblical heroes.[59] In doing so, they must "interpret" the words of the Bible as if they were reading "paragraphs of a law book."

Of course Old Testament scripture was not entirely clear. We noted that Luther first employed the concept of calling, in its *this-worldly* sense, in a translation of a passage from Jesus Sirach [Ecclesiasticus, or The Wisdom of Ben Sira]. According to its entire mood of devotion, however, and despite its Hellenic influences, this book belongs among the most traditional sections of the (expanded) Old Testament [the Apocrypha].[60] Characteristically, Jesus Sirach appears to possess, even today, a special attraction for Lutheran German peasants[61] and those broad streams of German Pietism more bound to Lutheranism.[62]

In light of their harsh either-or distinction between the Divine and depraved human beings, the Puritans criticized the Apocrypha as uninspired by God.[63] Among the canonical books, the Book of Job then became all the more central. On the one hand, it manifested a glorification of God's absolutely sovereign majesty, separate from all human standards—an idea highly congenial to Calvinist views. On the other, as breaks forth again in Job's concluding passages and combined with this idea of a majestic God, it presents a God who will, with certainty, bless His faithful—and will do so in this life, also in a material sense (as exclusively stated in this book).[64] Though of secondary importance to Calvin, this promise proved important for Puritanism. At the same time, the Puritan interpretation abandoned all Near Eastern quietism, which came to the fore in some of the most devotional verses of Psalms and Proverbs. Similarly, in his discussion of a passage in the First Letter to the Corinthians, Baxter interpreted away its traditional overtones. Doing so proved essential for his concept of the calling. In light of these developments, the Puritans all the more placed an emphasis upon those Old Testament passages that praised *formal correctness in terms of religious law* in one's conduct as constituting a sign of God's approval.

[Further interpretations also moved in this direction.] The Puritans opposed the theory that the law of Moses had lost its legitimacy with the founding of Christianity. They argued instead that only those passages relating to Jewish ceremonial or historically conditioned statutes were invalid. Otherwise this law, they maintained, as an expression of *lex naturae* [natural law], possessed its validity from eternity and therefore must be retained.[65] This interpretation allowed on the one hand the elimination of statutes not easily adaptable to modern life, and on the other a powerful strengthening of a spirit of self-righteous and dispassionate legality suitable to Puritanism's this-worldly asceticism. Once in place, this development enabled numerous related features of Old Testament morality to flow freely into ascetic Protestantism.[66]

* * *

Therefore, correctly understood, the repeated depiction of the basic ethical orientation of English Puritanism in particular, even by its contemporaries (as well as more recent writers), as "English Hebraism"[67] is fully appropriate. Nevertheless, one should not think of this English Hebraism as the Palestinian Judaism from the period of the Old Testament's origin. Rather, one should recall the later Judaism that developed gradually under the influence of formal-legal and Talmudic learning over many centuries. Even then one must be extremely cautious regarding historical parallels. The mood of ancient Judaism, which was by and large oriented toward an appreciation of life's spontaneity as such, was far removed from the specific uniqueness of Puritanism [see pp. 290–99].

Yet it should not be overlooked that Puritanism remained far distant as well from the economic ethic of medieval and modern Judaism in respect to features decisive for the development of the capitalist *ethos*. Judaism stood on the side of an "adventure" capitalism in which political or speculative motives were central. In a word, the economic ethic of Judaism was one of *pariah* capitalism.[68] By contrast, Puritanism carried the ethos of a rational, middle-class *company* and the rational organization of *work*. It took from Judaism's ethic only that which proved adaptable to this framework. [1920]

To chart out the characterological consequences of the penetration of life by Old Testament norms would be impossible in the context of this sketch (however stimulating a task, although until now it has not been adequately undertaken even for Judaism itself).[69] An analysis of the inner habitus of the Puritans in its entirety (*inneren Gesamthabitus*), in addition to the relationships already discussed, would also have to consider how it accompanied a grandiose rebirth of their belief in being the chosen people of God.[70] Just as even the mild-mannered Baxter thanks God for allowing him to be born in England and in the true church, and not elsewhere, this thankfulness for one's own blamelessness (which was caused by God's grace) penetrated the mood of life[71] of the Puritan middle class. It conditioned the formal rectitude and unbending character of these representatives of the heroic epoch of capitalism.

* * *

We can now seek to clarify those aspects of the Puritan conception of the calling and promotion of an ascetic *organization of life* that must have *directly* influenced the development of the capitalist style of life. As we have seen, asceticism turned with all its force mainly against the *spontaneous enjoyment* of existence and all the pleasures life had to offer.

This aspect of asceticism was expressed most characteristically in the struggle over the *Book of Sports* [1637].[72] James I and Charles I raised its arguments to the level of law in order explicitly to confront Puritanism, and Charles ordered the reading of this law from all pulpits. The fanatic opposition of the Puritans to the king's decree—on Sundays, certain popular amusements would be legally allowed after church services—arose *not* only on account of the resulting disturbance of the Sabbath day of rest. Rather, the more important source of this opposition was the fully premeditated disruption the decree implied of the ordered and organized life practiced by the Puritan saints. Moreover, the king's threat to punish severely every attack on the legality of these sporting activities had a single clear purpose: to banish this Puritan movement that, owing to its *anti-authoritarian ascetic* features, posed a danger to the state. Monarchical-feudal society protected the "pleasure seekers" alike against the crystallizing middle-class morality and the hostility to authority of the ascetic *conventicles*, just as today capitalist society seeks to protect "those willing to work" against the class-specific morality of workers and the trade unions hostile to authority.

In opposition to the feudal-monarchical society, the Puritans held firm to their most central feature in this struggle over the *Book of Sports*, namely, the principle of leading an organized life anchored in asceticism. Actually, Puritanism's aversion to sports was not a fundamental one, even for the Quakers. However, sports must serve a rational end, Puritanism insisted: they must promote the relaxation indispensable for further physical achievement. Hence, sports became suspect whenever they constituted a means for the purely spontaneous expression of unrestrained impulses. They were obviously absolutely reprehensible to the extent that they became means toward pure enjoyment or awakened competitive ambition, raw instincts, or the irrational desire to gamble. Quite simply, the enjoyment of life as if it were only *physical drives*, which pulls one equally away from work in a calling and from piety, was the enemy of rational asceticism as such. This enmity endured, regardless of whether the enjoyment of life presented itself in the form of monarchical-feudal society's sports or in the common man's visits to the dance floor or the tavern.[73]

Correspondingly, Puritanism's position toward those aspects of culture devoid of any direct relevance to religious matters was also one of suspicion and strong hostility. That is not to say that a sombre, narrow-minded scorn for culture was contained in Puritan ideals. Precisely the opposite holds, at least for the sciences (*Wissenschaften*), with the exception of Scholasticism, which was despised.[74] Moreover, the great representatives of Puritanism were deeply submerged in the humanism of the Renaissance; the sermons in the Presbyterian wing drip with references to classical antiquity,[75] and even the radicals (although they took offense at it) did not reject this humanist learning in theological polemics. Perhaps no country was ever so overpopulated with "graduates" as New England in the first generation of its existence. Even the satires of opponents, such as *Hudibras* [1663–78] by [Samuel] Butler [1612-1680], turn quickly to the armchair scholarship and sophomoric dialectics of the Puritans [see pp. 410–11]. Their learning *in part* goes together with the high religious esteem for knowledge that followed from the Puritans' rejection of the Catholic *fides implicita*.

Matters are distinctly different as soon as one moves into the arena of non-scientific literature[76] and to the realm of art, which appeals to the senses. Asceticism now blankets like a frost the life of merry old England. Its influence was apparent not only on secular festivals. The angry hatred of the Puritans persecuted all that smacked of "superstition" and all residuals of the dispensation of grace through magic or sacraments, including Christmas festivities, the may pole celebration,[77] and all unrestricted use of art by the church.

In Holland the survival of a public space within which the development of a masterful, often coarse and earthy, realistic art[78] could occur demonstrates in the end that the authoritarian regimentation of morality by the Puritans was not able to exercise a complete domination. The influence of court society and the landlord stratum, as well as members of the lower middle class who had become wealthy and sought joy in life, all contested the impact of Puritanism. This resistance took place after the short domination of the Calvinist theocracy had dissolved into a staid state church. As a consequence of this development, Calvinism in Holland suffered a distinct loss in ascetic energy. Thus its capacity to attract believers perceptibly declined.[79]

The theater was reprehensible to the Puritans.[80] As in literature and art, radical views could not survive once eroticism and nudity had been strictly banned from the realm of the possible. The notions of "idle talk," "superfluities,"[81] and "vain ostentation," all of which designated to the Puritans irrational, aimless, and thus not ascetic, behavior, and surely not conduct serving God's glory but only human goals, surfaced quickly. Hence, dispassionate instrumentalism was given a decisive upper hand over and against every application of artistic tendencies. This purposiveness was especially important wherever the direct decoration of the person was involved, as for example in respect to dress.[82] The foundation in ideas for that powerful tendency to render styles of life uniform, which today supports the capitalist interest in the "standardization" of production,[83] derived from the Puritans' rejection of all "glorification of human wants and desires."[84]

* * *

Certainly, in the midst of these considerations, we should not forget that Puritanism contained within itself a world of contradictions. It must be recognized that the instinctive awareness among Puritan leaders of the eternal greatness of art certainly transcended the level of art appreciation found in the milieu of the [feudalism-oriented] "cavaliers."[85] Furthermore, and even though his "conduct" would scarcely have found grace in the eyes of the Puritan God, a unique genius such as Rembrandt was, in the direction of his creativity, fundamentally influenced by his sectarian milieu.[86] These acknowledgments, however, fail to alter the larger picture: the powerful turn of the personality in an inward-looking direction (which the further development of the Puritan milieu could cultivate and, in fact, co-determined) influenced literature for the most part. Even in this realm, however, the impact of ascetic Protestantism would be felt only in later generations.

We cannot here investigate further the influences of Puritanism in all these ways. Nevertheless, we should note that *one* characteristic barrier always opposed ascribing legitimacy to the joy experienced from aspects of culture serving pure aesthetic pleasures or to the pure enjoyment of sports: *this pleasure should not cost anything.* Persons are only administrators of the cultural performances that the grace of God has offered. Hence, every dime expended for them must be justified, just as in the example of the servant in the Bible.[87] It remains doubtful at least whether any part of this money should be spent for a purpose that serves one's own pleasure rather than the glory of God.[88]

Who among us, whose eyes are open, has not seen manifestations of this outlook even at the present time?[89] The idea of a person's *duty* to maintain possessions entrusted to him, to which he subordinates himself as a dutiful steward or even as a "machine for producing wealth," lies upon his life with chilling seriousness. And as one's possessions become more valuable, the more burdensome becomes the feeling of responsibility to maintain them intact for God's glory and to increase their value through unceasing work—*if* the ascetic temper meets the challenge. The roots of this style of life also extend back to the Middle Ages (at least particular roots), as is true of so many components of the modern capitalist spirit.[90] This spirit, however, first found its consistent ethical foundation in the ethic of ascetic Protestantism. Its significance for the development of [modern] capitalism is obvious.[91]

* * *

Let us summarize the above. On the one hand, this-worldly Protestant asceticism fought with fury against the spontaneous *enjoyment* of possessions and constricted *consumption*, especially of luxury goods. On the other hand, it had the psychological effect of *freeing* the *acquisition of goods* from the constraints of the traditional economic ethic. In the process, ascetic Protestantism shattered the bonds restricting all striving for gain—not only by legalizing profit but also by perceiving it as desired by God (in the manner portrayed here). The struggle against the desires of the flesh and the attachment to external goods was *not*, as the Puritans explicitly attest (and also the great Quaker apologist, Barclay), a struggle against rational *acquisition*; rather, it challenged the irrational use of possessions. That which remained so familiar to feudal sensibilities—a high regard for the *external* display of luxury consumption—was condemned by the Puritans as a deification of human wants and desires.[92] According to them, God wanted a rational and utilitarian use of wealth on behalf of the basic needs of the person and the community.

Hence, this-worldly asceticism did *not* wish to impose *self-castigation* upon the wealthy.[93] Instead, it wanted that wealth to be used for necessary, *practical*, and *useful* endeavors. The notion of "comfort" [English in original], typically for the Puritans, encompasses the realm of the ethically permissible use of goods. Thus, it is naturally not by chance that one observes the development of the style of life attached to this notion, earliest and most clearly, precisely in those most consistent representatives of the Puritan life outlook: the Quakers. In opposition to the glitter and pretense of feudalism's pomp and display, which rests upon an unstable economic foundation and prefers a tattered elegance to low-key simplicity, the Puritans placed the ideal of the clean and solid comfort of the middle-class "home" [English in original].[94]

* * *

In terms of capitalism's *production* of wealth, asceticism struggled against greed. It did so in order to confront both the danger it presented to social order and its *impulsive* character. The Puritans condemned all "covetousness" and "mammonism," for both implied the striving for wealth—becoming rich—as an end in itself. Wealth as such constituted a temptation.

The nature of asceticism again becomes clear at this point. Its methodical-rational organization of life was the power "that perpetually wanted good and perpetually created evil,"[95] namely, evil in the manner conceived by asceticism: wealth and its temptations. For asceticism (together with the Old Testament and completely parallel to the ethical valuation of "good works") defined the pursuit of riches, if viewed as an *end* in itself, as the peak of reprehensibility. At the same time, it also viewed the acquisition of wealth, when it was the *fruit* of work in a vocational calling, as God's blessing. Even more important for this investigation, the religious value set on tireless, continuous, and systematic work in a vocational calling was defined as absolutely the highest of all ascetic means for believers to testify to their elect status, as well as simultaneously the most certain and most visible means of doing so. Indeed, the Puritan's sincerity of belief must have been the most powerful lever conceivable working to expand the life outlook that we are here designating as the spirit of capitalism.[96]

Moreover, if we now combine the strictures against consumption with this unchaining of the striving for wealth, a certain external result [that is, one with an impact outside the realm of religion] now becomes visible: *the formation of capital* through *asceticism's compulsive saving*.[97] The restrictions that opposed the consumption of wealth indeed had their productive use, for profit and gain became used as *investment* capital.

Of course, the strength of this effect cannot be determined exactly in quantitative terms. The connection became so apparent in New England, however, that it did not escape early on the eye of a historian as distinguished as John Doyle.[98] But it was also apparent in Holland, where a strict Calvinism ruled for only seven years. The greater simplicity of life that dominated the Dutch regions of ascetic Protestantism led, among the enormously wealthy, to an excessive desire to accumulate capital.[99]

Furthermore, it is evident that the hostility of Puritanism to all feudal forms of life must have inhibited to a measurable extent the tendency for middle-class fortunes to be used for the acquisition of noble status (which has existed in all epochs and countries, and even today remains significant in Germany). English writers on the mercantilism of the seventeenth century traced the superiority of Dutch over English capitalism back to the English practice (as in Germany) of regularly investing newly acquired fortunes in land. On this basis (for the purchase of land is not the only issue), newly wealthy persons sought to make the transition to feudal habits of life and to noble status. The result was clear: such land could not be used for capitalist investment.[100]

An esteem for *agriculture* was even present among the Puritans. Indeed, it constituted a particularly important arena for making a living (for example, in the case of Baxter) and was highly conducive to piety. Yet the Puritan engagement in agriculture diverged from feudalism: it involved productive farming rather than merely owning land as a landlord. In the eighteenth century, it was oriented more toward "rational" commercial farming than toward the acquisition of a country manor and entry into the nobility.[101]

Since the seventeenth century, the division between the "squirearchy," which were the **social carriers** of "merry olde England," and the Puritan circles, whose societal power varied across a broad spectrum, cut through English society.[102] Both streams—on the one hand a spontaneous and uncomplicated taking pleasure in life and on the other a strictly regulated, reserved self-control and ethical restraint—stand even today alongside each other in any portrait of the English "national character."[103] A similarly sharp polarity runs through the earliest history of North American colonization between the "adventurers," who wanted to build plantations with the labor of indentured servants and to live like feudal lords, and the middle-class frame of mind of the Puritans.[104]

As far as its power extended, the Puritan life outlook benefited under all circumstances the on-going trend toward a middle-class, economically *rational* organization of life. This outlook was, of course, far more important than the mere facilitating of the formation of capital. Indeed, it was the most substantial and, above all, single consistent social carrier of this middle-class mode of organizing life. Just this rational organization of life stood at the cradle of modern "economic man" (*Wirtschaftsmenschen*).[105]

* * *

Of course, these Puritan ideals of life failed to meet the challenge whenever the test—the "temptations" of wealth (which were well known even to the Puritans themselves)—became too great. We find the most sincere followers of the Puritan spirit very frequently among those in the middle class who operated small businesses, among farmers and the *beati possidentes* [those in possession of salvation]—all of whom must be understood as having been at the beginning of an *upwardly mobile* journey.[106] Yet we find that many in these groups were prepared quite frequently to betray the old ideals.[107] Such betrayal even occurred among the Quakers. The predecessor of this-worldly asceticism, the monastic asceticism of the Middle Ages, repeatedly fell victim to this same fate. Whenever the rational organization of the economy had fully developed its productive powers in the cloister milieu, which was characterized by a strict regulation of life as a whole and limited consumption, then the accumulated wealth was either used to acquire land and noble status (as occurred in the era before the Reformation) or it threatened the dissolution of monastic discipline. One of the numerous "reform movements" in monasticism had to intervene if this occurred. In a certain sense, the entire history of the religious orders reveals a constantly renewed struggle with the problem of the secularizing effects of wealth.

On a larger scale, the same is true for Puritanism's this-worldly asceticism. The powerful "revival" of Methodism, which preceded the flowering of English industrialism near the end of the eighteenth century, can be appropriately compared with the "reform movements" in the monastic orders. A passage[108] from John Wesley himself can be noted now, for it is well suited to stand as a motto for all that has been stated here. It indicates how the main figures in the ascetic movements were themselves completely aware of the apparently so paradoxical relationships presented here and understood these connections fully.[109]

> I fear, wherever riches have increased, the essence of religion has decreased in the same proportion. Therefore I do not see how it is possible, in the nature of things, for any revival of true religion to continue long. For religion must necessarily produce both industry and frugality, and these cannot but produce riches. But as riches increase, so will pride, anger, and love of the world in all its branches. How

then is it possible that Methodism, that is, a religion of the heart, though it flour-
ishes now as a green bay tree, should continue in this state? For the Methodists in
every place grow diligent and frugal; consequently they increase their possession of material goods. Hence they proportionately increase in pride, in anger, in
the desire of the flesh, the desire of the eyes, and the pride of life. So, although the
form of religion remains, the spirit is swiftly vanishing away. Is there no way to
prevent this continual decay of pure religion? We ought not to prevent people
from being diligent and frugal; *we must exhort all Christians to gain all they can, and
to save all they can; that is, in effect, to grow rich.* [Weber's emphasis] [1920]

(There follows the admonition that those who have "acquired all they can and
saved all they can" should also "give all they can"—in order to grow in grace
and to assemble a fortune in heaven.) In this passage from Wesley one sees the
connection, in all its details, illuminated in the analysis above.[110] [1920]

Exactly as Wesley noted here, the significance for economic development of
the powerful early religious movements was to be found mainly in the ascetic
effects of their *socialization*. To him, their full *economic* impact developed, as a
rule, only after the peak of their *pure* religious enthusiasm. As the paroxysms
of the search for God's kingdom gradually dissolved into the dispassionate
virtues of the vocational calling and the religious roots of the movement
slowly withered, a utilitarian orientation to the world took hold. In the popular imagination, if we follow [the Irish scholar of English and French literature
Edward] Dowden [1843–1913], "Robinson Crusoe"—the *isolated economic man*
(who is engaged in missionary activities in his spare time)—now took the
place of Bunyan's "pilgrims" scurrying through the "amusement park of vanity" on their solitary spiritual quest for God's kingdom.[111] If subsequently the
basic principle "to make the best of *both* worlds"[112] came to prevail, then, finally, as Dowden also observed, the clear conscience came to be ordered
among the series of possessions comprising the comfortable, middle-class
life (as is so beautifully expressed in the German adage about the "soft pillow").[113]

That which the religiously lively epoch of the seventeenth century bequeathed to its utilitarian heirs was above all a startlingly clear conscience—we can say without hesitation, *pharisaically* good—as concerns the
acquisition of money. Wherever lacking, the making of money was directed
exclusively by laws and conventions.[114] Now, with Puritanism, every residual of the medieval proverb *deo placere vix potest* [the merchant cannot be
pleasing to God] has disappeared.[115]

* * *

A specifically *middle-class vocational ethos* (*Berufsethos*) arose. Now the
middle-class employer became conscious of himself as standing in the full
grace of God and as visibly blessed by Him. If he stayed within the bounds
of formal correctness, if his moral conduct remained blameless, and if the
use he made of his wealth was not offensive, this person was now allowed
to follow his interest in economic gain—and indeed *should* do so. Moreover,
the power of religious asceticism made available to the businessperson dis-

passionate and conscientious workers. Unusually capable of working, these employees attached themselves to their work, for they understood it as bestowing a purpose on life that was desired by God.[116]

In addition, religious asceticism gave to the employer the soothing assurance that the unequal distribution of the world's material goods resulted from the special design of God's providence. In making such distinctions as well as in deciding who should be among the chosen few, God pursued mysterious aims unknown to terrestrial mortals.[117] Calvin had argued early on (in a passage frequently cited) that the "people"—the overwhelming majority of skilled and unskilled workers—would continue to obey God only if kept poor.[118] The Dutch (Pieter de la Court and others) "secularized" this statement; to them, most persons *worked* only if driven to do so by necessity. In turn, this formulation of a key idea regarding the functioning of the capitalist economy then merged into the plethora of theories on the "productivity" of low wages. Here again, and in full conformity with the developmental pattern we have repeatedly observed, as the religious roots of an idea died out a utilitarian tone then surreptitiously shoved itself under the idea and carried it further.

In the mendicant orders, medieval Catholicism had not only tolerated begging, but actually glorified it. Moreover, because they offered to the wealthy the opportunity for good works (the giving of alms), secular beggars were occasionally depicted as a "status group"—and valued, accordingly, more positively. This position appeared as late as the Anglican social ethic of the Stuarts [1615–1644], which stood spiritually very close to it. A formulation of severe laws on the treatment of the poor awaited the participation of the Puritans, who then fundamentally changed the old laws. This could occur because the Protestant sects and the strict Puritanical communities actually *did not know* begging in their midst [1920].[119]

* * *

Now let us turn away from the Puritan employer and briefly toward the other side, namely, the perspective of the worker. Zinzendorf's branch of Pietism, for example, glorified workers who were loyal to their callings, lived in accord with the ideals of the apostles, and never strove for gain—hence, workers endowed with the charisma of Christ's disciples.[120] Similar views were widespread, in an even more radical form, among the baptizing congregations in their early stages.

Of course, the entire corpus of literature on asceticism, which is drawn from almost *all* religions [East and West], is permeated with the point of view that loyal work is highly pleasing to God, even if performed for low wages by people at a great disadvantage in life and without other opportunities. *Here* Protestant asceticism added nothing new as such. It dramatically deepened, however, this point of view. In addition, it created the norm on which its impact *exclusively depended*: the psychological *motivation* that arose out of the conception of work as a *calling* and as the means best suited (and in the end often as the *sole* means) for the devout to become certain of their state of salvation.[121] Furthermore, on the other hand, in interpreting the employer's acquisition of money also as a "calling," Protestant asceticism formally ratified the exploitation of this particular willingness to work.[122]

It is obvious how powerfully the *exclusive* striving for the kingdom of God—through fulfillment of the duty to work in a vocational calling and through strict asceticism, which church discipline naturally imposed in particular upon the propertyless classes—must have promoted the "productivity" of work in the capitalist sense of the word.[123] For the modern worker, the view of work as a "vocational calling" became just as characteristic as the view of gain as a "vocational calling" became for the modern employer. New at the time, this situation was reflected in the keen observations on Dutch economic power of the seventeenth century by the insightful Englishman Sir William Petty [see p. 66]. He traced its growth back to the especially numerous "Dissenters" (Calvinists and Baptists) in Holland, who viewed *"work and the industrious pursuit of a trade as their duty to God."*[124]

* * *

The "organic" societal organization, in the form of the fiscal monopoly it assumed in the Anglicanism under the Stuarts [1603–1714] and especially in [Archbishop William] Laud's [1573–1645][125] conceptions, involved specific features. First, a coalition of state and church with the "business monopolists" arose. Second, this alliance became anchored in [Anglican] Christian social ethics.

The Puritans stood against this coalition. They passionately opposed *this* type of economy, one in which the state offered privileges to merchants, cottage industries, and colonial capitalism. Instead, a type of capitalism in which a person's competence and initiative-taking capacity provided the individualistic *motivation* for rational-legal acquisition was upheld by the Puritans. In England, where the industrial monopolies privileged by the state as a whole soon disappeared, Puritanism decisively participated in the creation of newly emerging industries. It did so in spite of and against the state's authoritarian powers.[126] [1920]

The Puritans [William] Prynne [1600–1669] and [Matthew] Parker [1504–74][127] rejected every common undertaking with "courtiers and operators" in the mold of large-scale capitalists, for they perceived such people as members of an ethically suspect class. Moreover, the Puritans did so on the basis of pride in their own superior middle-class business ethics (*Geschäftsmoral*). In turn, precisely this ethos constituted the true reason for the persecution of Puritans by large-scale capitalists. Even as late as [the eighteenth-century, the novelist Daniel] Defoe [1660–1731] suggested a struggle against Puritans. He sought to win this conflict by arguing in favor of boycotts against all businesses that changed banks and the cancellation of bank and stock accounts. [1920]

The contrast between the two types of capitalist conduct paralleled to a very great extent the religious contrasts. Even in the eighteenth century the opponents of the Puritans repeatedly satirized them as carriers of a "spirit of shopkeepers" and persecuted them as the ruin of old English ideals. The contrast between Puritan and Jewish economic ethics is also anchored *here* and even contemporaries (Prynne) knew that the former, and not the latter, was the middle-class economic ethic.[128] [1920]

* * *

Our analysis should have demonstrated that one of the constitutive components of the modern capitalist spirit and, moreover, generally of modern civilization, was the rational organization of life on the basis of the *idea of the calling*. It was born out of the spirit of *Christian asceticism*. If we now read again the passages from Benjamin Franklin cited at the beginning of this essay, we will see that the essential elements of the frame of mind described as the "spirit of capitalism" are just those that we have conveyed above as the content of Puritan vocational asceticism.[129] In Franklin, however, this "spirit" exists without the religious foundation, which had already died out.

The idea that modern work in a vocational calling supposedly carries with it an *ascetic* imprint is, of course, also not new. The limitation of persons to specialized work, which necessitates their renunciation of the Faustian multi-dimensionality of the human species, is in our world today the precondition for doing anything of value at all—that is, the "specialized task" and "foresaking" of multidimensionality irredeemably presuppose and mutually condition one another. *Goethe*, at the peak of his wisdom in his *Wilhelm Meister's Years of Travel* [1829] and in his depiction of Faust's final stage of life [1808], tried to teach us just this:[130] the middle-class way of ordering life, if it wishes to be guided at all rather than to be devoid of continuity, contains a basic component of asceticism. This realization for Goethe implied a resigned farewell to an era of full and beautiful humanity—and a renunciation of it. For such an era will repeat itself, in the course of our civilizational development, with as little likelihood as a reappearance of the epoch in which Athens bloomed.

The Puritan *wanted* to be a person with a vocational calling; we *must* be. For to the extent that asceticism moved out of the monastic cell and was carried over into the life of work in a vocational calling, and then commenced to rule over this-worldly morality, it helped to do its part to build the mighty cosmos of the modern economic order—namely, an economy bound to the technical and economic conditions of mechanized, machine-based production. This cosmos today determines the style of life of all individuals born into this grinding mechanism, and *not* only those directly engaged in economically productive activity. It does so with overwhelming force—and perhaps it will continue to do so until the last ton of fossil fuel has burnt to ashes. The concern for material goods, according to Baxter, should lie on the shoulders of his saints like "a lightweight coat that one can throw off at any time."[132] Yet fate allowed this coat to become a steel-hard casing (*stahlhartes Gehäuse*)[133] To the extent that asceticism undertook to transform and influence the world, the world's material goods acquired an increasing and, in the end, inescapable power over people—as never before in history.

Today the spirit of asceticism has fled from this casing, whether with finality who knows? Victorious capitalism, in any case, ever since it came to rest on a mechanical foundation, no longer needs asceticism as a supporting pillar. Even the optimistic temperament of the Enlightenment, asceticism's joyful heir, appears finally to be fading. And the idea of an "obligation to search for and then accept a vocational calling" now wanders around in our lives as the ghost of beliefs no longer anchored in the substance of religion. The person of today usually rejects entirely all attempts to make sense of a "fulfillment of one's calling" wherever this notion cannot be directly aligned with the highest spiritual and cultural values, or wherever, conversely, it must not be experienced subjectively simply as economic coercion. Then the person of today rejects entirely all attempts to make sense of it at all. The pursuit of gain, in the region where it has become most completely unchained and stripped of its religious-ethical meaning, the United States, tends to be associated with purely competitive passions. Not infrequently, these passions directly imprint this pursuit with the character of a sports event.[134]

No one any longer knows who will live in this casing and whether entirely new prophets or a mighty rebirth of ancient ideas and ideals will stand at the end of this prodigious development. *Or*, however, if neither, whether a mechanized ossification, embellished with a sort of rigidly compelled sense of self-importance, will arise. Then, indeed, if ossification appears, the saying might be true for the "last humans"[135] in this long civilizational development:

> narrow specialists without minds, pleasure-seekers without heart; in its conceit, this nothingness imagines it has climbed to a level of humanity never before attained.[136]

* * *

Here, however, we have fallen into the realm of value-judgments, with which this purely historical analysis should not be burdened. Nor should it be burdened by judgments rooted in faith. The further task is a different one: to chart the significance of ascetic rationalism.[137] The above sketch has only hinted at its importance.

Its significance for the content of a community-building, ethical *social policy* must now be outlined, that is, for the type of organization and the functions of social groups, ranging from the conventicle to the state. Having done that, we must analyze the relationship of ascetic rationalism to the ideals and cultural influences of humanistic rationalism.[138] Further, we must investigate the relationship of ascetic rationalism to the development of philosophical and scientific empiricism, to the unfolding of technology, and to the development of non-material culture (*geistige Kulturgüter*) in general.[139] Finally, we need to pursue the historical course of ascetic rationalism, beginning with the first signs of this-worldly asceticism in the Middle Ages and moving all the way to its dissolution in pure utilitarianism. We should then need to trace this development in its *historical* manifestations and through the particular regions of the expansion of ascetic religious devotion. Only after the completion of such investigations can the *extent* of ascetic Protestantism's civilizational significance be demarcated in comparison to that of other elements of modern civilization that can be changed and shaped in response to the actions of persons.

This study has attempted, of course, merely to trace ascetic Protestantism's influence, and the particular *nature* of this influence, back to ascetic Protestantism's motives in regard to one, however important, point.[140] The way in which Protestant asceticism was in turn influenced in its development and characteristic uniqueness by the entirety of societal-cultural conditions, and especially *economic* conditions, must also have its day.[141] For sure, even with the best will, the modern person seems generally unable to imagine *how* large a significance those components of our consciousness rooted in religious beliefs have actually had upon culture, national character, and the organization of life. Nevertheless, of course it can not be the intention here to set a one-sided spiritualistic analysis of the causes of culture and history in place of an equally one-sided "materialistic" analysis. *Both* are *equally possible*.[142] Historical truth, however, is served equally little if either of these analyses claims to be the conclusion of an investigation rather than its preparatory stage.[143]

2

**The Protestant Sects in America and
the Uniqueness of Western Rationalism**

INTRODUCTION

Stephen Kalberg

> *[The sects] . . . alone have been able, on the foundation of Protestantism, to instill an intensity of interest in religion in the broad middle class — and especially modern workers — that otherwise is found only, though in the form of a bigoted fanaticism, among traditional peasants. (p. 203)*

> *. . . it was...primarily the grandiose discipline, which held a middle position between the cloister and the factory, that presented the person with the choice to either work or perish. It was this discipline,* bound up *of course with religious enthusiasm and made possible* only *through it, that brought forth the amazing economic achievements of [the] sects. (p. 531; emph. in orig.)*

After returning from a two-month whirlwind tour of the United States in late November 1904, Max Weber finished *PE* and wrote a short essay on the Protestant sects (1985). Significantly revised and expanded in 1919 (2002b), these two studies comment directly on American society.[1]

Less scholarly than *PE*, they ("Sects") seek to reach a much broader audience. Informal in tone, they convey Weber's perspicacious observations as he travels through the Midwest, the South, the Middle Atlantic states, and New England. His commentary, however, should not be comprehended as offering merely fragmented "impressions of American life." Instead, Weber brings his audience up to date in respect to the status of Puritan beliefs in the United States 250 years after their origin. He focuses on two major themes.

First, *PE*'s argument is expanded in "Sects." These essays offer a subtle analysis of how a social-psychological dynamic distinct to the sect as a social organization accomplished two important tasks: it effectively conveyed the *ethical* action expected by the early Puritan Divines into the daily lives of the devout, and transferred consistently ascetic Protestantism's economic ethic into everyday conduct. As a consequence of this complex dynamic, the faithful became oriented systematically to work and the search for profit and material success.

Second, and although related to *PE*, Weber addresses a new realm: the political culture of the United States. Opposing stereotypes widespread throughout Europe, and especially in Germany, he refuses to depict American society as a "sandpile of atoms"—of individuals adrift and without viable connections. Rather, Weber sees a multitude of clubs, associations, and

---

1.   Although *PE* can be said to be a book about the religious tradition dominant in the United States, passages directly pertaining to this country are limited to the endnotes. Weber poured his analysis and observations largely into the two sect essays, as soon will become apparent. Both essays reprinted here are abridged. For the complete essays, see Weber, 1985; 2002b.

societies as prominent. Their origins could be traced back to the Protestant sects, he discovered.

Weber's observations paint a picture of American society as open and energetic, yet stable. Indeed, he sees the United States as a vibrant nation soon to embark upon a period of great power. However, differences vis-à-vis European industrial societies in respect to both economic and political cultures are prominent. German society in particular differed distinctly, Weber is convinced, and he seeks in "Sects" to demonstrate to his countrymen the firm roots of the American success story. Barely visible to highly secularized Europeans, a distinct configuration of religious values stood at the foundation of American growth and power, he holds. His treatment of these themes will be more easily understood after a brief summary of his sojourn in America.

THE BACKGROUND: THE AMERICAN JOURNEY

Invited to present a lecture at the famous St. Louis Universal Exposition and Congress of Arts and Science in late September 1904, Weber, accompanied by his wife Marianne, landed on August 30 on American shores. Their ship had steamed past the Statue of Liberty, and the Webers disembarked in lower Manhattan into the noisy din of the New World's "spirit of capitalism." A hectic two-month tour began. As apparent from Marianne's account, Weber threw himself into the social life of this "modern reality" and soaked up information from a vast diversity of sources. He listened well, told stories frequently, interacted in a leisurely manner with people from a wide variety of backgrounds, and posed questions incessantly.[2]

Weber's German travel companions remarked that his walking pace quickened and, after a long period of depression, his spirit became animated. New York's dynamism and the "fantastic stream" of people in this colossus enraptured him. His interest was lively and his curiosity insatiable, and he refused to countenance the stiff opprobrium of several of his German travel companions (see Rollman, 1993, pp. 367–68, 372–74). Weber had become immersed, as he wrote to his mother, in a rough and ready, raw and untamed society at the vanguard of the modern world. He "wished to appreciate everything and to absorb as much of it as possible" (Marianne Weber, 1975, p. 281; see pp. 280–83).[3]

After ten days of sightseeing throughout the teeming metropolis and intensive discussions with family friends, distant relatives, and many new acquain-

---

2.   Much of this section rests upon Marianne Weber's discussion of the journey. See 1975, pp. 279–304; see also the interesting studies by Roth (1985), Rollman (1993), Scaff (1998, 2005), and Mommsen (2000).

3.   Quotations are from Marianne Weber unless otherwise noted. The Webers were accompanied in New York by several colleagues, including Max's friends Werner Sombart and the distinguished theologian Ernst Troeltsch. He conveys Weber's admiration of New York: "Weber is splendid. He . . . talks much and educates me without interruption in the most interesting way. It is of great benefit to see with him this country of businesses. He, too, learns continuously from what he sees and attempts to work it through. But since he thinks *aloud* while doing so, it helps me" (Rollman, 1993, p. 368; see p. 372)

tances,[4] the peripatetic couple journeyed north along the Hudson River to Niagara Falls and then to Chicago, "the crystallization of the American spirit" (Marianne Weber, p. 285). He met with social reformers Jane Addams and Florence Kelley at Hull House[5] and attended a banquet at the University of Chicago (Rollmann, 1993, pp. 369–70, 375–76). Mixing awe and revulsion, he described in his letters a rugged city of ethnic stratification. Here the "guts" of modern capitalism were on open display, especially in its stockyards:

There is a mad pell-mell of nationalities: Up and down the streets the Greeks shine the Yankees' shoes for 5 cents. The Germans are their waiters, the Irish take care of their politics, and the Italians of their dirtiest ditch digging. With the exception of the better residential districts, the whole tremendous city — more extensive than London! — is like a man whose skin has been peeled off and whose intestines are seen at work. (Max Weber in Marianne Weber, p. 286)

Everywhere one is struck by the tremendous intensity of work—most of all in the "stockyards" with their "ocean of blood," where several thousand cattle and pigs are slaughtered every day. From the moment when the unsuspecting bovine enters the slaughtering area, is hit by a hammer and collapses, whereupon it is immediately gripped by an iron clamp, is hoisted up, and starts on its journey, it is in constant motion—past ever-new workers who eviscerate and skin it, etc., but are always (in the rhythm of the work) tied to the machine that pulls the animal past them. One sees an absolutely incredible output in this atmosphere of steam, muck, blood, and hides in which I teetered about together with a "boy" who was giving me a guided tour for fifty cents, trying to keep from being buried in the filth. There one can follow a pig from the sty to the sausage and the can. (Max Weber in Marianne Weber, p. 287)

A "magnificent wildness," Marianne writes of Chicago, co-existed with a "modern reality" that "indifferently swallowed up everything individual." Yet "... its gentle features ... bespoke a capacity for love as well as kindness, justice, and a tenacious desire for beauty and spirituality" (Marianne Weber, p. 287).

Weber presented his paper, "The Relations of the Rural Community to Other Branches of Social Science," in St. Louis to a small audience.[6] His wife was relieved: his first public lecture in more than six years was excellently delivered and well-received (Marianne Weber, pp. 290-91).[7] On this occasion Weber renewed his acquaintance with W. E. B. DuBois, who had

---

4. On the New York City visit, and in particular its connections to Weber's extended family, see Roth, 2005.
5. Marianne Weber described Kelley, the chief inspector in Illinois of factories, 1893–97, as "by far the most outstanding figure" the Webers met in America (see Marianne Weber, p. 302). They discussed, among many other topics, the opposition of capitalist entrepreneurs to workplace safety regulations and the negative impact of large-scale immigration upon the strength of labor unions. Kelley became the American editor of the journal Weber co-edited, *Archiv für Sozialwissenschaft und Sozialpolitik*.
6. This complex lecture is summarized by Ringer (see 2004, pp. 132–33) and Scaff (see 2005, pp. 38–39). It was retitled ("Capitalism and Rural Society in Germany"), edited, and published in English in full (Weber, 1946a, pp. 363–85) and in abridged form (Weber, 2005, pp. 142–46). On the conference generally, see Rollman, 1993.
7. Mommsen believes this was Weber's "first public appearance in more than four years" (2000, p. 103).

attended his lectures in the early 1890s in Berlin. Several years later he would describe him as "the most important sociological scholar anywhere in the Southern States, with whom no white scholar can compare" (1973, p. 312).[8]

Weber then journeyed west by train alone into "Indian country."[9] In Oklahoma, mainly through interviews, he investigated the ongoing partition of the native American land. Weber witnesssed how the juggernaut of American capitalism confronted directly, and conquered, the frontier:

> There were many ... things [here] of burning interest to Weber ... : the conquest of the wilderness by civilization, a developing city and the developing state of Oklahoma in an area that had until recently been reserved for the Indians. ... Here it was still possible to observe the unarmed subjugation and absorption of an "inferior" race by a "superior," more intelligent one, the transformation of Indian tribal property into private property, and the conquest of the virgin forest by colonists. Weber stayed with a half-breed. He watched, listened, transformed himself into his surroundings, and thus everywhere penetrated to the heart of things. (Marianne Weber, p. 291)[10]

The informality and friendliness of the Americans continued to impress the Webers, though also their sturdy individualism, mutual respect for one another, and "can-do" approach to even the most intractable problems. The "lightning speed" of capitalism's transformation of the prairie appeared to Weber incapable of losing momentum:

> [McAlester, Oklahoma] is a more "civilized" place than Chicago. It would be quite wrong to believe that one can behave as one wishes. In the conversations, which are, to be sure, quite brief, the courtesy lies in the tone and the bearing, and the humor is nothing short of delicious. Too bad, in a year this place will look like Oklahoma [City], that is, like any other American city. With almost lightning speed everything that stands in the way of capitalistic culture is being crushed. (Max Weber in Marianne Weber, p. 293)

The hyperactive quest for the sources of American life's fast pulse moved next to New Orleans. Weber observed black, white, and mulatto relations here first-hand. He would recall later, at a conference in Germany in 1911, his experiences and observations to support arguments against those who trumpeted the superiority of "the European race" (see 1971a; 1973; 2005, pp. 306–13; Winter, 2004). An emotional tour of the black college,

---

8. Weber encouraged DuBois to write an article for his journal (see DuBois, 1906). His attempt to arrange the translation into German and publication of DuBois's "splendid work," *The Souls of Black Folk*, failed, despite Weber's plan "to write a short introduction about [the] Negro question and literature." He had also intended to write an article on "the recent publications [on] the race problem in America." See Weber's letter in English to DuBois (Aptheker, 1973, p. 106). See also Scaff, 1998. On Weber's views on race, see 1971; 1973; 2005, pp. 297–314; Manasse, 1947; Peukert, 1989, pp. 92–101; Scaff, 1998, pp. 69–73; Winter, 2004.

9. Marianne Weber stayed in St. Louis. Traveling by train, they later met, on the way to New Orleans, in Memphis.

10. See the fascinating description of this aspect of Weber's journey by Scaff, 2005, pp. 85–109.

Tuskegee Institute, in Alabama,[11] followed: "What they found [here] probably moved them more than anything else on their trip. The great national problem of all American life, the showdown between the white race and the former slaves, could here be grasped at its roots" (Marianne Weber, p. 295).[12] To Weber, "the Americans are a wonderful people, and only the Negro question and the terrible immigration constitute the big black clouds" (Max Weber in Marianne Weber, p. 302). His general assessment would be soon offered in a letter to DuBois: "I am absolutely convinced that the 'color-line-problem' will be the paramount problem of the time to come, here and everywhere in the world."[13] His hope to return to the South "as soon as possible" was never fulfilled.

Distant relatives at the edge of the Blue Ridge Mountains in Mt. Airy, North Carolina, were then visited for several days. While observing an adult baptism ceremony, one of Weber's cousins scoffed when a young acquaintance stepped forward. Upon inquiry, the candidate's motives were revealed as suspect: he wished to open a new business in the neighborhood, Weber's cousin explained (pp. 186–87). Church membership, which was allowed only after scrutiny of the candidate's "good character," would offer solid evidence of his trustworthiness—and merchants who were known to offer fair deals and just prices would be preferred throughout the community over others.[14]

Brief visits to Washington, Baltimore, and Philadelphia ensued. Marianne's relatives hosted the travelers in a northern suburb of Boston in a modest home on a quiet street. They explored the city and attended a Harvard-Yale football game (see Marianne Weber, p. 301).[15] Weber probably met with Harvard's distinguished psychologist, William James (p. 190). America's colleges — "worlds by themselves" (Marianne Weber, p. 288)[16] — impressed the sojourners,[17] who perceived here "the tradition of the Pilgrim

---

11. Weber met, and later corresponded with, its founder, Booker T. Washington. He was familiar with his major writings. See Scaff, 1998, pp. 69–70.

12. "... the whites are bleeding to death because of this separation [in the South] intended as 'racial protection,' and the only enthusiasm in the South may be found among [the often nine-tenths white] Negro upper class; among the whites there is only random, knee-jerk hatred of the Yankees" (Max Weber in Marianne Weber, p. 296; transl. altered).

13. Letter to DuBois, November 17, 1904 (quoted in Scaff, 1998, p. 72). As Scaff notes (pp. 70–71), this was the position DuBois had earlier articulated. Weber had read the major works of DuBois (see Scaff, pp. 69–71).

14. Relatives who recalled Weber's visit to North Carolina were recently inverviewed. See Keeter, 1981. Marianne's general comment appears on the mark: "Unexpectedly Weber even here acquired illustrative material for his work: old and new forms of the social stratification of democratic society. In an elemental form he saw the life-forming effect of religious sects . . ." (Marianne Weber, p. 298; see also Weber's letter cited at pp. 288–89).

15. With their hosts, the Webers sat in a carriage in the end zone. However, they became bored and left at halftime.

16. "The whole magic of youthful memories attaches solely to this period. An abundance of sports, attractive forms of social life, infinite intellectual stimulation, and lasting friendship are the returns, and above all the education includes far more habituation to work than there is among our students" (Max Weber in Marianne Weber, p. 288).

17. Weber visited nearly all the major East Coast universities, including the campuses of Yale, Johns Hopkins, Brown, and Harvard. He "sometimes attended classes in order to observe American teaching methods" (Marianne Weber, p. 288).

fathers" (Marianne Weber, p. 288).[18] After an evening attending a play in Yiddish in a Jewish neighborhood in New York, the Webers departed on the nineteenth of November for Germany.

The journey yielded little for Weber's *PE* scholarship. He briefly visited libraries and archives at Columbia, Harvard, and Haverford College; however, he was unable to pursue research in depth. The visitors attended Quaker, Presbyterian, Methodist, Baptist, black Baptist, and Christian Science services (Marianne Weber, pp. 288–89, 300–01).[19]

Weber had been an avid international traveler since his teenage years.[20] During his lifetime the train grid in Europe became comprehensive, and his many journeys (see "Chronology") took him across the expanse of the continent from southern Italy to northern Scotland. The United States, however, left an indelible mark, and he referred often in later years in public lectures and writings to personal observations.[21] Most of his German colleagues were convinced that raw American capitalism threatened the ethical integrity of individuals, exploited workers systematically, and destroyed viable social ties, leaving people adrift and "atomized."[22] Weber, on the other hand, for the most part, embraced the United States, absorbed its heterogeneity, and perceived in this nation value-based ethical standards, an openness, and a stalwart sense of purpose lacking in Europe: ". . . for there was a youthfully fresh, confident energy, a force for good that was just as powerful as the evil forces" (Marianne Weber, p. 302).[23] Indeed, he wished to confront stereotypes of America widespread in Germany.[24] However, he feared, as will be discussed, a future "Europeanization" of the United States—a longer-term diminution of its economic growth and a gradual bureaucratizing of its political parties, economic organizations, and civil service. The outcome was evident to him: less egalitarianism, more social hierarchy, and less dynamism.

This eleven-week journey significantly influenced Weber's various writings on the sociology of religion, but also on political leadership, bureaucracies, democracy, race and ethnicity, and status groups and stratification. Moreover, he gained a more clear understanding of how past developments in the realm of religion lived on and penetrated into, in secularized forms, the present. Finally, he comprehended with even greater precision the ways in which modern industrial and urbanized societies differ. Surely

---

18. "[This tradition] still bound the young men to the ideal of chastity, prohibited smutty stories, and instilled into them a measure of chivalry toward women which was unknown to the average German of the day" (Marianne Weber, p. 288).

19. Weber comments in a long letter in detail on the Christian Science service. See Scaff, 1998, pp. 67–68.

20. On the extremely cosmopolitan character of Weber's far-flung family, see Roth, 2001, 2005.

21. On Weber's views of the United States generally, see Mommsen (1974), Roth (1985), Scaff (1998), Berger (1971), and Rollman (1993). On the influence on the young Weber of American Unitarianism and the Social Gospel movement, see Roth, 1997. On Weber's youthful readings on the United States, see Scaff, 2005, pp. 80–81; Roth, 2005, pp. 35–36. Weber's interest in America stretches back to his mid-teen years (see Weber, 1936, p. 29).

22. The letters home of Weber's friend and travel companion in New York, Werner Sombart, lamented "this dreadful cultural hell" and the "chamber of horrors of capitalism" (Lenger, 1994, pp. 148–49).

23. This sentence is from Marianne Weber.

24. Nonetheless, Weber also repeatedly depicted the widespread corruption in the "machine politics" of large American cities. See 1968, p. 1401; 1946b, pp. 107–11; Marianne Weber, p. 302.

his understanding of the particularity, and weaknesses, of German political culture was enhanced as a consequence of the knowledge of American political culture acquired during this journey.[25] The sojourn also appeared to have had an unequivocally salubrious effect on Weber's mental health: Marianne Weber "had the feeling she was bringing home a man restored to health" (Marianne Weber, p. 304). Weber's summary of the trip strikes similar chords:

> It cannot be said, of course, that the "scientific" results of the trip are equal to its expenses[26]. . . for my work in cultural history I did not see much more than where the things are that I ought to see, particularly the libraries I would have to use, which are scattered all over the country in little sects and colleges. Under these circumstances the trip can be justified in our present situation only from the general point of view of a widening of my scholarly horizon (*and* improving my state of health). . . . a year ago it would have been utterly impossible. . . . Stimulation and occupation of the mind without intellectual exertion simply is the only remedy. (Weber in Marianne Weber, p. 304)

"Sects" can now be introduced. Discussions of the ways its contours contrast with *PE* and of the crucial distinction between "church" and "sect" constitute indispensable preliminary steps.

BEYOND *THE PROTESTANT ETHIC*: THE PROTESTANT SECT

PE offers a detailed portrait of the Puritan cosmos of belief and meaningful action. By reference to the doctrine of Predestination and revisions undertaken by Baxter and other Puritan Divines, Weber's "essay in cultural history" provides an explanation for the intense orientation of the faithful to God and their this-worldly asceticism. The solitary salvation quest, pursued by the devout without assistance from church intermediaries and despite the fatalism implied by the Predestination decree, stands at the center of his discussion (see pp. 106–09). Through a fine-grained analysis, *PE* explores the eventual attachment of subjective meaning and ethical standards to certain practical and economic activities, as well as to a disciplined and organized life. The psychological rewards placed on action remain foremost. These large themes dominate his massive inquiry into the Protestant ethic's origins.

The process of testifying to one's salvation status assumed significant new contours in the course of the eighteenth century. It moved away from Puritans engaged in a lonely attempt to orient their activities to God and to

---

25. Weber's notion of "plebiscitory democracy," which he wished to introduce into Germany and which contrasted European-style political parties rooted in ideology to American-style parties anchored in the appeal of individual leaders, appears taken directly from the American model.
26. The trip's total cost: $1,700. Weber's honorarium for speaking at the St. Louis Congress was $500. See Scaff, 2005, p. 82.

create "evidence" of their salvation, Weber holds, and toward believers situated deeply within a *social* milieu—namely, in the American *Protestant sect*.[27] Hence, he now expands his analysis beyond *PE*'s question — How can the faithful prove their devoutness *before God*? — to an investigation of how they testify to their sincere belief *in sects before men* (p. 198). Although the devout drew upon an internal strength in order to lead "the moral life" and remained focused on God, the sect's strict monitoring and unrelenting pressure to conform also significantly influenced the activity of members, Weber now argues. This tightly knit group cultivated and sustained the doctrinal-based ethical action and methodical-rational organization of life originally expected by the Puritan Divines.

He explores how ideas and values are efficiently "implemented" because of the impact of the Protestant sect. This "social carrier" (*Träger*) of ideas and values, by inculcating the beliefs and psychological rewards enunciated by the Puritan cosmos, confirmed and conveyed *systematically* to believers the ethical conduct analyzed in *PE*. The sect's influence contributed mightily to the spirit of capitalism in this way. To Weber, "Both aspects were mutually supplementary and operated in the same direction: they helped to set free the 'spirit' of modern capitalism—that is, its specific *ethos*: the ethos of the modern *middle classes*" (pp. 198–99).

How did the sect contribute to the expansion of ethical action in the economy life-sphere and even to the methodically organized life? Weber's pivotal distinction between "sect" and "church" must first be noted. His multivalent social-psychological analysis can be then considered.

SECT AND CHURCH

A church implies to Weber an inclusive, "sacred corporation." Members are born into it. As a "universal institution" and a "trust fund of eternal blessings . . . offered to everyone," the church allows its "grace [to] shine over all," the righteous and unrighteous alike. This organization officially monopolizes and mediates all sacred values on behalf of a "universalism of grace" (p. 188; 1968, p. 1164).

Its task — to cultivate religious beliefs and conduct, and to seek to save each member's soul — often proves difficult. Because obligatory, church membership implies no particular individual spiritual and ethical qualities; even sinners and heretics fall within this organization's encompassing democratic mission. However, its priests and ministers possess a greater faith than the laity, and their elevated position in an elaborate hierarchy grants to them a special aura, or "office charisma"—and hence a clear authority to subject the sinner to the church's discipline and to address *all* salvation concerns and specific violations. Through the Confessional priests

---

27.   "The major domicile of the sects is the United States" (1968, p. 1206).

are guardians of the church's "trust fund," and defend the "ethical suffi-
ciency of all those . . . enrolled under [its] institutional authority" (pp.
187–188, 201–02; 1968, p. 1164; 1946e, p. 288). Weber has mainly Catholicism
in mind here, but also the Lutheran church.

Sects, as voluntary communities composed exclusively of persons with
demonstrated "religious qualifications," diverge distinctly. Admission
occurs only after a probationary period in which the candidate's sincerity
of belief and moral character are scrutinized. This examination *must* take
place, sect members insist, for God's majesty would be insulted and dis-
honored by the presence of the sinful at the Lord's Supper. The "black
sheep" must be excluded for His wrath will strike unless the "qualified [are
separated] from the unqualified" (1968, pp. 1204–06). Were debts promptly
paid? Were visits to a tavern frequent? Dancing? Was card-playing or gambling evident among admission candidates? Were the childhood years disorderly? A wide-ranging investigation was indispensable, for a sincerity
of character must be evident: potential members must have avoided frivolities, flaws, and blemishes (1968, pp. 1205–06).

Moreover, the conviction of sect members that God must be obeyed more
than men, and strictly, places a clear demand upon behavior: it must be unequivocally oriented to God's will and in full accord with the sacred
Word—it must be "righteous." Acting as a firm community and on behalf
of appropriate conduct, the entire sect disciplined members, unlike
churches, which disciplined in an authoritarian manner through a clergy
(1968, pp. 1204–05).

Hence, members view themselves as belonging to a religious elite.[28]
"Ethical purity" and a capacity to live "the clean life" constitute central
themes, and the exemplary conduct of the faithful is now displayed in the
"visible church" (pp. 187–88, 193, 202). Finally, outside a "salvation institution" and cut off from religious officials empowered to administer special means of dispensation, believers are left entirely on their own:

> The idea that the individual, on the basis of the religious qualifications be-
> stowed upon him by God, decided on his salvation status exclusively on his
> own was important. . . . Only the believer's practical conduct mattered: his be-
> havior "proved and testified" to his faith and alone provided a *sign* that he
> stood on the road to salvation. (pp. 203–04)

Weber concludes that churches and sects influenced the action of believers in quite differing ways owing to these variations.[29] More effective in in-
stilling sincere faith, the sect disciplined the devout to a unique degree of
intensity on behalf of an ethical posture, he contends—all the more so ow-

---

28. "The sect is a group whose very nature and purpose precludes universality and requires the free
   consensus of its members, since it aims at being an aristocratic group, an association of persons
   with full religious qualification" (1968, p. 1204).

29. In seventeenth- and eighteenth-century America, Baptists, Quakers, Methodists, Mennonites,
   and Presbyterians all constituted, according to Weber, sects.

ing to the absence of a forgiving priest or minister endowed by an organization with a direct connection to God. Heterogeneous social-psychological dynamics were here at work. The far greater capacity of sects to mold and shape activity — to "breed" ethical qualities — is a theme of pivotal centrality to Weber. It must now be addressed.

THE SECT'S SOCIAL-PSYCHOLOGICAL DYNAMIC: "HOLDING YOUR OWN" INDIVIDUALISM, CONFORMITY, AND THE METHODICAL-RATIONAL ORGANIZATION OF LIFE

The sect expected the faithful to adhere to high standards and strict ethical codes. This organization's strong influence became manifest in several ways, Weber argues.

First, as a consequence of selective admission procedures, sect membership itself legitimized and guaranteed one's good character. This "certificate of moral qualification," combined with the believer's focus upon God, clearly defined every transgression: a "fall from grace" had occurred rather than a random and forgivable lapse. The sect, however, having banished Catholicism's mechanism — the Confession — to address sinfulness, lacked the institutionalized means to relieve internal distress (pp. 187–88, 198). A qualitative strengthening of the necessity for the faithful to act *constantly* in a righteous manner was the result, according to Weber.

Second, the sect's self-governing feature also enhanced its remarkable capacity to call forth ethical activity. The exercise of discipline and authority in this group was distinct from the exercise of discipline and authority in churches, according to Weber: although less centralized and authoritarian in the sects because now in the hands of laymen, it became, for this reason, more thorough and encompassing. Any misstep would surely be revealed.[30]

Third, the definition of the American sect as an exclusive organization of pure believers implied that expulsion would follow immediately upon any exposure of "poor character." This harsh treatment involved an intolerable situation for the expelled, Weber emphasizes: through its innumerable activities (church suppers, Sunday school, charitable activities, team sports, Bible study groups, etc.), the sect not only shaped members efficiently and hence provided a guarantee of appropriate socialization, but also monopolized the believer's social life. Those excluded for "dishonorable conduct" immediately "[suffered] . . . a kind of social boycott" and a collapse of their entire social existence (pp. 195, 197; 200; 1968, p. 1206). The necessity to "hold one's own" under the watchful eyes of peers — to testify unceasingly through ethical conduct to one's membership among the elect — now became intensified, as did the sect's capac-

---

30.   This feature of the sect in particular, Weber contends, lends to it a monitoring capacity that rivals that of the monastic order. See pp. 195–98.

ity to mold action: "The most powerful individual interest of social self-esteem [was put] in the service of this breeding of traits" (p. 198).[31]

Fourth, Weber refers to a related social-psychological dynamic to further explain the unique capacity of the Protestant sects to cultivate and sustain ethical activity. The faithful, as a consequence of the selection of members on the basis of moral qualities, were viewed as persons of great integrity and even trustworthiness within their geographical regions. As the sect — largely for this reason — acquired social prestige, supervision of behavior among the devout became further intensified: for the sect's favorable reputation must be maintained. In other words, to the degree that social honor within the larger community became salient, members became subject to enhanced conformity pressures to uphold "good moral character" standards. A shaping of an ethical posture also took place in this manner, Weber contends. Indeed, by engaging the entire person and bestowing both social honor and esteem,[32] the sect had the effect, especially in contrast to the authoritarianism of churches, of disciplining believers to cultivate ethical action to a unique degree of intensity: "According to all experience there is no stronger means of breeding traits than through the necessity of holding one's own in the midst of one's associates" (p. 198; see pp. 195–96; 1968, p. 1206). Weber saw here a source of American initiative-taking and the American notion of self-respect.

Fifth, and finally, the sect constituted a functional, even "impersonal" (*sachliche*) group: it was oriented above all *to tasks* in service to God's greater glory and to the construction of His kingdom. By promoting "the precise ordering of the individual into the instrumental task pursued by the group," this "mechanism for the achievement of . . . material and ideal goals" circumscribed affect-laden and tradition-laden relationships among the faithful. Emotion-based interaction did not prevail in the sect,[33] nor did a warm and comfortable, sentimental mode of interaction rooted in familiar and longstanding traditions.[34] In addition, all residue of any "mystical total es-

---

31.　"Hold one's own" is the usual translation of *sich behaupten*. It implies, within a constituted group, a maintenance and defense of an individual's social — and ethical — standing vis-à-vis one's peers. "Prove your mettle" conveys today the same idea in routinized form, as does the notion that persons should "measure up" to the task at hand. While *within* a group, members do not "lose themselves" to or "dissolve" into the group; rather, and despite interaction in this cohesive group of a degree of intensity that otherwise would insure an orientation exclusively to others, a focus upon an ethical standard remains. While an unequivocally positive connotation is bestowed upon "holding your own" in the United States, persons from cultures uninfluenced by a tradition of this-worldly asceticism may well view this degree of individualism with scepticism—namely, as dangerously close to egocentrism.

32.　Those who conducted themselves in an exemplary fashion according to the expectations of peer sect members received from them a clear message: you are honorable and accepted. This unequivocal and unmediated bestowal of social esteem must have served to elevate the devout psychologically and to counterbalance any residual inclination toward fatalism deriving from the doctrine of Predestination. Interestingly, whereas the religious context here determined that approval from one's fellows implied a symbolic dimension ("you are saved"), cohesive groups in the secularized twentieth century could bestow only the *caput mortuum*, or routinized, form of approval: "you are well liked." This tension between the person in search of approval (and hence conforming to group norms) and the person holding his own inside the group, by adhering to ethical standards, endures in American society to the present.

sence floating above [the believer] and enveloping him" was banished (p. 492, note 34; p. 204).[35]

A halo never encompassed the sect—one into which the believer could merge amid a sacred glow. Rather, an orientation by the individual to tasks in service to God and high standards of ethical conduct reigned. Stalwart believers, evaluated exclusively by reference to the "religious qualities evident in [their] conduct," constantly attended to the necessity of holding their own (p. 204). To Weber, and despite the typically intense interaction among members, a cultivation of deep emotional ties with others and an immersion into the group failed to occur. "Association" (*Vergesellschaftung*) with others, and sociability, characterized interaction.[36]

In sum, in juxtaposing an unceasing orientation to activities and tasks, intense conformity pressures, and a hold-your-own individualism, sects pulled the devout away from emotion-oriented relationships, tradition-oriented sentimentality, and all inclinations to attribute a sacred aura to groups. However, far from abandoning believers to the flux and flow of an interest-oriented utilitarianism ("practical rationalism"), or to an endless random and nihilistic drift, the sect immediately took firm hold of the faithful and bound them tightly within its own social-psychological dynamic—one that actively cultivated, sustained, and rejuvenated ethical action.

Weber's position in "Sects" must be repeated. The *methodical-rational* organization of life typically found among ascetic Protestants arose not only from the individual's lonely quest to create "evidence" of his salvation and the psychological rewards placed upon ethical action by the Puritan Divines, as charted in *PE*, but also from the efficient "implementation" of this systematically organized life in the Protestant sect. Indeed, the requirement of this group — to insure that only the morally qualified participate in communion — can be understood as itself giving an impetus to the congregation's many social activities, for they enabled the indispensable monitoring of members' conduct.[37] To Weber, "The sect and its derivations are one of [America's] unwritten but vital constitutional elements, since they shape the individual more than any other influence" (1968, p. 1207).

Nonetheless, and although pivotal, his social-psychological analysis of the ways in which this organization confirms and promotes manifold ethical action among the faithful constitutes merely a preliminary step for

---

33. In this regard Weber notes Puritanism's condemnation of personal wants and desires (*Kreaturvergötterung*) — for their satisfaction competes with the believer's loyalty to God — as denying legitimacy to a focus upon the person and all privatized concerns. See p. 493, n. 39.

34. Toennies' famous *Gemeinschaft—Gesellschaft* (1957) dichotomy was well known to Weber. He is here explicitly taking an antagonistic position (see p. 204).

35. Weber has here in mind both Catholicism and Lutheranism. Because enveloped by a mystical aura, members of these churches are absolved of an urgent necessity to hold their own. He is critical of this mode of group formation, which he found to be widespread in the Germany of his times (see Mommsen, 1974, pp. 80–81).

36. "Sociation" offers also an adequate translation of *Vergesellschaftung*.

37. This point, unmentioned in Weber's texts, has been inferred.

Weber. His major purpose must be kept in mind: to investigate how the sects bolstered the penetration into believers of *the Protestant ethic*:

> [The sects placed] ... *individual* motives and personal self-interests ... in the service of maintaining and propagating the "middle class" Puritan ethic, with all its ramifications. This is absolutely decisive for its penetrating and for its powerful effect. (p. 198)

We must now turn away from the social psychology that anchored the extreme *intensity* of the Puritan's ethical action to a discussion of the *direction* taken by the devout to "certify moral qualities." Examined above, the Protestant ethic's major features can be reviewed here only briefly. The expansive vibrancy of this economic ethic, even vis-à-vis longstanding tradition and the practical rationalism of daily life, now becomes fully visible to Weber, as does its energetic capacity to mold believers' activity distinctly and comprehensively.

FROM THE SOCIAL PSYCHOLOGY OF ETHICAL ACTION TO THE PROTESTANT ETHIC OF THE AMERICAN SECTS

How does the ethical action cultivated in the sect, he queries, relate to a vocational ethic? How does it underpin and intensify action systematically oriented to work and the search for profit and material success? According to Baxter's revisions, the Puritan devout could convince themselves of their favorable salvation status *only* through a continuous focus on labor in a calling, profit, and the accumulation of wealth. The social-psychological dynamic of admonition and discipline emanating from the American sects, Weber holds, pushed action decisively in these directions—that is, toward the Protestant ethic.

Members of sects, all of whom claimed elect salvation status, must testify in daily life to their good moral character: integrity, honesty, and trustworthiness must be apparent. In addition, entrepreneurialism, reliable service to customers, fixed and fair prices, and the prudent management of money and credit all evidenced, in a manner visible to an entire community as well as to sect members, sincere belief and a dedication to one's vocational calling. Competence and success demonstrated "approved qualities"; they testified to one's devotion and membership among the saved (pp. 193–94, 202).

Moreover, as a consequence of the "certificate of moral qualification" provided by sect membership, all who participated in dishonest commercial practices became subject to an onerous social stigma. Indeed, the businessperson's awareness that unethical conduct would be followed by expulsion from the sect, and hence the disappearance of all further opportunities for credit, intensified the ethical premium placed upon economic transactions (p. 188). Weber perceives the sect's capacity to monitor "appropriate" behavior as central for the development of ascetic Protestantism's economic ethic:

> Unqualified integrity, evidenced by, for example, a system of fixed prices in retail trade, strong management of credit, avoidance of all "worldly" consumption and every kind of debauchery, in short, life-long sober diligence in one's "calling," appears as the specific, indeed, really the *only* form by which one can demonstrate his qualification as a Christian and therewith his moral legitimation for membership in the sect. (p. 201; emph. in original)[38]

In these ways, high standards of conduct accompanied methodical work and the search for wealth and profit. Rewards were apparent—as were punishments. Sect members in search of bank loans and financial opportunities of various sorts were viewed as creditworthy,[39] and the devout came to be perceived as honest merchants who could be trusted even with the customer's money. A halo of respectability replaced the traditional view of the businessperson as an unethical and manipulative figure.[40] A "social existence" was established. And this aura *had to* be maintained, for otherwise potential customers would abandon their preference for sect members and a boycott would occur (pp. 186, 193–94, 201–2; 1968, pp. 1204–06). Both business and social reputations were at stake. Specifically American forms of social trust, social status, and respectability developed.

The impact of the Protestant sect upon the Protestant ethic in this manner proved significant, Weber argues. Another feature of this organization, already mentioned, is emphasized in this respect also. The sect, because it encouraged among members an instrumental orientation to tasks in service to God and because its major features precluded a merging of the faithful into a "mystical total essence," remained a functional and impersonal organization. To Weber, just the suspicion that accompanied any cultivation of deep emotional ties on the one hand, and all merging of the individual into the group amid a "sacred glow" on the other hand, facilitated a further ordering of believers into its overarching tasks and coordination of labor. Formal legal equality, abstract norms, and bureaucratization, as well as modern capitalism's purposeful mode of utilizing persons and the "lifestyle in [its] . . . middle classes," were here foreshadowed: ". . . this-worldly asceticism . . . and the specific discipline of the sects bred the capitalist spirit and the rational "professional" (*Berufsmensch*) who was needed by capitalism" (p. 492, n. 34; pp. 204, 415).[41]

---

38. Weber lists, for example, the business practices Methodists held to be forbidden. See p. 194.
39. This aspect of membership in a sect — the moral legitimation of members — did not obstruct geographical mobility if only because entry into a new community could be gained easily; namely, by a letter from the pastor of one's home church. Such a "letter of introduction" immediately overcame the normal suspicion of newcomers and, moreover, established their honesty, respectability, and creditworthiness. See 2002b, p. 254, n. 34; 1968, p. 1206; see also Weber's letter (Marianne Weber, 1975, p. 299). (Weber would argue that consideration of just such *religious* legacies must be included in all explanations for the high rates of geographical mobility in the United States today.)
40. "Business ethics" in the United States here finds its point of origin. This phrase is viewed widely in Europe as an oxymoron.
41. On the pathway from this impersonal utilization of the individual in the Protestant sect to the Enlightenment, see p. 415.

For all these reasons, the Protestant sects intensified the orientations to economic action expected by Baxter and the Puritan Divines. They *directed* believers in a systematic manner toward profit, the accumulation of wealth, and work in a vocation: "the 'proven' Christian is the person who is proven in his 'calling,' particularly the businessman who from a capitalist standpoint is capable" (p. 200). To Weber, only the rigorous organizing of life that occurred in "the ascetic sects could legitimate and put a halo around the economic 'individualist' impulses of the modern capitalist ethos" (p. 199; see pp. 194, 197–98).[42] Capitalism today would look quite differently if it had been devoid of ". . . the universal diffusion of these qualities and principles of a methodical way of life . . . maintained through these religious groups" (190).[43]

However, Weber also argued that the Protestant ethic proved fleeting. It increasingly developed into a secular ethic as the eighteenth and nineteenth centuries unfolded. We arrive again at the spirit of capitalism.

THE NINETEENTH CENTURY: THE SPIRIT OF CAPITALISM OF CLUBS, SOCIETIES, AND ASSOCIATIONS

As noted, Weber contends that the Protestant ethic began to lose its specifically religious foundation in many regions of the United States as early as the mid-eighteenth century. Represented by Benjamin Franklin, a spirit of capitalism now appeared: a configuration of values directly indebted to ascetic Protestantism. However, this spirit had been stripped of all supernatural justification.

Despite this shift to "secular" values, the "sect spirit," manifest in later carrier organizations, lived on throughout the nineteenth century, Weber argues. Community-oriented clubs, societies, and voluntary associations now cultivated and conveyed the spirit of capitalism. He perceived, for example, as discussed, the many businessmen's groups particularly pervasive in the United States — the Lions, Rotary, and Kiwanis associations, for

---

42. Weber's quotation marks indicate his skepticism toward Adam Smith's solitary "economic man." The sources for this individualism are not located, as Smith maintained, in a secular and utilitarian pursuit of private interests and the consequent development of particular skills (see p. 480, n. 8). Rather, its complex, and *supernatural*, origins are to be discovered in Calvin's doctrine of Predestination, revisions by the Puritan Divines, and the American sects, Weber contends. Moreover, modern individualism is not related exclusively to the faithful standing isolated before God and responsible exclusively to him; in addition, a *community*-oriented task is central: the creation of God's kingdom and the initiative and energy placed into motion by the urgency of this undertaking. Finally, Smith's "economic man," according to which a "natural propensity to truck, barter, and exchange" characterizes individuals, must be acknowledged — rather than "natural" — as a legacy of the particular Calvinist individualism widespread in Smith's eighteenth-century Scotland, Weber insists.

43. Weber offers even a further summary statement of his overall theme: "*My* question concerns the origins of that *ethical* 'style of life' internally 'adequate' to the 'capitalism' stage of economic development; this style of life meant the victory of capitalism in the human 'soul'" (Weber, 2001, p. 50; transl. altered).

example — as direct legacies. Membership, which occurred through selection processes and involved a close monitoring of activities, constituted a "badge of respectability" that established one's good character, trustworthiness, and social honor as a "gentleman" (pp. 191–94; 1968, pp. 1206–07).

> The modern position of the secular clubs and societies with recruitment by ballot is largely the product of a process of *secularization*. Their position is derived from the far more exclusive importance of the prototype of these voluntary associations, to wit, the sects. (p. 192)

> . . . large numbers of "orders" and clubs of all sorts have begun to assume in part the functions of the religious group. Almost every small businessman who thinks something of himself wears some kind of badge in his lapel. However, the archetype of this form, which *all* use to guarantee the "honorableness" of the individual, is indeed the ecclesiastical community. (2005, p. 288; transl. altered; emph. in orig.; see pp. 189–90)

These "straight derivatives, rudiments, and survivals of those conditions which once prevailed in all ascetic sects" are apparent in "all walks of American life," Weber maintains (p. 197; 1968, p. 1206; see 1972, pp. 173-4).[44] In the form of a vocational ethos that oriented action methodically toward work, the search for profit, and the acquisition of wealth, the values of the Protestant sects permeated entire communities and offered nourishment first to a spirit of capitalism and then to modern capitalism. For Weber, "[these associations] . . . served to diffuse and to maintain the bourgeois capitalist business ethos among the broad strata of the middle classes . . . " (p. 190).

Weber's complex argument must be summarized. He opposes vehemently, against the prevalent intellectual currents of his time, all explanations that trace Franklin's secular spirit of capitalism and the economic ethic of nineteenth-century businessmen's clubs alone back to "practical activity" and the utilitarian pursuit of economic and political interests. Only "adventure capitalism" developed in this manner. A more complex conceptual framework is required to explain the origins of *modern* capitalism, Weber holds, not least owing to the unusual resilience of the traditional economic ethic. The anchoring of a *methodical-rational* organization of life in a configuration of *ethical values*, and the necessity for believers to testify to their elect salvation status *before God*, proves indispensable for its banishment. In addition, Weber's investigations emphasize, a carrier organization must form to inject these values, on the basis of a particular social-psychological dynamic, rigorously into the daily lives of the devout.

---

44. "... [religous institutions are] the most characteristic features of American life, as well as the most fateful factors for a deep inner transformation. Up to now it was the orthodox sects here that gave to all of life its special character. All sociability, all social cohesion, all agitation in favor of philanthropic and ethical and even political concerns (such as the campaign against corruption) are held in their grasp" (letter of September 20 from the United States; from Scaff, 1998, p. 66).

Holding their own within tightly knit Protestant sects, the faithful demonstrated their moral character *before men*.

These organizations prove crucial in this way to Weber's argument. They conveyed, far more efficiently than the admonitions of Richard Baxter, Puritanism's economic ethic *into the worlds* of labor and commerce. Moreover, albeit transformed, the sects endured: manifest in the eighteenth and nineteenth centuries in secular form, their economic ethic penetrated directly into arrays of associations, clubs, and societies. These new carrier groups cast the direct successor of the Protestant ethic — the spirit of capitalism — through generations and even into the twentieth century.

Here our overview of the American sects' broad influence, according to Weber's analysis, upon the economic culture of the United States comes to a conclusion, as does our discussion of the intertwining of *PE* and "Sects." Only an acknowledgment of the complementary character of these writings captures his full Protestant ethic thesis. The second major theme in "Sects" explores a subject of endless fascination to Weber: the political culture of American society. His oft-repeated phrase organizes his analysis: "American society is not a sandpile."

AMERICAN POLITICAL CULTURE: "AMERICAN SOCIETY IS NOT A SANDPILE"

With great energy and a sweeping thrust, American society perpetually formulates groups and associations, Weber contends. Endless "exclusivities" are characteristic rather than, as widely believed in Europe during his time, "sandpiles" of individuals lacking substantive connection to each other. The causal significance of ascetic Protestantism and the sect heritage must again be acknowledged, for "the tremendous flood of social groupings, which penetrate all corners of American life, are constituted according to this model 'sect'" (p. 204).

Weber is all too aware that his German readers, accustomed to equating urbanization and industrialization with the disappearance of religion, will scarcely comprehend this feature of American society. In part, he addresses his skeptical audience by recounting personal observations that illustrate its comprehensive devoutness (see pp. 186–88). He confronts in addition the exploration of the differences between feudal and industrial societies by Ferdinand Toennies in *Gemeinschaft und Gesellschaft* (1957). Values and traditions had offered the foundation for groups in premodern *Gemeinschaften* (*communities*), Toennies maintained; however, because of capitalism's effective banishment of religion and traditions, groups in *Gesellschaften* (*societies*) became grounded exclusively in interests, whether political or economic—and were unstable. Moreover, because capable of providing only "impersonal" connections across persons and groups of persons, interests remained incapable of creating substantive relationships, let alone viable communities. Consequently, social instability pervaded modern societies and, because of a prevalence of instrumental calculations, relationships were harsh, impersonal, and manipulative, he insisted.

Weber announced a principled challenge. Group formation in that nation viewed in Europe as at the vanguard of modern capitalism — the United States — occurred often *in reference to values*, he held. Modern capitalism had pushed aside neither ascetic Protestantism nor its legacy organizations. On the contrary, religion remained significant and provided a value-based foundation for these organizations. Indeed, it stood at the core of the expansive group formation that distinguished the American political culture and precluded its depiction as a sandpile of atomized individuals. How does Weber comprehend this uniquely energetic capacity to form groups? Some elements of his argument are already familiar to us.[45]

The purpose of Puritan devotion — to serve God by creating on earth His noble and righteous kingdom — oriented the faithful away from personal desires and in a distinct direction: toward this supreme Being and His tasks. A loyalty to His purposes must prevail and this allegiance was monitored. Moreover, because behavior deemed righteous, ethical, and trustworthy testified to "God's strength within," and therefore to a favorable salvation status (for He would not favor with strength just anyone), the saved — now visible — recognized a common sincerity and devoutness. On this basis they gravitated toward one another without fear and formed congregations:

> On the one hand, the idea that the individual, on the basis of the religious qualifications bestowed upon him by God, decided on his salvation exclusively on his own was important....only the believer's practical conduct mattered: his behavior "proved and testified" to his faith and alone provided a *sign* that he stood on the road to salvation. On the other hand, this very notion — the individual could testify to his salvation through his righteous behavior — formulated the foundation for the social knitting together of the congregation. (pp. 203–04; emph. in original)

"This individualism," Weber contends, "produced an eminent power to form *groups*" (p. 203). For these same reasons, he insists, believers began distinctly to turn away from a cultivation of the private realm's deep personal relationships; a veritable circumscribing of the emotions took place. To the same extent a focusing upon impersonal tasks more easily occurred, as did a cooperation among persons sharing a purpose and an activity. And individuals oriented to common goals fit better into groups than individu-

---

45.   This section examines Weber's view of American society by emphasizing Puritanism's capacity to form groups *in general*. Its further energetic empowerment — to create viable civil associations and a *civic sphere* — also counteracts any historical developments in American society toward the European nightmare: atomized individuals without viable social ties. This aspect of Weber's analysis has been explored elsewhere. That discussion, by investigating the creation of God's kingdom and the formation of the congregation, and the manner in which the congregation's values became generalized into the larger community, complements the analysis to follow (see Kalberg, 1997, pp. 212–16; 2003; 2005). Weber's disparate writings on this theme have been compiled at Weber, 2005, pp. 277–89, 273–76. On the way in which Weber sees work, in the American context, as assisting the formation of groups, see Kalberg, 2001b, pp. 187–88; 2002.

als bound to emotions, Weber contends. A social lubricant had congealed, and "groups became mechanisms" on behalf of *goals*: the overarching aim to build God's kingdom bestowed legitimacy upon them. Individuals experienced a clear pressure to fit into the group, and their "dedication to the group" enhanced its solidarity (pp. 107–08; 492, n. 34; 204, 493–94).

Once formed, these groups put a self-sustaining dynamic into motion, Weber holds. A functional and impersonal mode of interaction prevailed — association — that facilitated a focus on tasks and promoted the "precise ordering" of the individual into the project pursued by the group, despite a level of regular and even intense interaction (p. 204). Moreover, this "sociation" mode proved well suited both for a continued orientation by the faithful to ethical standards and a surveillance of sect members' behavior. Hence, the ethical responsibility of individuals acknowledged within the sect could now move even more to the forefront. Indeed, it enhanced group solidarity, as did the demeanor of the faithful: trusting, respectable, and decent.

> . . . the tying together of the internal isolation of the individual (which means that a maximum of his energy is deployed externally) with his ability to form social groups having the most stable cohesion and maximum impact at first was realized most fully on the soil of the formation of the sects. (Weber, 2005, p. 285; transl. altered)

In this way, remarkably, the systematic interaction of believers *with the supernatural* realm called forth extensive group-forming skills and innumerable "exclusivities" in Colonial America and the United States. All explanations that focus on the utilitarian and pragmatic orientations of persons in the immediate present must be rejected.[46] The "old sect spirit," rather than having disappeared under the onslaught of homogenizing industrialization and urbanization, Weber argued against Toennies, lived on. It remained influential in the nineteenth century despite secularization and, because of its group-formation capacities, created an American political culture far distant from a "sandpile of unconnected individuals" (p. 204). Innumerable clubs, societies, and associations now monitored the behavior of applicants and selected by ballot those of "good moral character." In addition, *vis-à-vis* the organization's ethical standards, the individual must hold his own under the watchful eyes of his fellows. And membership, as had admission into the sect, continued to signify a claim to respectability, decency, and status. The club's lapel pin visibly legitimated social honor and integrity, Weber saw, and membership proved indispensable for social acceptance in a community (p. 200). To him, "American democracy is not a sandpile of unrelated individuals but a

---

46.   This is the focus of Tocqueville. He comprehends the "nimbleness" of the Americans to form groups as originating out of egalitarianism, which putatively sets free the "commercial passions," and a subsequent recognition by persons of common economic interests. Once the personal skills that assist formulation of groups in this arena congeal, they are then utilized on behalf of the formation of groupings in the political sphere. See Tocqueville, 1945, pp. 123–27; Kalberg, 1997, pp. 212, 216–18.

maze of highly exclusive, yet absolutely voluntary sects, associations and clubs, which provide the center of the individual's social life" (p. 440; see p. 203; 1968, p. 1207).

Hence, rather than "the open door," exclusivities permeated American society in this manner. This "tremendous flood of social groupings," which accounts for the uniqueness of the American experiment, remained invisible to Weber's highly secularized German compatriots. Their imaginations could not grasp the continued stamp of religious belief upon modern political and economic cultures.

Weber confronted in "Sects" German stereotypes of America in these ways. In doing so, he offered a portrait of a dynamic society oriented, even "in this secular age," significantly toward standards and arrays of ethical values. His concerns related to the West's pluralistic pathways into the modern era.

On the one hand, Weber wished to persuade Germans to become self-critical in respect to their own society. It was fast becoming overly bureaucratized and stratified, he believed, and hence too socially stagnant to produce the pluralistic conflict that sustains ethical action. Was the "atomized" *Gesellschaft* Toennies and others saw on the horizon a particularly *German* vision, he queried, one that sprang from political, economic, and cultural constellations specifically German (see Kalberg 1987, 2001b, 2003)? On the other hand, Weber argued against the many contemporary schools of thought that defined "modernity" in a monolithic manner: namely, as an epoch, as a result of urbanization, industrialization, bureaucratization, and modern capitalism, that homogenized nations into similar — even indistinguishable — "structures" and societies. His attention to American ascetic Protestantism and the social psychology of the sect convinced him that the United States, with respect to both its economic and political cultures, had pursued a heterogeneous course quite unlike its European counterparts.

Although Weber's message on these themes is clear, his occasional remarks to the contrary should not be neglected. Even while attending to the uniqueness of the United States and insisting upon its unusual developmental pathway, his investigations perceive also an ominous homogenizing tendency *across* industrial nations—one that will in due course, he contends, influence even the United States. A "Europeanization" is underway: as the new world moves away from a "youthful" capitalism, as its vast frontier becomes settled, and as legacies from the Protestant sects vanish completely, American society will be enveloped by the slow, yet unceasing, bureaucratization already in motion in Europe, he maintains. A more organized economy with greater specialization of tasks and occupations, more firm social hierarchies, and a specialist civil service trained for administrative duties will appear. Groups will become more closed, and rigid lines of social status will appear (pp. 193–94, 198–99; Weber, 1971b, p. 197; see Roth, 1985, pp. 221–25; Mommsen, 1971).

Nonetheless, "Sects," as well as *PE* and Weber's other major texts, as will become apparent, demonstrate vividly the many ways in which *ethical values* vary across the West's economic and political cultures. They must be acknowledged as influential, he asserts; indeed, they contributed substantively, in the form of varying "economic ethics," to the shaping of the distinct routes taken in Europe and America into the modern era. And their role in molding the contours of present-day industrial societies must not be neglected. Again, Weber's analysis rejects forcefully those approaches that examine historical change and the present by reference alone to power, domination, utilitarian calculations, and economic and political interests. Also opposed are all schools of linear thought that proclaim inevitable and evolutionary change in history. As a comparative-historical sociologist oriented to cases rather than "developmental laws" (see Kalberg, 1994b, pp. 81–84), he investigated how the pathways of nations diverged despite a common experience of urbanization, bureaucratization, industrialization, and modern capitalism. Their distinct religious traditions, he maintains, in part account for this variation.[47]

"PREFATORY REMARKS": THE POST-*PE* WRITINGS AND THE TRANSITION TO MODERN WESTERN RATIONALISM

Weber's thinking on the relationship between religious belief and economic activity became radically comparative after *PE* and "Sects." He began a series of studies around 1910 on the religions of China (Confucianism and Daoism), India (Hinduism and Buddhism), and ancient Israel (Judaism) (1951, 1952, 1958). First published separately in article form in the *Archiv für Sozialwissenschaft und Sozialpolitik* in 1916 and 1917, these investigations were later given the title Economic Ethics of the World Religions (EEWR) and prepared in 1919 and 1920 for publication in book form. The complete, three-volume enterprise, which placed *PE* and the later sects essay (pp. 185–99) at its beginning, was published after Weber's death in 1920 under the title *Collected Essays in the Sociology of Religion*.[48] "Prefatory Remarks" ("PR"), the general introduction to this treatise, was penned late in

---

47. This theme, in respect to *PE* and "Sects," has been the general focus here. A further theme cannot be addressed, namely, his analysis of the rise of modern democracy. *PE* and "Sects" would play pivotal parts in any reconstruction of this analysis.

48. Weber lived to complete revisions only on *PE*, "Sects," and *The Religion of China: Confucianism and Taoism* (1951). Two analytic essays were also included: "The Social Psychology of the World Religions" (1946e), which is the introduction to the EEWR series, and "Religious Rejections of the World" (1946c), which is placed after the investigation of Confucianism and Taoism and before the study of Hinduism and Buddhism (1958). It offers a masterly and sweeping analysis of modern Western rationalism, and hence doesn't fit well into this series (although it could have been placed at the end). *Collected Essays* remained incomplete. Weber had planned to write chapters on the religions of ancient Egypt, Phoenicia, Babylonia, and Persia, and volumes on Islam, ancient Christianity, and Talmudic Judaism.

1919.[49] As the concluding selection to the readings on the Protestant ethic thesis, it introduces major aspects of Weber's post-1908 writings — EEWR, *E&S*, *GEH*, and *AG* — and defines *modern Western rationalism* (see pp. 223–29).

"PR" conveys the expanded *conceptual* framework of these works. First, rather than being oriented exclusively to the religion life-sphere, it outlines a multicausal methodology. An array of spheres (rulership, law, the economy, and religion) and their interactions constitute Weber's focus. *E&S*, EEWR, and *GEH* combine *ideas and interests*, thereby investigating "both sides of the causal nexus." Second, Weber's research turns prominently to the question of whether powerful groups form to cultivate beliefs and to serve as the *social carriers* of a religion's economic ethic. Third, these treatises, by constantly situating single groups in configurations of groups, attend to *social contexts*. Finally, as noted, an expansive comparative thrust now characterizes Weber's investigations. Frequent comparisons to China, India, and the Middle East isolate uniqueness, define group boundaries, and evaluate causes.

In addition, "PR" significantly expands the *thematic* framework of *PE* and "Sects." Instead of scrutinizing further aspects of the West's religious development, Weber's post-*PE* works seek to examine the origins of modern capitalism in the West by reference to Western rationalism and modern Western rationalism. These central concepts define the multiple groups that became allied in configurations in the West to form deep contexts of groups both conducive to the rise of capitalism and favorable to its metamorphosis into modern capitalism. They also demarcate the West vis-à-vis Chinese rationalism, the rationalism of India, and the rationalism of the Middle East—civilizations that did not give birth to modern capitalism.

The opening pages of "PR" offer Weber's inventory of the ways in which the West diverged from other major civilizations. No other passage in his works summarizes the "characteristic features" of modern Western rationalism so forcefully and succinctly.

---

49. This essay was given the title "Author's Introduction" in the earlier translation by Talcott Parsons. Placed in his volume before *PE*, generations of readers of *PE* have incorrectly viewed this essay as an introduction to *PE* (despite a partial explanation by Parsons).

THE PROTESTANT SECTS
AND THE SPIRIT OF CAPITALISM[1]

From: Pp. 302–22 in *From Max Weber*, edited and translated by H. H. Gerth and C. Wright Mills. Translation slightly revised by Stephen Kalberg (New York: Oxford University Press; 1946). Endnotes omitted; footnotes abridged.

For some time in the United States a principled "separation of state and church" has existed. This separation is carried through so strictly that there is not even an official census of denominations, for it would be considered against the law for the state even to ask the citizen for his denomination. We shall not here discuss the practical importance of this principle of the relation between religious organizations and the state. [2] We are interested, rather, in the fact that scarcely two and a half decades ago the number of "persons without church affiliation" in the U.S.A. was estimated to be only about 6 percent; and this despite the absence of all those highly effective psychological **premiums** which most of the European states then placed upon affiliation with certain privileged churches and despite the immense immigration to the U.S.A.

It should be realized, in addition, that church affiliation in the U.S.A. brings with it incomparably higher financial burdens, especially for the poor, than anywhere in Germany. Published family budgets prove this, and I have personally known of many burdened cases in a congregation in a city on Lake Erie, which was almost entirely composed of German immigrant lumberjacks. Their regular contributions for religious purposes amounted to almost $80 annually, being paid out of an average annual income of about $1,000. Everyone knows that even a small fraction of this financial burden in Germany would lead to a mass exodus from the church. But quite apart from that, nobody who visited the United States fifteen or twenty years ago, that is, before the recent Europeanization of the country began, could overlook the very intense church-mindedness which then prevailed in all regions not yet flooded by European immigrants. Every old travel book reveals that formerly church-mindedness in America went unquestioned, as compared with recent decades, and was even far stronger. Here we are especially interested in one aspect of this situation.

---

1.   This is a new and greatly enlarged draft of an article published in the *Frankfurter Zeitung*, Eastern 1906, then somewhat enlarged in the *Christliche Welt*, 1906, pp. 558 ff., 577 ff., under the title, "Churches and Sects." [see following pp. 200–04]. I have repeatedly referred to this article as supplementing *The Protestant Ethic and the Spirit of Capitalism*. . . .

2.   The principle is often only theoretical; note the importance of the Catholic vote, as well as subsidies to confessional schools.

Hardly a generation ago when businessmen were establishing themselves and making new social contacts, they encountered the question: "To
what church do you belong?" This was asked unobtrusively and in a manner that seemed to be apropos, but evidently it was never asked accidentally. Even in Brooklyn, New York's twin city, this older tradition was
retained to a strong degree, and the more so in communities less exposed to
the influence of immigration. This question reminds one of the typical
Scotch *table d'hôte*, where a quarter of a century ago the continental European on Sundays almost always had to face the situation of a lady's asking,
"What service did you attend today?" Or, if the Continental, as the oldest
guest, should happen to be seated at the head of the table, the waiter when
serving the soup would ask him: "Sir, the prayer, please." In Portree (Skye)
on one beautiful Sunday I faced this typical question and did not know any
better way out than to remark: "I am a member of the *Badische Landeskirche*
[Church of the State of Baden] and could not find a chapel of my church in
Portree." The ladies were pleased and satisfied with the answer. "Oh, he
doesn't attend any service except that of his own denomination!"

If one looked more closely at the matter in the United States, one could
easily see that the question of religious affiliation was almost always posed
in social life and in business life which depended on permanent and credit
relations. However, as mentioned above, the American authorities never
posed the question. Why?

First, a few personal observations [from 1904] may serve as illustrations.
On a long railroad journey through what was then Indian territory, the author, sitting next to a traveling salesman of "undertaker's hardware" (iron
letters for tombstones), casually mentioned the still impressively strong
church-mindedness. Thereupon the salesman remarked, "Sir, for my part
everybody may believe or not believe as he pleases; but if I saw a farmer or a
businessman not belonging to any church at all, I wouldn't trust him with
fifty cents. Why pay me, if he doesn't believe in anything?" Now that was a
somewhat vague motivation.

The matter became somewhat clearer from the story of a German-born
nose-and-throat specialist, who had established himself in a large city on
the Ohio River and who told me of the visit of his first patient. Upon the
doctor's request, he lay down upon the couch to be examined with the [aid
of a] nose reflector. The patient sat up once and remarked with dignity and
emphasis, "Sir, I am a member of the ___ Baptist Church in ___ Street." Puz-
zled about what meaning this circumstance might have for the disease of
the nose and its treatment, the doctor discreetly inquired about the matter
from an American colleague. The colleague smilingly informed him that
the patient's statement of his church membership was merely to say: "Don't
worry about the fees." But why should it mean precisely that? Perhaps this
will become still clearer from a third happening.

On a beautiful clear Sunday afternoon early in October I attended a baptism ceremony of a Baptist congregation. I was in the company of some relatives who were farmers in the backwoods some miles out of M. (a county

seat) in North Carolina. The baptism was to take place in a pool fed by a brook which descended from the Blue Ridge Mountains, visible in the distance. It was cold and it had been freezing during the night. Masses of farmers' families were standing all around the slopes of the hills; they had come, some from great distances, some from the neighborhood, in their light two-wheeled buggies.

The preacher in a black suit stood waist deep in the pond. After preparations of various sorts, about ten persons of both sexes in their Sunday-best stepped into the pond, one after another. They avowed their faith and then were immersed completely—the women in the preacher's arms. They came up, shaking and shivering in their wet clothes, stepped out of the pond, and everybody "congratulated" them. They were quickly wrapped in thick blankets and then they drove home. One of my relatives commented that "faith" provides unfailing protection against sneezes. Another relative stood beside me, and being unchurchly in accordance with German traditions, he looked on, spitting disdainfully over his shoulder. He spoke to one of those baptized, "Hello, Bill, wasn't the water pretty cool?" and received the very earnest reply, "Jeff, I thought of some pretty hot place (Hell!), and so I didn't mind the cool water." During the immersion of one of the young men, my relative was startled.

"Look at him," he said. "I told you so!"

When I asked him after the ceremony, "Why did you anticipate the baptism of that man?" he answered, "Because he wants to open a bank in M."

"Are there so many Baptists around that he can make a living?"

"Not at all, but once being baptized he will get the patronage of the whole region and he will outcompete everybody."

Further questions of "why" and "by what means" led to the following conclusion: Admission to the local Baptist congregation follows only upon the most careful "probation" and after closest inquiries into conduct going back to early childhood (Disorderly conduct? Frequenting taverns? Dance? Theatre? Card Playing? Untimely meeting of liability? Other frivolities?) The congregation still adhered strictly to the religious tradition.

Admission to the congregation is recognized as an absolute guarantee of the moral qualities of a gentleman, especially of those qualities required in business matters. Baptism secures to the individual the deposits of the whole region and unlimited credit without any competition. He is a "made man." Further observation confirmed that these, or at least very similar phenomena, recur in the most varied regions. In general, *only* those men had success in business who belonged to Methodist or Baptist or other *sects* or sectlike **conventicles**. When a sect member moved to a different place, or if he was a traveling salesman, he carried the certificate of his congregation with him; and thereby he found not only easy contact with sect members but, above all, he found credit everywhere. If he got into economic straits through no fault of his own, the sect arranged his affairs, gave guarantees to the creditors, and helped him in every way, often according to the Biblical principle, *mutuum date nihil inde sperantes* [Lend, expecting nothing in return] (Luke 6:35).

The expectation of the creditors that his sect, for the sake of their prestige, would not allow creditors to suffer losses on behalf of a sect member was not, however, decisive for his opportunities. What was decisive was the fact that a fairly reputable sect would only accept for membership one whose "conduct" made him appear to be morally qualified beyond doubt. It is crucial that sect membership meant a certificate of moral qualification and especially of business morals for the individual. This stands in contrast to membership in a "church" into which one is "born" and which lets grace shine over the righteous and the unrighteous alike. Indeed, a church is a corporation which organizes grace and administers religious gifts of grace, like an endowed foundation. Affiliation with the church is, in principle, obligatory and hence proves nothing with regard to the member's qualities. A sect, however, is a voluntary association of only those who, according to the principle, are religiously and morally qualified. If one finds voluntary reception of his membership, by virtue of religious *probation*, he joins the sect voluntarily. It is, of course, an established fact that this selection has often been very strongly counteracted, precisely in America, through the proselyting of souls by competing sects, which, in part, was strongly determined by the material interests of the preachers. Hence, cartels for the restriction of proselyting have frequently existed among the competing denominations. Such cartels were formed, for instance, in order to exclude the easy wedding of a person who had been divorced for reasons which, from a religious point of view, were considered insufficient. Religious organizations that facilitated remarriage had great attraction. Some Baptist communities are said at times to have been lax in this respect, whereas the Catholic as well as the Lutheran churches were praised for their strict correctness. This correctness, however, allegedly reduced the membership of both churches.

Expulsion from one's sect for moral offenses has meant, economically, loss of credit and, socially, being declassed.

Numerous observations during the following months confirmed not only that church-mindedness *per se*, although still (1904) rather important, was rapidly dying out; but the particularly important trait, mentioned above, was definitely confirmed. In metropolitan areas I was spontaneously told, in several cases, that a speculator in undeveloped real estate would regularly erect a church building, often an extremely modest one; then he would hire a candidate from one of the various theological seminaries, pay him $500 to $600, and hold out to him a splendid position as a preacher for life if he would gather a congregation and thus preach the building terrain "full." Deteriorated churchlike structures which marked failures were shown to me. For the most part, however, the preachers were said to be successful. Neighborly contact, Sunday School, and so on, were said to be indispensable to the newcomer, but above all association with "morally" reliable neighbors.

Competition among sects is strong, among other things, through the kind of material and spiritual offerings at evening teas of the congregations. Among genteel churches also, musical presentations contribute to this competition. (A tenor in Trinity Church, Boston, who allegedly had to sing on Sundays *only*, at that time received $8,000.) Despite this sharp competition, the sects often maintained fairly good mutual relations. For instance, in the service of the Methodist church which I attended, the Baptist ceremony of the baptism, which I mentioned above, was recommended as a spectacle to edify everybody.

In the main, the congregations refused entirely to listen to the preaching of "dogma" and to confessional distinctions. "Ethics" alone could be offered. In those instances where I listened to sermons for the middle classes, the typical bourgeois morality, respectable and solid, to be sure, and of the most homely and sober kind, was preached. But the sermons were delivered with obvious inner conviction; the preacher was often moved.

Today the kind of denomination [to which one belongs] is rather irrelevant. It does not matter whether one be Freemason,[3] Christian Scientist, Adventist, Quaker, or what not. What is decisive is that one be admitted to membership by "ballot," after an *investigation* and an ethical *probation* in the sense of the virtues which are at a premium for the inner-worldly asceticism of Protestantism and hence, for the ancient Puritan tradition. Then, the same effect could be observed.

Closer scrutiny revealed the steady progress of the characteristic process of "secularization," to which in modern times all phenomena that originated in religious conceptions succumb. Not only religious associations, hence sects, have this effect on American life. Sects exercised this influence, rather, in a steadily decreasing proportion. If one paid some attention it was striking to observe (even fifteen years ago) that surprisingly many men among the American **middle classes** (always outside of the quite modern metropolitan areas and the immigration centers) were wearing a little badge (of varying color) in the buttonhole, which reminded one very closely of the rosette of the French Legion of Honor.

When asked what it meant, people regularly mentioned an association with a sometimes adventurous and fantastic name. And it became obvious that its significance and purpose consisted in the following: Almost always the association functioned as a burial insurance, besides offering greatly varied services. But often, and especially in those areas least touched by modern disintegration, the association offered the member the (ethical) claim for brotherly help on the part of every brother who had the means. If he faced an economic emergency for which he himself was not to be blamed, he could make this claim. And in several instances that came to my notice at the time, this claim again followed the very principle, *mutuum date nihil inde sperantes*, or at least a very low rate of interest prevailed. Apparently, such claims were willingly recognized by the members of the brotherhood. Furthermore—and this is the main point in this instance—membership was again acquired through balloting after investiga-

---

3. An Assistant Professor of Semitic languages in an eastern university told me that he regretted not having become "master of the chair," for then he would go back into business. When asked what good that would do the answer was: As a traveling salesman or seller he could present himself in a role famous for respectability. He could beat any competition and would be worth his weight in gold.

tion and a determination of moral worth. And hence the badge in the buttonhole meant, "I am a gentleman patented after investigation and probation and guaranteed by my membership." Again, this meant in business life above all, tested *credit worthiness*. One could observe that business opportunities were often decisively influenced by such legitimation.

All these phenomena, which seemed to be rather rapidly disintegrating—at least the religious organizations—were essentially confined to the middle classes. Some cultured Americans often dismissed these facts briefly and with a certain angry disdain as "humbug" or backwardness, or they even denied them; many of them actually did not know anything about them, as was affirmed to me by William James. Yet these survivals were still alive in many different fields, and sometimes in forms which appeared to be grotesque.

These associations were especially the typical vehicles of social ascent into the circle of the entrepreneurial middle class. They served to diffuse and to maintain the bourgeois capitalist business ethos among the broad strata of the middle classes (the farmers included).

As is well known, not a few (one may well say the majority of the older generation) of the American "promoters," "captains of industry," of the multi-millionaires and trust magnates belonged formally to sects, especially to the Baptists. However, in the nature of the case, these persons were often affiliated for merely conventional reasons, as in Germany, and only in order to legitimate themselves in personal and social life—not in order to legitimate themselves as businessmen; during the age of the Puritans, such "economic supermen" did not require such a crutch, and their "religiosity" was, of course, often of a more than dubious sincerity. The middle classes, above all the strata ascending with and out of the middle classes, were the bearers of that specific religious orientation which one must, indeed, beware viewing among them as only opportunistically determined.[4]

Yet one must never overlook that without the universal diffusion of these qualities and principles of a methodical way of life, qualities which were maintained through these religious communities, capitalism today, even in America, would not be what it is. In the history of any economic area on earth there is no epoch, [except] those quite rigid in feudalism or patrimonialism, in which capitalist figures of the kind of Pierpont Morgan, Rockefeller, Jay Gould, et al. were absent. Only the technical *means* which they used for the acquisition of wealth have changed (of course!). *They* stood and they stand "beyond good and evil."[4] But, however high one may otherwise evaluate their importance for economic transformation, they have never been decisive in determining what economic **frame of mind** was to dominate a given epoch and a given area. Above all, they were not

---

4.   "Hypocrisy" and conventional opportunism in these matters were hardly stronger developed in America than in Germany where, after all, an officer or civil servant "without religious affiliation or preference" was also an impossibility. And a Berlin ("Aryan!") Lord Mayor was not confirmed officially because he failed to have one of his children baptized. Only the *direction* in which conventional "hypocrisy" moved differed: official [state civil service] careers in Germany, business opportunities in the United States.

the creators and they were not to become the bearers of the specifically Occidental middle class frame of mind.

This is not the place to discuss in detail the political and social importance of the religious sects and the numerous similarly exclusive associations and clubs in America which are based upon recruitment by ballot. The entire life of a typical Yankee of the last generation led through a series of such exclusive associations, beginning with the Boys' Club in school, proceeding to the Athletic Club or the Greek Letter Society or to another student club of some nature, then onward to one of the numerous notable clubs of businessmen and the middle class or finally to the clubs of the metropolitan plutocracy. To gain admission was identical to a ticket of ascent, especially with a certificate before the forum of one's sense of self-worth; that is, to gain admission meant to have "proved" oneself. A student in college who was not admitted to any club (or quasi-society) whatsoever was usually a sort of pariah. (Suicides because of failure to be admitted have come to my notice.) A businessman, clerk, technician, or doctor who had the same fate usually was of questionable ability to serve. Today, numerous clubs of this sort are bearers of those tendencies leading toward aristocratic status groups which characterize contemporary American development. These status groups develop alongside of and, what has to be well noted, partly in contrast to the naked plutocracy.

In America mere "money" in itself also purchases power, but not social honor. Of course, it is a means of acquiring social prestige. It is the same in Germany and everywhere else; except in Germany the appropriate avenue to social honor led from the purchase of a feudal estate to the foundation of an entailed estate and acquisition of titular nobility, which in turn facilitated the reception of the grandchildren into aristocratic "society." In America, the old tradition respected the self-made man more than the heir, and the avenue to social honor consisted in affiliation with a genteel fraternity in a distinguished college, formerly with a distinguished sect (for instance, Presbyterian, in whose churches in New York one could find soft cushions and fans in the pews). At the present time, affiliation with a distinguished club is essential above all else. In addition, the kind of home is important (in "the street" which in middle-sized cities is almost never lacking) and the kind of dress and sport. Only recently descent from the Pilgrim fathers, from Pocahontas and other Indian ladies, et cetera has become important. This is not the place for a more detailed treatment. There are masses of translating bureaus and agencies of all sorts concerned with reconstructing the pedigrees of the plutocracy. All these phenomena, often highly grotesque, belong in the broad field of the Europeanization of American "society."

In the past and up to the very present, it has been a characteristic precisely of the specifically American democracy that it did *not* constitute a formless sand heap of individuals, but rather a buzzing complex of strictly exclusive, yet voluntary associations. Not so long ago these associations still did not recognize the prestige of birth and *inherited* wealth, of the office and educational diploma; at least they recognized these things to such a low degree as has only very rarely been the case in the rest of the world. Yet, even so, these associations were far from accepting anybody with open arms as an equal. To be sure, fifteen years ago an American farmer would not have led his guest past a plowing farmhand (American born!) in the field without making his guest "shake hands" with the worker after formally introducing them.

Formerly, in a typical American club nobody would remember that the two members, for instance, who play billiards once stood in the relation of boss and clerk. Here equality of gentlemen prevailed absolutely. This was not always the case in the German-American clubs. When asking young German merchants in New York (with the best Hanseatic names) why they all strove to be admitted to an American club instead of the very nicely furnished German one, they answered that their (German-American) bosses would play billiards with them occasionally, however not without making them realize that they (the bosses) thought themselves to be "very nice" in doing so. To be sure, the American worker's wife accompanying the trade unionist to lunch had completely accommodated herself in dress and behavior, in a somewhat plainer and more awkward fashion, to the middle class lady's model.

He who wished to be fully recognized in this democracy, in whatever position, had not only to conform to the conventions of middle class society, the very strict men's fashions included, but as a rule he had to be able to show that he had succeeded in gaining admission by ballot to one of the sects, clubs, or fraternal societies recognized as sufficiently legitimate, no matter what kind. And he had to maintain himself in the society by proving himself to be a gentleman. The parallel in Germany consists in the importance of the *Couleur*[5] and the commission of an officer of the reserve for *commercium* [commercial exchange] and *connubium* [intermarriage], and the great status significance of qualifying to give satisfaction by duel. The thing is the same, but the direction and material consequence characteristically differ.

He who did not succeed in joining was no gentleman; he who despised doing so, as was usual among Germans, had to take the hard road, and especially so in business life. But note above. Entry into an American club (in school or later) is always the decisive moment for the loss of German nationality.

However, as mentioned above, we shall not here analyze the social significance of these conditions, which are undergoing a profound transformation. First, we are interested in the fact that the modern position of the secular clubs and societies with recruitment by ballot is largely the product of a process of *secularization*. Their position is derived from the far more exclusive importance of the prototype of these voluntary associations, to wit, the sects. They stem, indeed, from the sects in the homeland of genuine Yankeedom, the North Atlantic states. Let us recall, first, that the universal and equal franchise within American democracy (of the Whites! for Ne-

---

5. Student fraternity, comparable to a "Greek letter society."

groes and all mixtures have, even today, no de facto franchise) and likewise the "separation of state and church" are only achievements of the recent past, beginning essentially with the nineteenth century. Let us remember that during the colonial period in the central areas of New England, especially in Massachusetts, full citizenship status in the church congregation was the precondition for full citizenship in the state (besides some other prerequisites). The religious congregation indeed determined admission or non-admission to political citizenship status.[6]

The decision was made according to whether or not the person had **testified** to his religious qualification through conduct, in the broadest meaning of the word, as was the case among all Puritan sects. The Quakers in Pennsylvania were not in any lesser way masters of that state until some time before the War of Independence. This was actually the case, though *formally* they were not the only full political citizens. They were political masters only by virtue of extensive gerrymandering.

The tremendous social significance of admission to full enjoyment of the rights of the sectarian congregation, especially the privilege of being admitted to the *Lord's Supper*, worked among the sects in the direction of breeding that ascetist professional ethic which was adequate to modern capitalism during the period of its origin. It can be demonstrated that everywhere, including Europe, the religiosity of the ascetist sects has for several centuries worked in the same way as has been illustrated by the personal experiences mentioned above for [the case of] America.

When focusing on the religious background of these Protestant sects, we find in their literary documents, especially among those of the Quakers and Baptists up to and throughout the seventeenth century, again and again jubilation over the fact that the sinful "children of the world" distrust one another in business but that they have confidence in the religiously determined righteousness of the pious.

Hence, they give credit and deposit their money only with the pious, and they make purchases in their stores because there, and there alone, they are given honest and *fixed prices*. As is known, the Baptists have always claimed to have first raised this price policy to a principle. In addition to the Baptists, the Quakers raise the claim, as the following quotation shows, to which Mr. Eduard Bernstein drew my attention at the time:

> But it was not only in matters which related to the law of the land where the primitive members held their words and engagements sacred. This trait was remarked to be true of them in their concerns of trade. On their first appearance as a society, they suffered as tradesmen because others, displeased with the peculiarity of their manners, withdrew their custom from their shops. But in a little time the great outcry against them was that they got the trade of the country into their hands. This outcry arose in part from a strict exemption of all commercial agreements between them and others and *because they never asked two prices for the commodities they sold.*

---

6.   In the colony of Massachusetts the church was formally a completely autonomous corporation. It admitted, however, only citizens for membership. On the other hand, affiliation with the church was a prerequisite of citizenship. . . .

The view that the gods bless with riches the man who pleases them, through sacrifice or through his kind of conduct, was indeed diffused all over the world. However, the Protestant sects consciously brought this idea into connection with this kind of religious conduct, according to the principle of early capitalism: "Honesty is the best policy." This connection is found, although not quite exclusively, among these Protestant sects, but with this continuity and consistency it is found *only* among them.

The whole typically middle class ethic was from the beginning common to all ascetic sects and conventicles, and it is identical with the ethic practiced by the sects in America up to the very present. The Methodists, for example, held to be forbidden:

(1) To make words when buying and selling ("haggling").
(2) To trade with commodities before the custom tariff has been paid on them.
(3) To charge rates of interest higher than the law of the country permits.
(4) 'To gather treasures on earth' (meaning the transformation of investment capital into 'funded wealth').
(5) To borrow without being sure of one's ability to pay back the debt.
(6) Luxuries of all sorts.

But it is not only this ethic, already discussed in detail [7] which goes back to the early beginnings of asceticist sects. Above all, the social premiums, the means of discipline, and, in general, the whole organizational basis of Protestant sectarianism with all its ramifications reach back to those beginnings. The survivals in contemporary America are the derivatives of a religious regulation of life which once worked with penetrating efficiency. Let us, in a brief survey, clarify the nature of these sects and the mode and direction of their operation.

Within Protestantism the principle of the "believer's church" first emerged distinctly among the Baptists in Zürich in 1523–24. This principle restricted the congregation to "true" Christians; hence, it meant a voluntary association of really sanctified people segregated from the world. . . .

In Protestantism the external and internal conflict of the two structural principles—of the "church" as a compulsory association for the administration of grace, and of the "sect" as a voluntary association of religiously qualified persons—runs through the centuries from Zwingli [1484–1531] to Kuyper [1837–1920] and Stöcker [1835–1909]. Here we merely wish to consider those consequences of the voluntarist principle which are practically important in their influence upon conduct. In addition, we recall merely that the decisive idea of keeping the Lord's Supper pure, and therefore excluding unsanctified persons, led also to a way of treating church discipline among those denominations which failed to form sects. It was

---

7.   In *The Protestant Ethic and the Spirit of Capitalism.*

especially the predestinarian Puritans who, in effect, approached the discipline of the sects.

The central social significance of the Lord's Supper for the Christian communities is evidenced in this. For the sects themselves, the idea of the purity of the sacramental communion was decisive at the very time of their origin. Immediately the first consistent voluntarist, Browne, in his "Treatise of Reformation without tarying for anie" (presumably 1582), emphasized the compulsion to hold communion at the Lord's Supper with "wicked men" as the main reason for rejecting Episcopalianism and Presbyterianism. The Presbyterian church struggled in vain to settle the problem. . . .

The entire church history of New England is filled with struggles over such questions: who was to be admitted to the sacraments (or, for instance, as a godfather), whether the children of non-admitted persons could be baptized (even the Brownist petition to King James of 1603 protested against this), under what clauses the latter could be admitted, and similar questions. The difficulty was that not only was the worthy person allowed to receive the Lord's Supper, but he *had* to receive it. Hence, if the believer doubted his own worth and decided to stay away from the Lord's Supper, the decision did not remove his sin. The congregation, on the other hand, was jointly responsible to the Lord for keeping unworthy and especially reprobated persons away from communion, for purity's sake. Thus the congregation was jointly and especially responsible for the administration of the sacrament by a worthy minister in a state of grace. . . .

Where the [congregations] were too large for this, either conventicles were formed, as in Pietism, or the members were organized in groups, which, in turn, were the bearers of church discipline, as in Methodism. The extraordinarily strict moral discipline of the self-governing congregation constituted [a further] principle. This was unavoidable because of the interest in the purity of the sacramental community (or, as among the Quakers, the interest in the purity of the community of prayer). The discipline of the asceticist sect was, in fact, far more rigorous than the discipline of any church. In this respect, the sect resembles the monastic order. The sect discipline is also analogous to monastic discipline in that it established the principle of the novitiate.[8] In contrast to the principles of the official Protestant churches, persons expelled because of moral offenses were often denied all intercourse with the members of the congregation. The sect thus invoked an absolute boycott against them, which included business life. Occasionally the sect avoided any relation with non-brethren except in cases of absolute necessity. And the sect placed disciplinary power predominantly into the hands of laymen. No spiritual authority could assume the community's joint responsibility before God. The weight of the lay elders was very great even among the Presbyterians. However, the Independents, and even more, the Baptists signified a struggle against the domination of the community by theologians. In exact correspondence this struggle led naturally to the

---

8.   In all probability among all sects there existed a period of probation. Among the Methodists, for example, it lasted for six months.

clericalization of the lay members, who now took over the functions of moral control through self-government, admonition, and possible excommunication. The domination of laymen in the church found its expression, in part, in the quest for freedom of the layman to preach (liberty of prophesying). In legitimizing this demand, reference was made to the conditions of the early Christian community. This demand was not only very shocking to the Lutheran idea of the pastoral office but also to the Presbyterian idea of God's order. The domination of laymen, in part, found its expression in an opposition to any professional theologian and preacher. Only charisma, neither training nor office, should be recognized.[9]

The Quakers have adhered to the principle that in the religious assembly anyone could speak, but he alone should speak who was moved by the spirit. Hence no professional minister exists at all. To be sure, today this is, in all probability, nowhere radically effected. The official "legend" is that members who, in the experience of the congregation, are especially accessible to the spirit during service are seated upon a special bench opposite the congregation. In profound silence the people wait for the spirit to take possession of one of them (or of some other member of the congregation). But during service in a Pennsylvania college, unfortunately and against my hopes, the spirit did not take hold of the plainly and beautifully costumed old lady who was seated on the bench and whose charisma was so highly praised. Instead, undoubtedly by agreement, the spirit took hold of a brave college librarian who gave a very learned lecture on the concept of the "saint."

To be sure, other sects have not drawn such radical conclusions, or at least not for good. However, either the minister is not active principally as a "hireling," holding only honorific position, "or else he serves for voluntary honorific donations. [10] Again his ministerial service may be a secondary occupation and only for the refunding of his expenses;[11] or he can be dismissed at any time; or a sort of missionary organization prevails with itinerant preachers working only once in a while in the same "circuit," as is the case with Methodism. Where the office (in the traditional sense) and hence the theological qualification were maintained, such skill was considered as a mere technical and specialist prerequisite. However, the really decisive quality was the charisma of the state of grace, and the authorities were geared to discern it. . . .

Internally, among the sect members, the spirit of early Christian brotherliness prevailed, at least among the early Baptists and derived denominations; or at least brotherliness was demanded.[12] Among some sects it was considered taboo to call on the law courts.[13] In case of need, mutual aid was

---

9.   Already Smyth in Amsterdam demanded that when preaching the regenerate must not even have the Bible in front of him.
10.   The latter was demanded for all preachers in the Agreement of the People of 1 May 1649.
11.   Thus the local preachers of the Methodists.
12.   The Westminster Confession (XXVI, I) establishes the principle of *inner and external* obligation to help one another. The respective rules are numerous among all sects.
13.   The Methodists have often attempted to sanction the appeal to the secular judge by expulsion. On the other hand, in several cases, they have established authorities upon which one could call if debtors did not pay promptly.

obligatory. Naturally, *business* dealings with nonmembers were not inter-
dicted (except occasionally among wholly radical communities).

Yet it was self-understood that one preferred the brethren.With the
Methodists this is expressly prescribed. From the very beginning, one finds
the system of certificates (concerning membership and conduct), which
were given to members who moved to another place. The charities of the
Quakers were so highly developed that in consequence of the burdens in-
curred their inclination to propagandize was finally crippled. The cohesiveness of the congregations was so great that, with good reason, it is said
to be one of the factors determining New England settlements. In contrast
to the South, New England settlements were generally compact and, from
the beginning, strongly urban in character.[14]

It is obvious that in all these points the modern functions of American sects
and sectlike associations, as described in the beginning of this essay, are revealed as straight derivatives, rudiments, and survivals of those conditions
which once prevailed in all asceticist sects and conventicles. Today they are de-
caying. Testimony for the sectarian's immensely exclusive "pride in caste" has
existed from the very beginning.[15]

Now, what part of this whole development was and is actually decisive
for our problem? Excommunication in the Middle Ages also had political
and civic consequences. Formally this was even harsher than where sect
freedom existed. Moreover, in the Middle Ages only Christians could be
full citizens. During the Middle Ages it was also possible to proceed
through the disciplinary powers of the church against a bishop who would
not pay his debts, and, as [the historian of the Middle Ages] Aloys Schulte
[1857–1941], has beautifully shown, this possibility gave the bishop a credit
rating over and above a secular prince. Likewise, the fact that a Prussian
Lieutenant was subject to discharge if he was incapable of paying off debts
provided a higher credit rating for him. And the same held for the German
fraternity student. Oral confession and the disciplinary power of the
church during the Middle Ages also provided the means to enforce church
discipline effectively. Finally, to secure a legal claim, the opportunity provided by the oath was exploited to secure excommunication of the debtor.

In all these cases, however, the forms of behavior that were favored or tabooed through such conditions and means differed totally from those
which Protestant asceticism bred or suppressed. With the lieutenant, for instance, or the fraternity student, and probably with the bishop as well, the
enhanced credit rating certainly did not rest upon the breeding of personal
qualities suitable for *business*; and following up this remark directly: even
though the effects in all three cases were intended to have the same direction, they were worked out in quite different ways. The medieval, like the
Lutheran church discipline, first, was vested in the hands of the ministerial

---

14.   Doyle, in his work which we have repeatedly cited [see *PE*, ch. IV, note 10], ascribes the indus-
      trial character of New England, in contrast to the agrarian colonies, to this factor.

15.   Cf., for example, Doyle's comments about the status conditions in New England, where the fami-
      lies bearing old religious literary tradition, not the "propertied classes," formed the aristocracy.

officeholder; secondly, this discipline worked—as far as it was effective at all—through authoritarian means; and, thirdly, it punished and placed premiums upon concrete *individual* acts.

The church discipline of the Puritans and of the sects was vested, first, at least in part and often wholly, in the hands of laymen. Secondly, it worked through the necessity of one's having to hold one's own; and, thirdly, it bred or, if one wishes, selected *qualities.* The last point is the most important one.

The member of the sect (or conventicle) had to have qualities of a certain kind in order to enter the community circle. Being endowed with these qualities was important for the development of rational modern capitalism, as has been shown in the first essay.[16] In order to hold his own in this circle the member had to *prove* repeatedly that he was endowed with these qualities. They were constantly and continuously bred in him. For, like his bliss in the beyond, his whole social existence in the here and now depended upon his "testifying" to his belief. The Catholic confession of sins was, to repeat, by comparison a means of *relieving* the person from the tremendous internal pressure under which the sect member in his conduct was constantly held.

According to all experience there is no stronger means of breeding traits than through the necessity of holding one's own in the circle of one's associates. The continuous and inconspicuous ethical discipline of the sects was, therefore, related to authoritarian church discipline as rational breeding and selection are related to ordering and forbidding.

In this as in almost every other respect, the Puritan sects are the most specific bearers of the inner-worldly form of asceticism. Moreover, they are the most consistent and, in a certain sense, the only consistent antithesis to the universalist Catholic Church—a compulsory organization for the administration of grace. The Puritan sects put the most powerful individual interest of social self-esteem in the service of this breeding of traits. Hence *individual* motives and personal self-interests were also placed in the service of maintaining and propagating the "middle class" Puritan ethic, with all its ramifications. This is absolutely decisive for its penetrating and for its powerful effect.

To repeat, it is not the ethical *doctrine* of a religion, but that form of ethical conduct upon which *premiums* are placed that matters. Such psychological rewards operate through the form and the condition of the respective goods of salvation. And such conduct constitutes "one's" specific "ethos" in the sociological sense of the word. For Puritanism, that conduct was a certain methodical, rational way of life which—given certain conditions—paved the way for the "spirit" of modern capitalism. The premiums were placed upon "testifying" oneself before God in the sense of attaining salvation—which is found in *all* Puritan denominations—and "testifying" oneself before men in the sense of socially holding one's own within the Puritan sects. Both aspects were mutually supplementary and operated in the same

---

16.   *The Protestant Ethic and the Spirit of Capitalism.*

direction. They helped to set free the "spirit" of modern capitalism—that is, its specific *ethos*: the ethos of the modern *middle classes*.

The ascetic conventicles and sects formed one of the most important historical foundations of modern "individualism." Their radical break away from patriarchal and authoritarian bondage,[17] as well as their way of interpreting the statement that one owes more obedience to God than to man, were especially important.

Finally, in order to understand the nature of these ethical effects, a comparative remark is required. In the *guilds* of the Middle Ages there was frequently a control of the general ethical standard of the members similar to that exercised by the discipline of the ascetic Protestant sects. But the unavoidable difference in respect to the effects of guild and of sect upon the economic conduct of the individual is obvious.

The guild united members of the same occupation; hence it united *competitors*. It did so in order to limit competition as well as the rational striving for profit which operated through competition. The guild trained for "civic" virtues and, in a certain sense, was the bearer of middle class "rationalism" (a point which will not be discussed here in detail). The guild accomplished this through a "subsistence policy" [market-restrictive policies designed to guarantee its economic foundation] and through [**economic**] **traditionalism**. In so far as guild regulation of the economy gained effectiveness, its practical results are well known.

The sects, on the other hand, united men through the selection and the breeding of ethically qualified *fellow believers*. Their membership was not based upon apprenticeship or upon the family relations of technically qualified members of an occupation. The sect controlled and regulated the members' conduct *exclusively* in the sense of formal *righteousness* and methodical asceticism. It was devoid of the purpose of a material subsistence policy which handicapped an expansion of the rational striving for profit. The capitalist success of a guild member undermined the spirit of the guild—as happened in England and France—and hence capitalist success was shunned. But the capitalist success of a sect brother, if legally attained, testified to his worth and his state of grace, and it raised the prestige and the propaganda chances of the sect. Such success was therefore welcome, as the several statements quoted above show.

The organization of free labor in guilds, in their Western medieval form, has certainly—very much against their intention—not only been a handicap but also a precondition for the capitalist organization of labor, which was, perhaps, indispensable. But the guild, of course, could not give birth to the modern middle class capitalist *ethos*. Only the methodical way of life of the ascetic sects could legitimate and put a halo around the economic "individualist" impulses of the modern capitalist ethos.

---

17.   The formation of congregations among ancient Jewry, just as among early Christians, worked, each in its own way, in the same direction (among Jewry the decline of the social significance of the SIB, as we shall see, is conditioned thereby, and Christianity during the early Middle Ages has had similar effects).

"CHURCHES" AND "SECTS" IN NORTH AMERICA: AN ECCLESIASTICAL SOCIOPOLITICAL SKETCH

From: *Sociological Theory* 3 (1985): 7–10. Translated by Colin Loader; slightly revised by Stephen Kalberg.

The considerable development of ecclesiastical communal life in the United States is a phenomenon that strikes all but the most superficial visitor.... The American who is "modern," or wants to be regarded as modern, becomes increasingly embarrassed when, in conversation with Europeans, the ecclesiastical character of his country is discussed. However, ...

In areas of the United States where the old relationships are still strong and where there is still only minor differentiation among purposive social groups *(Zweckverbände)*, the religious congregation (the initial and most universal community) still embraces almost all "social" interests in which the individual participates beyond his own doorstep. Not only instructional presentations, church suppers, Sunday school, and all imaginable charitable institutions, but also the most diverse athletic activities (football practice and the like), are offered by the church congregation; and time is allotted, circumstances permitting, for announcements of these activities at the end of the church service. A man, who in earlier times was publicly excluded for dishonorable conduct or who today is quietly dropped from the rolls, suffers therewith a kind of social boycott. He who stands outside of the church has no social "connection." The guarantee of *social* qualities which is included in church membership is still important. ...

The basic premise *of all* varieties of ascetic Protestantism (radical Calvinist, Baptists, Mennonites, Quakers, Methodists and the ascetic branch of continental Pietism), that only proving oneself in life, especially in the activity to which one is called *(Berufsarbeit)*, provides the certainty of rebirth and exculpation, always forces one down the same path—the "proven" Christian is the person who is testifying in his "calling" *(Berufsmensch)*, particularly the businessman who from a capitalist standpoint is capable. Christianity of this stamp was one of the prime educators of the "capitalist" person. As early as the seventeenth century Quaker writers rejoiced over the visible grace of God, which also brought the "children of the world" as customers to Quaker businesses, because they could be certain to find in the latter reliable service, fixed prices, etc. And it is the constitution of the religious communities as "sects" in the specific sense of the word, then, that played and (as stated)—even today, a certain extent still plays—a role in this "pedagogical" achievement.

And just what is this meaning [of the word "sect"]? And accordingly what is a "sect" in contrast to a "church" within the sphere of Western Christianity?

* * *

Neither the simple limitation of the number of followers—the Baptists are one of the largest of all Protestant denominations—nor the statutory feature of a lack of "recognition," i.e., privileged position, for the church by the state—which in America is shared by all denominations—can be considered decisive *in themselves*. Of course we know that the *size* of a social group exercises the most decisive influence on its internal structure. And the canonical limitation of the size of the unity, the congregation, to such dimensions that all members *personally* know one another and, therefore, can judge and supervise their "probation" reciprocally has always been a fundamental Baptist principle. A form of this principle was also found in genuine Methodism in the cultivation of the so-called class meetings in which members practice (originally weekly) a kind of reciprocal examination through confessions, just as it was in the small communities *(ecclesiolae)* of Pietism.

One needs only to see the Berlin Cathedral to know that the most consequential form of the Protestant "spirit" is alive not in [this] caesaro-papist state hall but rather in the small chapels of the Quakers and the Baptists, which lack such mystical ornamentation. Conversely, the considerable expansion of the followers of Methodism, which exhibits in its various forms a singular mixture of "church-like" and "sect-like" principles, clearly has fostered the unquestionable predominance of the former today. The basic fact of smallness in and by itself stands in close connection with the sect's inner "essence," but yet *is not* that essence itself. With regards to the church-state relationship, naturally the "churches" and "sects" share the factual absence of state "recognition." The real distinction between the two types likewise is that what for the "churches" (Lutheran and Reformed as well as Catholic) is "chance" and in its entire structure *contrary* to principle, conversely for the "sect" constitutes an emanation of a religious idea. The "separation of church and state" is a dogmatic axiom for all of the sects arising from the great, popular Baptist movement and is at least a structural principle for the radical pietistic communities (Calvinist Independents and radical Methodists).

A church sees itself as an "institution" *(Anstalt)*, a kind of divine endowed foundation *(Fideikomissstiftung)* for the salvation of individual souls who are *born into it* and are the *object* of its efforts, which are bound to the "office" in principle. Conversely, a "sect" (the terminology used here has been created *ad hoc* and would not be used by the sects in discussing themselves) is a voluntary community of individuals purely on the basis of their religious *qualification*. The individual is *admitted* by virtue of a voluntary resolution by both parties. The historically given forms of the religious communal life (here as always) are not examples that perfectly conform to the conceptual dichotomy.

One always has to ask simply in what *respect* a concrete denomination corresponds to or approaches one "type" or the other. However, one can always perceive the fundamental contrast in the basic ideas. Whereas the baptismal ceremony itself, exclusively on the basis of the voluntary resolution of *adult* followers, was the adequate symbol for the "sect-like" character of the Baptist community, the intrinsic falsity of the "confirmation" (whose postponement beyond the childhood years even Stoecker is known to advocate) demonstrates the intrinsic contradiction of the allegiance, which is only formally "spontaneous," to the structure of our [Lutheran and Catholic] "churches." The latter, as such, can basically never go beyond the not-so-"naive" peasant conception: the priest, as administrator of the divine foundation, must be *more* faithful than the rest of the congregation and also must be capable of such due to a special dispensation of grace. The "universalism" of the "churches" allows their light to shine on both the righteous and the unrighteous. Only a rebellion against authority that is expressed as a public and obstinate impenitence will lead to "excommunication."

The community of the "chosen few" remains the "invisible church," whose composition is known only to God. The "purity" of its membership is a vital question for the genuine "sect." In the formative period of the pietistic sects, the driving impulse was the continuous deep fear of having to participate in the Lord's Supper with a "reprobate," or even to receive it from the hand of a reprobate, an official "hireling," whose conduct did not bear the sign of being chosen. The "sects" see themselves as a religious "elite," which sees the "invisible church" displayed in plain sight in the community of "proven" members. The intervention of the religiously unqualified into the sects' internal affairs (especially every relationship undertaken by the holders of worldly power) was necessarily intolerable to them. The principle that "one must obey God above men," whose various interpretations and explanations in a certain sense incorporate the whole cultural mission of Western European Christianity, acquires here its specific anti-authoritarian character.

From: Pp. 284–86 in *Max Weber: Readings and Commentary on Modernity*, edited by Stephen Kalberg. Translated by Colin Loader; revised by Stephen Kalberg (Oxford: Blackwell, 2005).

The exclusive appraisal of a person purely in terms of the religious qualities evidenced in his conduct necessarily prunes feudal and dynastic romanticism from its roots. To be sure, the aversion to all kinds of idolatry was neither confined to the "sects" in our technical sense, nor has it been immediately characteristic of *all* communities constituted along the lines of the sect. It is much more an attribute of the religiosity whose essence is *ascetic* and, in the case of the Calvinist Puritans, is a direct consequence of the idea of predestination. In light of the dreadful earnestness of this idea of predestination, all offering of "God's grace" by earthly institutions had to crumble into nothing but a blasphemous swindle.

To be sure, however, this frame of mind only reached its fullest expression in the naturally anti-authoritarian climate of the sects. If, by their strict avoidance of all oaths of allegiance that were courtly [feudal] or stemmed from court life, the Quakers took upon themselves not only the Crown of Martyrs but also the much heavier burden of everyday derision, then this stand came from the conviction that those oaths of allegiance should be made to God alone and that it is an insult to His majesty to accord them to people. The unconditional rejection of all such demands of the state that went "against one's conscience" and the demand that the state recognize "freedom of conscience," as the inalienable right of the individual were conceivable from the position of the sect only as an overt *religious* claim. This claim reached its logical conclusion in the Quaker ethic, one of whose guiding principles was that what is duty for one can be forbidden to another, when the voice of one's own carefully explored *conscience* implied engaging in the action for the former and abstaining from it for the latter. The autonomy of the individual [in the sect] is anchored not to indifference but to religious positions; and the struggle against all types of "authoritarian" arbitrariness is elevated to the level of a religious duty.

In the time of its heroic youth [in the sects], this individualism produced an eminent power to form groups. The "church's" universalism, which goes hand in hand with ethical moderation, stands in contrast to the sect's propagandism, which is paired with ethical rigorism. Again, the latter reaches its logical conclusion in the Quaker ethic with the idea that God can spread his "inner light" also to those upon whom the Gospel has never been urged. The religiously qualified individual, rather than objectified contracts and traditions, is seen as the bearer of a revelation which continues eternally without ever being attained. The "invisible" church, therefore, is *larger* than the "visible" sect and its task involves assembling its members. . . . The sect [on the other hand], is a naturally "particularistic" organization, but its religiosity is one of the most unique and viable forms completely unlike all traditional, "popular" religiosity. . . .

* * *

[The sects] . . . alone have been able, on the foundation of Protestantism, to instill an intensity of interest in religion in the broad middle class—and especially modern workers—that otherwise is found only, though in the form of a bigoted fanaticism, among traditional peasants. And here the significance of the sects expands beyond the religious realm. American democracy, for example, acquired its own dynamic form and unique imprint exclusively from them.

On the one hand, the idea that the individual, on the basis of the religious qualifications bestowed by God, decided on his salvation status exclusively on his own was important. That is, magical sacraments were devoid of utility for one's salvation; only the believer's practical conduct mattered: his behavior "proved and testified" to his faith and alone provided a *sign* that he stood on the road to salvation. On the other hand, this very notion—the individual could testify to his salvation through his righteous behavior—formulated the foundation for the social knitting together of the congregation. Indeed, the tremendous flood of social groupings, which penetrate all corners of American life, are constituted according to this "sect" model.

Those who imagine "democracy" to be rooted in a mass of people fragmented into atoms, such as our [German] Romantics love to do, are making a fundamental mistake—at least as concerns the American democracy. "Atomization" results far more from bureaucratic rationalism than from democracy; hence it will not be eliminated by an imposition from above of "stratified formations," as the Romantics hope. American society in its genuine form—and here my remarks explicitly concern also the "middle" and "lower" strata—was never such a sandpile, nor even a building where everyone who sought to enter found open, undiscriminating doors. Rather, it was, and is, saturated with "exclusivities" of all sorts. Wherever this earlier situation still remains, the individual firmly acquires a foundation under his feet, at the university and in business, only when he succeeds in being voted into a *social organization* (earlier almost without exception a church, today an organization of a different sort) and manages, within this organization, to *hold his own*. The old "sect spirit" holds sway with relentless effect in the internal character of these organizations.

Sects are "artefacts" of "societies" *(Gesellschaften)* rather than "communities" *(Gemeinschaften)*, in the terminology of Ferdinand Tonnies, In other words, they are based upon neither "tender and sentimental" feelings nor do they strive to cultivate "sentimental values" [see pp. 194–5, n. 34]. Rather, by integrating himself into them, the individual seeks in these organizations to hold *his own*. Lacking totally is the undifferentiated "sentimentality" and companionability commonly found in a spontaneous manner among peasants—without which, as Germans believe, a sense of community cannot be cultivated. Instead, the cool *matter-of-factness* characteristic of association promotes the precise ordering of the individual into the instrumental task pursued by the group, whether a football team or a political party.

Nonetheless, this integrating of the individual in no way signifies a weakening of the necessity for the individual constantly to be concerned to hold his own. On the contrary, his task *to "testify himself"* actually becomes directly incumbent upon him only at the point when he moves *inside* the group and into the circle of his fellows. For this reason, the social organization to which the individual belongs never becomes something *organic*—that is, a mystical total essence floating above him and enveloping him. Rather, in a manner entirely conscious to the individual, social organizations *always* become mechanisms for the achievement of his own material and ideal *goals*.

PREFATORY REMARKS TO COLLECTED ESSAYS IN THE SOCIOLOGY OF RELIGION (1920)

From: "Vorbemerkung". Pp. 1–16 in *Gesammelte Aufsätze Zur Religionssoziologie I*. Translated by Stephen Kalberg. Tübingen: Mohr/Siebeck, 1972.

Any heir of modern European culture will, unavoidably and justifiably, address universal-historical[1] themes with a particular question in mind: What combination of circumstances led in the West, and only in the West, to the appearance of a variety of cultural phenomena that stand—at least as we like to imagine—in a historical line of development with *universal* significance and empirical validity?

Science, developed to the stage that we today recognize as "valid," exists only in the West. Empirical knowledge, reflection on the world and the problems of life, philosophical and theological wisdom of the deepest kind, extraordinarily refined knowledge and observation—all this has existed outside the West, above all in India, China, Babylon, and Egypt. Yet a fully developed systematic theology appeared only in Hellenic-influenced Christianity (even though some beginnings were apparent in Islam and a few sects in India). And despite empirical knowledge, Babylonian and every other type of astronomy lacked a mathematical foundation (rendering the development, in particular, of Babylonian astronomy all the more astonishing), which would be provided only later by the Greeks.

A further product of the Hellenic mind, the idea of **rational** "proof," was absent from geometry in India. This mind also first created mechanics and physics. Moreover, although the natural sciences in India were quite well developed as concerns observation, they lacked the rational experiment, which was essentially a product of the Renaissance (although beginnings can be found in the ancient world). The modern laboratory was also missing in the natural sciences developed in India. For this reason, medicine in India, which was highly developed in terms of empirical technique, never

---

1. Stemming originally from the German polymath Johann Gottfried von Herder (1744–1803), "universal history" (*Universalgeschichte*) came to refer in the nineteenth century to a mode of German historiography that avoided specialist studies and instead attempted to offer a synthesizing portrait of an entire historical epoch or area of culture. See, for example, Theodor Mommsen on ancient Rome, Jacob Burckhardt on the Italian Renaissance, and Ernst Troeltsch on Christianity. The term does not imply "world history" [sk].

acquired a biological and, especially, a biochemical foundation. A rational chemistry was absent from all regions outside the West.

The scholarly writing of history in China, which was very advanced, lacked the rigor of Thucydides [*ca.* 460–400 B.C.E.].[2] Precursors of Machiavelli [1489–1527] existed in India, yet all Asian theorizing on the state omitted a systematic approach comparable to Aristotle's, as well as rational[3] concepts in general. A rational jurisprudence based on rigorous juridical models and modes of thinking of the type found in Roman law, and the Western law indebted to it, was absent outside the West, despite all beginnings in India (School of Mimamsa)[4] and the comprehensive codification of law in the Near East especially—and in spite of all the books on law written in India and elsewhere. A form of law similar to Canon law cannot be found outside the West.

Similar conclusions must be drawn for art. The musical ear, apparently, was developed to a more refined degree among peoples outside the West than in the West to this day; or, at any rate, not less so. The most diverse sorts of polyphonic music have expanded across the globe, as did also the simultaneous playing of a number of instruments and singing in the higher pitches. All of the West's rational tone intervals were also widely calculated and known elsewhere. However, unique to the West were many musical innovations. Among them were rational, harmonic music (both counterpoint and harmony); formation of tone on the basis of three triads and the major third;[5] and the understanding of chromatics and enharmonics since the Renaissance harmonically and in rational form (rather than by reference to distance). Others were the orchestra with the string quartet as its core and the organization of ensembles of wind instruments; the bass accompaniment; and the system of musical notation (which made possible the composition and rehearsal of modern works of music and their very survival over time). Still other innovations were sonatas, symphonies, and operas (although organized music, onomatopoeia, chromatics, and alteration of tones have existed in the most diverse music as modes of expression). Finally, the West's basic instruments were the means for all this: the organ, piano, and violin.

[The situation is similar in architecture.] As a means of decoration, pointed arches existed outside the West, both in the ancient world and in Asia. Presumably, the juxtaposition of pointed arches and cross-arched

---

2. Thucydides of ancient Greece is best known for his history of the Peloponnesian War (431–404 B.C.E.). Weber refers to his attempt to record events and occurrences as they empirically took place; hence he interviewed direct observers, avoided speculative interpretations and reference to supernatural forces ("the will of the gods"), and sought to offer an "objective" account. He was the first historian to do so [sk].

3. "Rational" here implies to Weber "rigor" and a "systematic aspect" (as also in the next paragraph and throughout). The term does not imply "better." See Kalberg, (1980) [sk].

4. A religious-philosophical school in India that developed out of the pre-Hindu Vedas (seventh century B.C.E.). It emphasized that salvation could be attained though the performance of certain ritualized good works [sk].

5. "Major third" (*harmonische Terz*) refers to the distance on the piano keyboard from note "c" to "e." Use of these notes together formed a harmonious sound that was used frequently in classical composition [sk].

vaults was not unknown in the Middle East. However, the rational utilization of the Gothic vault as a means to distribute thrust and to arch over variously formed spaces and, above all, as a principle of construction for large monumental buildings and as the foundation for a *style* that incorporated sculpture and painting, as was created in the Middle Ages—all this was missing outside the West. A solution to the weight problem introduced by domes was also lacking outside the West, even though the technical basis for its solution was taken from the Middle East. Every type of "classical" **rationalization** [6] of the entire art world—as occurred in painting through the rational use of both linear and spatial perspective—was also lacking outside the West, where it began with the Renaissance.

Printing existed in China. Yet a printed literature intended *only* to be printed and made possible exclusively through printing—"daily newspapers" and "periodicals," mainly—originated only in the West.

Universities of all possible types existed also outside the West (China and the Islamic world), even universities that look externally similar to those in the West, especially to Western academies. A rational and systematic organization into scientific disciplines, however, with trained and specialized professionals (*Fachmenschentum*), existed only in the West. This becomes especially evident if these disciplines are viewed from the vantage point of whether they attained the culturally dominant significance they have achieved in the West today.

Above all, the cornerstone of the modern state and modern economy—specialized *civil servants*—arose only in the West. Only precursors of this stratum appeared outside the West. It never became, in any sense, as constitutive for the social order as occurred in the West. The "civil servant," of course, even the civil servant who performs specialized tasks, appeared in various societies, even in ancient times. However, only in the modern West is our entire existence—the foundational political, technical, and economic conditions of our being—absolutely and inescapably bound up in the casing (*Gehäuse*) of an *organization* of specially trained civil servants. No nation and no epoch has come to know state civil servants in the way that they are known in the modern West, namely, as persons trained in technical, commercial, and, above all, legal areas of knowledge who are the social carriers of the most important everyday functions of social life.

[And what about the state?] The organization of political and social groups on the basis of *status* has existed historically on a broad scale. Yet the *Ständestaat* in the Western sense—*rex et regnum*—has appeared only in the West.[7] Moreover, parliaments of periodically elected "representatives," with demagogues and party leaders held responsible as "ministers" to parliamen-

---

6. "Rationalization" can be equated with "systematization." See the article cited in note 3 [sk].
7. A succinct translation of these German and Latin phrases does not capture that which Weber wishes to convey here, namely, the manner in which the Western *Ständestaat* involved, uniquely, a precarious balancing of powers between the ruler, a cohesive aristocracy, and powerful, municipally based political actors. Hence, it implied temporary alliances and a rudimentary division of powers, an arrangement that was a precursor to the division of powers in the modern constitutional state. See Weber, 1968, pp. 1085-87 [sk].

tary procedures, have come into existence only in the West. This remains the case even though "political parties," of course, in the sense of organizations oriented to the acquisition of political power and the exercise of influence on political policy, can be found throughout the world. The "state," in fact, as a political institution (*Anstalt*) operated according to a rationally enacted "constitution" and rationally enacted laws, and administered by civil servants possessing *specialized* arenas of competence and oriented to rules and "laws," has existed with these distinguishing features only in the West, even though rudimentary developments in these directions have crystallized elsewhere.

The same may be said of that most fateful power of our modern life: [modern] *capitalism.*

A "drive to acquire goods" has actually nothing whatsoever to do with capitalism, as little as has the "pursuit of profit," money, and the greatest possible gain. Such striving has been found, and is to this day, among waiters, physicians, chauffeurs, artists, prostitutes, corrupt civil servants, soldiers, thieves, crusaders, gambling casino customers, and beggars. One can say that this pursuit of profit exists among "all sorts and conditions of men" [Sir Walter Besant],[8] in all epochs and in all countries of the globe. It can be seen both in the past and in the present wherever the objective possibility for it somehow exists.

This naive manner of conceptualizing capitalism by reference to a "pursuit of gain" must be relegated to the kindergarten of cultural history methodology and abandoned once and for all. A fully unconstrained compulsion to acquire goods cannot be understood as synonymous with capitalism, and even less as its "spirit." On the contrary, capitalism *can* be identical with the *taming* of this irrational motivation, or at least with its rational tempering. Nonetheless, capitalism is distinguished by the striving for *profit*, indeed, profit is pursued in a rational, continuous manner in companies and firms, and then pursued *again and again*, as is *profitability*. There are no choices. If the entire economy is organized according to the rules of the open market, any company that fails to orient its activities toward the chance of attaining profit is condemned to bankruptcy.

* * *

Let us begin by *defining terms* in a manner more precise than often occurs. For us, a "capitalist" economic act involves first of all an expectation of profit based on the utilization of opportunities for *exchange*; that is, of (formally) *peaceful* opportunities for acquisition. Formal and actual acquisition through violence follows its own special laws and hence should best be placed, as much as one may recommend doing so, in a different cat-

---

8. The German editor, Johannes Winckelmann, attributes this phrase to the progressive English social critic, novelist, biographer, urban historian, and philanthropist, Sir Walter Besant (1836–1901). [sk].

egory.[9] Wherever capitalist acquisition is rationally pursued, action is oriented to *calculation* in terms of capital. What does this mean?

Such action is here oriented to a systematic utilization of skills or personal capacities on behalf of earnings in such a manner that, at the close of business transactions, the company's money *balances*, or "capital" (its earnings through transactions), exceed the estimated value of all production costs (and, in the case of a longer lasting company, *again and again* exceed costs). It is all the same whether goods entrusted to a traveling salesman are involved and he receives payment through barter, so that the closing calculation takes place in goods, or whether the assets of a large manufacturing corporation (such as buildings, machines, cash, basic materials, and—partly or entirely—manufactured goods) are weighed against its production costs. Decisive in both situations is that a *calculation* of earnings in money terms takes place, regardless of whether it is made on the basis of modern accounting methods or primitive, superficial procedures. Both at the beginning of the project and at the end there are specific calculations of balances. A starting balance is established and calculations are carried out before each separate transaction takes place; at every stage an instrumental assessment of the utility of potential transactions is calculated; and, finally, a concluding balance is calculated and the origin of "the profit" ascertained.

The beginning balance of the *commenda* transaction [see ch. 2, note 15] involves, for example, a designation of the amount of money agreed upon by both parties regarding what the relevant goods *should* be worth (assuming they have not already been given a monetary value). A final balance forms the estimate on the basis of which a distribution of profit and loss takes place. Calculation lies (as long as each case is rational) at the foundation of every single activity of the *commenda* partners. However, an actual exact accounting and appraisal may not exist, for on some occasions the transaction proceeds purely by reference to estimates or even on the basis of traditions and conventions. Indeed, such estimation appears in every form of capitalist enterprise even today wherever circumstances do not require more exact

---

9. As in regard to a number of other points, I am here also taking a position in opposition to our honorable master, Lujo Brentano [see *Die Anfänge des modernen Kapitalismus* (Munich: Akademie der Wissenschaften, 1916)]. We disagree primarily on terms, though also on substantive matters. It does not seem to me helpful to bring together under the same category heterogeneous factors, such as earning a living through seizing booty and earning a living through managing a factory. It appears to me even less helpful to designate every striving to acquire *money* (in contrast to other forms of acquisition) as a "spirit" of capitalism. If one refers to this "spirit" in this manner, the concept loses all precision; if one brings heterogeneous factors together under one category, it becomes impossible to clarify what is specific to Western capitalism vis-à-vis other forms of capitalism. "The money economy" and "capitalism" are also placed far too closely together in Georg Simmel's *Philosophie des Geldes* (1900) [*The Philosophy of Money*, translated by Tom Bottomore and David Frisby (London: Routledge & Kegan Paul, 1978)], to the detriment also of the substantive analysis. That which is *specific* to the West—the rational organization of work—moves strongly into the background in Werner Sombart's writings, above all in the more recent edition of his fine major work, *Der moderne Kapitalismus* [Leipzig: Duncker & Humblot (2nd edition), 1916–17]. Instead, placed in the foreground are development forces that have been effective throughout the world and not only in the West.

calculation. These points, however, relate only to the *degree* of rationality of capitalist acquisition.

Important for the formation of the *concept* of capitalism is only that economic action is decisively influenced by the *actual* orientation to a comparison of estimated monetary expenses with estimated monetary income, however primitive in form the comparison may be. Now in this sense we can see that, insofar as our documents on economies have reached into the distant past, "capitalism" and "capitalist" enterprises, at times with only a moderate degree of rationalization of capital accounting, have existed in *all* the world's civilizations.

In other words, "capitalism" and "capitalist" enterprises have been found in China, India, Babylon, Egypt, the ancient Mediterranean, and medieval Europe, as well as in the modern West. Not only entirely isolated enterprises existed in these civilizations; rather, also businesses are found completely oriented to the continuous appearance of new companies and to a continuity of "operations." This remained the situation even though trade, over long periods, did not become perpetual, as it did in the West; instead, it assumed the character of a series of separate enterprises. A business context—the development of different "branches" for business—congealed only gradually and only slowly influenced the behavior of the *large-scale* commercial traders. At any rate, the capitalist enterprise has been an enduring, highly universal, and ancient organization. Also capitalist businessmen, not only as occasional entrepreneurs but as persons oriented permanently to business, have been ancient, enduring, and highly universal figures.

* * *

The West, however, has given birth to types and forms of capitalism (as well as to directions for its unfolding) that have provided the foundation for the development of capitalism to an extent and significance unknown outside the West. Merchants have engaged in wholesale and retail trade, on a local as well as international scale, throughout the world. Businesses offering loans of every sort have existed widely, as have banks with the most diverse functions (although for the most part functions essentially similar to those of Western banks of the sixteenth century). Sea loans,[10] *commenda*, and *kommandit* [11] types of businesses and formal associations have been widespread. Wherever the financing of public institutions through *currency* has occurred,[12] financiers have appeared—in Babylon, ancient Greece, India, China, and ancient Rome. They have financed above all wars, piracy, and all types of shipping and construction projects; as entre-

---

10. The sea loan, which originated in Mediterranean antiquity and became used widely in the Western Middle Ages, was a response to the unusually high danger of shipping by sea and the attempt by borrowers (who had purchased the goods on credit) and creditors to distribute the risk of total loss: the borrower agreed to pay to the creditor an extremely high interest rate (perhaps 30 percent) in exchange for which the creditor assumed liability for the goods in the event of loss. See Weber, *General Economic History* (New Brunswick: Transaction Books, 1981), pp. 204–06 [sk].

11. A type of company that limits liability for owners in respect to both damage caused by faulty products and injuries suffered by employees [sk].

12. In contrast to barter [sk].

preneurs in colonies they have served the international policy goals of nations. In addition, these *adventure* capitalists have acquired plantations and operated them using slaves or (directly or indirectly) forced labor; they have leased land and the rights to use honorific titles; they have financed both the leaders of political parties standing for re-election and mercenaries for civil wars; and, finally, as "speculators" they have been involved in all sorts of money-raising opportunities.

This type of entrepreneur—the adventure capitalist—has existed throughout the world. With the exception of trade, credit, and banking businesses, his money-making endeavors have been mainly either of a purely irrational and speculative nature or of a violent character, such as the capture of booty. This has taken place either through warfare or the continuous fiscal exploitation of subjugated populations.

Promoter, adventure, colonial, and, as it exists in the West, modern finance capitalism can be characterized often, even today, in terms of these features. This becomes especially apparent whenever capitalism is oriented to warfare, although it holds even in periods of peace. Single (and only single) components of large-scale international commerce today, as in the past, approximate adventure capitalism.

In the *modern* era the West came to know an entirely different type of capitalism. Absent from all other regions of the globe, or existing only in preliminary developmental stages, this capitalism appeared side-by-side with adventure capitalism and took as its foundation the rational-capitalist[13] organization of (legally) *free labor*. With *coerced* labor, a certain degree of rational organization had been attained only on the plantations of antiquity and, to a very limited extent, on the ancient world's *ergasteria*.[14] An even lesser degree of rationality was reached in agricultural forced-labor enterprises generally, the workshops of medieval manors, and in manor-based cottage industries utilizing the labor of serfs at the dawning of the modern era [see pp. 377–79]. Outside the West, free labor has been found only occasionally. Even the existence of actual "cottage industries" has been documented with certainty only rarely outside the West. And the use of day laborers, which naturally can be found everywhere, did not lead to manufacturing and not at all to a rational, apprenticeship-style organization of skilled labor of the type practiced in the West's Middle Ages. This must be said despite a very few, very unusual exceptions, and even these diverged significantly from the modern Western organization of industrial work in companies (especially from those companies that, through support from the state, held market monopolies).

However, the rational organization of industrial companies and their orientation to *market* opportunities, rather than to political violence or to irratio-

---

13. Again, Weber is using "rational" in the sense of a systematic, organized, disciplined, and economically-efficient manner of organizing work [sk].

14. *Ergasteria* are shops, separate from the private residence, where workers perform their labor. They vary widely, from the bazaar, which combines the place of work and the place of sale, to the factory. Central in all cases is that an entrepreneur prescribes the conditions of work and pays wages. See Weber, *General Economic History*, pp. 119, 162 [sk].

nal speculation, does not constitute the only distinguishing mark of Western capitalism. The modern, rational organization of the capitalist industrial firm would not have been possible without two prior important developments: (1) the *separation of the household from the industrial company*, which absolutely dominates economic life today, and, connected closely to this development, (2) the appearance of rational *accounting*.

The spatial separation of the place of labor or sales from the place of residence can be also found elsewhere (in the Oriental bazaar and in the *ergasteria* of other cultures). Capitalist associations with accounting procedures separate from personal accounts existed in East Asia as well as in the Middle East and the ancient world. Nonetheless, compared to the modern situation in which company operations are fully independent, these examples show only very limited beginnings. This remained the case above all because the *internal* preconditions for independent business operation—rational *accounting* methods and a *legal* separation of company wealth from personal wealth—were either entirely absent or developed only to preliminary stages.[15] Instead, outside the West, industry-oriented endeavors tended to become simply one component of the feudal manor's *household* activities (the *oikos*). [The economic historian of antiquity Karl Johann] Rodbertus [1805–65] has already noted that all developments toward the *oikos* deviated distinctly from the route taken by capitalist activity in the West. Indeed, as he argues, and despite a number of apparent similarities, the *oikos* stood starkly in opposition to the Western pathway.[16]

* * *

All these particular aspects of Western capitalism, however, in the end acquired their present-day significance as a result of their connection to the capitalist organization of *work*. Even what one is inclined to call "commer-

15. Of course the contrast should not be understood as absolute. Rational, *permanent* businesses grew out of politically-oriented (above all tax farming-based [see ch. 2, note 16]) capitalism as early as antiquity in the Mediterranean and Middle East regions, although also in China and India. Moreover, their accounting, which is known to us only in miserable fragments, may have had a "rational" character. Finally, politically oriented "adventure" capitalism has been closely connected to rational, industrial capitalism with respect to the historical origin of modern *banks*, which for the most part originated out of businesses that were motivated by *political* and military considerations, even as late as the Bank of England [in 1694]. The contrast between the individualism of [its founder William] Paterson, for example, a typical "promoter," and the individualism of members of this Bank's board of trustees (which provided the distinguishing imprint on its long-term policies—the Bank very quickly became known as The Puritan Usurers of Grocers' Hall) ["promoter" and "Grocers' Hall" appear in English in the original] is characteristic of the close connection between politically oriented adventure capitalism and rational, industrial capitalism. Just as illustrative is the collapse, on the occasion of the South Sea Bubble [1720; see pp. 382–83; *General Economic History*, pp. 289–90], of the policies of this "most solid" Bank. In sum, the contrast between adventure and rational capitalism is of course a fluid one. Yet it is *there*. A rational organization of *work* was created as little by the titan promoters and financiers as—again, in general and with specific exceptions—by the typical carriers of finance and political capitalism: the Jews. Rather, the rational organization of *work* was created by (as an ideal type!) entirely different people. [See above, pp. 141–59].
16. Rodbertus created the term *oikos* for antiquity's large-scale household economies. To him, all economies of the ancient Mediterranean were *oikos* economies. See Weber, 1968, pp. 381–84, 1009–10; *Agrarian Sociology of Ancient Civilizations* (1976), pp. 42–43 [sk].

cialization"—the development of stocks and bonds and the systematization, through stock markets, of speculation—must be seen as taking place
in the context of a capitalist organization of labor. All this, even the development toward "commercialization," if it had been possible at all, would
never have unfolded to anywhere near the same proportion and dimension
if a capitalist-rational organization of work had been lacking. Hence, all of
these new factors would never have significantly influenced the social
structure and all those problems associated with it specific to the modern
West. Exact calculation, the foundation for everything else, is possible only
on the basis of *free* labor.[17]

And as the world outside the modern West has not known the rational
organization of work, it has also not known, and for this reason, rational *socialism*. Now, of course, just as history has experienced a full spectrum of
types of economies—ranging from those, on the one hand, oriented to city
development and city-organized food supply policies, mercantilism, the
social welfare policies instituted by princes, the rationing of goods, a thorough regulation of the economy, and protectionism—and on the other hand
to *laissez-faire* theories (also in China), the world has also known socialist
and communist economies of the most diverse sorts. State socialist (in [an-
cient] Egypt) and cartel-monopolistic versions of socialism can be found, as
can types of communism more rooted in (a) heterogeneous consumer organizations, (b) private sphere values of intimacy and the family, (c) religious
values, and (d) military values.

However (despite the existence everywhere at one time or another of
guilds and brotherhood corporations, various legal distinctions between
cities and provinces in the most diverse form, and cities that granted specific market advantages to particular groups), just as the concept of "citizen" is entirely missing except in the West and the concept of "bourgeoisie"
is completely absent outside the modern West, so also the notion of a "proletariat" as a *class* is absent. Indeed, it could not appear outside the West
precisely because a rational organization *of free labor* in *industrial enterprises*
was lacking. "Class struggles" between strata of creditors and debtors, between those who owned land and those who did not (whether serfs or ten-
ant sharecroppers), between persons with economic interests in commerce
and consumers or owners of land—all these conflicts have existed for centuries in various constellations. Yet even the struggles typical in the West's
medieval period between domestic industry entrepreneurs and their wage
workers [the putting-out system] are found elsewhere only in a rudimentary form. The modern opposition between large-scale industrialists, as
employers, and free workers paid a wage is completely lacking outside the
West. And thus a situation of the type known to modern socialism also
could not exist.

---

17. Weber discusses the inefficiencies of slave labor elsewhere. See, for example, *The Agrarian Sociology*, pp. 202–09, 357; *General Economic History*, p. 132 [sk].

* * *

Hence, for us, as we investigate the universal history of civilizations, and even if we proceed by reference exclusively to issues directly related to the economy, the central problem in the end *cannot* be the unfolding of capitalist activity everywhere and the various forms it took. That is, our concern cannot be whether it appeared more as adventure capitalism, commercial capitalism, or a capitalism oriented to the opportunities for profit offered by war, politics, and state administration. Rather, the central problem must ultimately involve the origin of *middle class* *industrial* capitalism with its rational organization of *free labor*. Or, rendered in the terms of cultural history: The central problem must ultimately concern the origin of the Western middle class and its particular features. Of course, this theme is closely interwoven with the question of the origin of the capitalist organization of labor. Yet it is naturally not exactly the same—for the simple reason that a "middle class," in the sense of a stratum of people, existed before the development of this specifically Western capitalism anchored in the capitalist organization of labor. However, obviously this was the case *only* in the West.

Now evidently the capitalism specific to the modern West has been strongly influenced above all by advances in the realm of *technology*. The nature of the rationality of modern Western capitalism is today determined by the calculability of factors that are technically decisive. Indeed, these factors are the foundation for all more exact calculation. In turn this calculability is rooted fundamentally in the characteristic uniqueness of Western science, and especially in the natural sciences grounded in the exactness of mathematics and the controlled experiment [see pp. 446–48].

The development of these sciences, and the technology that is based upon them, acquired—and continues to acquire—pivotal invigorating impulses from opportunities offered by capitalism. Market opportunities, that is, as rewards, are connected to the economic applications of these technologies. [see pp. 377–91] However, it must also be emphasized that the origin of Western science cannot be explained by the availability of such economic opportunities. Calculation, even with decimals, existed also in the algebra of India, where the decimal system was discovered. Yet in India it never led to modern calculation and accounting methods; this mode of calculation was first placed into *operation* only in the West's developing capitalism. Similarly, the origin of mathematics and physics was not determined by economic interests, yet the *technical* application of scientific knowledge was. Important for the quality of life of the broad population, this application was conditioned by economic rewards—and these crystallized precisely in the West. These rewards, however, flowed out of the particular character of the West's *social* order. It must then be asked: From *which* components of this unique social order did these rewards derive? Surely not all of its features have been of equal importance.

The rational structure of *law* and administration has undoubtedly been among the most central elements of this social order. This is the case for the simple reason that modern-rational industrial capitalism, just as it requires calculable technical means in order to organize work, also needs a calculable law and administration that function according to formal rules. Of course adventure capitalism and a trade-based capitalism oriented to speculation, as well as all types of capitalism determined by political considerations, can well exist without calculable law and administration. However, a rational industrial firm—with fixed capital and reliable *calculation*, and operating in a private economy—is not possible without this type of law and administration.

Yet this type of law and administration, in *this* degree of legal-technical and formal perfection, was placed at the disposal of the economy and its development *only* in the West. Hence, one must ask: What was the source of this type of law in the West? Undoubtedly, in addition to other circumstances, *also* economic interests paved the way for the rule of a stratum of jurists who were professionally trained in rational law and who, in a disciplined and regular manner, practiced and administered law. This is evident from every investigation. Yet these economic interests were not the exclusive, or even the primary, causal forces in the rise of this stratum to importance. Moreover, economic interests did not of themselves *create* this type of law. Rather, entirely different powers were active in respect to this development. And why then did capitalist interests not call forth this stratum of jurists and this type of law in China or India? How did it happen that scientific, artistic, and economic development, as well as state-building, were not directed in China and India into those tracks of *rationalization* specific to the West?[18]

* * *

The issue in all of the cases mentioned above evidently involves a characteristic aspect of a specifically formed "rationalism" of Western civilization. Now this word can be understood as implying a vast spectrum of matters [see pp. 241–45, 251].[19] There is, for example, "rationalization" of mystical contemplation, that is, of a type of behavior that is specifically "irrational" if viewed from the perspective of other realms of life.[20] Similarly, there may be rationalization of the economy, technology, scientific work,

---

18. This sentence is central to Weber's entire argument. It succinctly captures the theme he has been developing over the last few pages: Major historical developments must be understood as occurring in reference to a series of causal forces, and the effect of single factors—such as economic interests—can be ascertained only after an investigation of how they are situated within a context of forces (above referred to as a "social order"). On the "contextual" and "conjunctural" character of causal analysis in Weber's comparative-historical sociology, see Kalberg, 1994b, pp. 98–102, 151–92 [sk].

19. Weber adds at this point in the text: "As the later analyses will repeatedly make clear." This is a reference to the volumes and essays that follow this essay in the German edition, including *PE*, *The Religion of China*, *The Religion of India*, and *Ancient Judaism*. (see pp. 183–84) [sk].

20. By "other realms of life" Weber has in mind the arenas of the economy, law, or rulership. Because "activity in the world" is valued as worthwhile and meaningful in these realms, the mystic's withdrawal through contemplation is seen as meaningless, or "irrational."The reverse also holds true. See 1946c, pp. 325–26; 1968, pp. 541–51 [sk].

education, warfare, administration, and the practice of law. One may further "rationalize" each one of these arenas from vantage points and goals of the most diverse sort and ultimate orientations. What may appear "rational" viewed from one angle may appear "irrational" when viewed from another.

Hence, we must note that rationalizations have occurred in the various arenas of life in highly varying ways and in all circles of cultural life. It is necessary, in order to identify the ways in which the multiple rationalization paths have characteristically varied according to cultural and historical factors, to assess *which* arenas have been rationalized and in what directions [see pp. 87–88]. Again, important here above all are the special *characteristic features* of Western rationalism and, within this particular type of rationalism,[21] the characteristic features of modern Western rationalism. Our concern is to identify this uniqueness and to explain its origin.

Every such attempt at explanation, recognizing the fundamental significance of economic factors, must above all take account of these factors. However, the opposite line of causation should not be neglected if only because the origin of economic rationalism depends not only on an advanced development of technology and law but also on the capacity and disposition of persons to **organize their lives** in a practical-rational manner. Wherever magical and religious forces have inhibited the unfolding of this organized life, the development of an organized life oriented systematically toward *economic* activity has confronted broad-ranging internal resistance. Magical and religious powers, and the belief in them anchored in ethical notions of duty, have been in the past among the most important formative influences upon the way life has been organized. This is our subject in the collected and enlarged essays that follow.

* * *

Two older essays have been placed at the beginning of this collection on the sociology of religion: [*The Protestant Ethic and the Spirit of Capitalism* and "The Protestant Sects and the Spirit of Capitalism"].[22] By reference to *one* important point, both attempt to shed light on that aspect of the problem normally most difficult to understand: the influence of certain religious ideas on the origin of an "economic **frame of mind**," that is, on the "ethos" of an **economic form**. This theme will be addressed by offering an example of the connections between the modern economic ethos and the rational

---

21. In the volumes that follow in the German edition (see note 19), Weber will refer repeatedly to, for example, "Chinese rationalism," "the rationalism of India," and "the rationalism of the Middle Ages" [sk].
22. Weber is referring to the German edition. *PE* and "The Protestant Sects" essay are placed at the beginning of the three-volume study [sk].

economic ethic of ascetic Protestantism. Thus, these two essays investigate only *one* side of the causal relationship.[23]

The later essays, which constitute the **Economic Ethics of the World Religions** [EEWR] series, attempt to explore *both* causal relationships[24] to the extent necessary for the discovery of points of *comparison* with the West's development, which will later be analyzed further.[25] They do so by offering an overview of the relationships between, on the one hand, the most important religions and the economy, and on the other hand, between the most important religions and the social stratification in their milieu. Only in this way will it be at all possible to pursue a relatively clear line of causal *attribution* that enables a determination of which components of the religion-defined Western economic ethics (that are characteristic for them and do not appear in non-Western economic ethics) became causal forces.

Thus, no claim is made that the EEWR essays seek to serve as something close to a comprehensive analysis of civilizations, albeit in an ever so compressed form. Rather, in respect to every theme, they intentionally and insistently emphasize that which stood—and stands today—in *contrast* to the line of development of Western civilization. They are, in other words, on the occasion of a depiction of the Western pathway of development, [as in *The Protestant Ethic and the Spirit of Capitalism*], entirely oriented to what seems to be important from the vantage point of *such contrasts*. No other mode of procedure appeared possible in light of [the] particular goal [here to determine the causal effect of the characteristic components of the economic ethics of Western religions]. Nonetheless, in order to avoid misunderstanding, the limitations of these studies must be explicitly noted at the outset.

In yet another manner the uninitiated, if not also others, must be warned against overestimating the significance of these analyses. To area specialists on China, India, or Egypt, as well as to experts on Semitic culture, these studies will offer no new research findings. It can only be hoped that these specialists discover nothing *essential* to the subject here that must be judged as objectively *incorrect*. The author cannot know to what extent he has succeeded in coming as close to this ideal, at least, as a non-specialist might be at all capable. It is certainly completely obvious that a person dependent on translations, and, moreover, forced to orient himself in a specialist literature (that is frequently highly debated and on which he cannot arrive at independent judgments) in order to use and evaluate a massive amount of documentary and literary material, has every reason to think of the value of

---

23. Namely, the side of the causal relationship involving the influence of "internal factors," that is, ideas and values [sk].

24. Namely, the "other" side of the causal relationship, that is, in Weber's terms the causal role of "interests," or "external factors." Hence Weber's famous formulation: "ideas and interests (see p. 241) [sk].

25. Weber did not live to write a systematic volume on this subject. Innumerable short statements that compare the development of the West to that of China and India are found throughout his substantive works. See, for example, pp. 252–56, 259–63, 275–89, 361–64, 397–99; 1968, pp. 809–38, 1064–69, 1108–09, 1236–65; 1927, pp. 315–37; 1978, pp. 282–83 [sk].

his achievement in very modest terms. This is all the more the case because the number of available translations of the actual "source" material (that is, inscriptions and documents) in part to this day (especially for China) remains very small in proportion to that which exists in the original and is important. The completely *provisional* character of these essays follows from all these factors, especially for those sections that concern Asia.[26]

Only the specialist is entitled to render a final judgment on these investigations. Moreover, these studies were written only because, understandably, analyses by specialists oriented to the particular goal enunciated above and undertaken from the special angle pivotal here did not hitherto exist. Indeed, they are destined, far more so and in a different sense from specialized studies, soon to become "out-of-date"—although this, in the end, can be said of every scientific study [see Weber, 2005, p. 321]. Nonetheless, however hazardous, an encroachment into other social science disciplines cannot be avoided when one pursues such comparative themes. Yet one must acknowledge the consequence of doing so: a sense of deep resignation regarding the degree of one's success.

Fashion and the yearning of intellectuals today [1920] easily leads to the conclusion that the specialist can be pushed aside or, in order to please a public in search of a "show," humiliated by being reduced to the level of a subordinate worker. Almost all of the sciences are indebted to dilettantes for achievements of some sort, and often for the contribution of quite valuable vantage points. However, science would come to an end if dilettantism became its operating principle. Whoever wishes a "show" should best visit the cinema; it will offer, even in literary form, a massive schedule of events touching on just this thematic complex.[27] Nothing stands more distant from the dilettante's frame of mind than the completely dispassionate analyses offered in these (according to my intention) strictly empirical investigations.

And, I would like to add, those who wish to hear a "sermon" should visit a **conventicle**. Not a single word will be expended on behalf of the relative *value* of the civilizations compared here.[28] It is true that the path of human destiny deeply scars the breast of each person who glances at even a short historical epoch. But all will be better off keeping their insignificant personal commentaries to themselves, just as one does when standing before an ocean vista and towering mountain peaks—unless one knows oneself to be called and endowed with the gift of artistic expression or prophetic powers. In most other cases the loquacious discus-

---

26. Also the remains of my knowledge of Hebrew are entirely unreliable.

27. I need not note that attempts such as those on the one hand by Karl Jaspers, in his book *Psychology of World Views (Psychologie der Weltanschauungen)*[Berlin: Springer, 1919], or on the other hand by [Ludwig] Klages [*Charakterology* (Leipzig: Barth 1910; Bonn: Bouvier, 1976–1979)], and similar studies, do not fall into this category. These investigations can all be distinguished from what is here attempted by reference to their differing point of departure. This is not the place for a critical confrontation. [The Klages volume had a large influence among conservative and nationalist groupings that would later support German fascism.]

28. For Weber's more succinct formulations of the tasks and limits of science, see "Science as a Vocation" 1946d, pp. 138–39, 145–48, 150–51 [sk].

sion of "intuition" only veils a lack of distance upon the beauty of nature—which must be judged no differently than a lack of distance upon persons.

* * *

It needs to be justified how it came about that, on behalf of the goals pursued here, the author did not use *ethnographic* research to anywhere near the extent (in light of its present-day development) naturally indispensable for a fully convincing analysis, especially of religious devoutness in Asia. This omission occurred not only because there are limitations to the human capacity for work. Rather, it appeared permissible mainly because our concern here must necessarily be the contexts for the religion-determined ethic of those strata that constituted the "carriers of culture" in their respective geographical regions. The influences exerted by *their* particular mode of organizing life concern us. Now it is completely correct that these influences, in their particularity, can actually be comprehended accurately only if the ethnographic-anthropological record is utilized.

Hence, it is explicitly conceded and emphasized that a deficiency exists on this score and that ethnographers may legitimately raise objections to these studies. I will hope to be able to rectify this omission in part when I turn to a systematic treatment of the sociology of religion [see 1968, pp. 399–634]. However, given the limited purposes of the Economic Ethics of the World Religions series, such an undertaking would have moved beyond the framework of its analysis. These investigations had to be content with attempting to unveil, as far as possible, the points of *comparison* to our *major* Western religions.

Finally, the *anthropological* side of the problem should also be considered. If we again and again discover in the West, and *only* in the West, specific *types* of rationalizations (and also in arenas of life [such as religion, the economy, and law] that seemingly developed independently from one another), then naturally a certain assumption appears plausible: heredity is playing a decisive role. The author confesses that he is inclined, personally and subjectively, to estimate highly the importance of biological heredity. However, despite the significant achievements of anthropological research at this time, I do not see any manner of exactly comprehending, or even hinting at in terms of probabilities, the share of heredity—namely, according to its extent and, above all, type and points of impact—in the development investigated *here*.

As one of its major tasks, sociological and historical research will have to reveal as many as possible of those influences and causal chains that are satisfactorily explainable as reactions to the effect of [biological] fate on the one hand and that of social milieu on the other. Only then, and only when, in addition, the comparative study of racial neurology and psychology moves beyond its rudimentary beginnings of today (which are promising in many ways, if one examines the discrete studies), can one *perhaps* hope for satisfactory results even for the problem studied here.[29] Yet any development in this direction appears to me for the time being not to exist and any referral to "heredity" would be, it seems to me, tantamount to both a premature abandonment of the extent of knowledge perhaps possible *today* and a displacement of the problem onto (at this time still) unknown factors.

---

29. Many years ago an excellent psychiatrist expressed the same opinion to me.

3

Demarcating the Uniqueness of the West Through Comparisons

Magic and the Economic Ethics of the World Religions

INTRODUCTION

Stephen Kalberg

> *Neither religions nor men are open books. They have been historical rather than logical or even psychological constructions devoid of internal contradictions. (pp. 240–50.)*
>
> *Behind the [varieties of belief was] a stand regarding something in the actual world which was experienced as specifically "senseless."' Thus, the demand has been implied: that the world order in its totality is, could, and should somehow be a meaningful "cosmos." (p. 242)*

In *PE*, Weber rejects the view that the origin of the Protestant ethic can be found in an intensification of utilitarian action. Instead, an extreme rationalization of action in reference to a wide-ranging constellation of religious values anchored the ascetic Protestant's vocational ethos, he insists. As a consequence of urgent salvation concerns, life became rigorously organized *from within*; ethical standards guided this believer. The Puritan's *methodical-rational organization of life* implied a unique world mastery posture capable of accelerating significantly economic development.

The readings in Section 3 turn to Weber's comparative studies of the world religions: Confucianism, Hinduism, Buddhism, Islam, Judaism, and Christianity.[1] His three-volume Economic Ethics of the World Religions (EEWR; see p. 183) and his systematic chapter on the sociology of religion in *Economy and Society* (1968, pp. 399–640) serve as major texts. The selections below outline Weber's project. Two themes are pivotal.

First, Weber stresses that a rationalization of the believer's conduct occurs only on the basis of a prior weakening of magic. As he extends his horizon to encompass the world religions, "demagification" (*Entzauberung*) becomes a major focus: the posture of each religion vis-à-vis sorcery must be delineated, he holds. Was magic shattered in the West's ethical universe more comprehensively than in the East's? Whereas the charismatically endowed *virtuoso* devout universally escaped the influence of sorcery, *lay* believers managed to do so *only* in the West. This conclusion proved key for an understanding of the particular course followed by the rationalization of action in the religion life-sphere in the West, Weber contends.

Second, he now wishes to assess, through an array of comparative experiments across cases, whether Puritanism can be said to be unique. After painstaking research, Weber concluded that Confucianism, Hinduism,

---

1. See pp. 238–40. Although "world religion" status is not accorded to them, Weber discusses also in some detail Jainism and Daoism. See 1951, pp. 173–213; 1958, pp. 193–203.

Buddhism, ancient Judaism, Islam, ancient Christianity, and Catholicism failed to influence the economic activity of believers in a manner similar to Puritanism. Hence, these religions never placed an impulse into motion toward modern capitalism. Moreover, all failed to give birth to a methodical-rational organization of life directed *toward* the world.

These themes — the more widespread weakening of magic in the West, the broader societal influence in the West of a rationalization of action process emanating from the religion arena, and the uniqueness of the modern economic ethic carried by Puritanism — intertwine deeply in Weber's texts. His cross-civilizational comparisons revealed their linkage. Indeed, one of *PE*'s major conclusions — the Protestant ethic's origin must be sought outside the realm of utilitarian, interest-based activity — is now substantiated: a rationalization of action process in the religion domain constituted a major source. Its long-range course was characterized by a disruption of both magic and utilitarian action and the subsequent extension of ethical action — and eventually methodical-ethical action — *into* the world.

These pivotal themes must now be addressed. Each contributes to Weber's "religion *and* world" explanation of the rise of Western rationalism, modern Western rationalism, and modern capitalism.

SALVATION PATHS, DEMAGIFICATION, AND THE VIRTUOSO AND LAY DEVOUT EAST AND WEST

Weber's EEWR investigations led to a significant conclusion: the world religions opposed magic with different degrees of intensity and effectiveness. Searching for explanations, he examined their multiple lay and virtuoso salvation paths. To what extent, he queries, did the laity remain immersed in sorcery? What causes in the West drove a uniquely strong "demagification process"? Taking India at this point as his major comparative case, Weber pondered Hinduism and Buddhism in their classical forms. Did the salvation path each defined for the virtuosi devout — *mysticism* — effectively cast an ethical orientation *across* strata, thereby weakening magic's hold upon lay believers? Conversely, in the West the major salvation pathways confronted magic in entirely different, and more effective, ways, Weber discovered. Exploration of this variation revealed distinctions of great significance in the ethical universes of India and the West. These differences will highly influence the capacity of the world religions to give birth to economic ethics.

The East: Mysticism, the Ethical Orientation "Away from the World," and the Failure to Confront Magic

Mysticism appeared as a major salvation path in India whenever believers perceived the supernatural realm as an incorporeal and immanent ethical

Being. Here impersonal rules were believed to govern the cosmos in general. The mystic sought redemption through immersion into the All-One instead of, as in the West, an alignment of daily action with the ethical demands of an anthropomorphic God.

This merging in India with the "supreme and wise order" could occur only if the believer managed to silence and control all inner natural rhythms and drives. A comprehensive meditation regimen, energetic concentration, and an evacuation of the consciousness facilitated the thoroughgoing break from everyday life prerequisite to a "rest in God" and "possession" of the immanent Being. "Entrance into the profound and blissful tranquility and immobility of the All-One" provided an emotional unity of knowledge and volitional mood. Amid an ecstasy of mystic illumination, this "absolute Oneness" assured the faithful of their state of grace (1946c, pp. 325–26; 1946e, p. 282; 1968, pp. 536, 545–46; 1958, p. 332). How did this salvation-striving interact with magic?

As a result of the mystic's aim to flee from the world and to merge into the incorporeal God, all worldly activity became devalued. Mysticism, for this reason, as well as its systematic character, stood strongly opposed to sorcery. Nonetheless, because absolute "flight from the world" mattered most, the devout tolerated all earthly "irrationality"; hence, they avoided an active confrontation with magic. Moreover, mysticism's salvation goal — immersion into the All-One — could be attained only by those few in possession of virtuoso religious qualifications, and this tiny minority could scarcely influence India's all-pervasive magic. Finally, this believer's *own* redemption comprised his exclusive concern rather than God's will. For all these reasons, Weber concludes, mysticism never uprooted the lay devout from their immersion in sorcery and age-old tradition; they were left untouched. How does this comparative case shed light on sorcery's weakening, and even banishment, in the West?

Mainline salvation-striving in the Western ethical universe opposed mysticism's flight from the world, Weber contends. Both virtuoso and lay devout remained *in* the world in the West; they attempted to implement *on earth* the ethical commandments of a monotheistic God. To serve His glory, all believers were commanded to transform action, whether more traditional, affectual, or means-end rational, into ethical action pleasing to Him—for His kingdom must be constructed in the here and now. Thus, a direct confrontation with magic's random and a-ethical character ensued.

Weber stresses that the manifold ethical action carried by ascetic Protestantism must be understood as only the last stage in a long-range rationalization of action process distinct to Western salvation religions. Any investigation of Puritanism's uniqueness and origins must not neglect this larger religious terrain—namely, the reforms initiated *earlier* than those undertaken by John Calvin and Richard Baxter. Indeed, the roots of the Protestant ethic extend even farther into the past than the other-worldly asceticism of medieval Catholic monks, he maintains. The demanding monotheistic God of ancient Judaism, once adopted in moderated form by ancient Christianity, proved crucial. Importantly for Weber's attempts to isolate the particularity of Western rationalism and its developmental pathway, this deity stood in stark contrast to the immanent and impersonal Being widespread in India (p. 248; see 1946c, pp. 324–26).

Ancient Judaism and early Christianity enunciated paths toward redemption quite different from Puritanism's, as well as from those prevalent in India. Through the introduction of ethical action *in* the world, albeit fragmented at times, all Western religions persistently confronted magic—*also* among the lay devout. After conducting a series of rigorous comparisons to India, Weber concluded that redemption religions in the West, in this respect, were singular.

The West: The Confrontation with Magic and the Introduction of Ethical Action Among the Lay Devout

Judaism and Christianity infrequently called forth among believers a sustained flight from the world. Instead, their several salvation paths generally placed psychological premiums upon "practical-ethical" action. Indeed, they did so to such an extent that magic, to varying degrees, was suppressed.

Pivotal was the heightened capacity of these religions, largely as a result of the more intense form taken by the problem of theodicy under monotheism, to develop doctrines, according to Weber (see 1968, pp. 460–63). Moreover, once anchored socially with Catholicism in the Middle Ages in congregations and cultivated through pastoral care, the *ethical* action demanded by these doctrines and the anthropomorphic God expanded effectively beyond small elites. Orienting action *to* the world, the certainty of salvation quest pulled *also* the lay faithful away from sorcery. This occurred more broadly wherever, as in the West, churches, congregations, and pastoral care were present.

Hence, long before ascetic Protestantism, precedents were formulated for manifold ethical action, a full eradication of magic, a subjugation of the practical-rational way of life, and a modern economic ethic. Action oriented to the supernatural realm over millennia underwent a "rationalization process" away from magic and ritual and toward methodical ethical action. The banishing of the traditional economic ethic, and the ushering in of a world mastery ethos, took place only on the basis of this methodical-rational organization of life, Weber holds. Highly influential, as will become apparent, was a dilemma indigenous to the realm of religion that endowed it with a degree of autonomy: the quandary of unjust suffering.[2] Ancient Judaism, in conjunction with early Christianity, cast the major imprint upon the West's worldview. Weber's comparative investigations reveal a singularly broad expansion of ethical action in the West beyond the virtuoso devout.

How did ancient Judaism direct salvation-striving *to* the world and effectively confront sorcery? The nature of its God in part determined magic's sheer ineffectiveness. As a universal and sovereign Lord who had ascended to "an absolutely supramundane supremacy," the warrior Deity Yahwe of the Old Confederacy (1180–1004 B.C.E.) became endowed with omnipotence, omniscience, and consummate ethical qualities—and became established as far too mighty to be manipulated or coerced by magicians.[3] In addition, this monotheistic Divinity operated within an *ethical* universe: as a God of just ethical compensation, He offered grace only when His commandments were upheld. Thus, the earthly fortune of individuals followed as the "fruit of their doing" (1952, pp. 301–09). Finally, the ethical absolutism of ancient Judaism's prophets stood in a relationship of strict antagonism to sorcery's fluctuating and instrumental character (1952, pp. 222, 394, 298, 394; 1968, p. 424).

Heeding Yahwe's demands, charismatic prophets placed psychological rewards upon ethical action. To the same extent all less rational orientations to the supernatural realm — to orgiastic ecstasy, dream interpretation, the Baal fertility cult, fragmented ritual, and magic — were attacked and devalued. Furthermore, in denying the ethical meaning of misfortune, sorcery implied that blind chance, fate, or bad luck explained worldly events and suffering rather than Yahwe's Will, as the prophets proclaimed. Hence, representing a disloyalty to ancient Judaism's awesome God, magic became viewed by these heroic figures as "irrational." Its practice was abhorred as a mortal sin (p. 245; 1952, pp. 334–35, 394; 1927, p. 322).[4]

Talmudic Judaism (537 B.C.E to 70 C.E.) constricted sorcery further. The spontaneous nature of all magic opposed the vigilant self-control and attention to the sacred Laws demanded by rabbis. Grace could not be acquired through the performance of magical sacraments of any sort, they insisted. Indeed, the Talmud stood in a relationship of strict antagonism to such "irrational" salvation-seeking methods, all of which threatened the pious Jew's attempt to study the sacred Law and to practice dutifully a correct deportment on its behalf. The Talmud judged all sorcery as an "abomi-

---

2.   It must be emphasized that Weber's analysis departs from an understanding of religion as a bounded arena infused by indigenously arising questions (the problem of suffering and the problem of theodicy) and dilemmas associated with the ordering of the believer's "relations to the transcendent realm." Religion-oriented action, although always located within configurations of political and economic interests, as well as power constellations, must not be reduced to external determinants. He sees patterns of action fully independent of the other significant arenas of life: the rulership, economy, law, status groups, and family domains (see pp. 238–41; 1968, pp. 399–639; Kalberg, 1994b, pp. 149–50). Why did undeserved suffering occur so frequently? What accounted for the endurance of misery? Why did it so often appear randomly? What were its origins? What explanations render hardship plausible and what ideas define the supernatural realm? Answers to these queries explained religion's appeal and led to the demarcation of a *sphere* of action (see 1968, pp. 399–439, 518–29; 1946e, pp. 271–77). On the "autonomy" of the religion sphere's development, see Kalberg, 1990, 2001a, 2004.

3.   For a reconstruction of Weber's complex analysis of monotheism's rise in ancient Israel, see Kalberg, 1994a.

4.   Whereas comprehended earlier as the violation of external ritual, *sin* now became understood as a fully internalized attitude wholly antagonistic to Yahwe's demands. See 1952, pp. 291–92, 327–28, 332.

nable and blasphemous" means of interaction with Yahwe (1952, pp. 394–97; 1968, p. 562).

The entire course of Western history was influenced, Weber holds, once early Christianity adopted ancient Judaism's hostility to magic and its *directing* of the search for salvation *toward* the world.[5] Puritanism, which also opposed sorcery, stood directly within the "track" laid down by ancient Judaism (pp. 107, 114–15).

As in Judaism, sorcery proved an ineffective mode of interaction with *ancient Christianity's* powerful God. Most important for the believer in search of redemption was an ethic of brotherhood and compassion, the actions of the savior, belief in the savior, and faith in God. Juxtaposed with a coherent ethos of universal love, these salvation paths — through a savior and through faith — introduced a degree of ethical action, Weber maintains. Moreover, unlike classical Hinduism and Buddhism, ancient Christianity addressed its message against elites and explicitly toward "the masses" (1968, pp. 557–58). This was evident in the vigorous protests of Jesus Christ against the obscurantism of Talmudic scholarship, the emphasis it placed upon the study of the Law rather than upon faith, its comprehensive ritualism, and the elitism of ancient Judaism's rabbis (1968, p. 512). Christ's prophecy extolled the faith of the unlearned pious — the artisans, the craftsmen, and the inhabitants of small towns — against the Law's scholarly interpretation. Medieval Catholicism, by placing clear expectations upon the lay believer to undertake ethical action *in the world*, took over this posture. It also rationalized action away from magic.

However greatly *Catholicism's* salvation paths for lay and virtuoso believers varied, identical claims were placed upon *all* devout with respect to behavior toward others. Compassion, unconditional forgiveness, the endurance of injustice, and a "turning of the other cheek" constituted central ingredients. Following ancient Christianity, Catholicism bestowed — because God willed the good of humanity as a whole — psychological premiums upon a "universalist brotherhood" that transcended the barriers of place, tribe, kin, and class. Both the monastery and a powerful and organized group — the church — sought to institute this brotherly ethic among all believers.

Catholicism's ethical action resulted from the linkage of participation in the Church's sacraments with the belief that only those free from sin — the ethically pure in the sight of God — could be saved. The Church's emphasis upon the performance of good works also pulled the lay devout toward ethi-

---

5.   ". . . in considering the condition of Jewry's development, we stand at a turning point of the whole cultural development of the West and the Middle East. Quite apart from the significance of the Jewish pariah people in the economy of the European Middle Ages and the modern period, Jewish religion has world-historical consequences. Only the following phenomena can equal those of Jewry in historical significance: the development of Hellenic intellectual culture; for Western Europe, the development of Roman law and of the Roman Catholic church resting on the Roman concept of office; the medieval order of estates; and finally, in the field of religion, Protestantism. [Protestantism's] influence overthrows this order but develops its institutions" (1952, p. 5; transl. altered).

cal action, for particular actions could be added to or subtracted from the ethical "account" of those in search of redemption (pp. 113–16; 1968, p. 533).

Finally, ethical action among the faithful was also strengthened by the *congregation*, which Weber sees as unique to the West. It required that the lay devout interact as "brothers in the faith." In this organization, the lay brethren stood under a *single ethical* standard, namely, an ethos of universal inclusion. For all these reasons the Catholic Church opposed fragmented sorcery vehemently—even though, as Weber quickly points out, magic found its way into various aspects of its practice.

In sum, Weber's comparative investigations revealed that ancient Judaism, ancient Christianity, and medieval Catholicism called forth a type of action oriented *to* the world that stood in a relationship of radical antagonism to magic— ethical action. These world religions did so in ways far more intensely than the salvation religions of India—albeit incompletely compared to Puritanism. Furthermore, in respect to the extent to which the lay devout remained immersed in magic, Weber's comparative studies indicated that the Western religions varied greatly from Buddhism and Hinduism: *all* believers were expected in the West to orient their activity toward ethical values. He insists that a singular demagification process was visible in the religion domain even in the West's ancient and medieval epochs, as were clear precedents for Puritanism's manifold ethical action.

However, as noted, these diverging capacities of salvation paths in India and the West to confront sorcery, and then to rationalize practical action in the direction of ethical action, constituted to Weber only one important development. He isolated, through his comparative research, the religion-based causes for the West's singular historical pathway by reference also to a further pivotal theme: the extent to which salvation religions in the East and West formulated economic ethics. Weber's urgent query can now be addressed: did a *modern* economic ethic oriented *to* the world *and* grounded in *manifold* ethical action appear only in the West?

THE ECONOMIC ETHICS OF THE WORLD RELIGIONS

The readings in Section 3 investigate the economic ethics of Confucianism, Hinduism, Buddhism, Islam, ancient Judaism, ancient Christianity, and medieval Catholicism. By reference to worldviews, doctrines, and salvation paths, Weber examines the activities that became salient and subjectively meaningful to believers. Were psychological premiums, he queries, in a particular religion awarded to action *in* the world *and* a *methodical* ethos? Did religions other than Puritanism direct believers to practical activity and a modern economic ethic? Through rigorous comparisons, Weber seeks to isolate similarities and differences across the world religions in respect to their influence upon the action of the devout. These "mental experiments" demarcate again the uniqueness of ascetic Protestantism.

The East and Middle East: Flight from the World and Ritualism

Manifold ethical action could not arise from *Confucianism*. An "unbroken unity" of magic and a "purely magical worldview" prevailed. Whereas the Puritan felt compelled by religious duty toward his God to assess all human relationships in reference to the Deity's grand design and His standards, the Confucian fulfilled his religious obligation "within organically given, personal relations." This world religion's emphasis upon familial piety opposed directly all impersonal consideration of personal relationships. Piety toward "concrete, living or dead persons" comprised the Confucian's duty; absent were psychological premiums upon the fulfillment of functional tasks (pp. 279–80; 1946c, p. 350; 1968, pp. 484, 1053).

Confucianism lacked not only the understanding of economic success as testimony to one's state of grace, but also the entire notion of methodical-ethical action directed comprehensively "from within" and oriented to world mastery on behalf of a monotheistic God's commandments. The "gentleman ideal" of Confucianism — which proclaimed that persons must not be "tools" and that specialized training, as well as vocational work, could not serve the goal of universal self-perfection — opposed the introduction of modern forms of economic organization. Despite "sobriety and thriftiness combined with acquisitiveness and regard for wealth," the unfolding of an economic ethic similar to that of ascetic Protestantism was precluded (pp. 285–86, 288–89).

Owing to its "adjustment to the world" ethos, Confucianism proved powerless to initiate action that challenged the authority of clan patriarchs and established a "community of faith" in opposition to a "community of blood." Business confidence remained grounded in the strong personal relationships of familial and clan groupings rather than the "ethical qualities" of persons as demonstrated in impersonal, vocational work (pp. 281, 287). Hence, Confucianism failed to give birth to a modern economic ethic capable of forming an independent thrust antagonistic to the clan-based economy.

Weber examined the economic ethics of *Hinduism* in its Classical (600 B.C.E. to 700 C.E.) and Restoration (700–1200 C.E.) eras, as well as virtuoso and lay, forms. The doctrines he explored never threatened the caste-based, traditional economic ethic at India's core. Even his detailed analysis of Hinduism's metamorphosis, as it became transformed from a religion of virtuosi and intellectuals in its earliest era to one adapted in India's Middle Ages to the magic and ritual widespread among the masses, failed to discover psychological premiums upon action oriented to the economy (see 1958, pp. 291–328). To Weber, assessment of this salvation religion's economic ethos involved basically two investigations: an identification of the consequences for action of the virtuoso's mystical quest for salvation directed away from the world, and an examination of the purely ritual search for redemption, as pursued by the overwhelming majority of Hindus, through "caste ethics."

The salvation-striving of the virtuoso Brahmin — who devalued the world and sought, following the mysticism salvation path, to withdraw from it — never introduced an economic ethic. All terrestrial activity and attempts to change earthly relationships to conform to values drew this believer inexorably into the *karma* chain of insufferable and unending rebirth—and thus led away from redemption. The aim of the virtuosi faithful to extricate themselves from this-life concerns, to silence the inner drives, and to submerge into the All-One in an ecstasy of unity could be realized only through a "turning away" from and "flight from" mundane existence (see p. 257).

For the laity, on the other hand, adherence to caste ritual — *dharma* — alone promised attainment of their redemption goal: rebirth into a higher caste. Lives became regimented comprehensively "from without" and the violation of *dharma* defined the only notions of "sin" and "evil" (p. 261; 1968, pp. 530, 561). Weber held further that attempts to escape the eternal cycle of rebirth and death carried out by the Hindu Restoration's magicians, whether more meditative or orgiastic-ecstatic, also precluded the awarding of psychological incentives to economic activity of any sort (p. 266; 1946e, p. 284). Finally, because judged as devoid of meaning, participation in trade, moneylending, and profitable pursuits were reserved for the "ignorant." Rigid ritual often prevented the educated from using their learning on behalf of a vocation.

A small segment of each caste's practical ethics pertained to economic action, either directly or indirectly, Weber maintains. However, premiums were bestowed upon means-end rational or rigidly traditional action rather than either a spirit of capitalism or ethical action aimed to transform the world on behalf of divine commandments. That both virtuoso and lay believers "accepted this world as eternally given, and so the best of all possible worlds," provided the most fundamental doctrinal presupposition for Hinduism's "organic, traditionalistic ethic of vocation, similar in structure to medieval Catholicism's, only more consistent" (p. 265; 1968, p. 599).[6]

A bestowing of psychological premiums upon a modern economic ethic, particularly of the type found in ascetic Protestantism, was far removed from lay Hinduism. Without such incentives, even the extreme evaluation of riches and money in India, as in China, proved incapable of introducing a modern economic ethic. Whether for lay or virtuosi devout, methodical-ethical action in the world, economic or otherwise, never testified to salvation from the end-

---

6.   "The caste system tends to perpetuate a specialization of labor of the handicraft type, if not by positive prescription, then as a consequence of its general spirit and presupposition. . . . Each caste nourishes its feeling of worth by its technically expert execution of its assigned vocation" (1968, p. 436).

"... no motivation toward a rational-methodical control of life flowed from Buddhist, Daoist, or Hindu piety. Hindu piety in particular . . . maintained the strongest possible power of tradition since the presuppositions of Hinduism constituted the most consistent religious expression of the "organic" view of society. The existing order of the world was provided absolutely unconditional legitimation in terms of the mechanical operation of a proportional retribution in the distribution of power and happiness to individuals on the basis of their merits and failures in their earlier lives" (pp. 265–66).

less wheel of *karma* rebirth and compensation. Signs of the Hindu's salvation could not be derived from the integrity and success of economic activity, as occurred for the Puritan devout (pp. 257, 261–62, 266–67).

Buddhist virtuoso mystics attained gnostic knowledge — the experiencing of the "quietness and inwardness of God" — only when they minimized activity by withdrawing from everyday mundane interests, practical routines, satisfactions, and temptations. Believers remained resigned and indifferent to the institutions of the world. Terrestrial success was viewed as devoid of all significance for redemption and as a distraction from the goal of serving as a "vessel" of the ethical Being (pp. 248–49; 1946c, pp. 325, 342; 1968, pp. 548–50).

Hence, and although the virtuosi could not fully avoid action, action *in* the world could never testify to one's salvation. Premiums were bestowed upon contemplation — that is, action consistent with the attempt to merge into the impersonal All-One — rather than upon practical action. This action, and especially every consistent rationalization of action, was perceived as antagonistic to the Buddhist's salvation goal of fleeing from the wheel of endless reincarnation. All realms of this-worldly conduct, including any methodical-rational or goal-directed action that might oppose economic traditionalism, were denied meaning (see 1958, p. 213). The Puritan's orientation toward a secular vocational ethic and economic affairs diametrically opposed Buddhism's world rejection and salvation through mystical illumination.

Islam, a world religion founded by warrior strata, commanded above all belief by the devout in Allah, recognition of Him as the one true God, and acceptance of Mohammed as his prophet. In addition, a series of "practical commandments" must be upheld: to pray five times daily, to fast during Ramadan, to undertake at least one pilgrimage to Mecca, to attend services weekly, and to offer assistance to the poor. Usury, gambling, alcohol, unclean foods, private feuds, and illegitimate forms of sexual behavior were prohibited. Taxes for warfare must be paid (see p. 301; 1968, pp. 564, 570, 1185).

These practical commandments defined the behavior required of the faithful. A confrontation with the "basic and ultimate problem of the relationship between a religious ethic and worldly domains" never crystallized in overt form (1968, pp. 564, 599). Religious ethics that aimed to define a range of activity *in the world as devout* never unfolded in Islam. Accordingly, specific modes of behavior, such as the Catholic's "good works" or the Puritan's methodical organization of life around work, never acquired psychological premiums. A belief in Allah and the prophets "adequately secured" the fate of the individual in the world beyond (see 1968, pp. 564, 599).

This remained the case even though Islam shared the idea of predestination with Calvinism—and here this idea had led eventually to a systematic approach to economic activity. An ascetic, manifold control of conduct in daily life — either in monasteries or "in the world" — proved unnecessary in Islam, and the practical commandments never demanded a rigorous organization of the believer's economic life (pp. 302–03; 1968, pp. 569). Rather than taking the salvation fate of the individual in the next world, the predestination decree, or the ascetic quest of the individual for personal salvation as its focus, as did Puritanism, traditional Islam defined "the uncommon events of this world, and above all such questions of whether . . . the warrior for the faith would fall in battle" (p. 303), as of primary concern. Ritualistic demands and fatalism came to the forefront rather than religious dogma and ethical action *in* the world. Hence, magic was not rigorously suppressed (1968, pp. 431, 575).

The continuous development of doctrine in ancient Judaism, ancient Christianity, and medieval Catholicism led to a devaluation of the world and a type of asceticism that, with Puritanism, sought to acquire — through ethical action — comprehensive mastery over daily life's practical rationality. On the other hand, Islam's basic tenet — above all belief in the power of its God — had the effect of curtailing the development of religious dogma that might lead to a devaluation of this world and eventually to severe ethical requirements in opposition to the utilitarianism of daily life. The promises of Islam pertained to this world: "exalt worldly goods" and their enjoyment. A systematic vocational ethic empowered to break through economic traditionalism could never arise from these promises, according to Weber—despite a "certain sobriety in the conduct of life that unfolded out of this religion's sexual and ritual commandments." Moreover, the petty bourgeois stratum of artisans, traders, and craftsmen in Islamic lands mainly carried a dervish religion containing orgiastic, and mystical elements, and hence practiced a "thoroughly traditionalistic ethic of everyday life" (p. 302; 1968, p. 1191). In spite of occasional manifestations of asceticism, ". . . this was the asceticism of a military caste [and] certainly . . . not a middle-class ascetic systematization of the conduct of life. . ." (pp. 302).

For these reasons, Weber contends, Islam's economic ethic starkly opposed Puritanism's. He sees it as "purely feudal" and as one of "accommodation" to the world. The West contrasted massively, he holds, to the ethical universes of both the East and Middle East: ethical action *in* the world came to the forefront. However, only rarely in the West, Weber maintains, was a connection between an overt search by the devout for salvation certainty and economic activity established. Another turn toward ancient Judaism, early Christianity, and Catholicism will reveal that Puritanism constituted a unique case.

The West: The Salience of Activity in the World for the Salvation of Virtuoso and Lay Believers

How can the contours of *ancient Judaism's* economic ethic be characterized? The intensive involvement of the Jews over the centuries in a wide variety of commercial activities would appear to support the hypothesis that this world religion placed psychological premiums upon economic endeavors.

Moreover, as noted above, the search for redemption in ancient Judaism awarded incentives to this-worldly action. Finally, fully detached from magic as well as all irrational procedures, the action of the devout, in conforming to ritual-ethical laws, called forth an "alert wakefulness" and rigid self-control. To Weber: ". . . the disciplining of thought resulting from the tremendously intensive Jewish instruction in the Torah and its casuist interpretation has no doubt been beneficial to the rational economic ethos" (1968, p. 1201).

Nonetheless, several observations led him to ponder whether this extensive business involvement signified an ethos similar to that of ascetic Protestantism. Most important, economic activities by Jews never included an "organization of industrial production in domestic industry and in a factory system," and entrepreneurs never employed workers in a manner that facilitated the emergence of a "modern and distinctively industrial bourgeoisie of any significance" (p. 292). In general, Weber contends that the adventure and political capitalism of the Jews had no decisive influence on the *rational* organization of production characteristic of *modern* capitalism.

Indeed, after scrutinizing the attitudes of Jews toward wealth and riches, he concludes that a traditional economic ethic prevailed—even though profit legally acquired could be viewed as a sign of God's "gracious direction," "personal favor," and "Divine blessings." The notion of the calling in Talmudic Judaism never acquired a secure religious foundation, as in Puritanism, Weber maintains.[7] Furthermore, because of the absence of a predestination notion, economic activity, and the capacity of believers to undertake incessant labor, could never be regarded in Judaism as certification of a state of grace (see p. 14).

A "neighborly ethic" prevailed in *ancient Christianity*. Mutual assistance was extended in times of need and the devout were obligated to practice brotherly love. *All* persons with whom, by chance, the faithful came into contact were to be treated in accord with this ethic—not only friends and intimates. Indeed, through Jesus and St. Paul, the ethic of neighborliness became an ethic of universal love. A cultivation of these qualities and the actions of a savior proved most important for the believer's grace. Moreover, the "excess" of grace accumulated by the redeemer, as a consequence of his extraordinary achievements, could be distributed to others. All depended upon the strength of his charismatic endowment. A connection in ancient Christianity of the believer's conduct to economic activity appeared remote to Weber.

Catholicism, as ancient Christianity, legitimized viable fraternization among "unknown others," monitored relationships based upon personal bonds, and stood clearly antagonistic, according to Weber, to the capitalist economy—where an impersonal calculation of profit and an orientation to

---

7.   ". . . economic activity could never furnish the setting for a religious 'proving' of one's self. If God 'blessed' his own with economic success, it was not owing to their having 'proven' themselves in economic activity; rather, it was because the pious Jew had lived in a manner pleasing to God *outside* of this activity. . . . [T]he area of proving one's piety . . . for Jews lay in a quite different realm than that of the economy" (1952, p. 345).

market-oriented laws predominated over an ethical orientation to persons. Functional relationships, such as those between the holders of mortgages and the debtors of the banks that issued these mortgages, could not be regulated by a consistent brotherly ethos. Hence, Catholicism viewed every development toward the market economy and modern capitalism with profound suspicion. The modern marketplace's thoroughly impersonal economic transactions, the remoteness of the market's objective laws from brotherliness, and capitalism's treatment of persons in regard to their potential to facilitate an instrumental and smooth exchange of goods—all this formed the root cause for Catholicism's condemnation of rational profit-making, commercial enterprises, and all attachment to money and goods.[8] A modern economic ethic appeared quite foreign to this world religion (p. 434; 1946c, p. 331; 1968, pp. 583–85; 1927, pp. 357–58).

In sum, another "Puritanism" could not be located. Weber discovered neither an economic ethos that linked the crucial question of the believer's salvation to systematic work, a search for profit, and a vocational ethos generally, nor salvation paths that directed manifold ethical action *toward* the world. In India, psychological premiums were placed upon the methodical ethical "action" of the virtuosi devout, yet its orientation was decisively *away* from the world. Even the awarding of incentives by ancient Judaism, early Christianity, and medieval Catholicism to ethical action *in* the world normally failed to systematize activity.[9] With the exception of Judaism, an explicit orientation among the devout to economic activity appeared even more rare. Weber's studies indicated the singularity of ascetic Protestantism.

CONCLUSION: THE UNIQUENESS OF THE WEST'S SALVATION RELIGIONS

Ancient Judaism, early Christianity, and medieval Catholicism directed the believer's action toward the world. Moreover, all forcefully opposed magic and called forth a degree of *this*-worldly ethical action, even among their lay devout, more effectively than occurred with Confucianism, Hinduism, Buddhism, or Islam. However, these Western salvation religions provided redemption to the faithful *without* either awarding psychological premiums to manifold ethical action or directing salvation-striving toward the Puritan's world mastery ethos. They lacked, in other words, the capacity to organize life *methodically*—a rigorous element that, Weber maintains, proved indispensable for the birth of a modern economic ethic, the shattering of the traditional economic ethic, and the suppression of the practi-

---

8.   "The devout Catholic, as he went about his economic affairs, found himself continually behaving — or on the verge of behaving — in a manner that transgressed papal injunctions. His economic behavior could be ignored in the confessional only on the principle of *rebus sic stantibus* [the existing sins can be neglected], and it could be permissible only on the basis of a lax, probabilistic morality" (pp. 293–94).

9.   The Catholic monk's methodically organized life was in the monastery "outside the world."

cal-rational way of life. His exhaustive comparative investigations yielded a clear conclusion: this-worldly asceticism alone managed to do so. Puritanism's systematic ethical action organized the believer's life comprehensively *and* produced a vocational ethos.

In this rigorous manner Weber's "empirical experiments" isolated ascetic Protestantism's singularity *and* its long-range roots. Ancient Christianity had confirmed the "worldly" direction for salvation-striving established by Judaism's monotheism: the believer's *conduct* proved decisive for redemption. Henceforth, the Western faithful could attain a certainty of their salvation *only* through daily activity. For this reason, Weber insists, the action of the devout can never be comprehended as exclusively utilitarian in nature. Instead, it implied a salvation-relevant, value-grounded, and nonempirical dimension—and thus an *intensification* of conduct, Weber insists. Despite the significant historical presence of sects that cultivated mysticism throughout Western history, a complete "world rejection" — a "world fleeing" search for an "escape from the senseless mechanism of the 'wheel' of existence" — could not move into the mainstream of the Western religious tradition (1958, p. 373).[10]

These conclusions can also be rendered in a slightly different vein. On behalf of a quest to acquire salvation certainty, Puritanism's this-worldly ascetics, as the Hindu and Buddhist mystics, aimed to substitute a conscious and methodical directing of life toward the supernatural realm for a dependence upon utilitarian action and the empirical world. However, unlike mysticism, and also unlike ancient Judaism, early Christianity, and medieval Catholicism, this-worldly asceticism awarded psychological premiums to manifold ethical action *in* everyday life.[11] A comprehensively *disciplined believer* completely scornful of "irrational" sorcery, attributing meaning to economic activity, and systematically focused on work and profit, now marched onto the West's historical stage (pp. 266–67).

Puritanism's "practical-ethical" faithful, far more capable of calling forth significant social transformations than great political actors, powerful economic elites, or technical inventions, Weber maintains, formulated cohesive congregations throughout several societies in the sixteenth and seventeenth centuries. Comprised of extremely dedicated believers, churches and sects influenced societies far and wide, pushed social change, rejected age-old traditions, and assisted the birth of modern capitalism, he contends.

Before presenting the readings on the economic ethics of the world religions, Section 3 offers selections that define several of Weber's key EEWR terms, such as economic ethic, social carriers, stereotyped sacred law, and mysticism. These writings also "locate" belief within social contexts.

---

10.   "If even [the German mystic] Meister Eckehart [1260–1328] occasionally expressly placed Martha above Mary, he did so ultimately because he could not realize the pantheist experience of God, which is peculiar to the mystic, without entirely abandoning all the decisive elements of the Western belief in God and creation" (1946e, p. 286; transl. altered). [Martha is active in the world, while her sister Mary observes the world passively; see Luke, 10:42.]

11.   This, of course, is the this-worldly asceticism of Puritanism. The *other-worldly* asceticism practiced by monks "outside" the world in monasteries also "orders daily life"—yet only in the cloister. See pp. 116–18.

They first do so by addressing a fundamental query in his sociology of religion: how influential are carrier groups upon the formation of a religion's teachings? To become broadly effective, messages from prophets and salvation doctrines must be "carried" by cohesive strata, classes, or organizations—and these groups, Weber contends, influence strongly the content of teachings. After a religion's initial period of charismatic inspiration, "in the long run an elective affinity between spiritually prescribed conduct and the socially conditioned way of life of status groups and classes asserts itself" (1968, p. 1180; see pp. 1179–93). As social groups form to carry them, the announcements of prophets become embedded in everyday life and "routinized"—that is, increasingly influenced by the ideal *and* material interests of these carriers (pp. 240, 243).

> The various great ways of leading a rational and methodical life have been characterized by irrational presuppositions, which have been accepted simply as "given" and which have been incorporated into such ways of life. What these presuppositions have been is historically and socially determined, at least to a very large extent, through the uniqueness of those strata that have been the carriers of the ways of life during its formative and decisive period. (p. 242; see also Kalberg, 1994b, pp. 108–11)

In addition, the broader social context must be scrutinized, Weber holds in these readings. Entire configurations of "world" groups — in the rulership, the economy, and law spheres, for example — influence a religion's founding and formation, he contends, as do stratification contexts and power. Finally, great variation exists depending upon a religion's *internal* organization. He particularly attends to the question of whether congregations developed.

However, and despite the impact of social contexts, Weber emphasizes the importance of recognizing a religion's enduring confrontation with the *purely religious* conundrum: those perpetual dilemmas that surround the problems of suffering and theodicy. The substantively new *religious* truths offered by the ideas and personal revelations of charismatic prophets, disciples, mystics, and ascetics must not be downplayed, he maintains. Every ethic "receives its stamp primarily from religious sources and, first of all, from the content of its annunciation and promise" (p. 240). "The rational elements of a religion, its doctrine, also have an autonomy . . . " (p. 242), he insists.

Weber's masterful summary of the "decisive differences" between the Eastern and Western notions of salvation concludes this opening selection of readings.

Although ancient Judaism and early Christianity can be clearly identified as having laid down the tracks within which the Western journey unfolded, Weber knew well that the route had been uneven, unpredictable, and far from linear. Religion *and* world had to interact in favorable configurations. Only then would Western rationalism and modern Western rationalism establish the indispensable deep contexts capable of sustaining capitalism's growth and transformation into modern capitalism. Weber's complex *ideas and interests* analysis come to the forefront in the readings in Section 4.

MAIN CONCEPTS: ECONOMIC ETHICS, SOCIAL CARRIERS, SACRED LAW, AND THE ETHIC OF CONVICTION

From: Pp. 267–70, 279–81 in *From Max Weber,* edited and translated by H. H. Gerth and C. Wright Mills; revised by Stephen Kalberg (New York: Oxford University Press, 1946).

B y "world religions," we understand the five religions or religiously determined systems of life-regulation which have known how to gather *multitudes* of confessors around them. The term is used here in a completely value-neutral sense. The Confucian, Hinduist, Buddhist, Christian, and Islamist religious ethics all belong to the category of world religion. A sixth religion, Judaism, will also be dealt with. It is included because it contains historical preconditions decisive for understanding Christianity and Islamism, and because of its historic and autonomous significance for the development of the modern economic ethic of the West—a significance, partly real and partly alleged, which has been discussed frequently recently.[1] References to other religions will be made only when they are indispensable for the historical context.

What is meant by the "economic ethic" of a religion will become increasingly clear during the course of our presentation. This term does bring into focus the ethical theories of theological compendia; for however important such compendia may be under certain circumstances, they merely serve as tools of knowledge. The term "economic ethic" points to the *practical impulses for action* which are founded in the psychological and pragmatic contexts of religions. The following presentation may be sketchy, but it will make obvious how complicated the structures and how many-sided the conditions of a concrete economic ethic usually are. Furthermore, it will show that externally similar forms of economic organization can be united with very different economic ethics and, according to the unique character of their economic ethics, how such forms of economic organization may produce very different historical effects. An economic ethic is not a simple "function" of a form of economic organization; and just as little does the reverse hold, namely, that economic ethics unambiguously stamp the form of the economic organization.

---

1. See pp. 14, 291–92. Weber is here referring to his friend the economic historian Werner Sombart (1863–1941). See his *The Jews and Modern Capitalism* (New York: Collier Books, 1962) and *Die deutsche Wirtschaft im 19. Jahrhundert* (Berlin: G. Bondi, 1903). [sk]

No economic ethic has ever been determined solely by religion. In the face of man's attitudes towards the world—as determined by religious or other (in our sense) "inner" factors—an economic ethic has, of course, a high measure of autonomy. Given factors of economic geography and history determine this measure of autonomy in the highest degree. The religious determination of life-conduct, however, is also one—note this—only one, of the determinants of the economic ethic. Of course, the religiously determined way of life is itself profoundly influenced by economic and political factors operating within given geographical, political, social, and national boundaries. We should lose ourselves in these discussions if we tried to demonstrate these dependencies in all their singularities. Here we can only attempt to peel off the directive elements in the life-conduct of those social *strata* which have most strongly influenced the practical ethic of their respective religions. These elements have stamped the most characteristic features upon practical ethics, the features that distinguish one ethic from others; *and,* at the same time they have been important for the respective economic ethics [see 1968, pp. 479–80].

By no means must we focus upon only one stratum. Those strata which are decisive in stamping the characteristic features of an economic ethic may change in the course of history. And the influence of a single stratum is never an exclusive one. Nevertheless, as a rule one may determine the strata whose styles of life have been at least predominantly decisive for certain religions. Here are some examples, if one may anticipate:

Confucianism was the status ethic of men with literary educations who were characterized by a secular rationalism. They lived off prebends [pensions or endowments in land]. If one did not belong to this *cultured* stratum he did not count. The religious (or if one wishes, irreligious) status ethic of this stratum has determined the Chinese life-conduct far beyond the stratum itself.

Earlier Hinduism was borne by a hereditary caste of cultured literati. Remote from any office, they functioned as a kind of ritualist and spiritual group of advisers for individuals and communities. They formed a stable center for the orientation of the status stratification, and they placed their stamp upon the social order. Only Brahmans, *educated* in the [ancient sacred] Veda [texts], formed, as bearers of tradition, the fully recognized religious status group. And only later a non-Brahman status group of ascetics emerged by the side of the Brahmans and competed with them. Still later, during the Indian Middle Ages, Hinduism entered the plain. It represented the ardent sacramental religiosity of the savior and was borne by the lower strata with their plebeian mystagogues [who, as officials, revealed mysteries].

Buddhism was propagated by strictly contemplative, mendicant monks, who rejected the world and, having no homes, migrated. They alone were full members of the religious community; all others remained religious laymen of inferior value: objects, not subjects, of religiosity.

During its first period, Islamism was a religion of world-conquering warriors, a knight order of disciplined crusaders. They lacked only the sexual asceticism of their Christian copies of the age of the Crusades. But during the Islamic Middle Ages, contemplative and mystical Sufism[2] attained at least an equal standing under the leadership of plebeian technicians of orgiastics. The brotherhoods of the petty bourgeoisie grew out ot Sufism in a manner similar to the Christian Tertianans, [the lay order of Franciscans], except they were far more universally developed.

Since the Exile, Judaism has been the religion of a civic "pariah people." We shall in time become acquainted with the precise meaning of the term [see below, p. 293, and 1958, pp. 11–13]. During the Middle Ages Judaism fell under the leadership of a stratum of intellectuals who were trained in literature and ritual, a peculiarity of Judaism. This stratum has represented an increasingly quasi-proletarian and rationalist petty-bourgeois intelligentsia.

Christianity, finally, began its course as a doctrine of itinerant artisan journeymen. During all periods of its external and internal development it has been a quite specifically urban, and above all a civic, religion. This was true during Antiquity, during the Middle Ages, and in Puritanism. The city of the West, unique among all other cities of the world—and a middle class, in the sense in which it has emerged only in the West—has been the major theatre for Christianity. This holds for the piety [of the unruly spirits or *pneumata*] of the ancient religious community, for the mendicant monk orders of the High Middle Ages, and for the [Protestant] sects of the Reformation up to Pietism and Methodism.

It is not our thesis that the specific nature of a religion is a simple "function" of the social situation of the stratum which appears as its characteristic carrier, or that it represents the stratum's "ideology," or that it is a "reflection" of a stratum's material or ideal interest-situation. On the contrary a more basic misunderstanding of the standpoint of these discussions would hardly be possible.

However incisive the social influences, economically and politically determined, may have been upon a religious ethic in a particular case, it receives its stamp primarily from religious sources and, first of all, from the content of its annunciation and its promise. Frequently the very next generation reinterprets these annunciations and promises in a fundamental fashion. Such reinterpretations adjust the revelations to the needs of the religious community. If this occurs, then it is at least—again, as a rule—the case that religious doctrines are adjusted to *religious needs*. Other spheres of interest could have only a secondary influence; often, however, such influence is very obvious and sometimes it is decisive.

For every religion we shall find that a change in the socially decisive strata has usually been of profound importance. On the other hand, the type of a religion, once stamped, has usually exerted a rather far-reaching

---

2.   A Mohammedan mysticism originating in Persia during the eighth century. It developed an elaborate symbolism, much used by poets [G&M].

influence upon the life-conduct of very heterogeneous strata. In various ways people have sought to interpret the relationship between religious ethics and interest-situations in such a way that the former appear as mere "functions" of the latter. Such interpretation occurs in so-called historical materialism—which we shall not here discuss—as well as in a purely psychological sense [see 1968, pp. 468–517].

* * *

The various religious or magical states that have given their psychological stamp to religions may be systematized according to very different points of view. Here . . . we merely wish to indicate quite generally the following.

The kind of empirical state of bliss or experience of rebirth that is sought after as the supreme value by a religion has obviously and necessarily varied according to the character of the stratum which was its most important carrier. The chivalrous warrior class, peasants, trade- and occupation-oriented classes, and intellectuals with literary education have naturally pursued different religious tendencies. As will become evident, these tendencies have not by themselves determined the psychological character of religion; they have, however, exerted a very lasting influence upon it. The contrast of warrior and peasant strata to intellectual and business strata is of special importance. Of these groups the intellectuals have always been the exponents of a rationalism which, in their case, has been relatively theoretical. The trade classes (merchants and skilled laborers) have been at least possible exponents of rationalism of a more practical sort. Rationalism of either kind has borne very different stamps, but has always tended to exert a great influence upon the religious posture [see below 1946e, pp. 282–84; 1968, pp. 468–517].

Above all, the uniqueness of the intellectual strata in this matter has been in the past of the greatest importance for religion. . . . [It] was the work of the intellectuals to sublimate the possession of sacred values into a belief in "salvation."

The conception of the idea of salvation as such is very old if one understands by it a liberation from distress, hunger, drought, sickness, and ultimately, from suffering and death. Yet salvation attained a specific significance only where it expressed a systematic and rationalized "world view" and a stand in reference to it. For the meaning as well as the intended and actual psychological quality of salvation has depended upon such a world view and such a stand. Not ideas, but material and ideal interests, directly govern a person's activity. Yet very frequently the "world views" that have been created by "ideas" have, like switchmen, determined the tracks along which action has been pushed by the dynamic of interest. "From what" and "for what" one wished to be "saved" and, let us not forget, could be saved, depended upon one's world view.

There have been very different possibilities in this connection; One could wish to be saved from political and social servitude and lifted into a Messianic realm in the future of this world; or one could wish to be saved from being defiled by ritual impurity and hope for the pure beauty of psychic and bodily existence. One could wish to escape being incarcerated in an impure body and hope for a purely spiritual existence. One could wish to be saved from the eternal and senseless play of human passions and desires and hope for the quietude of the pure beholding of the divine. One could wish to be saved from radical evil and the servitude of sin and hope for the eternal and free benevolence in the lap of a fatherly god. One could wish to be saved from peonage under the astrologically conceived determination of stellar constellations and long for the dignity of freedom and partaking of the substance of the hidden deity. One could wish to be redeemed from the barriers to the finite, which express themselves in suffering, misery and death, and the threatening punishment of hell, and hope for an eternal bliss in an earthly or paradisical future existence. One could wish to be saved from the cycle of rebirths with their inexorable compensations for the deeds of the times past and hope for eternal rest. One could wish to be saved from senseless brooding and events and long for the dreamless sleep.

Many more varieties of belief have, of course, existed. Behind them always lies a stand towards something in the actual world which is experienced as specifically "senseless." Thus, the demand has been implied: that the world order in its totality is, could, and should somehow be a meaningful "cosmos." This quest, the core of genuine *religious rationalism,* has been borne precisely by strata of intellectuals. The avenues, the results, and the efficacy of this metaphysical need for a meaningful cosmos have varied widely. . . .

The various great ways of organizing a rational and methodical life have been characterized by irrational presuppositions, which have been accepted simply as "given" and then incorporated into these organized lives. What these presuppositions have been is historically and socially determined, at least to a very large extent, by the unique features of those strata that have been the carriers of the rational-methodical life during its formative and decisive period. The *interest* situation of these strata, as determined socially and psychologically, has made for their uniqueness, as we here understand it.

From: Pp. 286–87 in *From Max Weber,* edited and translated by H. H. Gerth and C. Wright Mills; revised by Stephen Kalberg (New York: Oxford University Press, 1946).

The rational elements of a religion—its "doctrine"— also have an autonomy: for instance, the Indian doctrine of Kharma, the Calvinist belief in predestination, the Lutheran justification through faith, and the Catholic doctrine of sacrament. The rational religious pragmatism of salvation, flowing from the nature of the images of God and of the "world view," have under certain conditions had far-reaching consequences for the formation of a practical way of life.

These comments presuppose that the nature of the desired sacred values has been strongly influenced by the nature of the external interest-situation and the life-conduct corresponding to it of the ruling strata—and thus by social stratification itself. But the reverse also holds: wherever the direction of the whole way of life has been methodically rationalized, it has been profoundly determined by the ultimate values toward which this rationalization was oriented. These values, and positions taken in reference to them, were thus *religiously* determined. That is, they have not always, or exclusively, been decisive; however, they have been decisive in so far as an *ethical* rationalization held sway, at least so far as its influence reached. As a rule these religious values have been *also*, and often entirely, decisive. . . .

From: Pp. 367–70, 304 in *Wirtschaft und Gesellschaft: Religiöse Gemeinschaften* [*Max Weber Gesamtausgabe (MWG)* I/22-2], edited by Hans G. Kippenberg. Translated by Stephen Kalberg. (Tübingen: Mohr/Siebeck, 2001). [*Economy and Society*, pp. 576–79, 528]

The more a religion of salvation has been systematized and internalized in the form of an ethic of conviction, the greater becomes its tension with worldly realities. This tension appears in a less consistent fashion, and less as a matter of principle, so long as the religion has a ritualistic or legalistic form. Its effect in this form is essentially the same as magic. That is, a salvation religion generally speaking begins by assigning inviolable sanctity to those conventions passed down to it—since all the followers of a particular god are interested in avoiding the wrath of the deity and thus in punishing any violation of the norms upheld by him. Consequently, once an injunction has achieved the level of a divine commandment, it rises out of the circle of alterable conventions into the rank of sanctity. From this point on, the regulations formulated by the religion are regarded, like the arrangements of the cosmos as a whole, as eternally valid: although they can be interpreted, they remain unalterable unless the God himself reveals a new commandment.

In this stage, the religion exerts a stereotyping effect on all legal institutions and social conventions in the same way that symbolism stereotypes specific major aspects of a culture and magical taboos stereotype basic relationships between human beings and gods. The sacred books of the Hindus, Muslims, Parsees, and Jews, and the classical books of the Chinese, treat legal statutes in precisely the same way that they address ceremonial and ritual norms. The law is "sacred" law. The dominance of law that has been stereotyped by religion constitutes one of the most important barriers to the rationalization of the legal order—and hence to the rationalization of the economy.

Conversely, a sudden or a gradual revolution of massive scale may take place, even in the daily rhythm of life and particularly in the realm of the economy, wherever ethical prophecies break through stereotyped magical or ritual norms. Of course there are limits to the power of religion in both directions. It is by no means true that religion is always the driving element when it is found together with social change. Furthermore, in particular, religion nowhere creates from the outset economic conditions; rather it creates economic change only if existing relationships and constellations of interests have already introduced certain possibilities of — or even powerful drives toward — such economic change. Any general formula that articulates the substantive power of the various developmental components, and the type of their "adjustment" to each other, cannot be offered.

The needs of economic life make their influence felt. This takes place when either a reinterpretation of the sacred commandments or a casuistically motivated circumvention of them occurs. On occasion it also takes place when, in the normal course of ecclesiastical dispensation of penance and grace, the sacred commandment is eliminated for simple and practical reasons. An example would be the elimination within the Catholic church of so important a provision as the prohibition against usury even *in foro conscientiae* [in the conscience of the judge]; this occurred without an explicit abrogation, which would have been impossible. Probably the same transformation will take place in the case of another forbidden practice, *onanismus matrimonialis*, viz., the limitation of offspring to two children per family.

The frequent ambiguity or silence of religious norms with respect to new problems and practices like the aforementioned, which occurs in the natural course of things, results on the one hand in the unmediated juxtaposition of absolutely unalterable stereotypes with, on the other hand, extraordinary capriciousness and utter unpredictability with respect to the validity of a particular application of these stereotypes. Thus, in dealing with the Islamic *shar'iah* it is virtually impossible to assert what is the practice today in regard to any particular matter. The same confusion obtains with regard to all sacred laws and ethical injunctions that have a formal ritualistic and casuistical character, above all the Jewish law.

However, a systematization of religious duties in the direction of an ethic based on inner religious "conviction" (*Gesinnungsethik*) produces a situation that is fundamentally different in essence. Such systematization breaks through the stereotypization of individual norms in order to bring about a "meaningful" total relationship of life conduct to the goal of religious salvation. Moreover, an inner religious conviction does not recognize any "sacred law," but only a "sacred inner consciousness"—and this consciousness can sanction different maxims of conduct according to the situation. It is hence elastic and capable of accommodation. Depending on the direction of life it engenders, it may produce revolutionary consequences from within instead of exerting a stereotyping effect.

But it acquires this ability to revolutionize at the price of an essentially intensified and "internalized" dynamic. The inherent tension between the religious postulate and worldly realities does not in truth diminish, but rather increases. With the increasing systematization and rationalization of social relationships and of their substantive contents, the external compensations provided by the teachings of theodicy are more and more replaced by the struggles of the separate autonomous spheres of life [law, the economy, rulership] against the requirements of religion—and hence these struggles shape the "world." To the same extent that the religious need becomes intense, the "world" becomes all the more formed as a problem. . . .

The religious ethic penetrates deeply into the societal spheres of life to very different degrees. The decisive aspect of this ethic is not here the intensity of its attachment to magic and ritual or the distinctive character of religion generally, but above all its position in principle toward the world generally. To the extent that a religious ethic organizes the world from a religious perspective into a systematic, rational cosmos, its ethical tensions with the world's societal spheres are likely to become sharper and more principled. This is the more true the more the spheres in turn are systematized according to their own internal laws. A religious ethic originates that is oriented to the rejection of the world—and this ethic by its very nature completely lacks any of that stereotyping character of sacred laws. Precisely the tension which this ethic of world rejection carries into relationships with the world's spheres becomes a strongly dynamic developmental element.

* * *

Our concern is with the quest for salvation, whatever its form, essentially insofar as it produced certain consequences for *practical behavior* for daily life. It is most likely to acquire such an overt orientation to the world as a result of a *conduct of life* which is determined specifically by religion and given coherence by some central meaning or manifest goal. In other words, a quest for salvation in any religious group has the strongest chance of exerting practical influences when there has arisen, out of religious motivations, a systematization of practical action resulting from an orientation to unified values. The goal and significance of such life-conduct may remain altogether oriented to the world beyond, or it may focus on this world, at least in part. In the particular religions, this has occurred in exceedingly diverse fashion and in different degrees—and even within each religion there are corresponding differences among its various adherents. Moreover, the religious systematization of the conduct of life has, in the nature of the case, certain limits insofar as it seeks to exert influence upon economic action. Finally, religious motivations, especially the hope of salvation, *need not* necessarily acquire any influence at all upon the manner of the conduct of life, particularly the mode of economic conduct. Yet they may do so to a quite considerable degree.

From Pp. 328–30 in *From Max Weber,* edited and translated by H. H. Gerth and C. Wright Mills; revised by Stephen Kalberg (New York: Oxford University Press, 1946).

Wherever prophecies of salvation have created groups with a purely religious foundation, the first power with which they have come into conflict has been the natural sib. The tribe has had to fear devaluation by prophecy. Those who cannot be hostile to members of the household, to father and to other, cannot be disciples of Jesus, "I came not to send peace, but a sword" (Matthew x, 34) was said in this connection and, it should be noted, solely in this connection. The preponderant majority of all religions have, of course, regulated the inner-worldly bonds of piety. Yet the more comprehensive and the more inward the aim of salvation has been, the more it has been taken for granted that the faithful should ultimately stand closer to the savior, the prophet, the priest, the father confessor, and the brother in the faith than to natural relations and to the matrimonial community.

Prophecy has created a new social community particularly where it became a soteriological religion of congregations. Thereby the relationships of the sib and of matrimony have been, at least relatively, devalued. The magical ties and exclusiveness of the sibs have been shattered, and within the new community the prophetic religion has developed a religious ethic of brotherliness. This ethic has simply taken over the original principles of social and ethical conduct which the "association of neighbors" had offered, whether it was the community of villagers, members of the sib, the guild, or of partners in seafaring, hunting, and warring expeditions. These communities have known two elemental principles: first, the dualism of in-group and out-group morality; second, for in-group morality, simple reciprocity: "As you do unto me I shall do into you."

From these principles the following have resulted for economic life: For in-group morality the principled obligation to give brotherly support in distress has existed. The wealthy and the noble were obliged to loan, free of charge, goods for the use of the propertyless, to give credit free of interest, and to extend liberal hospitality and support. Men were obliged to render services upon the request of their neighbors and, likewise, on the lord's estate without compensation other than mere sustenance. All this followed the principle: your want of today may be mine of tomorrow. This principle was not, of course, rationally *weighed*; rather it played an emotional part. Accordingly, higgling in exchange and loan situations, as well as permanent enslavement resulting, for instance, from debts, were confined to out-group morality and applied only to outsiders.

The religiosity of the congregation transferred this ancient economic ethic of neighborliness to the relations among brethren of the faith. What had previously been the obligations of the noble and the wealthy became the fundamental imperative of all ethically rationalized religions of the world: to aid widows and orphans in distress, to care for the sick and impoverished brother of the faith, and to give alms. The giving of alms was especially required of the rich, for the holy minstrels and magicians, as well as the ascetics, were economically dependent upon the rich.

The principle that constituted the communal relations among the salvation prophecies was the suffering common to all believers. And this was the case whether the suffering actually existed or was a constant threat, whether it was external or internal. The more the idea of salvation was comprehended as rational and the more it became sublimated into an ethic of conviction, the more the commands that arose out of the reciprocity ethic of the neighborhood became, as a consequence, intensified externally and internally. Externally, such commands rose to a communism of loving brethren; internally they rose to the attitude of *caritas*, love for the sufferer *per se*, for one's neighbor, for human beings, and finally for the enemy. The barrier to the bond of faith and the existence of hatred in the face of a world conceived to be the locus of undeserved suffering seem to have resulted from the same imperfections and depravities of empirical reality that originally caused the suffering.

Above all, the peculiar euphoria of all types of sublimated religious ecstasy operated psychologically in the same general direction. From being "moved" and edified to feeling direct communion with God, ecstasies have always inclined men towards the flowing out into an objectless acosmism of love. In religions of salvation the profound and quiet bliss of all heroes of acosmic benevolence has always been fused with a charitable realization of the natural imperfections of all human doings, including one's own. The psychological tone as well as the rational, ethical interpretation of this inner attitude can vary widely. But its ethical demand has always lain in the direction of a universalist brotherhood, which goes beyond all barriers of societal associations, often including that of one's own faith.

The religion of brotherliness has always clashed with the orders and values of this world, and the more consistently its demands have been carried through, the sharper the clash has been. The split has usually become wider the more the values of the world have been rationalized and sublimated in terms of their own laws. And that is what matters here.

From: Pp. 288–94 in *From Max Weber,* edited and translated by H. H. Gerth and C. Wright Mills; revised by Stephen Kalberg (New York: Oxford University Press, 1946).

The religious virtuosos saw themselves compelled to adjust their demands to the parameters offered by everyday-life religiosity in order to acquire and maintain ideal and material mass patronage. The nature of their accommodations have naturally been of major significance for the manner of religion's influence upon everyday life. In almost all Eastern religions the virtuosos allowed the masses to remain stuck in magic-permeated tradition. Hence, their influence has been infinitely smaller than occurred in those cases where religion undertook ethically and generally to rationalize everyday life. This remains the case in the East even where religion has been directed precisely and exclusively at the masses.

In addition to the relationship between the religiosity of the virtuosos and the masses, the unique nature of the concrete religiosity of the virtuosos was itself of decisive importance for the development of the organization of life of the masses. It has therefore also been central for the economic ethic of the religion concerned. Indeed, this uniqueness resulted in the end from the virtuoso–mass relationship. For the religion of the virtuoso has been not only a genuinely "exemplary"–practical religiosity; in addition, various possibilities arose, according to the organization of life this religiosity prescribed for this figure, for the creation of a rational ethic of everyday life. This relation of virtuoso religion to daily life, which is the arena for the economy, has especially varied according to the particular *sacred values* such religions strove for.

No bridge has led from religion to the practical action of daily life wherever the sacred values and the salvation paths of a virtuoso religion contained a contemplative or orgiastic-ecstatic character. Economic action in such cases was considered religiously inferior, as was all other action in the world. In addition, psychological motives for world action could not be — even indirectly — derived from the Habitus esteemed as the supreme religious posture. In its internal essence, contemplative and ecstatic religiosity has been particularly hostile to the economy. Mystic, orgiastic, and ecstatic experience is extraordinary: it leads away from everyday life and from all means-end action. Such experience is *therefore* deemed to be "holy."

Hence, a deep abyss separates the "layman's" organization of life in these religions from that of the community of virtuosos. The rule of the virtuoso status group inside the religious community readily shifts then into the pathway of a magical anthropolatry: the virtuoso is directly worshipped as a saint or, at a minimum, as a layman, as a means of assisting mundane success or religious salvation and as a mechanism of purchasing his blessing and his magical powers. As the peasant was to the landlord, so the layman was to the Buddhist and Jainist *bhikshu* [wandering mendicant monks]: ultimately sources of tribute that allowed virtuosos to avoid performing the mundane work that would endanger their salvation and to live entirely for religious salvation.

Nonetheless, the organization of life of the layman could still undergo a certain ethical regulation, for the virtuoso is the layman's spiritual adviser, his father confessor, and *directeur de l'ame* [director of the soul]. Hence, he frequently exercises a powerful influence over the religiously "unmusical" layman. However, this influence might not be in the direction of his (the virtuoso's) own religious way of life, but instead in the direction of unconnected ceremonial, ritual, and conventional practices. For action in this world to the virtuoso remained in principle religiously insignificant and lay in precisely the opposite direction of his religious striving. In the end, unlike the charisma of the genuine magician, which serves others, the charisma of the pure "mystic" completely serves himself alone.

Everything has been completely otherwise where religiously qualified virtuosos, striving to shape life in the mundane world according to the will of a God, came together into an ascetic sect. To be sure, two preconditions had to be in place for this to occur in any genuine sense. First, the highest sacred value must not be of a contemplative character; that is, it must not consist on the one hand of a unification with a supra-mundane being who, in contrast to the world, lasts forever, or on the other hand in a mystical union (*unio mystica*) based in orgiasticism or apathetic ecstasy. These pathways lead away from the real world, for they lie beyond it and too distant from daily life activity. Second, as far as possible, such a religiosity must have banished the purely magical or sacramental character of the *means* of salvation—for these means also always devalue worldly action as at best relative in its religious significance. They do so by linking the decision regarding salvation to the success of processses *not* of a rational-everyday nature.

If one disregards the small rational sects found throughout the world, only the great churches and sects of ascetic Protestantism in the West called forth both a disenchantment (*Entzauberung*) of the world and a displacement of the path to salvation away from a contemplative "flight from the world" to an active, ascetic "shaping of the world through work" (*Weltbearbeitung*). These developments took place only on the basis of a reciprocal interaction of Western religiosity's quite distinct and purely historically-determined destinies. In part the influence of its social environment was important, above all the stratum decisive for this religiosity's development [urban civic strata]. However, just as strongly, the genuine character of Western religion played a central role: the transcendental God and the specificity of the means and paths of salvation as historically determined first by Israelite prophecy and the Torah doctrine. . . .

A magic-based route toward salvation is precluded wherever the religious virtuoso is placed into the world as an "instrument" of his God. In this case the demand is placed upon the believer that he "testify" to his status as being called by God — namely, as among the saved — through the ethical quality of his action in the world's spheres—and *only* in this manner. This implies that the virtuoso must actually testify to his salvation to himself. The "world" as such, regardless of how completely it now becomes de-valued by religion and rejected as merely the realm of the physical and a vessel of sin, is all the more affirmed psychologically as the arena within which the action demanded by God — in a "vocational calling" — takes place. Although inner-worldly asceticism rejected the world in the sense that it scorned and tabooed, as competitors to the kingdom of God, the values of dignity and beauty, of beautiful delirium and the magnificient dream, of power utilized for purely secular ends and the purely secular pride of heroes, it nonetheless refused to flee from the world into contemplation. On the contrary, inner-worldly asceticism wanted ethically to rationalize the world to bring it into accordance with God's commandments.

Indeed, for this reason inner-worldly asceticism remained oriented to the world in a manner particularly more penetrating than the direct "affirmation of the world" typical of the unbroken humanity, for instance, of Antiquity and lay Catholicism. The state of grace, and of being among the chosen, experienced by the religiously qualified, was testified to precisely in everyday life—not, to be sure, in everyday life as given, but in methodical-*rationalized* daily activity in service to the Lord. Everyday action, intensified into a vocational calling, became testimony to one's salvation. And it was the Western sects of religious virtuosi that formed the methodical rationalization of life-conduct, including also economic action. Unlike Asia's communities of contemplative, orgiastic, or apathetic ecstatics, these [Western] sects have not constituted mechanisms for the longing to escape from the senselessness of inner-worldly activity.

The most varied transitions and combinations existed between these polar opposites of other-worldly mysticism and inner-worldly asceticism, for neither religions nor men are open books. They have been historical, rather than logical or even psychological constructions devoid of internal contradictions. Very often they contained a series of motives that would have, if followed out consistently, run up against one another, indeed even to the extent of diametrical opposition. Rather than the rule, "consistency" was here the exception. Even the salvation paths and sacred values were, on a regular basis, not straightforward. Even the search for God by the monks of ancient Christianity and the Quakers retained very strong contemplative aspects. Nonetheless, the entire content of their religiosity — above all their transcendental God of creation and manner of insuring the certainty of the believer's salvation — again and again directed the devout toward the path of action.

The Buddhist monk, on the other hand, also acted. However, owing to the ultimate orientation of his quest for salvation toward a flight from the "wheel" of rebirths, his action fled from every consistent *inner-worldly* rationalization. In the Western Middle Ages the religious penetration of everyday life was carried by the sectarians and other brotherhoods, and these organizations found their counter-images in the — even more universally developed — brotherhoods of Islam. Even the strata typical of such brotherhoods in the West and in Islam were identical: the petty bourgeoisie and especially artisans. Yet the spirit of their respective religiosity was very different. Viewed externally, numerous Hindu religious communities appear to be "sects" indistinguishable from the religious communities of the West. The sacred value, however, and the manner in which salvation was mediated, pointed in radically opposed directions.

A further accumulation of illustrations need not occur here. We wish rather to consider the most important of the world religions separately. Neither in this respect nor any other can they be simply arranged into a chain of types, each of which signifies a new "stage." Rather, they constitute historical individual cases of a highly complex nature. When taken all together, they exhaust only a few of the possible combinations that could conceivably be formed out of the relevant — and very numerous — individual factors.

Hence, we are not concerned in the following discussions in any way with a *systematic* "typology" of religion. Yet neither do they constitute a purely historical presentation. Rather, they must be viewed as "typological"—namely, in the sense that they consider what is important in a typical manner in the historical realities of the religious ethics in respect to their connection with the widely diverging frames of minds oriented to the economy. Other aspects will be neglected. Hence, these presentations nowhere claim to offer a fully well-rounded picture of the religions discussed here. Those features unique to the individual religions *in contrast to* other religions, but which *at the same time* are important for the connections we wish to establish, must be brought out strongly. . . .

Furthermore, it should be noted that we are here essentially interested in the features of a religion that are important for its economic ethic from a particular vantage point: the way in which they are related to economic rationalism. More precisely, our concern is with the manner in which features of a religion relate to the specific type of economic rationalism that began to dominate, as a partial manifestation of the West's particular civic rationalization of life, since the sixteenth and seventeenth centuries.

We must from the outset remember again that "rationalism" can signify very different themes. . . . That is, our concern — the rationalization of life-conduct — can take on unusually varied forms.

Confucianism, in the sense of an absence of all metaphysics and almost all residuals of an anchoring in religion, is rationalist—indeed to such an extent that it stands at the outer boundaries of that which one can identify as a "religious" ethic. Simultaneously, in the sense of an omission and rejection of all non-utilitarian standards, Confucianism is more rationalist and sober than any other ethical system with the possible exception of Jeremy Bentham's. Nonetheless, this world religion, despite enduring real and apparent analogies, remains extraordinarily different from Bentham's utilitarianism and from all other types of practical rationalism in the West. The highest aesthetic ideal of the Renaissance was "rational" in the sense of the belief in a valid "canon," and its view of life was rational in its rejection of traditional ties and its belief in the power of the *naturalis ratio*. These features of the Renaissance remained despite the presence of elements of platonizing mysticism. In a completely different manner, namely, as a "systematic ordering," "rational" are also the methods of mortificatory asceticism, magical asceticism—and, in its most consistent forms as found, for example, in yoga or the later Buddhist manipulations using prayer machines—contemplation.

In part in the same manner (that is, an orientation to a formal methodology) and in part differently (that is, "rational" in the sense of a distinction between the normatively "valid" and the empirically given), were in general all types of practical ethics systematically and clearly oriented to firm salvational goals. It is this distinction, as a type of rationalization process, that interests us in the following discussions. . . .

The author, must, however, in order to pursue this course of research, take the liberty of proceeding "unhistorically" in the sense that the particular religions will be presented in a manner systematically essentially more unified than they ever appeared in the flow of their development. An entire series of contrasts that live within the separate religions — ones that concern both developments at the outset on the one hand and branching off developments on the other — must be left aside. This means that the features of importance to us will be, compared to the actual reality, presented frequently with greater logical consistency and with less attention to developmental detail.

If carried out in an arbitrary manner, this simplification would *then* yield a "false" historical picture. However, this is not the case, at least not intentionally. Rather, the emphasis has continuously been placed much more on those features in a religion's entire picture that were decisive for the formation of its *practical* organization of life. Throughout, those features that *distinguish* the religion under investigation vis-à-vis other religions [will be] stressed.

From: "The Decisive Differences Between Eastern and Western Salvation." Pp. 332–40 in *Wirtschaft und Gesellschaft: Religiöse Gemeinschaften* [*MWG I22-2*], edited by Hans G. Kippenberg. Translated by Stephen Kalberg. (Tübingen: Mohr/Siebeck), 2001) [*Economy and Society*, pp. 551–56]

The decisive historical difference between the predominantly Eastern and Asian types of salvation religion and those found primarily in the West is that the former essentially culminate in contemplation and the latter in asceticism. For our purely empirical study, the great significance of this distinction is not at all altered by the fluid nature of this difference: recurrent combinations of mystical and ascetic characteristics demonstrate that these heterogeneous elements may merge, as in, for example, the monastic religiosity of the West. The effects upon action constitute our concern.

In India even the highly ascetic procedure for attaining salvation as that of the Jain monks culminated in a purely contemplative and mystical ultimate goal. And in Eastern Asia Buddhism became the characteristic religion of salvation.

On the other hand, in the West, apart from the few representatives of a distinct Quietism, which belongs to the modern period, even explicitly mystical religions regularly become altered into an active, and then of course mainly ascetic, pursuit of virtue. To be more precise, there occurred along the pathway an internal selection of motivations which above all favored active conduct and, usually, asceticism. Neither the mystical contemplation of St. Bernhard [of Clairvaux; 1090–1153], nor Franciscan spirituality, nor the contemplative strains among the Baptists and the Jesuits, nor even the emotional storms of Zinzendorf prevented either the community or often even the individual mystic from awarding priority to action and testifying to salvation through activity, even though ranging to very different degrees from pure asceticism to a limited contemplation. In the end Meister Eckehart placed Martha above Mary, despite Christ's preference (see p. 236, note 10).

However, to a certain degree this salvation-striving was specific to Christianity from the outset. Even then, at a time when all types of irrational charismatic and spiritual offerings were believed to be the decisive indication of sanctity, a distinctive answer had already been given by Christian apologetics: the divine origin of the spiritual achievements of Christ and his followers could be distinguished from all achievements of Satanic or demonic origin by the morality of the faithful—and this morality itself testified to its divine source. The devout from India could not answer in this way.

Many reasons account for this fundamental difference. The following should be noted:

1. The concept of a transcendental, absolutely omnipotent God, which implies the complete subordination and creaturely character of the world created by Him out of nothing, arose in the Near East and was imposed on the West. Consequently, any methodical striving for salvation

and any genuinely mystical possession of God, at least in any strict sense, was permanently precluded: this striving could be perceived only as a blasphemous deification of merely creaturely beings. The salvation path to the ultimately pantheistic consequences of mysticism was "blocked"; it was always viewed as heterodox. All salvation must repeatedly take on the character of an ethical "justification" before God. Ultimately only some sort of active conduct in the world would allow this justification and demonstrate one's belief. Even for the mystic [in the West], a "certification" of the actually divine quality of the mystical possession of salvation (as assessed by the mystic himself) could be arrived at only through the path of activity.

However, activity in turn introduced into mysticism paradoxes, tensions, and the prevention of an ultimate union with God. This was spared to India's mysticism. For the Western mystic, the world is a "work" which has been "created" and is not simply given for all eternity, not even in its more firm aspects, as are those for the Asian mystic. Consequently, in the West mystical salvation could not be found simply in the consciousness of an absolute union with a supreme and wise "order of things" as the only true "being." Nor, on the other hand, could a work of divine origin ever be regarded in the West as involving absolute world rejection, as occurred with the flight from the world characteristic in India.

2. This contrast [between Asian and Western salvation religions] is related also to the character of Asiatic salvation religions as pure religions of intellectuals who never abandoned the "meaningfulness" of the empirical world. For the Buddhist there was actually a way leading directly from "insight" into the ultimate consequences of the *karma* chain of causality to illumination, and from there to a unity of "knowledge" and action. This way remained forever closed to every religion that faced the absolute paradox of a perfect God's "creation" of a permanently imperfect world. Indeed, the intellectual mastery of the world leads in this latter type of religion away from God rather than toward him. From the practical point of view, those instances of Western mysticism that have a purely philosophical foundation stand closest to the Asiatic type.

3. Further to be considered in accounting for the basic distinction between Western salvation religions and the salvation religions of India are various practical issues. Particular emphasis must be placed on the Roman West's unique development and maintenance of a rational law, for various reasons yet to be explained. In the West the relationship of man to God became, in a distinctive fashion, a sort of legally definable relationship of subjection. Indeed, the question of salvation can be settled by a sort of legal process, a method which was later distinctively developed by [the Benedictine monk] Anselm of Canterbury [1033–1109].

Such a legalistic procedure of achieving salvation could never be adopted by the religions [of India] which posited an impersonal divine power or which posited, instead of a God standing above the world, a God standing within a world that is self-regulated by the causal chains of *karma*. Nor could the legalistic direction be taken by religions teaching concepts of Dao, belief in the celestial ancestor gods of the Chinese emperor, or, above all, belief in the Asiatic popular gods. In all these cases the highest form of piety took a pantheistic form and, in terms of their practical impulses, turned piety toward contemplation.

4. Another aspect of the rational character of a methodical procedure for achieving salvation was in origin partly Roman, partly Jewish.

The Greeks, in spite of the reluctance of the urban patriciate to embrace the Dionysiac intoxication cult, positively valued ecstasy, both the acute orgiastic type involving divine intoxication and the milder form of euphoria awakened mainly by rhythm and music. They saw it as assisting an awareness in humans of the uniquely divine. Even the ruling stratum among the Greeks experienced, from the childhood years, this mild form of ecstasy. A stratum in possession of great social prestige, such as the office nobility in Rome, was lacking in Greece since the dominance [in the seventh and sixth centuries B.C.E.] of hoplite [heavily-armed foot soldiers] discipline. Social stratification in Greece was in all respects less developed and less feudal.

In Rome [on the other hand], where nobles comprised a rational office-holding stratum of increasing prestige and where single families possessed entire cities and provinces as client holdings, ecstasy was completely rejected. Like the dance, it was perceived as completely improper and unworthy of a nobleman's honor. This is obvious even from the terminology employed in Rome to translate the Greek word for ecstasy (*ekstasis*) into Latin: *superstitio*. The performance of cultic dances occurred only in the oldest colleges of priests and, as a round of dances, only among the *fratres arvales* [Arval brotherhood]—and then typically only behind closed doors after the departure of the community.

Dance and music were regarded by the Romans as indecent; hence, in these arenas Rome remained completely unproductive. Naked exercises in the *gymnasion* [elite schools], which the Spartans had created as arenas for these activities, were similarly viewed as unseemly. The Roman Senate prohibited the Dionysiac cult of intoxication. The rejection of all types of ecstasy by Rome's world-conquering military-official aristocracy, and of all orientation by individuals to methodical procedures for the attainment of salvation — which corresponds closely to the equally strong antagonism of the Chinese bureaucracy toward all methodologies of salvation — was thus one of the sources [of the West's] strictly empirical rationalism infused with a practical-political orientation.

As they developed, Western Christian communities found this rationalism and opposition to ecstasy to be firmly entrenched on all essentially Roman territory. The Roman Christian community in particular adopted these Roman elements in a conscious and consistent manner. Whether charismatic prophecy at the beginning or the greatest innovations in church music later, it refused to accept in all cases irrational elements into its religion or culture. And this Roman Christian community was infinitely weaker than the Hellenistic East and the community of Corinth in regard to both theological thinkers and, as the sources appear to suggest, every type of manifestation of the spirit (*pneuma*). Nonetheless, and just for this reason, a dispassionate practical rationalism, the most important legacy of Rome to the Christian church, almost everywhere set the tone for a dogmatic and ethical systematization of belief, as is well known.

The development of the methods for salvation in the West continued along similar lines. The ascetic requirements of the old Benedictine regulations [for living] and the reforms of Cluny [910] are, when measured by the standards of India and the ancient East, extremely modest and obviously adapted to novices recruited from the higher social circles. However, it is precisely in the West that *labor*, as a sanitized-ascetic means, comes to the forefront as the essential characterisic.

This emphasis became intensified in the entirely methodical regulations of the Cistercians [founded 1098], a monastic order that cultivated the most rational simplicity of living. Even the mendicant monks, in contrast to their monastic counterparts in India, were forced into the service of the hierarchy and compelled, shortly after their appearance in the West, to serve rational goals: preaching, the supervision of heretics, and systematic charity, which in the West was developed into a routinely functioning organization. Finally, the Jesuit order completely expelled all the unsanitized elements of the older asceticism and introduced the most completely rational disciplining of the believer for the purposes of the church. This development is obviously connected with the next point we are to consider.

5. The Western [Catholic] church is a unified rational organization with a monarchical head and the control of piety in a centralized manner. That is, at its head is not only a personal transcendental God, but also a terrestrial ruler of enormous power who actively regulates the lives of his subjects.

Such a figure is lacking in the religions of Eastern Asia, partly for historical reasons, partly because of the nature of the religions in question. Even Lamaism [in Tibet], which is strictly organized, does not have the rigidity of a bureaucracy.... The Asiatic hierarchs in Daoism, and the other hereditary patriarchs in sects in China and India, were always partly mystagogues, partly the objects of anthropolatric veneration, and partly — as in the cases of the Dalai Lama and Panchen Lama — the chiefs of a completely monastic religion of magical character. The other-worldly asceticism of monks, which transformed undisciplined troops into a rational bureaucracy of office, was systematized only in the West increasingly into a methodology of active and rational life-conduct.

Moreover, only in the West was the additional step taken — by ascetic Protestantism — of transferring rational asceticism into the life of the world. The inner-worldly order of dervishes in Islam cultivated a planned procedure for achieving salvation, but this procedure, for all its variations, was oriented ultimately to the mystical quest for salvation of the Sufis. Deriving out of sources from India and Persia, this search of the dervishes for salvation possessed orgiastic, spiritualistic, or contemplative characteristics in different instances rather than "asceticism" in the special sense of that term which we have employed. People from India have played a leading role in dervish orgies as far afield as Bosnia.

The asceticism of the dervishes is not, like that of ascetic Protestants, a religious "ethic of vocation," for the religious achievements of the dervishes have very little relationship to their secular occupations; at best secular vocations have a purely external relationship to the planned procedure of salvation. Even so, the procedure of salvation might exert indirect effects on one's occupational behavior. The simple, pious dervish is, other things being equal, more reliable as a craftsman than a nonreligious man in the same way that the pious Parsee prospers as a businessman because of his strict adherence to the rigid injunction to be honest.

But an unbroken unity integrating in systematic and principled fashion an ethic of vocation in the world with assurance of religious salvation was the unique creation of the ethic of vocation of ascetic Protestantism alone. Furthermore, only in this ethic does the world, despite all its creaturely imperfections, possess unique and religious significance as the object through which believers fulfill their duties by rational behavior according to the will of an absolutely transcendental God. The very existence of this other-worldly rational and sober, purposive and success-oriented, action is itself the sign that God's blessing rests upon it.

This inner-worldly asceticism had a number of distinctive consequences not found in any other religion. It placed a series of demands upon the believer: not celibacy, as in the case of the monk, but the avoidance of all erotic "desire"; not poverty, but the elimination of all idle and exploitative enjoyment of unearned wealth and income, and the avoidance of all feudal, sensuous, ostentatious display of wealth; not the ascetic death-in-life of the cloister, but an alert, rationally controlled life-conduct; and the avoidance of all surrender to the beauty of the world, to art, or to one's own moods and emotions.

The manifest goal of this asceticism was the disciplined and methodical organization of life. Its typical representative was the "man of a vocation," and its unique result was the rendering of social relationships impersonal and ones of sociation only. This transformation was the unique result of the West's this-worldly asceticism—an asceticism that stands in opposition to the salvation paths offered by all other religions of the world.

INDIA: HINDUISM AND BUDDHISM

A. HINDUISM

From "Hindu Doctrine and Ritual." Pp. 24–25 in *The Religion of India*. Translated and edited by Hans H. Gerth and Don Martindale; slightly revised by Stephen Kalberg. (New York; The Free Press, 1958.)

. . . [The heretical sects] . . . tear the individual away from his ritualistic duties, hence from duties of the caste of his birth, and thus ignore or destroy his *dharma*. When this occurs the Hindu loses caste. And since only through caste can one belong to the Hindu community, he is lost to it. *Dharma*, that is, ritualistic duty, is the central criterion of Hinduism.

Hinduism is primarily ritualism, a fact implied when modern authors state that *mata* (doctrine) and *marga* (holy end) are transitory and "ephemeral"—they mean freely elected—while *dharma* is "eternal"—that is, unconditionally valid.

The first question a Hindu asks of a strange religion is not what is its teaching *(mata)* but its *dharma*. The Christian *dharma* of a Protestant is, for the Hindu, something positive in baptism, communion, church attendance, rest on Sunday and other Christian festivals, the table prayer. These observances would be acceptable to the members of all good Hindu castes with the exception of communion. When administered in either of its forms communion requires the drinking of alcohol, and compulsory table community with noncaste fellow-Christians. Moreover, the negative aspects of the Christian *dharma*—that, for example, it permits Christians to eat meat, particularly beef, and drink hard liquor—stamp it as the *dharma* of impure barbarians (*mlechha dharma*).

What, then, is the content of *dharma* to a Hindu? We learn that *dharma* differs according to social position and, since it is subject to "development," which is not absolutely closed and completed, *dharma* depends upon the caste into which the individual is born. With the split of old into new castes *dharma* is specialized. Through the advance of knowledge *dharma* can be further developed. . . .

Dharma depends first on sacred tradition, the adjudication, the literary and rationally developed learning of the Brahmans. Just as in Islamism, Judaism, and early Christianity, there is no "infallible" doctrinal authority of definite priestly office because the Brahmans represent no hierarchy of officials. The everyday *dharma* of the caste derives its content, in large measure, from the distant past with its taboos, magical norms, and witchcraft. Hindu *dharma*, however, is more extensively and in practice more significantly an exclusive product of the priesthood and its literature than the present-day ritualistic commandments of the Catholic Church. This fact has had important consequences for Hinduism.

* * *

From: "The Sects and Their Redemption Religiosity." Pp. 521–26 in *Die Wirtschaftsethik der Weltreligionen: Hinduismus und Buddhismus* [*MWG I/20*], edited by Helwig Schmidt-Glintzer. Translated by Stephen Kalberg. Tübingen: Mohr/Siebeck, 1996. [*The Religion of India*, pp. 326–28]; endnotes omitted.

Let us once more make clear which "spiritual" elements, aside from caste ties and the domination of the guru over the vast majority of believers, established Hinduism's traditional economic and social features.

Among the intellectual stratum, in addition to the authoritative bond to caste, above all common to all orthodox and heterodox Hindu thinking was the dogma on the unchangeableness of the order of the world. The devaluation of the world, which every salvation religion called forth, could here only take the form of an absolute flight from the world. The primary means on behalf of this flight, rather than active asceticism, could be only mystical contemplation.

The prestige of this salvation path — as the highest of all — was never actually diminished by the plethora of distinct ethical teachings in India. The extraordinary and irrational features of the means it offered toward salvation endured—namely, either those of an orgiastic nature (which therefore turned, in an entirely unmediated fashion, in directions opposed to every methodical organization of life) or those rational in respect to their methodicalness but irrational in respect to their goal. However, the "vocational" performance required, in the most consistent manner by the Bhagavadgita, for example, was "organic"—namely, strictly traditional. Hence, [devoid of asceticism], the salvation path remained open to a [world-fleeing] mystical influence, and activity became activity in the world yet never activity of the world. No Hindu would imagine that economic success in his vocation, and his loyalty to his vocation, could constitute signs of his salvation status. More importantly, no Hindu would evaluate a rational transformation of the world to accord with abstract principles as the execution of a god's will. And no Hindu would then initiate corresponding action.

Just in this context it must always be recognized that the stratum in India past and present of intellectuals proper was quite thin. This must be noted also of the strata of those interested in "salvation" in any rational manner. The population as a whole, at least among Hindus today [1916], knew nothing of "salvation" (*moksha, mukhti*). The expression was hardly known, and surely not the meaning. It must always have been roughly this way, with the exception of short periods of time. The masses of believers strove for — and do now — crude, and purely this-worldly, sacred interests, the execution of imprecise magic-based formulae, and the enhancement of one's reincarnation opportunities. Even the [Hindu] sects failed to influence the "masses" proper. Surely they do not do so today. . . .

The vast body of Hindus . . . understood "salvation" (*mukhti*) as a favorable rebirth. This occurs, according to the old Hindu soteriology, as a consequence of the believer's own actions rather than as a result of God's. From his local village god the Hindu expected rain and sunshine, and assistance regarding daily life problems was expected from his family god—for example, the regional gods Mailar Linga or Keda Linga (fetish). A "confession"-oriented socialization by gurus, understood by the laity as advisors, never existed: even though gurus knew ritual-based formulae, the vast lay majority found their Brahman-based theology quite incomprehensible.

The gap between the religion of the intellectuals and the daily life needs of the vast majority of believers becomes evident precisely here. The assignment of persons to a sect depended upon the Brahman guru, for he alone understood its character. Lay believers, however, never felt bound to a particular denomination. Rather, as in the ancient world, Apollo or Dionysus were worshipped according to the occasion. . . .

The sects, with their religion of salvation, offered — and offer — an opportunity for a mostly middle class group, advised by intellectuals, to acquire the salvation of the intellectual stratum through the power of contemplation. To be sure, as [*The Religion of India*] has concluded, it does not follow that the uniqueness of the intellectual's religion and its promises possessed no enduring indirect influence on the organization of life of the masses. Rather, this influence existed to a high degree.

However, its effect was never to operate in a manner that brought forth among lay believers a this-worldly methodical rationalization of life-conduct; instead, precisely the opposite was usually the case. Wealth, and especially money, enjoy an almost inestimable prestige in the proverbs of India. Yet, in addition to the alternative options — enjoyment of wealth for oneself or giving it away — there exists another: the loss of wealth. Hinduism, rather than initiating a drive toward the rational accumulation of wealth and the high estimation of money, created irrational opportunities to accumulate for magicians and soul shepards, and fees and benefits for mystagogues and intellectual strata oriented either toward ritual or a soteriology of salvation.

The modern "reform" movements inside Hinduism, such as the "Brahmo Samaj" community much discussed in Germany or the (perhaps more importantly) "Arya Samaj" community, are mainly a concern of the intellectual stratum, especially of that part of this group cultivated by, or at least imprinted by, European influences. Their history belongs in this [discussion of Hinduism's economic ethic] as little as does a discussion of the Anglo-Indian university. Bred by this university, politicians and journalists became the social carriers of a gradually developing — in the Western sense of the word — modern Indian nationalism.

Emerging in a country characterized by a fragmentation of groups into countless castes, sects, and language and racial groups in relationships of bitter enmity, this nationalism is fundamentally alien to the India to be described [in the readings that follow]: a people anchored deeply to traditions and the soil. On the other hand, European nationalism expands only on the foundation of a unified middle class together with a national literature oriented to it and, above all, with a press. This middle class generally assumes the prior development of a somehow unified (externally) conduct of life, however achieved. Yet the India of the historical Hinduism we have been discussing [in *The Religion of India*] must be seen as directly opposite of all this.

From: "The General Character of Asiatic Religion." Pp. 331–33, 336–39, 340, 342–43 in *The Religion of India*, translated and edited by Hans H. Gerth and Don Martindale; slightly revised by Stephen Kalberg. (New York: The Free Press, 1958)

Asia and that is to say, again, India is the typical land of intellectual struggle singly and alone for a *Weltanschauung,* in the particular sense of the word for the "meaning" of life and the world. It can be maintained here—and in light of the incompleteness of our discussion we must be satisfied with an incomplete certification—that in the area of thought concerning the "meaning" of the world and life there is throughout nothing which has not in some form already been conceived in Asia.

Each, according to the nature of its own apprehension, unavoidably (and as a general rule, actually all genuine Asiatic and that is Indian, soteriology) found gnosis to be the single way to the highest holiness, and at the same time, however, the single way to correct the practice. Therefore, in no way is the proposition so close to all intellectualism more self-evident: that virtue is "teachable" and right knowledge has quite infallible consequences for right practices. In the folklore itself, for example, of [the later lay and non-orthodox] Mahayanism, which plays a role for the pictorial arts somewhat similar to our biblical history, it is everywhere the self-evident presupposition. According to the circumstances, only wisdom provides ethical or magical power over the self and others. Throughout the "teaching," this "knowledge" is not a rational implement of empirical science such as made possible the rational domination of nature and man as in the West. Rather, it is the means of mystical and magical domination over the self and the world: gnosis. It is attained by an intensive training of body and spirit, either through asceticism or, and as a rule, through strict, methodologically-ruled meditation.

That such knowledge, in the nature of the case, remained mystical in character had two important consequences. First was the formation by the soteriology of a redemption aristocracy, for the capacity for mystical gnosis is a charisma not accessible to all. Second, and closely connected, is its acquisition of an asocial and apolitical character. Mystical knowledge is not, at least not adequately and rationally, communicable. Thus Asiatic soteriology always leads those seeking the highest holy objectives to an other-worldly realm of the rationally unformed and, on account of this lack of form, to a realm of divine seeing, having, possessing, and being possessed by a holiness—a bliss apart from this world. However, through the attainment of gnosis, it can be acquired in this life. It was conceived by all the highest forms of Asiatic mystical belief as "emptying." This is an emptying of experience of materials of the world. This corresponds throughout to the normal significance of mysticism; in Asia it is only carried to its logical conclusions. The devaluation of the world and its drives is an unavoidable psychological consequence of this. It is the meaning-content of mystical holy possession which rationally cannot be further explained.

This mystically experienced holy circumstance, rationally interpreted, takes the form of the opposition of peace to restlessness. The first is "God" and the second is specifically creature-like, and therefore, finally, either illusory or still soteriologically valueless, bound by time and space and transitory. Its most rational interpretation, which was dominant throughout Asia, of the experientially-conditioned inner-attitude to the world was conditioned by the Indian *samsara* and *karma* teachings.

Through these Indian doctrines the soteriologically devalued world of real life won a relatively rational meaning. According to the most highly developed rational representations, the world was dominated by the laws of determinism. Especially in the Japanese form of Mahayanistic teaching, causality in our sense appears in external nature. In the fate of the soul the ethical value-determinism of *karma* obtained. From it there was no escape other than flight, by means of gnosis, into that otherworldly realm. Thereby, the fate of the soul could simply take the form of an "extinction," or as a circumstance of eternal, individual rest the form of a dreamless sleep. Or it could take the form of a circumstance of an eternal peaceful state of holy feeling in the countenance of god, or as a reception into divine individuality.

Similarly, the idea that "eternal" punishment or rewards in the future could be assigned for transitory deeds of transient beings on this earth, and indeed, through the power of arrangement of a simultaneously all-powerful and good God, is for all genuine Asiatic thought absurd, appearing spiritually subaltern, and so it will always appear. Thereby, however, disappeared the powerful emphasis which, as already noted, the soteriology of the Western doctrine of the beyond placed upon the short span of this life. World indifference was the expected posture, regardless of whether it took the form of a flight from the world or the form of being in the world yet indifferent to its activity—that is, a proving of oneself *against* the world and one's own activity rather than a proving of oneself in the world and through one's own activity.

Whether the highest holiness is personally or, naturally, as a rule, impersonally represented—and this is for us not without importance—is a matter of degree rather than kind. The implications of the rare, however still occasionally occurring, super-worldliness of a personal God was not carried through. Decisive for this was the nature of the striving for holy values. This was finally determined by the fact that thought about the meaning of the world formed a soteriology corresponding to the needs of literary strata. . . .

* * *

This most highly anti-rational world of universal magic also affected everyday economics. There is no way from it to rational, inner-worldly life conduct. . . .

A rational practical ethic and life methodology did not emerge from this magical garden which transformed all life within the world. Certainly the opposition of the sacred and the secular appeared—that opposition which in the West historically conditioned the systematic unification of life-conduct, described in the usual manner as "ethical personality." But the opposition in Asia was by no means between an ethical God and the power of "sin," the radical evil which may be overcome through active life-conduct. Rather, the aim was to achieve a state of ecstatic Godly possession through orgiastic means, in contrast to everyday life where God was not felt as a living power. Also, the goal involved an accentuation of the power of irrationality, which the rationalization of inner-worldy conduct precisely restricted. Or the aim was the achievement of apathetic-ecstatic Godly possession of gnosis in opposition to everyday life, the abode of transient and meaningless drives. This, too, represents an orientation that is both extra-worldly and passive—and thereby, from the standpoint of inner-worldly ethics, irrational and mystical, leading away from rational conduct in the world.

Where the inner-worldly ethic was systematically "specialized," with great consequences and with sufficient, workable, soteriological premises, in practice, for the corresponding relations in the Hindu inner-worldly caste ethic, it was simultaneously traditionally and ritually absolutely stereotyped. Where this was not the case, indeed, traces of "organismic societal theories" appeared—however, without psychologically workable premises for the corresponding practical behavior. Consequently, a psychologically workable systematization was lacking.

The laity, to which the gnosis and also the highest holiness is denied or which it refuses itself, is handled ritually and traditionally in terms of its everyday interests. The unrestricted lust for gain of the Asiatics in large and in small is notoriously unequalled in the rest of the world. However, it is precisely a "drive for gain" pursued with every possible means including umversal magic. It was lacking in precisely that which was decisive for the economics of the West: the refraction and rational immersion of the drive character of economic striving and its accompaniments in a system of rational, inner-worldly ethic of behavior, e.g., the "inner-worldly asceticism" of [ascetic] Protestantism in the West. Asiatic religion could not supply the presuppositions of inner-worldly asceticism. How could it be established on the basis of a religiosity which also demanded of the laity life as a Bhagat, as a holy ascetic, not simply as an ancient ideal goal but a contemporary existence as a wandering beggar during workless times of his life in general—and not without consequences[1]—as a religiously recommended service?

In the West the establishment of a rational, inner-worldly ethic was bound up with the appearance of thinkers and prophets who developed a social context on the basis of political problems which were alien to the Asiatic cultures; these were the political problems of civic status groups of the city without which neither Judaism nor Christianity nor the development

---

1. In India, April was the time for the assumption of a life of wandering mendicancy as a ritual duty for the members of the lower castes.

of Hellenic thought is conceivable. The establishment of the "city," in the Western sense, was restricted in Asia, partly through sib power which continued unbroken, partly through caste alienation.

The interests of Asian intellectuality, so far as it was concerned with everyday life, lay primarily in directions other than the political. When political intellectuals, such as the Confucians, appeared they were aesthetically cultivated literary scholars and conversationalists (also in this sense salon-men) rather than politicians. Politics and administration represented only their prebendary [stipend] subsistences; in practice these were usually conducted through subaltern helpers.

The orthodox or heterodox Hindu and Buddhist educated classes, by contrast, found the true sphere of their interests quite outside the things of this world. This was in the search for a mystic, timeless salvation of the soul and the escape from the senseless mechanism of the "wheel" of existence. In order to be undisturbed in this, the Hindu avoided the fineness of the aesthetic gesture. . . .

The Daoistic Wu wei, the Hinduistic "emptying" of consciousness of worldly relations and worldly cares, and the Confucian "distance" of the spirit from preoccupation with fruitless problems, all represent manifestations of the same type. The Western ideal of active behavior—be it in a religious sense concerning the beyond, be it inner-worldly—centrally fixes upon "personality." To all, highly developed Asian intellectual soteriology this could only appear either as hopelessly one-sided philistinism or as barbaric greed for life. Where it is not found in the beauty of the traditional, refined, salon-sublimated gesture, as in Confucianism, it is found in a realm beyond this world, namely one that offers salvation from the transitory. One's highest interests are oriented to this realm; from it the "personality" acquires its dignity.

In the highest, and not only orthodox Buddhist conception, salvation is called "nirvana." Neither grammatically nor actually would it be thinkable that this—as popularly often is done—be equated with "nothing." From the aspect of the "world" and seen from it, it could only be "nothing." But from the standpoint of the holy doctrine, the holy circumstance is quite different and very positively evaluated. However, it must not be forgotten that the striving for success of the typical Asian holy man is centered in "emptying," and that each positive holy circumstance of unspeakable, death-defying, this-worldly holiness is in the first place only evaluated as a positive complement of success. However, success is not always achieved. In fact, to actually attain [this] possession of the godly was the high charisma of the blessed. However, how do things stand with the great mass that never attains it? For them, in a very practical sense, "the end was nothing, the movement everything"—a movement in the direction of "emptying.". . .

The lack of economic rationalism and rational life methodology in Asia is, so far as other than psychological-historical causes play a part, pre-eminently conditioned by the continental character of the social order as developed in terms of the geographic structure. Western culture was throughout established on the basis of the foreign or transient trade: Babylon, the Nile delta, the ancient polls, and the Israelite Confederation were dependent on the caravan traffic of Syria. It was different in Asia. . . .

* * *

Wherever an intellectual stratum attempted to establish the "meaning" of the world and the character of life and—after the failure of this unmediated rationalistic effort—to comprehend the "meaning" of the world and life through experience, indirect rationalistic elements were taken into consideration. It was led somehow into the field of the world beyond of formless Indian mysticism. And where, on the other side, a status group of intellectuals rejected such world-fleeing efforts and, instead, consciously and intentionally pursued the charm and worth of the elegant gesture as the highest possible goal of inner-worldly consummation, it moved, in some manner, toward the Confucian ideal of cultivation.

Out of both these components, crossing and jostling one another, however, an essential part of all Asiatic intellectual culture was determined. The conception that, through simple behavior addressed to the "demands of the day," one may achieve salvation—which lies at the basis of all the specifically Western significance of "personality"—is alien to Asia. This is as excluded from Asiatic thought as the pure factual rationalism of the West, which practically tries to discover the impersonal laws of the world.

They were, indeed, protected by the rigid ceremonial and hieratic stylization of their life-conduct from the modern Western search for the individual self in contrast to all others—the attempt to take the self by the forelock and pull it out of the mud, forming it into a "personality." To Asia this was an effort as fruitless as the planned discovery of a particular artistic form of "style." Asia's partly purely mystical, and partly purely inner-worldly aesthetic goal of self-discipline, could take no other form than an emptying of experience of the real forces of experience. As a consequence of the fact that this lay remote from the interests and practical behavior of the "masses," they were left in undisturbed magical bondage. . . .

The appearance of [an ethic of everyday life for lay believers] in the West, —above all, in the [ancient] Near East—with the extensive consequences borne with it, was conditioned by highly particular historical constellations. If they had been absent, despite differences of natural conditions, development there could easily have taken the course typical of Asia, particularly of India.

B. BUDDHISM

From: "The Other-Worldliness of Buddhism and Its Economic Consequences." Pp. 627–30 in *Economy and Society*, edited by Guenther Roth and Claus Wittich; translated by Ephraim Fischoff; revised by Roth, Wittich and Stephen Kalberg (Berkeley: The University of California Press, 1978).

At the opposite extreme from religious ethics preoccupied with economic affairs in the world stands the ultimate ethic of world-rejection: the concentration upon mystical illumination of authentic ancient *Buddhism* (naturally not the completely altered manifestations Buddhism assumed in Tibetan, Chinese, and Japanese popular religions). Even this most world-rejecting ethic is "rational" in the sense that it produces a constantly alert control of all natural instinctive drives, though for purposes entirely different from those of inner-worldly asceticism.

Salvation is sought, not from sin and suffering alone, but also from ephemeralness as such; escape from the wheel of *karma*-causality into eternal rest is the goal pursued. This search is, and can only be, the highly individualized task of a particular person. There is no predestination, but neither is there any divine grace, any prayer, or any religious service. Rewards and punishments for every good and every evil deed are automatically established by the *karma*-causality of the cosmic mechanism of compensation. This retribution is always proportional, and hence always limited in time. So long as the individual is driven to action by the thirst for life, he must experience in full measure the fruits of his behavior in ever-new human existences. Whether his momentary situation is animal, heavenly, or hellish, he necessarily creates new chances for himself in the future. The most noble enthusiasm and the most sordid sensuality lead equally into new existence in this chain of individuation. (It is quite incorrect to term this process transmigration of souls, since Buddhist metaphysics knows nothing of a soul.)

This process of individuation continues on as long as the thirst for life, in this world or in the world beyond, is not absolutely extinguished. The process is but perpetuated by the individual's impotent struggle for his personal existence with all its illusions, above all the illusion of a unified distinctive soul and "personality."

All rational purposive activity is regarded as leading away from salvation, except of course the subjective activity of concentrated contemplation, which empties the soul of the thirst for the world's goods and every connection with worldly interests. The achievement of salvation is possible for only a few, even of those who have resolved to live in poverty, chastity, and unemployment (for labor is purposive action), and hence in mendicancy. These chosen few are required to wander ceaselessly—except at the time of the heavy rains—freed from all personal ties to family and world, pursuing the goal of mystical illumination by fulfilling the injunctions relating to the correct path *(dharma)*.

When such salvation is gained, the deep joy and tender, undifferentiated love characterizing such illumination provides the highest blessing possible in this existence, short of absorption into the eternal dreamless sleep of *Nirvana,*the only state in which no change occurs. All other human beings may improve their situations in future existences by adhering to the *dharma* prescriptions and by avoiding major sins in this existence. Such future existences are inevitable, according to the *karma* doctrine of causality, because the ethical account has not been straightened out—the thirst for life has not been "abreacted," so to speak. For most people, therefore, some new individuation [re-incarnation] is inevitable when the present life has ended. Nonetheless, truly eternal salvation remains to them unavoidably closed.

There is no path leading from this only really consistent position of world-flight to any economic ethic or to any rational social ethic. The "mood of pity," which is universal and extends to all creatures, cannot be the carrier of any rational action and in fact leads away from it. This mood of pity is the logical consequence of contemplative mysticism's position regarding the solidarity of all living, and hence transitory, beings. This solidarity follows from the common *karma*-causality which overarches all living beings. In Buddhism, the psychological basis for this universal pity is the religion's mystical, euphoric, universal, and acosmistic love.

Buddhism is the most consistent of the salvation doctrines produced before and after by the intellectualism of educated Indian strata. Its cool and proud emancipation of the individual from life as such, which in effect stood the individual on his own feet, could never become a salvation faith spread broadly across a society. Buddhism's influence beyond the circle of the educated was due to the tremendous prestige traditionally enjoyed by the *shramana*, i.e., the ascetic, who possessed magical and anthropolatric traits. As soon as Buddhism became a missionizing religion rooted broadly, it duly transformed itself into a savior religion based on *karma* compensation and, guaranteed by devotional techniques, cultic and sacramental grace, and deeds of mercy, hopes for the world beyond. Buddhism now exhibited a natural tendency to welcome purely magical notions.

In India itself. Buddhism succumbed, among the upper classes, to a renascent philosophy of salvation based on the Vedas; and it met competition from Hinduistic salvation religions, especially the various forms of Vishnuism, from Tantristic magic, and from orgiastic mystery religions, notably the *bhakti* piety (love of god). In Lamaism, Buddhism became the purely monastic religion of a theocracy which controlled the laity by ecclesiastical powers of a thoroughly magical nature. Wherever Buddhism was diffused throughout east Asia, its original form underwent striking transformation as it competed and entered into diverse combinations with Chinese Daoism, thus becoming the region's typical mass religion. It distributed grace and salvation, and thus offered a religion in opposition to the life submerged in this world and the ancestral cult.

At all events, no motivation toward a rational-methodical control of life flowed from Buddhist, Daoist, or Hindu piety. Hindu piety in particular, as we have already suggested, maintained the strongest possible power of tradition since the presuppositions of Hinduism constituted the most consistent religious foundation of the "organic" view of society. The existing order of the world was provided absolutely unconditional legitimation in terms of the mechanical operation of a proportional retribution in the distribution of power and happiness to individuals on the basis of their merits and failures in their earlier lives.

All these widespread religions of Asia left room for the "acquisitive drive" of the tradesman, the interest of the artisan in "sustenance" (*Nahrungs-Interesse*), and the traditionalism of the peasant. These popular religions also left uncontested both philosophical speculation and the conventional status-oriented life patterns of privileged groups. These status-oriented patterns of the privileged evinced feudal characteristics in Japan; patrimonial-bureaucratic, and hence strongly utilitarian, features in China; and a mixture of knightly, patrimonial, and intellectualistic traits in India. None of these mass religions of Asia provided the motives or orientations for a *rational*-ethical shaping of a terrestrial world to accord with divine commandments. Rather, all accepted this world as eternally given, and so the best of all possible worlds. The only choice open to the sages, who possessed the highest type of piety, was whether to accommodate themselves to the Dao, the impersonal order of the world and the only specifically divine aspect, or to save themselves from the inexorable chain of causality by passing into the only eternal being: the dreamless sleep of Nirvana.

"Capitalism" existed on the soil of all these religions, of the same kind as in Western Antiquity and the Western medieval period. But there was no development toward *modern* capitalism, nor even *any stirrings* in that direction. Above all, there evolved no "capitalist spirit," in the sense that is distinctive of ascetic Protestantism. To attribute to the Hindu, Chinese, or Muslim merchant, trader, artisan, or coolie a weaker "acquisitive drive" than the ascetic Protestant is to fly in the face of the facts. Indeed, the reverse would seem to be true, for what is distinctive of Puritanism is the rational and ethical limitation of the "quest for profit."

There is no proof whatever that a weaker natural "endowment" for technical economic "rationalism" was responsible for the actual difference in this respect. At the present time, all these people import this "commodity" as the most important Western product, and whatever impediments exist result from rigid traditions, such as existed among us in the Middle Ages, not from any lack of ability or will. Such impediments to rational economic development must be sought primarily in the domain of religion, insofar as they must not be located in purely political conditions (the internal structures and forms of domination, with which we shall deal later).

Only ascetic Protestantism completely eliminated magic and the other-worldly quest for salvation that took as its highest form an intellectualist, contemplative illumination. It alone created the religious motivations for seeking salvation primarily through immersion in one's worldly vocation *(Beruf)*. This Protestant stress upon the methodically rationalized fulfillment of one's vocational responsibility was diametrically opposite to Hinduism's strongly traditionalistic concept of vocations. For the various popular religions of Asia, in contrast to ascetic Protestantism, the world remained a great enchanted garden, in which the practical way to orient oneself, or to find security in this world or the next, was to revere or coerce the spirits and seek salvation through ritualistic, idolatrous, or sacramental procedures. No path led from the magical religiosity of the non-intellectual strata of Asia to a rational, methodical control of life. Nor did any path lead to that methodical control from the world accommodation of Confucianism, from the world-rejection of Buddhism, from the world-conquest of Islam, or from the messianic expectations and economic pariah law of Judaism.

CHINA: CONFUCIANISM

From: "The Confucian Life Orientation" and "The Traditionalist Character of Chinese Orthodoxy." Pp. 152–54, 156–61, 208 in *The Religion of China*, translated and edited by Hans H. Gerth; revised by Stephen Kalberg (New York: The Free Press, 1958); endnotes omitted.

Confucianism, like Buddhism, consisted only of ethics. This *Dao* corresponded to the Indian *dharma*. However, in sharp contrast to Buddhism, It exclusively represented an inner-worldly morality of *laymen*. Confucianism meant adjustment to the world, to its orders and conventions. Ultimately it represented just a tremendous code of political maxims and rules of social propriety for cultured men of the world. This was in still greater contrast to Buddhism.

The cosmic orders of the world were considered fixed and inviolate and the orders of society were but a special case of this. The great spirits of the cosmic orders obviously desired only the happiness of the world and especially the happiness of man. The same applied to the orders of society. The "happy" tranquillity of the empire and the equilibrium of the soul should and could be attained only through its ordering into the internally harmonious cosmos. If success did not occur, human lack of reason and, above all, disorderly leadership of state and society were to be blamed. Thus, in a nineteenth century edict the prevalence of bad winds in a province was traced to negligence in certain police duties, namely, in surrendering suspects and unduly drawing out trials. This had caused the spirits to become restless.

The charismatic conception of imperial power and the unity of order in the cosmos with order in society determined this basic assumption. Everything depended upon the behavior of the officials responsible for the leadership of a society conceived as one large, patrimonially ruled community. The monarch should deal with the uneducated mass of the people as children. His primary duties were to care for officialdom materially and spiritually, and to maintain good and respectful relations with them.

The common person best served Heaven by developing his own true nature, for in this way the good within every person would unfailingly appear. Thus, everything was an educational problem, and the educational aim was the development of the self from one's natural endowment. There was no radical evil.

One has to go back to the third century BCE to find philosophers who taught the heterodox doctrine of the original wickedness of the person. There were only faults, and these were the result of deficient education. Certainly the world—and the social world in particular—was, as it were, just as imperfect as man. Evil demons existed alongside the good spirits; however, given respectively the educational level of man and the charismatic quality of the ruler, the world was as good as could be. The orders of the world were a product of the purely natural development of cultural needs and the unavoidable division of labor—and collisions of interests that followed from it. According to the ruler's down-to-earth conceptions, economic and sexual interests were the basic impulses of human action. Hence, creatural wickedness and a "state of sin" did not constitute the reasons for coercive power or social inequality; rather, their existence was simply accepted as a necessity: in a very pragmatic manner, a simple economic reality—the scarcity of the means of subsistence in proportion to continuously increasing needs—was viewed as explaining this coercion and social subordination. Out of this situation a war of all against all would follow were it not for coercive power. Therefore, in principle the coercive order *per se*, the differentiation of property, and the struggles of economic interests were not in any sense perceived as problems.

Although the school developed a cosmogony, Confucianism was in large measure bereft of metaphysical interest. . . .

* * *

The conventionally educated man will participate in the old ceremonies with due and edifying respect. He controls all his activities, physical gestures, and movements as well with politeness and with grace in accordance with the status mores and the commands of "propriety," a basic concept (!) of Confucianism. The sources like to dwell on describing the Master as one who moved about with perfect elegance, a man of the world who knew how to greet all participants according to rank and according to the most intricate forms of etiquette. "Cultivated man"—"princely," or "noble" man—is a central concept which recurs in many transmitted statements of the master. He is a man who is both inwardly and, in relation to society, harmoniously attuned and poised in all social situations, be they high or low; he behaves accordingly and without compromising his dignity. Controlled ease and correct composure, grace, and dignity in the sense of a ceremonially ordered court-salon characterize this man.

In contrast to the passion and ostentation of the feudal warrior in ancient Islam, we find watchful self-control, self-observation, and reserve. Above all, we find repression of all forms of passion, including that of joy, for passion disturbs the equilibrium and the harmony of the soul. The latter is the root of all good. However, detachment does not, as in Buddhism, extend to all desire but to all irrational desire, and it is not practiced as in Buddhism for the sake of salvation from the world but for the sake of integration into the world. The Confucian ethic, of course, had no idea of salvation, and the Confucian had no desire to be "saved," either from the migration of souls or from punishment in the beyond. Both ideas were unknown to Confucianism.

The Confucian wished neither for salvation from life, which was affirmed, nor salvation from the social world, which was accepted as given. He thought of prudently mastering the opportunities of this world through self-mastery. He desired neither to be saved from evil nor from a fall of man, of which he knew nothing. Rather, he wished harmoniously to be "saved" from nothing except the undignified barbarism of social rudeness. Only the neglect of piety, the one basic social duty, could constitute "sin" for the Confucian. . . .

Residues of feudalism still inhere rather strongly in Chinese status ethics. Piety (*HSIAO*) toward the feudal lord was enumerated along with piety toward parents, superiors in the hierarchy of office, and office-holders generally, for the identical principle of *HSIAO* applied to all of them. In substance, feudal allegiance was transferred to the patronage of relationships of officials. And the basic character of allegiance was patriarchical, not feudal. The absolutely primary virtue, constantly inculcated in children, was filial piety toward parents. In case of conflict, piety preceded all other virtues.

No man's conduct met the test of the master until his way of mourning his parents was observed. In a patrimonial state where filial piety was transferred to all relations of subordination, it can be readily understood that an official—and Confucius for a time was a [state] minister—would consider filial piety as the virtue from which all others issue. Filial piety was held to provide the test and guarantee of adherence to unconditional discipline, the most important status obligation of bureaucracy. . . .

Thrift must not be positively valued. We see that the attitude toward things economic, here as in every status ethic, is a problem of consumption and not of work. It is not worthwhile for a "superior" man to learn economic management; actually it is not proper for him to do so. This does not result from a principled rejection of wealth *per se:* on the contrary, a well-administered state is the state in which people are ashamed of their poverty. In a poorly administered state people are ashamed of their wealth which in some cases might have been dishonestly acquired in office. There were only reservations concerning the acquisition of wealth. Economic literature was a literature of mandarins. . . .

The master considered acquisitiveness a source of social unrest. Obviously, he meant the rise of the typical, pre-capitalist class conflict between the interests of the buyers or the monopolists and the consumers' interests. Naturally, Confucianism was predominantly oriented toward a consumers' policy. Still, hostility toward economic profit was quite remote, as it was also in the popular mind. Extortionist and unfair officials, especially tax and other petty officials, were bitterly chastized on the stage, but not much seems to have been made of the accusations or mockery of merchants and usurers. The hostile wrath of Confucianism toward Buddhist monasteries led to Emperor Wu Tsung's campaign of annihilation in the year 844. But Confucianism primarily justified itself by the argument that the monasteries distracted people from useful work. Actually, as we have seen, "currency policy"played a role in this.

Economic activity is highly appreciated throughout orthodox literature. Confucius, too, might strive for wealth, "even as a servant, with whip in hand" (Legge, p. 198), if only the success of the endeavor were fairly guaranteed. But the guarantee does not hold and this fact leads to the one really essential reservation concerning economic acquisitiveness: namely, the poise and harmony of the soul are shaken by the risks of acquisitiveness. Thus, the position of the office prebendary appears in ethically hallowed form. It is the one position becoming to a superior man because the office alone allows for the perfection of personality. [The main disciple of Confucius], Mencius [Meng-tzu; 372–289 B.C.E.) reasons that without permanent income the educated man can be of constant mind only with difficulty, and the people not at all. Economic, medical, priestly income represent the "little path." This leads to professional specialization, a very important point and closely connected with what has been said above. The cultured man, however, strives for that university which in the Confucian sense education alone provides and which the office precisely requires. This view characterizes the absence of rational specialization in the official functions of the patrimonial state.

Yet, as in politics Wang An-shih's attempted [money economy and trade monopoly] reforms [1077] indicated specialization so in literature it was recommended that specialized competencies of officials in the modem bureaucratic manner replace the traditional universality of official business, which no single man could possibly master. The old educational ideal of the Chinese, however, stood in sharp contrast to these functional demands and, concomitantly, to the execution of a functional administrative rationalization in the manner of our European mechanisms.

The Confucian aspirant to office, stemming from the old tradition, could hardly help viewing a specialized, professional training of European stamp as anything but a conditioning in the dirtiest Philistinism. This was undoubtedly the locus of much of the important resistance to "reform" in the Western sense. The fundamental assertion—"a cultured man is not a tool"—meant that he was an end in himself and not just a means for a specified useful purpose. The all-around educated Confucian "gentleman," as Dvorak has translated the term *chun-tzu*, or the "princely man," supported a status ideal of cultivation that was directly opposed to the socially oriented Platonic ideal.

The Platonic ideal was established on the soil of the polis and proceeded from the conviction that man can attain fulfillment by being good at only one task. There was even stronger tension between the Confucian ideal and the vocational concept of ascetic Protestantism. Confucian "virtue" based upon a command of many talents—that is, on self-perfection—was greater than the riches to be gained by one-sided specialization. Not even in the most influential position could one achieve anything in the world without the virtue originating from education. And vice versa, one could achieve nothing, no matter what one's virtue, without an influential position. Hence, rather than seeking profit, the "superior" man coveted such a position.

Such, in brief, are the basic propositions concerning the attitude to vocational life and property, generally ascribed to the master.

$$* * *$$

. . . The Confucian belief in predestination, which differs in meaning from the Puritan belief in predestination is oriented to a personal God and his omnipotence. Also the Puritan firmly and clearly rejects the benevolence of providence; however, in doing so he looks out for himself in the beyond. In Confucianism, on the other hand, neither the cultured nor the common man bothered about the beyond. The cultured Confucian's one interest beyond death was that his name be honored; to protect this honor he had to be prepared to endure death. Confucian rulers and generals indeed knew how to die proudly when Heaven was against them in the high gamble of war and human destiny. They knew better how to die than their Christian colleagues, as we in Germany know. The strongest motive for high-minded deportment known to Confucianism may well have been this specific sense of honor, which characterized a cultured man and was linked essentially to a man's accomplishments—not to this birth. In this regard the Confucian way of life was oriented to status and not to *bourgeois* values in the sense of the West.

This implies that such an ethic of intellectuals was necessarily limited in respect to its influence upon the broad masses. The local and the social differences in education were enormous. The traditional and hitherto strong subsistence economy was maintained among the poorer strata of the people by a masterful art of thrift (in the sense of consumption). The most unbelievably intensive thrift was unequaled anywhere else in the world. It was possible only given a way of life that precluded any substantive relationship of the masses to the gentleman ideals of Confucianism. Here, as elsewhere, only the gestures and external forms of behavior of the ruling stratum could be generally adopted by those outside this stratum.

From: "Confucianism and Daoism." Pp. 204–06 in *The Religion of China*, translated and edited by Hans H. Gerth; revised by Stephen Kalberg (New York: The Free Press, 1958); endnotes omitted.

. . . it was decisive for the adherence of mercantile circles to Daoism that their special god of *wealth*, the vocational god of the merchants, was cultivated by the Daoists. Daoism brought quite a number of such special deities to a position of honor. Thus the hero of the imperial troops was canonized as a god of war; student deities, gods of erudition and especially gods of longevity were honored.

As with the Eleusian mysteries the center of gravity for Daoism was its promise of health, wealth, and happy life in this world and in the beyond. In theory, the spirits held out rewards and punishments for all deeds, be it in this world or in the beyond; be it for the actor or, in contrast to the doctrine of migration of souls, his descendants. The promises of a beyond were especially attractive to a large public. For both the Daoist and the Confucian, it was implicitly understood that, just as "correct living" is decisive for the individual's behavior, so the "correct living" of the prince is decisive for the fate of the realm and the cosmic order. Therefore Daoism, too, had to raise ethical demands. However, its unsystematic beginnings toward connecting the fate in the beyond with an *ethic* remained unsuccessful.

Naked magic, never seriously confronted by the stratum educated in Confucianism, was rampant again and again. For this reason, and in the way described, Daoist doctrine was increasingly developed as sacramental therapy, alchemy, macrobiotics, and a technique for gaining immortality. . . .

Daoism, in its effects, was essentially even more traditionalist than orthodox Confucianism. Nothing else could be expected from its magically oriented technique of salvation, nor from its sorcerers: their entire economic existence made them directly interested in conserving tradition, and especially the historically-transmitted demonology. Hence, it is not surprising to find ascribed to Daoism the explicit and principled formulation: "Do not introduce innovations."

In any case not only was there no path leading from Daoism to a rational method of life, be it inner or other-worldly, but Daoist magic necessarily became one of the most serious obstacles to such a development. For laymen the genuine ethical imperatives in later Daoism were substantially the same as those in Confucianism; while the Daoist expected from their fulfillment personal advantages, the Confucian expected rather the good conscience of the gentleman. While the Confucian operated with the polar opposites "right" and "wrong," the Daoist, like all magicians, operated rather with "clean-unclean." Despite the interest in immortality and in rewards and punishments in the beyond, the Daoist retained athis- worldly orientation like the Confucian. . . .

Confucianism strictly rejected the emotional ecstasy to be found only among the popular magicians, the apathetic ecstasy among the Daoists, and every form of monastic asceticism. In general, all magic was rejected as "irrational" in this psychological sense.

Neither in its official state cult nor in its Daoist aspect could Chinese religiosity produce sufficiently strong motives for a religiously oriented life for the individual, such as the Puritan method represents. Both forms of religion lacked even the traces of Satanic force of evil against which the pious Chinese, whether orthodox or heterodox, might have struggled for his salvation. The truly Confucian wisdom of life was "civic" in the sense that officialdom possessed an optimist rationalism. It had its superstitious elements, as is the case with all enlightenment. As a "status" religion it was a morale of literary intellectualism whose specific note was pride in education. . . .

CONFUCIANISM AND PURITANISM

From: Pp. 226–48 in *The Religion of China*, translated and edited by Hans H. Gerth; translation revised by Stephen Kalberg (New York: Simon and Schuster, 1951).

We can now [at the end of *The Religion of China*] best place the above analysis in the context of our vantage points by clarifying the relationship of Confucian rationalism — and this phrase is appropriate — to that rationalism closest to us geographically and historically: Protestant rationalism.

The stage of rationalization represented by a religion can be identified above all by two yardsticks: the extent to which *magic* has been eradicated and the extent to which the relationship between God and the world is characterized by a systematic unity. Depending upon this relationship, the believer's own ethical relationship to the world may also be brought into a rigorous unity. These two yardsticks stand, by the way, in many ways in a relationship of internal interwovenness.

In respect to the banishment of magic, ascetic Protestantism, in its various manifestations, represents the last stage. Its most characteristic forms have most completely driven out magic. Even in sublimated forms — in the sacraments and in its symbols — magic has been swept away. This occurred to such an extent that the strict Puritans allowed even the corpse of a loved one to be buried without formalities. Doing so insured the complete elimination of every "superstition"—that is, in this context, a severing of all trust in magical manipulations.

The complete *demagification of the world* was *only* here carried through with complete consistency. This did not mean freedom from what we today normally view as "superstitiousness"; witch trials also flourished in New England. Still, while Confucianism left untouched the *positive* significance of magic for salvation, Puritanism came to consider all magic as *devilish*. Here only the rational-ethical remained of religious value: action according to God's commandments and proceeding only from a frame of mind sanctified by God.

Finally, it should be perfectly clear from [*The Religion of China*] that a rational economy and technology of the modern Western variety was simply precluded in the magic garden [in China] of heterodox doctrine (Daoism). Partly as a cause and partly as an effect of these elemental forces, *all natural scientific knowledge was lacking* [in this earlier epoch]: the power of chronomancers [offering advice regarding the propitious day and time for activity], geomancers [regarding the spirits], hydromancers [regarding rainfall], meteoromancers [regarding the weather], and a crude and abstruse universist conception of the unity of the world held sway. Moreover, Daoism was interested in the income, fees, and pension [prebendal] opportunities from state offices, the bulwark of the magic tradition. Furthermore, the preservation of this garden of magic belonged among the most pivotal aspects of Confucian ethics. However, *internal* reasons prevented any weakening of Confucian power.

In strongest contrast to Confucianism's unmediated relation to the things of this world, the Puritan ethic called forth a tremendous and moving tension with the "world." As we shall see further in detail, every religion that opposes the world on the basis of rational-ethical imperatives finds itself, at some point, in a state of tension with the world's irrationalities. These tensions set in at very different points in the various religions; and the nature and intensity of the tension varied depending largely on metaphysical promises as given by particular paths to salvation. We must note that the degree of religious devaluation of the world is not identical with the degree of its rejection in *actual practice*.

Confucianism . . . was (in intent) a rational ethic that reduced tension with the world to an absolute minimum. This was true in respect to its religious devaluation as well as to its practical rejection of the world. The world [for the Confucian] was the best of all possible worlds; human nature was disposed to the ethically good. People, in this as in all things, differed in degree; however, being of the same nature and surely capable of unlimited perfection, all were in principle capable of fulfilling the moral law. A philosophical-literary education based upon the old classics was the universal means of self-perfection. The only sources of bad habits were insufficient education and its main cause: an insufficient economic livelihood. Such vices, and especially those of the government, because they caused the unrest of (purely magically conceived) spirits, were the essential reason for all misfortunes.

The right path to salvation consisted in adaptation to the eternal and supra-divine orders of the world — to Dao — and thus to the social demand to live together that followed out of the cosmic harmony. Hence, above all, pious conformism to the fixed order of secular powers was required. The corresponding ideal for each person involved the formation of the self as a many-sided, harmoniously balanced personality—in this sense each person was a microcosm [of the cosmic harmony]. For the Confucian ideal person — the Gentleman — "grace and dignity" were expressed in fulfilling traditional obligations. Thus, the cardinal virtue and goal — self-perfection — meant ceremonial and ritualist propriety in all circumstances of life. The appropriate means to this aim were watchful, rational self-control and the repression of irrational passions, for these would cause poise to be shaken.

The Confucian, however, never desired "salvation"—except from the barbaric lack of education. As rewards for virtue, he expected only long life, health, and wealth in this world and the retention of his good name in the next world. As for the genuinely Hellenic man [of classical Greece], all transcendental anchorage of ethics, all tension between the commandments of a transcendent God and a creatural world, all orientation toward a goal in the beyond, and all conceptions of radical evil were absent. [Under Confucianism], he who complied with the decrees, which were set for the man of average ability, was free of sin.

Where such presuppositions were taken for granted, Christian missionaries tried in vain to awaken a feeling of sin. An educated person in China would simply refuse to be continually burdened with "sin." Indeed, this notion is usually felt as rather shocking and lacking in dignity by cultivated intellectuals everywhere. Usually this stratum seeks to replace it with conventional, feudal, or aesthetically formulated routinizations ("indecent" or "not in good taste"). Certainly there were sins; however, these consisted in the field of ethics of offenses against traditional authorities, parents, ancestors, and superiors in office hierarchies. For the rest, there were magically dangerous violations of inherited customs, traditional ceremonies, and, finally, stable societal conventions. All were of equal standing. "I have sinned" corresponded to the infringement upon a convention: "I beg your pardon."

Asceticism, contemplation, mortification, and escape from the world were not only unknown in Confucianism; they were also despised as parasitism. All forms of congregational and salvation religiosity were either directly persecuted and eradicated or considered a private affair and held in low esteem. This corresponded to the treatment of the orphic priests by the noble Hellenic men of the classical era.

The Confucian ethic of unconditional affirmation of and adaptation to the world presupposed the unbroken and continued existence of purely magical religion. It applied even to the position of the emperor: on the basis of his personal qualities, he was responsible for the good conduct of the spirits and hence the occurrence of rain and good harvest weather. Purely magical religion applied also to ancestor worship, which was fundamentally equally widespread among both official and popular religions. And it applied to unoffical (Daoist) magical therapy and the other remaining forms of animistic coercion of spirits, namely, the anthropolatric [worship of persons] and herolatric [worship of heroes] beliefs in functional deities.

The educated Confucian, just as the educated Hellene, viewed magic with a mixture of skepticism and occasional submission. However, most Chinese, influenced by Confucianism in respect to their manner of organizing their lives, believed in an unmediated manner in magical representations. Like old Faust in relation to the beyond, the Confucian would say: "Fool who turns his eyes blinking in that direction." However, he would also, again with Faust, have to offer a qualification: "If only I could remove magic from my pathway . . . " [*Faust*, Part II, Act 5, midnight]. Even high civil servants, educated in the old Chinese manner, rarely hesitated to show devout respect for arbitrary and nonsensical miracles.

A tension with the "world" never arose [in China] because ethical prophets, worshipping a transcendent God who placed ethical *demands* upon believers, were completely absent as far as memory reaches. The "spirits" articulating such demands (mainly for respect for contracts) do not constitute substitutes, for here a *particular* obligation was always involved: to uphold an oath or other duty. This obligation was placed under the spirit's protection, and hence it varied distinctly from the internal formation of the personality *as such* and its organizing of life [as demanded by ethical prophets].

The leading intellectual stratum — civil servants and candidates for offices — consistently supported the preservation of the tradition of magic, and especially animistic ancestor worship, as absolutely necessary for the peaceful maintenance of bureaucratic authority. They also suppressed all upheavals stemming from religions of salvation. The only salvation allowed, in addition to Daoist divination and grace through the performance of sacraments, was that practiced by Buddhism's monks. As pacifist and thus unthreatening, their practical effect in China, as we will see [see Weber, 1958, p. 269], was to enrich and nuance the soul's impressive inward expanse. Buddhism otherwise served as a further source for magical-sacramental grace and tradition-strengthening ceremonies.

Hence, the significance of this ethic of intellectuals for the broader population necessarily has its limitations. First, local, and above all social, distinctions in regard to education were enormous. Among the poorer strata, the traditional and strongly subsistence-oriented pattern of consumption until modern times was maintained by an incredible and unusual thriftiness (in consumption matters). Nowhere surpassed, this frugality precluded any internal connection to Confucianism's Gentleman ideals.

Only the gestures and forms of the ruling stratum's external conduct could become, as everywhere, generally diffused. The decisive influence of the educated stratum upon the organization of life of the *general population* was channeled in all likelihood above all negatively: on the one hand a complete blocking of the sources for a religion of prophecy occurred, and on the other hand an eradication of almost all orgiastic elements in China's animistic religiosity took place. It must be possible that at least a part of those character traits some discuss as Chinese racial qualities are co-determined by these factors. Today, certainly, even specialists can say nothing certain regarding how far the influence of biological "heredity" extends. However, for us an observation easily made, and confirmed by well-known sinologists, is important: the farther one moves backward in history the more *similar* the Chinese and Chinese civilization (in those features of importance to us here) appear to that which is found in the West. The old popular beliefs, the old anchorets [religious hermits], the oldest songs of the [classical book of songs] *Shih Ching*, the old warrior kings, the opposing positions in the philosophical schools, the feudalism, and the beginnings of capitalism in the Warring States era [403–221 B.C.E.]—all this appears to us as far more closely related to Western development than as characteristic features of Confucian China. Hence, one must consider the possibility that many Chinese traits readily considered as innate were products of purely historically conditioned, civilizational influences. . . .

A true prophecy creates a systematic orientation to the conduct of life. Its direction is from inside the person outward to *one* value-based standard. The norm it establishes stands then against the "world" and endeavors ethically to form the world.

Confucianism involved just the opposite situation: adaptation to the world and its conditions. However, an optimally adjusted person — that is, one who rationalizes his life-conduct *only* to the extent necessary for adaptation — does not constitute a systematic unity; rather, he is composed of a combination of useful single qualities. The animistic conceptions in Chinese popular religion, which perpetuate the idea of the individual's multiple souls, could almost serve as a symbol of this situation.

Wherever all attempts to reach out to a world beyond fail [as in Confucianism], an autonomous counterweight against the world remains absent. A domestication of the masses and the Gentleman's dignified bearing could thereby arise. Nonetheless, the style it provided to the organization of life remained characterized by essentially negative features: it could not allow the birth of a striving, emanating from inside the person, toward integration of one's life-conduct into a whole, namely, a striving we associate with the concept "personality." Life for the Confucian remained a series of events rather than a unity methodically placed under a transcendental goal.

The contrast between this social-ethical position of Confucianism and all Western religious ethics was insurmountable. It might appear that some patriarchal features of the ethos formed by [Thomas] Aquinas [1225–1274 C.E.], and even Lutheran ethics, resembled Confucianism. However, this conclusion would be superficial: the Confucian system of radical optimism vis-à-vis the mundane world eradicated fundamentally the pessimistic tension between this world and the transcendent determination of the person. It did so more radically than any other religion. Even Christianity, which intertwined with the [economic, political, and legal] orders of the world in an extremely tight compromise, failed to do so to the same extent.

Completely absent in the Confucian ethic was any tension between nature and deity, ethical demand and human inadequacy, a consciousness of sin and a need for salvation, conduct on earth and compensation in the next life, and religious duty and sociopolitical reality. Thus, absent also was any leverage to influence the organization of life through coherent dynamics unconnected to given traditions and conventions. Rather, by far the strongest power influencing life-conduct was family piety, which rested upon the belief in spirits. This piety ultimately facilitated and controlled the strong cohesion of the sib organizations and the cooperative associations, which can be understood as extended families organized around division of labor principles. In its way, this firm cohesion was completely motivated by religion: the strength of this genuinely Chinese mode of organizing the

economy extended approximately as far as these person-oriented associations, and they were regulated by piety.

In the sharpest contrast stood the Puritan ethic, which rendered impersonal the believer's tasks. The Chinese ethic developed the strongest motives inside the circle of naturally growing, *person*-based organizations (or
organizations assimilated to or modeled after them). Under Puritanism,
however, religious duty vis-à-vis a transcendental and other-worldly God
led to the evaluation of all relationships to one's fellow human beings —
even, and especially, to intimates — as mere means. This situation manifested a frame of mind that had reached beyond organic [family-based] relationships. In contrast, the religious duty of the pious Chinese instructed
him to act exclusively *inside* organically given personal [family and clan] relationships.

Mencius rejected the universal "love of humankind" with the comment
that, if implemented, piety and justice would be dissolved; only animal life
is without fathers and brothers, he argued. For the Confucian in China, substantive duties always and everywhere involved piety to actual (living or
dead) people who stood close to him in the given order of things. A duty to a
transcendent God never appeared, and hence a duty vis-à-vis a sacred "cause"
or "idea" never arose[1]—for the *Dao* was neither. Rather, it embodied simply
binding *traditional ritual*; its decree was not "activity," but "emptiness."

Undoubtedly these personalistic barriers against abstract and impersonal relationships possessed for Confucianism's economic ethic a considerable significance; namely, they constituted obstacles to objectifying
rationalization. Persons possessed always the tendency to bind themselves
to the sib group and to companions bound to groups similar to the clan—in
any case to "persons" instead of to functional tasks ("enterprises"). As this
entire discussion has indicated, precisely this tendency was connected
most intimately with the religiosity of the Chinese and with those barriers it
established against rationalization. And the ruling cultivated stratum maintained these obstacles in the interest of preserving their own position. If all
trust — the foundation for all business relationships — remains anchored in
purely personal familial or semi-familial relationships, as occurred in a very
prominent manner in China, very considerable significance for the economy follows.

The large achievement of ethical religions, and above all the ethical and
ascetic sects of Protestantism, was the *breaking assunder* of the sib ties. These
religions established an overarching community of faith and a common
ethical organization of life in opposition to a community of *blood*, even to a
large extent in opposition to the family. From the point of view of the economy, *business confidence now became founded upon the ethical qualities* of the individual—and these were testified to in one's impersonal, vocational work.
The official and exclusive rule of a convention-based lack of candor, and of
the singularly significant need to maintain face under Confucianism, must

---

1. Weber is seeing the latter as a secularized form of the former [sk].

be presumably — here there are no measurement methods — rated fairly high in regard to their implications for the economy, for the result was the universal distrust of all against all.

Confucianism and the Confucian frame of mind, deifying "wealth," could favor *political*-economic measures (as did also the cosmopolitanism of the Renaissance in the West). However, at this point one can observe the limited significance of economic *policy* as opposed to an economic *frame of mind*. In no other civilized country has material welfare *ever* been so exalted as the supreme good as in China (see deGroot, 1910, p. 130). The political-economic views of Confucianism were comparable to those of our Cameralists [managers of state property]. The oldest document of Chinese political economy (as reprinted in Chavannes, 1895–1905) is a tract by the Confucian [historian] Ssu-ma Ch'ien [145–90 B.C.E.] on the "balance of trade"; here the usefulness of *wealth*, including riches acquired through trade, is emphasized. Economic *policy*, which alternated between fiscal and laissez-faire measures, was never intentionally antichrematistic [opposed to the acquisition of riches]. Businessmen were "despised" in our Middle Ages to the same degree as in China, and *are* as well even today by the intellectuals.

Nonetheless, [as noted], an economic *frame of mind* is never created out of economic *policy. The profits of traders in the Warring States period were political* profits acquired from state functionaries. The large mining companies were in search of gold. However, no intermediate link from Confucianism and its ethic, which remained anchored as firmly as Christianity's, led to a *middle class, methodical organization of life.* Yet *this* is the issue. Completely unintentionally, Puritanism created *this* methodical conduct. This odd reversal of the "natural," which seems odd only upon first, superficial glance, teaches us about the paradox of unintended consequences. This lesson concerns the relationship of people and fate: the *consequences* of action in relation to its *intention.*

[Compared to Confucianism], *Puritanism* constitutes the radically opposite example regarding a rational posture toward the world. A completely linear concept, as we earlier noted, does not here stand at the forefront. In practice, the true meaning of the *ecclesia pura* referred to the community that participated in the Lord's Supper: it was purged of all morally suspect participants. . . . Viewed broadly, Puritanism refers to the morally rigorous, Christian-ascetic lay communities in general. It includes the Baptist, Mennonite, Quaker, ascetic Pietist, and Methodist communities. . . .

Unusual to these communities, compared to Confucianism, was a rationalization of the world. In contrast to [the mystic's] flight from the world, [in Puritanism] rationalization occurred in spite of — or indeed because of — an ascetic rejection of the world. Because there can be no difference among persons in respect to their wickedness vis-a-vis God, all are as such equally condemned and ethically absolutely inadequate. Hence, the world is a vessel of sin. Adaptation to its vain habits and ways would constitute to the believer a sign of his condemnation, and self-perfection in the Confucian manner would be tantamount to idolatrous blasphemy. And riches and a devotion to their enjoyment would be a major temptation, reliance on philosophy and a literary education would constitute sinful creaturely pride, and all trust in the coercion through magic of spirits and gods would not only be despicable superstition, but also an audacious insult to God. All that reminded one of magic, and every residual legacy from ritualism and the power of priests, would have to be eradicated. The majority of ascetic sects were without salaried and professional ministers; Quakerism, in theory, abjured appointed preachers. Absent from the small and well-lit Quaker meeting halls were any traces of religious symbols.

People were held to be equally sinful by nature. This remained the case even though their religious opportunities were not equal; instead, they were highly unequal—and for all time rather than in the short run. This situation resulted either from arbitrary predestination (as with the Calvinists, the particular Baptists, the Whitefield Methodists, and the reformed Pietists) or differing capacities for the spiritual life. Finally, inequality of religious opportunity resulted also from the varying intensity, and hence success, of the striving to achieve salvation. Decisive with the old Pietists was the act of conversion, whether a "penitance struggle" or a "breakthrough" [see pp. 23–30]; for others rebirth was differently constituted. However, and despite these differences, the providential, inscrutable, and undeserved "free" grace given by a transcendent God governed. Thus, although only one shaping influence upon virtuoso religiosity, the belief in predestination was by far the most consistent and dogmatic.

Only a few of the *massa perditionis* [masses condemned to perdition] were called upon to attain the holy, whether they alone were destined for it by virtue of a predestination of yore, or whether all (according to the Quakers this included non-Christians) had received the offer. However, only a small group capable of seizing it could reach the goal. According to some Pietist doctrines, salvation was offered only once in a lifetime; according to others (the so-called Terminists), it was offered once and for all [see p. 126]. People always had to testify to their capacity to grasp the holy. Hence, everything was directed to God's free grace and one's destiny in the next life, and this life was viewed as either a valley of tears or only a temporary station along the way. However, everything that occurred in this brief life-span, just for this reason, became awarded with an enormous significance. [Thomas] Carlyle's [1795–1881] words capture this situation: "Millennia had to pass before you came to life, and other millennia silently wait for you to begin with this your life."[2]

The emphasis upon this short life did not result owing to the possibility that salvation could be attained through one's own achievements. This option remained foreclosed. Instead, the calling to salvation could be recognized by the believer only partly, and above all only through the consciousness of a central and unified relationship between this — his short — life and the transcendental God and His will: namely, through the con-

---

2.   The source of the quote remains unidentified [sk].

sciousness of a "sanctification." In turn, as is the case with all active asceticism, sanctification could testify to itself only through activities desired by God—that is, through activities to which He gives His blessing, namely, ethical action. Hence, ethical action itself — for this action gives to the believer certainty that he is God's tool — provides certainty of salvation.

In this manner a rational-ethical methodicalness to life acquired the strongest conceivable psychological premium. Only the life emanating from a unified core and oriented to firm and ordered foundational principles could be considered a life pleasing to God. Even though a naive surrender to [pleasures] unconditionally led away from salvation, the world and human beings were nonetheless God's creation. He had created all persons and placed specific demands on them (according to the Calvinist ideas) "for His glory." No matter how wicked people might be, He wanted to see His honor realized through a taming of sin and, possibly, also suffering. He wished to place all sin and suffering into a rational order and to subject them to an ethical discipline. To "work the works of Him who sent me, while it is day" [John 9:4] here became a duty. Far from ritual-based, the works given in this manner were rational-ethical in nature.

The contrast to Confucianism is clear. Both ethics possessed their irrational anchorages: in magic and in the ultimately inscrutable decisions of a transcendent God. The inviolability of tradition followed from magic: the anger of the spirits could be avoided only if the tried and proven magical means, and ultimately all traditional forms of organizing life, remained unchanged. On the other hand, the contrast between a transcendent God and an ethically irrational world populated by condemned human beings, yielded a situation in which tradition remained absolutely unsanctified and believers confronted a truly endless task: perpetual labor on behalf of an ethical-rational subduing and mastering of the existing world (that is, labor on behalf of rational-impersonal "progress"). Here the task to rationally transform the world stood opposed to the Confucian adaptation to the world.

Confucianism demanded a constant and vigilant self-control on behalf of a maintenance of the dignity of the all-sided, completely perfected, cosmopolitan person; in contrast, Puritan ethics required a constant and vigilant self-control on behalf of a methodical concentration upon God's will. Completely intentionally, the Confucian ethic left people either in rudimentary and naturally developed [e.g., the family, the clan] personal relationships or in given superordination and subordination relationships. It ethically glorified these — and only these — relationships, and knew in the end exclusively social duties between persons created by personal obligations of piety—namely, those from prince to servant, from higher civil servant to lower civil servant, from father and brother to son and brother, from teacher to pupil, and from friend to friend.

To the Puritan ethic, however, just these personal relationships were somewhat suspect. They concerned human beings alone, and under all circumstances the relationship to God took priority for the Puritans. Even though such personal relations were allowed to exist (as long as they did not violate God's laws) and the Puritans managed to ethically regulate them, this suspicion endured. Overly intensive idolatrous relations *per se* were by all means to be avoided. Trust in others, and precisely in those closest to one by nature [in the family], would endanger the soul. Thus, the Calvinist Duchess Renate d'Este might curse her next of kin if she knew them rejected by God (through arbitrary predestination).

From this, very important practical differences between the two ethical conceptions resulted—even though we shall designate both religions as rationalist in their practical turns and although both reached "utilitarian" conclusions. These differences did not alone result from the autonomous lawfulness (*Eigengesetzlichkeit*) of political-rulership structures. In part the cohesion of the sibs in China importantly also resulted from these structures. Nonetheless, political and economic organizations were themselves thoroughly tied to personal relations. To a striking degree all these organizations (relatively) lacked rational matter-of-factness, impersonal rationalism, and the features of an abstract, impersonal, purposive association. Hence, especially in the cities, actual "communities" were absent in China, as well as purely impersonal and purposive economic and managerial forms of association and organization.

Enterprises of this sort almost never originated from purely Chinese roots. All social action remained engulfed in and conditioned by purely personal, above all kinship, relations in China. This applied also to occupational associations. In contrast, Puritanism rendered everything impersonal and dissolved everything into a rational "enterprise" and purely impersonal "business" relationships. It placed rational law and contract in the position that, in China, was held by all-powerful tradition, local custom, and the concrete personal favor of the official.

A further element appears of even greater importance. In conjunction with China's tremendous population density, a "calculating" and self-sufficient frugality of unrivaled intensity developed under the influence of a world-affirming utilitarianism and belief in the ethical value of wealth as a universal means of moral perfection. The shopkeeper haggled over and calculated every penny and counted his cash register receipts daily. Money, and interests related to money, according to reliable travel reports, seemed to constitute the topic of discussion to a degree rarely seen.

However, it remains very striking that, out of this unending and intensive economic activity, and the often decried crass "materialism," those large and *systematic* business concerns of a rational nature presupposed by modern capitalism did not arise, at least in the arena of economic activity. Organizations of this type have remained foreign in China except where they have been taught: namely, in those areas (for example, Canton) influenced in the past by foreigners or in those areas now under the imprint of the incessant advance of Western capitalism.

Indigenously, the forms of a politically oriented capitalism arose (especially, it appears, in those periods when political divisions existed): office-based usury, emergency loans, wholesale trade, and, where industry developed, the *ergasteria* (including larger workshops [see p. 211, n. 14]). All of this appeared in late Antiquity in the West, in Egypt, and in the Islamic regions. More recently, there has also arisen the usual economic dependency upon the merchant and consumer. In general, however, the Chinese lacked the strict organization of the *sistema domestica* [putting-out system; see pp. 377–79], such as existed even during the late Middle Ages in the West. And in spite of the intensive internal and — for a time at least — considerable foreign trade, there existed no middle class capitalism of the modern, or even late Medieval, type.

There were no rational forms of the sort that developed in the Western late Medieval period, and surely no science-based, European-capitalist, industrial "enterprises." Furthermore, there was no formation of "capital" in the European manner. (Chinese capital, which played a part later given more modern opportunities, was predominently the capital of mandarins— capital acquired through extortion practices connected to offices.) A rational-methodical manner of organization of concerns in the European mold, a genuinely rational organization of commercial news services, and a rational money system were also absent. Lacking was a money economy the equal of that found in Ptolemaic Egypt [323–30 B.C.E.]. Legal institutions, such as those that regulated firms, commercial companies, and monetary and security exchanges, existed only in rudimentary stages. (Essentially these beginnings were characterized by incomplete technical development.) Typical also was a highly limited utilization, for purely economic ends, of innumerable technical inventions.[3] Finally, lacking was a technically developed system for commercial communication, accounting, and bookkeeping.

Thus, in spite of the almost complete absence of slavery (a consequence of the Empire's pacification), conditions very similar to those of Mediterranean Antiquity are found. In other ways the situation in China was even more distant from the "spirit" of modern capitalism and its institutions than was Western Antiquity. Nonetheless, and despite heresy trials in China, in comparison at least to Calvinist Puritanism there was considerable religious tolerance. A far-reaching free trade in commodities, freedom of mobility, freedom of occupational choice, and freedom of methods of production also existed. And all tabooing of the shopkeeper spirit was absent.

Nevertheless, all of this did not allow modern capitalism to arise in China. In this typical land of profiteering, one can see that "acquisitiveness," high and even exclusive esteem for wealth, and utilitarian "rationalism" have as such nothing to do with *modern* capitalism. The Chinese lower

---

3. For example, the lesser development of mining (which was a reason for currency crises), the failure to utilize coal for the production of iron (*in spite of* the presumed knowledge of the coking process), and the increasing restriction of maritime commerce to domestic navigation in traditional forms, and along traditional routes, are not to be traced back to defects in the *technical* capacity or talent for invention among the Chinese. This is crystal clear. Rather, *feng shui*, divination of various sorts, and fee and pension interests — products of magic and the state's form — were decisive.

middle class and middle class businessman (and also the big businessman who adhered to the old traditions) ascribed success and failure, as did the Puritans, to divine powers. However, in China these outcomes were attributed to the (Daoistic) god of wealth and never constituted a sign of one's state of grace. They were understood as consequences of magically significant or ceremonially significant service or violations. Attempts were undertaken for this reason to re-establish equilibrium through ritual "good works."

The Chinese lacked that which characterized the classical Puritan: the central, religiously determined, and rational-methodical organization of life that originated from within. Economic success for the Puritan was not an ultimate goal or end in itself, but a means of testifying to a state of grace. The Chinese lacked the Puritan's conscious closing off of himself from the impressions and influences of the "world"—a world the Puritan sought to control, just as he did himself, by means of a definite and one-sided rational effort of will. He was taught to *suppress* the petty *acquisitiveness* that destroys all methodicalness in the rational enterprise—an acquisitiveness that distinguishes the conduct of the Chinese shopkeeper. Foreign to the Confucian was the particular restriction and repression of natural impulse[4] brought about by the strict volitional and ethical rationalization that had socialized the Puritan.

The Confucian restriction of freely expressed and basic impulse was of a different nature. His watchful self-control aimed to maintain the external gesture and dignity of manner—to keep "face." This self-control was of an aesthetic and essentially negative nature. Dignified "deportment" in itself, devoid of a specific content, was prestigeful and desired. The equally vigilant self-control of the Puritan oriented itself to a positive aim — a certain socially esteemed mode of conduct — and, beyond this, to an inward goal: the systematic mastery of one's own nature, which was regarded as wicked and sinful. The consistent Pietist would take inventory through a sort of bookkeeping practiced daily. Even an *Epigone* such as Benjamin Franklin kept to this practice, for the transcendent, omniscient God saw into one's internal disposition. The world to which the Confucian adapted, on the other hand, gave priority to the graceful gesture.

Striving simply for a dignified countenance, the Confucian Gentleman distrusted others as generally as he believed others distrusted him—and this distrust handicapped all credit and business operations. It contrasted with the Puritan's trust, especially his trust, when in the marketplace, in the absolutely unshakeable and religion-determined uprightness of his fellow believer. Faced with the creatural wickedness of the world and of human beings, especially those in high places, this trust just sufficed to prevent his profoundly realistic and thoroughly unrespecting pessimism from becoming a hindrance to the acquisition of credit—which was indispensable for capitalist commerce. It merely caused him to assess dispassionately the ob-

---

4. On this theme see the very good remarks in the writings of Ludwig Klages [1899].

jective external and internal capacities of the partner and to take stock of the constancy of motives necessary for conducting business according to the principle "honesty is the best policy." The Confucian's word offered a beautiful and polite gesture as an end in itself; the Puritan's word constituted an impersonal, short, and absolutely reliable, business-like communication: "Yea, yea; Nay, nay: for whatsoever is more than these cometh of evil" [Matthew 5:37].

The thriftiness of the Confucian was narrowly circumscribed by the status decorum of the Gentleman. The Confucians struggled against the excessive thrift found in the mystically determined humility of [the Founder] Lao-tzu [ca. 380–320] and some other Daoists. For the Chinese lower middle classes, thrift meant hoarding, a practice fundamentally comparable to the peasant's way of hoarding wealth in his stocking: it served to insure burial rites and one's good name, as well as the honor and enjoyment from possession *per se*. This was typical where asceticism had not yet prevented the enjoyment of wealth.

However, for the Puritan, possessions were as great a temptation as for the monk. His income, just as for the monasteries, was a secondary result and sign of successful asceticism. As John Wesley remarked: "We have no choice but to recommend that people be pious, and that means," as an unavoidable effect, "getting rich." But the dangerous nature of riches for the pious individual was obviously the same as it had been for the monasteries. Wesley expressly focused upon the observed and apparent paradox between the world's great capacity to acquire goods even while rejecting the world [see pp. 153–54].

For the Confucian, as a statement handed down by the Master expressly teaches, wealth was the most important means for a *virtuous* — that is, dignified — life, and the precondition for a dedication of oneself to self-perfection. Hence, inquiries regarding the means to improve people was answered with the axiom "enrich them"—for only the rich could live according to rank and station. However, for the Puritan, income was an unintended result and an important sign of virtue. The expenditure of wealth for purposes of personal consumption could easily fall into an idolatrous surrender to the world. Confucius would not as such disdain the acquisition of riches, yet wealth seemed precarious and hence might upset the equilibrium of the cultured soul. All genuinely market-oriented and vocational work constituted, to him, the activity of narrow-minded, specialized experts.

Regardless of his social usefulness, this person could *not* be elevated to the point of true dignity, according to the Confucian. Above all, the "cultured man" (Gentleman) could not be "a tool." In his adapting to the world and searching for self-perfection, he must be an end unto himself and never a means toward an abstract goal. The core of Confucian ethics rejected professional specialization, the modern bureaucracy run by experts, and specialized educational training. Crucially, Confucianism opposed all training oriented to the market and the acquisition of goods. Puritanism placed against this "idolatrous" maxim — "acquire goods" — the task of testifying to belief in one's vocational life and in the world's delimited and impersonal tasks.

The Confucian was the person with a literary education. More precisely, he possessed book knowledge—knowledge of the *written* word in the highest form. Confucianism was as foreign to the Hellenic elevation and cultivation of speech and conversation as it was to the energy of rational action, whether expended in military or economic affairs.

Most Puritan denominations, on the other hand, albeit with varying intensity, opposed a philosophical-literary education, for it conflicted with their grounding in the Bible, which remained indispensable. (The Bible was cherished as a sort of middle class book of rules and managerial teachings.) Thus, while the highest ornament of the Confucian, philosophical-literary education for the Puritan was an idle waste of time and a danger to religion. To him, scholasticism and dialectics, Aristotle and his schools, were a horror and a menace. Hence, Spener [see p. 123–28], for instance, preferred mathematically founded Cartesian rational philosophy. Useful and pragmatic knowledge, especially if empirically based, of the natural sciences and geography, as well as the dispassionate clarity of realistic thinking and specialized expert knowledge, were first cultivated in an organized manner as educational ends by Puritans. In Germany, Pietist circles in particular furthered this mode of education.

Such knowledge was the only avenue toward knowledge of God's glory and the divine providence embodied in His creation. In addition, this knowledge served as a means of rationally mastering the world in one's vocation and rendering to Him, for His honor, that which He is due. Hellenism and the core of the Renaissance at its height were equally distant from both Confucianism and Puritanism, although in different ways.

The indispensable "ethical" qualities of the modern capitalist entrepreneur were:

- a radical concentration on God-ordained purposes;
- [practice of] the relentless practical rationalism of the ethic of asceticism;
- [utilization of] methodical and impersonal procedures in business management;
- a horror of illegal, political, colonial, booty, and monopoly types of capitalism dependent upon the favor of princes and persons, and an orientation to a dispassionate, strict legality and the tamed rational energy of routine enterprise;
- [practice of] the rational calculation of the technically best way;
- and a practical solidity and focus upon goals instead of, as characteristic of the old artisan craftsman, a traditional pleasure in a centuries-old skill and the product's beauty.
- The devout worker's special willingness to work must also be mentioned.

The relentlessly and religiously systematized utilitarianism unique to rational asceticism — to a life "in" the world and yet not "of" it — has helped to create these superior rational skills and thus the "spirit" of the vocational man. This, in the last analysis, was denied to Confucianism. The Confucian organization of life was rational; however, unlike Puritanism, it was determined from without rather than from within. The contrast can teach us that mere moderation and frugality, combined with "acquisitiveness" and regard for wealth, were far from representing and far from releasing the "capitalist spirit" in the sense found specifically, in the modern economy, in the person oriented to a vocation.

The typical Confucian utilized his own, and his family's, savings in order to acquire a literary education and to arrange tutelege for the examinations. Thus, he gained the basis for a high status life. The typical Puritan earned a great deal, spent little, and reinvested, out of an ascetic compulsion to save, his income as capital in rational-capitalist companies. "Rationalism" — and this is our second lesson — was embodied in the spirit of both ethics. But only the Puritan rational ethic, with its *transcendent* orientation, brought the *this*-worldly economic rationalism to its consistent conclusion. This happened *because* nothing was further from the conscious intentions of the Puritan: this-worldly work was simply an expression of the striving to reach a transcendental goal. Because the Puritans "alone had striven for God and his justice" [Matthew 6:33], the world became, in accord with God's promises, Puritanism's domain.

Here lies the basic difference between the two kinds of "rationalism." Confucian rationalism meant rational adaptation to the world, while rational *mastery* of the world characterized Puritan rationalism. Both the Puritan and the Confucian were "dispassionate." However, the rational features of the Puritan were founded in a mighty emotion that the Confucian lacked completely. An unbreakable link between Western asceticism's rejection of the world and its opposite — namely, its eagerness to dominate the world in the name of a transcendental God — grounded this emotion, which also inspired the monk in the West.

Asceticism's imperatives were directed to the monk and, in variant and softened form, to the world. No greater antagonism existed than that between the Confucian ideal of gentility and the idea of a "vocation." The "princely" man was an aesthetic value and was therefore *not* a "tool" of a god. However, the genuine Christian — the other-worldly and this-worldly ascetic — wished to be nothing other than a tool of his God: for here he exclusively sought his dignity. And because this is what he wanted to be, he was a useful instrument to transform and master the world rationally.

V

JUDAISM

From: "Judaism and Capitalism" and "Jewish Rationalism vs. Puritan Asceticism." Pp. 611–23, 1203–04 in *Economy and Society,* edited by Guenther Roth and Claus Wittich; translated by Ephraim Fischoff and revised by Roth, Wittich, and Stephen Kalberg (Berkeley: The University of California Press, 1978).

Judaism, in its postexilic [after 538 B.C.E.] and particularly its Talmudic form, belongs among those religions that are in some sense "accommodated" to the world. Judaism is at least oriented to the world in the sense that it does not reject the "world" as such but only rejects the prevailing social rank order in the world.

. . . [Judaism's] religious promises, in the customary meaning of the word, apply to this world, and any notions of contemplative or ascetic world-flight are as rare in Judaism as in Chinese religion and in Protestantism. Judaism differs from Puritanism only in the *relative* (as always) absence of systematic asceticism. The "ascetic" elements of the early Christian religion did not derive from Judaism, but emerged primarily in the heathen Christian communities of the Pauline mission. The observance of the Jewish "law" has as little to do with "asceticism" as the fulfillment of any ritual or tabooistic norms. . . .

Judaism did not forbid the uninhibited enjoyment of life or even of luxury as such, provided that the positive prohibitions and taboos of the law were observed. The denunciation of wealth in the prophetic books, the Psalms, the Wisdom literature [Job, Proverbs, Ecclesiastes, Wisdom, Sirach], and subsequent writings was evoked by the social injustices which were so frequently perpetrated against fellow Jews in connection with the acquisition of wealth and in violation of the spirit of the Mosaic law. Wealth was also condemned in response to the arrogant disregard of the commandments and promises of God, and finally in response to the rise of temptations to laxity in religious observance. To escape the temptations of wealth is not easy, but is for this reason all the more meritorious: "Hail to the man of wealth who has been found to be blameless."

Moreover, since Judaism possessed no doctrine of predestination and no comparable idea producing the same ethical effects, incessant labor and success in business life could not be regarded or interpreted in the sense of certification, which appears most strongly among the Calvinist Puritans and which is found to some extent in all ascetic Protestant religions, as shown in John Wesley's remark on this point [see pp. 153–54]

Of course a certain tendency to regard success in one's economic activity as a sign of God's gracious direction existed in the religion of the Jews as in the religions of the Chinese and the lay Buddhists and generally in every religion that has not turned its back upon the world. This view was especially likely to be manifested by a religion like Judaism, which had before it very specific promises of a transcendental God together with very visible signs of this God's indignation against the people he had chosen. It is clear that any success achieved in one's economic activities while keeping the commandments of God could be, and indeed had to be, interpreted as a sign that one was personally acceptable to God. This actually occurred again and again. But the situation of the pious Jew engaged in business was altogether different from that of the Puritan, and this difference remained of practical significance for the role of Judaism in the history of the economy. Let us now consider what this role has been.

In the polemic against Sombart's book, one fact should not have been seriously questioned, namely that Judaism played a conspicuous role in the unfolding of the modern capitalistic system. However, this thesis of Sombart's book needs to be made more precise. What were the distinctive economic achievements of Judaism in the Middle Ages and in modern times? We can easily list: moneylending, from pawnbroking to the financing of great states; certain types of commodity business, particularly retailing, peddling, and produce trade of a distinctively rural type; certain branches of wholesale business; and trading in securities, above all the brokerage of stocks. To this list of Jewish economic achievements should be added: money-changing; money-forwarding or check-cashing, which normally accompanies money-changing; the financing of state agencies, wars, and the establishment of colonial enterprises; tax-farming (naturally excluding the collection of prohibited taxes such as those directed to the Romans); banking; credit; and the floating of bond issues.

But of all these businesses only a few, though some very important ones, display the *forms*, both legal and economic, characteristic of *modern* Western capitalism (as contrasted to the capitalism of ancient times, the Middle Ages, and the earlier period in Eastern Asia). The distinctively modern legal forms include securities and capitalist associations, but these are not of specifically Jewish provenience. The Jews introduced some of these forms into the West, but the forms themselves have perhaps a common Oriental (probably Babylonian) origin, and their influence on the West was mediated through Hellenistic and Byzantine sources. In any event they were common to both the Jews and the Arabs. It is even true that the specifically modern forms of these institutions were in part Western and medieval creations, with some specifically Germanic infusions of influence. To adduce detailed proof of this here would take us too far afield. However, it can be said by way of example that the Exchange, as a "market of tradesmen," was created not by Jews but by Christian merchants.

Again, the particular manner in which medieval legal concepts were adapted to the purposes of rationalized economic enterprise, i.e., the way in which partnerships *en commandite, maone,* privileged companies of all kinds and finally joint stock corporations were created,[1] was not at all dependent on specifically Jewish influences, no matter how large a part Jews later played in the formation of such rationalized economic enterprises. Finally, it must be noted that the characteristically modern principles of satisfying public and private credit needs first arose *in nuce* on the soil of the medieval city. These medieval legal forms of finance, which were quite un-Jewish in certain respects, were later adapted to the economic needs of modern states and other modern recipients of credit.

Above all, one element particularly characteristic of modern capitalism was strikingly—though not completely—missing from the extensive list of Jewish economic activities. This was the organization of *industrial* production *(gewerbliche Arbeit)* in domestic industry and in the factory system. How does one explain the fact that no pious Jew thought of establishing an industry employing pious Jewish workers of the ghetto (as so many pious Puritan entrepreneurs had done with devout Christian workers and artisans) at times when numerous proletarians were present in the ghettos, princely patents and privileges for the establishment of any sort of industry were available for a financial remuneration, and areas of industrial activity uncontrolled by guild monopoly were open? Again, how does one explain the fact that no modern and distinctively *industrial* bourgeoisie of any significance emerged among the Jews to employ the Jewish workers available for cottage industry, despite the presence of numerous impoverished artisan groups at almost the threshold of the recent period?

All over the world, for several millennia, the characteristic forms of the capitalist employment of wealth have been state-provisioning, tax-farming, the financing of colonies, the establishment of great plantations, trade, and moneylending. One finds Jews involved in just these activities, found at all times and places but especially characteristic ot Antiquity, just as Jews are involved in those legal and entrepreneurial forms evolved by the Middle Ages but not by them. On the other hand, the Jews were (relatively) or altogether absent from the new and distinctive forms of modern capitahsm and the rational organization ot labor—especially production in an industrial enterprise of the factory type, The Jews evinced the ancient and medieval business frame of mind which had been and remained typical of all genuine traders, whether small businessmen or large-scale moneylenders, in Antiquity, the Far East, India, the Mediterranean littoral area, and the West of the Middle Ages: the will and the wit to employ mercilessly every chance of profit: "for the sake of profit to ride through Hell even if it singes the sails." But this frame of mind is far from distinctive of *modern* capitalism, as distinguished from the capitalism of *other* eras. Precisely the reverse is true. Hence, neither that which is new in the modern economic *system* nor

---

1. On the *commenda* and the *commandite,* see Weber, *General Economic History,* ch. 17, "Forms of Commercial Enterprise." The *maone* comprised various types of associations employed in Italian cities for the running of a fleet or the exploitation of an overseas colony [Roth].

that which is distinctive of the modern economic *frame of mind* is specifically Jewish in origin.

The ultimate principal reasons for this fact—that the distinctive elements of modern capitalism originated and developed quite apart from the Jews—are to be found in the special character of the Jews as a pariah people and of their religion. Their pariah status presented purely external difficulties impeding their participation in the organization of industrial labor. The legally and factually precarious position of the Jews hardly permitted continuous and rationalized industrial enterprise with fixed capital, but only trade and, above all, dealing in money.

Also of fundamental importance was the subjective ethical situation of the Jews. As a pariah people, they retained the double standard of morals which is characteristic of primordial economic practice in all communities: what is prohibited in relation to "one's brothers" is permitted in relation to strangers. It is unquestionable that the Jewish ethic was thoroughly traditionalistic in demanding that Jews exhibit an attitude of "support" toward fellow Jews. Although the rabbis made concessions in these matters, as Sombart correctly points out, even in regard to business transactions with fellow Jews, this amounted merely to concessions to laxity and those who took advantage of them remained far behind the highest standards of Jewish business ethics. In any case it is certain that such behavior was not the realm in which a Jew could testify to his religious merit.

However, for the Jews the realm of economic relations with strangers, particularly economic relations prohibited in regard to fellow Jews was largely an area of radical indifference. This is of course the primordial economic ethic of peoples everywhere. That this should have remained the Jewish economic ethic was a foregone conclusion, for even in Antiquity the stranger confronted the Jew almost always as an "enemy." All the well-known admonitions of the rabbis enjoining trust especially toward Gentiles could not change the fact that the religious law prohibited taking usury from fellow Jews but permitted it in transactions with non-Jews. Nor could the rabbinical counsels alter the fact, which again Sombart has rightly stressed, that a lesser degree of *exemplary* legality was required by the law in dealing with a stranger, i.e., an enemy, than in dealing with another Jew, in such a matter as taking advantage of an error made by the other party.

In fine, no proof is required to establish that the pariah condition of the Jews, which we have seen resulted from the promises of Yahweh and the resulting incessant contempt of the Jews by Gentiles, led to a situation in which the Jews could not react otherwise than by perpetually retaining a different business morality for relations with strangers than with fellow Jews.

Jewish Rationalism versus Puritan Asceticism. Let us summarize the mutual relatedness in which Catholics, Jews, and Protestants found themselves in regard to economic acquisition. The devout Catholic, as he went about his economic affairs, found himself continually behaving—or on the verge of behaving—in a manner that transgressed papal injunction. His economic behavior could be ignored in the confessional only on the principle of *rebus sic stantibus* [the existing sins can be neglected], and it could be permissible only on the basis of a lax, probabilistic morality. To a certain extent, therefore, the life of business itself had to be regarded as dubious or, at best, as not positively favorable to God.

The inevitable result of this Catholic situation was that pious Jews were encouraged to perform economic activities among Christians which, if performed among Jews, would have been regarded by the Jewish community as unequivocally contrary to the law—or at least as suspect from the point of view of Jewish tradition. At best these transactions were permissible on the basis of a lax interpretation of the Judaic religious code, and then only in economic relations with strangers. Never were they infused with positive ethical value.

Thus, the Jew's economic conduct appeared to be permitted by God, in the absence of any formal contradiction with the religious law of the Jews, but ethically indifferent, in view of such conduct's correspondence with the average evils in the society's economy. This is the basis of whatever factual truth there was in the observations concerning the inferior standard of economic legality among Jews. That God crowned such economic activity with success could be a sign to the Jewish businessman that he had done nothing clearly objectionable or prohibited in this area and that indeed he had held fast to God's commandments in *other* areas. But it would still have been difficult for the Jew to testify to his ethical merit by means of characteristically modern business behavior.

But this was precisely the case with the pious Puritan. He could testify to his religious merit through his economic activity because he did nothing ethically reprehensible, he did not resort to any lax interpretations of religious codes or to any double moralities, and he did not act in a manner that could be indifferent or even reprehensible in the general realm of ethical validity. On the contrary, the Puritan could testify to his religious merit precisely in his economic activity. He acted in business with the best possible conscience, since through his impersonal and legal behavior in his "business activity" he was objectifying the rational methodicalness of his completely organized life. He legitimated his ethical pattern in his own eyes, and indeed within the circle of his community, by the extent to which the absolute—not relativized—unassailability of his economic conduct remained beyond question.

No actually pious Puritan—and this is the crucial point—could have regarded as pleasing to God any profit derived from usury, exploitation of another's mistake (which was permissible to the Jew), haggling and sharp dealing, or participation in political or colonial exploitation. Quakers and Baptists believed their religious merit to be testified to before all mankind by such practices as their fixed prices, their absolutely reliable business relationships with everyone, and their unconditionally legal transactions completely lacking all thirst for money. They believed that precisely such practices promoted the irreligious to trade with them rather than with their

own kind, and to entrust their money to the trust companies or limited liability enterprises of the religious sectarians rather than to those of their own
people—all of which made the religious sectarians wealthy, even as their
business practices testified them before their God.

By contrast, the Jewish law applying to strangers, which, in practice was
the pariah law of the Jews, enabled them, nothwithstanding innumerable
reservations, to engage in dealings with non-Jews which the Puritans rejected violently as showing an acquisitive thirst. Yet the pious Jew could
combine such a frame of mind with strict legality, with complete fulfillment
of the law, with all the inwardness of his religion, with the most sacrificial
love for his family and community, and indeed with pity and mercy toward
all God's creatures. For in view of the operation of the laws regarding
strangers, Jewish piety never in actual practice regarded the realm of permitted economic behavior as one in which the genuineness of a person's
obedience to God's commandments could be proven. The pious Jew never
gauged his inner ethical standards by what he regarded as permissible in
the economic context. Just as the Confucian's ideal of life was the gentleman who had undergone a comprehensive education in ceremonial esthet-
ics and literature and who devoted lifelong study to the classics, so the Jew
set up as his ethical ideal the scholar learned in law and casuistry and the intellectual continuously immersed in sacred writings and commentaries at
the expense of his business, which he very frequently left to the management of his wife. . . .

The economic behavior of the Jews simply moved in the direction of least
resistance which was permitted them by these legalistic ethical norms. This
meant in practice that the "acquisitive drive," which is found in *all* strata
and nations, was here directed primarily to trade with strangers, that is,
"enemies". . . .

In all his other dealings, as well as those we have just discussed, the
Jew—like the pious Hindu—was inhibited by scruples concerning his Law.
As [Julius] Guttmann has correctly emphasized, genuine study of the Law
could be combined most easily with the occupation of moneylending,
which requires relatively little continuous labor.[2] The outcome of Jewish le-
galism and intellectualist education was the Jew's "methodical life" and his
"rationalism." It is a prescription of the Talmud that "A man must never
change a practice." Only in the realm of economic relationships with
strangers, and in no other area of life, did tradition leave a sphere of behavior that was (relatively) indifferent ethically. Indeed, the entire domain of
things relevant before God was ruled by tradition and its interpretation
rather than a rational, self-oriented, presuppositionless, and goal-oriented
action derived from a "natural law." The "rationalizing" effect of the Jewish
fear of God's Law is thoroughly pervasive, but entirely indirect.

"Awake" and always internally secure, under control, and calm—these
qualities were found among Confucians, Puritans, Buddhist and other

---

2.   See Julius Guttmann, "Die Juden und das Wirtschaftsleben," *AfS*, vol. 36 (1913), pp. i49ff. This is
a critique of Sombart's book (Wittich).

types of monks, Arab sheiks, and Roman senators, as well as among Jews. But the basis and significance of self-control were different in each case. The alert self-control of the Puritan flowed from the necessity of subjugating, in order to secure certainty of his own salvation, all creaturely impulses to a rational and methodical plan of conduct. Self-control appeared to the Confucian as a personal necessity which followed from his disesteem for plebeian irrationality—the disesteem of an educated gentleman who had received classical training and had been bred along lines of propriety and dignity. On the other hand, the self-control of the devout Jew of ancient times was a consequence of a preoccupation with the Law in which his mind had been trained, and of the necessity of his continuous concern with the Law's precise fulfillment.

The pious Jew's self-control received a characteristic coloring and effect from the situation of being piously engaged in fulfilling the Law. The Jew felt that only he and his people possessed this law, for which reason the world persecuted them and imposed degradation upon them. Yet this law was binding; and one day, by an act that might come suddenly at any time but that no one could accelerate, God would transform the social structure of the world, creating a messianic realm for those who had remained faithful to His law. The pious Jew knew that innumerable generations had awaited this messianic event, despite all mockery, and were continuing to await it. This produced in the pious Jew a certain "wakefulness." But since it remained necessary for him to continue waiting in vain, he nurtured his feelings of self-esteem by a meticulous observance of the law for its own sake. Last but not least, the pious Jew had always to stay on guard, never permitting himself the free expression of his passions against powerful and merciless enemies. This repression was inevitably combined with . . . the inevitable effect of the feeling of "ressentiment" which derived from Yahweh's promises and the resulting unparalleled sufferings of this people.

These circumstances basically determined the "rationalism" of Judaism, but this is not "asceticism" in our sense. To be sure, there are "ascetic" traits in Judaism, but they are not central. Rather, they are by-products of the law or products of the peculiar tensions of Jewish piety. In any case, ascetic traits are of secondary importance in Judaism, as are any indigenous mystical traits. We need say nothing more here about Jewish mysticism, since neither cabalism, Chassidism, or any of its other forms—whatever symptomatic importance they held for Jews—produced any significant motivations toward practical behavior in the economic sphere. . . .

Above all, lacking in Judaism was the decisive hallmark of "inner-worldly" asceticism: a unified relationship to the world from the point of view of the individual's certainty-of-salvation-striving (*certitudo salutis*), which nurtures all else. Again in this important matter, ultimately decisive for Judaism was the pariah character of the religion and the promises of Yahweh. A this-worldly ascetic management of the world, such as that characteristic of Calvinism, was the very last thing of which a traditionally pious Jew would have thought. He could not think of methodically controlling the present world, which was so topsy-turvy because of Israel's sins, and which could not be set right by any human action but only by some free miracle of God that could not be hastened. He could not take as his "mission," as the sphere of his religious "vocation," the bringing of this world and its very sins under the rational norms of the revealed divine will, for the glory of God and as an identifying mark of his own salvation.

The Pious Jew had a far more difficult destiny to overcome than did the the Puritan, who could be certain of his "election" to the world beyond. It was incumbent upon each Jew to make peace with the fact that the world would remain contradictory to the promises of God as long as God permitted the world to stand as it is, and to be content if God sent him grace and success in his dealings with the enemies of his people, toward whom he must act soberly and legalistically in fulfillment of the injunctions of the rabbis. This meant acting towards non-Jews in an "objective" or impersonal manner, without love and without hate, solely in accordance with what God permits.

The frequent assertion that Judaism required only an external observance of the Law is incorrect. Naturally, this is the average tendency; but the requirements for real religious piety stood on a much higher plane. In any case, Judaic law fostered in its adherents a tendency to compare individual actions with each other and to compute the net result of them all. This conception of man's relationship to God as a bookkeeping operation of single good and evil acts with an uncertain total (a conception which may occasionally be found among the Puritans as well) may not have been the dominant official view of Judaism. Yet it was sufficient, together with the double-standard morality of Judaism, to prevent the development with Judaism of a methodical and ascetic orientation to the conduct of life on the scale that such an orientation developed in Puritanism. It is also important that in Judaism, as in Catholicism, the individual's activities in fulfilling particular religious injunctions produced his own chances of salvation. However, in both Judaism and Catholicism, God's grace was needed to supplement human inadequacy, although this dependence upon God's grace was not as universally recognized in Judaism as in Catholicism.

This ecclesiastical provision of grace was much less developed in Judaism, after the decline of the older Palestinian confessional (*teshubah*), than in Catholicism. In practice, this resulted in the Jew's having a greater religious responsibility for himself. This responsibility for oneself and the absence of any mediating religious agency necessarily made the Jewish organization of life more systematic and personally responsible than the corresponding Catholic organization of life. Still, the methodical control of life was limited to Judaism by the absence of the distinctively ascetic motivation characteristic of Puritans and by the continued presence of Jewish internal morality's traditionalism, which in principle remained in place. To be sure, there were present in Judaism numerous single stimuli toward practices that might be called ascetic, but the unifying force of a basically ascetic religious motivation was lacking. The highest form of Jewish piety is found in the religious "mood" *(Stimmung)* and not in active behavior. How could it be possible for the Jew to feel that by imposing a new rational order upon the world he would become the human executor of God's will, when for the Jew this world was thoroughly contradictory, hostile, and—as he had known since the time of Hadrian [76-138 ACE]—impossible to change by human action? This might have been possible for the Jewish freethinker, but not for the pious Jew. . . .

The Puritans, like Paul, rejected the Talmudic law and even the characteristic ritual laws of the Old Testament, while taking over and considering as binding—for all their variation—other expressions of God's will witnessed in the Old Testament. As the Puritans took these over, they always conjoined norms derived from the New Testament, even in matters of detail.

The Jews who were actually welcomed by Puritan nations, especially the Americans, were not pious orthodox Jews but rather Reformed Jews who had abandoned orthodoxy, Jews such as those of the present time who have been trained in the Educational Alliance, and finally baptized Jews. These groups of Jews were at first welcomed without any ado whatsoever and are even now welcomed fairly readily, so that they have been absorbed to the point of the absolute loss of any trace of difference. This situation in Puritan countries contrasts with the situation in Germany, where the Jews remain—even after long generations—"assimilated Jews." These phenomena clearly manifest the actual "kinship" of Puritanism to Judaism. Yet precisely the non-Jewish element in Puritanism enable Puritanism to play its special role in the development of the modern economic frame of mind, and also to carry through the aforementioned absorption of Jewish proselytes, which was not accomplished by nations with other than those with Puritan orientations.

* * *

Judaism and Capitalism. Wherever the Jews appeared, they were the agents of the money economy, especially (and in the High Middle Ages exclusively) of the loan business, but they also engaged widely in commerce. For the development of cities they were as indispensable to German bishops as to Polish nobles. Their prominent, and often dominant, participation is established with regard to the purveying and loan transactions of the early modern states, the founding of colonial companies, the colonial and slave trade, trade in cattle and agricultural goods, and in particular for the modern stock market trade in securities and for the floating of new issues.

It is a different question whether the Jews can be assigned a major role in the development of modern capitalism. The following must be considered: Capitalism living from loan usury, or from the state, its credit and supply needs, and from colonial exploitation, is nothing specifically modern. These are features which modern Western capitalism has *in common* with the capitalism of Antiquity, the Middle Ages and the modern Orient. In comparison to Antiquity (and the Near East and Far East), modern capitalism is characterized by the capitalist organization of *production,* and here the Jews have not had a decisive influence. Moreover, the frame of mind of the unscrupulous big financier and speculator can be found at the time of the prophets no less than during Antiquity and the Middle Ages. The decisive institutions of modern trade—the legal and economic forms of securities as well as the stock markets—have a Romanic and Germanic origin. However, the Jews contributed to giving the [stock] exchange its present importance.

Finally, the typical Jewish commercial "spirit," insofar as one can speak of it concretely, has general Middle Eastern characteristics, in part even petty-bourgeois features that are unique to the precapitalist age. With the Puritans the Jews have in common the purposive legitimation of formally legal profit, which is considered a sign of Divine blessings, and the idea of the calling, although it does not have as strong a religious foundation as in Puritanism. The most important influence of the Jewish Law upon the modern "capitalist" ethic was perhaps the fact that its legalistic ethic was absorbed by the Puritan ethic and thus put into the context of modern-"bourgeois" economic morality.

VI

THE MIDDLE EAST: ISLAM

From: "The This-Worldliness of Islam and its Economic Ethics." Pp. 623–27, 574 in *Economy and Society,* edited by Guenther Roth and Claus Wittich, translated by Ephraim Fischoff and revised by Roth and Wittich; slightly revised by Stephen Kalberg (Berkeley: The University of California Press, 1978).

Islam, a comparatively late product of Near Eastern monotheism, in which Old Testament and Jewish-Christian elements played a very important role, "accommodated" itself to the world in a sense very different from Judaism. In the first Meccan period of Islam [prior to 622 A.C.E.], the eschatological religion of Mohammed developed in pietistic urban conventicles which displayed a tendency to withdraw from the world. But in the subsequent developments in Medina and in the development of the early Islamic community, the religion was transformed into a national-Arabic religion and then into a status-oriented warrior religion. Those followers whose conversion to Islam made possible the decisive success of the prophet were consistently members of powerful families.

The religious commandments of the holy war were not directed in the first instance to the purpose of conversion. Rather, the primary purpose was war "until they (the followers of alien religions of the book) will humbly pay the tribute (*jizyah*)" i.e., until Islam should rise to the top of this world's social scale, by exacting tribute from other religions. This is not the only factor that stamps Islam as the religion of rulers. Military booty is important in the statutes, in the promises, and above all in the expectations characterizing particularly the most ancient period of the religion. Even the ultimate elements of its economic ethic were purely feudal. The most pious adherents of the religion in its first generation became the wealthiest, or more correctly, enriched themselves with military booty—in the widest sense—more than did other members of the faith.

The role played by wealth accruing from spoils of war and from political aggrandizement in Islam is greatly opposed to the role played by wealth in the Puritan religion. The Muslim tradition depicts with pleasure the luxurious raiment, perfume, and meticulous beard-coiffure of the pious. The saying that "when god blesses a man with prosperity he likes to see the signs thereof visible upon him"—made by Mohammed, according to tradition, to well-circumstanced people who appeared before him in ragged attire—stands in extreme opposition to any Puritan economic ethic and thoroughly corresponds with feudal conceptions of status. This saying would mean, in our language, that a wealthy man is obligated "to live in keeping with his status." In the Koran, Mohammed is represented as completely rejecting every type of monasticism *(rakhaniya)*, though not all asceticism, for he did accord respect to fasting, begging, and penitential mortification. . . .

. . . Islam was never really a religion of salvation; the ethical concept of salvation was actually alien to Islam. The god it taught was a lord of unlimited power, although merciful, the fulfillment of whose commandments was not beyond human power. An essentially political character marked all the chief commandments of Islam: the elimination of private feuds in the interest of increasing the group's striking power against external foes; the proscription of illegitimate forms of sexual behavior and the regulation of legitimate sexual relations along strongly patriarchal lines (actually creating sexual privileges only for the wealthy, in view of the facility of divorce and the maintenance of concubinage with female slaves); the prohibition of usury; the prescription of taxes for war; and the injunction to support the poor.

Equally political in character is the distinctive religious obligation in Islam, its only required dogma: the recognition of Allah as the one God and of Mohammed as his prophet. In addition, there were the obligations to journey to Mecca once during a lifetime, to fast by day during the month of fasting, to attend services once a week, and to observe the obligation of daily prayers. Finally, Islam imposed such requirements for everyday living as the wearing of distinctive clothing (a requirement that even today has important economic consequences whenever savage tribes are converted to Islam) and the avoidance of certain unclean foods, of wine, and of gambling. The restriction against gambling obviously had important consequences for the religion's attitude toward speculative business enterprises.

An individual quest for salvation and mysticism were alien to ancient Islam. The religious promises in the earliest period of Islam pertained to this world. Wealth, power, and glory were all martial promises, and even the world beyond is pictured in Islam as a soldier's sensual paradise. Moreover, the original Islamic conception of "sin" has a similar feudal orientation. The depiction of the prophet of Islam as "devoid of sin" is a late theological construction, scarcely consistent with the actual nature of Mohammed's strong sensual passions and his explosions of wrath over very small provocations. Indeed, such a picture is foreign even to the Koran, just as it is to the period after Mohammed's transfer to Medina: he lacked any sort of "tragic" sense of sin.

Rather, the original feudal conception of sin remained dominant in orthodox Islam: "sin" is a composite of ritual impurity, ritual sacrilege *(shirk,* i.e., polytheism), disobedience to the positive injunctions of the prophet; and the violation of status prescriptions by infractions of convention or etiquette. Islam displays other characteristics of a distinctively feudal spirit: the obviously unquestioned acceptance of slavery, serfdom, and polygamy; the disesteem for and subjection of women; the essentially ritualistic character of religious obligations; and finally, the great simplicity of religious requirements and the even greater simplicity of the modest ethical requirements.

Islam was not brought any closer to Judaism and to Christianity in decisive matters by such Islamic developments as the rise of theological and juristic casuistry, the appearance of both pietistic and enlightenment schools of philosophy (following the intrusion of Persian Sufism, derived from India), and the formation of the order of dervishes (still today strongly under Indian influence). Judaism and Christianity were specifically bourgeois-urban religions, whereas for Islam the city had only political importance. A certain sobriety in the organization of life might also be produced by the nature of the official cult in Islam and by its sexual and ritual commandments. The petty-bourgeois stratum was largely the carrier of the dervish religion, which was disseminated practically everywhere and gradually grew in power, finally surpassing the official ecclesiastical religion. This type of religion, with its orgiastic and mystical elements, with its essentially irrational and non-mundane character, and with its official and thoroughly traditional ethic of everyday life, became influential in Islam's missionary enterprise because of its great simplicity. It directed the organization of life into paths whose effect was directly opposed to the methodical control of life found among Puritans, and indeed, found in every type of asceticism oriented toward world mastery.

Islam, in contrast to Judaism, lacked the requirement of a comprehensive knowledge of the law and lacked that intellectual training in casuistry which nurtured the "rationalism" of Judaism. The ideal personality type in the religion of Islam was not the scholarly scribe (*Literat*), but the warrior. Moreover, Islam lacked all those promises of a messianic realm upon earth which in Israel were linked with meticulous fidelity to the law, and which—together with the priestly doctrine of the history, election, sin and dispersion of the Jews—determined the fateful pariah character of the Jewish religion

To be sure, there were ascetic sects among the Muslims. Large groups of ancient Islamic warriors were characterized by a trend toward "simplicity"; this prompted them from the outset to oppose the rule of the Umayyads [661–750 A.C.E]. The latter's merry enjoyment of the world was understood as a decline in comparison to the rigid discipline of the encampment fortresses in which Umar had concentrated Islamic warriors in the conquered domains; in their stead there now arose a feudal aristocracy. But this was the asceticism of a military caste, of a martial order of knights, not of monks. Certainly it was not a middle-class ascetic systematization of the conduct of life. Moreover, it was effective only periodically, and even then it tended to merge into fatalism. We have already spoken of the quite different effect which is engendered in such circumstances by a belief in providence, Islam was diverted completely from any really methodical organization of life by the advent of the cult of saints, and finally by magic. . . .

* * *

. . . Islamic predestination knew nothing of the "double decree"; it did not dare attribute to Allah the predestination of some people to hell, but only attributed to him the withdrawal of his grace from some people, a belief which admitted man's inadequacy and inevitable transgression. Moreover, as a warrior religion, Islam had some of the characteristics of the Greek *moira* [Fate] in that it developed far less the specifically rational elements of a world order and the specific determination of the individual's fate in the world beyond. The ruling conception was that predestination determined, not the fate of the individual in the world beyond, but rather the uncommon events of this world, and above all such questions as whether or not the warrior for the faith would fall in battle. The religious fate of the individual in the next world was held, at least according to the older view, to be adequately secured by the individual's belief in Allah and the prophets, so that no demonstration of salvation in the conduct of life is needed. Any rational system of ascetic control of everyday life was alien to this warrior religion from the outset, so that in Islam the doctrine of predestination manifested its power especially during the wars of faith and the wars of the Mahdi. The doctrine of predestination tended to lose its importance whenever Islam became more civilized, because the doctrine produced no planned procedure for the control of the workaday world, as did the Puritan doctrine of predestination.

VII

THE WEST: ANCIENT CHRISTIANITY AND CATHOLICISM

From: "Jesus' Indifference to the World." Pp. 630–33 in *Economy and Society*, edited by Guenther Roth and Claus Wittich; translated by Ephraim Fischoff and revised by Roth, Wittich, and Stephen Kalberg (Berkeley: The University of California Press, 1978).

The second great religion of "world-rejection," in our special sense of the term, was early Christianity, at the cradle of which magic and belief in demons were also present. Its savior was primarily a magician, and his magical charisma was an ineluctable source of his particular self-esteem. But the absolutely unique religious promises of Judaism rendered a special contribution to the distinctive character of early Christianity. It will be recalled that Jesus appeared during the period of the most intensive messianic expectations. Still another factor contributing to the distinctive message of Christianity was its reaction to the unique concern for erudition in the Law characteristic of Jewish piety.

Christianity arose in opposition to this legalistic erudition as a *non*-intellectual's proclamation directed to non-intellectuals, to the "poor in spirit." Jesus understood and interpreted the "law," from which he wished to remove not even a letter, in a fashion common to the lowly and the unlearned, and the pious folk of the countryside and the small towns. All understood the Law in their own way and in accordance with the needs of their own occupations, in contrast to the Hellenized, wealthy and upper-class people and to the erudite scholars and Pharisees trained in casuistry. . . .

Jesus' distinctive self-esteem did not come from anything like a "proletarian instinct." Rather, it arose from the knowledge that the way to God, because of his oneness with the Godly patriarch, necessarily led through him. His self-esteem was grounded in the knowledge that he, the non-scholar, possessed both the charisma requisite for the control of demons and a tremendous preaching ability, far surpassing that of any scholar or Pharisee. This self-esteem involved the conviction that his power to exorcise demons was operative among the people who believed in him, even if they be heathens. In his home town and his own family, among the wealthy and high-born of the land, the scholars, and the legalistic virtuosi—among none of these did he find the faith that gave him his magical power to work miracles. He did find such a faith among the poor and the oppressed, among publicans and sinners, and even among Roman soldiers.

It should never be forgotten that *these* charismatic powers were the absolutely decisive components in Jesus' self-esteem concerning his messiahship. These powers were the fundamental issue in his "woe" over the Galilean cities and in his angry curse upon the recalcitrant fig tree. His feeling about his own powers also explains why the election of Israel became ever more problematical to him and the importance of the Temple ever more dubious, while the rejection of the Pharisees and the scholars became increasingly certain to him.

Jesus recognized two absolutely "mortal sins." One was the "sin against the spirit" committed by the scriptural scholar who disesteemed charisma and its bearers. The other was unbrotherly arrogance, such as the arrogance of the intellectual toward the poor in spirit when the intellectual hurls at his brother the exclamation "Thou fool!" This anti-intellectualist rejection of scholarly arrogance and of Hellenic and rabbinic wisdom is the "status" and highly specific "element" of Jesus' message. In general his message is far from being a simple proclamation for everyone and all the weak of the world. True, the yoke is light, but only for those who can once again become as the children. In truth, Jesus set up the most tremendous requirements for salvation and his proclamations make salvation available only to an aristocracy of believers.

Nothing was further from Jesus' mind than the notion of the universalism of divine grace. On the contrary, he directed his whole preaching against this notion. *Few* are chosen to pass through the narrow gate, to repent, and to believe in Jesus. God himself renders unrepenting the others and hardens their hearts, and naturally it is the proud and the rich who fall victim to this fate. Of course this element is not new, since it can be found in the older prophecies. The older Jewish prophets had taught that, in view of the arrogant behavior of the highly placed, the Messiah would be a king who would enter Jerusalem upon the beast of burden used by the poor. This implies no "social equalitarianism." Jesus lodged with the wealthy, who were ritually reprehensible in the eyes of the [Jewish] virtuosi of the law, and when he bade the rich young man give away his wealth, Jesus expressly enjoined this act only if the young man wished to be "perfect," i.e., a disciple. Complete severing of all ties to the world, from family as well as possessions, such as we find in the teachings of the Buddha and similar prophets, was required [by Jesus] only of disciples. Yet, although all things are possible for God, continued attachment to riches (Mammon) constitutes one of the most difficult impediments to salvation into the Kingdom of God —for attachment to Mammon diverts the believer from that on which all exclusively depends: religious salvation.

Jesus nowhere explictly states that preoccupation with wealth leads to unbrotherliness. But this notion is at the heart of the matter, for the announced commandments definitely contain the primordial ethic of mutual help characteristic of neighborhood associations of poorer people. The chief difference is that in Jesus' message acts of mutual assistance were systematized into an ethic of conviction involving a fraternalistic sentiment of love and the commandment of mutual help was construed universalistically—that is, extended to everyone. All become "neighbors."

Indeed, the notion of mutual help was intensified into an acosmistic paradox on the basis of the axiom that God alone can and will reward. Unconditional forgiveness, unconditional charity, unconditional love even of enemies, unconditional suffering of injustice without requiting evil by force—these religious demands for heroism could have been products of a mystically conditioned acosmism of love. But it must not be overlooked, as it so often has been, that Jesus combined acosmistic love with the Jewish notion of retribution. God alone will one day compensate, avenge, and reward. Man must not boast of his virtue in having performed any of the aforementioned deeds of love, since his boasting would pre-empt his subsequent reward. To amass treasures in heaven one must in this world lend money to those from whom no repayment can be expected; otherwise, there is no merit in the deed. A strong emphasis upon the just equalization of destinies was expressed by Jesus in the legend of Lazarus and elsewhere. From this perspective alone, wealth is already a dangerous gift.

But Jesus held in general that what is most decisive for salvation is an absolute indifference to the world and its concerns. The kingdom of heaven, a realm of joy upon earth, utterly without suffering and sin, is at hand; indeed, this generation will not die before seeing it. It will come like a thief at night; it is already in the process of appearing among mankind. One makes one's way with riches instead of becoming obsessed with them; let man render unto Caesar that which is Caesar's—for what is the importance of profit in such matters? Let man pray to God for daily bread and remain unconcerned for the morrow. No human action can accelerate the coming of the kingdom, but man should prepare himself for its coming.

Although this message did not formally abrogate [Judaic] law, it did place the emphasis throughout upon the type of frame of mind. The entire content of the law and the prophets was condensed into the simple commandment to love God and one's fellow man, to which was added the one far-reaching proposition that the genuine frame of mind is to be judged by its fruits: it is testified to through conduct.

From: "Salvation Through Institutional Grace." Pp. 560–63 in *Economy and Society*, edited by Guenther Roth and Claus Wittich; translated by Ephraim Fischoff and revised by Roth, Wittich, and Stephen Kalberg (Berkeley: The University of California Press, 1978).

Wherever institutional grace operates consistently, three basic principles are involved. The first is *extra ecclesiam nulla salus:* salvation cannot be obtained apart from membership in a particular institution vested with the control of grace. The second principle is that it is not the personal charismatic qualification of the priest which determines the effectiveness of his distribution of divine grace; rather, the office within the institution does so. Third, the personal religious qualification of the individual in need of salvation is altogether a matter of indifference to the institution which has the power to distribute religious grace. That is, salvation is universal; it is accessible not only to the religious virtuosi. Indeed, the religious virtuoso may easily fall into spiritual danger with respect to chances of salvation and the genuineness of his religious profession—and actually cannot fail to fall into this danger—if, instead of relying ultimately on institutional grace, he seeks to attain grace by his own unaided power, treading his own pathway to God.

In this theory, all human beings are capable of finding salvation if they but obey god's requirements enough for the accession of grace distributed by the church to suffice for their attainment of salvation. The level of personal ethical accomplishment must therefore be made compatible with average human qualifications, and this in practice means that it will be set quite low. Whoever can achieve more in the ethical sphere, i.e., the religious virtuoso, may thereby, in addition to insuring his own salvation, accumulate good works for the credit of the institution—which will then distribute them to those in need of good works.

The viewpoint we have just described is the specific attitude of the *Catholic* church and determines its character as an institution of grace, which developed throughout many centuries but has been fixed since the time of Gregory the Great [538–594]. In practice, however, the viewpoint of the Catholic church has oscillated between a relatively magical and a relatively ethical-soteriological orientation

The manner in which the dispensation of charismatic and institutional grace influences the organization of life depends upon the preconditions attached to the granting of the means of grace. There are similarities here to ritualism, to which sacramental and institutional grace dispensation show a close elective affinity: Every type of actual dispensation of grace by a person, regardless of whether his authority derives from personal charismatic gifts or his official status within an institution, has the net effect of weakening the ethical demands upon the believer, just as does ritualism. The dispensing of grace always entails an inner *release* of the person in need of salvation; it consequently facilitates his capacity to bear guilt and, other things being equal, it largely spares him the necessity of developing an ethically systematized pattern of life. The sinner knows that he may always receive absolution by engaging in some occasional religious practice or by performing some religious rite.

It is particularly important that sins remain discrete actions, against which other discrete deeds may be set up as compensation or penance. Hence, value is attached to concrete single acts rather than to a total personality pattern—produced by asceticism, contemplation, or eternally vigilant self-control, a pattern that must constantly be testified to and determined anew. A further consequence is that no need is felt to attain the *certitudo salutis* by one's own powers. Thus, this mechanism, which may in other circumstances have such significant ethical consequences, recedes in importance. The believer's organization of life by the official—whether father confessor or spiritual director—empowered to distribute grace (a control that in certain respects is very effective), is in practice very often cancelled by the circumstance that there is always grace remaining to be distributed anew.

Certainly the institution of the confessional, especially when associated with penances, is ambivalent in its effects, depending upon the manner in which it is implemented. The poorly developed and rather general method of confession which was particularly characteristic of the Russian church, frequently taking the form of a collective admission of iniquity, was certainly no way to effect any permanent influence over the organization of life. Also the confessional practice of the early Lutheran church was undoubtedly ineffective. The catalog of sins and penances in the Hindu sacred scriptures makes no distinction between ritual and ethical sins, and enjoins ritual obedience (or other forms of compliance which are in line with the status interests of the Brahmins) as virtually the sole method of atonement. As a consequence, the pattern of organizing everyday life could be influenced by these religions only in the direction of traditionalism. Indeed, the sacramental grace of the Hindu *gurus* even further weakened any possibility of ethical influence.

The Catholic church in the West carried through the Christianization of Western Europe with unparalleled force, by virtue of an unexampled system of confessionals and penances, which combined the techniques of Roman law with the Teutonic conception of fiscal expiation *(Wergeld)*. But the effectiveness of this system in developing a methodical-rational life was quite limited, even apart from the inevitable threat caused by this loose system of dispensation. Even so, the influence of the confessional upon conduct is apparent "statistically," as one might say, in the impressive resistance to the two-children-per-family system among pious Catholics, though the limitations upon the power of the Catholic church in France are evident even in this respect.

A tremendous historical influence was actually exerted by the absence in Judaism and ascetic Protestantism of anything like the confessional, the dispensation of grace by a human being, or magical sacramental grace. This historical influence favored the development of an ethically rationalized formation of life *(ethisch rationalen Lehensgestaltung)* in both Judaism and ascetic Protestantism, despite their differences in other respects. These religions provide no opportunity, such as the confessional or the purveyance of institutional grace, for obtaining release from sins. Only the Methodists maintained at certain of their meetings—the so-called "assemblages of the dozens"—a system of confessions which had even comparable effects, and in that case the effects were in an altogether different direction. . . .

Institutional grace, by its very nature, ultimately and notably tends to make obedience a cardinal virtue and a decisive precondition of salvation. This of course entails subjection to authority, either to the institution or the charismatic personality who distributes grace. In India, for example, the *guru* may on occasion exercise unlimited authority. In such cases the organizing of life is not a systematization from within, radiating out from a center which the person has achieved; rather, it is nurtured from some center outside the self. The content of the organization of life is not apt to be pushed in the direction of ethical systematization, but rather in the reverse direction. Nonetheless, such external authority, however, increases the elasticity of concrete sacred commandments and thus makes it easier to adjust them in practice to changed external circumstances, albeit with a different effect than the ethic of conviction. . . .

Thus, the ultimate religious value [according to this salvation path] is pure obedience to the institution, which is regarded as inherently meritorious, rather than concrete and substantive, ethical duty, or the virtuoso's self-achieved methodical-ethical actions. Wherever salvation through institutional grace is carried through consistently, the sole principle integrating organization of life is a formal humility of obedience. This produces, like mysticism, a characteristic quality of "brokenness," or humility, in the pious. . . .

4

The Rise of Modern Capitalism

The Western Rationalism and Modern Western Rationalism Deep Contexts

INTRODUCTION

Stephen Kalberg

And why then did capitalist interests not call forth this stratum of jurists and this type of law in China or India? How did it happen that scientific, artistic, and economic development, as well as state-building, were not directed in China and India into those tracks of rationalization specific to the West? (p. 215)

The origin of economic rationalism depends not only on an advanced development of technology and law but also on the capacity and disposition of persons to organize their lives in a practical-rational manner. Wherever magical and religious forces have inhibited the unfolding of this organized life, the development of an organized life oriented systematically toward economic activity has confronted broad-ranging internal resistance. (p. 216)

Max Weber is widely viewed as a sociologist who demonstrated in *PE* Puritanism's important role in giving birth to modern capitalism. In fact, his works *do* offer an analysis of the rise of modern capitalism. This classic study, however, sought only to establish an elective affinity linkage between a Protestant ethic and a spirit of capitalism. A series of later treatises, almost entirely neglected by *PE*'s critics, offers Weber's discussion of modern capitalism's development: *Economy and Society (E&S)*, Economic Ethics of the World Religions (EEWR), and *General Economic History (GEH)*. These massive works investigate in great detail "both sides" of the causal nexus. If modern capitalism's origins and expansion are to be understood, Weber argues emphatically, a *multi*causal approach is required.

Ideas — beliefs and values[1] — are described in *E&S*, EEWR, and *GEH* as influential *only* when sustained by favorable constellations of "external" developments, especially in the law, economy, and rulership life-spheres. The Protestant ethic's impact resulted not only from its salvation path and economic ethic, Weber contends, but also from arrays of groups in these major arenas. Even cohesive religious doctrines acquired influence only with the crystallization of a conducive "interests" milieu, and the rationalization of religion-oriented action away from magic depends in Weber's sociology upon the presence of viable and facilitating *world* configurations. Do coherent strata, classes, and organizations congeal to carry beliefs? Is their expansion assisted by interacting groups oriented to rulership, laws, and the marketplace? Do congregations ap-

---

1.   See note 7, p. xi above.

pear as social carriers? Ideas *and* interests — religion *and* world — must be investigated, he contends.[2]

Critics of *PE* have also infrequently acknowledged Weber's insistence that capitalism's birth and transformation into modern capitalism never followed a straight pathway. As is apparent in particular from *E&S* and *GEH*, many twists and turns appeared along the way. Seemingly firm lines of development were often disrupted and then cast in unexpected directions—if only because, he maintains, multiple groups with firm boundaries at times interwove and at other times fell into relations of severe conflict. Weber consistently opposes all who perceive an inevitable evolutionary drift to history and a linear progression spanning the West's unfolding (see p. 550, n. 142).

To him, the rise of the West involves above all the rise of modern capitalism. Section 4 focuses on its origins and growth as presented in the post-*PE* writings. However, although his various texts offer the methodological tools, broad concepts, and empirically based investigations indispensable for a comprehensive treatment, his oeuvre lacks a coherent and rigorous analysis. A discrete study is absent; indeed, his writings on this theme remain fragmented and scattered. Section 4 assembles his discussion in a coherent fashion. Its selections bring together central texts from his treatises *E&S*, EEWR, and *GEH* on the origins and expansion of modern capitalism. All diverge substantially from *PE*.

Weber's differentiated picture of modern capitalism's route will here come into focus. On the one hand, unlike *PE*'s "ideas" framework, a multicausal, comparative, context-sensitive, and configurational methodology is apparent in these later writings; on the other hand, two broad-ranging concepts — "Western rationalism" and "modern Western rationalism" — become pivotal.[3] They now replace and broaden *PE*'s focus upon the religious origins of the spirit of capitalism. These methodological and thematic shifts enable Weber's sociology to identify the arrays of background groups that sustained capitalism's expansion and its transformation into modern capitalism.

The remainder of this introduction provides a synthetic reading of the selections that follow and further writings from *E&S*, EEWR, and *GEH*.[4] It seeks in this manner to *reconstruct* Weber on this theme. Constellations of ideas *and* interests come to the forefront, as do the *many* ways in which groups, as social carriers of ideas and interests, become formed into configurations that establish *deep contexts*. His notion of a civilization's overarching *track* will also be emphasized.

---

2.   Collins in particular has acknowledged Weber's complex analysis of the rise of modern capitalism (1981). His reconstruction of "Weber's last theory of capitalism," however, varies from this chapter in many ways. Of foundational significance is the choice of sources: whereas Collins exclusively relies upon *GEH* as his post-*PE* text, this chapter utilizes also *E&S* and EEWR.

3.   These terms are noted on occasion in *PE*. However, they belong to Weber's 1919–20 revisions and are not in the original 1904–05 version.

4.   Also included is a selection from Weber's *Agrarian Sociology of Ancient Civilizations* (1976 [1909]). This analysis excludes a consideration of religion.

Attention to these central themes and methodological axioms will allow investigation of how, according to Weber, Western rationalism and modern Western rationalism provided the clusters of diverse groups that sustained capitalism's rise in the West and drove its metamorphosis into modern capitalism. Furthermore, in order to isolate the West's uniqueness and the causes behind its developmental pathway, this chapter — again, following Weber — continuously offers comparisons and contrasts to China, India, and the Middle East. His post-*PE* methodological and thematic alterations must be first addressed.[5]

THE DIVERGENCE FROM *PE* AFTER 1910: METHODOLOGICAL AND THEMATIC DEVELOPMENTS

PE charts the religious sources at the foundation of the spirit of capitalism. Its causal direction is evident: from ideas to interests. EEWR also examines beliefs and values—those of the great religions. Their influence upon the conduct of the devout, as in *PE*, is illuminated.

However, unlike *PE*, EEWR also pursues the *world* side of Weber's ambitious agenda: this three-volume study investigates the economies of China, India, and ancient Israel, their cities and dominant stratification, and their types of rulership and law. All shaped, he contends, the various constellations of groups that assisted the birth of the world religions and influenced their expansion or circumscription. Hence, EEWR combines ideas and interests. *E&S* and *GEH* also manifest, in their wide-ranging chapters, this attention to "both sides." All three post-*PE* treatises reject a focus upon a single causal direction and aspire to fulfill the agenda announced at the end of *PE*: to juxtapose ideas and interests on an equal footing (p. 159; see 1968, p. 341). Viewed through the lens of his entire corpus, *PE*'s exclusive orientation to beliefs and values must be seen as the exception.

All three of Weber's later volumes also focus on groups in constellations and the ways in which, from those constellations, contexts are formed. Especially in the EEWR and *E&S* volumes, configurations of "religion" groups become embedded in clusters of "world" groups oriented, for example, to rulership, market forces, and laws. Conversely, arrays of "world" groups become embedded in constellations of "religion" groups.[6] And groups in coalitions, Weber contends, often create further configurations of groups—that is, further contexts. New groups are then promoted or circumscribed depending upon features of existing arrays of groups. In this

---

5.   This chapter may appear to offer a detailed rendering of Weber's argument. In fact, it touches only upon highlights. Readers are referred to *E&S*, EEWR, and *GEH*. It is hoped that this rendering captures the major tenor of his investigations.

6.   I will hold to this statement even though it should also be clearly noted that most chapters in the EEWR volumes treat ideas and interests separately rather than contextually. These aspects of Weber's analysis are mainly apparent in innumerable paragraphs throughout EEWR and in the "Social Psychology of the World Religions" essay (1946e).

way, Weber traces, throughout his post-*PE* sociology, *deep* contexts and their impact. And, as a consequence of this later orientation to groups and their locations amid multitudes of groups, tension, power, and conflict stand at the very core of *E&S*, EEWR, and *GEH*—though also the possibility that unconnected groups may share basic features and peacefully form elective affinity alliances.

This major difference between *PE* and the post-1909 writings must be understood as only one among several methodological distinctions. In addition, cross-civilizational comparisons are frequent throughout EEWR, *E&S*, and *GEH*. Weber extended his research, in order to isolate uniqueness, demarcate group boundaries, and evaluate causal effectiveness, to the ancient and medieval Middle East, the ancient Mediterranean, and the full histories of China, India, and the West. His innumerable comparative experiments further revealed to him the many ways in which groups become situated in deep contexts of groups. For example, in discusssing in "PR" the origins exclusively in the modern West of a type of law based upon formal rules and administered by a stratum of specially trained jurists (and hence a type of law that provided the stability and calculability indispensable for complex economic transactions and, in this way, served the interests of businessmen), Weber queries: "Why then did capitalist interests not call forth this stratum of jurists and this type of law in China or India?" (p. 215).

Finally, *PE*'s emphasis on the impact of the past upon the present is elongated even farther by *E&S*, EEWR, and *GEH*. Weber's analysis of the rise of modern capitalism now extends back to emissary prophets in ancient Israel and to the monotheism of ancient Judaism and ancient Christianity. As will be discussed below, Roman law and the guilds in Italy's politically autonomous city-states in the Middle Ages also laid down sociologically significant antecedents, as did the uniquely Western understanding of the lord–vassal contract under feudalism and the Catholic church's "office charisma" and Canon law.

Perhaps most unexpected to us today is Weber's repeated attention to the ways in which magic in the past had universally influenced activity. Its weakening and then banishment, with Puritanism, proved unique to the West. Sorcery endured over millennia in many other regions and civilizations—and, central to Weber, placed firm obstacles against economic development. His post-*PE* texts teach that the roots of the present can be traced even to epochs far preceding the sixteenth century's Reformation.

In sum, after 1910 Weber's methodological framework became significantly altered as a result of his attention to comparative experiments, a variety of life-spheres, a multitude of coherent and causally effective groups, the interaction of groups in configurations, the formation of deep contexts, and the impact of the extreme long-range past upon the present. He insists in *E&S*, EEWR, and *GEH* that an understanding of modern capitalism's complex origins, unique trajectory, and uneven expansion requires a sophisticated methodology.

A *thematic* focus broader and deeper than *PE*'s investigation of the religious sources of the spirit of capitalism is also necessary. In this regard, *E&S*, *EEWR*, and *GEH* again diverge qualitatively from *PE*. *Western rationalism* and *modern Western rationalism*, and the innumerable groups that played central roles in their formation, move now to the forefront. These concepts serve a major purpose: they acknowledge and capture the broad supporting milieux of groups indispensable for modern capitalism's rise and development. On the other hand, for Weber, Chinese rationalism, the rationalism of India, the rationalism of the ancient Near East, and the rationalism of Western antiquity acknowledge and capture different milieux, ones lacking a strong capacity to facilitate modern capitalism. How should the "rationalism" of a civilization be understood?

Whereas a single life-sphere — religion — oriented the entire *PE* study, *E&S* and *EEWR* chart out, as noted, an expanded conceptual framework: the economy, rulership, and law life-spheres became primary, as well as the religion sphere. The family, the clan, status groups, and a typology of cities are also central in these treatises. In his comparative research Weber utilizes all of these arenas and concepts, often in combinations. Indeed, taken together they form a loose *orientational grid* that serves his wide-ranging investigations. As an analytic yardstick, or standard for comparison, this large matrix assists researchers to identify empirically significant contours and parameters in the specific civilization under investigation: major life-spheres and their major groups, developmental stages within spheres and their major groups,[7] carrier groups (classes, organizations such as the family or clan, and status groups), and types of cities. It also allows demarcation of a civilization's major combinations and configurations of life-spheres, carrier groups, and types of cities. Thus, by defining arrays of major groups and group patterns, this analytic grid enables isolation of a civilization's empirical uniqueness.

This broadened, post-*PE* conceptual framework articulates a pivotal feature of Weber's comparative sociology. Civilizations, rather than to be comprehended as a series of interest calculations by individuals and the random flow of power, are comprised of innumerable clusters of groups in possession of relatively firm boundaries. Instead of arbitrary or free-floating, groups crystallize regularly — despite frequently high levels of cross-group conflict — and then sustain themselves, Weber maintains, in reference to existing constellations of groups—namely, group *contexts*. Furthermore, on the basis of multitudes of groups and their formation into configurations, civilizations develop. They do so in reference to a *track*: once multiple groups have formulated clusters and deep contexts, continuity and direction becomes manifest. Civilizations then unfold along specifiable pathways, struggling along the way against opposing groups.

---

7. The salvation paths in the sphere of religion (through a savior, an institution, ritual, good works, mysticism, and asceticism), the types of law ("primitive," traditional, natural, and logical-formal), the types of economies (natural, money, planned, market, and capitalist), and the types of authority (charismatic, patriarchal, feudal, patrimonial, and bureaucratic). See Kalberg, 1983; 1990; 1994b, pp. 149–50; 2001a.

An internal coherence, substance, and momentum characterizes each: to Weber, a *rationalism*.[8]

After numerous comparative experiments conducted in order to isolate uniqueness, delineate group boundaries, and evaluate potential causes, Weber concluded that Western rationalism's unique constellation of groups formulated a facilitating deep context of ideas *and* interests *conducive* to the growth of capitalism. He also concluded that modern Western rationalism offered the indispensable deep context of groups favorable to capitalism's transformation into modern capitalism.

Although Weber locates certain roots in Antiquity, Western rationalism's sources congealed mainly in the Middle Ages (476–1050 C.E.). Certain groups in particular life-spheres, groups specific to certain developmental stages within these spheres, carrier groups generally, and types of cities became allied and manifest in constellations of groups that sustained capitalism's expansion in this era, he contends. After an intermediate period of slower economic growth, additional groups concatenated in the seventeenth and eighteenth centuries to support capitalism's further development. And in the nineteenth century an unusual juxtaposition of groups gave birth to modern Western rationalism—which established in Weber's analysis the deep context necessary for industrial capitalism's expansion. His investigations of the civilizational rationalisms of China, India, the Middle East, and the ancient West led to a different conclusion: outside the West the clusters of groups and deep contexts that cultivated modern capitalism's rise were absent. These themes remain focal throughout Section 4's readings.

In sum, *E&S*, EEWR, and *GEH* argue that a comparative and context-sensitive mode of analysis oriented to multiple causes, configurations of groups, and deep contexts proves indispensable for the comprehension of modern capitalism's rise in the West. All linear, monocausal, and acontextual research designs are rejected firmly. Indeed, on the basis of the conceptual innovations apparent in these works, Weber's comparative query can be formulated more precisely: How did particular constellations of groups *in the West*, oriented above all toward specific salvation paths, types of cities, modes of organizing the marketplace, and forms of law and rulership — that is, toward Western rationalism and eventually modern Western rationalism — call forth, cultivate, and sustain modern capitalism? The selections below elucidate Weber's position: modern capitalism appeared in the eighteenth and nineteenth centuries as a consequence of unique mixtures at this time of "world" and "religion" groups that traced their roots back to the Middle Ages, and even to Antiquity.

Only a partial summary can be offered here of his vastly detailed investigations on the capacities of Western rationalism and modern Western ratio-

---

8. Nonetheless, Weber insists that civilizations must not be *conceptualized* as juggernauts, nor as organic and structurally unified. Of course *empirically*, during certain epochs and as a consequence of identifiable causes, civilizations may become rigid and "ossified." In this regard, he notes postclassical China and ancient Egypt.

nalism to supply the indispensable background building blocks for the rise of modern capitalism.

His emphasis upon deep contexts will be apparent throughout. We first turn to Western rationalism. Contrasts to the rationalism of China, India, and the Middle East will be discussed frequently in order to isolate the West's unique historical journey and specific causes for its development.

WESTERN RATIONALISM'S TRACK I: INDEPENDENT CITIES, CHRISTIANITY, LAW, AND CITIZENS IN THE WESTERN MIDDLE AGES

The West's historical route, Weber insists, cannot be comprehended as a progressive, linear, and unhindered advance from the Middle Ages to the present. Nonetheless, he maintains that Western rationalism's long-range unfolding proceeded in reference to a unique track, one that juxtaposed ancient Judaic and Christian monotheism, ancient and medieval Roman law, and distinct ancient and medieval urban areas. If Christianity's merger with a unique type of city in the Middle Ages had not occurred, this world religion would have developed in a different manner, Weber argues—with fateful consequences for Western history (see 1968, pp. 472; 1952, pp. 3–5). Innumerable comparisons to China, India, and the Middle East led him to this conclusion. Western rationalism's trajectory would also have varied if major impulses toward politically independent cities, Roman law, and a congregationalist religion had been curtailed.

Emanating from early Christianity, the medieval city and its guilds, and Roman law, Western rationalism's powerful universalistic thrusts weakened the authority of the clan, the tribe, and ethnic groupings. Anchored also in this city's cultivation of citizenship, these impulses confronted and challenged the severe insider–outsider and friend–enemy dualisms typical of these groupings. They also contested magic and traditional forms of rulership.

How did Western rationalism originate and acquire clear contours in the cities of the Middle Ages? Weber offers a fine-grained portrait; only its major features can be noted. Contrasts to China and India throw into relief this city's uniqueness and, in the process, serve to delineate the boundaries of Western rationalism.

Unlike the urban areas of Antiquity, which developed on the foundation of political and military groups, the cities of the Middle Ages were grounded in the economy and its growth, Weber holds. However, he distinguishes sharply between southern and northern European municipalities. While sea-trading commerce unfolded in the southern urban areas dominated by a stratum of wealthy patrician nobles (Venice, Genoa), the northern cities (Cologne) were based more thoroughly upon profits acquired through the production of goods and retail trade. This "inland industrial city[9] "is . . . one of the crucial factors inseparably linked with [modern capitalism's] . . . rise" (1968, p. 1323; see pp. 372–73).[10]

The shaping of this urban area's economy by capitalism became manifest in a variety of ways. As specialized products and new forms of production were introduced, trade volume came to greatly outstrip the ancient West's, especially across nonlocal and international markets. Consumer demand increased dramatically, and slave labor, which had hindered the efficient utilization of capital in the ancient era, was no longer used. Rooted in competition, capitalist free enterprise grew slowly but steadily. The urban workplace, characterized by a differentiated division of labor and systematic production processes, largely replaced the rural *oikos* (p. 213; 1976, p. 394). However, Western rationalism must not be viewed only in reference to this high level of wealth, Weber contends. Rather, a deep context of interacting multiple groups, only a few of which were directly oriented to the economy, must be acknowledged.

The political consequences of this wealth were significant. As their economic strength grew, residents of the inland industrial city eventually sought to sever all ties with a powerful rural nobility and to establish politically autonomous, even democratic, urban areas. Importantly, as warfare between patrician cities continued, the noble clans found it necessary, unlike in China and India, to arm the lower classes—ultimately transfering political power to them. Moreover, the capacity of urban artisans to produce goods, particularly for military endeavors, led to yet greater wealth. These classes soon proved capable of protecting their interests against the urban patrician clans and of forming autonomous corporate groups, or *guilds*. In possession of social, political, and economic power, these groups organized free craftsmen and artisans on a large scale and oriented the medieval city "immeasurably much more than any city of Antiquity . . . towards acquisition through rational economic activity" (1968, p. 1362). To Weber, "modern capitalism created the conditions of its growth on the soil of the medieval organization of commerce and industry, . . . utilizing tracks and legal forms created by the guilds" (p. 373; see p. 370; 1968, p. 1347; 1927, pp. 327–30).

He emphasizes that the guilds acquired legal rights and great social importance. Their capacity to call forth *confraternization* was also central. As "functional associations," membership "transcended existing status contrasts" (p. 370). Rather than from particular groups, whether classes, status groups, clans, or tribes, members were recruited on the basis of competence. Once formed, these organizations constituted the foundation for a

---

9. Or "producer city" (*Gewerbestadt*).

10. This city of middle-class entrepreneurs motivated by material interests and in pursuit of profit through markets, rather than through the conquest of new territories, stood in stark contrast to the city of antiquity: even before the appearance of any forms of capitalist organization, the medieval city was much closer to the development of modern capitalism than was the ancient *polis*. (see pp. 371–74). Ancient capitalism must be viewed as political capitalism, Weber insisted, and "modern capitalism [never] developed on the basis of the ancient city" (1968, p. 1323; see pp. 1332, 1346, 1351–55; see below, pp. 373–74; see also 1927, pp. 327–29, 334–36; 1976, pp. 40–60).

new and autonomous "separate community"—one which possessed wealth and, as a consequence of its military independence from both feudal lords in the countryside and patrician nobles in the cities, acquired political power. Thus, a subordinate social position could not be accepted. "The urban citizenry . . . usurped the right," Weber maintains, "to dissolve the bonds of seigneurial [feudal] rulership; this was the great — in fact, the *revolutionary* — innovation which differentiated the Western cities from all other cities" (1968, p. 1239; see pp. 370–72 ; 1927, pp. 324–26).

The guilds' political independence, economic means, and fundamentally democratic character transformed the inland industrial city. Administrative districts and juridical organs were formulated; a legal status separate from the rulership of the great rural and urban clans was acquired. Endowed with political rights and an economic policy-making role, this city *commune* "became an institutionalized association, autonomous and autocephalous, an active 'territorial corporation'; . . . [and] urban officials . . . became officials of this institution" (*Anstalt*) (p. 375; see 1968, p. 1323). Significantly to Weber, although found also in the ancient Western city, these features existed nowhere else.[11] Weber holds that a central cornerstone of Western rationalism had been laid with this "urban revolution" (pp. 375–76; 1951, p. 14).

China, India, and the Middle East

His comparative research demarcated these features of Western rationalism and their uniqueness. Although Weber noted the great financial strength of the guilds in India and China, a "decisive difference" remained—namely, the crucial capacity to oppose rulers militarily. The Chinese geopolitical configuration — the necessity of river regulation and irrigation projects gave birth to royal bureaucracies — opposed the transformation of a stratum of armed men into a commune of citizens (1951, pp. 14–15, 17–20, 76).[12] Collectivities of urban citizens never effectively challenged the dominance of clan associations in China[13] and castes in India in order to introduce confraternization among

---

11. The city's political independence led to the creation of commune-specific courts. Moreover, as members of an independent legal entity, citizens of the city commune began to create their own laws and even to elect lay judges. It was expected that the law would be applied uniformly. A flood of new codifications of civil and trial law appeared, and the creation of legal organs both secured individual rights and provided the mechanisms for citizens to conduct court proceedings—very often against aristocrats. On behalf of a broad agenda aimed at the equalization of classes, urban residents challenged arrays of legal inequalities that had bestowed privileges upon the feudal clans, whether urban or rural. All of these developments were arrested in China, India, and the Middle East. As Weber notes: "The rise of the medieval autonomous and autocephalous city association . . . is a process that differs in its very nature not only from the development of the Asian city but also from that of the ancient polis" (see pp. 371–72, 375–76; 1968, pp. 1315, 1325; 1927, pp. 318, 326).

12. Weber contrasts the medieval and Egyptian, as well as Asian, cities on several occasions. See 1968, pp. 1226–69, 1237–40, 1260–61.

13. "Revolts of the urban populace, which forced the officials to flee into the citadel, have always been the order of the day. But they always aimed at removing a concrete official or a concrete decree, especially a new tax—never at gaining a [legal] charter which might, at least in a relative way, guarantee the freedom of the city. This was hardly possible along Western lines because the fetters of the sib were never shattered. The new citizen, above all the newly rich ones, retained their relations to the native place of his sib and its ancestral land and temple. Hence, all ritually and personally important relations with the native village were maintained" (1951, p. 14).

city inhabitants and corporate bodies capable of executing legally binding contracts.[14]

Cities of the Middle East under Islamic rule in the medieval period reached a stage of development comparable to the Western ancient city, Weber contends. In both, urban patrician clans, in possession of military training and power grounded in wealth from trade, ownership of land, enslaved debtors, and purchased slaves, retained a "rather unstable autonomy" over patrimonial rulers and their administrative officials. Nonetheless, despite their strength, they never became consolidated into a "city patriciate"—namely, into an association of kinship groups capable of uniting an urban area into an independent commune.[15] Moreover, although merchant and artisan guild associations occasionally undertook organized action, urban citizens as a "collective" never did so. Such an incorporated, and politically autonomous, association that included a municipal financial administration and independent military power was lacking. Hence, an "association of burghers based on religious and secular equality before the law, *connubium*, commensality, and solidarity against non-members" could not arise (1968, p. 1241). Such a city was unknown: "The city commune in the full meaning of the word appeared as a mass phenomenon only in the West" (1968, p. 1226; see also pp. 1227–48; see below, pp. 374–75 in this volume; 1951, pp. 15, 20, 93).

Why was this the case? Trade associations, because discovered universally, possessed an "essentially indirect" effect, Weber argues (1968, p. 1258; see 1951, pp. 14–15, 16–19). Instead:

> For the development of the medieval city into an organization association two circumstances were of central significance: on the one hand, the fact that at a time when the economic interests of the citizens urged them toward an institutionalized association (*anstaltsmässige Vergesellschaftung*) this movement was *not* frustrated by the existence of magical or religious barriers, and on the other hand the *absence* of a rational administration enforcing the interests of a larger political association. (p. 376)

Weber addresses the latter theme in a succinct manner: rural nobles never possessed the administrative capacity — "a trained apparatus of officials able to meet the need for an urban administration" (1968, p. 1351) — to exercise political rulership over the cities. The sheer capacity of magic or religious barriers to obstruct change must be examined in more detail. The weakening of sorcery in the West will prove foundational to Western rationalism.

---

14. "... ordinarily there existed [in China and India] no association which could represent the commune of citizens as such. The very concept of an urban burgher and, in particular, a specific status qualification of the citizen was completely lacking. It can be found neither in China nor in Japan or India, and only in abortive beginnings in the Near East" (1968, pp. 1228–29; transl. altered).

15. Although empowered to settle conflicts in their favor, even the most wealthy guilds never developed into a "guild regiment" or "citizen stratum" capable of forming laws and exercising political authority. The military power of noble families, which was based upon slave troops, was decisive in blocking the establishment of strong and militarized guilds, Weber maintains. See 1968, p. 1233.

Christianity I: The Decline of Magic

As a consequence of Christianity's requirement that believers focus their lives around ethical teachings, all orientations to magic and ritual became weakened. This development in the religion sphere ultimately assisted the expansion of cities during the West's Middle Ages, Weber saw.

Unlike the religions of Asia, both ancient Judaism and early Christianity turned seekers of salvation *toward* the world. Their monotheistic and omniscient God required nothing less: His commandments must be upheld *amid* daily activity. Moreover, as noted above, this injunction held for the charismatically endowed — prophets and immediate disciples — *and* the lay faithful. And the unity of God's decrees, once combined with an unquestioned recognition of His omnipotence, diminished and degraded magic and ritual—for their incapacity to influence the supernatural realm now became apparent. As articulated forcefully by charismatic figures, His commandments must be practiced. For salvation, prophets demanded *ethical* action amid mundane activities.

Weber charted out the further implications of the "turn toward the world" by believers: confronted by the *meaningfulness* of religion-oriented action, the devout experienced the random ebb and flow of routine life as lacking. Religion now also contested directly, in addition to magic and ritual, all patterning of activity around practical concerns and utilitarian calculations—all "practical rationality." Hence, daily life heretofore untouched by religion was more and more penetrated by it, and the importance of *the world* — and ethical activity *in* the world — became intensified for lay and virtuosi devout alike. All *flight from* the world became stigmatized as meaningless and irrelevant to the salvation quest (1946c, pp. 326–28).

Weber stresses the central significance for Western rationalism of Christianity's emphasis upon ethical action and weakening of magic and ritual: insider–outsider dualisms, so common and unbending among clans, tribes, and ethnic groups and regularly "stereotyped" by magic and ritual, could now be directly contested and, in some cases, abolished. This *confraternization* breakthrough struck a firm blow against all ritual-based exclusiveness, which "had already begun to wane in the ancient city, . . . [and] was never strong [in medieval Europe]. . . . Sibs soon lost all importance as constitutencies of the city" (1968, p. 1243). To Weber, a direct contrast to China is evident: "In consequence of [the persistence of reliance upon magic] the power of the clans could not be broken, as happened in the West through the development of the cities and of Christianity" (1927, p. 339).

In addition, in keeping with St. Peter's pronouncements at Antioch, the ideals and values of this salvation religion were *universalistic*: "We are *all* God's children." Loyalties to clans, tribes, and ethnic groups, as well as invidious distinctions of all sorts, must be laid aside—for *all* were connected to the Christian God through the soul. Allegiance to Him was expected even over duties to the family (pp. 246–47). These developments established central components to Western rationalism and distinguished it from the rationalisms of China, India, and the Middle East.

Christianity II: The City, the Formation of the Congregation, and the Further Weakening of Clan Ties

A further development in the religion life-sphere contributed greatly to Western rationalism and, eventually, to the rise of modern capitalism, Weber contends: medieval Catholicism's formation of congregations (see 1968, pp. 452–67). Christianity's declaration that clan, tribal, and ethnic ties were devoid of meaning for the believer's relationship to the supernatural not only weakened the magical and ritual practices specific to these group-ings; in addition, this axiom contested invidious dualisms and then united "unknown others" *as believers* into a single organization. The congregation, within which this new *confraternization of faith* could take place, played a central part in this urban religion of salvation. An "equality of believers" reigned, and a universal compassion, brotherhood, and love for one's neighbor must be evident among all Christians (1951, pp. 37–38; 1968, pp. 1243, 1247).

The congregation served in this manner to mediate between and connect persons of diverse clan, tribal, and ethnic backgrounds. Believers who "joined the [city's] citizenry as individuals" rather than as members of ritu-ally sanctioned groups could now associate with one another freely—in-deed even on the basis of economic and political interests. Activity oriented to work and profit, and the formation of organizations designed to pursue economic endeavors, could occur simply as goal-oriented activity. Whether in guilds of artisans or trade organizations, economic interests in "free asso-ciations" could be pursued, as well as coalitions across heretofore separate groupings. "In dissolving clan ties," Weber argues, "[the Christian religion] importantly shaped the medieval city" (p. 375). These features of Christian-ity also, for example, supplied central preconditions for the birth of *individ-ual* households and *individual* heads of households (1968, pp. 1243–49).

Unlike under Chinese rationalism, where kinship bonds reinforced by magic-anchored ancestor worship prevailed, capitalist activity in the West could now expand more in reference to the laws of the market. Indeed, the enduring authority of the clan in China and a centralized patrimonial offi-cialdom, which "stood directly over the artisan and small peasant," op-posed the rise of an urban, entrepreneurial middle class (1951, p. 83). The caste system in India also constricted severely the arena of market freedom. And Islam in the Middle East, characterized as a "religion of a conquering army of tribes and clans" in its early period, never really overcame the divi-siveness of Arab tribal and clan ties." Cities in the Middle East remained "typical clan towns all through the Middle Ages and almost up to the pres-ent" (p. 375; 1968, pp. 1231–32).

In sum, to a far greater degree than occurred in China, India, and the Middle East, a configuration of developments uprooted magic in the West and weakened insider–outsider dichotomies rooted in clans, tribes, and ethnic groups. Orientations to monotheism and the quest for ethical salvation played an influential part, especially when interwoven with politically independent cities. Here craft guilds developed and independently carried confraternization, further surmounting invidious dualisms.

To Weber, the deep context of multiple groups that constituted Western rationalism was becoming demarcated—namely, a distinct configuration of groups that proved conducive to the birth of a coherent class of urban artisans organized in guilds and oriented to the marketplace. Absent these background developments, economic growth would not have been sustained, Weber is convinced. Economic interests in China, India, and the Middle East proved incapable of doing so as a consequence of the quite different constellations of groups and deep context shaped by Chinese rationalism, the rationalism of India, and the rationalism of the Middle East (see p. 215). Crucial in the West, Weber saw, was a unique juxtaposition of "world" and "religion": although Christianity's capacity to confront and weaken clan, tribal, and ethnic ties provided a foundational precondition for urban artisans to join together in *associative* relationships in the city commune, a reciprocity in fact reigned, he contends:

> ... it is highly unlikely that Christianity ... could have developed as it did apart from an "urban" community life, ... [which] greatly facilitated the renewed reception of [the destruction of all taboo barriers between kin groups], the concept of office, and the concept of the community as a compulsory organization (*Anstalt*) and as an impersonal and incorporated structure that serves goals. (1968, p. 472; transl. altered).

Further features of the Middle Ages and High Middle Ages (*ca.* 1050–1450) proved distinct and also contributed to Western rationalism. Their appearance during Western antiquity and in China, India, and the Middle East was blocked. Roman law and Canon law provided key additional components to Western rationalism. In the end, they enhanced economic growth.

Roman Law and Canon Law

Roman law arose during the Middle Ages in the Italian city-states. It broke clearly from all "primitive law" anchored in magic and ritual, Weber holds. It also contrasts in a striking manner to "all law produced by the East and by Hellenic culture" (1968, p. 978).

Roman law's "legal formalism" and foundation in statutes marked a dramatic shift away from all modes of ad hoc folk justice rooted in the extraordinary qualities of charismatic figures. Moreover, owing to a reliance upon reason, Roman law stood opposed to all "lawfinding" oriented to unknowable supernatural forces. Rules of evidence now came to dominate over magically effective formulas; law acquired a strongly analytical nature and became viewed as enacted by persons in groups. Systematic categories were utilized and Roman legal thinking followed the rules of logic. Formal procedures and coherent legal doctrines developed; deductive arguments were derived from ultimate legal principles. The formal training of jurists commenced and a division of power between political administrators and judges arose (see pp. 404–05; 1968, pp. 795–98, 853–54, 1313; 1927, pp. 339–40). With Roman law, the "Western world had at its disposal a formally organized legal system. . . . Officials trained in this law were superior to all others as technical administrators" (p. 404; see 1968, p. 797).

Weber's orientational matrix identified here a crucial intertwining of the law and rulership life-spheres. Patrimonial emperors, ruling over large territories in the central and northern territories of Europe in the High Middle Ages, were the social carriers of this systematization of law: it served their attempts to establish legal uniformity, unity, and cohesion across their domains. Moreover, an "immanent need of patrimonial monarchical administration" was apparent, namely, the necessity for monarchs to "eliminate . . . the supremacy of [feudal] privileges" (1968, p. 846). Indeed, "the stronger and more stable the monarch's power," the more the law became unified and systematized. Hence, further social carriers — "officials" — revived and rendered available the more formalized aspects of Roman law. The practice of law as a profession expanded (see 1968, p. 853).

Ultimately, legal justice in the medieval West came to be characterized by a "juristically formal character" and a high degree of codification rather than by a "patriarchal administration of justice in accordance with standards of substantive welfare and equity," as occurred under patrimonial empires elsewhere (see 1968, pp. 241, 853). Roman law, "with the exception of England, northern France, and Scandinavia, . . . conquered all of Europe from Spain to Scotland and Russia." It cast its shadow forcefully down through the centuries to the logical-formal law of the present (1968, p. 855).[16]

Nonetheless, and although Roman law established one of Western rationalism's crucial cornerstones, Weber maintains that the law arena never pursued a linear advance. Rather, for centuries Roman law was contested. Popular assemblies and folk justice remained widespread. And feudal law, rooted in personal rights and special privileges and devoid of a universalistic thrust, opposed Roman law in the countryside. Moreover, patrimonial rulership in the West also promoted a notion of substantive justice — a social welfare ideal — that clashed with Roman law's emphasis upon formal procedures and universalism. The monarch's mission vis-à-vis his subjects — the "good king" must serve as the guardian of his people and protect their general welfare, especially against privileges claimed by feudal nobles — stood opposed to a sharp separation of ethics, law, and administration. Decisions under patrimonial law were often rendered on a case-by-case basis and by reference to a social-ethical ideal rather than, as in

---

16.   Roman law failed to make significant inroads in medieval England (see 1968, pp. 890–92). England's common law was oriented to the concrete case as such, whereas Roman legal thought aimed to apply to "legal propositions" derived through logical deduction from statutory texts.

Roman law, to codes, statutes, and formal standards.[17] An unlikely source offered support for Roman law: the Catholic Church's Canon law.

The Catholic church attained a level of development and influence a few centuries after its founding that precluded a continued distantiation from secular authorities. "Compelled to seek relations" with them, it sought to strengthen its position by drawing upon "a rational body of ideas" compatible with the value-based position of the church in respect to ethical action and social justice—namely, Stoic philosophy's notion of natural law. For the same reasons, the "most formal components" of Germanic law were appropriated. And the rational aspects of Roman law continued to influence the administration of the church (1968, pp. 828–30). Indeed, the "sober practical rationalism" of ancient Roman law, which directly opposed all orgiastic and ecstatic modes of interacting with the supernatural realm, was "the most important legacy of [ancient Rome] to Christianity" (p. 255).

The relationship between the church and the universities thrust the development of Canon law in the same direction. Uniquely, "the structure of the Western medieval university separated the teaching of both theology and secular law from that of Canon law and thus prevented the growth of such theocratic hybrid structures as developed elsewhere" (1968, p. 828). A "clear dualism" between sacred and secular law became strengthened, and this division itself allowed each type of law to develop formally rational procedures further.

Weber sees that Canon law's manner of organizing relations to the supernatural influenced doctrinal controversies regarding the problem of theodicy. The church's increasing subordination to a "monocratic," or single, authority proved also significant. A firm obstacle was now placed against severe doctrinal polarization and fragmentation: an infallible, single authority *did* exist and *did* arbitrate disputes.[18] Consequently, and despite great vigor and a continuous expansion of church dogma, pivotal debates concerning unjust suffering and the problem of theodicy generally remained within the church's jurisdiction. "A considerable degree of hierocratic development, especially the existence of an autonomous office hierarchy and education [within the church]," proved central, Weber maintains, to "the development of all systematic theology" (1968, p. 1175).

He notes the long-range influence of the Catholic church, as an organization, just in this regard. Influenced by the Roman concept of office, characteristic of this church was a "rigorously rational hierarchical organization" and "rationally defined bureaucratic offices" implying responsibility at each level. More than in any other religious community, legislation was rationally enacted—not least because, Weber contends, administrators in this "first institution" were not merely narrowly trained, secular specialists in the law. Rather, because they labored in an institution directly connected to God, their mission transcended both narrow legal issues and self-interests—and

---

17.   Weber sees this contradiction — between a notion of substantive justice and formal procedures — as inherent to patrimonialism and patrimonial law. See 1968, pp. 856–59.

18.   Unlike in both the Eastern Christian and Russian Orthodox churches.

must be executed rationally. Moreover, a religious aura surrounded, and legitimated, each office. This "office charisma" separated the organization from the particular office incumbent, and endowed each position in the hierarchy with an inviolable dignity and trust. These central features of the Catholic church's internal structure, Weber contends, established clear precedents on the road toward modern capitalism's characteristic organization: the bureaucracy (p. 398; see 1968, pp. 828–29; 1952, p. 5).

These components of Western rationalism are also rendered more precise through comparisons. Their uniqueness becomes more vivid.

The Law: Comparisons to China, India, and the Middle East

As a consequence of all these developments, a far more rationalized version of law distinguished Western rationalism than could be found elsewhere. A "rational judicial system," trial procedures designed to acquire evidence systematically, and "continuous lawmaking on the basis of rational jurisprudence" could not be found outside the West (p. 398).[19] Moreover, as theocratic elements in legal thinking in the East lost their hegemony, the practice of law never became incorporated into a secular, oath-bound legal entity (such as occurred in the city of the Middle Ages) or carried by a stratum of professionally trained jurists; rather, it remained "essentially patriarchal" (1968, p. 845). And absent in the East was the development of law by priests and theologians in an ecclesiastical institution characterized by "organs of rational lawmaking": the Councils, the bureaucracies of the dioceses, the Curia, and the Papacy (1968, p. 792). Instead, legal development was generally carried by priests attached to the royal courts of rulers—thereby uniting secular and sacred realms of justice. The formation of an independent status group of secular specialists in the law was excluded.

Under Islam, for example, jurists were theologians. On the basis of their intimate knowledge of the *hadiths*, which describe the exemplary living of the prophet Mohammed and his disciples, these lawmakers responded to concrete inquiries. Although also — as the jurist in the West standing in the Roman law tradition — an "officially licensed legal consultant," the *mufti* (lawmaker) acquired his knowledge of the law from a school explicitly oriented to the teachings of Islam. Teaching, which remained "predominantly theological," became a "routinized recitation of fixed sentiments" in universities (1968, p. 821).

Weber discovered from his comparative studies that Islamic law located its legitimation in the infallibility of the founder Mohammed and in agreements among the founding prophets. Sacred texts — the Koran and Sunna — compiled law. He argues that the arbitrariness and unpredictability of patrimonial rulership in the Middle East invigorated a subjugation to sa-

---

19. Weber offers a succinct formulation in regard to law in India: "The unusual importance of trade in India would lead one to believe that a rational law of trade, trading companies, and enterprise might well have developed. However, [and] . . . while partially formalistic, Indian justice and the law of evidence were basically irrational and magical. . . . Ritually relevant questions could only be decided by ordeals. In other questions the general moral code, unique elements of the particular case, tradition (particularly), and a few supplementary royal edicts were employed as legal sources" (1958, p. 365).

cred law. In turn, "the theoretical rigidity and immutability of...shariah [law] was 'corrected' by judges through subjective and often quite unpredictable interpretation" (1968, p. 1096). Decisions were frequently rendered according to local custom, yet the perpetual intervention of religious decrees prevented a systematization of secular guidelines. Hence, justice was often administered in a dualistic — religious and secular — manner, yet neither body of law favored juridical unification, consistency, and rationalization. Interpretations became fixed ("stereotyped") over time.

Furthermore, Islam's application of law to the Muslim alone, rather than also to non-Muslims, strengthened legal particularism. A universal law of the land (*lex terrae*), and formal rationality rooted in secular postulates and statutes, could not develop amidst the "vagueness and precariousness of sacred law" and the varying interpretations of theologian-jurists. Nor could either the domain of law as such or legal development acquire independence, as occurred under Western rationalism. Thus, a theocratic *kadi*-justice, which operated on a case-by-case basis and in reference to nonlegal axioms, prevailed over a unified, calculable, and predictable law: "In Islam . . . the validity of . . . commercial norms did not derive from enactment [through legal processes] or from stable principles of a rational legal system" (1968, p. 822). Hence, despite the influence of ancient philosophy, and its pronounced emphasis upon logic, there prevailed a sacred law rooted in "traditional observance" and procedurally less rational than Canon law. In the Islamic world "all beginnings of rational juristic thinking" were contained and tamed by theological thought (1946b, p. 93; 1968, pp. 799–800, 810–11, 821–22).

The extent of formal rationality found in Western rationalism's Roman and Canon law proved unique, Weber holds. This "two-fold rationalization of action procedure from the profane and spiritual sides" pushed the West forward, on a winding pathway, to the logical-formal procedures of modern Continental law (1927, p. 340; 1968, pp. 790–91, 799). However, also distinct to the West was a strong differentiation — a "clear dualism" of spheres of jurisdiction — between the spiritual and the secular. A public space became delineated within which secular monarchs and parliaments could legitimately form law, impose law, and systematize its procedural elements to ever higher degrees of formal rationality—unlike in India and China.

The severe tension indigenous to Western rationalism between the secular and spiritual realms, and the ensuing competition, in part *itself* drove legal development in the Middle Ages and High Middle Ages, Weber contends. This antagonism laid a cornerstone that contributed manifestly, particularly in later centuries, to the dynamic tension and competition — or "structural heterogeneity" — across major domains typical of Western rationalism and largely absent from the rationalisms of China, of India, and of the Middle East. A vivid passage on China charts a series of crucial differences:

> No estate of jurists existed because there was no advocateship in the Western sense. It was absent because the patrimonialism of the Chinese welfare state,

with its weak office authority, could not comprehend the *formal* development of secular law.... The tension between sacred and secular law was completely absent.... Chinese patrimonialism, after the unification of the empire, had neither to reckon with powerful and indomitable capitalist interests nor with an autonomous estate of jurists [as in the West]. But it had to recognize the sanctity of tradition, which alone guaranteed the legitimacy of patrimonialism, and to acknowledge the limited intensity of its administrative organization. Therefore, not only did formal jurisprudence fail to develop, but a systematic, substantive, and thorough rationalization of law was never attempted. In general, the administration of law retained the nature which usually characterizes *theocratic* welfare justice. (1951, pp. 148–50; transl. altered; see p. 328; 1968, p. 845)

Origins of the Modern State

A variety of groups that contributed to the formation of Western rationalism in the Middle Ages indirectly called forth, Weber insists, a large-scale modern organization: the state. As manifest in "formal juristic thinking" and the organization of law in general, Roman modes of thought served as an early precursor. In addition, the city of the Middle Ages was "inseparably linked" with the rise of the state. It constituted a "crucial" antecedent, Weber holds, owing both to its independent and self-governing status and its capacity, especially once a symbiotic relationship with Christianity had developed, to weaken the clan (1968, pp. 259, 714–15, 1323; 1927, p. 339).

This interlocking under Western rationalism of Christianity and independent cities circumscribed the power of the clan, as well as of clan charisma, to penetrate into and dominate a vast variety of social groups. Weber is convinced that this interweaving also helped sustain an expansion of individualism and egalitarianism—both of which then assisted the development of the bourgeoisie. This class would become a pivotal social carrier of the modern state and formal legal equality, for its economic interests both supported the extension of a demarcated *political* community and carried the pacification indispensable for trade.[20]

Simultaneously, the binding contract, as formulated under feudalism in the countryside, introduced an important precedent for the modern state. At the foundation of this form of rulership stood the notion that the holder of a fief would be, in return for services rendered (including service in the lord's army if necessary), guaranteed a social position. Hence, this "bilateral contract" implied more than a granting of privileges by the lord and an economic exchange; pivotal issues of social status were involved. Weber saw that this encompassing of the lord–vassal relationship by a "separation

---

20. "... the political community ... obtains a powerful and decisive support from all those groups which have a direct or indirect economic interest in the expansion of the market community.... Economically, ... the groups most interested in pacification are those guided by market interests, especially the citizens of the towns, as well as all those who are interested in river, road, or bridge tolls and in the tax-paying capacity of their tenants and subjects. These interest groups expand with an expanding money economy. Even before the political authority imposed public peace in its own interest, it was they who, in the Middle Ages, attempted, in cooperation with the church, to limit feuds and to establish temporary, periodical, or permanent leagues for the maintenance of public peace" (1968, pp. 908–09; see below pp. 403–04).

of powers" contract restrained arbitariness and discretion, holding them within predictable boundaries. Political power was regulated in this manner to such an extent that, Weber contends, feudalism "turned ... into an approximation of the *Rechtsstaat* [constitutional state]": "As the basis of the distribution of political power," the feudal contract anticipated constitutionalism, "at least in a primitive fashion" (1968, p. 1082).[21]

A brief summary of the Western rationalism of the Middle Ages and High Middle Ages must be offered. Its marked tension — or "structural heterogeneity" — between *world* and *religion* will be scrutinized. This discussion then turns to the Reformation. Once again, contrasts to the rationalisms of China, India, and the Middle East serve to illuminate the uniqueness of Western rationalism—namely, its formation of a deep context of multiple groups conducive to the rise of modern capitalism.

WESTERN RATIONALISM'S TRACK II: THE WEST'S STRUCTURAL HETEROGENEITY AND THE REFORMATION

Theologians and priests systematized in the Western Middle Ages and the High Middle Ages the message of Christianity's founder and rendered it comprehensible to larger populations. As persons oriented to this religion's values gave birth to and sustained the Roman Catholic Church, an organization quite distinct from the ancient charismatic community arose. The earlier epoch's salvation paths — through faith and through a savior — were now placed alongside two further redemption routes: through the institution of the church and through good works. Performance of prescribed sacraments and rituals, regular Confession, and occasional good works offered an affirmative answer to the central query: "Am I among the saved?" Importantly, magic became now permanently subordinate to the question of salvation and the ideal of ethical action. And the church, having established its own law and hierarchies of authority, became incorporated and politically autonomous. Furthermore, although apart from the world, it existed *within and oriented to* the world. Finally, as a delineated community legitimated by its ethos of charity, compassion, universal love, and inclusion, Catholicism opposed vehemently the insider–outsider dualisms of clans, tribes, and ethnic groups. It also stood against all exchange relationships oriented to the market's impersonal laws, for they could not be, because impersonal, regulated to the same extent by ethical claims (pp. 426–30).

The political and legal autonomy of Catholicism in the West must be understood as linked unequivocally to its *location* in incorporated cities,

---

21. On the crucial differences between Western feudalism and Japanese feudalism and the feudalism of the Middle East, see 1968, pp. 1074–77, 1105. Whereas the feudalism of the Middle East lacked the "personal fealty of the vassal," Japanese feudalism (although including an ethos of personal allegiance) lacked manors and fiefs. Hence the uniqueness of Western feudalism.

Weber holds. As discussed, these urban areas had, unusually, established independence from feudal and patrimonial rulers. Often organized into guilds, their *citizens* engaged in forms of self-governance separate from clan, tribal, and ethnic loyalties and uninfluenced by magic and ritual. These city-based developments found support from a salvation religion opposed to magic and in favor of confraternization and a universalistic ethos of compassion: Christianity. The effect of the juxtaposition of all these groups was manifest: urban economic activity was influenced far more now by city-anchored legal statutes and laws, and the trader's skills and business interests, than by magical practices or clan, tribal, and ethnic loyalties. Hence, here again a world–religion interaction characterized Weber's multicausal and contextual-configurational analysis of Western rationalism's origins and substance. Puritanism's "world mastery" frame of mind and modern economic ethic must be understood as existing within this broader ideas *and* interests context—namely, within Western rationalism's constellation of groups (see Nielsen, 2005).

Hinduism and Buddhism, in requiring ethical action only of elites, diverged radically from Christianity. Moreover, the ethical search for redemption by their virtuosi devout was directed *away* from daily life activities; a *flight from* the world was pursued. Any attempt to uphold ethical standards *in* the world was perceived as meaningless for salvation. Thus, the supernatural realm in India never directly confronted the religious practices anchored in magic and ritual widespread among the broader population. Furthermore, an ethos that, on the basis of universal claims, contested clan, tribal, and ethnic insider–outsider dualisms remained absent. And the caste system, once entrenched, foreclosed all patterning of daily life by reference to universalistic ideals. A religious halo never sanctified utilitarian activity. Weber renders these crucial differences succinctly:

> The unrestricted lust for gain of the Asiatics . . . was a "drive for gain." It was pursued with every cunning means and with the assistance of a universal mechanism: magic. It was lacking precisely that which was decisive for the economy of the West: the refraction and rational modulation of the *drive* character of the striving for goods and its alignment into a system, namely a rational, this-worldly ethic of action. Protestantism's "inner-worldly asceticism" . . . in the West had managed to accomplish just this. The development of religion in Asia was lacking the presuppositions for doing so. . . . In the West the establishment of a rational, this-worldly ethic was bound up with the appearance of thinkers and prophets who developed out of a social context alien to Asiatic civilization. This context consisted of the *political* problems engendered by the *city*'s status groups—without which neither Judaism nor Christianity nor the development of Hellenic thought is conceivable. The origin of the "city" in the Western sense was inhibited in Asia partly through the sustained power of clans [China] and partly through caste alienation [India]. (1958, pp. 337–38; transl. altered; see 1927, pp. 312–14)

Finally, neither of India's salvation religions of "world indifference" and "world flight" helped to create politically autonomous institutions that carried their own forms of law. For this reason also the utilitarian and practical rationality of daily life was never contested and pushed aside. And, unlike under Western rationalism, political rulers remained largely unchallenged by religious organizations.

Far greater patterned tension reigned under Western rationalism than appeared in the ancient West or in China, India, or the Middle East. Rooted in a pluralism of antagonistic life-spheres, conflicts in the Western Middle Ages far excelled in intensity and duration those that arose in more unified civilizations rooted in the dominance of either caesaropapism or theocratic rulership. Antagonisms between a relatively autonomous church — or "hierocratic power" — and secular political elites were severe (1968, p. 1174; see also pp. 1173–81; 1946e, p. 288). Whereas a state-appointed clergy lacking an autonomous "office hierarchy" remained frequent in the East, an unusual openness characterized the "less unified" West, Weber holds, and a "Western hierocracy lived in a state of tension with the political power and constituted its major restraint" (p. 398). A "structural heterogeneity" became constituent to Western rationalism, and it spurred a political and economic dynamism that contrasted starkly with the relative structural homogeneity widespread in non-Western civilizations. "In the West," he holds, "rulership was set against rulership, legitimacy against legitimacy, one office charisma against the other" (p. 398). Indeed, the *world* (the economy, rulership, and law spheres) and *religion* antagonism *itself* introduced "a strongly dynamic element into the West's unfolding" (1968, pp. 578–79).

Weber sees the Reformation as constituting the last major component of Western rationalism. It will eventually have, he is convinced, a strong impact upon the development of capitalism. A further unique interaction of ideas and interests is again apparent.

The Reformation: World and Religion Tensions

Weber insists that the Reformation's new religious movements arose not only from the abstract syntheses of theological postulates formulated by religious intellectuals. Distinct social, rulership, economic, legal, stratification, family, and power groupings significantly influenced the religion domain in this era, he maintains. The Reformation "was certainly codetermined by economic factors" (1968, p. 1196) and the decisive weakening of Papal authority had "political reasons":

[It] lost ground because of the caesaropapist inclinations and secularizing tendencies of the princes who had strengthened their power tremendously through administrative rationalization, and after the ecclesiastic tradition became discredited in the eyes of the intellectual circles and the noble and bourgeois strata. (1968, p. 1196)

Moreover, facilitating contexts, constituted from particular rulership and economic groups, had to be in place for Calvinism and the other ascetic Protestant sects and churches to arise: "The ascetic varieties of Protestantism have prevailed wherever the bourgeoisie was a social power, and the least ascetic churches of the Reformation, Anglicanism and Lutheranism, wherever the nobility or the princes had the upper hand" (1968, p. 119; see also pp. 471–72; pp. 431–34; 1927, pp. 356–69; 1958, pp. 337–38).

As the Reformation spread, lay believers increasingly communicated with ministers and theologians on a regular basis in reference to scriptural standards rather than age-old tradition, clan loyalties, or Catholicism's hierocratic authority. In turn, the Protestant clergy, as a result in part of the intense competition across varieties of churches and sects in the sixteenth and seventeenth centuries, more and more acknowledged "lay rationalism." Weber points out that Puritanism in England, arising out of a politically powerful middle class, "became saturated with [a plebeian] intellectualism." As an empowered laity demanded answers to the problem of suffering and the predestination conundrum, ministers and theologians responded—at times even adjusting doctrine (p. 411; 1968, p. 467).[22]

Pastoral care expanded as this dynamic unfolded. It was pushed along by an unusual command of scripture among the lay devout, their uncertainty regarding salvation in light of the harshness of the Predestination doctrine, and the practical — even economic — concerns of church and sect elites. In contrast to China and India, where "pure religion[s] of intellectuals" maintained hegemony and "priestly labors of systematization concerned themselves more and more with the most traditional, and hence magical, forms of religious notions and practices" (1968, p. 466), a widespread lay rationalism in the West often initiated dramatic and urgent dialogues among theologians and the clergy. At stake was the salvation of anxiety-plagued believers. Whereas the faithful in the East remained "submerged in magic," this post-Reformation dynamic in the West uprooted the devout even more from magic and ritual and pushed conduct more urgently toward ethical action *in* the world. Ascetic Protestantism's orientation to work, profit, wealth, and a vocational ethos eventually crystallized.

This examination of the West's overarching track, independent cities, citizenship, Christian doctrine, Roman and Canon law, the modern state's origins, the Reformation, lay rationalism, and structural heterogeneity has sought to define the configuration of groups that comprised the unique contours of Western rationalism in the Middle Ages and High Middle Ages. Contrast cases — the rationalisms of China, of India, and of the Middle East — have been referred to throughout in order to demarcate Western rationalism's substance and boundaries precisely. An array of causes behind its development have been identified.

The facilitating context of ideas and interests for a "take-off" toward modern capitalism, it would appear, was in place by the High Middle Ages. A firm alliance — the coalition of early Christianity's monotheism, universalism, and

---

22.   On this unique interaction between the laity, the clergy, and theologians, see 1968, pp. 452–67.

world-oriented salvation-striving with guild craftsmen in autonomous cities — had weakenend the hold of magic and surmounted clan, tribal, and ethnic dualisms to a significant extent by the Middle Ages and to a degree qualitatively greater than had occurred in China, India, or the Middle East. Both Roman law and Canon law had contributed to this development; ethical action oriented *toward* daily activities arose on a widespread basis in the Western cities. Western rationalism assumed quite distinct contours and parameters.

However, Weber rejects the view that capitalism expanded from the Middle Ages and the High Middle Ages in a linear manner to modern capitalism. History's flow never pursued a straight line, he contends; "market-irrational" groups often held firm—even despite the powerful push given by the Protestant ethic. Indeed, an array of groups became allied in opposition to capitalism's growth. And powerful barriers were erected against its transformation into modern capitalism, whether in the form of patrimonial empires struggling against politically independent and incorporated cities in the High Middle Ages, the scorn of feudalism's ethos for all systematic pursuit of wealth, Catholicism's traditional economic ethic and struggle against capitalist entrepreneurs, certain "market-irrational" aspects of patrimonial rulership, or the English monarchy against industrious Puritans. Ideas and interests interact in multiple and unpredictable ways, Weber is convinced.

Although the Middle Ages gave birth to an "urban revolution" and a period of dynamic capitalism, this era proved an *intermezzo* of high economic growth between the ancient world and the patrimonial rulers of the fifteenth, sixteenth, and seventeenth centuries, Weber maintains. As their empires became dominant to varying degrees in the different European countries, Western rationalism's parameters shifted. *Modern* capitalism, carried significantly by ascetic Protestantism and the spirit of capitalism, will crystallize, Weber holds, only with the weakening of these great empires and a further concatenation of many groups in configurations: modern Western rationalism.

THE PATRIMONIAL EMPIRES: ABSOLUTISM, MERCANTILISM, AND THE DECLINE OF THE URBAN REVOLUTION

The cross-sphere conflicts and severe structural heterogeneity of the Middle Ages and High Middle Ages proved short-lived as defining features of the Western developmental pathway and Western rationalism. Patrimonial empires expanded across much of Europe. Amid centralization, would a slow, but steady, societal ossification follow?

Rulers extended hegemony over large territories. Kings amassed military power and created complex administrative organizations, hence whittling away the military, judicial, and economic independence of cities.

Legal prohibitions were placed upon citizens of the urban areas, and the independent power of most cities to tax was eliminated. This patrimonial subjugation decreased the economy's growth and weakened the guilds (1968, pp. 1328–30, 1351). Weber identifies several specific causes for the economic and political decline of the medieval city.

The Putting Out System

The putting-out economy[23] gradually replaced production by urban craftsmen in guilds. Experienced merchants with access to markets began hiring workers in their own homes on a contract basis. Labor could now be more thoroughly organized and exploited than under the guild mode of production. The beginnings of an entrepreneurial middle class were apparent.

Although its extent and tempo varied enormously from country to country (see 1927, pp. 153–59), and even though the old and the new modes of production existed for centuries side by side, the domestic system gradually won out. England led the way, followed by France, which moved decidedly toward this "cottage" industry in the fourteenth century. It expanded widely as market-savvy merchants developed buying monopolies, delivered raw materials to workers in their homes, exercised control in respect to quality and scheduling over the production process, provided workers with the necessary tools, and established monopolies over the marketing and distribution of products. Wherever this mode of production expanded, the power of the guilds, which anchored the medieval city's economic and political power, was disrupted, hence weakening the autonomy of urban areas.

The domestic system proved unique to Western rationalism, Weber contends. Workers were elsewhere often unable freely to enter into contracts, and frequently their mobility was restricted by the necessity to perform ritualistic and magical acts. In China the dominance of clan-based production methods, and the distribution of the product only to the kinship group, constituted a strong barrier to its growth. Merchants were prevented in India from controlling the means of production owing to its caste-based, hereditary location—and hence a subjugation of craftsmen could not occur (see 1927, pp. 160–66).

The Decline of Feudalism

Weber saw feudal authority as precarious owing to the unstable anchorage of the vassal's obedience. While a relationship of loyalty underpinned the following of commands, possession by vassals and subvassals of administrative authority over demarcated territories implied the constant possibility of aggrandizement and usurpation of the ruler's domination. For stability to endure, the voluntary component — the "feudal ethos" of personal allegiance — must be continuously cultivated and strengthened. Conflict remained "chronic" (see 406–09; 1968, pp. 255–62, 1078–88).

---

23.   This economy is also referred to as the "domestic system" and "cottage industry."

The lord's wish to place his rulership on a more secure footing led repeatedly to attempts to create a directly subordinate administrative staff. These efforts frequently were successful in Europe—and feudalism more and more became transformed into patrimonial rulership. The necessity for tighter administrative control, amid warfare across competing regions and then among patrimonial "states," furthered this development. The push by jurists interested in legal reliability and the search by an expanding bourgeoisie for cross-regional economic stability did so as well.

Feudalism gradually lost out to expanding patrimonial kingdoms. In addition, exploitation and control of the cities intensified as absolutist monarchies commenced a period of intense competition and empire-building. In possession of large armies and utilizing officials trained to administer extended areas, rulers throughout Europe in the fifteenth, sixteenth, and seventeenth centuries succeeded in eroding the autonomy of the city communes. Western rationalism's urban revolution came to an end. Democracy and citizenship in the cities was suppressed in the process (1968, p. 1351).[24]

The Rise of Patrimonial Empires and Mercantilism

The advance of large-scale administrative organizations and rulership over huge territories occurred as patrimonialism bestowed economic privileges upon new groupings of entrepreneurs with roots in the putting-out system. In exchange for fees or profit sharing, the awarding of monopolies and private trade rights to "state commercial enterprises" and specific craft organizations became widespread practices.

Moreover, patrimonial rulership's antagonism to the formal rationality of the marketplace proved less intense than feudalism's; indeed, Weber saw even an elective affinity between certain aspects of patrimonialism's ethos and the market economy. Far more tolerant of upward mobility, trade, new property formation, and the search for riches than their feudal counterparts, patrimonial rulers and officials viewed status barriers as placing limitations upon acquisition and trade. To Weber: "The 'financier' is . . . feasible under almost all conditions of rulership, especially under patrimonialism." Western rationalism's "Age of Mercantilism," in which a direct relationship between the state and capital congealed, had commenced. Now patrimonialism's economic achievements only enhanced its capacity to maintain hegemony over the urban areas (see pp. 381–83, 397; 1968, pp. 1091–94, 1097–99).

A larger dynamic came into play to alter Western rationalism in the sixteenth and seventeenth centuries: princes and monarchs across Europe became engaged in ruthless competition for political power and the resources of the new world. "Ever more capital for political reasons, and because of the expanding money economy," was required (1968, p. 353). Precisely this competition, which Weber saw as unique to the West in this epoch, endowed the alliance between the state and an expanding class of merchants, financiers, and colonial adventurers with a special firmness and intensity.

---

24.   For further causes, see 1968, pp. 257–59, 971, 1089.

These emerging states promoted financial rationalization, introduced an expanded money economy, and "created the largest opportunities for modern capitalism," Weber holds (see p. 397).

Mercantilism's Opposition to Modern Capitalism

Once again, a linear unfolding to modern capitalism could be envisaged. However, according to Weber, this *political* capitalism never introduced *modern* capitalism. Twists and turns characterized its origins. Indeed, patrimonialism's mercantilism in the end opposed the growth of the market. Due to its person-oriented values, patrimonialism's ethos stood in a relationship of antagonism to the market's formal rationality. Moreover, because of its claim to legitimacy, this ethos remained more oriented to the welfare and loyalty of subjects than to the revolutionary changes placed into motion by the widening powers of business-oriented groups and the growth of the marketplace (pp. 408–09). Finally, the frequent tensions between the ruler, his court, and local officials created instability antagonistic to the growth of formal rationality.

In general, the "spirit of patrimonial administration" sought to preserve the traditional economic ethic; it "is alien to and distrustful of capitalist development" (p. 408). Even where great wealth was obtained, the proclivity of patrimonialism to immobilize riches through monopolies opposed a high degree of formal rationality (1968, pp. 1091, 1094–98). How then, Weber queries again, did Western rationalism give birth to modern capitalism?

THE SEVENTEENTH AND EIGHTEENTH CENTURIES: TECHNOLOGY, SCIENCE AND RELIGION, THE FACTORY, AND COMMERCIALIZATION

Despite the growth of great patrimonial empires, Western rationalism continued to be characterized by a certain structural heterogeneity conducive to economic activity. By the end of the sixteenth century, trade and economic development in general had increased to a heretofore unequaled extent. Compared to the ancient world, China, India, and the Middle East, a greater dynamic of competing groups and a political situation of relative openness existed. All in all, an entrepreneurial middle class planted deep roots and gradually expanded its power during the sixteenth, seventeenth, and eighteenth centuries. Weber maintains that technology, science, the factory, and new commercialization mechanisms (such as the stock market) played pivotal parts in this expansion. Only a brief overview can be offered.

The Role of Technological Change

Although an entire series of technological innovations in the West contributed to the growth of modern capitalism, Weber contends that an independent causal weight cannot be attributed to them. Indeed, in the ancient world capitalism developed in the absence of technological advance—even "one could say simultaneous with the cessation of technical progress." The view that "certain *technical* 'achievements' constituted the obvious origin of capitalist development" must be seen as a "popular error" (p. 447; 1976, pp. 353–54).

Weber's reluctance to endow technology with a clear causal capacity derives from his sociology's general proclivity to view single groups in configurations of groups. He then emphasizes the decisive role of the social context. Did the milieu — Western rationalism's salvation paths, forms of rulership and law, status groups, cities, and economic forms — facilitate or constrain the impact of a specific innovation? Did "the development of . . . technology . . . acquire pivotal invigorating impulses from opportunities offered by capitalism" (p. 214)?[25] Did a specific context singularly configure a facilitating milieu, thereby enabling innovations to take hold and have an impact? While "the origin of mathematics and physics was not determined by economic interests," Weber maintained, the *technical* applications of scientific knowledge were (p. 214). Even the influence of warfare upon the unfolding of modern capitalism and the demand for luxury goods depended upon a social context, he held, as evident from an examination of comparative cases (see pp. 389–90).

The Influence of Science: Material-Technological Interests and Religious Belief

Science began to play a part in the unfolding of modern capitalism in England when market forces became capable of offering sustained incentives to inventors, according to Weber. In the form of technological innovations, the application of science would lessen production costs, it was widely hoped. An entirely new, and more systematic, *motivation* was created among inventors and scientists quite different from Leonardo's: "science meant the path to *true* art" (2005, p. 325; see below pp. 390–91). With the expansion of markets, the question of whether an invention possessed "practical" utility became pivotal.

However, Weber refuses to see a "feverish pursuit of invention" as driven alone by material incentives. The social context was more complex, he insists; religious belief also proved again salient (see p. 516, n. 169). He rejects at the outset a view widespread among his colleagues: devoutness must be understood as an obstacle to the development of empirical science. Instead, the origin of modern natural science was intimately *interwoven* with religious faith, Weber maintains, particularly with Puritanism. Indeed, "most of the natural science heroes in England from the seventeenth century right up until [Michael] Faraday [1791-1867] and [James] Maxwell" [1831–1879] were sincere believers (p. 447; 1946d, p. 141).[26]

---

25. See Weber's many examples (pp. 389–91).
26. Weber notes that Catholic thinkers formed the early foundations of the modern natural sciences. However, the methodical connecting of science with practical goals "was principally 'Protestant,' " (p. 447). See Merton, 2001, pp. 628–82.

He is convinced that the religious dimension played a significant part in linking scientific innovation and the expansion of the economy in seventeenth- and eighteenth-century England. Above all, Puritan scientists sought to unveil God's will through an exploration of the universe's natural laws—and this quest frequently yielded knowledge that could be placed relatively easily into the service of new technologies. Hence, the natural sciences assisted economic growth in a more *practical* manner than in earlier epochs—and, given previous technological innovations, did so at a critical time for the economy's growth. Finally, the religious component in the motivational configuration of Puritan scientists inserted a *methodical* — "and not just occasional" — component into this interlocking of scientific innovation and economic growth (see p. 447, 516 [n. 169]; 2005, pp. 325, 340). Western rationalism acquired a further pivotal and unique component with this interweaving of science and religion.

The Rise of the Factory

Factories are centers of production that bring together a concentration of freely contracted workers under one roof. Nonhuman sources of power — machines — are typical, as is capital accounting. On the basis of mechanization, tasks are specialized and labor is organized, coordinated, and disciplined. An elaborate differentiation of functions, and their rational organization in reference to questions of technical efficiency, characterizes the factory's division of labor. A continuity of operations prevails.

This manner of organizing work stands in contrast to the putting-out system in two ways: the factory centralized labor and accumulated fixed capital to a far greater extent; it also appropriated land, tools, installations, and means of production to one owner. Thus, far higher degrees of efficiency accompanied the organization of labor and a more exact calculation of costs became possible. In the eighteenth century the factory gradually displaced the putting-out system (see p. 384; see also 1927, pp. 163, 169–73; 1968, pp. 117, 135; 1976, p. 44).

Largely because of its requirement for a large supply of free and mobile labor, the factory rarely appeared before the eighteenth century and infrequently outside the West. The requisite supply of labor proved difficult to assemble in India, and the perception by castes of each other as "impure" hindered easy cooperation on the factory floor. Moreover, each caste held to its own set of rituals, rest breaks, and holidays. In China, the cohesiveness of clans in villages limited the supply of mobile labor and fostered "communal clan" workshops rather than factories. Similarly, the scarcity of unfree labor created obstacles to factory development in Antiquity and the Middle Ages in the West.[27] On the other hand, Western rationalism assembled arrays of groups that assisted the birth of the factory, including a "mechanization of technology," a type of science oriented to practical innovations, and ascetic Protestantism's vo-

---

27. On these countries and this epoch, see pp. 370–376; 1976, p. 44.

cational ethos. A strong push in the direction of modern capitalism ensued, Weber contends (pp. 384–85; 1927, p. 184).

Commercialization

The economies of England, the American colonies, and the early United
States witnessed a broad-ranging commercialization in the eighteenth and
nineteenth centuries, and even earlier. This development "involved . . . the
appearance of paper representing shares in enterprise and, secondly, paper
representing rights to income, especially in the form of state bonds and
mortgage indebtednss" (p. 379). Large sums of capital were raised from the
publicly held stock company, which arose out of early war-financing activities and the large colonizing companies of the sixteenth and seventeenth
centuries (pp. 379–80).

Western rationalism's economies continued to grow and to introduce
systematizing mechanisms. The wholesaler became distinct from the re-
tailer in the eighteenth century, and soon introduced new commercial entities: wholesale trade, the auction, consignment trading, and buying on
commission, for example (see 1927, pp. 292–93). The standardization and
quantification of units increasingly allowed speculation upon, and exchange of, commodities. Futures trading, and especially the building of the
railroads, unchained the "speculative urge," and soon various goods,
grains, and colonial products were "drawn into the circle of exchange speculation in the nineteenth century" (1927, p. 294). The appearance of newspapers and commercial organizations facilitated the growth of speculative
and wholesale trade. Finally, the construction of turnpikes and railroads
boosted economic growth enormously.[28]

Despite the concatenating influence of facilitating groups and conducive
social contexts provided by Western rationalism, *modern* capitalism had not
yet appeared.[29] Exclusive reference to political, economic, scientific, and
organizational constellations fails, Weber holds, to account for its rise. And
neither types of law nor types of rulership rooted in formal rationality had
yet crystallized. Both facilitated greatly the growth of modern capitalism
by providing predictability to economic transactions and allowing
long-range calculation, he insists. Far from being linear, twists and turns
characterized modern capitalism's advance.

The Protestant ethic, which introduced a methodical-rational organization of life oriented toward world mastery, assisted the transformation of
England's political capitalism into modern capitalism. Placed on the de-
fensive, mercantilism was largely banished in the eighteenth century.
Weber stresses, of course, the capacity of the ascetic devout to *direct* energy vigorously and in a sustained manner toward wealth, profit, and

---

28. The importance of railroads is evident to Weber: "For economic life in general, and not merely
     for commerce,". . . the railway is the most revolutionary instrumentality known to history"
     (1927, p. 297).
29. The above discussion, as noted, has attempted to draw attention to major groups rather than
     to be comprehensive.

work in a vocational calling. The search by the faithful for signs of their salvation status, the ways heretofore purely utilitarian activities became sanctified, the newfound clear conscience of the entrepreneur in search of profit, and the necessity to testify to belief through ethical conduct proved sociologically significant, he insists. By rationalizing action radically and introducing *practical-ethical* action, ascetic Protestantism disrupted and replaced both the *practical-rational* organization of life and the traditional economic ethic. Patterned action more methodical and intense than utilitarian calculations had been required to do so. This *directed* life endowed the organization of labor in factories with a systematic aspect, promoted the introduction of new technologies into the workplace, and facilitated the birth of a broad-based middle class of entrepreneurs and industrious workers, Weber contends.

The conflict between mercantilism's political capitalism and the Puritan ethos, and the subsequent victory of Puritanism, were pivotal episodes in the history of modern capitalism's unfolding in England, according to Weber. The patrimonial empires proved unable to sustain an entrepreneurial spirit, although capable of awakening one. A modern economic ethic, which stimulated the expansion of the market in a variety of ways, appeared only with ascetic Protestantism. Western rationalism's various groups now gradually became more tightly interwoven and nourished each other reciprocally—weakening market-irrational substantive rationalities. The free market expanded and the preconditions for a maximum degree of formal rationality of capital accounting began to fall into place (see 1968, pp. 161–64). Calling forth indigenous types of formal rationality, configurations of groups in several major life-spheres lent strong support to modern capitalism's development, Weber emphasizes. Modern Western rationalism then embarked upon the stage of history.

MODERN WESTERN RATIONALISM'S CONCATENATING GROUPS: FORMAL-LOGICAL LAW, THE MODERN STATE, AND BUREAUCRATIC RULERSHIP

If to congeal and endure, modern capitalism required a further array of groups arranged in a supportive constellation. As a result of unique juxtapositions, eighteenth- and nineteenth-century developments introduced predictability and stability into the marketplace. Its capacity to give birth to high degrees of capital accounting is sustained in this epoch by a modern type of law, a modern state, and bureaucratic rulership. Formal rationality grounded these central components of modern Western rationalism.

Modern capitalism "operates best" wherever embedded in a legal order that functions in a calculable manner in reference to rational rules. Objective regulations, statutes, and laws universally applied provide systematized and unambiguous procedures. This type of legal order offers, for example, a secure method for transferring legal claims and a firm basis for the constant expansion of market exchanges (1927, p. 343; 1968, pp. 1394–95). Indeed, according to Weber: "The tempo of modern business communication requires a promptly and predictably functioning legal system, i.e., one which is guaranteed by the strongest coercive power" (1968, p. 337; see also p. 1095). Hence, as the market expands, modern capitalism:

> . . . favored the monopolization and regulation of all "legitimate" coercive power by *one* universalist institution with a monopoly over the legitimate use of force (*Zwangsanstalt*) — the state — and the disintegration of all particularist, status-determined and other coercive structures based mainly upon economic monopolies (1968, p. 337; transl. altered; emph. in original).

In addition to the modern state, modern Western rationalism is significantly constituted from bureaucratic rulership. It also offers a supportive milieu to modern capitalism's formal rationality, Weber contends. While not necessarily efficient, the modern bureaucracy nonetheless far surpasses traditional and charismatic forms of rulership in sheer organizational capacity, the performance of tasks, and formal rationality.[30] A standardized execution of duties and an orientation to rules, prescriptions, and regulations characterizes action within bureaucracies rather than an orientation — favoring or disfavoring — to persons.[31]

This organization's modes of procedure, which ultimately provide rationally debatable "reasons" for every administrative act, enables business to take place at an impersonal level and in a predictable fashion (1968, pp. 956, 1095). The stability and continuity indispensable for economic planning and the operation of large industrial enterprises is provided. Moreover, the status ethic of the manager — disciplined, uncorruptable, and reliable — tends to further sustain modern capitalism's demand for calculability. The "matter of factness" (*Sachlichkeit*) of the professionally trained expert, his view of knowledge as "useful" in a technical sense, and his formal rationality "tended already . . . in the direction of the private economic rationalism of the middle class strata" (1968, p. 847; transl. altered). "In its modern stages of development," Weber maintains, "capitalism requires the bureaucracy" (1968, p. 224; see pp. 956, 1095).

---

30. The secondary literature has too often argued that Weber viewed this form of rulership as "efficient" as such. His orientation instead is toward the question of the organization of labor and the bureaucracy's technical superiority (the performance of administrative tasks) *in comparison to* the charismatic, patrimonial, feudal, and patriarchal types of rulership. He is well aware of "red tape."
31. It should be again recalled that Weber is here constructing an ideal type. See Glossary.

MODERN WESTERN RATIONALISM AND MODERN CAPITALISM'S AUTONOMY

Called Western rationalism by Weber, configurations of groups in the Middle Ages commenced the meandering story of modern capitalism's origin and development. For the West's uniqueness and track, pivotal were above all the growth of citizenship in politically independent cities, guild-based city economies, Christianity's ethos of universal compassion, the confraternization cultivated by both religious congregations and guilds, Roman law and Canon law, feudalism's notion of contract, the weakening of magic and insider–outsider dualisms anchored in clans, tribes, and ethnic groups, and the office charisma developed by the Catholic church.

Weber saw these various groups as interacting off each other and forming configurations of groups. Contexts crystallized from juxtapositions of interests and ideas. Western rationalism acquired continuity, an internal coherence, and a developmental direction—one that would offer to capitalism a context conducive to its growth. Nonetheless, a linear line of "progress" from capitalism to modern capitalism cannot be ascertained, he insists.

Capitalism experienced significant circumscription in the fifteenth, sixteenth, and seventeenth centuries because of the centralizing powers of absolutist patrimonial empires, feudalism's particularism and opposition to the middle class outlook, and Catholicism's traditional economic ethic. Nonetheless, on the basis of a favorable constellation of interacting world *and* religion groups, capitalism resumed its steady expansion in the eighteenth century. Technological innovations, modern science, the methodical application of new technologies, the organization of a workforce into factories, and the introduction of new commercialization mechanisms interacted in supportive ways. Clusters congealed that gave vibrancy to and sustained Western rationalism's tracks. The presence of a distinct and large group — ascetic Protestants — systematically in pursuit of profit and motivated to labor in a methodical manner, Weber contends, provided a significant impulse along the winding pathway to modern capitalism. The Protestant sects endowed the Puritan ethic in the United States with an unusual dynamism and served as its effective social carrier. Businessmen's clubs and a variety of civic associations cultivated a spirit of capitalism several generations later.

Only an acknowledgment of ideas *and* interests allows consideration of the full configuration of groups — Western rationalism's deep context — that gave rise to, facilitated, and nourished capitalism along its long journey, Weber insists. It eventually unfolded in the eighteenth and nineteenth centuries into an additional array of groups that further cultivated Western rationalism's track: modern law, the modern state, and the modern bureaucracy. This multidimensional context — modern Western rationalism — also proved conducive to the economy's growth. It assisted the entrepreneur and businessman to fulfill indispensable tasks: to calculate, in reference to the free market, actual costs and to introduce technical efficiency. Capitalism became transformed into modern capitalism. The twists and turns that marked capitalism's expanse and metamorphosis become apparent, according to Weber, only if the facilitating group configurations that constituted Western rationalism and modern Western rationalism are acknowledged.

In his many investigations of Western rationalism, and in his comparative research into the rationalisms of China, India, and the Middle East, Weber analyzed how powerful groups opposed to the efficient functioning of the market's laws gradually declined only in the West: for example, feudalism's aristocracy, Catholicism's traditional economic ethic, and mercantilism. Only then could the "free market," an impersonal "spirit of calculation," a technically refined formal rationality, and capital accounting become widespread, he held.

In the nineteenth century, the rules of commercial accounting and efficient management began to dominate action oriented to the market in several Western nations. Rather than an ethos of universal compassion, or ethical claims, decision-making in the economy life-sphere more and more occurred exclusively by reference to the laws of the market, assessments of net income, and the struggle of interests, Weber contends. Capitalism now pursued unhindered, with "market freedom," its *own* laws—those of the marketplace. And noncompliance with its formal rationality implied direct consequences: "The growing impersonality of the economy on the basis of association in the marketplace follows its own impersonal lawfulness, disobedience to which entails economic failure and, in the long run, economic ruin" (1968, p. 585; transl. altered, see below, pp. 426–27).

This reconstruction of capitalism's expansion and transformation has revealed Weber's sociology as an empirical sociology of deep contexts. For this reason alone it rejects unilinear views of history and all depictions of the West's pathway as one of metaphysical and unceasing progress. Crucial crossroads appeared frequently, he maintains. At times, Western rationalism's constellations of groups failed to push the unfolding of the economy toward modern capitalism; at other times a qualitative leap in this direction was sustained by concatenating groups; at still other times a course taken proved only much later, once a variety of groups had shifted and new configurations had formed, a spur to modern capitalism. Even initiatives favoring capitalism's growth conveyed by powerful carrier groups often faded from the landscape—crushed, at least temporarily, by centralizing, even bureaucratizing, tendencies. Not least, the sheer tension between ethical standards articulated within the religion life-sphere on the one hand and daily life's practical rationality and the formal rationality dominant in the rulership, economy, and law domains on the other may *itself*, Weber emphasizes, place dynamic and unpredictable thrusts into motion (pp. 86–88; 1976, p. 366; 1968, pp. 578–79; 1946c, pp. 328–30; Kalberg, 2001a).

This extensive introduction to Section 4's readings has sought to convey how, in Weber's post-*PE* writings, social groups formed configurations of groups in the West that provided deep contexts — Western rationalism and modern Western rationalism — favorable to capitalism's expansion and development to modern capitalism. However, a further goal has also been central: to convey the many ways that, for Weber, constellations of groups from the distant past repeatedly cast long shadows—indeed, even into the immediate present. Western rationalism's origins must be located in part even in the ancient world.

This overview has also attempted to capture the multicausality at the foundation of Weber's sociology. Causality perpetually "shifts" across a range, above all, of economic, rulership, religious, legal, clan, tribal, and status-related groups, as well as in relation to discrete historical occurrences, Weber contends. A "final resting point" — whether, for example, the economy or the religion sphere — can never be identified (pp. 215–16; 1968, p. 341).[32] Hence, his analysis of the rise of modern capitalism rejected, as noted, the Marxian formula articulated by his colleague and friend, Werner Sombart: the modern economic ethic is best understood as an outgrowth of capitalism's development (pp. 86–88). "Economic forms" prove incapable of giving birth to economic ethics, Weber emphasized repeatedly. Nonetheless, whether manifest as guild-based capitalism, the putting-out system, or mercantilism, these forms, he holds, *must* be included in any analysis that purports to explain modern capitalism's origin and expansion. And the *economic and political interests* of major groups within each economic form, and their pursuit of sheer power, must also be acknowledged and their causal weight investigated. However, Weber also insists that the "other side" must not be lost in the process. As noted, the development of technological innovations utilized by market-based capitalism, for example, was accelerated by the religious beliefs of ascetic Protestant scientists.

Weber's multicausal, context-specific, configurational, and comparative methodology maintains that *both* "internal" and "external" causes must be scrutinized (see Kalberg, 1994b). However, it also contends that the *reciprocal* interactions of ideas and interests must be acknowledged in order to establish causality. Religious congregations in the cities of the Middle Ages, for example, overcame traditional insider–outsider dualisms and turned believers effectively, as members of a *new* community *of belief*, toward universal values. This transformation then assisted confraternization elsewhere: guilds and commerce could now include heretofore excluded groups. Yet Weber moves in the reverse causal direction as well: guilds themselves recruited members on the basis of skills rather than particularistic criteria—and hence facilitated Christianity's attempt to introduce universalistic ethics.

---

32.   "I would like . . . to protest against the notion recently mentioned here that there is something — whether technology or whether the economy — that constitutes the 'ultimate' or 'final' or 'actual' cause of something else. If we look at the causal chain, we will see that it runs always from technological to economic and political things and then from political to religious and then economic factors, etc. At no point do we find a resting point. And that conception of historical materialism, which is not found infrequently, that the 'economic factor', in whatever way and in whatever sense it may be formulated, can be seen as the 'final' cause in the array of causes—this view is, in my opinion, completely finished as a scientific proposition" (1988, p. 456).

His identification of the many deep context groups Western rationalism and modern Western rationalism provided to sustain capitalism and modern capitalism rested upon his highly comparative methodology. *Only* through large-scale comparisons to China, India, and the Middle East that isolate uniqueness, he contends, can Western rationalism's trajectory be delimited. How did capitalism's contours and course in other civilizations vary from its contours and course in the West? Weber's fine-grained and multicausal investigations repeatedly explore the ways constellations of interacting groups formed contexts and even *tracks*—ones along which the economy developed in singular directions.

Variations of great magnitude are revealed, indeed, to such an extent that a widely held view of Weber's sociology is discredited: if only an "equivalent" for the Protestant ethic had appeared, China and India would early on have pursued the West's path of economic modernization (see pp. 215–16). His multicausal, context-sensitive, configurational, and group-based analyses teach that the investigation of such large questions requires utilization of a far more sophisticated research design—one that attends, in comparative perspective, to the causal potential of *multiple* groups and their unique interactions.[33]

Weber's explorations reveal many East–West differences. Western rationalism's structural heterogeneity must again be recalled. These regular antagonisms across the rulership, law, economy, and religion spheres became significant and pivotal. First apparent during the Middle Ages, they assumed a qualitatively broader and more enduring form than appeared in Chinese rationalism, the rationalism of India, and the rationalism of the Middle East. Indeed, this pluralism of conflict became intense and widespread. However, rather than calling forth in the West debilitating fragmentation over the long run, this heterogeneity introduced dynamism—a societal dynamism seldom discovered elsewhere. It distinguished Western rationalism and proved important both for its transformation into modern Western rationalism and for capitalism's metamorphosis into modern capitalism, Weber maintains.

How, briefly, does he perceive today's capitalism (see pp. 34–35)? Characterized by a domination of formal, practical, and theoretical rationality, a high utilization of scientific innovations, and a bureaucratization of the labor force, modern capitalism has expanded into the far corners of many societies. Weber appreciates its economic achievements: a large share of the population experiences a standard of living in these societies heretofore unknown. He queries, however, whether capitalism today will allow values, and especially *public sphere ethical* values, to continue in a viable manner to

---

33.   Weber's studies manifest a comparative thrust not only with respect to this overarching theme. He seeks to isolate and explain the uniqueness of the route toward modern capitalism followed in the West *and* to define precisely the ways in which the pathways followed by several Western nations varied. A homogeneity of development is not evident. Despite significant "Western" similarities, Weber identified separate routes toward modern capitalism in Germany, France, England, and the United States. This complex analysis cannot be explored here. See Kalberg 1987, 1992, 2001b, 2003, 2005.

orient action. Will they survive exclusively as dead legacies (*caput mortuum*), namely, as a religious heritage lacking active social carriers and a binding character—and hence of restricted influence? What type of human being (*Menschentyp*) *can* then become representative (p. 88; see 1949, p. 27; 2001, p. 106)? Under modern Western rationalism, ethical action might abandon the realms of work and politics, become problematic, and recede into privatived realms, he fears. Or will new prophets and new world views appear on new landscapes to sustain new constellations of ethical values (p. 158; Weber, 2005, pp. 270–71)?

COMPARATIVE CASES: CHINA AND INDIA

A. CHINA: THE CHINESE EMPIRE, DEEP KINSHIP TIES, SIB FETTERS UPON THE ECONOMY, AND THE PATRIMONIAL STRUCTURE OF LAW

From: Pp. 1047–51 in *Economy and Society,* edited by Guenther Roth and Claus Wittich, translated by Roth and Wittich; revised by Stephen Kalberg (Berkeley: The University of California Press, 1978; endnotes abridged).

In the Chinese empire . . . the power of patrimonial officialdom was based on river regulation, especially canal construction—but primarily for transportation, at least in northern and central China—, and on tremendous military fortifications. These projects were only possible through intensive utilization of compulsory labor and through the use of warehouses for storing payments in kind. Officials drew their benefices, and the army its equipment and provisions, from these warehouses.

In addition, the patrimonial bureaucracy benefitted from the even more complete absence of a landed nobility than was the case in Egypt. In historical times there were no liturgical ties, which perhaps had existed for a period in the past or whose introduction may once have been attempted; this could be inferred from certain traces visible in traditions and some legacies. At any rate, *de facto* freedom of mobility and of vocational choice—both officially did not really exist—does not seem to have been permanently restricted in the historical past. In practice some impure vocations were hereditary. Otherwise there is not a trace of a caste system or of other status hereditary privileges, apart from an unimportant titular ennoblement which was granted for several generations. In the main, patrimonial officialdom was confronted only by the sibs as an autochthonous [indigenous] power, aside from merchant and craft guilds as they are found everywhere. The sibs, whose elders retained a very effective power position in the villages, were bound together within the narrower circle of the family by ancestor worship and within the broader circle through common surnames in the case of exogamy.

Because of the tremendous expansion of the empire, and the small number of officials relative to the size of the population, the Chinese administration was neither intensive nor was it centralized under the average ruler. The directives of the central agencies were treated by subordinate offices as discretionary rather than binding. Here as everywhere under such circumstances officialdom was obliged to take into account the resistance of traditionalism, whose bearers were the sib elders and the occupational guilds, and somehow to arrive at an accommodation with these powers so that it could function at all.

On the other hand, and despite the tremendously tenacious power of these forces, the government apparently succeeded not only in creating a rather uniform officialdom, as far as its general character was concerned, but also prevented its transformation into a stratum of territorial lords or feudal barons whose power rests on local notability and who are therefore independent of the imperial administration. This was accomplished even though here too officials like to use legally and illegally acquired wealth for investment in land and even though the Chinese ethic prescribed closed bonds of loyalty between the candidate for office and his teachers, and office-holders and their superiors. Especially the institution of patronage and the officials' close relation to their sib were bound to create a tendency toward hereditary office baronies with a permanent clientele.

It seems that such incipient baronies emerged time and again; above all, tradition glorified feudalism as the historically original institution and the classic writings consider the *de facto* hereditability of ranking offices as the normal state of affairs, as they do the right of the highest-ranking officials to be consulted before the appointment of colleagues. To vitiate the recurrent tendencies toward office appropriation and to arrest the formation of a fixed clientage and the rise of office monopolies on the part of local *honoratiores*, the imperial patrimonial regime employed the usual measures: brief office tenures, exclusion from appointment in areas in which the official's sib is entrenched, and surveillance by spies (the so-called censors).

In addition, the imperial regime introduced something new: for the first time in history there appeared official qualifying examinations and official certificates of conduct. Qualification for rank and office came to depend in theory exclusively, and largely in practice, upon the number of examinations successfully passed. Confirmation in office and promotion or demotion were based upon the official's conduct reports, a resumé of which was periodically published until recently, together with the enumeration of reasons, roughly in the manner of the quarterly grade reports of a German *Gymnasiast* [elite high-school student]. From a formal viewpoint this constitutes the most radical application of bureaucratic objectivity possible and therefore an equally radical break with typical patrimonial office-holding, which rests on the ruler's personal discretion and favor.

It is true, of course, that benefices still could be bought and that personal patronage remained important, but feudalization, appropriation and the attachment of a clientele to an office (*Amtsklientel*) were contained—negatively by the intensive competition and distrust which isolated the officials, and positively by the increasingly universal acceptance of the social prestige which the educational patents imparted. As a result, the status conventions of the officials took on those features of an educational aristocracy which have since characterized Chinese life so distinctly. These conventions were specifically bureaucratic, had a utilitarian orientation, were formed by classical education, and considered as highest virtues the dignity of gesture and the maintenance of "face."

Nevertheless, Chinese officialdom did not develop into a modern bureaucracy, for the functional differentiation of spheres of jurisdiction was carried through only to a very limited extent in view of the country's huge size. Technically, this low degree of differentiation was feasible because the whole administration of the pacified empire was a civilian administration. Moreover, the relatively small army constituted a separate body and . . . measures other than the division of jurisdiction guaranteed the officials' compliance.

But the empirical reasons for refraining from jurisdictional differentiation were more substantive. The specifically modern concept of the functional organization (*Zweckverband*) and of specialized officialdom, a concept which was so important in the course of the gradual modernization of the English administration, would have run counter to everything characteristically Chinese and to all the status orientations of Chinese officialdom. For the educational achievements, controlled by the examinations, did not impart professional qualifications but rather their exact opposite. The mastering of the calligraphic art, stylistic perfection, and convictions properly oriented to the classes were of paramount importance in passing the essay tests; their themes were sometimes reminiscent of the traditional patriotic and moral essay topics in our secondary schools.

The examination really was a test of a person's cultural level and established whether he was a gentleman, not whether he was professionally trained. The Confucian maxim that a refined mind was not a tool—the ethical ideal of universal personal self-perfection, so radically opposed to the Western notion of a specific vocation—stood in the way of professional schooling and specialized competencies, and time and again prevented their general application. This accounts for the specifically patrimonialist and anti-bureaucratic orientation of this administration, which in turn explains its "extensive" [decentralized] character and its technical backwardness.

But China was also that country which had oriented status privileges more exclusively toward a conventional and officially patented literary education. To this extent it was formally the most perfect representative of the modern, pacified and bureaucratized society whose monopolies of benefices on the one hand, and specific status structure on the other, rest everywhere on the prestige of patented education. It is true that the beginnings of a bureaucratic ethos and philosophy can be found in some Egyptian documents, but only in China was a bureaucratic philosophy, Confucianism, systematically elaborated and brought to theoretical consistency. . . .

The unity of Chinese culture is essentially the unity of that status group which is the bearer of the bureaucratic classic-literary education of a Confucian ethic with its ideal of gentility. . . . The utilitarian rationalism of this status ethic is firmly restricted by the acceptance of a traditional magical religiosity and of its ritual code as a component of the status convention, and in particular by the acceptance of the duty of filial piety toward ancestors and parents. Just as patrimonialism has its genesis in the piety of the children of the house toward the patriarch's authority, so Confucianism bases the subordination of the officials to the ruler. of the lower to the higher-ranking officials, and particularly of the subjects to the officials and the ruler, on the cardinal virtue of filial piety. The typically Central and East European patrimonial notion of the "father of the country" (*Landesvater*) is similar, as is the role which filial piety plays as the foundation of all political virtues in strictly patriarchal Lutheranism. Confucianism, however, elaborated this complex of ideas much more consistently.

This development in Chinese patrimonialism was of course aided by the lack of a landowning seigneurial stratum and thus of a group of local notables capable of exercising political authority. In addition, it was made possible by the far-reaching pacification of the empire since the completion of the Great Wall, which for many centuries diverted the invasion of the Huns to Europe. Ever since expansive drives had been aimed only at territories which could be held in subjection by a relatively small professional army.

Toward subjects the Confucian ethic developed a theory of the welfare state which was very similar to, but much more consistent than, that of the patrimonialist theoreticians of the West in the age of enlightened absolutism [1600–1789] and also that of the theocratically and spiritually accentuated edicts of the Buddhist king Asoka [250–180 B.C.E. in India]. Yet the practice was different: despite some traces of mercantilism, the patrimonial regime interfered only for compelling reasons with the numerous local feuds of the sibs and villages. Economic intervention was nearly always fiscally motivated. Wherever this was not the case, the attempt [to control centrally] usually foundered on the recalcitrance of the interested groups and the inevitable extensiveness of the administration. In normal times this seems to have led to a far-reaching restraint of the political authorities toward the economy, a restraint which very early found support in theoretical laissez-faire principles. Within the sibs the educational prestige of the examined candidate for office, to whom all sib members turned for advice and, if he held office, for patronage, overlapped with the traditional authority of the elders, whose decisions remained usually decisive in local matters.

* * *

From: Pp. 84–88, 95–97, 100–04 in *The Religion of China*, translated and edited by Hans H. Gerth. Translation and revised by Stephen Kalberg, (New York: The Free Press, 1951).

The Absence of Capitalist Relationships.   In the Warring States era [260 B.C.E–220 A.C.], in which competition for political power prevailed, capitalism developed in China to a considerable extent. As elsewhere under similar conditions, this politically conditioned capitalism of money-lenders and suppliers for princes, who operated with high rates of profit, was common among patrimonial states. In addition, mining and trade are noted in the literature as sources for the accumulation of wealth. Multimillionaires apparently existed, calculated in copper, during the Han dynasty [206 B.C.E.–220 A.C.E.].

However, China's political unification into a world empire, as occurred also when Imperial Rome unified the *orbis terrarum* [known world], led apparently to a decline of this type of capitalism essentially anchored in the state and its competition with other states. Nonetheless, a purely market-based capitalism oriented to an unhindered exchange of goods was maintained in an embryonic stage. Of course, within industrial enterprises, businessman visibly held sway over technical experts—even in those businesses . . . organized in a more cooperative and solidarity fashion. This conclusion is apparent even from the normal ratios within business organizations for the distribution of profits. And evidently the speculative gains from inter-regional industries were often quite considerable.

Hence, the old classical prestige attached to agriculture in China—as an actually sacred violation—failed to hinder the placing of the opportunity for profit in industry higher than the opportunity for profit in agriculture. This was the case even as early as the first century ACE (and accounts were similar to those in the Talmud). Nor did the esteem of agriculture prevent trade from acquiring the highest prestige.

Nonetheless, this situation never signified a point of departure for the development of modern capitalism. Precisely its characteristic institutions, which had developed in the flourishing middle class in the West's medieval cities, were either absent in China or indicated quite different contours. Missing in China were the legal forms and the sociological underpinnings of the capitalist "enterprise": namely, its rational depersonalization of business transactions. In unmistakable beginning forms, these features were already present in the commercial law of the Italian city-states. On the other hand, a point of departure in China in the distant past for the unfolding of personal credit—the joint liability of members in the clan—failed to unfold further; it survived in tax law and criminal law only.

Further developmental stages were also absent in China. To be sure, associations of heirs, organized as household partnerships on behalf of a common pursuit of profit, developed among the propertied strata. And these partnerships were not unlike the family associations out of which, in the West (at least in Italy), the "public trading company" emerged. Nonetheless, in China, the economic meaning was characteristically different.

As is usually the case in the patrimonial state, he who was formally an *official*, and actually a tax farmer, had the best opportunities to assimilate wealth. . . . [And] retired officials invested their fortunes, more or less legally acquired, in landholdings. The sons, in order to preserve their wealth and influence, remained in hereditary partnerships as co-heirs and, in turn, raised the means enabling some members of the family to study [to become members of the literati]. Since these members had the opportunity of entering remunerative offices, they, in turn, were usually expected to enrich the co-heirs and provide sib members with public offices. In this manner, through political accumulation of property, there developed a stratum of land magnates who leased lots. This (albeit unstable) patriciate bore neither a feudal nor a bourgeois stamp, but speculated in opportunities for the purely political exploitation of office.

Hence, as is characteristic of patrimonial states, the accumulation of wealth, and especially landed wealth, was not primarily a matter of rational profit-making. In addition to trade, a system of internal booty capitalism prevailed which also led to the investment of money in land. For, as noted above, the officials made their fortunes by speculating in taxes, that is, by arbitrarily defining the exchange rate of the currency in which the tax obligations had to be calculated.

Examination degrees also constituted a claim to the feed from this trough. Accordingly, the examinations were always distributed anew among the provinces, though it was exceptional to restrict them to a fixed quota. Thus, cessation of examinations in a district was a most effective economic sanction for the participating distinguished families. It is clear that this sort of acquisitive familial community pointed in a direction opposite to the development of rational economic corporate enterprises.

Above all, this community was held together by rigid kinship bonds. This brings us to the discussion of the significance of the sib associations.

The Sib Association. The kinship group, which was practically insignificant in the Western Middle Ages, was completely retained in China in the administration of the smallest political units as well as in the operation of economic associations. Indeed, the sib developed to an extent unknown elsewhere—even in India. The patrimonial rule from above clashed with the sibs' strong counterbalance from below.

To the present day, a considerable proportion of all politically dangerous "secret societies" has consisted of sibs. The villages were often named after the sib exclusively or predominantly represented in the village. At times the villages were confederations of sibs. The old boundary marks indicate that the land was not allotted to individuals but to sibs. The cohesiveness of the sibs was important in maintaining this condition.

The village head—often a salaried man—was elected from the sib numerically most powerful. "Elders" of the sib stood beside him and claimed the right to depose him. The individual sib, with which we must deal first, claimed the right to impose sanctions on its members and enforced this claim, however little modern public authorities officially acknowledged it. Only domestic authority and the jurisdiction of the imperial sib over its members were officially recognized.

The cohesion of the sib undoubtedly rested wholly upon the *ancestor cult*. The sib withstood the ruthless encroachments of the patrimonial administration, its mechanically constructed liability associations, its resettlements, its land repartitions, and the classification of the population in terms of *ting*, or employable *individuals*. The ancestor cult was the only "folk-cult" that was not managed by the caesaropapist government and its officials. Rather, the head of the household, as the house priest, managed it with the assistance of the family. Undoubtedly it was a classical and ancient folk-cult. Even in the "men's house" of archaic militarist times, ancestral spirits seem to have played a role. . . .

In historical times the most fundamental belief of the Chinese people has been to ascribe power to ancestral spirits—not exclusively but predominantly to the spirits of one's ancestors. Ritual and literature testify to belief in the ancestral spirits and to their role as mediators of the descendant's wishes before the Spirit or God of Heaven. Furthermore, it was believed absolutely necessary to satisfy the spirits and to win their favor with sacrifices. The ancestral spirits of the emperors were of almost equal rank with the following of the Heavenly Spirit. A Chinese without male descendants, indeed, had to resort to adoption and, if he failed to do so, the family undertook a posthumous and fictitious adoption on his behalf. This was done less in his interest than in their own concern to be at rest with his spirit.

The social consequences of these all-pervasive ideas are evident in the enormous support gained by patriarchal power and in the reinforcement of sib cohesion. In Egypt, not the *ancestral* cult but the cult of the *dead* dominated everything, and there sib-cohesion was broken under the influence of bureaucratization and fiscalism just as it was broken later in Mesopotamia. In China, the influence of the sib was maintained and grew to equal the power of political rulers. . . .

* * *

Sib Fetters Upon the Economy.　　It was necessary to reach agreement with [a local committee], a firmly cohesive stratum of village notables, wherever any change whatsoever was to be introduced, such as raising the traditional taxes. Otherwise the state official was just as certain of meeting stubborn resistance as were the landlord, lessor, employer, and in general any "superior" outside of the sib. The sib stood unified in support of any member who felt discriminated against and the joint resistance of the sib, naturally, was incomparably more efficacious than a strike by a freely formed trade union in the West. In this fact alone, "work discipline" and the free market selection of labor, which have characterized the modern large enterprise, have been thwarted in China. And this has been true of all rational administration along Western lines. The strongest counterweight to officials educated in literature was a-literate *old age per se*: No matter now many examinations the official had passed, he had to obey unconditionally the completely uneducated sib elder in the traditionally fixed affairs of the sib.

In practical terms, a considerable measure of usurped and conceded self-government faced the patrimonial bureaucracy—on the one hand, there were the sibs and on the other hand organizations of the village poor. The rationalism of the bureaucracy was confronted with a resolute and traditionalistic power which, on the whole and in the long run, was stronger because it operated continuously and was supported by the most intimate personal organizations. Moreover, any innovation could call forth magic evils. Above all, fiscal innovations were suspect and met with sharp resistance. No peasant would here have believed in the idea of "impersonal" motives, and in this he was quite similar to the Russian peasants in Tolstoy's *Resurrection* [1900]. Besides, the influence of the sib elders was mostly decisive for the acceptance or rejection of religious innovations, which is of special concern to us. Naturally, and almost without exception, their weight tipped the balance in favor of tradition, especially when they suspected a threat to ancestral piety. This tremendous power of the strictly patriarchical sib was, in truth, the carrier of the much discussed "democracy" of China, which had nothing whatsoever in common with "modern" democracy. It was rather the expression, first, of the abolition of feudalism's status groups; second, of the extensiveness of patrimonial bureaucratic administration; and third, of the unbroken vigor and pervasive power of the patriarchical sibs.

Economic organizations that went beyond the scope of the individual establishment rested almost wholly upon actual or copied personal sib relationships. First we wish to consider the community of the *tsung-tsu*. This sib organization owned, in addition to the ancestral temple and the school building, sib houses for provisions and implements for the processing of rice, for the preparation of conserves, for weaving, and for other domestic industries. Possibly a manager was employed. Apart from that, the *tsung-tsu* supported its members in need through mutual aid and free or cheap credit. Thus, it amounted to a sib and cumulative household community that had been expanded into a producers' cooperative.

Conversely, in the cities there were, in addition to the shops of individual artisans, specific entrepreneurial communities. Small-capitalist in nature, these were organized as communal workshops [*ergasterian*] with an intensive division of manual labor. Furthermore, technical and commercial management were often specialized and profits were distributed partly according to capital shares and partly according to special commercial or technical services. Similar arrangements have been known in Hellenistic antiquity and the Islamic Middle Ages. It seems that such establishments in China were found especially to facilitate joint sustaining of the slack period in seasonal industries and, of course, to facilitate credit and the specialization of productive work.

These ways of establishing large economic units had, in their social aspects, a specifically "democratic" character. They protected the individual against the danger of proletarization and capitalist subjection. From a purely economic point of view, however, such domination could creep in through high investments by absentee capitalists and through the superior power and higher profit shares enjoyed by employed sales managers.

On the other hand, the putting-out system, which introduced capitalist domination in the West, was apparently confined until the present to the various forms of purely factual dependence of the artisan on the merchant. Only in individual trades did it advance to the level of domestic work with interspersed shops for finishing work and a central sales bureau. At present [in China] the putting-out system has developed on a significant scale in trades working for distant markets. As we have seen, it may well have been decisive that there was extremely little opportunity, owing to the strength of the sib group, of *coercing* the services of dependent workers and getting them to deliver on time in prescribed quantity and quality. Apparently, large private capitalist factories can scarcely be traced historically. Probably no factories producing mass consumer goods existed, since there was no steady market for them. Except for silk, which could be marketed, the textile industry could hardly compete with the domestic industry even in distant places. Long-distance trade, however, was monopolized by the silk caravans of the imperial *oikos* [household]. . . .

* * *

The Patrimonial Structure of Law.　A number of reasons—mostly related to the *structure* of the state— can be seen for the fact that capitalism failed to develop.

In the patrimonial state, the typical ramifications of administration and judiciary created a realm of unshakable sacred tradition alongside a realm of prerogative and favoritism. Especially sensitive to these political factors, *industrial* capitalism was impeded by them in its development. Rational and *calculable* administration and law enforcement, necessary for industrial development, did not exist. Be it China, India, or Islam, in general, wherever rational enactment and adjudication of law had not triumphed, the *dictum* was *Willkür bricht Landrecht*: [Privileges have precedence over the law of the land]. However, this dictum could not benefit the development of capitalist legal institutions, as it had done in the Western Middle Ages. On the one hand, the cities lacked corporate political autonomy and, on the other, decisive legal institutions—fixed and guaranteed by privilege—did not exist. Yet it was exactly with the assistance of these combined principles that all the legal schemata appropriate to capitalism were created in the Western Middle Ages.

To a large extent the law was no longer a norm valid from the remote past and no longer "found" by magical means alone. Imperial administration of the Western Middle Ages enacted statutes *en masse*, and legal provisions were distinguished, at least technically, by the relatively brief and business-like form. Criminal law, as J. F. Kohler [1849-1919] has emphasized, knew a considerable sublimation of legal facts and took "the frame of mind" into consideration.

This contrasted to the patriarchical instructions and admonitions of the Buddhist monarchs of India whose ethical and administrative decrees resembled some of the Chinese statutes. The Chinese statutes were also systematically collected in the *Ta Ch'ing Lü Li*.[1] But there were few, and only indirectly pertinent, legal acts covering subject matter most important for commerce in our sense. No "fundamental freedoms of the individual" were guaranteed. In one case among the Warring States (the state of Ch'en, 536 A.C.E.), the rationalism of the literati officials found expressions in a codification of the laws engraved on metal plates. But, according to the Annals, when the question was

---

1.　Laws and Rules of the Ch'ing Dynasty, 1647.

discussed among the literati stratum, a minister [Shu Hsiang] of the state of Ch'n successfully objected: "If the people can read, they will despise their superiors." The charismatic prestige of the educated patrimonial bureaucracy seemed endangered and these power interests never again allowed such an idea to emerge.

Though formally under separate secretaries for taxation and for justice, administration and law were not actually separated. The mandarin official, in patrimonial fashion, hired domestic servants at his own expense for both police work and minor office duties. The basically anti-formalist and patriarchical character of mandarin administration is unmistakable—offensive deportment was punished even without specific documentation.

Most significant was the intrinsic character of adjudication. Patrimonialism, being ethically oriented, always sought substantive justice rather than formal law. Hence, in spite of the traditionalism, there was no *official* collection of precedents because legal formalism was rejected and, above all, because there was no central court, as in England. The local "shepherd" [civil servant] of the official knew the precedents. In following tried models, as advised, the judicial procedure of the Chinese official corresponded externally to the use of *"similia"* among our junior judges. What is absence of clear knowledge in the latter case was extreme value in China.

For the most part, the administrative edicts of the Emperor were couched in the pedagogical form specific to papal bulls of the Middle Ages but without a similarly precise legal content. The best know statutes codified ethical rather than legal norms and excelled in literary erudition. For example, even the second last Emperor announced in the *Peking Gazette* that the decree of a remote ancestor had been found and would be published in the near future as a code of conduct. Insofar as it was oriented to orthodoxy, the whole imperial administration was controlled by an essentially theocratic board of literati. This was the oft-mentioned "Academy" (*Hanlin Yüan*) which safeguarded Confucian orthodoxy and perhaps corresponded to a congregation of the papal *Curia*. Accordingly, legal administration remained largely "kadi" [interference by the wise man] and possibly "cabinet justice" interference by the prince]. . . .

This was also the case of the judicial relation between English sheriffs and the lower classes. But in England, in order to transact the fortunes important for capitalism, there was the law of precedent with its corresponding bail system of justice. It had been created under the steady influence of the interested parties—whose influence was guaranteed through the recruitment of judges from among lawyers. While not rational, this law was *calculable,* and it made extensive contractual autonomy possible.

The advocate, in the Western sense, however, found no home in patriarchal Chinese justice. Sib members, possibly educated in literature, functioned as lawyers for their kin. Otherwise an untrustworthy consultant made out written documents. This phenomenon was characteristic of all specifically patrimonial states, particularly the theocratic and ethico-capitalistic states of Eastern stamp. That is, in addition to non-capitalist sources of accumulated wealth, such as the pure political office and tax prebend, a political capitalism of suppliers to the state and tax farmers flourished. Under certain conditions this capitalism celebrated true booms. Furthermore, a purely commercial "market"-oriented capitalism of middlemen developed.

However, the rational industrial capitalism specific to modern [Western] development originated nowhere under this régime. Capital investment in an industrial "firm" is far too sensitive to such irrational rule, and too dependent upon the possibility of calculating the steady and rational operation of the state machinery, to emerge under this type of Chinese administration. But why did this administration and judiciary *remain* so irrational from a capitalist point of view? *That* is the decisive question. We have become acquainted with some of the interests which played a part, but they deserve closer attention.

Just as capitalism lacked a judiciary independent of substantive individual- ization and arbitrariness, so it also lacked political prerequisites. To be sure, the feud was not lacking. On the contrary, the whole of Chinese history is replete with great and small feuds, including the numerous struggles of individual villages, associations, and sibs. Since the pacification of the World Empire, however, there has been no rational *warfare* and, what is more important, no armed peace during which several *competing* autonomous states constantly prepare for war. Capitalist phenomena thus conditioned through war loads and commissions for war purposed did not appear (see pp. 397–8).

The particularized state authorities of the West had to *compete* for freely mobile capital in Antiquity (before the World Empire), as well as during the Middle Ages and modern times. As in the Roman Empire, following the unification of the Chinese Empire, political competition for capital disap- peared. The Chinese Empire also lacked overseas and colonial relations and this handicapped the development of those types of capitalism *common* to Western Antiquity, the Middle Ages, and modern times. These were the varieties of booty capitalism, represented by colonial capitalism and by Mediterranean overseas capitalism, connected with piracy. While the barri- ers to overseas expansion partly depended on the geographical conditions of a great inland empire, they *resulted* in part, as we have seen, also from the general political and economic character of Chinese society.

Rational, firm-based capitalism, which in the West found its specific locus in industry, has been handicapped not only by the lack of a formally guaran- teed law, a rational administration and judiciary, and by the ramifications of a system of prebends, but also, basically, by the lack of a particular *frame of mind*. Above all it has been handicapped by conduct rooted in the Chinese "ethos" and carried by a stratum of officials and aspirants to office. This brings us to our central theme [the economic ethos of Confucianism; see above pp. 268–89).

From: Pp. 1062–63 in *Economy and Society,* edited by Guenther Roth and Claus Wittich, translated by Roth and Wittich; slightly revised by Stephen Kalberg (Berkeley: The University of California Press, 1978).

The "extensive" and intermittent administration by the justices of the peace [in England] seems to be reminiscent of the Chinese administration. It had some of the same external characteristics. The same appears true of the way in which the central authorities intervened: either for demarcated individual cases and then often successfully, or in an abstract manner through very general directives—which often had little more than suggestive value. But the difference is tremendous.

It is true that here as there the decisive state of affairs is the same: The patrimonial-bureaucratic administration is confronted by local authorities with whom it must somehow reach an accommodation in order to carry on its operations. However, in China the educated administrative officials face the elders of the sibs and the guild associations, whereas in England the professionally trained judges face the educated *honoratiores* of the land-owning gentry. The Chinese *honoratiores* are the educated who have been prepared for an administrative career through a classical-literary training; they are benefice-holders and aspirants to benefices, and therefore on the side of the patrimonial-bureaucratic power. By contrast, in England the core of the gentry was a free status group of large landowners. They were empirically trained on the job to rule over retainers and workers, and came to be humanistically educated. Such a stratum did not exist in China, which represents the purest type of patrimonial bureaucracy that is unencumbered (as far as this is possible) by any counterweight and, at the same time, has not yet been refined into a modern, specialized officialdom.

From: Pp. 248–49 in *The Religion of China,* translated and edited by Hans H. Gerth; revised by Stephen Kalberg (New York: Simon & Shuster, 1951).

The Chinese in all probability would be quite capable, probably more capable than the Japanese, of *assimilating* capitalism which has technically and economically been fully developed in the modern civilization regions. It is obviously not a question of deeming the Chinese "naturally ungifted" for the demands of capitalism. But, compared to the West, the varied conditions which externally favored the origin of capitalism in China did not suffice to *create* it. Likewise, capitalism did not originate in Western or Near Eastern Antiquity, or in India, or where Islamism held sway. Yet in each of these areas different and favorable circumstances seemed to facilitate its rise.

Many of the circumstances which could or had to hinder capitalism in China similarly existed in the West and assumed definite shape in the period of modern capitalism. There were the patrimonial traits of Western rulers, their bureaucracy, and the fact that the money economy was unsettled and undeveloped. The money economy of Ptolemaic Egypt was carried through much more thoroughly than it was in fifteenth or sixteenth century Europe. Circumstances which are usually considered to have been obstacles to capitalist development in the West had not existed in China for thousands of years. Such circumstances as the fetters of feudalism, landlordism, and, in part also, the guild system were lacking there. Moreover, a considerable part of the various trade-restricting monopolies, which were characteristic of the West, did not apparently exist in China. Also, in the past, China knew time and again the political conditions arising out of preparation for war and warfare between competing states.

In ancient Babylon and in Antiquity there were conditions conducive to the rise of political capitalism which the modern period also *shares* with the past. One could believe that the later decline of this essentially political orientation toward the accumulation of wealth and profit would have the effect of offering more favorable opportunities to a specifically modern capitalism oriented to the free market—roughly in the way that, in the recent period, the near complete absence of mobilization for warfare in northern America offered the most open space for the development of advanced capitalism.

Political capitalism was common to Western Antiquity until the time of the Roman emperors, to the Middle Ages, and to the East. The pacification of the Empire explains, at least indirectly, the non-existence of political capitalism, but it does not explain the non-existence of modern capitalism in China. To be sure, the basic characteristics of the "frame of mind"—in this case the practical stand toward the world—were deeply co-determined by political and economic destinies. Yet, in view of their autonomous laws, one can hardly fail to ascribe to this stand effects strongly counteractive to capitalist development.

B. INDIA: CLAN TIES, GUILDS, CASTES, AND TRADITIONALISM

From: Pp. 33–39, 49–54, 111–14, in *The Religion of India*, translated and edited by Hans H. Gerth and Don Martindale; slightly revised by Stephen Kalberg (New York: Simon & Shuster), 1958; endnotes abridged.

Caste and Guild. "Guilds" of merchants, and of traders who figured as merchants by selling their own produce, as well as "craft guilds," existed in India during the period of the development of cities and especially during the period in which the great salvation religions originated [600–400 B.C.E.]. As we shall see, the salvation religions and the guilds were related. The guilds usually emerged within the cities, but occasionally they emerged outside; survivals are still in existence. During the period of the flowering of the cities, the position of the guilds was quire comparable to that occupied by guilds in the cities of the medieval West.

The guild association (the *mahajan,* literally, the same as *popolo grasso* [businessman]) face the prince on one hand and on the other, the economically dependent artisans. These relations were about the same as those of the great guilds of literati and of merchants with the lower craft-guilds (*popolo minuto*) of the West. In the same way, associations of lower craft-guilds [blacksmith, carpenter, stone mason, etc.] existed in India (the *panch*). Moreover, the liturgical guild of Egyptian and late Roman character was perhaps not entirely lacking in the emerging patrimonial states of India.

The uniqueness of the development of India lay in the fact that these beginnings of guild organization in the cities led neither to the city autonomy of the Western type nor, after the development of the great patrimonial

states, to a social and economic organization of the territories corresponding to [the economic historian Gustav Schmoller's] "territorial economy"
of the West. Rather, the Hindu caste system, whose beginnings certainly
preceded these organizations, became paramount. In part, this caste system entirely displaced the other organizations; in part, it crippled them—it
prevented them from attaining any considerable importance. The "spirit"
of this caste system, however, was totally different from that of the merchant and craft guilds. . . .

First, that which is partly an exception and partly an occasional consequence for the occupational association is truly fundamental for the caste:
the magical distance between castes in their mutual relationships.

In 1901 in the "United Provinces" roughly ten million people (out of a total of about forty million) belonged to castes with which physical contact is
ritually polluting. In the Madras Presidency, roughly thirteen million people (out of about fifty-two million) could infect others even without direct
contact if they approached within a certain, though varying, distance. On
the other hand, the merchant and craft guilds of the [Western] Middle Ages
acknowledged no ritual barriers whatsoever between the individual guilds
and artisans, apart from the aforementioned small stratum of people engaged in opprobrious trades. Pariah peoples and pariah workers (for example, the knacker and hangman), by virtue of their special positions, come
close sociologically to the unclean castes of India. And there were factual
barriers restricting the connubium between differently esteemed occupations, but there were virtually no ritual barriers [in the West], such as are absolutely essential for caste. Within the circle of the "honorable" people,
ritual barriers to commensalism were completely absent; but such barriers
belong to the basis of caste differences.

Furthermore, caste is essentially hereditary. This hereditary character
was not, and is not, merely the result of monopolizing and restricting the
earning opportunities to a definite maximum quota, as was the case among
the absolutely closed guilds of the West. . . . The guild of the West, at least
during the Middle Ages, was regularly based upon the apprentice's free
choice of a master and thus it made possible the transition of the children to
occupations other than those of their parents, a circumstance which never
occurs in the caste system. This difference is fundamental. Whereas the clo-
sure of the guilds toward the outside became stricter with diminishing income opportunities, among the castes the reverse was often observed,
namely, they maintained their ritually required way of life, and hence their
inherited trade, most easily when income opportunities were plentiful.

Another difference between guild and caste is of even greater importance. The occupational associations of the medieval West were often engaged in violent struggles among themselves, but at the same time they
evidenced a tendency towards fraternization. The *mercanzia* [business-man's
court] and the *popolo* [interest organization of the common people] in Italy,
and the "citizenry" in the north, were regularly organizations of the occupational associations. The *capitano del popolo* [leader] in the south and, fre-

quently though not always, the Bürgermeister in the north were heads of oath-bound organizations of the occupational associations, at least according to their original and specific meaning. Such organizations seized political power, either legally or illegally. Irrespective of legal forms, the late medieval city *in fact* rested upon the fraternization of its economically active citizenry. This was at least the case where the political form of medieval city implied fraternization, its most important sociological characteristic.

As a rule the fraternization of the citizenry was carried through by the fraternization of the guilds, just as the ancient *polis* in its innermost being rested upon the fraternization of military associations and sibs. Note that the base was "fraternization." It was not of secondary importance that every foundation of the Western city, in Antiquity and the Middle Ages, went hand in hand with the establishment of a cultic community of citizens. Furthermore, it is of significance that the common meal of the *prytanes* [city councillors], the drinking rooms of the merchant and craft guilds, and their common processions to the church played such a great role in the official documents of the Western cities, and that the medieval citizens had, at least in the Lord's Supper, commensalism with one another in the most festive form. Fraternization at all times presupposed commensalism; it must be ritually possible. The caste order precluded this.

Complete fraternization of castes has been and is impossible because it is one of the constitutive principles of the castes that there should be at least ritually inviolable barriers against complete commensalism among different castes. As with all sociological phenomena, the contrast here is not an absolute one, nor are transitions lacking; yet it is a contrast which in essential features has been historically decisive. . . .

Let us now consider the West. In his letter to the Galatians (11:12, 13ff.) Paul reproaches Peter for having eaten in Antioch with the gentiles and for having withdrawn and separated himself afterwards, under the influence of the Jerusalemites. "And the other Jews dissembled likewise with him." That the reproach of dissimulation made to this very Apostle has not been effaced indicates, perhaps just as clearly as the occurrence itself, the tremendous importance this event had for the early Christians. Indeed, this shattering of the ritual barriers against commensalism meant a destruction of the voluntary ghetto, which in its effects is far more broad-ranging than any compulsory ghetto. It meant the destruction of Jewry as a pariah people, a situation that was ritually imposed upon this people.

For the Christians it meant the origin of Christian "freedom," which Paul celebrated triumphantly again and again; for this freedom meant the universalism of Paul's mission, which cut across nations and status groups. The elimination of all ritual barriers of birth for the community of the eucharists, as realized in Antioch, was, in connection with the religious preconditions, the hour of conception of the Western "citizenry." This is the case even though its birth occurred more than a thousand years later in the revolutionary *conjurationes* [oath-bound fraternization] of the medieval cities. For without commensalism—in Christian terms, without the Lord's

Supper—no oathbound fraternity and no medieval urban citizenry would have been possible. . . .

Even if there are no antagonisms of economic interests, a profound estrangement usually exists between the castes, and often deadly jealousy and hostility as well, precisely because the castes are completely oriented towards social rank. This orientation stands in contrast to the occupational associations of the West. Whatever part questions of etiquette and rank have played among these associations, and often it has been quite considerable, such questions could never have gained the religiously anchored significance which they have had for the Hindu. . . .

[T]he castes excluded every solidarity and every politically powerful fraternization of the citizenry and of the trades. If the prince observed the ritual traditions and the social pretensions based upon them, which existed among those castes most important for him, he could play off the castes against one another—which he did. Moreover, he had nothing whatever to fear from them, especially if the Brahmans stood by his side. Accordingly, it is not difficult even at this point to guess the political interests which had a hand in the game during the transformation to monopoly rule of the caste system (see Kalberg 1994b, pp. 177–92).

This shift steered India's social structure—which for a time apparently stood close to the threshold of European urban development—into a course that led far away from any possibility of such a development. In these world-historical differences the fundamentally important contrast between "caste" and "guild," or any other "occupational association," is strikingly revealed. . . .

* * *

Caste and Sib. There remains to be examined still another important unique aspect of Indian society intimately interrelated with the caste system. The heightened significance of the *sib*, as well as the formation of castes, belongs to the fundamental traits of Indian society. The Hindu social order, to a larger extent than anywhere else in the world, is organized in terms of the principle of *clan charisma*. "Charisma" means that an extraordinary, at least not generally available, quality adheres to a person. Originally charisma was thought of as a magical quality. "Clan charisma" means that this extraordinary quality adheres to sib members per se and not, as originally, to a single person.

We are familiar with residues of this sociologically important phenomenon particularly in the hereditary "divine right of kings" of our [Western] dynasties. To a lesser degree the legend of the "blue blood' of a nobility, whatever its specific origin, belongs to the same sociological type. Clan charisma is one of the ways personal charisma may be "routinized" (that is, become a part of everyday social experience). . . .

In India a [certain] belief won out: that charisma is a quality attached to the sib per se, and that the qualified successor or successors should be sought within the sib. This led to the *inheritance* of charisma, which originally had nothing to do with heredity. The wider the spheres to which magical belief applied, the more consistently developed such beliefs became, the wider, in turn, the possible field of application of clan charisma. Not only heroic and magico-cultic abilities, but any form of authority, came to be viewed as determined and bound by clan charisma. Special talents—artistic and craft— fell within the sphere of clan charisma. In India the development of the principle of clan charisma far surpassed what is usual elsewhere in the world. . . .

The strongest expression of clan charisma was in the sphere of authority. In India the "hereditary" transmission of authority—that is, on the basis of family ties—was normal. The further back one traces, the more universal the institution of the "hereditary" village-headship is found to be. Merchant and craft guilds and castes had "hereditary" elders; anything else was normally out of the question. So self-evident was priestly, royal, and knightly office charisma that free appointment of successors to office by patrimonial rulers, like the free choice of urban occupations, occurred only during upheavals of the tradition or at the frontiers of social organization before the social order was stabilized. . . .

The economic effects of sib integration through magical and animistic beliefs in China was described in [*The Religion of China*]. In China the charismatic glorification of the sib, shattered by patrimonial rulership's examination system, had economic consequences similar to those in India. In India, the caste organization, and the extensive caste autonomy and the autonomy of the guild, which was still greater because it was ritually unfettered, placed the development of commercial law almost completely in the hands of the interest groups themselves. The unusual importance of trade in India would lead one to believe that a rational law of trade, trading companies, and enterprise might well have developed.

However, if one looks at the legal literature of the Indian Middle Ages one is astonished by its poverty. While partially formalistic, Indian justice and the law of evidence were basically irrational and magical. Much of it, because of hierocratic influence, was formless in principle. Ritually relevant questions could only be decided by ordeals. In other questions the general moral code, unique elements of the particular case, tradition (particularly), and a few supplementary royal edicts were employed as legal sources. . . .

The details of later legal practice, to be sure, were adequate to serve trading needs. However, they hardly promoted trade on their own. The quite considerable capitalistic development which occurred in the face of such legal conditions can be explained only in terms of the power of guilds. They knew how to pursue their interests by use of boycott, force, and expert arbitration. However, in general, under conditions such as those described, the circumscription of credit relationships to the sib had to remain the normal state of affairs.

The principle of clan charisma also had far-reaching consequences out-side the field of commercial law. Because we are prone to think of Western feudalism primarily as a system of socio-economic ties, we are apt to over-look its particular origins and their significance. Under the compelling mil-itary needs of the time of its origins, the feudal relationship [in the West] made a *free contract* among *sib strangers* basic for the faith-bound relation between the lord and his vassals. Increasingly feudal lords developed the in-group feeling of a unitary status group. They developed eventually into the closed hereditary estate of chivalrous knights. We must not forget that this grew on the basis of sib estrangement among men who viewed them-selves not as sib, clan (phratry), or tribe members, but merely as status peers.

Indian development took quite a different turn. It is true that individual enfeoffment of retainers and officials with land or political rights occurred. Historically, this is clearly discernable. But it did not give the ruling stratum its stamp, and feudal status formation did not rest on land grants. Rather, as Baden-Powell [in *The Indian Village Community*, 1896] has correctly empha-sized, the character of Indian developments was derived from sib, "clan" (phratry), and tribe. . . .

In India the charismatic head of the phratry distributed conquered land, manorial prerogatives among fellow-sib members, and open fields among the ordinary men of the phratry. The conquering classes must be conceived of as a circle of phratries and sibs of lords dispersing over the conquered ter-ritory under the rule of the tribe.

Prerogatives were enfeoffed by the head of the phratry (*raja*) or, where one existed, by the tribal king (*maharaja*), only as a rule for his agnates [male line]. It was not a freely contracted relationship of trust and allegiance [as in the West]. Fellow sib members claimed this grant as a birthright. Each con-quest produced, in the first place, new office fiefs for the immediate and ex-tended sib of the king. Conquest was, therefore, the *dharma* of the king.

However minimal in the particular case the differences compared to the West would seem to be, this contrast accounts for ancient India's distinctive structure of secular rulership. No matter how often individual charismatic upstarts and their freely recruited followings shattered the firm structure of the sibs, the development always returned to its firm course: a charismatic clan organization of tribes, phratries, and sibs. Among the [Indo-European] Aryans, [who conquered northern India *ca* 1000–500 B.C.E.], the ancient sac-rificial priests, even at the time of the early Vedas [800–600 B.C.E.], had be-come a distinguished priestly nobility. The various sibs of this nobility divided according to hereditary routines, tasks, and appropriate clan cha-risma into hereditary "schools." Given the primacy of magical charisma claimed by these schools, they and their heirs—the Brahmans—became the primary propagators of this principle throughout Hindu society.

It is clear that the magical charisma of the clans contributed greatly to the establishment of the firm structure of magical caste estrangement, actually containing it *in nuce*. On the other hand, the caste order served greatly to stabilize the significance of the sib. All strata that raised claims to distinction were required to fall into line according to the pattern established by the ruling castes. The exogamous [external] marriage order was based on the sib. Social situation, ritual duty, way of life, and occupational position in the end were determined by the charismatic clan principle, which extended to all positions of authority. As clan charisma carried the caste, so the caste, in turn, carried the charisma of the sib.

* * *

Caste and Traditionalism.   We are now in a position to enquire into the effects of the caste system on the economy. These effects were essentially negative and must rather be inferred than inductively assessed. Hence we can but phrase a few generalizations. Our sole point is that this order by its nature is completely traditional and anti-rational in its effects. The basis for this, however, must not be sought in the wrong place.

Karl Marx had characterized the peculiar position of the artisan in the Indian village—his dependence upon fixed payment in kind instead of upon production for the market—as the reason for the specific "stability" of the Asiatic peoples. In this, Marx was correct.

In addition to the ancient village artisan, however, there was the merchant and also the urban artisan; and the latter either worked for the market or was economically dependent upon merchant guilds, as in the West. India has always been predominantly a country of villages. Yet the beginnings of cities were also modest in the West, especially inland, and the position of the urban market in India was regulated by the princes in many ways "mercantilistically"—in a sense similar to the territorial states [in the West] at the beginnings of the modern era. In any case, insofar as social stratification is concerned, not only the position of the village artisan but also the caste order as a whole must be viewed as the bearer of stability. One must not, however, think of this effect too directly. One might believe, for instance, that the ritual caste antagonisms had made impossible the development of "large-scale enterprises" with a division of labor in the same workshop, and might consider this to be decisive. But such is not the case.

The law of caste has proved just as elastic in the face of the necessities of the concentration of labor in workshops as it did in the face of a need for a concentration of labor and service in the noble household. All domestic servants required by the upper castes were ritually clean. . . The principle "the artisans's hand is always clean in his occupation" is a similar concession to the necessity of being allowed to have fixtures made or repair work done; and to have personal services or other work performed by wage workers or by itinerants not belonging to the household. Likewise, the workshop (*ergasterion*) was recognized as "clean."

Hence, no ritual factor would have stood in the way of jointly using different castes in the same large workroom, just as the ban upon interest during the Middle Ages, as such, hindered little the development of industrial capital, which did not even emerge in the form of investment for fixed interest. The core of the obstacle did not lie in such particular difficulties, which every one of the great religious systems in its way has placed, or has seemed to place against the development of the modern system. The core of the obstruction was rather embedded in the "spirit" of the whole system.

In modern times it has not always been easy, but eventually it has been possible to employ Indian caste labor in modern factories. And even earlier it was possible to exploit the labor of Indian artisans capitalistically in the forms usual elsewhere in colonial areas, after the finished mechanisms of modern capitalism had been imported from Europe. Even if all this has come about, it must still be considered extremely unlikely that the modern organization of industrial capitalism would ever have *originated* on the basis of the caste system. A ritual law, according to which every change of occupation and every change in work technique may result in ritual degradation, is certainly not capable of giving birth to economic and technical revolutions from within itself, or even of facilitating the first germination of capitalism in its midst.

Great in itself, the artisan's traditionalism was necessarily heightened to the extreme by the caste order. Commercial capital, in its attempts to organize industrial labor on the basis of the putting-out system, had to face an essentially stronger resistance in India than in the West. The traders themselves, in their ritual seclusion, remained in the shackles of the typical oriental merchant class, which by itself has never created a modern capitalist organization of labor. . . .

Today [1916–1920] a considerable tempo in the accumulation of wealth is singularly evident among castes which were formerly considered socially degraded or unclean, and which therefore were especially little burdened with (in our sense) "ethical" expectations addressed to themselves. In the accumulation of wealth, such castes compete with others which formerly monopolized the positions of scribes, officials, or collectors of farmed-out taxes, as well as similar opportunities for politically determined earnings typical of patrimonial states. Some of the capitalist entrepreneurs also derive from the merchant castes—yet these entrepreneurs could keep up with the castes of literati only to the extent to which they acquired the "education"today necessary. The training for trade is among entrepreneurs in part so intense—as far as the reports allow for insight—that their specific "gift" for trading must by no means rest upon any "natural disposition."[1] However, we have no indication that by themselves they could have created the rational industrial enterprise of modern capitalism.

Modern capitalism undoubtedly would never have originated from the circles of the completely traditionalist Indian trades. The Hindu artisan is nevertheless famous for his extreme industry; he is considered to be essen-

---

1. That ancient castes with strong occupational mobility often drift into occupations whose demands on "natural disposition" form the greatest psychological contrast imaginable to the previous mode of activity, but which stand close to one another through the common usefulness of certain forms of knowledge and aptitudes acquired through training, speaks against imputations of "natural disposition." Thus, the frequent shift . . . from the ancient caste of surveyors—whose members naturally know the roads very well—to the chauffeur may be referred to among many similar examples.

tially more industrious than the Indian artisan of Islamic faith. And, on the whole, the Hindu caste organization has often developed a very great intensity of work and of property accumulation within the ancient occupational castes. The intensity of work holds more for handicraft and for individual ancient agricultural castes. By the way, the Kunbis (for instance, those in South India) have acquired considerable wealth, and today even in modern forms.

Modern industrial capitalism, in particular the factory, made its entry into India with direct and strong incentives under the British administration. But comparatively speaking, how small is the scale and how great the difficulties.

THE ANCIENT AND MEDIEVAL CITIES IN THE WEST: FRATERNIZATION, INCORPORATION, AND THE DISSOLUTION OF CLAN TIES

From: Pp. 338–58 in *The Agrarian Sociology of Ancient Civilizations,* translated by R. I. Frank; slightly revised by Stephen Kalberg (London: New Left Books, 1976).

There were obviously many differences among medieval cites, and yet one can make this generalization: the Mediterranean coastal cities, in which commercial interests and commercial wealth were dominant, were the closest in type to the large cities of Antiquity, while the (secondary) purely agricultural cities were most similar to the small cities of Antiquity; however, the industrial cities of the Middle Ages were very different in type from the ancient *polis*. . . . It is clear, for example, in these industrial cities a new kind of labor structure developed, based on the social power of the guilds and the guild organization of production. This was the first time free labor was organized on a large scale. In Antiquity the first steps towards this had been taken, but nothing reached completion. . . .

There was . . . one basic difference. The mass of free and unfree workers in medieval cities formed functional associations which *transcended* existing status contrasts in their memberships and which were the seed from which sprang autonomous communities with clearly defined liberties. So it came about that those who paid taxes from the proceeds of their work or their land constituted the medieval city, whereas in Antiquity it was the aristocrats alone. At least such was the situation in that type we call the "industrial inland city," and in particular in all those cities where the guilds gained dominant influence. . . .

. . . the differences between the typical medieval city and the typical ancient *polis* remain fundamental. Above all the crucial point is that in Antiquity the position of industry—social as well as economic—did *not improve* as wealth increased, nor did it *ever* reach the commanding importance which industry enjoyed in the medieval cities. Furthermore, the specific characteristic of *modern* capitalist development, *industrial* capitalism, is based on legal forms which were created in the medieval "industrial" cities, forms which did *not exist* in the ancient *polis*. . . .

Whereas just as in the Middle Ages the artisans who produced goods needed for military supply formed corporate groups for electoral and military functions in the archaic *polis*, the organizations of craftsmen in the "classical" period of the ancient world had no importance whatever. It was only when the relative importance of commercial slavery declined that artisans' groups gained social importance. But even these lacked the legal rights typical of medieval guilds. . . .

. . . we see that in the Middle Ages the guilds became dominant in cities and forced aristocrats, in order to exercise political rights like everyone else, to enroll and submit to their taxes and regulations, whereas in Antiquity it was the village (. . . the *demos* in the Athenian Empire) which exercised similar compulsion. Again, whereas in Antiquity graded responsibilities for arming oneself were assigned to citizens according to the class of their land rentals, in the Middle Ages this was done according to guild membership. The difference is unusually striking, and suffices to demonstrate that the "medieval city"—that is, the type of city characteristic of the age—was in fundamental economic and social aspects constituted quite otherwise from the city of Antiquity. Even before the appearance of any forms of capitalist organization, the "medieval city" was much *closer* to the development of modern capitalism than was the ancient *polis*. . . .

Now the urban conflicts of the High Middle Ages (thirteenth and fourteenth centuries), centering round the opposition between *guilds* and great clans, can be compared to the struggles within the *polis* in the "Middle Ages" of Antiquity; the great issues in both were deprivation of political rights, oppression by fiscal authorities, and unfair disposition of common lands. However, there is this great difference: the core of the opposition in Europe's Middle Ages was not recruited from country *peasants* outside of the city, as in Antiquity, but from urban artisans. Then, once the effects of nascent capitalism were felt, the ensuing conflicts were not simply between richer and poorer or creditors and debtors, as in Antiquity. Rather, the further conflicts of economic interest developed, the sharper was the opposition between merchant and *artisan*, an opposition which in Antiquity had been of little significance. . . .

These differences point to a basic distinction between ancient and medieval urban development: the difference in residence and character of the *aristocracy* and *princes*. Whereas the ancient *polis* started its development as a *city* kingdom and then passed into the stage when the monarchy was ended by the city aristocracy, followed by the political emancipation of the countryside and its dominion over the city, medieval society was characterized by a rural *landed* aristocracy and kings and princes of a specifically agrarian type. Medieval urban development therefore consisted in the emancipation of *urban* citizens from manorial and legal dependence on these non-urban authorities. Here too, of course, one must not make distinctions absolute. . . .

This points to a further contrast: medieval cities steadily *expanded* their autonomy within the larger states of which they were part until well on in the fifteenth century, whereas Hellenistic and Roman cities steadily *lost* autonomy within their monarchical states. The reason for this difference is the contrasting *structures* of the states within which ancient and medieval cities were embedded. The monarchical state of Antiquity was or became a bureaucratic state. In Egypt, as early as the second millennium B.C.E., the royal clientele had grown into a universally dominant bureaucracy. This bureaucracy, along with [The Egyptian] theocracy, throttled the free *polis* in the ancient Near East, and the same happened in the later Roman Empire. In the medieval West the transformation of the ministeriales into a bureaucracy and the expansion of the power of territorial princes started in the thirteenth and was completed in the sixteenth, after which the autonomy of the cities was steadily reduced and then eliminated (the process began in the fifteenth century), and the cities were incorporated into the dynastic bureaucratic state. But before that, during all of the Early and High Middle Ages, towns had political space in which to develop their characteristic features, and in this period cities were not only centres of a money economy but also, because of their official responsibilities, of *administration*, ...

. . . The inland city of the Middle Ages was, despite all its emphasis on the military duties of citizens, from the beginning of bourgeois character and was more and more shaped by the peaceful pursuit of profit in the market. The medieval burgher was from the first much more motivated by material interests than his ancient counterpart could have been or wanted to be. . . .

. . . the basic problem: What is the origin of the later medieval and modern economic system—in a word, of modern capitalism? . . . We must examine the development of the *market*: how did consumer demand develop in medieval times for the industries later organized on capitalist lines? We must also consider the organization of *production*: how did the endeavor to exploit capital lead to the creation of organizations of "free" labor such as never existed in Antiquity?

Most of the manors were not suburban but *rural* structures, and they supported an *agrarian* ruling class—princes, free vassals, and their knightly ministeriales . . . The manors supported the medieval ruling class only in part with payments in kind; the large manors not even mainly with such payments. Indeed, kings, princes, and great vassals all wanted to use manor payments to gain profits from *commerce*. Thus the establishment of markets and cities was due to the desire of princes and barons to increase their income from fees and rents. . . .

At the end of the Middle Ages the average farmer was a peasant on a manor, normally subject only to traditional feudal dues, generally selling his goods in the nearby city, and himself the normal and secure consumer of the city's industrial products (since the city monopolized industry as much as possible and did all it could to suppress rural industries). The feudal army and the feudal state helped create the medieval peasantry and medieval city—both interested only in economic expansion.

These conditions provide the context in which modern *capitalism* transformed industry and agriculture by a process of gradual dissolution. *However*, one should not underestimate the system of liberties and rights, cooperatives, labor services, and staple and market privileges in establishing the basis of capitalist development. Above all there were the *price* regulations based on tradition or policy, which limited capital's drive for profits but nevertheless provided a basis for long-range calculation such as the bargaining of the Near East could not provide. It is clear that the medieval trade organization, as it developed with the theocratic and feudal world of the time, was one of the elements which made possible a commodity system amenable to planned calculation, just as the classes of free peasants and petty bourgeoisie—which were shaped by feudal organization—provided that large, *relatively* stable consumer market which modern capitalism needs for its products.

There was then a great difference between the development of the bourgeoisie and the peasant economy in medieval Western Europe and analogous developments in Antiquity. This was due in the first place to a *shift* in geographical setting, secondly to a great change in the *military* organization of the Middle Ages, which was caused by a great number of factors. The medieval army of knights made feudal social organization inevitable; then its displacement by mercenary armies, and later (beginning with Maurice of Orange [1567–1625]) by disciplined troops, led to the establishment of the modern state. . . .

Modern capitalism created the conditions for its growth on the soil of the medieval organization of commerce and industry. It did so in part *alongside* commerce and industry and in part within it. However, and despite all struggles against the guilds, modern capitalism also created the conditions of its growth by utilizing tracks and legal forms created by the guilds. For example: the *commenda* [see p. 210], a prevalent form of commerce from the time of Hammurabi down to the thirteenth century, was the origin of the limited liability company (only the first steps towards this were taken in Antiquity, and those were—characteristically—in connection with companies formed to assume state farming contracts). Again, in Antiquity the only enterprises based on joint liability were simple artisans' groups resembling the Russian cartel, but in later medieval law this has developed into sophisticated forms of trading and manufacturing companies. It was also in the later Middle Ages that the legal institutions were created for permanent capitalist enterprises in commerce and industry. . . .

As soon as capitalism became established in *industrial* production in the Middle Ages it started the process of *merging* the small workshops of artisans. First it organized sales and then purchase of raw materials. Next it inexorably moved towards the production process itself, gradually developing a more rationalized technology and establishing increasingly larger productive which were increasingly separated from the family. These large units were more and more created to further the concentration of workers and the division of labor. *Nothing* similar is known to us from Antiquity, at least as regards purely private industry. . . .

There was a further basic difference: in Antiquity the wars of the *poleis* down to the end of the Roman Republic [44 B.C.E.] generally meant that the losing state's property system would be annihilated and its territory would be subjected to massive confiscations and colonization. In this respect the *polis* acted like the German tribes of the *Völkerwanderung* (Great Migration; 375–570 A.C.E.). In the Middle Ages, on the other hand, despite knightly love of battle, and even more so in Early Modern times, an international community existed which can be called "pacified" in comparison with Antiquity. This is not to say that there was a quantitative decline in warlike activity; there was, rather, an increasing pacification of the elements engaged in private business and industry, in particular the cities and the bourgeoisie.

It is of course true that modern capitalism gained its largest profits from military contracts in medieval and modern times. But there was still something new: the capitalist organization of industrial production was based on the "pacification" mentioned above. Hence, despite all the vicissitudes of war and politics it maintained the continuity of economic development in which large feudal states, and—even more—the international church, had their share. . . .

From: Pp. 1243–44, 1248–50 in *Economy and Society,* edited by Guenther Roth and Claus Wittich, translated by Wittich; revised by Stephen Kalberg (Berkeley: The University of California Press, 1978); endnotes abridged.

A Prerequisite for Confraternization: Dissolution of Clan Ties.   In the West, taboo barriers similar to those of the Indian-Equatorial area were absent. Also missing were the magical totemic, ancestral, and caste props of the clan organization which, in Asia, impeded confraternization into a unified city corporation. A thorough totemism and the casuistic implementation of sib exogamy arose—certainly at a relatively late point in time—precisely in those areas where large-scale politico-military and, in particular, urban associations never developed. In the religions of Western Antiquity we find only traces of these phenomena, either as "residuals" or thwarted "beginnings."

The reasons for this, insofar as they are not specifically religious, can only be vaguely guessed. The mercenary soldiering and the piratical life of the early period, the military adventures, and the numerous inland and overseas colony foundations, inevitably leading to intimate permanent associations between tribal or even members of different clans, seem with equal inevitability to have broken the strength of the exclusive clan and magical ties. Even though in Antiquity clan ties were everywhere artificially reinstituted, for tradition's sake, by the division of newly founded communities into "clan" associations and phratries, it was not the sib association but the military association of the polis which now constituted the basic unit. The century-long wanderings of conquering warrior-associations of the Germanic tribes before and during the Great Migration, their mercenary soldiering and their war expeditions under elected leaders, must have resulted in an equal number of impediments to the rise of taboo and totemic ties. Even though they are said to have settled, wherever possible, on the basis of real or fictitious sibs, other forms of association were much more important. The legislative-judicial and military associations of the "hundreds,"[1] the "hide"-system[2] as the basis for the allocation of public burdens, later the relationship to a prince (following and vassaldom)—these were the decisive elements, and not some magical clan ties which never really developed, perhaps precisely because of these circumstances.

When Christianity became the religion of these peoples, who had been so profoundly shaken in all their traditions, it finally destroyed whatever religious significance these clan ties retained. Indeed, perhaps it was precisely the weakness or absence of such magical and taboo barriers which made the conversion possible. The often very significant role played by the parish community in the administrative organization of medieval cities is only one of many symptoms pointing to this quality of the Christian religion. In dissolving clan ties, it importantly shaped the medieval city. Islam, by contrast, never really overcame the divisiveness of Arab tribal and clan ties, as is shown by the history of internal conflicts of the early caliphate [661–750A.C.E.] In its early period it remained the religion of a conquering army of tribes and clans.

* * *

The Sworn Confraternization and the Rise of an Institutionalized Association. The Western city—and especially the medieval city, which for the time being shall be our only concern—was not only economically a seat of trade and the crafts, politically a fortress in the normal case and perhaps a garrison, administratively a court district; however, it was beyond all this also a sworn confraternity. In Antiquity the symbol of a confraternity was the joint election of the *prytaneis*.[3] In the Middle Ages the city was a sworn *commune* [community of citizens] possessing the legal status of an independent corporation , although this was attained only gradually. . . .

The city became an institutionalized association (*anstaltsmässige Vergesselschaftung*), autonomous and autocephalous (even though to varying degrees), and an active "territorial corporation"; urban officials, in the entirety or in part, became officials of this institution (*Anstalt*). It is of great importance for the development of medieval cities that, from the very beginning, the privileged position of the citizen was a right of the individual vis-à-vis outside parties. This was not only a consequence of the "personalist" approach to law common to both Antiquity and the Middle ages, . . . according to which the members of a group were considered to have—as a matter of group privilege—right to be dealt with under a common "objective" law.

Another source for this position of the citizen, especially for the Middle Ages, is to be sought . . . in survivals from the Germanic judicial system and,

---

1. The ancient principle of ordering among the Germanic tribes for legal meetings and army platoons. Weber here has in mind particularly the settling of warriors together in military groupings in the ancient city rather than in tribes or clans. See Weber, 1968, pp. 1290–91 [sk.].
2. According to the ancient German hide system, all fully qualified members of a village community possess the same property use rights to the village's fertile land [sk.].
3. City councillors. The point Weber . . . wishes to make here seems to be that in Antiquity the traditional or artificial "tribal" subdivisions of the cities were confraternities, but not the city as a whole, for the Attic prytans were delegations of the individual phylae (tribes). . . . [Wittich]

in particular, in the concept of the *Ding*-community. As an active member in that community—and that means serving as a judge in the *Ding* court—the citizen and member of a legally autonomous group himself creates the "objective" law to which he is subject. . . . A right of this type did not exist for those subject to the law of almost all cities of the world. (Only in Israel can traces of it be found. . .)

For the development of the medieval city into an organization, two circumstances were of central significance: on the one hand, the fact that, at a time when the economic interests of the citizens urged them toward an institutionalized association, . . . this movement was *not* frustrated by the existence of magic or religious barriers, and on the other hand the *absence* of a rational administration enforcing the interests of a larger political association. Even if only one of these conditions were present—as in Asia—the strongest common economic interests of the city inhabitants would have enabled them to achieve no more than transitory unification. The rise of the medieval autonomous and autocephalous city association, with its administrative council headed by the *Konsul, Majer* [mayor] or *Bürgermeister*, is a process that differs in its very nature from both the development of the Asian city and that of the ancient polis.

THE PUTTING-OUT SYSTEM, MODES OF FINANCING, MERCANTILISM, AND THE FACTORY

From: Pp. 287–89 in *Wirtschaftsgeschichte*. Translated by Stephen Kalberg (Munich and Leipzig: Duncker & Humblot, 1923). [*General Economic History*, pp. 158–61]

The Putting Out System. The precapitalist domestic industry of the West did not always, and never simply as a rule, develop out of the craft organization.[1] This occurred to the least extent in Germany and to a much greater extent in England. Rather, it quite commonly existed *side by side* with craft work, in consequence of the substitution of rural craft workers for urban, or of the fact that new branches of industry arose through the introduction of new raw materials, especially cotton. The crafts struggled against the putting-out system as long as they could, and longer in Germany than in England and France.

Typically, the stages in the growth of the domestic system are the following:

1) A purely factual buying monopoly of the entrepreneur in relation to the craft worker. This was regularly established through indebtedness; the entrepreneur, on the basis of his knowledge of the market as merchant, compels the worker to turn over his product to him exclusively. Thus, the buying monopoly is connected with a selling monopoly and a taking possession of the market by the entrepreneur; he alone knows where the products will finally stop.

2) Delivery of the raw material to the worker by the entrepreneur. This stage appears not infrequently (though also not on a regular basis) connected from the outset with the buying monopoly of the entrpreneur. It was attained in the West, but seldom elsewhere.

3) Control of the production process. The entrepreneur has an interest in this process because he is responsible for uniformity in the quality of the product. Hence, the delivery of raw material to the worker is often associated with a delivery of semi-complete products. Westphalian linen weavers in the nineteenth century had to, for example, complete beforehand a prescribed quantity of warp and yarn.

---

1. Weber uses here the terms domestic, putting out, cottage, and house industry synonymously. The "craft organization" had been dominant in the Medieval cities. [sk]

4) With this was connected not infrequently, but also not quite commonly, the provision of the tools by the entrepreneur. This practice obtained in England from the sixteenth century on, while on the continent it spread more slowly. In general these conditions were confined to the textile industry; there were orders on a large scale for looms for the entrepreneurs, who then turned them over to the weavers for rental. Thus, the worker was entirely separated from the means of production, and at the same time the entrepreneur strove to monopolize for himself the disposal of the product.

5) The entrepreneur took the step of combining several stages in the production process (also not very common; this occurred most likely in the textile industry): he bought the raw material and distributed it to the individual workman, in whose hands the product remained until finished. When this stage was reached, the craft worker again had a master, in quite the same sense as the craftsman on a feudal estate—except that in contrast with the latter he received a monetary wage and an entrepreneur, producing for the market, took the place of the aristocratic household.

The ability of the putting-out system to maintain itself so long rested on the *unimportance of fixed capital*: in weaving this consisted of the loom; in spinning, prior to the invention of mechanical spinning machines, fixed capital was even less significant. The capital remained in the possession of the independent worker and its constituent parts were decentralized; that is, they were not concentrated, as in a modern factory, and hence without special importance.

Although the domestic system was spread widely over the earth, this last stage – the provision of the tools and the detailed direction of production in its various stages by the entrepreneur — was reached comparatively seldom outside the Western world. As far as can be learned, no trace whatever of the system survived from Antiquity, although it was present in China and India. Wherever it dominated, the apprentice–master craftswork system continued to exist. Even the guild, with journeymen and apprentices, might remain, even though divested of its original significance. It became either a guild of home workers — not a modern labor organization but at most a forerunner of such — or, within the guild, a differentiation between wage workers and masters arose.

In the form of entrepreneurial control of unfree labor power, we find that the domestic industry spread over the world as feudal-manorial, monastic, and temple industry. As a free putting-out system it is found in connection with the industrial work of peasants—that is, peasants gradually become home workers producing for the market. . . . Indeed, dependence of urban as well as rural craft workers upon an employer (entrepreneur or "putter out") occurs. China especially affords an example, though the clan retails the goods produced by its members and the connection with clan industry obstructed the creation of a domestic industry. The castes in India blocked the complete subjugation of the craftsman by the merchant. Down to recent times, because hereditary only within castes, the merchant was unable to obtain possession of the means of production to the extent we find true elsewhere. Nonetheless, the domestic system in an elementary form developed here. The last and essential reason for its retarded development in these countries, as compared to Europe, is found in the presence in China and India of unfree workers and a magic-based traditionalism.

From: Pp. 279–85 in *General Economic History,* translated by Frank H. Knight and revised by Stephen Kalberg (New York: Simon & Schuster, 1927).

Modes of Financing. Commercialization involves, on the one hand, the appearance of paper representing shares in an enterprise and, on the other hand, paper representing rights to income, especially in the form of state bonds and mortgage indebtedness.

This development has taken place only in the modern Western world. Forerunners are indeed found in Antiquity in the share-commandite companies of the Roman *publicani,* who shared the profits with the public. But this is an isolated phenomenon and without importance for the provision for wants in Roman life. The picture presented by the economic life of Rome would not have been changed if it had been completely absent.

In modern economic life the issue of credit instruments is a means for the rational assembly of capital. Under this category belongs especially the company owned by stockholders. This represents a culmination of two different lines of development. In the first place, share capital may be brought together for the purpose of anticipating revenues. The political authority wishes to secure command over a definite capital sum or to know upon what income it may depend; hence it sells or leases its revenues to a stock company. . . .

This system implies that, in the place of the original situation (according to which any extraordinary state expenses were covered by compulsory loans from property owners, usually without interest and frequently never repaid), loans were given that appealed to the voluntary economic interests of the participants. Now, for the possessing classes, the state's conduct of war becomes a *business operation.* War loans bearing a high interest rate were unknown in Antiquity; if subjects were not in a position to supply the necessary means, the state had to turn to a foreign financier; his advances were secured by a claim against the spoils of war. If the war ended in defeat, his money was lost. The securing of money for state purposes, and especially for war purposes, by appeal to the general economic interest, was created first in the Middle Ages, especially in the cities.

Another, and economically more important form of association, is that for the purpose of financing commercial enterprises, although the development toward the form of association most familiar to us today—the stock company—only very gradually grew out of this beginning. Two types of such organizations are to be distinguished: first, large enterprises of an inter-regional character which exceeded the resources of a single commercial house; and second, international colonial enterprises.

For inter-regional enterprises which could not be financed by individual entrepreneurs, finance by groups was typical, especially in operations in cities in the fifteenth and sixteenth centuries. In part the cities themselves carried on inter-regional trade. However, for economic history the other case is more important: the city turned to the public and invited share participation in the commercial enterprise it organized. This was done on a considerable scale. When the city appealed to the public, the company thus formed became coerced to admit any citizen; hence, the amount of share capital was unlimited. . . .

Shareholders included not only merchants, but princes, professors, courtiers and, in general, the "public" in the strict sense—which participated gladly and to great profit. The distribution of the dividends was carried out in a completely irrational way according to the profit yield alone, and without reserves of any kind. All that was necessary was the collapse of authoritarian control for the modern stock company to appear in finished form.

The great colonization companies formed another preliminary stage in the development of the modern stock company. The most significant of these were the Dutch and English East India companies, although these were not yet stock companies in the modern sense. . . . Nonetheless, it was these great, successful companies that made the stock company widely known and popular. From them it was taken over by all the continental states of Europe. Stock companies created by the state and granted privileges came to regulate the conditions of participation in business enterprise in general, while the state itself, in a supervisory capacity, was involved in the most remote details of business activity. Not until the eighteenth century did the annual balance and inventory become established as principled procedures. Its recognition took place after many terrible bankruptcies.

Alongside the financing of state wants through stock companies stands *direct financing* by measures of the state itself. This begins with compulsory loans secured by a pledge of resources and the issue of certificates of indebtedness against anticipated revenues. The cities of the Middle Ages secured extraordinary income by bonds, pledging in return their fixed property and financial power. . . .

If one desires to understand the financial operations of a German city at the close of the Middle Ages, one must bear in mind that there was at that time no such thing as an orderly budget. The city, like the territorial lord, lived from week to week, as is done today in a small household. Expenditures were readjusted momentarily as income fluctuated.

The device of tax farming was of assistance in overcoming the difficulty of management without a budget. It gave the administration some security as to the sums to expect each year, and assisted it in planning expenditures. Hence, the tax farm operated as an outstanding instrument of financial rationalization, and was called into use by the European states first only occasionally—and then permanently. It also made possible the discounting of public revenues for war purposes, and in this connection achieved especial significance.

Rational administration of taxation was an accomplishment of the Italian cities in the period after the loss of their freedom [seventeenth century; see p. 397]. The Italian nobility is the first political power to order its finances in accordance with the principle of mercantile bookkeeping obtaining at the time, although this did not then include double entry. From the Italian cities the system spread abroad and came into German territory through Burgundy, France, and the Hapsburg states. It was especially the taxpayers who clamored to have the finances put in order.

A second point of departure for rational forms of administration was the English exchequer system, of which the word "check" is a last survival and reminder. This was a sort of checker board device by means of which the payments due the state were computed in the absence of the necessary facility with figures. Regularly, however the finances were not conducted through setting up a budget in which all receipts and disbursements were included; rather, a *special-fund system* was used. That is, certain receipts were designated and raised for the purpose of specified expenditures only. The reason for this procedure is found in the conflicts between the princely power and the prominent status groups. The latter mistrusted the princes and thought this the only way to protect themselves against having the taxes squandered for the personal ends of the ruler.

In the sixteenth and seventeenth centuries an additional measure, with the effect of rationalizing the financial operations of rulers, appeared in the monopoly strategies of the princes. In part they assumed commercial monopolies themselves and in part they granted monopolistic concessions, involving of course the payment of notable sums to the political authority. . . . The first example of monopoly concession was the attempt of the Emperor Frederick II [1194–1250] to establish a grain monopoly for Sicily. The policy was most extensively employed in England and was developed in an especially systematic manner by the Stuarts [1603–1649; 1660–1714]—and there also it first broke down, under the protests of Parliament. Each new industry and establishment of the Stuart period was . . . bound up with a royal concession and granted a monopoly. The king secured important revenues from the privileges, which provided him with the resources for his struggle against Parliament. But these industrial monopolies established for fiscal purposes broke down almost without exception after the triumph of Parliament [1649]. This in itself proves how incorrect it is to regard, as some writers have done, modern Western capitalism as an outgrowth of the monopolistic policies of princes. . . .

From: Pp. 347, 349–351 in *General Economic History,* translated by Frank H. Knight and revised by Stephen Kalberg (New York: Simon & Schuster, 1927); endnotes omitted.

Mercantilism.   The essence of mercantilism consists in carrying the point of view of capitalist industry into politics; the state is handled as if it consisted exclusively of capitalist entrepreneurs. External economic policy rests on the principle of taking every advantage of the opponent. Importing at the lowest price and selling much higher. The purpose is to strengthen the power of the state's capacity in its external relations. Hence, mercantilism signifies the formation of the modern state's power. This can be accomplished directly through increasing the income of the prince, and indirectly through increasing the tax paying power of the population. . . .

* * *

Mercantilism, in the sense of a league between the state and capitalist interests, had appeared under two aspects. One was that of status monopoly, which appears in its typical form in the policy of the Stuarts and the Anglican church—especially that of Bishop Laud [1573–1645], who was later beheaded. This system looked toward a hierarchical formation of the whole population in the Christian-Socialist sense, and a stabilization of status groups in order again to establish a Christian-oriented ethos of brotherly love. In the sharpest contrast to Puritanism, which saw every poor person as work-shy or as a criminal, its position toward the poor was more compassionate.

In practice, the mercantilism of the Stuarts was primarily oriented along fiscal lines. *New* industries were allowed to import only on the basis of a royal monopoly concession; and they were to be kept under the permanent control of the king with a view to fiscal exploitation. Similarly, although not so consistent, was the policy of Colbert [1619–1683] in France. He aimed at an artificial promotion of industries, supported by monopolies. . .

In England the royal and Anglican policy collapsed under the Long Parliament [1640–1653], owing to the Puritans. Their struggle with the king was pursued for decades under the war cry "down with the monopolies" which had been granted in part to foreigners and in part to courtiers—namely, monopolies and the colonies had been placed in the hands of royal favorites. The small entrepreneurial class—which in the meantime had expanded, especially within the guilds, though in part outside of them—resisted the royal monopoly policy. The Long Parliament deprived monopolists of the suffrage. The extraordinary obstinacy with which the economic spirit of the English people has striven against trusts and monopolies is expressed in these Puritan struggles.

The second form of mercantilism may be called *national*. It limited itself to the systematic protection of industries actually in existence, in contrast with the attempt to establish industries through monopolies.

Hardly one of the industries created by mercantilism survived the mercantilistic period. The economic creations of the Stuarts disappeared along with those of the Western continental states and those of Russia later. It follows that capitalist development was not an outgrowth of national mercantilism; rather, capitalism developed at first in England alongside its fiscal monopoly policy. The course of events was that a stratum of entrepreneurs, which had developed independently of the political administration, secured the systematic support of Parliament in the eighteenth century, after the collapse of the fiscal monopoly policy of the Stuarts. Here for the last time irrational and rational capitalism faced each other in conflict; that is, capitalism in the field of fiscal and colonial privileges and public monopolies, and capitalism oriented in relation to market opportunities developed from within on the basis of commercial achievements, by business interests themselves.

The point of collision of the two types was at the Bank of England. The bank was founded by Paterson, a Scotchman, a capitalist adventurer of the type called forth by the Stuarts' policy of granting monopolies. But Puritan businessmen also belonged to the bank. The last time the bank moved off course in the direction of speculative capitalism was in connection with the South Sea Company [see Weber, 1927, pp. 289–90].

Aside from this venture we can trace step by step the process by which the influence of Paterson and his group lost ground to the rationalist category of bank members—who were all directly or indirectly of Puritan origin or influenced by Puritanism [see p. 212].

Mercantilism further played the role that is familiar to us from the study of economic history. In England it finally disappeared when free trade was established. This was an achievement of the Puritan dissenters (Cobden and Bright) and their alliance with industrial interests now in a position to dispense with mercantilist protection.

From: Pp. 173–76, 302–12 in *General Economic History*, translated by Frank H. Knight and revised by Stephen Kalberg (New York: Simon & Schuster, 1927); endnotes omitted.

The Factory and the Development of Industrial Technique.   [I]t must be held at present, first, that the factory did *not* originate out of *craftwork* or at the expense of it; rather, at the beginning they developed alongside each other. The factory seized above all on new forms of production or new products, such as cotton, porcelain, colored brocade, substitute goods, or products which were not made by the craft guilds and with which they could compete. The extensive inroads by the factories in the sphere of guild work really belongs to the nineteenth century at the earliest, just as in the eighteenth century, especially in the English textile industry, progress was made at the expense of the domestic [cottage industry] system. Nonetheless, the guilds combated the factories and closed workshops growing out of them, especially on grounds of principle; the guilds felt threatened by the new method of production.

As little as out of craftwork did the factories develop out of the domestic system; rather, they similarly grew up *alongside* them. The volume of fixed capital was decisive in respect to the choice between the domestic system and the factory. Where fixed capital was not necessary the domestic system has endured down to the present; where it was necessary factories arose, though not out of the domestic system; an originally feudal or communal establishment would be taken over by an entrepreneur and used for the production of goods for the market under private initiative.

Finally, it is to be observed that the modern factory was not originally called into being by machines; however, there is a correlation relationship between the two. Machine industry made use originally of animal power; even Arkwright's first spinning machines in 1768 were driven by horses. The specialization of work and labor discipline within the workshop, however, formed a predisposing condition, even an impetus toward the increased application and improvement of machines. Premiums were offered for the construction of the new engines. Their principle—the lifting of water by fire—arose in the mining industry and rested upon the application of steam as the driving force. Economically, the significance of the machines lay in the introduction of systematic calculation.

The consequences which accompanied the introduction of the modern factory are extraordinarily far-reaching, both for the *entrepreneur* and for the *worker*. Even before the application of machinery, workshop industry meant the employment of the worker in a place separate both from his own dwelling and the dwelling of the consumer. There has always been concentration of workers in some form or other. In Antiquity it was the Pharaoh or the territorial lord who had products made to supply political or large-household needs. Now, however, the proprietor of the workshop became the master over workers and an entrepreneur producing for the market. The concentration of workers within the shop was, at the beginning of the modern era, partly compulsory; the poor, the homeless, and criminals were pressed into factories. In the mines of Newcastle the laborers wore iron collars down into the eighteenth century.

But in the eighteenth century itself the labor contract everywhere took the place of unfree work. It meant a saving in capital, since the capital requirement for purchasing the slaves disappeared. It also shifted the capital risk onto the worker, since his death had previously meant a capital loss for the master. Again, it removed responsibility for the reproduction of the working class, whereas slave-manned industry was wrecked on the question of the family life and reproduction of the slaves. The labor contract made possible the rational division of labor on the basis of technical efficiency alone, and although precedents existed, freedom of contract first made the concentration of labor in the shop the general rule. Finally, it created the possibility of exact calculation, which again could only be carried out in connection with a combination of the workshop with the nonslave, contracted worker.

In spite of all these conditions favoring its development, the workshop was and remained in the early period insecure; in various places it often disappeared again, as in Italy, and especially in Spain (where a famous painting of Velasquez portrays it to us), although later it is absent. Down into the first half of the eighteenth century it did not form an irreplaceable, necessary, or indispensable part in the provision for a society's general needs. One thing is certain: before the age of machinery, workshop industry with free labor was nowhere else developed to the extent that it was in the Western world at the beginning of the modern era. The reasons for the fact that elsewhere the development did not take the same course will be explained in what follows.

India once possessed a highly developed industrial technique, but here castes—impure to one another—stood in the way of development of the Western workshop. It is true that caste ritual did not go to the extent of forbidding of different castes to work together in the same shop; there was a saying—"the workshop is pure." However, if the workshop system could not here develop into the factory, the exclusiveness of caste is certainly in part responsible. Such a workshop must have appeared extraordinarily anomalous. Down into the nineteenth century, all attempts to introduce factory organization, even in the jute industry, encountered great difficulties. Even after the rigor of caste law had decayed, the absence of labor discipline stood in the way. Every caste had different rituals and different rest pauses, and demanded different holidays.

In China, the cohesion of the clans in the village was extraordinarily strong. Workshop industry is there communal clan economy. Beyond this, China developed only the domestic system. Centralized establishments were founded only by the emperor and great feudal lords, especially in the manufacture of porcelain by servile hand workers. Here the requirements of the contractor alone [held sway] and the market only to a limited extent (and generally on an unvarying scale of operation).

$$* * *$$

It is not easy to define accurately the concept of the factory. We think at once of the steam engine and the mechanization of "work," but the machine had its forerunner in what we call an "apparatus"—labor appliances which had to be utilized in the same way as the machine, but which, as a rule, were driven by water power. The distinction is that the apparatus works as the servant of people while with modern machines the inverse relation holds. The real distinguishing characteristic of the modern factory is in general, however, not the implements of work applied, but the concentration of ownership of the workplace, workplace tools, sources of power, and raw material in one and the same hand: that of the entrepreneur. This combination was only exceptionally met with before the eighteenth century.

Tracing the English development, which was key for the development of capitalism—although England occasionally followed the example of other countries, such as Italy—we find the following lines of development:

1. The oldest real factory which can be identified (though it was still driven by water power) was a silk factory at Derwent, near Derby, in 1719. It was conducted on the basis of a patent, the owner of which had stolen the invention in Italy. In Italy there had long been silk manufacture with various property relations. However, the product was oriented to luxury needs and belonged to an epoch which is not yet characteristic for modern capitalism. Nonetheless, this factory must be noted here because the implements of work, all material, and the product belonged to an entrepreneur.

2. The establishment of wool manufacture (1738) on the basis of a patent after the invention of an apparatus for running a hundred bobbins at once with the aid of water power.

3. The development of half-linen production.

4. The systematic development of the pottery industry through experiments in Staffordshire. Earthen vessels were produced under a modern division of labor and the application of water, power, and with the ownership of the workplace and implements by an entrepreneur.

5. The manufacture of paper, beginning with the eighteenth century; the development of the modern use of documents and of the newspaper constituted its permanent basis.

The decisive factor, however, in the triumph of the mechanization and rationalization of work was the fate of *cotton manufacture*. This industry was transplanted from the continent to England in the seventeenth century. There immediately began a struggle against the old national industry established in the fifteenth century, namely, wool. This struggle was as intense as that in which wool had previously been involved against linen. The power of the wool producers was so great that they secured restrictions and prohibitions on the production of half-linen, which was not restored until the Manchester Act of 1736. The factory production of cotton stuff was originally limited by the fact that, while the loom had been improved and enlarged, the spindle remained on the medieval level; hence, the necessary quantity of spun material was not available. A succession of technical improvements of the spindle after 1769 reversed this relation and, with the help of water power and mechanical aids, great quantities of usable yarn could be provided; however, it remained impossible to weave the same quantity with corresponding speed. This discrepancy was removed in 1785 through the construction of the power loom by Cartwright, one of the first inventors who combined technology with science and handled the problems of the former by reference to theoretical considerations.

Despite this revolution in the tools of work, the development might have stopped and modern capitalism, in its most characteristic form, might never have appeared. Its victory was decided by coal and iron. We know that coal had been consumed, even in the Middle Ages, as in London, Luttich and Zwickau. However, until the eighteenth century the technique was determined by the fact that smelting, and all preparation of iron, was done with charcoal. The deforestation of England resulted; Germany was saved from this fate by the circumstance that in the seventeenth and eighteenth centuries it was untouched by capitalistic development.

Everywhere the destruction of the forests brought industrial development to a standstill at a certain point. Smelting was only released from its attachment to organic materials of the plant world by the application of coal. It must be noted that the first blast furnaces appear as early as the fifteenth century; however, they were fed with wood and not used for private consumption but for war purposes, and in part also in connection with ocean shipping. In the fifteenth century, furthermore, the iron drill for the preparation of cannon barrels was invented. At the same time appeared the large heavy trip hammer, up to a thousand pounds weight, driven by water power, so that in addition to the handling of cast iron with the drill, mechanical forging was now also possible. Finally, in the seventeenth century the rolling process, in the modern sense of the word, was also applied.

Two difficult problems arose with further development. These congealed, on the one hand from the *danger of deforestation* and, on the other, from the perpetual bursting of water in the mines. The first question was the more pressing because, unlike the expansion of the textile industry, the English iron industry had shrunk step by step; at the beginning of the eighteenth century one had the impression it had reached its end. The solution was reached through the *coking* of coal, which was discovered in 1735, and the use of coke in blast furnace operation, which was undertaken in 1740. Another step forward was made in 1784 when the puddling process was introduced as an innovation. On the other hand, the threat to mining was removed by the invention of the steam engine. Crude attempts first showed the possibility of lifting water with fire and, between 1670 and 1770 and toward the end of the eighteenth century, the steam engine reached an advanced stage of serviceability, one which made it possible to produce the amount of coal necessary for modern industry.

The significance of the development just portrayed is to be found in three consequences. In the first place, coal and iron released technology, and hence productive possibilities from the limitations inherent to organic materials; from this time forward industry was no longer dependent upon animal power or plant growth. Through a process of exhaustive exploitation, fossil fuel, and through it iron ore, were brought up to the light of day and, by means of both, men achieved the possibility of extending production to a degree previously inconceivable. Thus, iron became the most important factor for the development of capitalism. What would have happened in regards to this economy or to Europe in the absence of this development we do not know.

The second consequence is that the mechanization of the production process through the steam engine liberated production from the *organic limitations of human labor.* Not altogether, it is true, for it goes without saying that labor was indispensable for the tending of machines. But the mechanizing process has always and everywhere been introduced with the definite end of releasing labor. Every new invention signifies the extensive displacement of craft workers by a relatively small labor force, one now oriented to machine supervision.

Finally, through the union with science, the production of goods was emancipated *from all the bonds of inherited tradition* and came under the dominance of the freely roving intelligence. It is true that most of the inventions of the eighteenth century were not made in a scientific manner; when the coking process was discovered no one suspected what its chemical significance might be. The connection of industry with modern science, especially the systematic work of the laboratories, beginning with [the chemist] Justus von Liebig [1803–1873], enabled industry to become what it is today, and hence brought capitalism to a full development.

The *recruiting of the labor force* for the new form of production, as it developed in England in the eighteenth century, resting upon the concentration of all the means of production in the hands of the entrepreneur, was carried out first by *means of compulsion,* though of an indirect sort. Here belongs especially the Poor Law and the Statute of Apprentices of Queen Elizabeth. These measures had become necessary in consequence of the large number of people rendered destitute by the revolution in agriculture and wandering about the country. Its displacement of the small, dependent peasant by large renters and the transformation of arable land into sheep pastures (although the latter has occasionally been overestimated) worked together constantly to reduce the amount of labor required on the land and to bring into being a surplus population, which was subjected to compulsory labor. Anyone who refused employment was thrust into a regimented workhouse and anyone who left a position without a certificate from the master craftsman or entrepreneur was treated as a vagabond. No unemployed person was supported except in the form of a compulsory entrance into the workhouse.

In this way the first labor force for the factories was recruited. With difficulty the people adapted themselves to the discipline of the work. But the power of the possessing classes was too great; they secured the support of the political authority through justices of the peace, who in the absence of binding law operated on the basis of a maze of instructions and largely according to their own dictates. Down into the second half of the nineteenth century they exercised an arbitrary control over the labor force and stuffed the workers into the newly arising industries.

From the beginning of the eighteenth century, on the other hand, begins the regulation of relations between entrepreneur and laborer, presaging the modern control of labor conditions. The first anti-trucking laws [in kind payments of workers] were passed under Queen Anne and George I. While during the entire Middle Ages the worker had struggled for the right to bring the product of his own labor to market, from now on legislation protected him against being paid for his work in the products of others and secured for him remuneration in money.

The second source of labor power in England was the small master [craftsman] class, the great majority of whom were transformed into a proletariat of factory laborers. Two great sources of demand appeared in the markets for the products of these newly established industries, namely war and luxury; the military administration and the luxury needs of court society.

The *military administration* became a consumer of the products of industry to the extent that great mercenary armies developed—indeed, consumption of products increased as army discipline and the rationalization of arms and all military technique progressed. In the textile industry the production of uniforms was fundamental, as they served by no means simply as an army perk; rather, they were a mechanism of discipline in the interest of unitary regimentation and in order to keep the soldiers under control. The production of cannon and firearms occupied the iron industry, and the provision of supplies did the same for trade.

In addition to the land army there was the navy; the increasing size of the war ships was one of the factors which created a market for industry. While the size of merchant ships had changed little before the end of the eighteenth century and, as late as 1750, the ships entering London were typically of about 140 tons burden, war ships had grown to a size of one thousand tons in the sixteenth century; in the eighteenth this became the normal burden. The demand of the navy, like that of the army, increased further with the growth in the number and extent of the voyages (and this also applies to merchant ships), especially after the sixteenth century. Down to that time the Levant cruise had normally occupied a year: at this time ships began to remain much longer at sea and at the same time the increasing magnitude of campaigns on land necessitated a more extensive provision with supplies, munitions, etc. Finally, the speed of ship building and of the construction of cannon increased with extraordinary rapidity after the seventeenth century.

Sombart has assumed that the standardized mass provision for war is among the decisive conditions affecting the development of modern capitalism. This theory must be reduced to its proper proportions. It is correct that annually enormous sums were spent for army and navy purposes; in Spain 70 percent of the revenues of the state went for this purpose and in other countries two-thirds or more. But we also find outside the Western world, as in the Mogul Empire and in China, enormous armies equipped with artillery (although not yet with uniforms), yet no impulse toward capitalist development followed. Moreover, even in the West the army needs were met to an increasing extent, developing in parallel with capitalism itself, by the military administration on its own account: in its own workshops and arms and munition factories. Capitalism proceeded along non-capitalistic lines.

Hence, it is a false conclusion to ascribe to war as such, through the army demands, the role of prime mover in the creation of modern capitalism. It is true that it was involved in capitalism, and not only in Europe; but this motive was not decisive for its development. Otherwise the increasing provision of army requirements by direct action of the state would again have forced capitalism into the background, a development which did not take place.

For the *luxury demand* of the court and the nobility, France became the typical country. For a time in the sixteenth century, the king spent 10 million livres a year directly or indirectly for luxury goods. This expenditure by the royal family and the highest social classes constituted a strong stimulus to quite a number of industries. The most important articles, aside from such means of enjoyment as chocolate and coffee, are embroidery (sixteenth century), linen goods (for the treatment of which ironing develops; seventeenth century), stockings (sixteenth century), umbrellas (seventeenth century), indigo dyeing (sixteenth century), tapestry (seventeenth. century), and carpets (eighteenth century). The two last named were the most important of the luxury industries with regard to the volume of the demand; they signified a *democratization of luxury.* This is the *crucial turn for capitalism.*

Court luxury existed in China and India on a scale unknown in Europe, yet no significant stimulus to capitalism or capitalist industry proceeded from this fact. The reason is that the provision for the Court's needs were arranged leiturgically through compulsory contributions. This system maintained itself so tenaciously that, down to our own time, Beijing peasants in the region have been obliged to furnish to the imperial court the same objects as 3000 years ago—although they did not know how to produce them and were compelled to buy them from producers. In India and China the army requirements were also met by forced labor and contributions in kind.

In Europe itself the leiturgical contributions of the East are not unknown, although they appear in a different form. Here the princes transformed workers in luxury industries into compulsory laborers by indirect means, binding them to their places of work by grants of land, long period contracts, and various privileges—although in France, the country which took the lead in luxury industries, this was not the case. Here the handicraft form of establishment maintained itself, partly under a putting-out organization and partly under a workshop system. Neither the technology nor the economic organization of the industries was transformed in any revolutionary way.

The decisive turn toward capitalism could come only from one source, namely, a *mass market demand,* which again could arise only in a small proportion of the luxury industries through the democratization of demand, especially along the line of production of substitutes for the luxury goods of the upper classes. While mass market demand is characterized by *price competition,* the luxury industries working for the court follow the handicraft principle of *competition in quality.* The first example of the policy of a state organization entering upon price competition is afforded in England at the close of the fifteenth century. The effort was made to undersell Flemish wool, an object which was promoted by numerous export prohibitions.

The *great price revolution of the sixteenth and seventeenth centuries provided a powerful lever* for the specifically capitalist tendencies to seek profit through lowering production costs and lowering the price. This revolution is rightly ascribed to the continuous inflow of precious metals, in consequence of the great overseas discoveries. It lasted from the 1530s to the time of the Thirty Years War [1618-1648]; however, it affected different branches of economic life in quite different ways. In the case of agricultural products an almost universal rise in price set in, making it possible for a transformation to production for the market. It was quite otherwise with the course of prices for industrial products. By and large these remained stable or rose in price relatively little—thus actually falling in comparison to the agricultural products. This relative decline was made possible only through a shift in technology and economics, and exerted pressure in the direction of increasing profit by repeated cheapening of production. Thus, the development did not follow the order that capitalism set in first and the decline in prices followed, but the reverse: first the prices fell relatively and then came capitalism.

The tendency toward rationalizing technology and economic relations, with a view to reducing prices in relation to costs, generated in the seventeenth century a feverish pursuit of new inventions. All the inventors of the period are dominated by the goal of cheapening production. The notion of perpetual motion as a source of energy is only one of many elements of this very widespread ferment.

The inventor as a type goes back much farther. But if one scrutinizes the constructions of the greatest inventor of pre-capitalist times, Leonardo da Vinci—for the controlled experimentation originated in the field of art and not that of science [see Weber, 2005, pp. 324–25]—one observes that his creations sought the rational mastery of technical problems as such rather than a cheapening of production costs. The inventors of the pre-capitalistic age worked empirically; their inventions had more or less the character of accidents. An exception is mining, and in consequence it is the problems of mining in connection with which conscious technical developments took place [see Weber, 1927, pp. 178–91].

A positive innovation for the invention process as such was the first rational *patent law*. This English law of 1623 contains all the essential provisions of a modern statute. Down to that time the exploitation of inventions had been arranged through a special grant in consideration of a payment; in contrast the law of 1623 limits the protection of the invention to fourteen years and makes its subsequent utilization by an entrepreneur conditional upon an adequate royalty for the original inventor. Without the stimulus of this patent law, the inventions crucial for the development of capitalism in the field of textile industry in the eighteenth century would not have been possible. . .

THE DEFINITION OF MODERN CAPITALISM, AND THE RELATIONSHIP OF FEUDALISM AND PATRIMONIALISM TO CAPITALISM

From: Pp. 238–40 in *Wirtschaftsgeschichte*. Translated by Stephen Kalberg (Munich and Leipzip: Duncker & Humblot, 1923). [*General Economic History*, pp. 275–78]

Capitalism exists wherever a production-oriented provision of the wants of a human group occurs — irrespective of what wants are involved — on the basis of an *enterprise*. A specifically rational capitalist firm is one in which capital accounting prevails. That is, here a production-oriented firm assesses its income-yielding capacity by calculation according to the methods of modern bookkeeping and the checking of balances. . . . It goes without saying that a single enterprise may be conducted along modern capitalist lines to the most widely varying extent; parts of the provision of wants may be organized in a capitalist manner and other parts on the handicraft or manorial patterns. . . .

In contrast with the greater part of the past, our everyday wants today are supplied through modern capitalism. . . . An entire *epoch* can be designated as typically capitalist only when the provision of wants is organized according to modern capitalism's features to such a predominant degree that, if we imagine this form of the economy as absent, the whole economic system will collapse.

While various forms of capitalism have confronted us in all periods of history, the provision of *daily wants* by modern capitalism is unique to the West. Even here it has existed only since the latter half of the nineteenth century. Whatever can be found otherwise of capitalist beginnings in earlier centuries constitutes in the end precursors only. Even the few capitalist businesses of the sixteenth century can be banished from the economic life of this era without causing fundamental change.

The most general precondition for the existence of modern capitalism is the existence of rational capital accounting as the norm for all large industrial undertakings concerned with the provision of daily wants. This accounting involves, . . . first, the appropriation of all physical means of production — land, buildings, machines, tools, etc. — as the disposable property of autonomous and private industrial enterprises. This is a phenomenon known only to our time; the army alone is the exception.

Second, modern capitalism involves freedom of the market; that is, the absence of irrational limitations on trading in the market. Such restrictions might be of a status character. Here a certain way of organizing life is prescribed for a group rigidly along status group lines. Further, a status group monopoly may exist, as, for example, if townsmen are not allowed to own a manorial estate or the knight or peasant is not permitted to participate in industry. In such cases neither a free labor market nor a free commodity market exists.

Third, capitalist accounting presupposes a *rational technology*; that is, one oriented to calculation to the largest possible degree, and this implies a mechanized technology in production, commerce, and transportation.

Fourth, rational capital accounting presupposes calculable law. The capitalist industrial organization, if it is to operate rationally, must be able to depend upon calculable adjudication and administration. Neither in the age of the Greek city-state (polis) nor in the patrimonial state of Asia, nor in Western countries down to the Stuarts, was this condition fulfilled. The royal "cheap justice," with its remissions by royal grace, introduced continual disturbances into the calculations of economic life. . . .

Free labor is the fifth feature. Persons must be present who are both legally available and economically coerced to sell their labor on the market without restrictions. It is in contradiction to the essence of [modern] capitalism, and the development of [modern] capitalism remains impossible, if such a propertyless statum is absent—namely, a class compelled to sell its labor in order to live. If only unfree labor is at hand, modern capitalism cannot exist. Rational capitalist calculation is possible only on the basis of free labor. Only where, as a consequence of the existence of workers who are voluntary in a formal sense, but actually under the compulsion of the whip of hunger, can the costs of products be unambiguously determined by agreement in advance.

The sixth and final condition is the commercialization of the economy. By this we understand the general use of commercial instruments to represent share rights in enterprises and in the ownership of property [see pp. 379–83].

In summary, under modern capitalism it must be possible to conduct the provision for wants exclusively through orientations to market opportunities and the calculation of profits. To the extent that commercialization is added to the other characteristics of capitalism, an enhancement of the significance of another factor not yet mentioned occurs; namely, speculation. Speculation acquires this significance only from the moment when property takes on the form of negotiable paper.

* * *

From: Pp. 1099-1103 in *Economy and Society*, edited by Guenther Roth and Claus Wittich, translated by Roth and Wittich; revised by Stephen Kalberg (Berkeley: The University of California Press, 1978); endnotes omitted.

The Formation and Distribution of Wealth under Feudalism.

The feudal order has a different effect upon the economy than does patrimonialism, which in part furthers and in part deflects modern capitalism. The patrimonial state offers the whole realm of the ruler's discretion as a hunting ground for accumulating wealth. Wherever binding tradition or stereotyped prescription does not impose strict limitations, patrimonialism gives free lein to the enrichment of the ruler himself, the court officials, favorites, governors, mandarins, tax collectors, influence peddlers, and the great merchants and financiers who function as tax-farmers, purveyors, and those offering credit. The ruler's favor and disfavor, grants and confiscations, continuously create new wealth and destroy it again.

In contrast, feudalism, with its closely delineated rights and duties, not only has a stabilizing effect upon the economy as a whole, but also upon the distribution of individual wealth. To begin with, *it* achieves this effect through its legal order The feudal association, and also the related patrimonial forms that have a stereotyped status structure, constitute a synthesis of purely concrete rights and duties. They amount to a "constitutional state" (*Rechtsstaat*) on the basis of "subjective" rights, not an "objective" legal framework. Instead of a system of abstract [state-based] rules, compliance with which permits the free use of economic resources to all, we find a congeries of acquired rights. These impede the freedom of acquisition and provide opportunities for capitalist acquisition only through the granting of further concrete privilege of the type that were generally at the foundation of the oldest manufactories. To be sure, in this manner capitalist acquisition gains a support which is steadier than the personal, changeable favors of patriarchal patrimonialism. However, the danger that the granted privileges will be disputed persists since older acquired rights remain untouched.

Capitalist development is handicapped even more by the economic foundations and consequences of feudalism. Land granted as a fief became immobilized, for in accord with his status the vassal's ability to discharge his obligations, to live in a knightly fashion, and to raise his children depended upon the holding together of his property. Hence, it was normally inalienable and indivisible. . . .

The feudal landlord or political ruler can be a capitalist producer or a person who provides credit to businesses—witness the [Japanese] *daimyos*. With the help of serf labor feudal landlords often established commercial enterprises, manorial home industries, and especially factories, for example in Russia. Therefore, the patrimonial foundation of feudalism implies by no means a necessary linkage with a natural [barter] economy. But partly for this very reason it impedes the unfolding of modern capitalism, which depends upon the development of mass purchasing power for industrial products: the frequently massive tributes and services of the peasants to the landlords or feudal magistrates confiscate much of their purchasing power, which could have contributed toward the creation of a market for industrial products.

The landlords' purchasing power, which derives from this confiscation, does not benefit mass-produced articles, upon which modern industrial capitalism largely depends; rather, it creates luxury demands, especially the consumption-oriented maintenance of personal servants. Moreover, since the manorial profit-making enterprises operate with forced labor and since in general the manorial household and craft enterprises utilize unpaid labor and hence waste manpower, they withhold labor from the free market and use it in a manner which largely fails to create capital—and sometimes simply consumes it. Insofar as these enterprises can compete with the urban trades because their workforce is paid little or nothing, wages cannot create mass purchasing power; and insofar as these enterprises cannot compete, in spite of this advantage, because of—and this is the rule—technological "backwardness," the manorial lord tries to impede the capitalist development of the urban trades through political repression.

In general, the feudal stratum tends to restrict the accumulation of wealth in bourgeois hands or at least to "declass" the *nouveaux riches*. This happened particularly in feudal Japan where eventually the whole foreign trade was greatly restricted, primarily in the interest of stabilizing the social order. In varying degrees similar phenomena can be observed everywhere. The social prestige of the manorial lords also motivates the *nouveaux riches* to invest their acquired wealth in a capitalist venture rather than in land in [the hope of rising] into the nobility. All of this impedes the formation of productive capital; this was very typical of the Middle Ages, especially in Germany

Thus feudalism more or less handicaps or diverts capitalist development; moreover, its strong traditionalism generally strengthens the authoritarian powers distrustful of all new social formations. However, the continuity of [feudalism's] legal order, which is after all much greater than in the non-stereotyped patrimonial state, may facilitate capitalist development. Where the bourgeois accumulation of wealth is not restricted as much as in Japan, it will be indeed slowed down, but whatever is lost in this way [under feudalism], especially in comparison with the vacillating economic opportunities in the patrimonial state, can eventually benefit the formation of a rational capitalist *system* as a result of a more gradual and continuous development—and can further its advance within the interstices of the feudal system.

Opportunities for individual acquisition were certainly much smaller in the Northern countries of the Western Middle Ages than for the officials and government purveyors of the Assyrian empire, the Caliphate and Turkey, or for the Chinese mandarins, or Spanish and Russian government purveyors and state creditors. But exactly because these choices were lacking [in Europe], capital flowed into the channels of purely bourgeois acquisition through the putting-out system and the manufactories. And the more successfully the feudal stratum prevented the intrusion of *nouveaux riches*, excluded them from offices and political power, socially "declassed" them and blocked their acquisition of aristocratic landed estates, the more it directed this wealth to purely bourgeois-capitalist uses.

Patrimonial Monopoly and Capitalist Privilege. Patriarchal patrimonialism is than much more tolerant than feudalism toward social mobility and the acquisition of wealth. The patrimonial ruler does not like independent economic and social powers, and therefore does not favor the rational enterprises based on the organization of labor; that is, on the trades. He also opposes status barriers among "subjects," except where liturgical ties exist [collective responsibility associations]. . . . For the rest, diverse circumstances determine the extent to which patrimonialism tends more toward monopolies of its own, and therefore toward hostility to private capitalism, or more toward direct privileges for capital. The two most important circumstances are political:

1) The very structure of patrimonial domination, whether estate-oriented or more patriarchal. In the former case the ruler is naturally more limited, *ceteris paribus*, in the free development of his own monopolies. Nevertheless, it is true that in modern times the West has known many monopolies by patrimonial rulers, much more so than China, at least during the same period; but it is also true that most of these monopolies were used only in the form of leases or licenses to capitalists—that is, in private capitalist fashion. Furthermore, the ruler's monopolies evoked a very effective response from the ruled. Such a strong reaction would have been scarcely possible under strictly patriarchal domination; to be sure, state monopolies—as Chinese literature too seems to confirm—have everywhere been resented. But most of the time they were [in China] hated by the consumers, rather than, as in the West, by the (bourgeois) producers.

2) . . . The privileges of private capital in patrimonial states were always the more developed the more the power competition of *several* states made it necessary for them to woo mobile money capital. Politically privileged capitalism flourished in Antiquity as long as several powers fought for ascendancy and survival. In China, too, it seems to have developed in this era. It flourished during the age of mercantilism in the West, when the modern power states entered upon their political competition. It disappeared in the Roman empire when the latter became a "world empire" and had only to protect frontiers. It was almost completely absent in the Chinese empire and relatively weak in the Oriental and Hellenistic world-empires—all the weaker the more these states were "universal"—and also in the [Muslim] Caliphate. Of course, not every competition for political power led to privileges for capital; this could only happen when capital formation was already under way. Conversely, pacification and the resulting decline of political demands for capital on the part of the great universal states eliminated the privileged position of capital. . . .

THE WEST'S CROSS-STATE COMPETITION VERSUS HIEROCRACY AND CAESAROPAPISM

From: Pp. 287-89 in *Wirtschaftsgeschichte*. Translated by Stephen Kalberg (Munich and Leipzig: Duncker & Humblot, 1923). [*General Economic History*, pp. 336–37]

... [The city's] ... administrative autonomy was progressively diminished. The English city of the seventeenth and eighteenth centuries had become a clique of guilds; it could claim only financial and social status significance. The German cities of the same period, with the exception of the imperial cities, were province-based entities (*Landstädte*). All rulership was imposed from above. This same development appeared even earlier in the French cities. On the occasion of the insurrection of the *comuneros*, the Spanish cities were conquered by Charles V [1685–1749]. The Italian cities were in the hands of the *signory* [nobles], and Russian cities never saw freedom in the sense it had been attained by the Western cities. Everywhere the cities were stripped of military, judicial, and commercial authority.

The old rights were as a rule formally unchanged. Nonetheless, the modern city in reality was deprived of its freedom as effectively as had happened in Antiquity with the establishment of the Roman dominion. However, in contrast to this era, the cities now came under the violence of competing national states engaged in perpetual peaceful and warfaring struggles for power.

These competitive conflicts created the largest opportunities for modern Western capitalism. Each separate state had to compete for mobile capital, and this situation prescribed to each the extent to which capital would assist the acquisition of power. Out of this alliance of the state with capital, created by necessity, arose the nation-wide citizenry in the modern sense of the word: the bourgeois middle class. Hence, it is the closed nation-state that provided the opportunity to capitalism for its continued existence. As long as the nation-state is not replaced by a world empire, capitalism will endure.

* * *

From: Pp. 1192–93 in *Economy and Society*, edited by Guenther Roth and Claus Wittich, translated by Roth and Wittich; revised by Stephen Kalberg (Berkeley: The University of California Press, 1978).

Hierocratic Rationalization and the Uniqueness of Western Civilization. The more favorable constellation for capitalist development that Western Catholicism offered (in comparison with these Eastern religions) was primarily due to the rationalization of hierocratic domination under-taken in continuation of ancient Roman traditions. This refers especially to the manner in which science and jurisprudence were developed. The Eastern religions preserved the unrationalized charismatic character of religiosity more than did the Western church; in part at least, this was a consequence of the purely historical fact that not they but the secular powers, whose paths they crossed, were the carriers of spiritual and social culture, and they always remained subject to caesaropapist control, Buddhism excepted.

The Eastern church lacks an hierocratic apparatus with a monocratic head. Since the catastrophe of Patriarch Nikon [1605–1681] and the aboli-tion of the patriarchal position during the reign of Peter the Great [1689–1725], the *Oberprokuror* has been the dominant figure of the Russian Holy Synod, a purely bureaucratic organization of state-appointed clerical dignitaries. . . . Hence, there is no infallible doctrinal authority: In Islam, Buddhism and the Eastern church the sole source of new knowledge is the *consensus ecclesiae*; in the two former cases this brought about considerable flexibility and growth potential, but also greatly impeded the rise of ratio-nal philosophical thought from developing out of theology.

Finally, there was no rational judicial system of the kind established by the Western ecclesiastic apparatus. The church created a trial procedure—inqui-sition—in order to obtain evidence in a rational manner, primarily for its own purposes; this, in turn, strongly affected the development of secular justice. There was also no continuous lawmaking on the basis of rational jurispru-dence, such as the Western church developed in part on its own and in part on the model of Roman law . . .

All in all, the specific developmental seeds of Western civilization car-ried within themselves a tension and unique balancing out between office charisma and monasticism on the one hand and, on the other, between po-litical power that is rooted in a status- and feudal-based contract state and a rationally and bureaucratically constituted hierocracy—which is inde-pendent of this state yet also intersects with it. At least from a sociological viewpoint the Western Middle Ages were much less of a *unified civilization* (*Einheitskultur*) than the Egyptian, Tibetan, and Jewish cultures after the hierocracy's victory, or than China since the triumph of Confucianism, Ja-pan—if we disregard Buddhism—since the victory of feudalism, Russia since the rise of caesaropapism and state bureaucracy, and Islam since the definite establishment of the Caliphate and the prebendalization of domi-nation; finally, even Hellenic and Roman civilizations were more unified than medieval Europe.

This generalization appears to be largely correct even though all these civ-ilizations were unified in a different sense. The alliance between political and hierocratic powers reached two high points in the West: The first time in the Carolingian empire [751–911] and during certain periods in which the Holy Roman Empire attained the height of its power; the second time in the few cases of Calvinist theocracy and, in strongly caesaropapist form, in the states of the Lutheran and Anglican Reformation and in the great unified states of the Counter-Reformation: Spain and Bossuet's France.

However, even during periods of co-operation Western hierocracy lived in a state of tension with the political power and constituted its major restraint; this contrasted with the purely caesaropapist or purely theocratic structures of Antiquity and the East.

In the West authority was set against authority, legitimacy against legitimacy, one office charisma against the other—yet in the minds of the rulers and ruled the ideal remained the unification of both political and hierocratic power. The person, however, did not have any legitimate sphere of his own *against* these two types of legitimate domination, with the exception of the independent family charisma in the clan state or the contractually guaranteed, direct or derived autonomy of the [feudal] vassal. The extent to which the state of Antiquity, hierocracy, the patrimonial state or caesaropapism assert their power over the individual . . . is a purely factual question, the answer to which depends primarily upon the survival interests of the ruling group and its form of organization. The point is that a legitimate limitation of authority in favor of the person as such did not exist.

VI

JURIDICAL FORMALISM AND THE RATIONAL STATE

From: Pp. 241–42 in Max Weber: *Readings and Commentary on Modernity,* edited by Stephen Kalberg. Translated by Max Rheinstein; revised by Guenther Roth and Claus Wittich; slightly revised by Stephen Kalberg (Oxford: Blackwell, 2005). [*Economy and Society,* pp. 811–14]

Juridical formalism enables the legal system to operate like a technically rational machine. Thus it guarantees to individuals and groups within the system a relative maximum of freedom, and greatly increases for them the possibility of predicting the legal consequences of their actions. Procedure becomes a specific type of pacified contest, bound to fixed and inviolable "rules of the game.". . . The modern theory . . . binds the judge to the motions of, and the evidence offered by, the parties and, indeed, the same principle applies to the entire conduct of the suit: in accordance with the principle of adversary procedure the judge has to wait for the motions of the parties. Whatever is not introduced or put into a motion does not exist as far as the judge is concerned; the same is true of facts which remain undisclosed by the recognized methods of proof, be they rational or irrational. Thus, the judge aims at establishing only that relative truth which is attainable within the limits set by procedural acts of the parties. . . .

. . . Formal justice guarantees the maximum freedom for the interested parties to represent their formal legal interests. But because of the unequal distribution of economic power, which the system of formal justice legalizes, this very freedom must time and again produce consequences which are contrary to the substantive postulates of religious ethics or of political expediency. Formal justice is thus repugnant to all authoritarian powers, theocratic as well as patriarchic, because it diminishes the dependency of the individual upon the grace and power of the authorities. To democracy, however, it has been repugnant because it decreases the dependency of the legal practice and therewith of individuals upon the decisions of their fellow citizens. Furthermore, the development of the trial into a peaceful contest of conflicting interests can contribute to the further concentration of economic and social power.

In all these cases formal justice, due to its necessarily abstract character, infringes upon the ideals of substantive justice. It is precisely the abstract character which constitutes the decisive merit of formal justice to those who wield the economic power at any given time and who are therefore interested in its unhampered operation, but also to those who on ideological grounds attempt to break down authoritarian control or to restrain irrational mass emotions for the purpose of opening up individual opportunities and liberating capacities. To all these groups nonformal justice simply represents the likelihood of absolute arbitrariness and subjectivistic instability. Among those groups who favor formal justice we must include all those political and economic interest groups to whom the stability and predictability of legal procedure are of very great importance; that is, particularly rational, economic, and political organizations intended to have a permanent character. Above all, those in possession of economic power look upon a formal rational administration of justice as a guarantee of "freedom," a value which is repudiated not only by theocratic or patriarchal-authoritarian groups but, under certain conditions, also by democratic groups. Formal justice and the "freedom" which it guarantees are indeed rejected by all groups ideologically interested in substantive justice. . . .

. . . [C]apitalist interests will fare best under a rigorously formal system of adjudication that applies in all cases and operates under the adversary system of procedure. In any case, adjudication by honoratiores inclines to be essentially empirical, and its procedure is complicated and expensive. It may thus well stand in the way of the interests of the bourgeois classes, and it may indeed be said that England achieved capitalist supremacy among the nations not because, but rather in spite, of its judicial system. For these very reasons the bourgeois strata have generally tended to be intensely interested in a rational procedural system and therefore in a systematized, unambiguous, and specialized formal law that eliminates both obsolete traditions and arbitrariness; here rights can have their source exclusively in general objective norms. Such a systematically codified law was thus demanded by the English Puritans, the Roman Plebeians, and the German bourgeoisie of the nineteenth century. . . .

From: Pp. 238–39, 240–41 in *Max Weber: Readings and Commentary on Modernity,* edited by Stephen Kalberg. Translated by Max Rheinstein and revised by Guenther Roth, Claus Wittich, and Stephen Kalberg (Oxford: Blackwell, 2005). [*Economy and Society,* pp. 695–96, 698–99]

In the past, special law arose normally as "volitive law" (*gewillkürtes Recht*), that is, from tradition, or as the agreed enactment of consensual groups (*Einverständnisgemeinschaften*), or rational associations. It arose, in other words, in the form of autonomously created orders. The maxim that "particularist law" (i.e., volitive law in the above sense) "breaks" (i.e., takes precedence over) the "law of the land" (i.e., the generally valid common law) was recognized almost universally, and it obtains even today in almost all legal systems outside the West, and in Europe, for example, to some extent for the Russian peasantry [before World War I].

The state insisted almost everywhere, and usually with success, that the validity of these special laws, as well as the extent of their application, should be subject to its consent; and the state did this in just the same manner in which it also transformed the towns and cities into heteronomous organizations endowed by it with powers it defined. In both cases, however, this was not the original state of affairs. For the body of laws by which a given locality or a group were governed was largely the autonomously arrogated creation of mutually independent groups or associated groups. The continuously necessitated adjustment between them was either achieved by mutual compromise or by imposition by those political or ecclesiastical authorities that happened at the given time to have preponderant power. . . .

Prior to the emergence and triumph of the purposive contract and of freedom of contract in the modern sense, and prior to the emergence of the modern state, every consensual group or rational association that represented a special legal order—and that therefore might properly be named a "law community" (*Rechtsgemeinschaft*)—was constituted in its membership on the one hand by such objective characteristics as birth, political affiliation, ethnicity or religious denomination, or on the other hand by mode of life or occupation. Finally, it could also arise through the process of explicit fraternization across groups of *persons*. The early situation . . . was that any "lawsuit" corresponding to our "trials" took place only in the form of reconciliation-proceedings between *different* groups (sibs) and their members. Within the group—that is, among the members of the group—patriarchal arbitration prevailed.

At the very origin of all legal history there thus prevailed, if viewed from the standpoint of the political power and its continuously growing strength, an important dualism; that is, a dualism of the autonomously created law between groups, and the norms determinative of disputes among group members. At the same time, however, another fact intruded into this apparently simple situation: namely, that the individual, even at the earliest stages of development known to us, often belonged to several groups rather than to just one.

But, nevertheless, the subjection to the special law was initially a strictly personal quality, a "privilege" acquired by usurpation or grant. Thus, it constituted a monopoly for its possessors, who, by virtue of this fact, became "comrades in law" (*Rechtsgenossen*). Hence, in those groups which were politically integrated by a common supreme authority, like the Persian empire, the Roman empire, the kingdom of the Franks, or the Islamic states, the body of laws to be applied to by the judicial officers differed in accordance with the ethnic, religious, or political characteristics of the component groups—for instance, legally or politically autonomous cities or clans. Even in the Roman empire, Roman law was at first the law for Roman citizens only, and it did not entirely apply in the relations between citizens and noncitizen subjects. The non-Moslem subjects of the Islamic states, and even the adherents of the four orthodox schools of Islamic law, live in accordance with their own laws. However, when the former resort to the Islamic judge rather than to their own authorities, he applies Islamic law, as he is not obliged to know any other. And, as in the Islamic state, the non-Moslems are mere "subjects.". . .

* * *

The ever-increasing integration of all persons and facts of the case into one compulsory institution—which today, at least, rests in principle on formal "legal equality"—has been achieved by two great rationalizing forces; that is, first, by the extension of the market economy and, second, by the bureaucratization of the activities of the organs of the consensual groups. They replaced that particularist mode of creating law which was based upon the private power of the granted privileges of monopolistically closed organizations; that means, they reduced the autonomy of what were essentially organized status groups in two ways: The first is the formal, universally accessible, but closely regulated autonomy of voluntary associations that may be created by anyone wishing to do so; the other consists in the grant to everyone of the power to create law of his own by means of engaging in private legal transactions of certain kinds.

The decisive factors in the transformation of the technical forms of autonomous legislation were, politically, the power-needs of the rulers and officials of the states as it was growing in strength and, economically, the interests of those segments of society that were oriented towards power in the market, i.e., those persons who were economically privileged in the formally "free" competitive struggle of the market by virtue of their position as property owners—an instance of "class position." If, by virtue of the principle of formal legal equality, everyone "without respect of person" may establish a business corporation or entail a landed estate, the *propertied* classes *as such* obtain a sort of factual "autonomy," since they alone are able to utilize or take advantage of these powers. . . .

From: Pp. 239–40 in *Max Weber: Readings and Commentary on Modernity*, edited by Stephen Kalberg. Translated by Stephen Kalberg (Oxford: Blackwell, 2005). [*Economy and Society*, pp. 903–04]

The modern position of political organizations rests on the prestige bestowed upon them by a specific belief held by their members in a special consecration, namely, in the "legitimacy" of that social action prescribed by these organizations. This prestige becomes greater wherever—and to the extent that—this social action involves physical coercion encompassing the power to dispose over life and death. A consensus regarding the actual legitimacy of this power to dispose over life and death is specific to political organizations.

This belief in the specific "legitimacy" of action oriented to a political organization can intensify—as is actually the case under modern circumstances—to the point where exclusively certain political groups (called "state") are viewed as ones, on the basis of their contracts with or permissions from some other groups, capable of "legitimately" exercising physical coercion. Accordingly, a system of casuistic statutes and rules, to which this specific "legitimacy" is imputed, exists in the fully developed political group for the purpose of exercising and threatening to exercise this coercion—namely, the "legal order." The political community, because it has in fact today normally usurped the monopoly forcefully to bestow—through physical coercion—respect for these statutes and rules, constitutes its single normal creator.

This guaranteeing of a "legal order" prominently by *political* force originated from a very long developmental process. Owing to pressures emanating from economic and organizational transformations, in this process other groups that appeared as carriers of their own coercive force lost their power over individuals. Either they disintegrated or became subjugated by action oriented to a political community. This resulted in a constriction of their coercive force or a managing of it. Yet, simultaneously, there developed constantly new interests that needed to be protected—yet found no politically guaranteed legal order to do so. A continuously expanding circle of interests, especially economic interests, would eventually find security only through those rationally ordered guarantees created by the political community. . . . In this process . . . all "legal norms" became—and are still becoming—the domain of states (*"Verstaatlichung"*).

From: Pp. 292–93 in *Wirtschaftsgeschichte*. Translated by Stephen Kalberg (Munich and Leipzig: Duncker & Humblot, 1923). [*General Economic History*, pp. 342–43]

The reception of Roman law was crucial only to the extent that it created *formal juristic thinking*. According to its structure every legal system is oriented either to formal-legalistic or substantive principles.

By substantive principles are to be understood utilitarian and justice considerations, such as, for example, those according to which the Islamic *kadi* practices his jurisprudence. While justice is oriented substantively in every theocracy and absolutist state, bureaucracies orient justice to formal-legalistic procedures. Frederick the Great [1712–1786] hated the jurists because they constantly applied his substantive decrees in a formalistic manner and hence transformed them into their own ends—results he disowned. In this connection (as in general) Roman law was the means of crushing substantive law in favor of a formal legal system.

However, this formal law is *calculable*. It occurred in [classical] China that the seller of a house, having fallen into poverty, would request lodging of the new owner. If the ancient Chinese command to provide assistance went unheeded, the spirits became disturbed—and hence the impoverished former owner was permitted a rent-free domicile. If laws were constituted in this fashion, capitalism could not function. Rather, it requires laws that can be depended upon with the same calculability as a machine. Ritualistic and magical considerations must be excluded.

The creation of law along these lines was achieved as a consequence of the coalition between the modern state and jurists for the purpose of achieving the state's claims to power. In the sixteenth century, the state had attempted for a period of time to ally itself with the Humanists. The first Greek *Gymnasien* [elite public schools] were founded on the belief that a [classical] education would qualify young men for careers as state officials—for political struggles were carried out to a great extent through the exchange of official documents, and hence only those in command of Latin and Greek could mediate the conflicts. This illusion proved short-lived, for it soon became apparent that the *Gymnasium*-educated were not on this basis capable of conducting politics. Recourse to jurists became then the final resort.

In China, where humanistically educated mandarins reigned, jurists remained unavailable to the monarch. The struggle among the different philosophical schools regarding the question of superior qualification for statecraft became resolved only with the triumph of orthodox Confucianism. Writers existed in India, but no trained jurists. Available in the West, on the other hand, was a formally organized system of law, the product of the Roman genius. Officials trained in this type of law were superior to all others as technical administrators. This situation is significant from the vantage point of economic history: the alliance between the state and formal jurisprudence indirectly favored capitalism.

From: P. 977 in *Economy and Society,* edited by Guenther Roth and Claus Wittich, translated by H. H. Gerth and C. Wright Mills and revised by Roth and Wittich; slightly revised by Stephen Kalberg (Berkeley: The University of California Press, 1978).

Reasons for the Differences in the Development of Substantive Law in Germany and England.

In Germany, primarily for political reasons, a socially powerful status group of notables was lacking. There was no status group which, like the English lawyers, could have been the carrier of the administration of a national law, and thereby could have raised national law to the level of a technology based on a standardized apprenticeship. Such a status group could have offered resistance to the intrusion of the technically superior training of the Roman-law jurists. It is not that Roman law was in its *substantive* provisions better adjusted to the needs of emerging capitalism; this did not decide its victory on the Continent. In fact, all legal institutions specific to modern capitalism are alien to Roman law and are medieval in origin.

Decisive was the rational *form* of Roman law and, above all, the technical necessity to place the trial procedure in the hands of rationally trained experts, which meant men trained in the universities in Roman law. This necessity arose from the increasing complexity of legal cases and the demands of an increasingly rationalized economy for a rational procedure to establish evidence to replace the ascertainment of the truth by concrete revelation or sacerdotal guarantee, which everywhere was the early means of proof. Of course, this situation was strongly influenced by structural changes in the economy. But this factor was efficacious everywhere, including England—where the royal power introduced the rational procedure for evidence primarily for the sake of the merchants.

The predominant reasons for the differences in the development of substantive law in England and Germany do not rest upon such economic differences. As is already obvious, these contrasts have sprung from the autonomous development of the respective structures of *domination*. In

England centralized justice and rule by notables; in Germany, absence of political centralization in spite of bureaucratization. Hence, England, which in modern times was the first and most highly developed capitalist country, thereby retained a less rational and less bureaucratic judicature. Capitalism in England, however, could quite easily come to terms with this because the nature of the court constitution and of the trial procedure up to the modern period amounted in effect to a far-going denial of justice to the economically weak groups. This fact, in association with the high time and money expenses of the system of real estate transfers—itself a function of the economic interests of the lawyer class—exerted a profound influence upon the agrarian structure of England in favor of the accumulation and immobilization of landed wealth.

VII

ETHOS AND EDUCATION UNDER FEUDALISM AND PATRIMONIALISM, CLERICAL EDUCATION, AND THE PURITANS' MASS INTELLECTUALISM

From: Pp. 1104–09 in *Economy and Society,* edited by Guenther Roth and Claus Wittich, translated by Roth and Wittich; revised by Stephen Kalberg (Berkeley: The University of California Press, 1978); endnotes omitted.

The structure of rulership affected the general habits of peoples more by virtue of the type of *frame of mind* it established than through the creation of [the] technical means of commerce. In this respect feudalism and patriarchal patrimonialism differ greatly. Both shaped strongly divergent political and social ideologies and, through them, a very different organization of life.

Especially in the form of free vassalage and of the fief system, feudalism appeals to "honor" and personal "fealty," freely assumed and maintained, as constitutive motives of action. . . . The combination of "honor" and "fealty" was only known. . . in Western feudalism and Japanese "vassalic" feudalism. Both have in common with Hellenic urban feudalism a special status socialization that aims at the inculcation of a *frame of mind* based on status "honor." However, in contrast to Hellenic feudalism they made the "vassal's fealty" the center of an outlook that perceives the most diverse social relationships—from Savior to the loved one — from this vantage point. The feudal association thus permeated the most important relationships with strictly personal bonds; their uniqueness also had the effect of centering the feeling of knightly dignity upon the cult of the personal. This contrasts violently with all impersonal and commercial relationships, which are bound to appear—and have always thus appeared—undignified and vulgar to the feudal ethic.

However, the antagonism toward commercial rationality also has a series of other roots. First, there is the specific military character of the feudal system, which eventually is transposed to the rulership structure. The typical feudal army is an army of knights, and this means that individual heroic combat, not the discipline of the large army, is decisive. The goal of military socialization is not, as in mass armies, drill for the sake of adaptation to an organized operation, but individual perfection in personal military skills. Therefore, one element finds a permanent place in training and the organization of life, which, as a form of developing qualities useful for life, belongs to the original energy of persons and animals, but is increasingly eliminated by every rationalization of life— the *game*. In feudal society it is just as little a "pastime" as in organic life; rather, it is the natural form in which the psycho-physical capacities of the organism are kept alive and supple. The game is a form of "training" which, in its spontaneous and unbroken animal instinctiveness, transcends any split between the "spiritual" and the "material," "body" and "soul"—even where it is sublimated through conventions.

Only once in the course of history did the game find a specifically artistic perfection, imbued with a natural spontaneity: in the feudal or semi-feudal Hellenic society of warriors as they appeared first in Sparta. The aristocratic status conventions among Western feudal knights and Japanese vassals, with their stricter sense for social distance and dignity, imposed a greater limitation on this kind of spontaneous freedom than existed under the (relative) democracy of the [ancient] citizenry of *hoplites* [soldiers]. But unavoidably the game also occupies a most serious and important position in the life of these knightly strata; it stands in the way, as its counterpole, of all economically rational action. However, this kinship with the artistic organization of life, which resulted from this aspect of the game, was maintained also directly by the "aristocratic" frame of mind of the dominant feudal stratum. The need for "ostentation," glamour and imposing splendor, for surrounding one's life with products which are not justified by utility but, in Oscar Wilde's sense, by their uselessness and hence their "beauty," is primarily a feudal status need and an important power instrument for the sake of maintaining one's own dominance through mass suggestion. "Luxury" in the sense of rejecting a purposive-rational orientation to consumption is for the dominant feudal strata nothing superfluous: it is a means of social self-assertion.

Finally, positively privileged feudal strata do not view their existence functionally, as a means for serving a "mission"; that is, as an "idea" that should be realized purposively. Their typical myth is the value of their "existence." Only the knightly fighter for the true faith has a different orientation, and wherever he was permanently dominant, most prominently in Islam, the free artistic game had only a limited importance.

At any rate, feudalism is inherently contemptuous of bourgeois-commercial utilitarianism and considers it as sordid greediness and as the life force specifically hostile to it. The feudal organization of life leads to the opposite of the rational economic frame of mind and is the source of that nonchalance in business affairs which has been typical of all feudal strata, not only in contrast to the middle class, but also to the peasants' proverbial "shrewdness." This solidarity of feudal society is based on a common socialization that inculcates knightly conventions, pride of status, and a sense of "honor." This socialization is opposed to the charismatic magic asceticism of prophets and heroes through its this-worldly orientation, to literary education through its warrior-heroic frame of mind, and to rational specialized training through its playful and artistic features. . . .

Typical of patrimonialism is the determined rise from rags, slavery, and lowly service to the ruler, to the precarious all-powerful position of the favorite. In the interest of his domination, the patrimonial ruler must oppose the status independence of the feudal aristocracy and the economic independence of the bourgeoisie. Ultimately, every autonomous dignity and any sense of honor on the part of the "subjects" must be suspected simply as hostile to authority. . . .

The only specific socialization system of patriarchal patrimonialism is administrative training, which alone provides the basis for a stratum that, in its most consistent form, constitutes an educated status group of the well-known Chinese type. However, education may also remain in the hands of the clergy as possessors of the skills useful for patrimonial administration, which needs accounting and clerical work unknown to feudalism. This happened in the Near East and in the Western Middle Ages. In this case education has a specifically literary character. Or eduction may involve a secular professional training in law, as in the medieval universities. Even in this case, however, it retains a literary orientation, and leads with increasing rationalization to specialization and to the ideal of a "vocation" typical of the modern bureaucracy.

Patrimonial education always lacks the features of playfulness and elective affinity to art, of heroic asceticism and hero worship, of heroic honor and heroic hostility to the impersonal utilitarianism and the enterprise—features which feudalism inculcates and preserves. Indeed, the [patrimonial] administrative "organization" (amtliche Betrieb) is an impersonal "business" (sachliches Geschäft): the official bases his honor not upon his "being," but on his "functions"; he expects advantages and promotion from his "services." The idleness, the games and the commercial nonchalance of the knight must appear to him as slothfulness and lack of efficiency. The status ethos adequate to the patrimonial official turns here into the tracks of the middle class business ethos. Even the philosophy of the ancient Egyptian officials, as we know it from exhortations by scribes and officials to their sons, has a distinctly utilitarian-bourgeois character. In principle, nothing has changed since, apart from the increasing rationalization and professional specialization in the development from patrimonial officialdom to modern "bureaucracy."

The main difference between the utilitarianism of the [patrimonial] officials and the specifically [modern] "middle class" ethos has always been the former's abhorrence of the acquisitive drive, which is natural for a person who draws a fixed salary or takes fixed fees, who is ideally incorruptible, and whose performance finds its dignity precisely in the fact that it is not a source of commercial enrichment. To that extent the "spirit" of patrimonial administration, interested as it is in public peace, the preservation of a traditional means of livelihood, and the satisfaction of subjects, is alien to and distrustful of capitalist development—which revolutionizes the given social conditions. This was true . . . most of all of the Confucian ethos and, to a moderate degree, everywhere, especially since resentment against the emergent autonomous economic powers became an additional factor.

Hence, it is no accident that specifically modern capitalism developed first in England where the rule of officials was minimized, just as under similar conditions ancient capitalism had reached its high point. This kind of resentment and the traditional position of the bureaucracy toward rational economic profit, which arose out of its orientation to status, eventually became the motives on which modern welfare state policies could rely—and which facilitated them, especially in the bureaucratic states [of Europe]. However, these motives also determined the limitations and the uniqueness of these policies.

From: Pp. 633–34 in *Wirtschaft und Gesellschaft: Herrschaft* (MWG I/22–24), edited by Edith Hanke. Translated by Stephen Kalberg (Tübingen: Mohr/Siebeck, 2005). [*Economy and Society*, p. 1145]

Clerical Education.   An example for the far-reaching "clericalization" of education is provided by the control of the Egyptian priests over the training of officials and scribes in this typically bureaucratic state. In numerous other cases in the Middle East, too, the priesthood controlled the training of officials, and — because it alone developed a rational educational system and provided the state with scribes and officials trained in rational thinking — education in general.

In the Western Middle Ages the education offered by the church and the monasteries, as the agents of every kind of rational instruction, was also of great importance. However, clerical-rational and knightly education co-existed, competed, and cooperated with one another in the West owing to the feudal and status character of the ruling stratum. They imparted to Western medieval man and the Western universities their specific character. In contrast, there was no counterweight to the clericalization of education in the purely bureaucratic Egyptian state. And, since they lacked the requisite Western contract-feudalism foundation [see pp. 394–95], the other patrimonial states of the East also failed to develop a specifically knightly education. Finally, completely depoliticized Jews, whose cohesion depended upon the synagogue and the rabbinate, developed in the West a major type of strictly clerical education.

Absent in the Hellenic polis and in Rome was not only a state bureaucracy, but also a priestly bureaucracy, one that might have created a clerical educational system. It was only in part a fateful historical accident that Homer, the literary product of a secular aristocracy highly lacking in respect for the gods — hence Plato's deep hatred against him — remained unchallenged as the major vehicle of the literary education and stood against any theological rationalization of the religious powers. Decisive was the complete absence of a clerical system of education.

In China, finally, the uniqueness of Confucian rationalism — its orientation to convention and its reception as the basis for education — was conditioned by the bureaucratic rationalization of the secular patrimonial officialdom and the absence of feudal powers.

From: Pp. 533–34 in *Wirtschaft und Gesellschaft Religiöse Gemeinschaften* (MWGI/22-2), edited by Hans G. Kippenberg. Translation by Stephen Kalberg (Tübingen: Mohr/Siebeck, 2005). [*Economy and Society*, pp. 513–15]

The Puritans' Mass Intellectualism.   A deciphering of the relationships between religion and intellectualism in medieval Christianity cannot be examined here. This religion, at any rate, was not oriented to intellectuals, at least to any sociologically relevant degree. Moreover, the strong effect of monastic rationalism existed at the level of general civilizational influences; it can be clearly isolated only through a comparison of Western and Asian monasticism. . . . [This is an important task because] the distinctive cultural influence of the church in the West located its foundation primarily in the particularity of its monasticism.

A lay religious intellectualism of a petit-bourgeois character, or of a paria intellectualism, was not known (to a relevant degree) in the Western medieval period; ocasionally it appeared among the sects. [On the other hand], the role of the highly educated strata in the development of the church is not a small one. Its influence in the Carolingian, Ottonic, and Salic-Staufen epoch [751–1258] approximated that of an imperial-theocratic cultural organization, as was the case in regard to the [strictly orthodox] Josephite monks in sixteenth-century Russia. The Gregorian Reform Movement [to strengthen Canon law and erect the independence of the papacy vis-à-vis secular authority], above all, and the power struggle on the part of the papacy, found their social carriers in an elite intellectual stratum and its ideology.

This stratum formed a common front against the feudal powers. The papacy, with the increasing expansion of university education, struggled to monopolize, on behalf of fiscal or simply patronage goals, the enormous number of beneficiaries. Economic support for this educated stratum was provided by benefices. An ever-growing group, these "beneficiaries" then turned against the papacy in what was at first an essentially economic and nationalistic interest in monopoly. Then, following the [so-called Western] Schism [1378–1417], these intellectuals opposed the papacy, also ideologically; they became the "carriers" of the conciliary reform movement, [which placed the ecumenical council above the pope], and later of Humanism. . . .

Especially in England, the Humanists demonstrated an intellectual scepticism and a rationalistic Enlightenment. There appeared as well a tender religious temper or, as in the [French] Port Royal [1635–1709] circles [of Jansenists], a frequently asceticism-based moralism.[1] In the earlier period in Germany, and also in Italy, they displayed an individualizing mysticism.

Yet these Humanist groupings were not up to the task of confronting the interest-based struggles rooted in existence and survival over political power and the economy—all of which, if not outright violent, were waged

---

1.   Cornelius Otto Jansen (1585–1638), a Dutch and French theologian, founded Jansenism. This movement inside the Catholic church in Holland and France opposed the Jesuits. It advocated a great moral rigorism and a return to the teachings of St. Augustine's ancient Christianity, especially its indifference to the world. Jansenists were persecuted in eighteenth-century France by the church as unorthodox [sk].

with demagogic means in an accepted way. Certainly at the very least classically educated theologian polemicists, and a similarly educated stratum of ministers, were needed by those churches that wished to place the ruling groupings and, above all, the universities, at their service. Inside Lutheranism, in keeping with its coalition with the nobility's power, this juxtaposition of religious activism and the educated stratum quickly led to a withdrawal, mainly into the theological seminaries.

Samuel Butler's [1612–1680] satirical poem, *Hudibras* [1663–78], still mocked the Puritans for their ostensible philosophical erudition. However, it was not the intellectualism of the elite stratum that endowed the Puritans, and above all the Baptist sects, with their indestructible power of resistance. Rather, decisive was the intellectualism of the plebeian and occasionally even the pariah classes—for Baptist Protestantism was in its first period a movement carried by wandering craftsmen or apostles. An intellectual stratum with clear boundaries, demarcated by conditions of life entirely its own, never existed among these Protestants. Instead, after the end of a short period of missionizing by wandering preachers, a middle class became saturated with intellectualism.

An unparalleled expansion of knowledge of the Bible and an interest in extremely abstruse and sublime controversies over dogma was characteristic in these seventeenth century Puritan circles. Indeed, these debates extended even deeply into the peasantry. This religious mass intellectualism would never again find its equal. Looking backward it can be compared only to late Judaism and the mass intellectualism of the Pauline missionary communities. In England, as opposed to Holland, parts of Scotland, and the American colonies, it soon became weakened after the [seventeenth-century] religious wars and after the spheres of power — and chances to acquire power — had been tested and appeared firm.

Nevertheless, it is from this period that the entire uniqueness of Anglo-Saxon elite intellectualism acquired its imprint: namely, its traditional orientation to and respect for a Deistic-rooted and Enlightenment-based religiosity. Although of varying degrees of mildness, it never developed to the point of anticlericalism (a theme we cannot pursue now). This Anglo-Saxon religiosity has been determined by the traditional position, and the moralistic interests, of a politically powerful middle class—and hence by a religious plebeian intellectualism [see 1968, pp. 507–8]. For this reason it offers the sharpest contrast to the development of the basically court-centered and elite education of the Latin countries, which stood in radical antipathy toward, or absolute indifference to, the church.

VIII

THE SECT, DEMOCRACY, TOLERANCE, FREEDOM OF CONSCIENCE, AND A COSMOS OF ABSTRACT NORMS

Pp. 1207–10 in *Economy and Society,* edited by Guenther Roth and Claus Wittich, translated by Roth and Wittich; revised by Stephen Kalberg (Berkeley: The University of California Press, 1978).

By virtue of the dictum that "We must obey God rather than men" [Acts 5:29], [the Church] hierocracy claimed an autonomous charisma and law of its own, found obedience, and firmly restrained the political power. On the basis of its *office* charisma, hierocracy protects those over whom it claims rulership against encroachment from other authorities, whether the interfering person be the political ruler, the husband, or the father. Since both the fully developed political [the state] and hierocratic powers raise universalist demands—that is, since each makes a claim to establish dominance over persons—their adequate relationship is a compromise and alliance on behalf of joint rulership, one in which their spheres of influence are mutually delimited. The axiom "separation of church and state" is feasible only if either of the two powers has in fact renounced its claim to dominate completely those areas of life that are in principle available to it.

In contrast to hierocracy, the *sect* opposes the charisma of office. The individual can exercise hierocratic powers only by virtue of his personal charisma, just as he can become a member only by virtue of a publicly established qualification, the most unambiguous symbol of which is the "rebaptism" of the Baptists—in reality, the baptizing of qualified adults. The services of the Quakers are a silent waiting in order to see whether the Divine spirit will come to a member on this day. Only he will speak up to preach or pray. It is already a concession to the need for regulation and order if those who have proven their qualification to preach the Word of God are put on special seats and are now compelled to help along the coming of the spirit by preparing sermons; this is done in most Quaker congregations. However, in contrast to all consistent "churches," all rigorous sects adhere to the principle of "lay preaching" and of "every member's priesthood." They do so even if they establish regular offices for economic and pedagogic reasons.

Wherever the "sects" character has been maintained in pure form, the congregation insists upon "direct democratic administration" and upon treating clerical officials as "servants" of the congregation. The internal elective affinity between the sect and the structure of democracy is already apparent in these structural principles of the sect. They also account for its unusual and highly important relationship to the political power. The sect is a specifically antipolitical, or at least apolitical, power. Since it must not raise universal demands and endeavors to exist as a voluntary association of qualified believers, it cannot enter into an alliance with the political power. If it concludes such an alliance, as did the Independents in New England, the result is an aristocratic political rule by the ecclesiastically qualified; this leads to compromises and to the loss of the particular sect character—witness the so-called Halfway Covenant [of the Congregational churches in 1662]. The greatest experiment of this kind was the abortive rule by Cromwell's Parliament of Saints.

The pure sect must stand for "tolerance" and "separation of church and state" for several reasons: because it is in fact *not* a universalist redemptory institution for the repression of sin and can scarcely withstand political—as little as hierocratic—control and reglementation; because no official power can dispense grace to unqualified persons and, hence, all use of political force in religious matters must appear senseless or outright diabolical; because the sect is simply not concerned with non-members; because, taking all this together, the sect just cannot be anything but an absolutely voluntary association if it wants to retain its innermost religious meaning and effectiveness. Therefore, the most consistent sects have always taken this position and have been the most genuine social carriers of the demand for "freedom of conscience."

Other groups, too, have favored freedom of conscience, but in a different sense [see pp. 510–511]. It is possible to speak of this freedom and of tolerance under the caesaropapist regimes of Rome, China, India, and Japan, since the most diverse cults of subjected or conjoined states were permitted and since no religious compulsion existed; however, in principle this freedom of conscience and tolerance is limited by the official state-cult of the political power, the cult of the emperor in Rome, the religious veneration of the emperor in Japan, and probably the emperor's cult of Heaven in China. Moreover, this tolerance had political—not religious—reasons, as did that of King William the Silent [1533–1584], Emperor Frederick II [1194–1250], or those manorial lords who used sect members as skilled labor, and the city of Amsterdam—where the sectarians were major social carriers of commercial life. Thus, economic motives here were decisive. But the genuine sect must demand the nonintervention of the political power and "freedom of conscience" for specifically religious reasons— the many transitional forms we will leave here aside intentionally.

A fully developed salvation institution—that is, one with universalist claims (a "church")—on the other hand, according to the particular faith, can concede "freedom of conscience" all the less. It claims to do so whenever it finds itself in a minority position—thereby demanding something for itself without, in principle, being able to grant it to others. "The Catholic's freedom of Conscience," as [Hermann] Mallinckrodt[1] stated in the Reichstag, "consists in being given the right to obey the pope." In other words, to act for himself in accord with *his own* conscience.

---

1.   1821–1874; founder of the Catholic Center Party and member of the Reichstag, 1866–71 [sk].

However, if they are strong enough, neither the Catholic nor the (old) Lutheran Church and, all the less so, the Calvinist and Baptist churches, recognize the freedom of conscience of *others*. These churches cannot act differently in view of their institutional commitment to safeguard the salvation of the soul or, in the case of Calvinists, to protect the glory of God.

By contrast, the consistent Quaker applies the principle of the freedom of conscience not only to himself but also to others, and rejects any attempt to compel those who are not Quakers or Baptists to act as if they belonged to his group [see above, p. 511]. Thus, the consistent sect gives rise to an inalienable and recognized "right" of the ruled—and, indeed, of every single ruled person—as against political, hierocratic, patriarchal, or any other type of power. Regardless of whether, as [Georg] Jellinek [see 1979] has argued probably convincingly, the "freedom of conscience" in this sense is the oldest "human right," surely it constitutes the most basic human right—because it encompasses the most far-reaching, indeed the entirety of, ethically conditioned action and freedom from coercion, especially from the state. In this form freedom of conscience was as unknown in Antiquity and the Middle Ages as it was, for example, in Rousseau's social contract theory, which endorsed the state's power to coerce religious belief.

The other "human," "civil," or "basic" rights were appended onto the freedom of conscience—above all the right to follow one's own economic interests. This latter right especially includes the right to pursue one's own economic interests, which includes the inviolability of individual property, the freedom of contract, and vocational choice. These economic rights exist within the limits of a system of guaranteed abstract laws that apply to everybody alike. All of these rights find their ultimate justification in the belief of the Age of Enlightenment in the workings of individual "reason": if left unimpeded, it would result in the at least relatively best of all worlds. This would occur owing to Divine providence and because the individual is best qualified to know his own interests. This charismatic glorification of "Reason" (which found its characteristic expression in its apotheosis with Robespierre) is the very last form charisma adopted in its fateful historical course.

It is also clear that these claims of formal legal equality and economic mobility paved the way for the destruction of all particular foundations of patrimonial and feudal legal orders in favor of a cosmos of abstract norms—and hence indirectly of bureaucratization. It is further clear that these claims facilitated in a very specific way the expansion of capitalism. The preconditions for capitalism to use, without hindrances, products and people were offered by the notions of human rights and basic rights, just as "this-worldly asceticism" (which the sects adopted, albeit for motives not entirely the same) and the type of discipline within the sects gave birth to the capitalist frame of mind and the rationally-acting "vocational man" needed by capitalism. The basic Rights of Man made it possible for the capitalist to use things and people freely, just as this-worldly ascetism—adopted with some dogmatic variations—and the specific discipline of the sects bred the capitalist spirit and the rational "professional" (*Berufsmensch*) who was needed by capitalism.

BUREAUCRATIZATION, DEMOCRACY, AND MODERN CAPITALISM

From: Pp. 211–12 in *Max Weber: Readings and Commentary on Modernity,* edited by Stephen Kalberg. Translated by Talcott Parsons; revised by Guenther Roth and Claus Wittich; slightly revised by Stephen Kalberg. (Oxford: Blackwell, 2005) [*Economy and Society,* pp. 223–24]

The Expansion of Bureaucracy into All Fields.   The development of modern forms of organization in *all* fields is nothing less than identical with the development and continual spread of bureaucratic administration. This is true of church and state, of armies, political parties, economic enterprises, interest groups, foundations, clubs, and many other organizations. The bureaucracy's development is, to take the most striking case, at the root of the modern Western state.

However many forms there may be which do not appear to fit this pattern, such as collegial representative bodies, parliamentary committees, soviets, honorary officers, lay judges, and what not, and however many people may complain about the "red tape," it would be sheer illusion to think for a moment that continuous administrative work can be carried out in any field except by means of officials working in offices. The whole pattern of everyday life is cut to fit this framework. If bureaucratic administration is, other things being equal, always the most [formal] rational type from a technical point of view, the needs of mass administration make it today completely indispensable. The choice in the field of administration is only that between bureaucratization or increasing dilettantism.

Those subject to bureaucratic control who seek to escape the influence of the existing bureaucratic apparatus find it normally possible to do so only by creating an organization of their own—yet this organization is equally subject to bureaucratization. Similarly the existing bureaucratic apparatus is driven to continue functioning by the most powerful interests, which are material and objective, but also ideal in character. Without it, a society like our own—with its separation of officials, employees, and workers from ownership of the means of administration, and its dependence on discipline and on technical training—could no longer function. The only exception would be those groups, such as the peasantry, still in possession of their own means of subsistence. Even in the case of revolution by force or of occupation by an enemy, the bureaucratic machinery will normally continue to function just as it has for the previous legal government.

From: "Einleitung." Pp. 124–25 in *Die Wirtschaftethik der Weltreligionen: Konfuzianismus und Taoismus (MWG* I/19), edited by Helwig Schmidt-Glintzer. Translated by Stephen Kalberg (Tübingen: Mohr/Siebeck, 1996).

Legal Rulership and Bureaucratic Rule.   With the triumph of *formalist* juristic rationalism, the *legal* type of rulership (*Herrschaft*) appeared in the West at the side of the long-surviving types of rulership [charismatic and traditional]. *Bureaucratic* rule was not and is not the only variety of legal rulership, but it is the purest. The modern state and municipal official, the modern Catholic priest and chaplain, and the officials and employees of modern banks and of large capitalist enterprises represent . . . the most important types of this structure of rulership.

The following characteristic must be considered decisive for our terminology: in legal rulership, submission does not rest upon the belief and devotion to charismatically gifted *persons*, such as prophets and heroes. Nor does it rest upon sacred tradition, or upon piety toward a *personal* lord and master who is defined by internally coherent traditions, or upon piety toward the possible incumbents of office fiefs and office prebends who are legitimized in their *own* right through privilege and conferment.

Rather, submission under legal authority is based upon an *im*personal bond to the generally designated functions that accompany a "duty of office." The official duty — like the corresponding right to exercise authority; that is, the "jurisdictional competence" — is firm and determined by *rationally established* norms (laws, decrees, and regulations). This occurs in such a way that the legitimacy of the rulership becomes the legality of the general *rule*, which is purposefully thought through, enacted, and announced in a formally correct manner.

From: Pp. 957–58 in *Economy and Society,* edited by Guenther Roth and Claus Wittich, translated by Roth and Wittich (Berkeley: The University of California Press, 1978).

The Bureaucracy's External Form.   The management of the modern office is based upon written documents (the "files"), which are preserved in their original or draft form, and upon a staff of subaltern officials and scribes of all sorts. The body of officials working in an agency, along with the respective apparatus of material implements and the files, makes up a *bureau* (in private enterprises often called the "counting house," or *Kontor*).

In principle, the modern organization of the civil service separates the bureau from the private domicile of the official and, in general, segregates official activity from the sphere of private life. Public monies and equipment are divorced from the private property of the official. This condition is everywhere the product of a long development. Nowadays, it is found in public as well as in private enterprises; in the latter, the principle extends even to the entrepreneur at the top. In principle, the *Kontor* (office) is separated from the household, business from private correspondence, and business assets from private wealth. The more consistently the modern type of business management has been carried through, the more are these separations the case. The beginnings of this process are to be found as early as the Middle Ages. . . .

Office management, at least all specialized office management—and such management is distinctly modern—usually presupposes thorough training in a field of specialization. This, too, holds increasingly for the modern executive and employee of a private enterprise, just as it does for state officials.

When the office is fully developed, official activity demands the *full working capacity* of the official, irrespective of the fact that the length of his obligatory working hours in the bureau may be limited. In the normal case, this too is only the product of a long development, in the public as well as in the private office. Formerly the normal state of affairs was the reverse: Official business was discharged as a secondary activity.

The management of the office follows *general rules,* which are more or less stable, more or less exhaustive, and which can be learned. Knowledge of these rules represents a special technical expertise which the officials possess. It involves jurisprudence and administrative or business management.

The reduction of modern office management to rules is deeply embedded in its very nature. The theory of modern public administration, for instance, assumes that the authority to order certain matters by decree—which has been legally granted to an agency—does not entitle the agency to regulate the matter by individual commands given for each case, but only to regulate the matter abstractly. This stands in extreme contrast to the regulation of all relationships through individual privileges and bestowals of favor, which . . . is absolutely dominant in patrimonialism, at least in so far as such relationships are not fixed by sacred tradition. . . .

From: P. 998 in *Economy and Society.* Translated by H. H. Gerth and C. Wright Mills; revised by Guenther Roth and Claus Wittich; slightly revised by Stephen Kalberg (Berkeley: The University of California Press, 1978).

The Separation of the Public and Private Spheres. Only with the bureaucratization of the state and of law in general can one see a definite possibility of a sharp conceptual separation of an "objective" legal order from the "subjective" rights of the individual which it guarantees, as well as that of the further distinction between "public" which, which regulates the relationships of the public agencies among each other and with the subjects, and "private" law which regulates the relationships of the governed individuals among themselves. These distinctions presuppose the conceptual separation of the "state," as an abstract bearer of sovereign prerogatives and the creator of legal norms, from all personal authority of individuals.

These conceptual distinctions are necessarily remote from the nature of *pre*-bureaucratic, especially from patrimonial and feudal, structures of rulership. They were first conceived and realized in urban communities; for as soon as their officeholders were appointed through periodic *elections,* the individual power-holder, even if he was in the highest position, was obviously no longer identical with the person who possessed authority "in his own right" [charismatic rulership]. Yet it was left to the complete depersonalization of administrative management by bureaucracy and the rational systematization of law to realize the separation of the public and the private sphere fully and in principle.

From: Pp. 201–02 in Max Weber: *Readings and Commentary on Modernity*, edited by Stephen Kalberg. Translated by H. H. Gerth and C. Wright Mills; revised by Guenther Roth and Claus Wittich; slightly revised by Stephen Kalberg. (Oxford: Blackwell, 2005). [*Economy and Society*, pp. 958–59]

The Ethos of Office. That the office is a "vocation" (*Beruf*) finds expression, first, in the requirement of a prescribed course of training, which demands the entire working capacity for a long period of time, and in generally prescribed special examinations as prerequisites of employment. Furthermore, it finds expression in that the position of the offical is in the nature of a "duty" (*Pflicht*). This determines the character of his relations in the following manner: Legally and actually, office holding is not considered ownership of a source of income, to be exploited for rents or emoluments in exchange for the rendering of certain services, as was normally the case during the Middle Ages and frequently up to the threshold of recent times; nor is office holding considered a common exchange of services, as in the case of free employment contracts. Rather, entrance into an office, including one in the private economy, is considered an acceptance of a specific duty of fealty to the purpose of the office (*Amtstreue*) in return for the grant of a secure existence. It is decisive for the modern loyalty to an office that, in the pure type, it does not establish a relationship to a *person*, like the vassal's or disciple's faith under feudal or patrimonial authority, but rather is devoted to *impersonal* and *functional* purposes. These purposes, of course, frequently gain an ideological halo from cultural values, such as state, church, community, party or enterprise, which appear as surrogates for a this-worldly personal ruler and which are embodied by a given group.

From: Pp. 198–200 in *Max Weber: Readings and Commentary on Modernity*, edited by Stephen Kalberg. Translated by H. H. Gerth and C. Wright Mills; revised by Guenther Roth and Claus Wittich; slightly revised by Stephen Kalberg. (Oxford: Blackwell, 2005). [*Economy and Society*, pp. 973–75]

The Technical Superiority of Bureaucratic Organization Over Administration by Notables. The decisive reason for the advance of bureaucratic organization has always been its purely *technical* superiority over any other form of organization. The fully developed bureaucratic apparatus compares with other organizations exactly as does the machine with non-mechanical modes of production. Precision, speed, unambiguity, knowledge of the files, continuity, discretion, unity, strict subordination, reduction of friction and of material and personal costs—these are raised to the optimum point in the strictly bureaucratic administration, and especially in its monocratic form. As compared with all collegiate, honorific, and avocational forms of administration, trained bureaucracy is superior on all these points. And as far as complicated tasks are concerned, paid bureaucratic work is not only more precise but, in the last analysis, it is often cheaper than even formally unremunerated honorific service.

Honorific arrangements make administrative work a subsidiary activity: an avocation and, for this reason alone, honorific service normally functions more slowly. Being less bound to schemata and more formless, it is less precise and less unified than bureaucratic administration—also because it is less dependent upon superiors. Because [under honorific arrangements] the establishment and exploitation of the apparatus of subordinate officials and clerical services are almost unavoidably less economical, honorific service is less continuous than bureaucratic administration and frequently quite expensive. This is especially the case if one thinks not only of the money costs to the public treasury—costs which bureaucratic administration, in comparison with administration by notables, usually increases—but also of the frequent economic losses of the governed caused by delays and lack of precision. Permanent honorific administration by notables is normally feasible only where official business can be satisfactorily transacted as an avocation.

With the qualitative increase of tasks the administration has to face, administration by notables reaches its limits—today even in England. Work organized by collegiate bodies, on the other hand, causes friction and delay and requires compromises between colliding interests and views. The administration, therefore, runs less precisely and is more independent of superiors; hence, it is less unified and slower. All advances of the Prussian administrative organization, for example, have been, and will in the future, be advances of the bureaucratic, and especially of the monocratic, principle.

Today, it is primarily the capitalist market economy which demands that the official business of public administration be discharged precisely, unambiguously, continuously, and with as much speed as possible. Normally, the very large modern capitalist enterprises are themselves unequalled models of strict bureaucratic organization. Business management throughout rests on increasing precision, steadiness, and, above all, speed of operations. This, in turn, is determined by the particular nature of the modern means of communication, including, among other things, the news service of the press. The extraordinary increase in the speed by which public announcements, as well as economic and political facts, are transmitted exerts a steady and sharp pressure in the direction of *speeding up the tempo of administrative reaction* towards various situations. The optimum of such reaction time is normally attained only by a strictly bureaucratic organization. (The fact that the bureaucratic apparatus also can, and indeed does, create certain definite impediments for the discharge of business in a manner best adapted to the individuality of each case does not belong in the present context.)

Bureaucratization offers above all the optimum possibility for carrying through the principle of specializing administrative functions according to purely objective considerations. Individual performances are allocated to functionaries who have specialized training and who, by constant practice, increase their expertise. "Objective" discharge of business primarily means a discharge of business according to *calculable rules* and "without regard for persons" [*sine ira as studio*].

"Without regard for persons," however, is also the watchword of the market and, in general, of all pursuits of naked economic interests. Consistent bureaucratic domination means the leveling of status "honor." Hence, if the principle of the free market is not at the same time restricted, it means the universal domination of the "class situation." That this consequence of bureaucratic domination has not set in everywhere proportional to the extent of bureaucratization is due to the differences between possible principles by which polities may supply their requirements.

However, the second element mentioned, calculable rules, is the most important one for modern bureaucracy. The uniqueness of modern culture, and specifically of its technical and economic basis, demands this very "calculability" of results. When fully developed, bureaucracy also stands, in a specific sense, under the principle of *sine ira as studio*. Bureaucracy develops the more perfectly the more it is "dehumanized" and the more completely it succeeds in eliminating from official business love, hatred, and all purely personal, irrational, and emotional elements which escape calculation. This is appraised as a special virtue by capitalism.

The more complicated and specialized modern culture becomes, the more its external supporting apparatus demands of the personally detached and strictly objective *expert*, in lieu of the lord of older orders who was moved by personal sympathy and favor, by grace and gratitude. The bureaucracy offers the structure demanded by the external apparatus of modern culture in the most favorable combination. In particular, only bureaucracy has established the foundation for the administration of a rational *law* conceptually systematized on the basis of "statutes," such as the later Roman Empire first created with a high degree of technical perfection. During the Middle Ages, the reception of this [Roman] law coincided with the bureaucratization of legal administration: The advance of the rationally trained expert displaced the old trial procedure, which was bound to tradition or to irrational presuppositions. . . .

From: Pp. 481–82 in *Wirtschaft und Gesellschaft: Herrschaft* (*MWG* I/22-24), edited by Edith Hanke. Translated by Stephen Kalberg (Tübingen: Mohr/Siebeck: 2005). [*Economy and Society*, pp. 1116–17]

Revolutionizing "From Without" and "From Within". . . . bureaucratic rationalization . . . can be a revolutionary power of the first magnitude in opposition to tradition—and it often has been. It revolutionizes, however, through *technical* means, as does in particular every transformation of the economy. Here, in principle, a metamorphosis "from without" takes place: conditions and life-spheres are first changed and then, from this point of origin, people. Thus, the bureaucracy brings about change in the sense that it dislocates the conditions of adaptation for people and eventually increases their opportunities to adapt, through a rational means-end procedure, to the external world.

In contrast, the power of charisma is based upon a belief in revelation and in heroes. It is rooted furthermore in an emotional conviction that charisma's manifestation — whether religious, ethical, artistic, scientific, political, or of whatever other type — is important and valuable. It rests upon heroism, whether expressed in the form of asceticism, warfare achievements, judiciary wisdom, magical grace, or however else. . . .

Rationalization proceeds in such a fashion that the broad masses of the led in the end accept or adapt themselves to the external, technical results of practical significance for their interests (as we "learn" the multiplication table and as too many jurists "learn" the techniques of law). Irrelevant to them is the substance of a creative person's ideas. This is meant when we say that rationalization and rationalized life-spheres revolutionize "from the outside." Charisma, conversely, if it has any specific effects at all, manifests its revolutionary power from within—from a central *metanoia* [change] of the frame of mind of the ruled. The bureaucratic sphere replaces merely the belief in the sanctity of norms, as given by tradition, by compliance with rationally enacted rules. This compliance is accompanied by the knowledge that these rules can be, if one has the necessary power, replaced by others. Hence, they are not "sacred."

In contrast, in its highest manifestations, charisma disrupts rules as well as traditions altogether and overturns directly all notions of sanctity. Instead of reverence for that which has always been, and is thus viewed as sacred, it enforces an inner subjugation to the unprecedented and absolutely unique—and therefore Divine. In this purely empirical and value-free sense charisma is indeed the specifically "creative," revolutionary power of history.

From: Pp. 209-11 in *Max Weber: Readings and Commentary on Modernity*, edited by Stephen Kalberg. Translated by H. H. Gerth and C. Wright Mills; revised by Guenther Roth, Claus Wittich, and Stephen Kalberg (Oxford: Blackwell, 2005). [*Economy and Society*, pp. 983-86]

Bureaucracy, Social Levelling, and Passive Democracy.

. . . Mass democracy, which makes a clean sweep of the feudal, patrimonial, and—at least in intent—the plutocratic privileges in administration, unavoidably has to put paid professional labor in place of the historically inherited "avocational" administration by notables. . . .

. . . The progress of bureaucratization within the state administration itself is a phenomenon paralleling the development of democracy, as is quite obvious in France, North America, and now in England. Of course, one must always remember the term "democratization" can be misleading. The *demos* itself, in the sense of a shapeless mass, never "administers" larger organizations; rather it is administered. What changes is only the way in which the executive leaders are selected and the measure of influence which the *demos*—or better, which social circles from its midst—are able to exert upon the content and the direction of administrative activities by means of "public opinion." "Democratization," in the sense here intended, does not necessarily mean an increasingly active share of the subjects in the rulership of the relevant social formation. This may be a result of democratization, but it is not necessarily the case.

We must expressly recall at this point that the political concept of democracy, deduced from the "equal rights" of the ruled, includes these further postulates: (1) prevention of the development of a closed "status group of officials" in the interest of accessibility to offices, and (2) minimization of the rulership of officialdom in the interest of expanding the sphere of influence of "public opinion" as far as practicable. Hence, wherever possible, political democracy strives to shorten the term of office through election and recall; it strives to do so by offering candidates without respect to expert and specialized certificates. Thereby democracy inevitably comes into conflict with the bureaucratic tendencies which have been produced by democracy's very fight against [feudal] notables.

The loose term "democratization" cannot be used here, in so far is it is understood to mean the minimization of civil servants' rulership in favor of the greatest possible "direct" rule of the *demos*—which in practice means the respective party leaders of the *demos*. The decisive aspect here—indeed it is rather exclusively so—is the leveling *of the ruled* in the face of the ruling and bureaucratically articulated group, which in its turn may occupy a quite autocratic position, both in fact and in form.

In Russia, the destruction of the position of the old seigneurial nobility through the regulation of the *mestnichestvo* (rank order) system and the consequent permeation of the old nobility by an office nobility [under Peter the Great] were characteristic transitional phenomena in the development of bureaucracy. In China, the estimation of rank and the qualification for office according to the number of examinations passed had similar significance, although with an—at least in theory—even more pronounced rigor. In France the Revolution and, more decisively, Bonapartism, have made the bureaucracy all-powerful.

In the Catholic church, first the feudal powers were eliminated and then all independent, local and intermediary powers. This was begun by Gregory VII [1073–85] and continued through the Council of Trent [1592] and the Vatican Council [1869–70], and it was completed by the edicts of Pius X [1903–14]. The transformation of these local powers into pure functionaries of the central authority was connected with the constant increase in the factual significance of the formally dependent *Kapläne* [auxiliary clergymen supervising lay organizations], a process which above all was grounded in the political party organization of Catholicism. Hence, this process meant an advance of bureaucracy and at the same time of "passive" democratization, as it were; that is, the leveling of the ruled. In the same way, the substitution of the bureaucratic army for the self-equipped army of notables is everywhere a process of "passive" democratization—in the sense in which this applies to every establishment of an absolute military monarchy in the place of a feudal state or of a republic of notables. . . .

From: Pp. 205–07 in *Max Weber: Readings and Commentary on Modernity,* edited by Stephen Kalberg. Translated by H. H. Gerth and C. Wright Mills; revised by Guenther Roth, Claus Wittich, and Stephen Kalberg. (Oxford: Blackwell, 2005). [*Economy and Society,* pp. 991–94]

Democracy and the Pure Power Interests of Bureaucracy . . . We must remember the fact, which we have encountered several times and which we shall have to discuss repeatedly, that "democracy" as such is opposed to the "rule" of bureaucracy, in spite and perhaps because of its unavoidable yet unintended promotion of bureaucratization. Under certain conditions, democracy creates palpable breaks in the bureaucratic pattern and impediments to bureaucratic organization. Hence, one must in every individual historical case analyze in which of the special directions bureaucratization has there developed.

For this reason, it must also remain an open question whether the *power* of bureaucracy is increasing in the modern states in which it is spreading. The fact that the bureaucratic organization is technically the most highly developed power *instrument* in the hands of its controller does not determine the weight that bureaucracy as such is capable or procuring for its own opinions in a particular social formation. The ever-increasing "indispensability" of the officialdom, swollen to the millions, is no more decisive on this point than is the economic dispensability of the proletarians for the strength of the social and political power position of that class (a view which some representatives of the proletarian movement hold). If "indispensability" were decisive, the equally "indispensable" slaves ought to have held this position of power in any economy where slave labor prevailed and, consequently, as freemen, as is the rule, shunned work as degrading.

Whether the power of bureaucracy as such increases cannot be decided *a priori* from such reasons. The drawing in of interest groups or other non-official experts, or the drawing in of lay representatives, the establishment of local, interlocal, or central parliamentary or other representative bodies, or of occupational associations—these *seem* to run directly against the bureaucratic tendency. How far this appearance is the truth must be discussed in another chapter. . . . In general, only the following can be said here:

The power position of a fully developed bureaucracy is always great, under normal conditions overpowering. The political "ruler" always finds himself, vis-à-vis the trained official, in the position of a dilettante facing the expert. This holds whether the "ruler," whom the bureaucracy serves, is the "people" equipped with the weapons of legislative initiative, referendum, and the right to remove officials; or a parliament elected on a more aristocratic or more democratic basis and equipped with the right or the *de facto* power to vote a lack of confidence; or an aristocratic collegiate body, legally or actually based on self-recruitment; or a popularly elected president or an "absolute" or "constitutional" hereditary monarch. . . .

Every bureaucracy seeks further to increase this superiority of the professional insider through the means of *keeping secret* its knowledge and intentions. Bureaucratic administration always tends to exclude the public and to hide its knowledge and action from criticism well as it can. Prussian church authorities now [1912] threaten to use disciplinary measures against pastors who make reprimands or undertake other regulatory measures accessible in any way to third parties, charging that in doing so the pastors become "guilty" of facilitating a possible criticism of the church authorities. The treasury officials of the Persian Shah have made a secret science of their budgetary art and even use secret script. The official statistics of Prussia, in general, make public only what cannot do any harm to the intentions of the power-wielding bureaucracy. This tendency toward secrecy is in certain administrative fields a consequence of objective nature: namely, wherever power interests of the given structure of rulership *toward the outside* are at stake, whether this be the case of economic competitors of a private enterprise or that of potentially hostile foreign groupings.

If it is to be successful, management of diplomacy can be publicly supervised only to a very limited extent. The military administration must insist on the concealment of its most important measures to the extent the significance of purely technical aspects increases. Political parties do not proceed differently. . . .

However, the pure power interests of the bureaucracy exert their efforts far beyond these areas of purely functionally motivated secrecy. The concept of the "office secret" is the specific invention of bureaucracy, and there are few things it defends so fanatically as this attitude; outside of the specific areas mentioned it cannot be justified with purely functional arguments. In facing a parliament, the bureaucracy fights, out of a sure power instinct, every one of that institution's attempts to gain through its own means (as, e.g., through the so-called "right of parliamentary investigation") expert knowledge from the interested parties. Bureaucracy naturally prefers a poorly informed, and hence powerless, parliament—at least insofar as this ignorance is compatible with the bureaucracy's own interests. . . .

Only the expert knowledge of private economic interest groups in the field of "business" is superior to the expert knowledge of the bureaucracy. This is so because the exact knowledge of facts in their field is of direct significance for economic survival. Errors in official statistics do not have direct economic consequences for the responsible official, but miscalculations in a capitalist enterprise are paid for by losses—perhaps by its existence. Moreover, the "secret," as a means of power, is more safely hidden in the books of an enterprise than it is in the files of public authorities. For this reason alone authorities are held within narrow boundaries when they seek to influence economic life in the capitalist epoch. Very frequently their measures take an unforeseen or unintended course or are made illusory by the superior expert knowledge of the interested groups. . . .

THE IMPERSONALITY OF THE MARKET AND DISCIPLINE IN THE MODERN CAPITALIST FACTORY

From: Pp. 251–52 in *Max Weber: Readings and Commentary on Modernity*, edited by Stephen Kalberg. Translated by Max Rheinstein; revised by Guenther Roth, Claus Wittich, and Stephen Kalberg (Oxford: Blackwell, 2005). [*Economy and Society*, pp. 635–37]

A market may be said to exist wherever there is competition, even if only unilateral, for opportunities of exchange among a plurality of potential parties. Their physical assemblage in one place, as in the local market square, the fair (the "long distance market"), or the exchange (the merchants' market), only constitutes the most consistent kind of market formation. It is, however, only this physical assemblage which allows the full emergence of the market's most distinctive feature, viz. haggling. . . . From a sociological point of view, the market represents a coexistence and sequence of rational associations, each of which is specifically ephemeral insofar as it ceases to exist with the act of exchanging the goods, unless a [legal] framework has been promulgated which imposes upon the transferors of the exchangeable goods the guaranty of their lawful acquisition and payments. . . or . . . quiet enjoyment. . . .

. . . Money creates a group by virtue of material interest relations and payments between actual and potential participants in the market. . . . Within the market group every act of exchange, especially monetary exchange, is not directed, in isolation, by the action of the individual partner to the particular transaction, but the more rationally it is considered, the more it is directed by the actions of all parties potentially interested in the exchange. The market group as such is the most impersonal relationship of practical life into which humans can enter with one another.

This is not due to that potentiality of struggle among the interested parties which is inherent in the market relationship. Any human relationship, even the most intimate, and even though it be marked by the most unqualified personal devotion, is in some sense relative and may involve a struggle with the partner, for instance, over the salvation of the soul. The reason for the impersonality of the market is its matter-of-factness, its exclusive orientation to the commodity. Where the market is allowed to follow its own autonomous tendencies, its participants do not look toward the persons of each other but only toward the commodity; there are no obligations of brotherliness or reverence, and none of those spontaneous human relations that are sustained by personal unions. They all would just obstruct the free development of the bare market relationship. Its specific interests serve, in their turn, to weaken the sentiments on which these obstructions rest.

Market behavior is influenced by a rational, means-end pursuit of interests. The partner to a transaction is expected to behave according to rational legality and, quite particularly, to respect the formal inviolability of a promise once given. These are the qualities which form the content of market ethics. In this latter respect the market inculcates, indeed, particularly rigorous outlooks. Violations of agreements, even though they may be concluded by mere signs, entirely unrecorded and devoid of evidence, are almost unheard of in the annals of the stock exchange. Such absolute depersonalization is contrary to all the ancient structural forms of human relationships. . . . [the family, the sib group, the tribe]

The "free" market—that is, the market which is not bound by ethical norms, with its exploitation of constellations of interests and monopoly positions and its haggling—is an abomination to every system of fraternal ethics. In sharp contrast to all other groups that always presuppose some measure of personal fraternization or even blood kinship, the market is fundamentally alien to any type of fraternal relationship. . . .

From: Pp. 384–85 in *Wirtschaft und Gesellschaft*, edited by Johannes Winckelmann. Translated by Stephen Kalberg (Tübingen: Mohr/Siebeck, 1976). [*Economy and Society*, pp. 638–40]

The Market Association. The freedom of the market is typically restricted by sacred taboos or monopolistic associations of status groups. Both prevent exchange with outsiders. Market groups directed a continuous onslaught against these limitations. The very existence of the market constitutes a temptation to share in the opportunities it provides for gain.

The process of appropriation by a monopolistic group may develop to the point at which the market becomes closed to outsiders; that is, the land, or the right to share in common land, has been appropriated. However, the growing differentiation of needs and of economic survival independent of land ownership allows a new situation: wants now need to be satisfied through external exchange. Moreover, the situation of fixed, hereditary appropriation normally creates a steadily increasing interest by individual parties in the opportunity to use their appropriated property for external exchanges with the highest bidders.

This development is quite analogous to that which causes inheritors of industrial enterprises almost always, in the long run, to establish a corporation. Doing so enables the selling of shares more freely externally. And the stronger an emerging capitalistic economy becomes, the greater will be efforts to bring the means of production and labor services into a market unencumbered by sacred or status bonds. Similarly, efforts will expand to emancipate opportunities to sell products from limitations imposed by the sales monopolies of status groups.

Capitalist interests are, in this manner, parties interested in the continuous extension of the free market. However, this remains the case only up to that point when some succeed, through the purchase of privileges from a political authority or simply through the power of capital, in acquiring for themselves a monopoly for the sale of their products or for the acquisition of their material means of production. They then close the market on their own behalf.

Thus, the full appropriation of all means of production follows once status group–based monopolies have been shattered. This takes place if those possessing a stake in capitalism are in a position to influence, for their own advantage, those groups which regulate the ownership of goods and the mode of their use. It also may occur where, within status-based monopolistic groups, dominant power is gained by those interested in the use of their appropriated property in the market. This development may proceed to the point where rights guaranteed (as acquired or to be acquired) by the coercive apparatus of the property-regulating group [a political organization] become limited to rights in material goods and contractual claims, including claims to contractual labor. All other appropriations, especially those of customers or those of status-based monopolies, are destroyed. This situation, which we call free competition, lasts until it is replaced by new monopolies not based on status restrictions, namely capitalist monopolies achieved in the marketplace through the power of property.

These capitalist monopolies differ from monopolies of status groups because they are determined by purely economically rational [market-rational] forces. By restricting either the scope of possible sales or the conditions under which they may occur, status group monopolies exclude market mechanisms — such as bargaining and rational calculation — from their field of action. Conversely, the monopolies rooted solely in the power of property rest on a mastery of market conditions through entirely rational calculations—and market procedures may in fact remain formally entirely free.

The purely economically conditioned monopolies are the ultimate result of the gradual elimination of those bonds that constituted limitations upon the formation of rational market prices: namely, those anchored in status considerations, the sacred, and traditions. Those who benefit from status group monopolies assert their power against the market; on the other hand, the market-rational monopolist rules through the market. Those interest groups enabled by formal market freedom to achieve power will be referred to as market-interested groups.

A particular market may be subject to frameworks autonomously agreed upon by market participants or imposed by any of a great variety of different groups, especially political or religious organizations. Such frameworks may involve restrictions upon market freedom: limits upon negotiation or competition. Or they may establish guarantees for the observance of market legality, especially the type of payments or means of payment. Finally, in periods of interlocal insecurity, these frameworks may be aimed at guaranteeing market peace.

Since the market existed originally as an association of persons from different groups, and who were therefore "enemies," the guaranty of peace was ordinarily left to divine powers. Supernatural forces also normally guaranteed the restrictions placed by rudimentary forms of law upon permissible modes of warfare. Very often market peace was placed under the protection of a temple; later it tended to be transformed into a source of revenue for the chief or prince.

Although goods exchange is the specifically peaceful form of acquiring economic power, it can obviously be associated with the employment of force. The seafarer of Antiquity and the Middle Ages was pleased to take without pay whatever could be acquired by force. Peaceful bargaining commenced only when a power of equal strength was confronted or after an assessment of advantages for future exchange opportunities otherwise threatened.

However, the significant extension of exchange relations has always developed in tandem with relative pacification. All of the "public peace" (*Landfrieden*) settlements of the Middle Ages served to further exchange interests. And the appropriation of goods through free, purely economically rational exchange . . . is the conceptual opposite of appropriation of goods by force of any kind, though especially by physical coercion—the regulated exercise of which is constitutive of the political community.

From: P. 253 in *Max Weber: Readings and Commentary on Modernity*, edited by Stephen Kalberg. Translated by Max Rheinstein and revised by Guenther Roth, Claus Wittich, and Stephen Kalberg (Oxford: Blackwell Publishing, 2005). [*Economy and Society*, pp. 1186–87]

The A–Ethical Market. . . . Most of the time the rulership of capital appears in such an "indirect" form that one cannot identify any concrete "ruler" and hence cannot make any ethical demands upon him. It is possible to advance ethical postulates and to attempt the imposition of substantive norms with regard to household head and servant, master craftsman and apprentice, manorial lord and dependents or officials, master and slave, or patriarchal ruler and subject. This is because their relationships are personal and since the expected services result from these postulates and norms, and constitute a component of them. Within wide limits, personal, flexible interests are operative here, and purely personal intent and action can decisively change the relationship and the condition of the person involved.

However, for the director of a joint-stock company, who is obliged to represent the interests of the stockholders as the proper rulers, it is very difficult to relate in this manner to the factory workers. It is even more difficult for the director of the bank that finances the joint-stock company, or for the mortgage holder in relation to the owner of property on which the bank granted a loan. Decisive here are the need for "competitive survival" and the conditions of the labor, money, and commodity markets. Hence, "matter-of-fact" considerations neither ethical nor unethical, but simply a-ethical, determine individual behavior and push impersonal forces between the persons involved.

From an ethical viewpoint, this "masterless slavery" in which capitalism ensnares the worker or the mortgagee is debatable only as an institution. However, in principle, the behavior of any individual—whether on the side of the ruling or the ruled, participant or non-participant—cannot be so questioned: it is prescribed in all relevant respects by objective situations. The penalty for non-compliance is extinction, and this would not be helpful in any way. Decisive is that this behavior has the character of a "service" on behalf of an *impersonal, matter-of-fact end.*

From: P. 136 in *Max Weber: Readings and Commentary on Modernity,* edited by Stephen Kalberg. Translated by Max Rheinstein and revised by Guenther Roth, Claus Wittich, and Stephen Kalberg (Oxford: Blackwell Publishing, 2005). [*Economy and Society,* p. 1156.]

An All-Encompassing Discipline. No special proof is necessary to show that military discipline is the ideal model for the modern capitalist factory, as it was for the ancient plantation. However, organizational discipline in the factory has a completely rational basis: with the help of suitable methods of measurement, the optimum profitability of the individual worker is regularly calculated like that of any material means of production.

On this basis, the American system of "scientific management" triumphantly proceeds with its rational conditioning and training of work performances, thereby approaching the highest yields from the plant's mechanization and discipline. The psycho-physical apparatus of persons is here completely adjusted to the demands of the outer world: the tools and the machines. In short, functions are imposed and the individual is shorn of his natural rhythm as determined by his organism. In line with the demands of the work procedure, he is attuned to a new rhythm through the functional specialization of muscles and through the creation of an optimal economy of physical effort.

This whole process of rationalization, in the factory as elsewhere and especially in the bureaucratic state machine, parallels the centralization of the impersonal implements of production in the power of the ruler. Thus, an all-encompassing discipline, with the rationalization of all political and economic satisfaction of needs, becomes manifest universally. As it develops inexorably, this discipline more and more restricts the importance of charisma and of individually differentiated conduct.

WEBER'S SUMMARY STATEMENTS ON *"THE PROTESTANT ETHIC* THESIS"

A. THE DEVELOPMENT OF THE CAPITALIST FRAME OF MIND (1919–1920)

From: Pp. 352–57, 367–69 in *General Economic History.* Translated by Frank H. Knight and revised by Stephen Kalberg (New York: Simon & Schuster, 1927).

It is a widespread error that the increase of population should be viewed as the decisive agent in the unfolding of Western capitalism. Karl Marx claimed, in opposition to this view, that every economic epoch has its own law of population. Although untenable in this general form, this position is justified in the present case.

The growth of population in the West proceeded most rapidly from the beginning of the eighteenth century to the end of the nineteenth. China experienced in the same period a population growth of at least equal degree—from 60 or 70 to 400 million (allowing for the inevitable exaggerations). This corresponds approximately to the increase in the West.

Nonetheless, the development of capitalism moved backward in China rather than forward, for the population increase took place in different strata than in the West, rendering China a swarming mass of peasants. The increase of a class, which corresponded to our proletariat, was involved only to the extent that a foreign market made possible the employment of coolies. ("Coolie" is originally an expression from India; it signifies neighbor or fellow member of a clan.) The growth of population in Europe did indeed favor the development of capitalism to the extent that the system, in a small population, would have been unable to secure the necessary labor force. In itself, however, it never called forth this development.

Nor can the *inflow of precious metals* be regarded, as Sombart implies, as the primary cause of the appearance of [modern] capitalism. It is certainly true that, in a given situation, an increase in the supply of precious metals may give rise to price revolutions, such as took place after 1530 in Europe. And if then other favorable conditions are present — a certain form of labor organization is crystallizing — the development of capitalism may be stimulated by the fact that large stocks of cash come into the hands of certain groups.

But the case of India proves that such an importation of precious metal will not alone bring about capitalism. In India, in the period of the Roman empire [44 B.C.E. to 476 A.C.], an enormous mass of precious metal — some 25 million *sestertii* annually — was collected in exchange for domestic goods. This inflow, however, gave rise to commercial capitalism to only a slight extent. The greater part of the precious metal disapppeared into the hoards of the rajahs instead of being converted into cash and applied to the establishment of enterprises of a rational capitalist character. This indicates that the tendency that results from an inflow of precious metal depends entirely upon the formation of the labor organization.

The precious metal from America, after the discovery, flowed largely to Spain; but there a decline of capitalist development took place parallel with the importation. There followed, on the one hand, the suppression of the *comuneros* [small towns] and the destruction of the commercial policies of the Spanish grandees and, on the other hand, the use of the money to meet military goals. Consequently, the stream of precious metal flowing through Spain scarcely touched it. Rather, it fertilized other countries that, since the fifteenth century, had been already undergoing a process of transformation in the organization of labor favorable to capitalism.

Hence, neither the growth of population nor the importation of precious metal called forth [modern] Western capitalism. The external conditions for the development of [modern] capitalism are, rather, first, geographical in character. In China and India the enormous costs of transportation, connected with their decisively inland commerce, necessarily formed serious obstructions for those classes in a position to make profits through trade and to use trading capital in the construction of a capitalist system. However, in the West the position of the Mediterranean as an inland sea, and the abundant interconnections through rivers, favored the development of international commerce.

Nonetheless, this factor must not be overestimated. The civilization of Antiquity was distinctively coastal. Here the opportunities for commerce were very favorable (thanks to the character of the Mediterranean Sea) in contrast to the Chinese waters with their typhoons—and yet no capitalism arose in Antiquity. Capitalist development, even in the modern period, was much more intense in [modern] Florence than in Genoa or Venice. Capitalism in the West was born in the industrial cities of the interior rather than in those cities which were centers of sea trade.

Military requirements were also favorable, though not as such. Instead, they were facilitating because of the special nature of the particular needs of the Western armies. Favorable also was the luxury demand, though again not in itself. In many cases it led to the development of irrational forms, such as small workshops in France and compulsory settlements of workers in connection with the courts of many German princes. In the last resort the groups which produced capitalism were bound up with the rational permanent enterprise, rational accounting, rational technology, and rational law—but again not these alone. Necessary complementary forces were the rational spirit, the rationalization of the conduct of life in general, and a rational economic ethic.

At the beginning of all ethics and economic relations is *traditionalism*, the sanctity of tradition, and the exclusive reliance upon trade and industry as inherited from the fathers. This traditionalism survives far down into the present; only a human lifetime ago it proved futile to double the wages, in the hope of inducing increased exertions, of an agricultural laborer in Silesia who cultivated a certain tract of land on a contract basis. He would simply have reduced by half the work expended: with this half he would have been able to earn twice as much as before (sic). This general incapacity and indisposition to depart from the beaten path is the motive for the maintenance of tradition.

Primitive traditionalism may, however, undergo essential intensification as a consequence of two circumstances. First, material interests may be tied up with the maintenance of tradition. When, for example, in China the attempt was made to change certain roads or to introduce more rational means or routes of transportation, the perquisites of certain officials were threatened. And the same was the case in the Middle Ages in the West and in the modern era with the introduction of the railroad.

Such special interests of officials, landholders, and merchants assisted decisively in restricting a tendency toward rationalization. Stronger still is the effect of the stereotyping of trade on magical grounds. Here a deep repugnance exists to undertaking any change in the established conduct of life because supernatural evils are feared. Generally some injury to economic privilege is concealed in this opposition, but its effectiveness depends on a general belief in the potency of feared magical processes.

Traditional obstructions are not overcome by the economic impulse alone. The notion that our rational and capitalist era is characterized by a stronger economic interest than other periods is childish; the moving spirits of modern capitalism are not possessed of a stronger economic impulse than, for example, an oriental trader. The unchaining of the economic interests alone has produced only irrational results. Men such as Cortez and Pizarro, who were perhaps its strongest embodiment, were far from having an idea of a rational economic life. If the economic impulse in itself is universal, it is an interesting question as to the relations under which it becomes rationalized and rationally tempered in such fashion as to produce rational institutions of the character of the [modern] capitalist enterprise.

Originally, two opposite postures toward the pursuit of gain existed in combination [see 1927, pp. 312–13]. Internally, there was attachment to tradition and to the relations of piety among fellow members of the tribe, clan, and house-community, with the exclusion of the unrestricted quest for gain within the circle of those bound together by religious ties. Externally there was absolutely unrestricted play of the spirit of gain in economic relationships—every foreigner is seen as an enemy in respect to whom ethical restrictions do not apply. Here the ethics of internal and external relations are categorically different. The course of development involves the bringing in of calculation into the traditional brotherhood, thereby displacing the old religious relationships.

As soon as accountability is established within the family community, and economic relations are no longer strictly communistic, there is an end to the naive trust and its repression of the economic impulse. This side of the development is especially characteristic of the West. At the same time there is a tempering of the unrestricted quest for gain with the adoption of economic interests into the internal [family] economy. The result is a regulated economic life with the economic impulse functioning within bounds.

In detail, the course of development has varied. . . . The final result is the unusual fact that the germs of modern capitalism must be sought in a region where officially a theory was dominant which was distinct from that of the East and of classical Antiquity and in principle strongly hostile to capitalism. The *ethos* of the classical economic morality is summed up in the old judgment passed on the merchant, which was probably taken from primitive Arianism: *homo mercator vis aut numquam potest Deo placere* (he may conduct himself without sin but cannot be pleasing to God). This proposition was valid down to the fifteenth century, and the first attempt to modify it slowly matured in Florence under pressure of the shift in economic relations. . . .

* * *

The development of the concept of the calling quickly gave to the modern entrepreneur a fabulously clear conscience—and also to industrious workers. The employer gave to his employees–as the wages for their ascetic devotion to the calling and for cooperating in his ruthless exploitation of them through capitalism—the prospect of eternal salvation. This prospect, in an age when ecclesiastical discipline took control of the whole of life to an extent inconceivable to us now, represented a reality quite different from any it has today.

The Catholic and Lutheran churches also recognized and practiced ecclesiastical discipline. But in the Protestant ascetic communities admission to the Lord's Supper was conditioned on ethical fitness, which in turn was identified with business honor—while no one inquired into the content of one's faith. Such a powerful, unconsciously refined organization for the production of capitalist individuals has never existed in any other church or religion; in comparison with it what the Renaissance did for capitalism shrinks into insignificance. Its practitioners occupied themselves with technical problems and were experimenters of the first rank. Experimentation, which began in the realms of art and mining, was taken over into science [see 2005, pp. 324–25].

The worldview of the Renaissance, however, determined the politics of rulers in a large measure, even though it failed to transform the soul of mankind, as did the innovations of the Reformation. Almost all the great scientific discoveries of the sixteenth and seventeenth centuries grew on the soil of Catholicism. Copernicus was a Catholic, and Luther and Melanchthon repudiated his discoveries. Scientific progress and Protestantism must not at all be unquestioningly identified. The Catholic church has indeed occasionally obstructed scientific progress; however, the ascetic sects of Protestantism have also wished to know little about pure science—except when it concerned the real needs of daily life. Conversely, Protestantism's unique achievement was to have placed science in the service of technology and the economy (see p. 447).

The religious root of modern humanity oriented to the economy is dead. Today the concept of the calling stands as a *caput mortuum* in the world. Ascetic religiosity has been displaced by a pessimistic, though by no means ascetic, view of the world, such as portrayed in [Bernard de] Mandeville's "fable of the bees" [1729]. Private vices are here understood as, under certain conditions, in service to the civic realm. With the complete disappearance of all the remains of the original enormous religious pathos of the sects, the optimism of the Enlightenment, which believed in the harmony of interests, appeared as the heir of Protestant asceticism in the field of economic ideas [see p. 158]. The princes and writers of the later eighteenth and early nineteenth centuries were guided by its hand.

Economic ethics arose against the background of the ascetic ideal, and now it has been stripped of its religious meaning. The working class, as long as the promise of eternal happiness could be held out to it, could accept its lot. When this consolation fell away, however, the appearance of society's strains and stresses became inevitable. They have grown uninterruptedly since then. This era had been reached by the conclusion of capitalism's early period At this point capitalism had reached the end of its early period and had embarked upon, in the nineteenth century, an age of iron.

B. A FINAL REBUTTAL TO A CRITIC OF "SPIRIT OF CAPITALISM" (1910)

Felix Rachfahl, a professor of German and Dutch history, challenged Weber's thesis in a heated exchange over a two-year period (1909–1910). His criticisms ranged widely. In particular, he deplored Weber's "idealism" and insisted that equivalents of ascetic Protestantism could be found in the Middle Ages. A full-scale rejection of Weber's analysis is necessary, he maintained (see Rachfahl, 1978).[1]

Almost one-half as long as *PE*, Weber's reply is original and not simply a summary of this volume's major points. It offers an array of formulations more precise than their *PE* counterparts. The "calling" is especially emphasized, as is *PE*'s argument regarding the Puritans' new "style of life." It is reprinted here in abbreviated form.[2]

1. For summaries of Rachfahl's general position, see Davis, 1978; Chalcraft and Harrington (Weber, 2001, pp. 55–59, 89–91); and Baehr and Wells (Weber, 2002, pp. 244–46).
2. Weber's further contributions to this first phase of "the Protestant ethic debate" (1907–1910) — his responses to each of the four articles authored by his critics Fischer and Rachfahl—are not otherwise included here. See Weber, 2001, 2002. This early debate has been examined, for example, by Fischoff (1944), Marshall (1982, pp. 36–40, 58–59, 137), Ray (1987, pp. 106–15), Lichtblau and Weiss (1993a), Lehmann (1987; 1993; 2005, pp. 9–22), and Chalcraft (2001, 2005).

From: "A 'Final Rebuttal' to a Critic of 'Spirit of Capitalism'" (1910). Pp. 107–20 in *The Protestant Ethic Debate: Max Weber's Replies to his Critics, 1907–10*, edited by David J. Chalcraft and Austin Harrington and translated by Harrington and Mary Shields; slightly revised by Stephen Kalberg (Liverpool: Liverpool University Press, 2001.) [Endnotes by Weber and the original editors abridged].

... in the present case of a very complex historical phenomenon, it was only possible to start from the concretely given and gradually attempt to elicit our concept by eliminating what is "inessential" from it, insofar as such concepts can only be formed through selection and abstraction. I therefore proceeded by first:

1. calling to mind examples of the remarkably strong congruence disputed as yet by no one between Protestantism and modern capitalism, and in particular capitalistic choice of occupation and capitalistic success. Then, by way of illustration, I

2. gave some examples of just those ethical life-maxims (Franklin) I see as testifying indubitably to the "capitalist spirit," posing the question of how they differ from other, particularly medieval, maxims. And then I

3. sought to *illustrate,* again through examples, how these spiritual attitudes relate *causally* to the modern capitalist economic system. This then

4. led me to the idea of the "calling," along with the unique and long-established elective affinity of Calvinism to capitalism (and also of Quakerism and similar sects), that Gothein in particular has noted. At the same time I

5 sought to demonstrate that our contemporary concept of vocation is in some way *religiously* based.

Then there arose ... the problem of how the various shadings of Protestantism relate to the idea of the calling, in its significance for the development of those *ethical* qualities among individuals that influenced their suitability for capitalism. This question of course only made sense if such religiously conditioned ethical qualities existed at all. At the time, I could only explain the *nature* of these qualities generally through examples. Therefore, to supplement what I had already said about the problem, I needed to demonstrate ever more thoroughly *that* such qualities did indeed exist among certain strands of Protestant ethics; *which* qualities these were; what *kinds* of Protestantism these qualities so fostered to such a high degree; and *how* they differed from those qualities of the medieval church and of other varieties of Protestantism that were in part acquired and absorbed and in part just tolerated.

In so doing, my actual treatment of the problem had to: (1), as far as was possible for a layman in theology, discover first the theoretical and dogmatic anchorage of the ethic among the various shades of Protestantism, in order to show that not merely secondary things were at issue having nothing to do with religious thought-contents; but also (2) accomplish something *very different* from this, namely, to elucidate the *practical-psy-*

chological motives for actual ethical *behaviour* contained in each of these unique shades of religiosity.

Rachfahl has still not once been able to grasp that these two questions concern *completely different things* (to say nothing of all his other distortions and superficialities). He has not grasped how important and interesting is the question (also from a practical standpoint) of what kind of ethical ideals were contained in the church *doctrines* of Catholicism, Luther, Calvin and others in their various similarities and differences, and of whether, as Rachfahl reports, church theory "expected" the same kinds of behaviour that ascetic Protestantism cultivated practically and psychologically "from the Catholic layman as well" (rather than just from monks). But nor has he seen that the answer to this question establishes *absolutely nothing* about whether the religious doctrine in question created in its adherents the *psychological vehicle capable of generating a type of behaviour* germane to that doctrine. (It may instead have created a quite different type of behaviour or perhaps one that pushed the doctrine in particular distinct directions.)

As I have said myself, one of course finds conscientious *work* by the layman in the world praised and recommended very regularly in all ages, both among ethical theorists and among preachers in the Middle Ages such as Berthold von Regensburg [1210–1272] and others (although early Christianity, by contrast, essentially shared antiquity's view of "work"—as [the theologian Adolf von] Harnack [1851–1930] has indicated in a short essay). Luther's sayings along the same lines are well known. There has certainly been no lack of teaching outside ascetic Protestantism about the blessing of secular work too. But what use is it if (as in Lutheranism) no *psychological premiums* are placed on these theoretical teachings being practised with methodical consistency? Or if (as in Catholicism) far greater premiums are placed on *quite different* kinds of behaviour? Or if, and moreover, through the form of confession, the individual is vouchsafed a means of spiritually unburdening himself of absolutely all kinds of transgressions against church commands over and over again?

In contrast to this, Calvinism and Baptism in their development since the late sixteenth century generated the thought of the necessity of ascetic *proof*—proof in life generally and especially in vocational life—as the subjective guarantee of the *certitudo salutis* (i.e. not as an *actual ground* of salvation but as one of the most important reasons for *knowing* one's salvation) [*nicht als Realgrund, sondern als einer der wichtigsten Erkenntnis-gründe der eigenen Bestimmung zur Seligkeit*] and they thereby created a very specific psychological premium for the ascetic methodical life practices they demanded, one whose effectiveness is not easily surpassed in *this* area.

This was the state of affairs I had to address in my writings, along with the methodical life practices it unleashed. I first had to explain the *characteristic* features of these practices and then their inner consistency and the absolute seamlessness with which they were lived out by every *individual* who grew up in the atmosphere these religious powers created—even if not *consciously*, of course.

That these motives also found powerful supports in the various social institutions of the churches and in other institutions influenced by the churches and sects I partly sought to indicate briefly in my *Archiv* essay and partly sought to illuminate more clearly in my outline in *Christliche Welt* [pp. 59–159] Let me recapitulate here. First, the central cultic act of Communion was very specifically emphasised in "ascetic" Protestantism. The thought that whoever does not belong to God's invisible church but still takes part in this act "eats and drinks in his own judgement" contains a pathos whose power today has been almost completely lost, even to most of the "Christians" among us. However, we can still vividly reconstruct it from the older generation's memories of its youth and from the remnants of ecclesiastical gravitas that we have, as it were, shunted into the corners (at least, as we look back at things today).

Ascetic Protestantism lacks (and by no means accidentally!) the institution of confession that afforded the Catholic *relief* from the pressure of such pathos-filled questions as the individual's qualification for election. And here too, as everywhere, the problem of whether one belonged to the qualified was answered for the Protestant, not, as for the medieval Catholic, through an adding up of guilt and merit which would be approximately balanced out and then possibly supplemented with ecclesiastical grace, but, as I showed quite specifically in ascetic Protestantism, through a rigid either—or of the whole *personality*, as manifested in the totality of the individual's ethical conduct of life. As I showed in detail, here alone—and again, infinitely more starkly than in Lutheranism—would the individual be confronted with his God and have to rely solely on himself and his state of grace, which he could only perceive from his *entire* conduct of life. And at the same time, his external structuring of life would be very much more subject to *control by his peers*: through the members of the congregation; whereas in Catholicism and Lutheranism it falls ultimately only to the representative of the "ministry" to settle with himself and the layman whether the individual is ready for Communion.

In Calvinism, the responsibility for "God's glory" not being dishonoured by the participation of someone patently "wearing" signs of exclusion from the elect concerns *every member* of the whole congregation—for worship of "God's glory" provided an unambiguous focus for the whole social life, with a power that was in *this* way quite foreign to the other large churches. It was these same laypeople who brought about the Kuyper schism [1892 in Holland], barely a generation ago (Kuyper himself was a lay elder), by demanding that Communion be refused to confirmands whom they believed did not qualify and had been examined by out-of-town preachers. What we see behind this ultimately is a protest against the principle that any authority that has no place in the concrete, self-correcting *congregation* of communicants should interfere in this question [of qualification] in any way—in a question that affects every single member of the congregation directly.

The immense social significance of these ways of thinking was revealed most clearly at that time in the New England churches, where the demand for an *ecclesia pura* and especially for a pure community of communicants directly created genuine "class differences," along with battles and compromises over the position of the "would-be Christians" concerning their entitlement to bring children for baptism and stand proxy for them, and such like.

If one examines the Protestant church ordinances and examines their development and, wherever possible, their practical implementation and reflects on their consequences, one is struck first by how much of that moral regimentation of life that was once given over to the ecclesiastical courts [*Sendgerichte*] in the Carolingian age, or was in the hands of the municipalities at the end of the Middle Ages, or in the hands of the royal police at the time of the territorial states, is here taken on by the church—in widely differing degrees, of course, and generally much more so in the Calvinist than Lutheran areas (for, as I indicated in my essay, express *submission* to church discipline on entry to the congregation was emphasized only *after* Calvin).

But, as I also stressed, what was, and still is in its vestiges to the present day, incomparably more predominant and effective was that kind of ethical "training" that the ascetic sects imposed on their members. I recounted something of this from contemporary observations of the United States in my *Christliche Welt* essay. The present process of secularisation in American life and the tremendous immigration of diverse elements will quickly wash away this legacy, and the ruthless "soul-fishing" in recruitment among the competing denominations weakens the intensity of their socialization achievements.

Nonetheless, only a little attention to these things suffices to make us see vividly the former importance of those phenomena from the remnants marking their legacy. I remind the reader of what I said in *Christliche Welt* about the function of the sects in economic life (gradually being replaced today by all kinds of purely secular organisations). I refer especially, for example, among numerous similar experiences, to the motive I was told for a young man's entering a Baptist congregation in North Carolina. This was that he was thinking of opening a bank, while on closer questioning it emerged that this was not so much a matter of his reckoning on Baptist custom in particular as on precisely that of the *non*-sectarians who greatly predominated in that area. The reason for this was that whoever wanted to be accepted for baptism there had to be prepared during his "catechumenate" [preparatory instruction for baptism] for an astonishingly systematic investigation of his conduct by the congregation, with inquiries into all his earlier places of residence [pp. 187–88].

Questions would be asked such as: ever frequented public houses? Ever drunk liquor? Ever played card games? Ever led an "unclean life"? Profligacy? Cheques not paid promptly? Or other debts? Any signs whatever of unreliability in business? And so on. If he was admitted, his credit-worthiness and qualification for business were thereby guaranteed, and he could then beat off any competitor not so legitimated—while, at the same time, any possible exclusion for bad behaviour meant his social excommunication, as always with the sects.[3] We find the same thing already developed 200 years ago.

---

3. In my article [pp. 200–04], I compared this creditworthiness with a German fraternity student's ability to "borrow." (In my time, it was possible for a student to live almost for free in Heidelberg after "gaining the ribbon" from his fraternity; and if you were a *Fuchs* [new member] you could record your debts with the Registrar.) I also noted a similarly specific creditworthiness of the clergy in the Middle Ages (where the threat of excommunication could be used as a sanction). Similar

Another example: the Quakers have always boasted of creating the "fixed prices" system, so important to capitalism, in place of oriental haggling. And indeed this is so. Historical research shows that, 200 years ago, the reason given for rhe flourishing of Quaker retail trading was that customers felt sure of this principle being adhered to, surer than any medieval or modern price regulation could make them. The Quaker congregation also stepped in when anyone began a business transaction for which he lacked the necessary capital or knowledge, or such like. And in the literature of all these sects one finds that soon after their emergence they would rejoice that the Lord was visibly blessing them, for "children of the world" were bringing their money to them (as deposit, as investment or in any other form) rather than to members of their own confession or non-members, because the sects would be sure to provide the requisite personal ethical guarantees. . . .

Let me only note further that, as everyone knows, until the last few decades the old-style Yankee—indeed *precisely* the *businessman*—simply could nor understand, and sometimes even today cannot understand, that a person should belong to no "denomination" at all (it does not matter which denomination: in this regard he is absolutely "intolerant"). Any such religious outlaw [English in original] would have been suspect to him, both socially and in business, *because* not ethically "legitimated." Until almost 15 years ago, even the tourist could be reminded of a similar outlook in Scotland and bourgeois English circles, particularly on Sundays.

Today, having escaped this once overwhelming necessity for religious legitimation, the businessman of the American middle classes instead has at his disposal various other organisations that are increasingly emerging. He typically supports his legitimation by having himself balloted into them so as to demonstrate certain "gentlemanly" qualities, and wears their "badge" in his buttonhole. (If one watches out for them, one sees such insignia on a massive scale, reminiscent ot the legion of honour rosette.)

As long as the true Yankee spirit ruled, American democracy was never a simple heap of sand composed of isolated individuals, even disregarding all the trusts and trade unions. To a great degree, it was a jumble of *exclusive* organisations, of which the prototype is the *sect,* and all of them demanded from their members and cultivated in them those qualities that go to make up the kind of business gentleman capitalism requires. Admittedly, someone in the position of Mr. Pierpont Morgan [1837–1913] has no such need of legitimation to fulfil his economic position. And in other ways too, things are quite different today. But the penetration of the specific "spirit" that fos-

---

3.   (continued) again is the often dubious creditworthiness of the modern young officer, where the sanction is possible dismissal. However, there is a sociologically highly significant difference here in that, in all these cases, creditworthiness is not demanded as a *subjective* quality of the *personality* like it is in the sects (through selection according to appropriate socialization). Only certain *objective* guarantees are increased (which is something the sects required in addition). The Methodists' characteristic "training" [English in orig.] for young people has disappeared, but it was once highly significant. The same is true for that characteristic custom of gathering in small groups for regular examination on the state of one's soul, i.e. for a kind of limited public confession. This of course denoted a completely different psychological *situation* from the Catholic confession behind the window grille since it involved personal equals grouping together.

tered these associations into the whole of life was certainly an extremely important precondition for modern capitalism to "take root," that is, for it to discover an adequate "lifestyle" among the broad stratum of the bourgeois middle classes and in the end also among the masses. Both groups became subordinate to its mechanisms, and hence their conduct was brought under modern capitalism's coercion.

Understandably, historians of Rachfahl's type have no idea of the scale of socialization necessary for this to occur.[4] And if anyone with the "common sense" Rachfahl trumpets so loudly comes to consider it "plausible" that this qualification of religious training for business life and this whole configuration of specifically business and religious credentials may possibly be a consequence of those religious communities developing in an already capitalist "milieu"—this person I must ask: why, then, did the Catholic Church *not* develop such a combination of attitudes and such a system of socialization so geared towards capitalism? Why did it not do so, either in the great centers of the Middle Ages like Florence where, God knows, capitalism was incomparably more "developed" than in the still sparsely settled farming area of western North Carolina I wrote about, or than in the largely subsistence-economy areas of the American colonies where this religious spirit took root well over 200 years ago? And why did Lutheranism not do so either? It was because [in the movements I described] a web of psychic meanings came to be woven out of quite unique moral and religious roots, offering *possibilities* for capitalist development.

It is true that the lifestyle cultivated by the ascetic communities with such immense energy also "rubbed off" onto that of *other competing* denominations in confessionally mixed areas, from the very beginning and increasingly with the ever greater permeation of economic life by the capitalist spirit, despite intense differences between them. This was so very early on for Dutch and American Lutheranism and even American Catholicism (while for German Lutheranism the older Pietism was the conduit, as is well known). Naturally, this process of "assimilation" only gradually lessened the differences between them and never fully erased them. However, as far as we can tell today, a movement towards the most consistent forms of Protestant asceticism (Calvinist in particular) almost always did

---

4. Socializing people to take a prevailing interest in "hard reality" is, as I indicated, an old and quite definitely religiously anchored principle of Pietist pedagogy. From the outset, we find something very similar among the Quakers and Baptists; and in the Reformed churches it is not uncommon today, for example in the preference for *Realschulen* and other similar types of school and in choice of vocation.[iv] These points are of immense importance for the connection between religious forms and modem capitalist development. The Reformation's familiar achievements *in general* are also undoubtedly significant for elementary school education, However, these last connections had their limits, for the achievements of the Prussian state in elementary education were *not* matched in the country of capitalism's greatest development: England. The "good elementary school" did *not as such* emerge in parallel with capitalist development. Incidentally, it is a quite dubious exaggeration to say, with Rachfahl, that no anxiety prevails or prevailed in Protestantism about increasing levels of education among ordinary people, especially where our good Protestant landowners east of the Elbe are concerned. In my essay I underlined the connection between certain denominational trends in schooling [p. 63]and the position taken towards *fides implicita*) [faith must be unquestioning].

occur, certainly at least among those groups that contained Protestants mixed in with them, and for that reason alone a mere statistic of true Calvinists among the Protestant emigrants could still be no argument against the significance of the ascetic forms of life. Contemporary discussions in Catholicism over how best to match the Protestants' economic superiority find their counterpart, in content if not style of expression, in some of Spener's remarks on the good progress of the Quakers. This motive has of course always been at work *tacitly* everywhere, just as in America today.

Leaving quite aside for the moment the *term* "inner-worldly asceticism," if one now asks finally whether I am justified in drawing a *substantive* parallel between this and Catholic monastic asceticism, I have no need to mention that Protestant ethical writers, especially in England, regularly quoted medieval devotional literature of monastic origin (Bonaventure [1221–1274] and others) in connection with the requirements I called "ascetic." But we can also compare much more simply than this. Monastic asceticism demanded chastity. Protestant asceticism (in my sense of the word) demanded chastity in marriage *as well*—in the sense of the elimination of "desire" and the restriction of sexual intercourse to the *rational* "natural purpose" of procreation as its only morally acceptable outlet.

At all events, these regulations were more than *mere* theorising. We know of certain Pietistic and Herrnhuter rules of this kind, and some strike us as directly unnatural today. On the other hand, attitudes to women in general have seen the *abolition* of the view of them as principally sexual vehicles—in contrast to Luther's residual peasant outlook.

Monastic asceticism also demanded poverty—and we know with what paradoxical consequences. Everywhere, the prosperity of the monasteries was viewed as the result of divine blessing—with the exception of certain strictly spiritual denominations that the popes treated with great suspicion—and indeed *was* in the greatest measure the *consequence* of their rational economy, alongside their endowments.

Similarly, I have set out the equally paradoxical consequences of the way in which Protestant asceticism for its part rejected both contented "satisfaction" with one's possessions and the pursuit of them "for their own sake." Monastic asceticism demanded independence from the "world" and condemned naive pleasure in particular. Protestant asceticism did likewise. Both also join up in their use of the *means* of "exercise" (for this is what the word "asceticism" means): strictly divided time; work; silence as a means of subduing the instincts; detachment from overly strong bonds to the flesh (dubiousness of overly intensive personal friendships and such like) and the renunciation of pleasure as such, whether "sensuous" pleasure in the narrowest sense or aesthetic—literary pleasure, and, in general, renunciation of all use of worldly goods not justifiable on *rational* grounds, for example hygiene.

I also pointed out at length that in the Middle Ages he who lived "methodically" specifically because of his *"calling"* was precisely the monk. Sebastian Franck's remark [see p. 118] . . . therefore shows rather more understanding of these things than my "critic." What distinguishes *ra-*

tional Protestant asceticism (in *my* sense of the word) from monastic asceticism is:

1. its rejection of all irrational ascetic means (and such means are also, incidentally, similarly rejected or limited by some of the more significant Catholic orders, particularly by the Jesuits);
2. its rejection of contemplation; and finally and most importantly
3. its change of direction towards inner-worldly asceticism; its working out of itself in the family and (ascetically interpreted) vocation, from which result the differences already mentioned and all others.

But if the kinds of "spirit" in each of these two contrasting principles of life regulation are *not* to be judged as inwardly and essentially parallel and akin to each other [*nicht als im innersten Wesen parallel und miteinander verwandt*], I do not know when one should ever speak of an "affinity" [*Verwandtschaft*].

As an aside, I will only mention how greatly the disappearance of the monasteries was regretted occasionally in Pietistic circles, along with that of the monastery-like organisations that were constantly recreated by these circles, and I refer further to what I wrote in my essay about Bunyan, for example. The inner tension and inner affinity between these two formations concerning the place of ascetic ideals in the total system of religious life arise ultimately from the reason already mentioned: from the fact that what for the monks counted as an *actual ground* of candidature for salvation signified for ascetic Protestantism a *cognitive ground* (that is, *a* cognitive ground but not *the* absolute or only ground, though probably the most important one). And as even modern "methodologists" (specifically historical methodologists) cannot always distinguish these two sets of facts, it is certainly not surprising that this Protestant "work holiness" often seemed to resemble Catholic elements like one egg to another—except that the seeds [of the eggs] came from different spiritual fathers and therefore developed very different inner structures.

To recapitulate the *dogmatic* foundations of inner-worldly asceticism here would be going too far. I must refer the reader wholly to my essay for this, where I also suggest, at least provisionally and hence very sketchily, that the question of whether these foundations were provided by the Calvinist doctrine of Predestination or by the Baptist movement's untheological dogmatics was not completely irrelevant to practical life orientation, despite all assimilation between them. But these in many ways very marked differences between them necessarily came second in this part of my project to what was common between them. It would be too much to go into detail here. Nonetheless, I must expressly reiterate that in empirically re-examining the question of whether those fundamental religious–psychological conditions had the specific effect on the *practice* of life I claimed they did, I adduced not textbooks of dogma or theoretical treatises on ethics but quite different sources.

The publications I singled out by Baxter and Spener in particular rested on pastoral work, essentially on answers to the inquiries of pastors on matters of concrete practical life. To the extent that they reflected *practical* life, these writings therefore represent a genre rather like the *responsa* of the Roman jurists to matters of appropriate practice in business and the law courts. Like the Roman jurists, these and similar works certainly also contained casuistic speculations, as did the Talmud—albeit on an enormous scale quite incomparable with the former—which likewise borrowed from once directly practical responses to problems. The form and context of these writings indicate where they draw from life—not always, of course, but fortunately often enough. And where they do so, *no* source matches them in authenticity and liveliness, except letters and, at best, autobiographies. Neither popular pamphlets and tracts nor sermons match them (though one may rightly use these last extensively *as a supplement* of course), nor any other literary products of the period (however important as a secondary source), nor finally even the quite superficial statements of confessional belonging of the various capitalist groups—especially if one leaves out of the picture the influence of the Protestant ascetic "atmosphere of life" on them. We are unfortunately very seldom lucky enough to see the meshing together of religious and capitalist interests in the workplace so clearly as in the case of the Kidderminster weavers I cited [see p. 529, note 22].

This is not to belittle in the slightest the importance of the works Rachfahl wishes to see. *But* only my approach is capable of disclosing the *specific direction* in which a particular colour of religiosity was able to develop—and this was what explicitly concerned me. This course of influence did not merely "intensify" some already present psychological outlook; it signified a *new* "*spirit,*" at least within the worldly sphere. From their religious lives, their religiously conditioned family traditions and religiously influenced lifestyle and surrounding world, these people developed a habitus that made them uniquely suited to meet the demands of early modern capitalism. In a nutshell, in the shoes of the entrepreneur whose "chrematism" made him feel at *most* "tolerated" by God, who like the native Indian trader today had to work off or make up for his *"usuraria pravitas,"* entered a new kind of entrepreneur who kept his good conscience intact.

The new entrepreneur was filled with a consciousness that Providence was showing him the path to profit not unintentionally, that he might tread this to the glory of God, that God was visibly blessing him in the increase of his profit and property, and that above all, as long as he achieved it by legal means, he could measure his worth by success in his calling—not only before men but before God—and finally that God had his purposes in selecting *him* for economic ascent and equipping him with the necessary means—unlike the others destined to poverty and hard labour, for good but unfathomable reasons.

This was the kind of entrepreneur who would make his way in "Pharisaic" certainty according to strict formal legality; for this he saw as the highest and only tangible virtue (since there was no such thing for him as "adequacy" before God). Alongside him stood the man of specific "readiness for work," in the person of the cottage-industry craftsman or worker, whose conscientiousness in his divinely willed "calling" made him conscious of his religious state of grace. These men's condemnation of the sin of idolatry of the flesh in sitting on one's laurels, enjoying pleasures and squandering money and time on things not useful for one's calling constantly drove them to make use of property acquired in their calling along the "vocational" path of capital investment (in the entrepreneur's case) or to pursue the course of "saving" and thereby possibly rising in the world (in the case of the "ethically" qualified propertyless).

What was decisive here was that vocation and innermost ethical core of personality remained in unbroken unity. However many isolated moves toward a practical vocational ethic one may find in the Middle Ages (and I have deliberately avoided speaking about this here) do not alter the fact that a "spiritual linkage" of this kind was simply *lacking* at that time. And in our times today, which place such specific value on "life" and "lived experience," and such like, an *inner dissolution* of this unity and a banning of the "vocational man" are as plain as can be. For a long time now, modern capitalism has no longer needed this supporting mechanism—and it is against this gear-like unceasing motion of modern capitalism that the modern sensibility I have just mentioned rebels, not only on social-political grounds but now precisely on account of its bondage to the "spirit" of vocational humanity [see pp. 157–58].

Admittedly, we do still find traces of a role for religious contents in capitalist development, as I repeatedly showed in my essay and elsewhere. We can see where industry continues to rely on those qualities of its personnel that arose out of this lifestyle often enough in the distribution of confessions across upwardly mobile foremen and white-collar workers, in contrast to ordinary workers, and likewise among entrepreneurs. Statistics will of course only reveal this for us once we have eliminated those contingencies that enter in through location (such as the presence of essential raw materials in a certain area) and through the inclusion of craftwork trades in the statistics. But on the whole, contemporary capitalism is, I repeat, most definitely and extensively emancipated from such moments.

In the period of early modern capitalism, by contrast, no one has so far thought to *doubt* that the Huguenots were linked to French bourgeois capitalism extremely closely and exported their typical commercial qualities *wherever* they emigrated in the late seventeenth century (after the revocation of the Edict of Nantes [1685]). They did so *not* only to countries with less-developed economies but also, *of all places,* to Holland where capital investment, as I have remarked already, was in part differently structured and in part tranquillised by rentier expenditure and social ostentation, albeit only in certain strata. In his review (though not now in his reply), Rachfahl denies that in the northern states of the U.S. bourgeois-capitalist development rested in a quite specific way on the likewise quite specifically conditioned Puritan lifestyle there, though he does admit such a link for England (albeit in his usual vague way). The English Romantics recognised just this correlation in Scotland[5] and, in Germany, [the economic historian Eberhard] Gothein [1853–1923] has already

---

5. Compare, for example, John Keats's letter to his brother Thomas (3 July 1818): "These churchmen" have turned Scotland into "colonies of savers and successful entrepreneurs" (in contrast to Ireland, whence he is writing).

ascertained these things, with a few examples added by me. I have offered reasons why ascetic Protestant forces in Holland working in *just the same* direction were in some degree crushed,[6] in keeping with the remarkable stagnation that set in to Holland's capitalist expansion fairly soon afterward (and not necessarily just its colonial expansion).[7]

This was due to a tangle of causes partly mentioned already, of which I scarcely dare claim to have noted even the most important so far. Just as with the economic life of certain medieval sects, all this has been known about largely since the seventeenth century, and so far no one who has taken any interest in the issue has doubted it. It is in fact *impossible* to contest, certainly least of all (for the reasons already given) by observations such as that, in Frankfurt, Dutch Lutheran immigrants existed alongside the Dutch Calvinist immigrants—however historically valuable these observations may be in themselves. I therefore merely *reminded* readers of these things in my essay. I now also *remind* them again that the many (though not *all*) Russian schismatics and sectarians, who held an essentially ascetic-*rational* outlook, showed quite similar economic behaviour as soon as they had outgrown their youthful otherworldly period. Here the most extreme combination of business acumen with ethical "world-rejection" was shown by the eunuch sect [the Skoptsy, a castration sect dating from the 1770s].

My essay had to rest content with *illustrations* of things well known already. . . . Further research into the power of the various confessions was not my concern, useful and necessary as it may be for specialized historical analysis of particular regions. However necessary (indeed, substantially *more necessary*) it may be to *compare* the various characteristics of the individual countries influenced by ascetic Protestantism (which alone will help explain evident differences in development), the most pressing questions for me lay and lie elsewhere. First, of course, I need to differentiate the various effects of Calvinist, Baptist, and Pietist ethics on lifestyle, much more deeply and in detail than had been done before. We must also investigate thoroughly the beginnings of similar development in the Middle Ages and early Christianity, as far as [Ernst] Troeltsch's works still leave scope for this—which will certainly require very intensive collaboration with theologians. Then we need to consider how best to explain, from the *economic* standpoint, that ubiquitous elective affinity of the bourgeoisie to a definite kind of lifestyle, showing up as it does always in different manifestations and yet always with a similar common root. And in particular, we need to study that specific affinity of the bourgeoisie to certain aspects of the religious lifestyle, the aspects that were most consistently exemplified by ascetic Protestantism.

---

6. However, these forces were not of course crushed by the predominant Arminianism (and even indifference) I mentioned among certain political élites. For just such allegiances are found elsewhere. In Holland it was the upper strata that most often strove (at least partially) to *relinquish* capitalist activity by "ennobling" their fortunes in manorial estates, like in England. . . .

7. Let there be no misunderstanding: this stagnation definitely had certain key political causes, in both foreign and domestic policy. But this should in no way exclude the relevance of that dispersion and fracturing of the ascetic life. Presently I am in no position to answer this question conclusively—and doubtless nor are others.

Numerous things have been said from many different quarters about this more general problem, but much more remains to be said—including, I believe, all that is fundamental. . . .

And finally, if anyone wanted to know my view of capitalism's probable fate (as an economic *system*) if we *imagined* the specifically modern elements of the capitalist "spirit" not having unfolded as they have . . , all one can honestly answer is that, in short, we don't know. However, those people – those nonspecialists, at least — who cannot disabuse themselves of the myth that certain *technological* "achievements" were the clear cause of capitalist development ought to be reminded of the broad features of this legacy. Ancient capitalism unfolded *in the absence* of technical "progress," indeed almost at the very moment technological advances were coming to an end. Technological advances in medieval continental Europe were not insignificant for the possibility of capitalist modernization, but were certainly no decisive "catalyst."

Objective factors, such as certain climatic variables influencing the conduct of life and labor costs, were important historical preconditions, along with other factors generated by the social-political organization of medieval society with its largely *inland culture* (in comparison with antiquity) and by the resultant unique character of the medieval city, especially the inland city, and its *burghers*. . . . An additional and specifically economic moment were certain new forms of trading organization (the cottage industries) which, compared with antiquty, were perhaps not absolutely new but were certainly new in structure, distribution, and significance.

The great process of development that *spans* the then still highly *fragile* career of capitalism today has been fulfilled by certain important objective-political and objective-economic *preconditions*. *Above all*, however, it has been fulfilled by the birth and nurturing of a rationalistic and antitraditionalistic "spirit" and by the rise of that whole type of human being who practically carried it forward, of which I have spoken. We must look, on the one hand, to the history of modern *science* and its practical effects on modern economic life and, on the other, to the history of the modern *conduct of life*—again in terms of its practical economic significance. I discussed the latter in my [*PE*] essay, and it is worth further discussion.

But the development of rational methodical *practices* in the conduct of *life* is clearly something fundamentally different from the development of *scientific* rationalism, and by no means simply given with the latter. The first touchstones of modern natural science sprang up in *Catholic* areas and in Catholic heads. What was principally "Protestant" was rather the methodical application of science to *practical* purposes, just as were certain specific principles of *methodical life* and the kind of affinity they seem to have shown to Protestant ways of thinking—but more detail on this would lead too far afield.

The error of regarding "devotion," however strict, as an *intrinsic* obstacle to the development of the *empirical* sciences at that time and later is proved in particular by most of the English heroes of the natural sciences from the seventeenth century to Faraday and Maxwell (indeed Faraday is still known to have *preached* in his sect's church in the nineteenth century). The *practical* and *methodical*, and not just occasional, enlisting of the natural sciences in the service of the economy has been a keystone for the rise of a "methodical life" in *general*, and to this must be added the decisive contributions of both the Renaissance and the Reformation, particularly in the direction I adumbrated.

If I am now asked in all honesty how *high* I rate the importance of the Reformation, my answer is that I rate it *very* highly indeed. I have constantly and scrupulously reflected on this question, and am not bothered that no "numerical" ratio exists for historical attribution here.

READING *THE PROTESTANT ETHIC*: THE TEXT AND THE ENDNOTES

Weber presents his major argument in Part I (Chapters 1–3) and in Section A of *PE's* Chapter 4. Here he examines Calvinism, which provides the most stark example for his thesis. He then draws all the threads together in a synthetic concluding chapter.

The student who wishes to acquire a higher level command of his thesis cannot avoid serious study of *PE's* abundant endnotes. Moreover, they are of great interest, both as documentary materials and in a wider sense: In dozens of insightful and sweeping commentaries, Weber draws out the frame of mind of the Puritans and contrasts their mode of organizing life to that of a variety of other groups. The many ways in which ascetic Protestantism introduced new values and a new "outlook" become evident in part through a detailed reading of the endnotes. This being said, many endnotes move beyond Weber's theme proper and render commentaries upon dozens of aspects of modern life in general that relate to Puritanism's legacies.

The endnotes, it must be noted, are longer than *PE's* text. In her biography of her husband, Marianne Weber maintains that Weber's numerous and lengthy responses to his critics (mainly Sombart and Brentano) in his 1919 revisions must be viewed as contributing significantly to *PE's* massive "scholarly apparatus." In general, she emphasizes, in light of the heated debate surrounding *PE* and the fact that Weber's "careful qualifications" had been often misunderstood, he wished to document his argument in an especially detailed manner. This "endnote inflation" made for the "monstrous" and "dualistic" form of *PE*: The reader is expected simultaneously to grasp from the text the most "surprising syntheses" and from the endnotes the "most painstaking scholarly documentation" (Marianne Weber, 1975, p. 336; transl. altered).

A short sampling of a number of Weber's major subjects in the endnotes will assist the reader to locate themes of particular interest. This section conveys only a rough sketch of their contents. one's vantage point.

Chapter 1

Endnotes 15 and 25, pages 460 and 461: On the work ethics of immigrants.

Chapter 2

Endnote 4, p. 463: On the differences between German and American sensibilities.

Endnote 10, page 464: The "rational" and "irrational" depend upon one's vantage point.

Endnote 12, pages 464–68: On the work ethic of the Middle Ages.

Endnote 17, page 468: Low wages and high profits do not call forth modern capitalism, as widely believed.

Endnote 18, pages 468–69: On how industries select new areas for relocation.

Endnote 28, page 470: The quality of aesthetic design declines with mass production techniques.

Chapter 3

Endnote 32, pages 484–85: Church membership is less central for an organizing of the believer's entire life than a religion's values and ideals.

Endnote 41, page 485: On the national pride of the English.

Chapter 4

Endnote 7, page 486: On the greater influence of salvation rewards upon action than rules for appropriate conduct.

Endnote 8, page 486: On the slowness of the interlibrary loan system in Germany.

——, page 487: On the denial in the United States of its sectarian past and a consequence for scholarship: Libraries have not retained documents relating to this past.

Endnote 29, page 491: On the different meanings encompassing the expression *individualism*.

Endnote 32, pages 491–92: On trusting friends and taking revenge.

Endnote 34, pages 492–95: On the uniqueness of social organizations in those cultures with a Puritan past.

Endnote 35, page 492: On how the anti-authoritarian character of Calvinism opposed the development of the welfare state.

Endnote 39, page 493: On the intensity of community-building when Calvinism constitutes a strong influence.

——, page 493: On the suspect character of purely feeling-based relationships.

——, page 493: On the Calvinist's striving to make the world rational.

——, page 494: On the overlap of Calvinism's view of the "public good" with that of classical economics.

——, page 494: On the comparative immunity to authoritarianism of political cultures influenced by Puritanism.

Endnote 43, page 494: On loving one's neighbor and the dying out of the "humanity" of the relations to "one's neighbor."

——, page 495: On the ideas behind Christian missionary activity and giving to charity.

Endnote 59, 498: On the "maintenance of a mystical-magical component in the Lutheran teachings on communion."

——, 498–99: That "mystical contemplation and a rational view of the calling do not exclude each other."

Endnote 74, page 500: Goethe on how one knows oneself.

Endnote 76, page 501: On why, for the Calvinist, fatalism follows logically from the doctrine of predestination; however, owing to "the insertion of the idea of 'conduct as testifying to one's belief,' " it does not follow *psychologically.*

——, page 501: On the great significance of a religion's *ideas.*

——, page 501: On William James' pragmatic view of religious ideas as an outgrowth of the world of ideas in his Puritan native land.

——, page 501: The ways in which a particular *type of idea* system both *directs* that which is "experienced" as religious and distinguishes the different world religions in regard to their ethical consequences.

Endnote 78, page 502: The Calvinist's mood of strictness, cold distance, and self-reliant isolation was lacking among lay Catholics in medieval times.

Endnote 81, pages 502–03: On the difference between good works and the transformation of conduct that follows from the influence of God's grace.

Endnotes 83 and 115, pages 503 and 506: On the checking-account manner of living (balancing out sins with good works, and vice-versa) and how this was no longer an option for the Puritans.

Endnote 92, page 504: On Puritanism's emphasis on "self-control" as one of the fathers of modern military discipline.

Endnote 95, page 504: On the emphasis on reason and the downplaying of the emotions among the Puritans.

Endnote 96, page 504: An *evaluation* of the religions discussed here is "distant from our concern"; the *effect* or religious "devotion on practical *behavior* is the only concern here."

Endnote 104, page 505: Rather than showing contrition for his sins, the Calvinist hates them and endeavors to overcome sinning through activity on behalf of God's glory.

Endnote 122, page 507: On the causes for the "*un*methodical character of the Lutheran organization of life."

——, page 508: On the origins of the general posture of resignation among the Germans and its impact on relationships.

Endnote 129, pages 510–11: On the religious origins in the West of the idea of tolerance.

Endnote 133, page 512: On the limitations of psychology, given its state of advancement, to assist Weber's research.

Endnote 138, pages 512–13: On our indebtedness to the idea of basic human rights (one source of which is Puritanism).

Endnote 169, page 516: On the predilection of ascetic Protestants for mathematics and the natural sciences, and, especially, physics (see also Ch. 5, note 83).

——, page 517: On the driving religious forces behind the scientific empiricism of the seventeenth century (see also Ch. 5, note 83).

——, page 517: On the implications that follow for the educational agenda of ascetic Protestantism.

Endnote 179, page 518: On how the systematic organization of life under Methodism can *not* be viewed as belonging "in a *general* line of development toward 'individualism'."

Endnote 190, page 519: On how Methodist emotionalism *perhaps* implies a stronger *ascetic* penetration of life than Pietism.

Endnote 197, page 521: On why the Anabaptists produced less theology "than would have been consistent with their principles."

——, page 521: Weber's criticisms of the distinguished theologian Ritschl on Anabaptism's collapse.

Endnote 199, page 522: On how to define a sect.

Endnote 206, page 523: On asceticism's hostility to authority.

——, page 523: On the uniqueness of democracy, even today, among peoples influenced by Puritanism (and the differences between these democracies and those that flowed out of the "Latin spirit").

——, page 523: On the "lack of respect" at the foundation of American behavior

Endnote 211, page 524: According to the Pietist Spener, owing to their reputations, the Quakers deserve to be envied.

Endnote 222, pages 525–26: The "truthfulness," "uprightness," and candor among Americans are all legacies of Puritanism. More "formalistic and cognitive," they vary from the German "honesty."

Chapter 5

Endnote 15, page 528: On the prohibition among the Puritans of "thoughtless speech."

——, page 528: On the "melancholy" of the Puritans.

Endnote 19, pages 528–29: On the origins of the observation that "the modern professional 'has no time'."

Endnote 20, page 529: Baxter on serving the common good.

Endnote 22, page 529: On Puritanism's view that proximity to a large city may enhance virtue.

Endnote 27, page 530: On the Puritan view of marriage and "the sober procreation of children," and the visible legacies of this view in Benjamin Franklin's "hygenic utilitarian" view of sexual intercourse.

——, page 531: On the part played by the baptizing churches and sects in protecting women's freedom of conscience.

Endnote 37, page 532: On Hinduism and economic traditionalism in India.

Endnote 39, page 532: On economic utilitarianism as deriving ultimately from an impersonal formulation of the "love thy neighbor" commandment.

Endnote 46, page 533: On how Pietists, Quakers, and Mennonites make profits and still remain pious—indeed, large profits may be a "direct *consequence* of pious uprightness."

Endnote 48, page 533: Milton's view that only the middle class (between the aristocracy and the destitute) can be the social carrier of virtue.

Endnote 49, page 533: Weber states his concern with *how* the religious orientations of believers exercise a practical effect upon their vocational ethic.

Endnote 52, page 534: On Calvin's prohibition of begging and the opposition of the Puritans to the "begging-letter system."

Endnote 54, page 535: On the American glorification of "business *success* and *acquisition* as a symptom of spiritual *achievement*," and the American lack of respect for inherited wealth.

Endnote 69, pages 536–37: Comparing Jewish and Puritan ethics (including economic ethics).

Endnote 78, page 539: On the adverse consequences for the development of art of the "Renaissance of the Old Testament" and the Puritan rejection of the deification of human wants and desires.

——, page 539: On experiencing the Puritan sensibility while standing in front of a Rembrandt painting.

Endnote 79, pages 539–40: On the lesser development of Protestant asceticism in Holland.

——, page 540: On the formality of the Dutch as a mixture of middle-class "respectability" and the consciousness of status among the aristocracy.

Endnote 81, page 540: On the Puritan rejection of indifference and adoption of an either-or alternative: "God's will or the vanity of the flesh."

Endnote 82, page 540: On the protests by the Quakers in Amsterdam against fashionable apparel.

——, page 540: The male apparel today is essentially the same as that of the Puritans.

Endnote 85, page 541: On the influence of Puritanism on the development of the natural sciences (see also Ch. 4, note 169).

Endnote 89, page 541: On the resistance of ascetic Protestants to culinary delights (oysters).

Endnote 91, page 542: On the two (very different) psychological sources of the wish to accumulate wealth.

——, page 542: A critical commentary in Sombart on the accumulation of wealth.

Endnote 94, page 542: To the Quakers, all "unconscientious" use of possessions must be avoided.

Endnote 96, page 543: On why Baxter "does not view matters through the eyes of the 'bourgeoisie'."

——, page 543: "For those whose conscience remains troubled wherever an economic . . . interpretation is omitted. . . ."

——, page 543: Economic development importantly influences the formation of religious ideas, yet ideas for their part carry "within themselves an autonomous momentum" and coercive power.

Endnote 97, page 543: Eduard Bernstein's view that asceticism is a middle-class virtue is correct, but incomplete.

Endnote 100, page 544: In the Dutch case in the latter half of the seventeenth century, "the superior power of inherited wealth broke the ascetic spirit."

Endnote 103, page 544: That the "character disposition" of the English was actually less predisposed toward an ascetic ethos than the "character disposition" in other countries.

Endnote 104, page 544: On the colonization of different New England regions by different groups of people.

Endnote 106, pages 544–45: Modern Western capitalism *characteristically* originated out of a "stratum of *small*-scale capitalists and *not* out of the hands of the great financial magnates."

Endnote 115, page 545–46: On Spener's support for engagement in business, despite the temptations involved, as "useful to the human species."

Endnote 116, page 546: The hiring of a "godly servant" is to be recommended, according to Baxter, for he "will do all your service . . . as if God Himself had bid him to do it." Weber notes that "the interests of God and the interests of employers here suspiciously interweave with one another."

Endnote 121, pages 546–47: An example of how Protestant asceticism socialized the masses to work.

Endnote 122, page 547: On the medieval craftsman's putative enjoyment of "that which he produced himself."

——, page 547: On Puritanism's glorification of work and capitalism's capacity today to coerce a willingness to work.

Endnote 126, page 547: On the origins in England of powerful public opposition to monopolies; on the belief that monopolistic barriers to trade violated human rights.

Endnote 129, pages 547–48: On the parallel development of the "lofty profession of spirituality" among Quakers and their "shrewdness and tact in the transaction of mundane affairs."

——, page 548: On how piety is conducive to the businessperson's success.

SUGGESTED FURTHER READING

A. THE PROTESTANT ETHIC THESIS AND THE PROTESTANT ETHIC DEBATE

Anthologies

Aronson, Perla and Edward Weisz, eds. 2007. *La vigencia del pensiamento de Max Weber a cien años de "la etica protestante y el espiritu del capitalismo."* Buenos Aires: Editorial Gorla.

Baehr, Peter, ed. 2005. "Max Weber's *Protestant Ethic and the "Spirit" of Capitalism*: A Centenary Special Issue." *Journal of Classical Sociology* 5 (March).

Besnard, Phillip, ed. 1970. *Protestantisme et Capitalisme: La controverse post-Weberienne.* Paris: Librairie Armand Colin.

Eisenstadt, S. N., ed., *The Protestant Ethic and Modernization.* London: Basic Books, 1968.

Green, Robert W., ed. 1973. *Protestantism, Capitalism, and Social Science: The Weber Thesis Controversy.* Lexington, MA: D.C. Heath.

Lehmann, Hartmut and Guenther Roth, eds. 1993. *Weber's Protestant Ethic: Origins, Evidence, Contexts.* Cambridge, UK: Cambridge University Press.

Losito, Marta, ed. 2006. *L'idea weberiana della modernita alla luce della globalizzazione.* Trento: Temi Editrice.

Martinez, Javier Rodriquez, ed. 2005. *En el centenario de la etica protestante y el espiritu del capitalismo.* Madrid: CIS.

Pina, Javier Rodriguez, ed. 2005. "La modernidad en la sociologia de Max Weber. Cien anos de polemica." *Sociologica* 20 (Sept.–Dec.).

Schluchter, Wolfgang and Friedrich Wilhelm Graf, eds. 2005. *Asketischer Protestantismus und der "Geist" des modernen Kapitalismus.* Tübingen: Mohr/Siebeck.

Seyfarth, Constans and Walter M. Sprondel, eds. 1973. *Seminar: Religion und gesellschaftliche Entwicklung—Studien zur Protestantismus-Kapitalismus. These Max Webers.* Frankfurt: Suhrkamp.

Swatos, William H. Jr., and Lutz Kaelber, eds. 2005. *The Protestant Ethic Turns 100: Essays on the Centenary of the Weber Thesis.* Boulder, CO: Paradigm Publishers.

Telos. 1988–89. "Symposium on Weber's *The Protestant Ethic*." Pp. 71–167 in *Telos: A Quarterly Journal of Critical Thought*, 78 (Winter). [See also *Telos*, Fall, 1989 (81).]

Max Weber Studies. 2001. "Issues of Translation." Edited by David J. Chalcraft and Sam Whimster. Vol. 2, 1 (November).

Symposium on Weber's *The Protestant Ethic*." 1988–89. Pp. 71–167 in *Telos: A Quarterly Journal of Critical Thought*, 78 (Winter). [See also *Telos*, Fall, 1989 (81).]

Books, Chapters, and Articles

Bendix, Reinhard. 1956. *Work and Authority in Industry.* Berkeley: The University of California Press.

Campbell, Colin. 1987. *The Romantic Ethic and the Spirit of Modern Consumerism*. Oxford, UK: Blackwell.

Chalcraft, David J. "Bringing the Text Back in: On Ways of Reading the Iron Cage Metaphor in the Two Editions of *The Protestant Ethic*." Pp. 142–63 in *Organizing Modernity*, edited by Larry Ray and Michael Reed. London: Routledge.

Collins, Randall. 1986. *Weberian Sociological Theory*. Cambridge, UK: Cambridge University Press.

Fulbrook, Mary. 1983. *Piety and Politics*. Cambridge, UK: Cambridge University Press.

Goldman, Harvey. 1988. *Max Weber and Thomas Mann: The Calling and the Shaping of the Self*. Berkeley: The University of California Press.

Holton, R. J. 1985. *The Transition from Feudalism to Capitalism*. New York: St. Martin's Press.

Landes, David S. 1998. *The Wealth and Poverty of Nations*. New York: Norton.

Lipset, Seymour Martin (1963, 1979) The First New Nation. New York: W.W. Norton.

Little, David. 1969. *Religion, Order and Law*. Chicago: The University of Chicago Press.

Marshall, Gordon. 1979. "The Weber Thesis and the Development of Capitalism in Scotland." *Scottish Journal of Sociology*, 3: 173–211.

——. 1980. *Presbyteries and Profits*. Oxford: Clarendon Press.

——. 1982. *In Search of the Spirit of Capitalism*. London: Hutchinson.

Nelson, Benjamin. 1969. *The Idea of Usury*. Chicago: The University of Chicago Press.

——. 1981. *On the Roads to Modernity: Conscience, Science and Civilizations*, edited by Toby E. Huff. Totowa, NJ: Rowman and Littlefield.

Poggi, Gianfranco. 1983. *Calvinism and the Capitalist Spirit*. Amherst, MA: The University of Massachusetts Press.

Silber, Ilana. 1993. "Monasticism and the 'Protestant Ethic': Asceticism, Rationality and Wealth in the Medieval West." *The British Journal of Sociology*, 44, 1: 103–23.

Swedberg, Richard. 1998. *Max Weber and the Idea of Economic Sociology*. Princeton, NJ: Princeton University Press.

Tawney, R. J. 1954 (1926). *Religion and the Rise of Capitalism*. New York: New American Library.

Troeltsch, Ernst. 1960 (1911). *The Social Teaching of the Christian Churches*, vols. I and II. Translated by Olive Wyon. New York: Harper Torchbooks.

Walzer, Michael. 1966. *The Revolution of the Saints: A Study in the Origins of Radical Politics*. London: Weidenfeld and Nicolson.

Zaret, David. 1985. *The Heavenly Contract: Ideology and Organization in Pre-Revolutionary Puritanism*. Chicago: The University of Chicago Press.

See also the many works directly on the Protestant ethic thesis cited at the editor's introduction (pp. 54–58) and the "Literature Cited" section (pp. 554–55).

B. MAX WEBER: LIFE AND WORK

Albrow, Martin. 1990. *Max Weber's Construction of Social Theory*. New York: St. Martin's Press.

Aronson, Perla and Eduardo Weisz. 2005. *Sociedad y Religión: Un siglo de controversias en torno a la nocion weberiana de rationalizacion*. Buenos Aires: Prometeo.

Bendix, Reinhard. 1962. *Max Weber: an Intellectual Portrait*. New York: Doubleday Anchor.

———. and Guenther Roth. 1971. *Scholarship and Partisanship*. Berkeley: University of California Press.

Beetham, David. 1974. *Max Weber and the Theory of Modern Politics*. London: George Allen and Unwin.

Colliot-Thelene, Catherine. 2001. *Etudes Weberiennes*. Paris: Presses Universitaires.

———. 2006. *La Sociologie de Max Weber*. Paris: LaDecouverte.

Hennis, Wilhelm. 1987. *Max Weber: Essays in Reconstruction*. London: Allen & Unwin.

Honigsheim, Paul. 1968. *On Max Weber*. New York: Free Press.

Huff, Toby and Wolfgang Schluchter, eds. 1999. *Max Weber and Islam*. New Brunswick, NJ: 1999.

Kalberg, Stephen. 2003. "Max Weber." Pp. 132–92 in *The Blackwell Companion to Major Social Theorists*, edited by George Ritzer. Oxford: Blackwell Publishers.

Kim, Sung Ho. 2004. *Max Weber's Politics of Civil Society*. Cambridge, UK: Cambridge University Press.

Löwith, Karl. 1982. *Max Weber and Karl Marx*. London: Allen & Unwin.

Mommsen, Wolfgang J. 1985. *Max Weber and German Politics, 1890–1920*. Chicago: University of Chicago Press.

———. 1989. *The Political and Social Theory of Max Weber*. Chicago: University of Chicago Press.

———. and Jürgen Osterhammel, eds. 1987. *Max Weber and His Contemporaries*. Boston: Unwin Hyman.

Nelson, Benjamin. 1974. "Max Weber's 'Author's Introduction' (1920): A Master Clue to His Main Aims." *Sociological Inquiry*, 44: 269–77.

Roth, Guenther. 2001. *Max Webers deutsch-englische Familiengeschichte*. 1800–1950. Tübingen: Mohr/Siebeck.

Ruano de la Fuente, Yolanda. 1996. *Racionalidad y conciencia tragica. La Modernidad segun Max Weber*. Madrid: Trotta.

Salomon, Albert. 1935. Max Weber's Sociology. *Social Research*, II, (Feb.): 60–73.

Schluchter, Wolfgang and Guenther Roth. 1979. *Max Weber's Vision of History*. Berkeley: University of California Press, pp. 11–64.

Schroeder, Ralph, ed. 1998. *Max Weber, Democracy and Modernization*. New York: St. Martin's Press.

Swedberg, Richard. 2004. *The Max Weber Dictionary*. Stanford, CA: Stanford University Press.

Tenbruck, Friedrich. 1999. *Das Werk Max Webers: Gesammelte Aufsätze zu Max Weber*, edited by Harald Homann. Tübingen: Mohr/Siebeck.

Turner, Bryan S. 1992. *Max Weber: From History to Modernity*. London: Routledge.

Weber, Marianne. 1975. *Max Weber: A Biographie*. Translated by Harry Zohn. New York: John Wiley & Sons.

Whimster, Sam and Scott Lash, eds. 1987. *Max Weber, Rationality and Modernity*. London: Allen & Unwin.

See also works cited in the "Literature Cited" section (pp. 554–55).

NOTES FOR *THE PROTESTANT ETHIC*

Chapter I

1. From the voluminous literature on this study I am citing only the most comprehensive criticisms. (a) Felix Rachfahl, "Kalvinismus und Kapitalismus," *Internationale Wochenschrift für Wissenschaft, Kunst und Technik* (1909), nos. 39–43. In reply, see my article, "Antikritisches zum 'Geist' des Kapitalismus," *Archiv für Sozialwissenschaft und Sozialpolitik* 30 (1910): 176–202. Rachfahl then replied in his "Nochmals Kalvinismus und Kapitalismus," 1910, nos. 22–25, of the *Internationale Wochenschrift*. Finally, my "Antikritisches Schlusswort" [Final Word], *Archiv* 31 (1910): 554–99. [These essays, and further "critical" comments and "anti-critical" responses by Weber (1907–10), have been collected into one volume. See *Max Weber: Die protestantische Ethik II*, edited by Johannes Winckelmann (Gütersloh: Gütersloher Verlag, 1978). Weber's responses to his critics are now available in English. See *The Protestant Ethic Debate: Max Weber's Replies to His Critics, 1907–1910*, edited by David Chalcraft and Austin Harrington (translated by Harrington and Mary Shields, Liverpool: Liverpool University Press, 2001). Weber occasionally refers in the notes below to "the critics" and to his "anti-critical" replies. These terms refer to this early debate.] (Brentano, in the criticism presently to be referred to, evidently did not know of this last phase of the discussion, as he does not refer to it.)

I have not incorporated anything in this edition from the rather unproductive (unavoidably) polemics against Rachfahl. He is an author whom I otherwise admire, but who has in this instance ventured into a field he has not thoroughly mastered. I have only added a few supplementary references from my anti-critical replies, and have attempted, in new passages and footnotes, to make impossible any future misunderstanding. (b) Werner Sombart, *Der Bourgeois* (Munich and Leipzig: Duncker & Humblot, 1913) [*The Quintessence of Capitalism* (New York: Howard Fertig, 1967)]. I shall return in the notes below to this volume. Finally, (c) Lujo Brentano in part 2 of the appendix to his Munich address (in the Academy of Sciences, 1913) on *Die Anfänge* [Beginnings] *des modernen Kapitalismus* [see note 15 below], which was published in 1916. [See ch. 3, excursus 2 on "Puritanism and Capitalism," pp. 117–57.] I shall also refer to this criticism in the notes in the proper places.

I invite anyone who may be interested to convince himself by comparison that in revision I have *not* left out, changed the meaning of, weakened, or added materially *different* statements to *a single essential sentence* of my essay. There was no occasion to do so, and the development of my argument will convince anyone who still doubts. Sombart and Brentano engaged in a more bitter quarrel with each other than with me. I consider Brentano's criticism of Sombart's book [published in 1911; translated in 1913 as *The Jews and Modern Capitalism* (New York: Burt Franklin)] in many points well founded, but often very unjust, even apart from the fact that Brentano does not himself seem to understand the real essence of the problem of the Jews (which is entirely omitted from this essay, but will be dealt with later). [See pp. 14, 233–34, 290–99; *Ancient Judaism* (New York: Free Press, 1952.)]

From theologians I have received numerous valuable suggestions in connection with this study. Its reception on their part has been in general friendly and objective, even when wide differences of opinion on particular points were apparent. This is all the more valuable to me since I would not have been surprised by a certain hostility toward the way in which these matters were necessarily treated here. What to a theologian is *valuable* in his religion naturally cannot play a very large part in this study. We are concerned with what, if *evaluated* from a religious point of view, are often quite external and unrefined aspects of religious life. These aspects, however, precisely because they were external and unrefined, have often had the strongest influence.

Another book that, besides containing many other themes, is a very welcome confirmation of and supplement to this essay, insofar as it addresses our problem, is the important work of [Ernst] Troeltsch, *The Social Teaching of the Christian Churches*, 2 vols. (New York: Harper & Row, 1960 [1911]). It treats the entire history of the ethics of Western Christianity from a very comprehensive, and unique, point of view. I here refer the reader to Troeltsch for general comparison, as I cannot refer to his work repeatedly in respect to particular points. Troeltsch is principally concerned with the *doctrines* of religion, while I am interested rather in the practical effect of religion. [entire note from 1920]

2.　The deviant cases are explained (not always but frequently) if we note that the religion of an industry's labor force is naturally, in the *first* instance, determined by the religion of the locality in which the industry is situated (that is, from which its labor is drawn). This circumstance often alters the impression given at first glance by statistics on religious affiliation, for instance in [the highly Catholic] state of North-Rhine Westphalia [Rheinprovinz]. Furthermore, figures can naturally be relied upon only if the particular occupations have become thoroughly specialized. Otherwise, in some situations, very large employers may be thrown together, under the category "proprietors of companies," with "master craftsmen," who work alone. Above all, the fully developed capitalism of *today*, especially so far as its broad, unskilled labor force is concerned, has become independent of any influence that religion *may* have had in the past. More on this point later.

3.　Compare, for example, Hermann Schell, *Der Katholizismus als Prinzip des Fortschrittes* (Würzburg: Andreas Gobel, 1899), p. 31, and Georg Freiherr von Hertling, *Das Prinzip des Katholizismus und die Wissenschaft* (Freiburg: Herder, 1899), p. 58.

4.　One of my students has thoroughly studied the most complete statistical material we possess on this subject: the denominational affiliation statistics of [the state of] Baden. See Martin Offenbacher, "Konfession und soziale Schichtung." *Eine Studie über die wirtschaftliche Lage der Katholiken und Protestanten in Baden* (Tübingen and Leipzig: Mohr, 1901), vol. 4, pt. 5, of the *Volkswirtschaftliche Abhandlungen der badischen Hochschulen*. The facts and figures used for illustrative purposes below all originate from this study.

5.　Germans (Protestants) and Poles (Catholics) lived side by side until World War II in what is today western Poland (Silesia) [sk].

6.　For example, in 1895 in [the state of] Baden, for every 1,000 Protestants a tax of 954,060 marks was collected for property that produced taxable income; 589,000 marks was collected for every 1,000 Catholics. It is true that the Jews, with more than four million marks for every 1,000 Jews, were far ahead of the rest. (For details see Offenbacher, *op. cit.*, p. 21.)

7.　On this point compare the whole discussion in Offenbacher's study.

8.　Offenbacher provides for Baden more detailed evidence also on this point in his first two chapters.

9.　As innumerable commentators have noted, *Herrschaft* is a particularly difficult term to translate. It implies both legitimate authority and a coercive, dominating component. I will employ (following the translation in Weber's major analytic work, *E&S*) "domination" and "rulership" synonymously throughout. This appears appropriate, as Weber occasionally uses the term *Autorität* (authority) in *The Protestant Ethic* volume [sk].

10.　The population of Baden was composed in 1895 as follows: Protestants, 37.0 percent; Catholics, 61.3 percent; Jews, 1.5 percent. The percentage of students who attended the *noncompulsory* schools [beyond the primary level] were, however, divided as follows (Offenbacher, p. 16 [Boldface from Weber.]):

	Protestant	Catholic	Jews
	Percent	Percent	Percent
Gymnasien	43	46	9.5
Realgymnasien	**69**	31	9
Oberrealschulen	**52**	41	7
Realschulen	49	40	12
Höhere Bürgerschulen ..	51	31	11
Average	48	42	10

[Moving from top to bottom of this table, the curricula in the schools move away from an emphasis on the classical liberal arts, including ancient languages, and toward modern languages, science, and mathematics. This school system was replaced with a three-track system in the 1950s. Weber's arithmetic is faulty. See Becker, 1997; Marshall, 1982, pp. 20–22]

The same proportions may be observed in Prussia, Bavaria, Württemberg, the German-speaking territories, and Hungary (see figures in Offenbacher, pp. 18 ff.).

11.   The figures in the preceding note indicate that Catholic attendance at secondary schools, which is regularly one-third less than the Catholic share of the total population, is exceeded, by a small percentage, *only* in the case of the *Gymnasien* (mainly as a result of preparation for theological studies). With reference to the subsequent discussion it may further be noted as characteristic that, in Hungary, those affiliated with the *Reformed* church exceed even the average Protestant [Lutheran] record of attendance at secondary schools. (See Offenbacher, p. 19, note.)

12.   For the figures see Offenbacher (p. 54) and the tables at the end of his study.

13.   This is especially well illustrated by passages in the studies of Sir William Petty [*Political Arithmetick* (London: Henry Mortlock, 1687)], (which will be referred to repeatedly later).

14.   Petty's occasional reference [to the contrary in] the case of *Ireland* is very simply explained by the fact that the Protestant stratum lived in Ireland only as absentee landlords. If his illustrations had meant to maintain more he would have been wrong (as is well-known), as is demonstrated by the position of the "Scotch-Irish." The typical relationship between Protestantism and capitalism existed in Ireland just as elsewhere. (On the Scotch-Irish see C. A. Hanna, *The Scotch-Irish*, 2 vols. [New York: Putnam, 1902].) [1920]

15.   This is not, of course, to deny that the historical-political, external situations had exceedingly important consequences. I shall show later that many Protestant sects were small and hence homogeneous minorities, as were actually all the *strict* Calvinists outside of Geneva and New England (even where they were in possession of political power). This [external situation] was of fundamental significance for the development of believers' entire orientation of life in the sects, and this orientation then reacted back upon the participation of the faithful in economic life.

That *migrants* from all the religions of the earth—from India, Arabia, China, Syria, Phoenicia, Greece, Lombardy, "cawerzische"—have universally been the social carriers, to other countries, of the *commercial education* in highly developed areas has nothing to do with our problem. (Brentano, in the essay I shall often cite, *Die Anfänge des modernen Kapitalismus* (Munich: Akademie der Wissenschaften, 1916) refers to his own family. But *bankers* of foreign extraction have existed at *all* times, and in all countries, as the social carriers of commercial experience and connections. These bankers are not unique to *modern* capitalism, and were looked upon with ethical mistrust by the Protestants [see below]. The case of the Protestant families from Locarno [Italy], such as the Muralts, Pestalozzi, and others, who migrated to Zurich, was different. They very soon became the social carriers of a specifically modern capitalist [industrial] development.) [1920]

16. Offenbacher, *op. cit.,* p. 68.

17. Weber is here referring to the French Huguenots [sk].

18. Weber refers here to those churches that take the early Christianity of the apostles as their ideal [sk].

19. Unusually acute observations on the characteristic uniqueness of the different religions in Germany and France, and the interweaving of their differences with other cultural elements in the conflict of nationalities in Alsace, are to be found in the excellent study by Werner Wittich, "Deutsche und französische Kultur im Elsass" [German and French Culture in Alsace-Lorraine], *Illustrierte Elsässische Rundschau* (1900; also published separately).

20. St. Francis lived in voluntary poverty and preached a doctrine of brotherly love and optimism [sk].

21. Naturally only *then*, we wish to make clear, if the *possibility* of capitalist development in the relevant area was *at all* present [1920].

22. Weber is here thinking of monks as entrepreneurial, as they often were in the High Middle Ages [sk].

23. On this point see, for instance, Dupin de St. André, "L'ancienne église réformée de Tours. Les membres de l'église," *Bulletin de la société de l'histoire du Protestantisme,* vol. 4 [1856], p. 10. Here again one could (and this idea will be appealing especially to those persons who evaluate this theme from the perspective of Catholicism) view the desire for *emancipation* from monastic control (or even control by the church) as the driving motive. But this view is opposed not only by the judgment of contemporaries (including Rabelais), but also, for example, by the qualms of conscience raised in the first national synods of the Huguenots (for example, 1st Synod, C. partic. qu. 10 in J. Aymon, *Synodes nationaux de s églises réformées de France* [1710], p. 10), as to whether a *banker* might become an elder of the church. Furthermore, and in spite of Calvin's unambiguous stand, repeated discussions took place in the same synods regarding the permissibility of taking interest. These discussions were occasioned by the questions of extremely conscientious members of the congregations. In part these discussions arose because a high percentage of church members were also participants in business and banking circles—and hence had a direct interest in these questions. These discussions arose, however, *at the same time* also because it was hoped by these circles that the wish to practice *usuraria pravitas* [depraved usury]—and to do so without supervision through the confession—could be considered as *not* central. (The same—see below—is true of Holland. Let it be said explicitly that the prohibition of the charging of interest by Canon law will play absolutely no part in *this* investigation.)

24. W. Eberhard Gothein, *Wirtschaftsgeschichte des Schwarzwaldes* [Economic History of the Black Forest], vol. 1 [Strasbourg: Trubner, 1892; reprinted in German in 1970 (New York: Burt Franklin)], p. 67.

25. The brief observations by Sombart relate to this point. See Sombart, *Der moderne Kapitalismus* (Leipzig: Duncker & Humblot [1902]), p. 380. Later, in by far the weakest (in my opinion) in respect [to the importance of Calvinism] to his larger studies, *The Quintessence of Capitalism* [see note 1], Sombart defended, unfortunately, a completely incorrect "thesis." I will return to it occasionally below [see notes 12 and 32 of ch. 2]. Sombart's study was influenced by the weak investigation by Franz Keller, *Unternehmung und Mehrwert* (Paderborn: Schriften der Görresgesellschaft, no. 12, 1912). Keller's volume contains many good observations (although they are not, in *this* respect, new). Nonetheless, his study remains *below* the standard set by other works of modern Catholic apologetics. [See note 32, ch. 2.] [1920]

26.   It has been thoroughly established that the simple fact of a change of residence is among the most effective means of intensifying labor (see note 15 above). The same Polish girl who at home was not to be shaken loose from her traditional laziness by any chance of earning money, however tempting, seems to change her entire nature and become capable of unlimited expenditures of energy when she becomes a migratory worker in a foreign milieu, such as [German] Saxony. The exact same transformation is manifest in the case of Italian laborers.

The socializing influence that occurs with movement into a higher "cultural milieu" is not here in the least the decisive factor (although it does, of course, play a part). This conclusion is evident if only because the same [intensification of work] occurs also wherever the *type* of work (such as agricultural labor) is the same in the foreign milieu as at home. Indeed, this intensification occurs despite the temporary decline in workers' standard of living (as a result of the accommodation, in the foreign milieu, in migrant labor camps) that would never be tolerated at home. The simple fact of working in completely unaccustomed and different surroundings breaks through the worker's traditional ways—and this new milieu is the "socializing" force. It is hardly necessary to note how much of American economic development is based upon such effects.

The similar significance of the Babylonian Exile for the Jews in ancient times is apparent (one would like to say, obvious in the inscriptions). The same is true for the Parsenes [today in Iran and Iraq, and reformed Zoroastrians known as followers of Mazdaism]. However, for the Protestants, as apparent even in the unmistakable differences among believers in the orientation to the economy in the Puritan New England colonies in contrast to Catholic Maryland, the Episcopal South, and denominationally mixed Rhode Island, the influence of unique religious factors is apparent. Indeed, this influence clearly indicates that religion plays an *independent* role. The same must be said of the Jain sect in India.

27.   It is well known to be, in most of its forms, a more or less *moderated* Calvinism or Zwinglianism. [1920]

28.   In Hamburg, which is almost entirely Lutheran, the *only* fortune going back to the seventeenth century is that of a well-known *Reformed* family. (This example was kindly called to my attention by Professor A. Wahl.) [1920]

29.   Hence, the assertion that such a connection [between Calvinism and the capitalist spirit] exists is not "new." E. de Laveleye [*Protestantism and Catholicism in Their Bearing upon the Liberty and Prosperity of Nations* (London: John Murray, 1875)] and Matthew Arnold [*St. Paul and Protestantism* (London: Smith, Elder, 1906)], among others, have addressed this connection. On the contrary, "new" is only its questioning, which is entirely unfounded. The task here is *to explain* this connection. [1920]

30.   Naturally, this does not mean that official Pietism, like other religious denominations, did not at a later date, as a result of [enduring] patriarchal proclivities, oppose certain "progressive" features of the capitalist economy (for example, the transition from cottage industry to the factory system). As we will often note, precisely that which a religion *strives for* as an ideal must be distinguished clearly from the actual *result* of the religion's influence upon the organization of its believers' lives.

(In a [recent] article I have offered my own examples, from a study of a factory in Westphalia, of the particular adaptability of Pietist workers. See "Zur Psychophysik der gewerblichen Arbeit" [On the Psychological-Physics of Industrial Work], reprinted in *Max Weber Gesamtausgabe* (Tübingen: Mohr 1995/1924), I/11, ed. by Wolfgang Schluchter, pp. 42–178.]) [1920]

31.   Knox was a leading Calvinist reformer in Scotland. Voët, a professor of Near Eastern languages in Holland, influenced significantly Pietist doctrine. Both are noted below. Calvin and Luther are discussed in depth in chapters 3 and 4 [sk].

Chapter II

1. Weber generally places the term *spirit* in quotation marks, although I have omitted them for ease of reading. By doing so he wishes (a) to express his awareness that controversy surrounded this term and (b) to emphasize that he is using it in this study in a specific and unique manner (and thus to distance his usage, above all, from that of the major figure of German Idealism, G. W. F. Hegel [1770–1831]) [sk].

2. Weber here alludes to a few central aspects of his sociological methodology: (a) historical concepts must refer to "historical individuals" (unique cases); (b) classificatory schemes (*genus proximum, differentia specifica*) are too abstract to capture uniqueness and hence are useful *only* as preliminary conceptual tools; (c) concepts do not "replicate reality," for "reality" varies depending on the investigator's particular research question (or "vantage point" upon reality); and (d) following from the above, concepts can be formulated only after an assessment by researchers of the "cultural significance" of potential constituent elements and a selection accordingly. All the above points are central to Weber's sociological methodology based on "subjective meaning," "interpretive understanding," and "ideal types." See "'Objectivity' in Social Science and Social Policy," in *The Methodology of the Social Sciences,* translated and edited by Edward A. Shils and Henry A. Finch (New York: Free Press, 1949). See also the "Basic Concepts" chapter in *E&S* (pp. 3–22). See Fritz Ringer, *Max Weber's Methodology* (Cambridge, MA: Harvard University Press, 1997); John Drysdale, "How Are Social-Scientific Concepts Formed? A Reconstruction of Max Weber's Theory of Concept Formation," *Sociological Theory* 14 (March 1996): 71–88 [sk].

3. The final [five short] passages are from *Necessary Hints to Those That Would Be Rich*, in *Works* (1736) [Sparks ed. (Chicago, 1882), vol. 2, p. 80]. The earlier are passages from *Advice to a Young Tradesman* (1748) (Sparks ed., vol. 2, pp. 87 ff.). [The italics in the text are Franklin's.] [sk]

4. This book, *Der Amerikamüde* (Frankfurt, 1855; Vienna and Leipzig, 1927), is well known to be a fictional paraphrase of Lenau's impressions of America. As a work of art, the book would today be somewhat difficult to enjoy. However, it is unsurpassed as a document of the differences (now long since blurred over) between German and American sensibilities; indeed, one could say, of the spiritual life of the Germans (which has remained *common* to all Germans since the German mysticism of the Middle Ages, despite all the differences between German Catholics and German Protestants) in contrast to Puritan-capitalist "can-do" energy. [See ch. 3.] [Italics in paragraphs one (*time*), two (*credit*), and four (the good *paymaster*) are Franklin's; the remainder are Weber's.]

5. Sombart has used this quotation as a motto for his section on "the genesis of capitalism" (*Der moderne Kapitalismus, op. cit.*, vol. 1 [see pp. 193–634], p. 193. See also p. 390).

6. Which obviously does not mean either that Jakob Fugger was a morally indifferent or an irreligious man, or that Benjamin Franklin's ethic is *completely* covered by the above quotations. It scarcely required Brentano's quotations (*Die Anfänge des modernen Kapitalismus, op. cit.*, pp. 151 f.) to protect this well-known philanthropist from the misunderstanding that Brentano seems to attribute to me. The problem is actually just the reverse: how could such a philanthropist come to write precisely *these sentences* (the especially characteristic form of which Brentano neglected to reproduce) in the manner of a moralist? [1920]

7. This way of formulating the problem constitutes the basis for our differences with Sombart. The very considerable practical significance of this difference will become clear later. It should, however, be noted here that Sombart has by no means neglected this ethical aspect of the capitalist employer. However, in his train of thought, capitalism calls forth this ethical aspect. We must, on the contrary, for our purposes, take into consideration the opposite hypothesis. A final position on this difference can only be taken up at the end of this investigation. For Sombart's view see *op. cit.*, vol. 1, pp. 357, 380, etc. His

reasoning here connects with the brilliant conceptualizations offered in [Georg] Simmel's *Philosophie des Geldes* [Leipzig: Duncker & Humblot, 1900] [*The Philosophy of Money* (London: Routledge, 1978)] (final chapter). I will speak later [see notes 12 and 32] of the polemics which Sombart has brought forward against me in his *The Quintessence of Capitalism*. At this point any thorough discussion must be postponed.

8. "I grew convinced that *truth, sincerity,* and *integrity* in dealings between man and man were of the utmost importance *to the felicity of life*; and I formed written resolutions, which still remain *in my journal book* to practise them ever while I lived. Revelation had indeed no weight with me as such; but I entertained an opinion that, though certain actions might not be bad because they were forbidden by it, or good because it commanded them, yet probably these actions might be forbidden *because* they were bad for us, or commanded *because* they were beneficial to us in their own nature, all the circumstances of things considered" [*Autobiography*, ed. by F. W. Pine (New York: Henry Holt, 1916), p. 112].

9. "I therefore put myself as much as I could out of sight and started it"—that is, the project of a library which he had initiated—"as a scheme of a *number of friends,* who had requested me to go about and propose it to such as they thought lovers of reading. In this way my affair went on smoothly, and I ever after practised it on such occasions; and from my frequent successes, can heartily recommend it. The present little sacrifice of your vanity will afterwards be amply repaid. If it remains *awhile* uncertain to whom the merit belongs, someone more vain than yourself will be encouraged to claim it, and then even envy will be disposed to do you justice by plucking those assumed feathers and restoring them to their right owner" [*Autobiography, ibid.,* p. 140].

10. Brentano *(op. cit.,* pp. 125; 127, note 1) takes this remark as an occasion to criticize the later discussion of "that rationalization and intensification of discipline" to which this-worldly asceticism has subjected men. That, he says, is a "rationalization" toward an "irrational" organization of life. This is in fact quite correct. Something is never "irrational" in itself but only from a particular "rational" vantage point. For the nonreligious person every religious way of organizing life is irrational; for the hedonist every ascetic organization of life is "irrational" even if it may be, measured against *its* ultimate values, a "rationalization." If this essay wishes to make any contribution at all, may it be to unveil the many-sidedness of a concept—the "rational"—that only appears to be straightforward and linear. [1920] [See below, pp. 215–16; see also Weber, 1946c, p. 326; 1946e, p. 293; Kalberg, 1980.]

11. In reply to Brentano's (*Die Anfänge des modernen Kapitalismus, op. cit.,* pp. 150 ff.) very detailed but somewhat imprecise apologia for Franklin, whose ethical qualities I have allegedly misunderstood, I refer only to this statement. It should have been sufficient, in my opinion, to render this apologia superfluous. [1920]

12. I will take this opportunity [1920] to interweave a few "anti-critical" remarks prior to embarking upon the main argument. Sombart (*The Quintessence of Capitalism, op. cit.,* note 1, ch. 1) occasionally argues on behalf of the indefensible assertion that this "ethic" of Franklin is a "word-for-word" repetition of some writings of that great and universal genius of the Renaissance, Leon Battista Alberti [1404–1472]. In addition to writing theoretical treatises on mathematics, sculpture, painting, architecture, and love (he was personally a woman-hater), he authored a four-volume treatise on the household (*Libri della famiglia* [*Book on the Family*]). (Unfortunately, I have not at this writing been able to acquire the new edition by G. Mancini [Firenze: Carnesecchi e Figli, 1908] and thus must use the older edition by Bonucci [Florence, 1843–49, 5 vols.].)

The passage from Franklin is printed above word for word [see pp. 70–71]. Where, then, are corresponding passages found in Alberti's work, especially the maxim that stands at the beginning—"time is money"—and the admonitions that follow it? As far as I know, the only passage that bears the slightest resemblance is found toward the end of the first book of *Della Famiglia* (ed. Bonucci, vol. 2, p. 353). Alberti speaks here in very general terms of money as the *nervus rerum* [major driving force] of the household, which, consequently, must be especially well-managed. These same terms are earlier found [in ancient Rome] in Cato when he writes *de re rustica* [*On Agriculture*].

Moreover, to treat Alberti, who always emphasized his descent from one of the most distinguished feudal families of Florence ("*nobilissimi cavalieri*"; *Della Famiglia*, in *ibid.*, pp. 213, 228, 247, etc. [Bonucci ed.]), as a man of "mongrel blood" (and filled with envy for the noble families owing to his illegitimate birth, which was to him not in the least socially disqualifying) is quite incorrect. Likewise, it is incorrect to argue that, as a businessman, he was excluded from association with the nobility.

Characteristic for Alberti is surely his recommendation to become engaged in *large* businesses, for these businesses alone are worthy of *nobile e onesta famiglia* [persons from noble and honest families] and *libero e nobile animo* [free and noble souls] (*ibid.*, p. 209). Moreover, large businesses require less labor (see *Del governo della Famiglia*, bk. 4, pp. 55, 116, in the edition published for the Pandolfini); *therefore*, a putting-out business for wool and silk is the best business. Furthermore, ordered and strict budgetary practices are recommended, in other words, an assessment of expenditures by reference to income. Hence, involved here is mainly a principle that concerns proper *budgeting* rather than a principle related to *acquisition* (as Sombart especially [as a specialist on this subject] should have recognized).

Similarly, in his discussion of the nature of money (*ibid.*), Alberti's concern is with the investment of *wealth* (money or *possessioni*) and not with the utilization of capital. All this is *santa masserizia* [prudent management], as represented in Alberti's book by the statements of "Gianozzo." As protection against the uncertainties of fate, he recommends the early habituation to continuous activity, which, by the way, alone maintains healthfulness in the long run (see *Della Famiglia*, pp. 73–74) *in cose magnifiche e ample* [in magnificent and grand affairs] (p. 192), and an avoidance of laziness, which always presents a threat to continued employment. Hence, as a precaution against the possibility of unexpected changes, [Alberti advises] the careful learning of skills appropriate to one's social status (however, every *opera mercenaria* [work motivated by a desire for material gain] is unsuitable to one's social status) (bk. 1, p. 209).

[An entire array of activities praised by Alberti would be] viewed by every Puritan as sinful "deification of human wants and desires": Alberti's idea of *tranquillità dell' animo* [peace of the soul], his strong tendency toward the Epicurean λάθε βιώσας (*vivere a sè stesso* [leading a self-sufficient life]; *ibid.*, p. 262), his special dislike of any office (as a source of unrest, as a place where enemies are created, and as a source of entanglement in corrupt business practices) (*ibid.*, p. 258), his idealizing of life in a country villa, his nurturing of self-confidence from thinking about his ancestors, and his consideration of the honor of his family (which, because of the importance of honor, should keep its fortune together, as is the Florentine custom, and not divide it up) as the decisive standard and purpose [for his business activity]. Indeed, in the eyes of Benjamin Franklin, all of these proclivities would have expressed (for he remained unacquainted with them) the pomposity of the aristocracy.

One should further note the high prestige of all endeavors that require a broad, liberal arts education (*industria* [diligent activity] is primarily oriented to literary and [broadly understood] scientific labor). This labor is viewed as the single endeavor actually worthy of the dignity of human beings. Basically, only the illiterate Gianozzo understands *masserizia*—in the sense of "rational budgeting" as the means to live independently from others and to avoid the fall into poverty—as equal in dignity to the tasks of the educated. Because of this perception, Gianozzo explains the origin of "rational budgeting" by reference to [the wisdom of] an old priest rather than by noting [its actual origins in] the ethic of medieval monks (see below).

One could place all of the above comments next to Benjamin Franklin's ethic and organized life (and, above all, that of his Puritan ancestors). In order to measure the depth of the differences one would note the orientation [on the one hand] of Renaissance literati [writers and scholars] toward a humanistic aristocracy, and [on the other] the orientation of the treatises and sermons of the Puritans toward the masses of a business-oriented middle class (more precisely, the *Commis* [merchants]). Alberti's economic rationalism, which is comprehensively supported by references to ancient authors, is in its essence most similar to the treatment of economic matters in the works of Xenophon (who remained unknown to him), Cato, Varro, and Columella (all of whom he quotes). However, especially in Cato and Varro, *acquisition* as such stands in the foreground in an entirely different way than is the case for Alberti. Furthermore, Alberti's (admittedly infrequent) discussions on the use of the *fattori*—the division of labor and discipline—to influence the unreliability of the peasants, etc., indeed sounds very much like a transposition of Cato's teachings on common sense, practical wisdom, and prudent behavior, acquired from the realm of the ancient slave-using household, onto the cottage industry and the manufacturing milieu, both of which are based upon free labor rather than slave labor.

When Sombart (whose referral to the ethic of the Stoics is quite incorrect) discovers economic rationalism as "developed to its greatest external consistency" as early as Cato, one must say that (if this description is correctly understood) he is not entirely incorrect. One can indeed bring together the *diligens pater familias* [conscientious family patriarch] of the Romans with the ideal of the *massajo* [prudent management] of Alberti under the same category. Characteristic for Cato, above all, is that a landed estate is valued and judged as an object for the *investment* of wealth. Nonetheless, the concept of *industria* [in Alberti] is differently shaded as a result of the influence of Christianity.

And here the difference becomes clear. In the concept of *industria*, which originates out of monastic asceticism and which was developed by monastic writers, lies the seed of an *ethos*. This ethos was fully developed later in the exclusively *this*-worldly asceticism (see below!) of Protestantism (*thus*, as will be often emphasized, a relationship [existed between the other-worldly asceticism of the monastery and ascetic Protestantism's this-worldly asceticism], although asceticism, by the way, was *less* closely related to the official church dogma of St. Thomas Aquinas than to the Florentine and Siennese mendicant-ethicists). This *ethos* of asceticism is lacking in Cato and also in Alberti's own writings. Instead, for both, the issue is one of common sense, practical wisdom, and prudent behavior rather than ethics. Franklin's writings also involve utilitarian considerations. However, the ethical element in the sermon to young merchants is entirely unmistakable. Moreover, it constitutes—and this is what matters to us here—that which is characteristic. A lack of carefulness in handling money signifies to him that one has, so to speak, "murdered" embryos which could have been used for the creation of capital. For this reason, such carelessness is also an *ethical* defect.

An inner affinity between the two (Alberti and Franklin) exists in fact only insofar as Alberti (who, although called pious by Sombart, actually—despite taking the sacraments and holding a Roman benefice [as mediated through the church], and with the exception of two colorless passages in his writings—*did not himself in any way*, like so many humanists, employ religious motives as points of orientation for the organization of life he recommended) had *not yet* related his recommendation for "economic efficiency" to religious conceptions, while Franklin *no longer* did so. Utilitarianism, as apparent in Alberti's preference for the wool and silk cottage industries as well as in his mercantilist social utilitarianism ("that many people should be given employment"; see Alberti, *ibid.*, p. 292), justifies, at least formally, economic activity in both of these arenas. Indeed, Alberti's writings on this subject offer a very appropriate example for that type of, so to speak, immanent economic "rationalism" that in fact exists as a "reflection" of economic conditions. Yet this interest of authors purely "in the thing itself" has been found everywhere and in all eras, and not less in the Chinese classical period [700–400 BCE] and in ancient

Greece and Rome than during the Renaissance and Enlightenment epochs. There can be no doubt that, just as in antiquity in the writings of Cato, Varro, and Columella, and as is the case also here with Alberti and his contemporaries, economic *ratio* [rationalism] was to a great extent developed out of the teaching of *industria*. However, how can one believe that such a *teaching* by the literati [educated stratum] could develop the power to radically transform life in the same manner as occurs when a religious belief places *salvation premiums* upon a specific (in this case, methodical-rational) way of organizing life?

[The utilitarian organization of life that follows from such teachings by the literati] looks quite different from a *religion*-oriented "rationalization" of the organization of life (and hence, in the process, eventually also of the conduct of economic activity). The contrast is visible in a number of (highly diverging) religious groupings, in addition to the Puritans of all denominations: the Jains [in northern India], the Jews, certain ascetic sects of the Middle Ages, [the followers of the pre-Reformation English theologian John] Wyclif [*ca.* 1320–84], the Moravian Brotherhood (an offshoot of the Hussite movement [which was influenced by Wyclif]), the Skoptsi and Stundists in Russia, and numerous religious orders.

The decisive point in regard to the distinction [between the religious groupings and the groupings oriented to utility] is that (if one may note this important point before commencing the argument) a religion-anchored ethic, and the behavior called forth by it, places completely specific, and as long as the religious belief remains viable, highly effective *psychological rewards* (not oriented to economic interests) upon this behavior; namely, rewards not available to Alberti's teachings on common sense, practical wisdom, and prudent behavior. Only to the extent that these rewards constitute an effective influence upon the believer's action (and they are often primarily influential—and this is the central point—in a significantly different *direction* from the influence of the theological *teachings*, for they also are only "teachings") do they acquire an independent (*eigengesetzlichen*) directional impact upon the organization of life, and, in this way, upon the economy. To state it clearly: this is actually the point of this entire essay. And I had not expected that this message would be so completely overlooked.

I will address on another occasion the relative welcoming of capitalism by theological ethicists of the High Middle Ages (in particular Anthony of Florence and Bernard of Siena, both of whom Sombart has likewise seriously misinterpreted). In any event, Alberti did not belong to this circle. And he took only the concept of *industria* from monastic lines of thought; this remains clear regardless of which mediating links came into play. Alberti, Pandolfini, and their kind are representatives of the frame of mind (although outwardly obedient) already emancipated spiritually from the traditional church. Indeed, despite all ties to the existing Christian ethic, they remained for the most part oriented to a "pagan" frame of mind with roots in Antiquity. Brentano believes that I have "ignored" the significance of precisely this frame of mind with respect to its significance for the development of modern teachings on the economy (and also on modern economic policy).

It is in fact correct that I did not address here *this* line of causality [and for a simple reason]: it did not belong in a study on the *Protestant ethic* and the spirit of capitalism. Far from attempting to deny its significance (which will be demonstrated at another time), I am rather (and for good reasons) of the opinion that the spheres of influence and directional influence of the "pagan" frame of mind were completely *different* from those of the Protestant ethic. (And the practical, and by no means insignificant, predecessors of this ethic were the sects [of the Middle Ages] and the Wyclif-Hussite ethic.) It was *not the organization of life* (of the rising middle class) that was influenced by the pagan frame of mind; rather, it influenced the policies of statesmen and princes. These two indeed partly, but by no means always, converging causal lines [—on the one hand the Protestant ethic and on the other hand the pagan frame of mind—] should at the outset be kept cleanly separate.

As concerns Benjamin Franklin, it must be noted that his tracts on the private economy (which were used in his time as basic readings in the schools) with respect to *this* point in fact belong to a category of works that have influenced *practical* life. In contrast, Alberti's massive works are hardly known outside of learned circles. However, I have explicitly cited Franklin as a man who stood completely beyond the Puritan regimentation of life; by his time, it had become considerably weaker. He remained as well uninfluenced by the English "Enlightenment" as a whole (which is often presented as having close ties to Puritanism). [entire note from 1920]

13.   Unfortunately Brentano (*op. cit.* [ch. 1, note 15]) has thrown every kind of striving for gain (regardless of whether peaceful or in warfare) into one pot. He has then defined the exclusive pursuit of *money* (instead of land) as that which is unique to "the capitalist" pursuit of gain (in contrast, for example, to the feudal striving for gain). He also opposes every further distinction, even though doing so could have led to clear concepts. In addition, he rejects the concept formulated here for the purpose of this investigation, the "spirit" of (modern!) capitalism (p. 131). He does so on the basis of an assertion incomprehensible to me: he contends that he has already included in his presuppositions that which should be proven. [1920]

14.   The observations of Sombart are relevant in every respect. See *Die deutsche Volkswirtschaft im neunzehnten Jahrhundert* [The German Economy in the Nineteenth Century (Berlin: Georg Bondi Publishers, 1903)], p. 123. I do not at all, in particular, need to emphasize—although this study goes back, with respect to its pivotal vantage points, to many of my earlier projects—how much the formulation of these vantage points is indebted to the simple existence of Sombart's manifold investigations and their acute formulations. This indebtedness remains also when Sombart's studies move along a pathway different from the one chosen here—in fact *precisely* when this occurs. Furthermore, those who feel stimulated time and again by Sombart's opinions to oppose strongly his views, and directly to reject some of his theses, are obligated to be aware of them.

15.   *Commenda* involved a contract in which one partner provided capital (money, or, for example, ships, merchandise, or equipment) and the other sought to render a profit for both parties from the capital. See Weber, *General Economic History*, pp. 206–07 [sk].

16.   Common in the ancient world, particularly in Rome and Egypt, tax farming involved the large landholder's farming out of the collection of public taxes to an entrepreneur. The latter paid a fixed fee to the lord and retained all sums collected above this fee. See *E&S*, pp. 965–66, 1045–46 [sk].

17.   Of course, we cannot here address the question of *where* these limitations lie, nor can we evaluate the well-known theory on the connection between high wages and the high productivity of labor. This theory was first suggested by [Thomas] Brassey [*Work and Wages* (New York: D. Appleton & Co., 1872)]. It was then formulated and upheld theoretically by Brentano [*Über das Verhältnis von Arbeitslohn und Arbeitszeit zur Arbeitsleistung* (Leipzig, 1875, 1893)] and simultaneously, historically and analytically, by [Gerhart] Schulze-Gaevernitz [*Der Großbetrieb* (Leipzig: Duncker & Humblot, 1892)]. The discussion was again opened by [Wilhelm] Hasbach's penetrating studies (see "Zur Charakteristik der englischen Industrie," in *Schmollers Jahrbuch* [1903, pp. 385–91, 417 ff.]), and is not yet finally settled. It is here sufficient for us to note (as is not, and cannot be, doubted by anyone) that low wages and high profits, as well as low wages and favorable opportunities for profit, do not simply go together with industrial development. That is, simply mechanical operations involving money do not at all call forth a "socialization" into a capitalist [economic] culture, and thereby the possibility of [the development of] a capitalist economy. All examples selected here are purely illustrative.

18.   Therefore, the importation, *even of capitalist* industries, has often not been possible without large emigration movements out of older culture areas. Sombart is correct in noting the contrast between, on the one hand, the "skills" of persons and the trade secrets of craftsmen, both of which take persons as their point of orientation, and scientific, objectified modern technology on the other. Nonetheless this distinction hardly existed

in the period of capitalism's origin. Indeed, the (so-to-speak) ethical qualities of the worker under capitalism (and, to a certain extent, also the ethical qualities of the employer) were often regarded, as a result alone of their scarcity, as more valuable than the craftsman's skills, which had become ossified in centuries-old traditionalism. And even industry today, when it selects a location to build, is not at all able to make this decision simply independently of the qualities a population has acquired as a result of longstanding traditions and socialization practices that have prepared it for intensive work. Corresponding to the ideas widespread in scientific circles today, this dependence upon the qualities of the local population, once first observed, is gladly attributed to hereditary racial qualities instead of to tradition and socialization. But to do so, in my view, is of very doubtful validity.

19.   See my "Zur Psychophysik der gewerblichen Arbeit." [See note 30, ch. 1.] [1920]

20.   The foregoing observations could be misunderstood. A well-known type of businessperson demonstrates a proclivity to lend support, for his own purposes, to the sentence "religion must be maintained among the people." This proclivity combines with the (earlier not infrequent) proclivity of broad circles (especially the Lutheran clergy, owing to its general sympathy for the authoritarian powers-that-be) to make themselves available to these powers as "secret police." Indeed, wherever able to do so, these circles labeled the [labor] strike as sinful and the unions as promoters of "greed," etc. These are occurrences that have nothing to do with the illustrations of concern to us here. The examples discussed in the text do not involve isolated instances. Instead, these illustrations point to very frequent occurrences that, as we will see, reappear in a recognizable and typical pattern.

21.   *Der moderne Kapitalismus, op. cit.,* vol. I, p. 62.

22.   *Ibid.,* p. 195.

23.   We are referring here, of course, to that *modern* rational *business* that is unique to the West, rather than to the capitalism of usurers, purveyors of warfare, traders in offices, tax farmers, large merchants, and financial magnates. This latter capitalism has, for 3,000 years, spread across the globe from China, India, Babylon, Greece, Rome, Florence, and into the present. See "Prefatory Remarks" [pp. 205–20]. [1920]

24.   The assumption (and this should be emphasized here) is by no means justified *a priori* that, on the one hand, the technique of the capitalist enterprise and, on the other, the spirit of "work as a vocational calling," which endows capitalism with its expansive energy, must have had their *original* sustaining roots in the same social groupings. Religious beliefs relate to social relationships in the same [imprecise] manner.

Historically, Calvinism was one of the social carriers of the socialization practices that gave rise to the "capitalist spirit." Yet, in the Netherlands, for example, those who possessed great fortunes were not predominately followers of the strictest Calvinism; rather, they were Arminians (for reasons that will be discussed later). In the Netherlands as well as elsewhere, the "typical" social carriers of the capitalist ethic and the Calvinist Church were persons from the upwardly mobile *middle* and *lower-middle* strata. The owners of businesses came out of these strata.

However, exactly this situation conforms very well with the thesis presented here. Persons who possessed great fortunes and large-scale merchants have existed in all epochs, yet a rational-capitalist organization of *industrial* work in a middle class first became known in the development that occurred between the Middle Ages and the modern period. [1920]

25.   On this point see the good Zurich dissertation by J. Maliniak (1913). [*Die Entstehung der Exportindustrie und des Unternehmerstandes in Zürich im 16. und 17. Jahrhundert* (Zürich: *Züricher volkswirtshaftliche Studien,* vol. 2, 1913).]

26.   These banks (*Notenbank*) issued their own currency. They are called "federal reserve banks" in the United States [sk].

27.   The following picture has been compiled "ideal typically" from different branches of the textile industry at a variety of locations [see pp. 377–79]. Of course, for the illustrative purpose served by this picture, it is irrelevant that the course of this revolution did not occur, in any of the examples we have in mind, in precisely the manner portrayed in this ideal-typical construct. [On the formation of the ideal type, Weber's central methodological tool, see 1968, pp. 19–22, and 1949, pp. 90–107.]

28.   Also for this reason it is no accident that this period—the beginning era of economic rationalism when German industry first began to flap its wings—is accompanied by, for example, a complete decline in the aesthetic design of the products commonly used in daily life. [1920]

29.   This is not to imply that movement in the supply of precious metals can be depicted as being without economic consequences. [1920]

30.   Weber here wishes to convey that a pattern of behavior in Germany different from the "American fascination"—the search for status in Germany through the acquisition of "landed estates and the patent of nobility"—does not constitute a viable alternative to the American situation. Rather, the German behavior "must be seen for what it is," namely, a legacy from the feudal past [sk].

31.   This refers to that type of employer *we* have made the object of our discussion here. We are not referring to any sort of empirical average. (On the "ideal type" concept see my essay [1949, pp. 90–107.].) [1920]

32.   This is perhaps the appropriate place briefly to address observations in the already cited book by Franz Keller (see note 25, ch. 1) and the observations by Sombart that relate to it (in *The Quintessence of Capitalism* [see note 1, ch. 1]), at least to the extent that they belong here. It is actually quite amazing that an author [Keller] criticizes a study in which the canonical prohibition of charging interest is *not at all mentioned* (except in *one* passing remark that had *no* relationship to the entire line of argument). Keller does so on the assumption that precisely this prohibition of interest (parallels to which are to be found in almost all religious ethics around the world) constitutes the distinguishing feature of the Catholic ethic as opposed to the ethics of the Reformation churches and sects.

One should really criticize only those studies that one has really read, or in those cases when their arguments, if read, have not already been forgotten. The struggle against *usuraria pravitas* [depraved usury] runs through Huguenot and Dutch church history of the sixteenth century. The Lombards (that is, the bankers) were often excluded from communion solely because they were bankers (see ch. 1, note 15). The more tolerant view held by Calvin (which, by the way, did not prevent the plan from including a usury litmus test in the first draft of the ordination regulations) was not victorious until [Claudius] Salmasius [1588–1653]. Hence, the opposition between the Catholic ethic and the ethics of Reformation churches and sects did not concern *this* issue [as Keller argues]; quite the contrary.

Still worse, however, are [Keller's] arguments that do rightfully belong here. Compared to the works of [Franz Xaver] Funk [*Zins und Wucher: Eine moraltheologische Abhandlung mit Berücksichtrgung des gegenwärtigen Standes der Kultur und der Staatswissenschaften* (Tübingen: Laupp'sche, 1868)] and other Catholic scholars (and Keller has not, by the way, in my opinion fully acknowledged the contribution of Funk or these scholars), and in opposition to the investigations of Wilhelm Endemann, which are today out of date in regard to details yet still remain fundamental [see *Studien in der Roman.-Kanon. Wirtschafts- und Rechtslehre, 1874–83* (Berlin: J. Guttentag; 2 vols., reprinted 1962)], they make a painful impression of superficiality.

To be sure, Keller has abstained from the excesses apparent in some remarks by Sombart (*The Quintessence of Capitalism*). Sombart notes that the "pious gentlemen" (referring basically to Bernhard of Siena and Anthony of Florence) "wished to excite the spirit of business in any way possible." [They wished to do so, Sombart argues,] by interpreting the prohibition against usury in a way that excluded the (in my terminology) "productive" investment of capital [from this prohibition]. Yet this manner of treating the prohibition against the taking of interest is hardly different from what has occurred across the entire world. Keller has kept his distance from such excesses. (Furthermore, Sombart places the Romans among the "heroic peoples," yet presumably—and this constitutes an irreconcilable contradiction, in view of his other books—sees economic rationalism as having developed "to its final consistency" as early as Cato [234–149 BCE]. This inconsistency is noted here only in passing. Nonetheless, it serves to indicate the quality of *The Quintessence of Capitalism*, a book "with a thesis" in the worst sense of this expression.)

Sombart has also completely distorted the significance of the prohibition against the taking of interest. This cannot be set forth here in detail. Its significance was earlier [in our scholarly research] often exaggerated, and later strongly underestimated; now (in an era of Catholic, as well as Protestant, millionaires) it has been turned upside down—for apologetic purposes. As is well known, and in spite of the grounding in the Bible (!) of a prohibition against the taking of interest, interest was not abolished until the last century. This took place by order of the *Congregatio Sancti Officii* [the highest judiciary body in the Catholic Church], yet only *temporum ratione habita* [for a limited period, and as a consequence of specific, this-worldly circumstances] and *indirectly*. That is, priests were prevented (because they wished to preserve their claims for obedience in the event of a re-institution of the right to take interest) from asking questions in the confessional about *usuraria pravitas*, for fear of unsettling the faithful.

Anyone who has even begun to undertake a thorough study of the extremely tangled history of the church's doctrine on usury cannot claim (in view of the endless controversies over, for example, the permissibility of purchasing bonds, the discounting of notes and various other contracts, and above all in light of the order of the *Congregatio Sancti Officii* mentioned above concerning a *municipal* loan) that the prohibition of taking interest concerned only emergency loans, that it had the purpose of "preserving capital," and, indeed, that it served "to aid capitalist businesses" [as Sombart does]. The truth is that the church began to reconsider the prohibition of interest only at a rather late time. The common forms of purely business investment, when this occurred, were *not* loans at fixed interest rates but the *foenus nauticum, commenda, societas maris*, and the *dare ad proficuum de mari* types of loans (loans made according to categories of risk, and shares of gain and loss were adjusted within fixed upper and lower limits within each category of risk). (In view of the nature of the employer's borrowing, loans *had* to be of these types.) Yet these loans were not defined as falling under the ban (although a few rigorous canonists disagreed).

However, when investment at a fixed rate of interest became possible and common, and discounting practices became widespread, these types of loans encountered clearly perceptible difficulties stemming from the prohibition against the taking of interest. Frequent punitive measures were taken against the merchant guilds (black lists were formed!). Nevertheless, even in these cases, the church proceeded [against the violators] in a *purely* legalistic-formal manner. In any event, the church did not, as Keller argues, exhibit any tendency to "protect capital."

Finally, the church's attitude toward capitalism, *to the extent* that it can be ascertained at all, on the one hand was determined by a traditional (and mostly more diffusely experienced) hostility against the encompassing power of capital; because *impersonal*, the ethical regulation of its flow was scarcely possible [see pp. 426–29] (as still reflected in Luther's comments on the Fuggers [a family of financial magnates] and on moneymaking as such). On the other hand, the church's attitude toward capitalism was determined by the necessity for accommodation.

Nevertheless, this theme does not belong here. As noted, the prohibition against taking interest and its destiny [in relationship to the Catholic Church] has, for us, at most only a symptomatic significance (and even in this regard only to a limited extent). [For a classic work on this theme written in the Weberian tradition, see Benjamin Nelson, *The Idea of Usury: From Tribal Brotherhood to Universal Otherhood* (Chicago: University of Chicago Press, 1969).]

The economic ethic of the Scots, and especially of certain fifteenth century mendicant theologians, primarily Bernhard of Siena and Anthony of Florence (hence, friar writers of a specifically rational *ascetic* orientation), undoubtedly deserves a separate treatment. In light of the major focus here, an examination of this economic ethic could take place only in a secondary fashion, which would not do justice to it. Moreover, if the attempt were nonetheless made, I would be forced here, in these "anti-critical" statements, to examine that which I wish to note later in discussing the *positive* relationship of the Catholic economic ethic to capitalism. Bernhard of Siena and Anthony of Florence go to great pains (and here they can be seen as precursors of many Jesuits) to legitimize the profit of the *merchant*; because (they argue) it constitutes a reward for the merchant's "industria" [industriousness], profit is ethically *permitted*. (Of course, obviously, even Keller cannot claim more.)

The concept and the high evaluation of *industria* obviously derives *ultimately* from monastic and mendicant asceticism. However, it also originates clearly from the concept of *masserizia* [see note 12], which Alberti borrowed from clerical sources (as he conveys to us through the words of Gianozzo). We will later address the way in which the monastic and mendicant ethic constitutes a precursor of the this-worldly ascetic denominations of Protestantism. (The beginnings of similar conceptions can be found in the ancient world with the Cynics, as is apparent from the tombstones in late Hellenic cemeteries [300–100 BCE], and—although as a consequence of entirely different social configurations—in Egypt.) That element that is decisive for us is *entirely lacking* in the ancient world (and with Alberti as well), namely, exactly what is characteristic for ascetic Protestantism, as we will note later: the conception of offering *testimony* to oneself of one's own salvation—that is, of offering the *certitudo salutis* [sense of being certain of one's salvation]—through the exercise of a vocational calling.

The psychological *reward* that ascetic Protestantism placed upon *industria* arose from this source (and is of necessity missing in Catholicism, for the simple reason that the means toward salvation in this religion were simply different). Ethical *teachings*, and their effects upon behavior, constituted the concern for these authors [whether Alberti, the Cynics, or the ancient Egyptians], whereas for the ascetic Protestant theologians, the issue involved practical motivations, as conditioned by the salvation interests of the faithful. Moreover, while the concern for Alberti, the Cynics, and the ancient Egyptians was one of *accommodation* [to the world as it exists], as is very easy to see, the issue for this-worldly asceticism involved [in respect to practical behavior] lines of argumentation deduced from direction-giving, internally consistent religious postulates. (Anthony of Florence and Bernard of Siena have, by the way, received from authors long ago better treatment than they received from F. Keller.) Furthermore, even these accommodations [to the world as it exists] by Alberti and the ancient authors, have remained, to the present day, controversial.

The significance of the ethical conceptions of early monasticism, as *symptomatic* [of the ascetic Protestant notion of offering testimony to one's salvation through a calling], should by no means be viewed as completely nonexistent. Nevertheless, the actual "beginnings" of the religious ethic that flowed into the *modern* concept of a *vocational calling* can be found in the [ascetic] sects and the unorthodox religious groupings. These early traces are primarily to be found in Wyclif, even though his significance is certainly highly overestimated by von Brodnitz (*Englische Wirtschaftsgeschichte* [vol. 1, 1918]). To him, Wyclif's influence had such a strong impact that Puritanism found nothing more to do. But all this cannot (and should not) be delved into here. We cannot conduct a parallel debate regarding the question of how, and to what extent, the Christian ethics of the Middle

Ages *actually* participated in creating the preconditions for the capitalist spirit. [entire note from 1920]

33.   The words μηδὲν ἀπελπίζοντες [without hoping for anything from it] (Luke 6:35), and the translation of the Vulgate, *nihil inde sperantes* [hoping for nothing from it], are presumably (according to Adelbert Merx) a misrepresentation of μηδένα ἀπελπίζοντες (or *neminem desperantes*) [do not despair regarding anyone (do not give up on anyone)]. These words decree the granting of loans to *all* brothers, including those who are indigent, and doing so without speaking at all about interest. The passage *Deo placere vix potest* [the merchant cannot be pleasing to God] is now thought to be of Arian origin (which is, for our argument, a matter of indifference). [1920]

34.   This school, which grew out of medieval Scholasticism, stood against Catholic orthodoxy [sk].

35.   We are instructed how, in this situation, a compromise with the prohibition of usury occurred, for example, in book I, section 65, of the statutes of the *Arte di Calimala* (at present I have only the Italian edition put out by Emiliani-Giudici, *Storia dei comuni Italiani* [Florence, 1866], vol. 3, p. 246). "Procurino i consoli con *quelli frati, che parrà loro, che perdono si faccia e come fare si possa il meglio per l'amore di ciascuno, del dono, merito o guiderdono, ovvero interesse per l'anno presente e secondo che altra volta fatto fue.*" In other words, the issue here concerns the attempt by guilds to find a way for their members, owing to their official position within the organization, to be exempt from the prohibition against usury. This must be done, however, it is noted, without undermining the church's authority. The instructions that follow, as well as those for the example immediately preceding (sect. 63)—to record all interest and profits as "gifts"—are very characteristic of the view of investment profit as amoral. The formation today by stock exchange traders of black lists against those who refuse to honor forward contracts on the basis of the margin defense (*Differenzeinwand*), [which renders unforceable a speculative agreement by revealing its illegality to the court], corresponds to the scorn for those [guild members in the Middle Ages] who pleaded before ecclesiastical courts on the basis of *exceptio usurariae pravitatis* [a legal defense that unveiled usury, and hence invalidated the contract in dispute and any obligation to pay interest. See 1968, pp. 1189–90 and Lutz Kaelber, "Max Weber on Usury and Medieval Capitalism," *Max Weber Studies* 4, 11 Jan, 2004: 51–75; see p. 60].

36.   On "practical rationalism" (and Weber's other types of rationalism), see Kalberg, 1980 [sk]

37.   We will discover that the "birth of the calling" did not follow *logically* from ascetic Protestantism's doctrine of predestination. On the contrary, despair and bleakness followed logically from this doctrine. The revisions formulated by Richard Baxter, which concerned the pastoral care of believers, introduced the "calling" of significance to Weber or, more precisely, the notion of testifying to one's belief through conduct. These revisions could not be deduced rationally from the doctrine of predestination. See p. 500, note 76) [sk].

Chapter III

1.   Of the ancient languages, only *Hebrew* has any similar concept—most of all in the word מְלָאכָה. It is used for priestly functions (Exod. 35:21; Neh. 11:22; 1 Chron. 9:13, 23:4, 26:30), for business in the service of the king (especially 1 Sam. 8:16; 1 Chron. 4:23, 29:6), for the service of a *royal* official (Esther 3:9, 9:3), of a *superintendent* of labor (2 Kings 12:12), of a slave (Gen. 39:2), of labor in the fields (1 Chron. 27:26), of *craftsmen* (Exod. 31:5, 35:21; 1 Kings 7:14), for traders (Ps. 107:23), and for worldly activity of any kind in the passage, Sirach 11:20, to be discussed later [on Jesus Sirach, see p. 536, note 60]. The word is derived from the root לאַךְ, to send, thus meaning originally a "task."

That it originated in the ideas current in Solomon's bureaucratic kingdom of serfs, built up as it was according to the Egyptian model, seems evident from the above references. In meaning, however, as I learn from A. Merx, this root concept had become lost even in antiquity. The word came to be used for any sort of "labor," and in fact became fully as colorless as the German *Beruf*, with which it shared the fate of being used primarily for mental functions. The expression חֹק, "assignment," "task," "lesson," which also occurs in Sirach 11:20, and is translated in the [pre-Christian Greek version of the Old Testament, the] Septuagint with διαθήκη, is also derived from the terminology of the bureaucratic regime of the time that enforced servitude, as is תְּבַל־יוֹם (Exod. 5:13; cf. Exod. 5:14), where the Septuagint also uses διαθήκη for "task." In Sirach 43:10 it is rendered in the Septuagint with κρίμα. In Sirach 11:20 it is evidently used to signify the fulfillment of *God's* commandments, being thus related to our "calling." On this passage in Jesus Sirach, reference may here be made to Smend's well-known book on Jesus Sirach [*Die Weisheit des Jesus Sirach* (Berlin: Georg Reimer, 1906)] on these verses and to his *Index zur Weisheit des Jesus Sirach* (Berlin, 1907) for the words διαθήκη, ἔργον, πόνος. (As is well known, the Hebrew text of the Book of Sirach was lost, but was rediscovered by Schechter, and in part supplemented by quotations from the Talmud. [See Solomon Schechter, *The Wisdom of Ben Sira* (New York: Macmillan, 1899.)] Luther did not possess it, and these two Hebrew concepts could not have had *any* influence on *his* use of language. See below on Prov. 22:29.) [1920]

In Greek there is no term corresponding in ethical connotation to the German or English words at all. Where Luther, quite in the spirit of modern usage (see below), translates Jesus Sirach 11:20 and 11:21, *bleibe in deinem Beruf* [stay in your calling], the Septuagint has at one point ἔργον, at the other, which however seems to be an entirely corrupt passage, πόνος (the Hebrew original speaks of the spark of divine help!). Otherwise in Antiquity τὰ προσήκοντα is used in the general sense of "duties." In the works of the Stoics, κάματος occasionally carries similar connotations, though its linguistic source is diffuse and insignificant (called to my attention by Albrecht Dieterich). All other expressions (such as τάξις, etc.) have no ethical connotations.

In Latin what we translate as "calling" (a person's specialized and sustained activity that is normally his source of income and thus, in the long run, the economic basis of his existence) is expressed, aside from the commonplace *opus* [work], with an ethical content somewhat related to that of the German word. This occurred either by *officium* (from *opificium*, which was originally devoid of an ethical dimension but later, especially in Seneca *De benef.*, bk. 4, p. 18, came to mean *Beruf*), by *munus* [duty] (derived from the compulsory obligations to the old civic community) or, finally, by *professio*. This last word was also characteristically used in this sense for public obligations, and was probably derived from the old tax declarations of the citizens.

It later came to be applied in the special modern sense of the liberal professions (as in *professio bene dicendi*). In *this* narrower meaning it had a significance in every way similar to the German *Beruf* (even in the more spiritual sense of the word, as is apparent when Cicero says of someone *non intelligit quid profiteatur*, in the sense of "he does not recognize his own profession"), except that it is, of course, definitely this-worldly and without any *religious* connotation. This is even more true of *ars*, which in Imperial times was used for handicraft. The Vulgate [see p. 536, note 60] translates the above passages from Jesus Sirach at one point with *opus*, at another (verse 21) with *locus*, which implies in this case something like social station. The addition of *mandatorum tuorum* derives from the ascetic Jerome. Brentano quite rightly notes this origin; however, he never calls attention, here or elsewhere, *precisely* to the fact that *mandatorum tuorum* was characteristic of the ascetic origin of the term (before the Reformation other-worldly, afterwards this-worldly). It is, by the way, uncertain from what text Jerome's translation was made. An influence of the old liturgical meaning of מְלָאכָת does not appear to be impossible.

In the Romance languages only the Spanish *vocación*, in the sense of an inner "call" to something, is found. This was carried over from the clerical office and its connotation partly corresponds to that of the German word. However, it was never used to mean "calling" in the external sense. In the Romance Bible translations, the Spanish *vocación* and the Italian *vocazione* and *chiamamento*, which otherwise have a meaning partly corresponding to the Lutheran and Calvinist usage to be discussed presently, are used only to translate the κλῆσις of the New Testament, which refers to the call of the gospel to eternal salvation (which in the Vulgate is *vocatio*). Oddly, Brentano, *op. cit.* [ch. 1, note 15], maintains that this fact, which I have myself adduced to defend my view, is evidence *for* the existence of the concept of the vocational calling in the sense that it had later. But it is nothing of the kind. κλῆσις should have been translated as *vocatio*. But where and when in the Middle Ages would it have been used in our sense? The fact of this translation, and the *lack* of any application of the word to a this-worldly connotation, *in spite of this translation*, makes the case.

Chiamamento is used in this manner along with *vocazione* in the Italian Bible translation of the fifteenth century, which is printed in the *Collezione di opere inedite e rare* (Bologna, 1887). On the other hand, the modern Italian translations use *vocazione*. The words used in the Romance languages for "calling," in the *external*, this-worldly sense of regular acquisitive activity, in contrast carry (as appears in all the dictionaries and from a report of my honorable friend, Professor Baist of Freiburg) no religious connotation whatever. This remains the case regardless of whether they are derived from *ministerium* or *officium* (both of which originally had a certain ethical dimension), or from *ars, professio* and *implicare* (*impiego*) (which entirely omitted an ethical dimension from the beginning). The passages in Jesus Sirach mentioned at the beginning, where Luther used *Beruf*, are translated as follows: in French verse 20 *office*, verse 21 *labeur* (a Calvinist translation); Spanish translations verse 20 *obra*, verse 21 *lugar* (following the Vulgate), recently *posto* (a Protestant translation). The Protestants of the Latin countries, since they were minorities, did not exercise (possibly did not even make the attempt) such a creative influence over their respective languages, as Luther did over the less highly rationalized (in an academic sense) German used in state offices.

2. However, the concept is developed only partially in the Augsburg Confession and only implicitly. Article XVI (ed. by Theodor Kolde [Gütersloh.: Bertelsmann, 1906], p. 43) teaches:

> For it is the case that the Gospel . . . does not stand against secular rulership, the police, and marriage; rather, the Gospel wishes that believers maintain the given rulership, police powers, and marriage as elements in God's order. Each in their own station in life, believers must practice Christian love and appropriate good works, each doing so *according to his calling.*

(The Latin: *et in talibus ordinationibus exercere caritatem* [and in such a status practice charity]: p. 42.) Thus, the consequence to be drawn is apparent: that people must obey the given authority. At least *primarily*, it is clear that the "calling" is understood as an *objective* order in the sense of the passage at 1 Cor. 7:20 ["Everyone should remain in the state in which he was called"]. And Article XXVII of the Augsburg Confession (Kolde, p. 83) discusses a "calling" (in Latin: *in vocatione sua*) only in connection with those statuses and positions ordained by God, such as the clergy, secular rulers, princes, and lords. Nonetheless, this is the case in German only in the concordance volume; in the main text the relevant sentence is omitted.

Only in Article XXVI (Kolde, p. 81) is the term "calling" used in a manner that encompasses the way the term is used today:

> . . . self-castigation should serve the purpose of maintaining the strength and health of the body (rather than earning of grace), for the body must not hinder persons

from that which they have been, according to their calling, commanded to do. (The Latin: *juxta vocationem suam.*)

3.   According to the lexicons, kindly confirmed by my colleagues Professors Braune and Hoops, the word *Beruf* (Dutch *beroep*, English *calling*, Danish *kald*, Swedish *kallelse*) does *not* occur in any of the languages that now contain it, in its present this-worldly sense, before Luther's translation of the Bible.

The Middle High German, Middle Low German, and Middle Dutch words, which *sound* like it, all *mean* the same as *Ruf* in modern German. They also include, and *especially* so, the idea of a "calling" (*Vokation*) of a candidate to an *ecclesiastical office* by those with the power of appointment. This is a special case, which is also often mentioned in the dictionaries of the Scandinavian languages. The word is also occasionally used by Luther in this sense.

However, even though this special use of the word [as referring to the formal appointment to a position] may have promoted its change of meaning, the modern conception of *Beruf* undoubtedly goes back linguistically to the Bible translations, especially by Protestants. Other beginnings are to be found, as we shall see later, only in [the mystic Johannes] Tauler [1300–61]. *All* the languages predominantly influenced by the *Protestant* Bible translations have the word. *All* languages for which this was not the case (such as the Romance languages) do not have the word, or at least not in its modern meaning.

Luther translates two quite different concepts with [the single] term *Beruf*. First the Pauline κλῆσις, in the sense of the call from God, to eternal salvation. See 1 Cor. 1:26; Eph. 1:18; 4:1, 4; 2 Thess. 1:11; Heb. 3:1; 2 Pet. 1:10. All these cases concern the *purely* religious idea of the call, as announced in the gospel, by the apostles; the word κλῆσις has nothing to do with this-worldly callings in the modern sense. The German Bibles before Luther's translation use *ruffunge* (that is, all early printed works in [my] Heidelberg [University] Library), and sometimes instead of *by God called* state *by God summoned*. Second, however, as we have already seen, Luther translates the words in Jesus Sirach discussed in the previous note (in the Septuagint ἐν τῷ ἔργῳ σου παλαιώθητι and καὶ ἔμμενε τῷ πόνῳ σου), with "beharre in deinem *Beruf*" [remain steadfast in your *calling*] and "bleibe in deinem *Beruf*" [stay in your *calling*] instead of "bleibe bei deiner *Arbeit*" [stay in your *work*]. The later (authorized) Catholic translations (for example that of Fleischütz; Fulda, 1781) have (as in the New Testament passages) simply followed him. Luther's translation of the passage in the Book of Sirach is, so far as I can see, the *first* case in which the German word *Beruf* appears in its present, *purely* this-worldly sense. (The preceding exhortation, verse 20, στῆθι ἐν διαθήκῃ σου, he translates *bleibe in Gottes Wort* [stay in God's word] although Sirach 14:1 and 43.10 show that, corresponding to the Hebrew חק, which—according to the citations to the Talmud—Sirach used, διαθήκη really did mean something similar to our calling, namely one's "fate" or "assigned task." [1920])

In its later and present sense the word *Beruf* did *not* exist in the German language. As far as I can see, it also did not exist in the works of the older Bible translators or preachers. The German Bibles before Luther rendered the passage from Sirach as *work*. [The Franciscan] Berthold of Regensburg [1210–1272], at the points in his sermons where today we would say *Beruf* [calling] uses the word *Arbeit* [work]. Thus, the usage was the same as in antiquity. The first passage I know in which *Beruf* is not used but nonetheless *Ruf* (as a translation of κλῆσις) is used, in the sense of purely worldly labor, is found in the fine sermon of the German mystic Tauler [see p. 44] on Ephesians 4 (*Works*, Basel edition, f. 117.5). It concerns peasants who cause trouble. To Luther, they would be better off "if only they would follow their own call (*Ruf*) rather than the [Catholic] clergy, who do not represent their own call." The word in this sense did not find its way into everyday speech. And although Luther's usage at first vacillates between *Ruf* and *Beruf* (see *Werke*, Erlangen edition, vol. 51, p. 51), a direct influence from Tauler is by no means certain (although Luther's [*The Freedom of a Christian* (Philadelphia: Muehlenberg Press, 1957

[1521])] is in many respects similar to this sermon of Tauler). But in the purely *worldly* sense of Tauler, Luther did *not* at the beginning use the word *Ruf*. (This position opposes [the distinguished Luther scholar, Heinrich Seuse] Denifle [1844–1905], *Luther und Luthertum* [1903], p. 163.)

Now evidently in the Septuagint the advice of Sirach contains (apart from the general exhortation to trust in God) no relationship to a specifically religious *valuation* of this-worldly work in a calling. The term πόνος, or toil, in the untenable second passage would be rather the opposite, were it not corrupted. What Jesus Sirach says corresponds simply to the exhortation of the Psalmist ("Dwell in the land, and *nourish yourself in a respectable manner*"—Psa. 37:3); this idea also comes out clearly in connection with the warning (verse 21) not to let oneself become enamored with the works of the godless, since it is easy for God to make a poor man rich. Only the opening exhortation to remain in the רְן (verse 20) has a certain relatedness to the κλῆσις of the gospel. Nevertheless, Luther did not here use the word *Beruf* for the Greek διαθήκης The bridge between Luther's two, seemingly quite unrelated, uses of the word *Beruf* is found in the first letter to the Corinthians and its translation.

In the usual modern editions, the whole context in which the passage stands is as follows, 1 Cor. 7:17–24 (English, King James version [American revision, 1901]):

> (17) Only as the Lord hath distributed to each man, as God hath called each, so let him walk. And so ordain I in all churches. (18) Was any man called being circumcised? Let him not become uncircumcised. Hath any man been called in uncircumcision? Let him not be circumcised. (19) Circumcision is nothing and uncircumcision is nothing; above all keep the commandments of God. (20) Let each man abide in that calling wherein he was called [ἐν τῇ κλήσει ἧ ἐκλήθη; this expression is undoubtedly from the Hebrew, as Privy Councillor Merx tells me—Vulgata: *in qua vocatione vocatus est* (in that calling he is called into)]. (21) Wast thou called being a bondservant? Care not for it; nay, even if thou canst become free use it rather. (22) For he that was called in the Lord being a bondservant is the Lord's freedman; likewise he that was called being free is Christ's bondservant. (23) Ye were bought with a price; become not bondservants of men. (24) Brethren, let each man, wherein he was called, therein abide with God.

The remark follows verse 29 that time is "short." Well-known commandments motivated by eschatological expectations follow: (31) to possess women as though one did not have them; to buy as though one did not have what one had bought, etc. Luther, in verse 20, following the older German translations, even in his 1523 exegesis of this chapter, renders κλῆσις with *call*, and interprets it as [related to] one's "status" (Erlangen edition, vol. 51, p. 51).

In fact it is obvious that the word κλῆσις in this passage, and *only* here, corresponds evidently to the Latin *status* and the German *Stand* (status of marriage, status of a servant, etc.). However, this usage of "status" is of course not, as Brentano assumes (*op. cit.* [ch. 1, note 15], p. 137), the same as *Beruf* in the modern sense. Brentano can hardly have read this passage, or what I have said about it, very carefully. A word that at least reminds us of *Beruf* (and it is etymologically related to ἐκκλησία, or an assembly which has been called) occurs in Greek literature (so far as the lexicons inform us) only once. It can be found in a passage from Dionysius of Halicarnassus. This word, which corresponds to the Latin *classis* (a word borrowed from the Greek) refers to those citizens who have been called to perform military service. Theophylaktos (eleventh-twelfth century) interprets 1 Cor. 7:20: ἐν οἴῳ βίῳ καὶ ἐν οἴῳ τάγματι καὶ πολιτεύματι ὢν ἐπίστευσεν [one should stay in the position one has been called into—in life, in *classes*, and in one's activities as a citizen]. (My colleague Professor Deissmann called my attention to this passage.)

Nonetheless, the modern *Beruf*, even in our passage, does *not* correspond to κλῆσις. Luther, however, having translated κλῆσις as *Beruf* in the eschatologically motivated exhortation—everyone should remain in his present status—naturally would, on account of the *objective similarity* of the exhortations alone when he later came to translate the Apocrypha [see p. 536, note 60], also use *Beruf* for πόνος to refer to the traditionalistic and anti-chrematistic advice given by Jesus Sirach, namely, that each should remain in his own occupation. (This is what is decisive and characteristic. As has been pointed out, the passage in 1 Cor. 7:17 does *not* use κλῆσις at all in the sense of *Beruf,* which implies a demarcated realm of achievements.)

In the meantime (or at about the same time), in the Augsburg Confession of 1530 the Protestant dogma regarding the uselessness of the Catholic attempt to surpass this-worldly morality was formulated. The expression "every person according to his calling (*Beruf*)" then became used (see previous note). This expression came to the forefront in Luther's translation. In addition, his translation also stressed his significantly increased estimation (which occurred at the beginning of the 1530s) of the *sacredness* of the order in which the individual is placed. This emphasis resulted, on the one hand, from Luther's increasingly clearly defined belief in the completely unusual character of divine rulership, even over the details of life; on the other hand, it resulted from his increasing proclivity to accept this-worldly orders as ones that God wishes to remain unchanged. *Vocatio,* in the traditional Latin, was used to designate the divine call to a *life* of holiness, especially in a monastery or as a priest. And now, under the influence of Luther's dogma, this term came to denote, for Luther, work in a this-worldly calling. For, while he now translated πόνος and ἔργον in Jesus Sirach as *Beruf* (for which earlier *only* the Latin analogies, which derived from the translations by *monks,* had been available), some years earlier, in translating Proverbs (see verses 22, 29), he had still translated the Hebrew מְלָאכָה, which anchored the ἔργον in the Greek text of Ecclesiastes. This Hebrew מְלָאכָת, in the same manner as the German *Beruf* and the Scandinavian *kald,* and *kallelse,* derived in particular from a *spiritual* notion of *Beruf.* Similarly, in other passages (Gen. 39:2), it was translated as *Geschäft* (Septuagint ἔργον, Vulgate *opus* [work]; in the English Bibles as *business,* and correspondingly in the Scandinavian and all the other translations before me).

Hence, the creation of the term *Beruf* by Luther in the sense in which we understand it today remained, for a time, entirely *Lutheran.* Because the Apocrypha [from which Luther had partly derived his concept] remained to the Calvinists entirely illegitimate, they accepted the Lutheran *concept* of a calling only later. They did so when the consequences of the development that placed the notion of an interest in "testifying to" one's belief came to the forefront. The Calvinists then sharply accentuated Luther's "calling." However, the Calvinists never had a corresponding *term* available to them from the first translations from the Romance languages [Spanish, French, and Italian]. Moreover, they never possessed the power to create such a word as an idiom in their own language, which was already too rigid and inflexible to allow for this possibility. [1920]

The concept of *Beruf* became integrated in its present sense into the secular literature as early as the sixteenth century. The Bible translators *before* Luther had used the word *Berufung* [appointment to a position] for the Greek κλῆσις (as, for example, in the Heidelberg translations of 1462–66 and 1485; the Eck translation of 1537 states *in dem Ruf, worin er beruft ist* [in the call, to which one is called]). Most of the later Catholic translations directly follow Luther. The first translation of the Bible in England, by Wyclif (1382), used *cleping* (the Old English word that was later replaced by *calling,* a borrowed term). This practice—of using a word that already corresponded to the later usage of the Reformation—is certainly characteristic of this type of Lollard ethics, [as practiced by followers of Wyclif]. On the other hand, Tyndale's translation of 1534 utilizes the idea in terms of *status:* "in the same *state* wherein he was called." This is the case also with the Geneva Bible of 1557. The official translation by Cranmer (1539) substituted *calling* for *state,* while the (Catholic) Bible of Rheims (1582), exactly like the Anglican court Bibles of the Elizabethan era, with their indebtedness to the Vulgate, characteristically return to "vocation."

Murray [unidentified] has already appropriately noted that Cranmer's Bible translation in England is the source of the Puritan conception of "calling" in the sense of *Beruf* (used in reference to trade). *Calling* is used in this sense as early as the middle of the sixteenth century. By 1588, "unlawful callings" are referred to, and "greater callings," in the sense of "higher" occupations, etc., are noted in 1603 (see Murray). Brentano's idea (*op. cit.*, p. 139) is highly remarkable. To him, because only a *free* man could engage in a *Beruf* in the Middle Ages, and freemen were *missing* at that time in the business-oriented vocations, *vocatio* was not translated as *Beruf*. For this reason, to him, this concept remained unknown. However, because the entire societal organization of medieval industry, in contrast to antiquity, rested upon free labor (and merchants, above all, were almost always free), I do not really understand this assertion.

4. Weber is here most likely referring to Johannes Tauler. See p. 44 [sk].

5. Compare the following paragraphs with the instructive discussion by K. Eger, *Die Anschauung Luthers vom Beruf* [*Luther's View of the Calling* (Giessen: J. Ricker, 1900)] Perhaps the only serious omission in this work, which almost all other theological writers also omit, concerns the analysis of the *lex naturae* concept. This discussion lacks adequate clarity. On this theme see the review by Ernst Troeltsch of Seeberg's *Dogmengeschichte*. Above all, see also the relevant sections in Troeltsch's *Social Teachings of the Christian Churches* [New York: Harper & Row, 1960 (1911) pp. 528–39].

6. [St. Thomas Aquinas interpreted Aristotle and synthesized numerous streams of ancient and medieval theology.] The stratification of people into social statuses and occupational groups is the work of divine *providence*, according to him. This stratification implies to him the existence of an objective societal *cosmos*. A *particular person's* decision to take up a particular "calling" (as we would say today, whereas Thomas speaks of *ministerium* or *officium*) results from *causae naturales* [natural causes]. To him:

> Haec autem diversificatio hominum in diversis officiis contingit primo ex divina providentia, quae ita hominum status distribuit, . . . secundo etiam ex causis naturalibus, ex quibus contingit, quod in diversis hominibus sunt diversae inclinationes ad diversa officia. . . . [This stratification of people into various occupations derives, firstly, from God's providence, according to which the positions people hold are allotted. This apportioning derives, secondly, from natural causes, for different proclivities toward the various occupations exist in different persons.] (See his Quaest. quodlibetal, bk. 7, Art. 17c.)

Pascal's evaluation of the "calling" is quite similar when he notes that *chance* decides the choice of a calling. See on Pascal, Adolf Köster, *Die Ethik Pascals* [Tübingen: H. Laupp, 1908]. Only the most closed of the "organic" religious ethics [in the sense of stable elements interrelated with one another in a firm manner]—those from India—are different in this respect. The contrast between the Thomistic and Protestant concepts of the calling are so obvious that we can, for now, refer simply to the quotation above [in the previous note]. (And, furthermore, the contrast of Catholicism to Lutheranism is clear, despite the close relationship in later Lutheranism, especially in regard to an emphasis upon the providential.) We will, at any rate, return later to Catholicism's notion of the calling. On Thomas, see Maurenbrecher, *Thomas von Aquinos Stellung zum Wirtschaftsleben seiner Zeit* [Leipzig: J.J. Weber, 1898]. Otherwise, Luther's agreement with Thomas, which appears to be the case in respect to a series of details, results in fact more from the influence upon Luther of the general teachings of the Scholastics, than from the teachings of Thomas in particular. According to the arguments of Denifle, Luther in fact appears to have been insufficiently acquainted with the works of Thomas. See Denifle, *op. cit.* [p. 180] (p. 501) and Walter Koehler, *Ein Wort zu Denifles Luther* [Tübingen: Mohr, 1904] (pp. 25f.).

7. In Luther's *The Freedom of a Christian, op. cit.*, (a) this-worldly duties are understood as involving a *lex naturae* (interpreted by Luther to mean the natural order of the world), and adherence to them is necessary owing to the "double" [good and evil] na-

tures of the human being. Hence, it follows (Erlangen edition 27, p. 188) that people are *in fact* bound to their bodies and to the social community. (b) In light of this situation, human beings (p. 196) will (and this point connects to the first as a *second* legitimation [for fulfillment of this-worldly duties]), *if* they are believing Christians, come to the conclusion that God's decision to grant salvation, which resulted from genuine love [of His children], must be remunerated by loving one's neighbor. This connection between "faith" and "love" is a very loose one. (c) However, it combines with the old ascetic legitimation of work (p. 190), namely as a mechanism that provides the "spiritual" person with mastery over the physical body.

Therefore, work (d) (and here the connection [with work as a mastery mechanism] is taken a step farther, and again the idea of *lex naturae*—now as natural morality—becomes valid, although in a different usage), a particular *drive*, one planted within the species by God (even with *Adam* [before the Fall]) and one which Adam held to "solely to please God." Finally (e) (pp. 161 and 199), in connection with Matthew 7:18 f., the idea appears that proficient work in a calling is a consequence of the new life that has been acquired, through faith, by the believer. Moreover, proficient work must have had this cause. Nevertheless, the decisive Calvinist idea—"the capacity to work itself constitutes an internal and external testifying to the person's devoutness"—has not yet developed [from this idea that proficient work derives from faith]. The utilization of such heterogeneous elements [five in all, as above] is explained by the powerful temperament that drives Luther's *The Freedom of a Christian*.

8.   "It is not from the benevolence of the butcher, the brewer, or the baker, that we expect our dinner, but from their regard to their own interest. We address ourselves, not to their humanity, but to their self-love; and never talk to them of our own necessities, but of their advantages" (*Wealth of Nations* [Dublin: Whitestone, 1776], bk. 1, ch. 2).

9.   This term refers to the major theological and philosophical teachings of the period 1000–1500. They were rooted in the authority of Christianity's founders on the one hand and Aristotle and his interpreters on the other [sk].

10.   "Omnia enim per te operabitur (Deus), mulgebit per te vaccam et servilissima quaeque opera faciet, ac maxima pariter et minima ipsi grata erunt" [Through you, God will sacrifice all. He will, through you, milk a cow, as he will also, through all, perform the most servile work. In addition, the smallest and largest tasks will each become welcome tasks.] (Luther, "Exegesis of Genesis," *Exegetica opera Latina*, edited by Christian S. Elsperger, vol. 7, p. 213 [Erlangen: Heyer, 1831]). The idea is found before Luther in [the major figure of early German mysticism] Tauler, who placed the spiritual and the worldly "callings," in terms of their value, in principle at an equal level. Luther and German mysticism share this position, one that contrasts to [Catholic] Thomism.

This contrast to Catholicism becomes manifest in that Thomas [Aquinas], in order firmly to retain the moral value of contemplation, though also because he was writing from the standpoint of a mendicant who must beg for a living, found it necessary to interpret Paul's maxim—"whoever does not work shall not eat"—in a certain way. Namely, Thomas viewed this maxim as imposed upon the human species as a whole (and actually, as *lege naturae* [through the law of nature], completely indispensable), rather than upon each person. This hierarchical variation in the prestige of work articulated by Thomas, from the *opera servilia* [servile tasks] of the peasants on up, is connected to the specific character of the Catholic mendicants; for material reasons, it was necessary for them to live in the towns. Such gradation was equally foreign to the German mystics and to Luther, the peasant's son. While attributing equal prestige to all occupations, both the mystics and Luther viewed the general stratification of the social order as willed by God. For the decisive passages in regard to Thomas Aquinas, see Maurenbrecher, *op. cit.* [note 6], pp. 65f.

11.   All the more astonishing is the belief by some scholars that such an innovation could have passed over the *action* of persons without the least effect. I confess, I don't understand this. [1920]

12.   Pascal believed that God's grace cannot be coerced or acquired; rather, it must be awaited [sk].

13.   "Vanity is so deeply embedded in the human heart that a camp-follower, a kitchen-helper, or a porter all boast and seek admirers . . . "(Faugeres, 1st ed., p. 208. cf. Koester, *op. cit.*, pp. 17, 136 ff.). On the principled position on the calling taken at Port Royal and by the Jansenists (which will be also briefly noted later), see now the excellent study by Dr. Paul Honigsheim, *Die Staats- und Soziallehren der französischen Jansenisten im 17ten Jahrhundert* [Darmstadt: Wissenschaftliche Buchhandlung, 1969 (1914)]. See especially pp. 138ff. Although printed separately, this volume belongs to Honigsheim's comprehensive study of the *Vorgeschichte der französischen Aufklärung* [*History Immediately Prior to the French Enlightenment*]. [1920]

14.   Because our knowledge can never give to us absolute certainty, "probabilities" must be assessed with respect to actions. If good reasons can be offered, action can be viewed as legitimate [sk].

15.   In regard to the Fuggers, Luther states: "It cannot be right and godly that, in the course of a single human life, such a large and regal fortune is accumulated." His view essentially expresses the [typical] peasant's mistrust of wealth. Similarly, Luther considers the purchase of stocks ethically suspect because they are "a newly discovered clever thing." In other words, because stocks are, to him, *incomprehensible*. This position is similar to the position of the modern clergy on investment in commodities. (See *Grosser Sermon vom Wucher* [Great Sermon on Usury], Erlangen edition, 20, p. 109.)

16.   Bankers were called *trapeziten* in ancient Greece. See Weber, *General Economic History*, p. 224 [sk].

17.   Hermann Levy develops the contrast appropriately. See *Die Grundlagen des ökonomischen Liberalismus in der Geschichte der englischen Volkswirtschaft* (Jena, 1912) [*English Liberalism* (London: Macmillan, 1913)]. Note also, for example, the petition of 1653 by the Levellers in Cromwell's army against monopolies and companies. See Samuel R. Gardiner, *History of the Commonwealth and Protectorate* [London: Longmans, Green & Co., 1894–1903], vol. 2, p. 179. On the other hand, [Archbishop William] Laud's regime [1629–1640] sought a "Christian-social" organization of the economy led by the monarchy and the church. The monarch expected political and fiscal-monopolistic advantages from this economy. The Puritans oriented their struggle against just such plans. [1920]

18.   An aristocrat, member of parliament, and strict Puritan, Cromwell led the opposition forces against the English monarchy in the English Civil War (1641–49) [sk].

19.   This statement can be best understood by reference to the example of the manifesto addressed to the Irish. With this document, in January, 1650, Cromwell opened his war of extermination against the Irish and answered the manifestos of the Irish (Catholic) clergy from Clonmacnoise of December 4 and 13, 1649. The pivotal sentences:

> Englishmen had good inheritances [manorial estates] (in Ireland, namely) which many of them *purchased with their money* . . . they had good leases from Irishmen for long time to come, *great stocks thereupon*, houses and plantations erected *at their cost and charge.* . . . You broke the union . . . at a time when Ireland was in perfect peace and when, through the *example of English industry, through commerce and traffic*, that which was in the nation's hands was better to them than if all Ireland had been in their possession . . . *Is God, will God be with you*? I am confident He will not.

This manifesto, which reminds one of editorials in the English press at the time of the Boer War [between England and South Africa, 1899–1902], is not unique for the reason that the "capitalist" interests of the English were defined as the legitimating reason for the war. This line of argument could very well have been likewise used in negotiations, for example, between Venice and Genoa over the extent of their respective spheres of influence in the Orient. (Strangely, and although I have emphasized this argument here, Brentano holds it against me; see *Die Anfänge des modernen Kapitalismus, op. cit.*, p. 142.) Rather, unique to this manifesto is that Cromwell legitimizes (with the deepest personal conviction, as everyone who knows his character will attest, and directly to the Irish themselves) the oppression of the Irish by calling upon God to note the circumstances; namely, that English capital had socialized the Irish to *work*. The manifesto is printed in Thomas Carlyle, *Oliver Cromwell's Letters and Speeches* [London: Chapman-Hall, 2nd ed., 1846]. It is reprinted in Samuel R. Gardiner, *op. cit.* pp. 163 f.

20.   A further exploration of this theme cannot be pursued here. See the writers cited in note 22 below.

21.   See the remarks in Adolf Jülicher's fine book, *Die Gleichnisreden Jesu* (Tübingen: Mohr, 1886–99), vol. 2, pp. 108f, 636.

22.   On the following see, above all, again the discussion in Karl Eger, *op. cit.* Also note Schneckenburger's fine work, which is even today not yet out of date: *Vergleichende Darstellung des lutherischen und reformierten Lehrbegriffs* (Stuttgart: J.B. Metzler, 1855). Christoph E. Luthardt's *Die Ethik Luthers in ihren Grundzügen* (Leipzig: Dorfling und Franke, 1866; only this edition is available to me) does not offer an analysis of the *development* (see p. 84). See further Reinhold Seeberg, *Lehrbuch der Dogmengeschichte* (Erlangen: A. Deichart, 1895–1898), vol. 2, pp. 262 ff. The article on *Beruf* in the *Realencyklopädie für protestantische Theologie und Kirche* is without value. It contains all sorts of rather shallow observations on everything imaginable, such as the women question, etc., instead of a scientific analysis of the concept and its origin.

From the national economics school's literature on Luther, I will refer here only to Schmoller's studies ("Zur Geschichte der Nationalökonomischen Ansichten in Deutschland während der Reformationszeit," *Zeitschrift für die gesamte Staatswiss.*, vol. 16 [1860]), [Heinrich] Wiskemann's prize essay [*Darstellung der in Deutschland zur Zeit der Reformation herrschenden nationalökonomischen Ansichten* (Leipzig: Jablonowskische Preisschrift, vol. 10], 1861), and the study by Frank G. Ward (*Darstellung und Würdigung von Luthers Ansichten vom Staat und seinen wirtschaftlichen Aufgaben, Conrads Abhandlungen*, vol. 21 [Jena, 1898]. As far as I can see, the literature on Luther on the occasion of the 400th anniversary of the Reformation (some of which is excellent) has not offered a significantly new contribution to *this* particular problem. Naturally, on Luther's social ethics (and the Lutheran social ethic) see the relevant sections of Troeltsch's *Social Teachings of the Christian Churches (op. cit.)*.

23.   *Auslegung des 7. Kap. des 1. Korintherbriefes* (1523, Erlangen edition, vol. 51, pp. 1f.). Here Luther still interprets the idea of the freedom "of every calling" before God, as alluded to in this Corinthians passage, to mean that (a) rules pertaining to the regulation of human beings should be repudiated (such as monastic vows, the prohibition of mixed marriages). He also interprets this passage (b) to imply that the fulfillment of customary, this-worldly duties to one's neighbor (which is in itself *indifferent* to God) should be intensified into a commandment *to love one's neighbor*. Actually, his central discussions concern, in view of the *lex naturae* dualism [see note 6 above], the question of the believer's just action before God (for example, at pp. 55, 56).

24.   Sombart correctly takes a passage from Luther as his motto for his presentation of the "craftsman spirit" (namely, a spirit of traditionalism):

> You must be prepared to seek, from such a business, nothing other than your basic sustenance. You can do so by calculating the amount of expected business, and then by being attentive to the cost of your room and board, the effort you must invest, and the potential dangers of your activity. Finally, you must attend to the pricing of your goods (whether higher or lower) in such a manner that you receive a wage for

your work and troubles. (Martin Luther, *Von Kaufhandlung und Wucher* [*On Business and Usury*], 1524)

Luther's basic approach here remains thoroughly in conformity with the writings of Thomas Aquinas.

25. A social revolutionary sect during Luther's time that wished to erect God's kingdom on earth. Its adherents supported a subjective piety based on feelings, adult baptism, and a strict church discipline [sk].

26. As early as Luther's letter to H. von Sternberg (where Luther states in 1530 that he is dedicating his exegesis of the 117th Psalm to Sternberg), the (lower) nobility "stratum" is viewed as founded by God, in spite of its moral degradation (Erlangen edition, vol. 40, p. 282). The decisive significance that the disturbances in Münster [see p. 525, note 214] had upon the development of this view are apparent from this letter (p. 282). See also Eger, *op. cit.*, p. 150.

27. Luther's polemics against a surpassing of the given order of things in the world through a withdrawal from the world into monasteries constituted the point of departure for his analysis in 1530 of the 111th Psalm, verses 5 and 6 (Erlangen edition, vol. 40, pp. 215–16). However, the *lex naturae* (in contrast to enacted law, which is manufactured by the emperor and jurists) is now clearly *identical* with *divine justice*: it is God's creation. Moreover, divine justice includes, in particular, the stratification of the people into *status groups* (p. 215). Luther emphasizes strongly here that the equality of status groups exists only before *God*.

28. As Luther taught especially in his *Von Konzilien und Kirchen* (1539) and *Kurzes Bekenntnis vom heiligen Sakrament* (1545).

29. The idea of the Christian's *testifying to his faith* in work in a vocational calling and in the organization of life remains, with Luther, in the background. This idea, so important for us, dominated Calvinism. A passage from Luther's *Von Konzilien und Kirchen* (1539, Erlangen edition, vol. 25, p. 3) indicates how far it remains in the background: "In addition to the seven major axioms" (by reference to which one recognizes the true church) "are now *several external signs* that allow one to recognize the holy Christian church . . . if we are not drunkards, and if we are not lascivious, proud, haughty, and ostentatious, but chaste, modest, and sober." According to Luther, these signs are not as certain as "the others" (doctrinal purity, prayer, etc.) "because heathens behaved in these ways, indeed to the extent that they occasionally have appeared more holy than Christians."

Calvin's own position, as will be discussed (unlike Puritanism's), was only slightly different. At any rate, Christians, according to Luther, serve God only *in vocatione* [*in* a vocation], not *per vocatione* [*for* a vocation] (Eger, *op. cit.*, pp. 117 ff.). The idea of *a testifying to belief*, on the other hand (more, nonetheless, in its Pietist than in its Calvinist manifestation), at least in incipient, fragmented forms, can be found in the German mystics, even though applied for them in a purely psychological manner. See, for example, the passage by Denifle cited by Reinhold Seeberg, *Lehrbuch der Dogmengeschichte, op. cit.* [note 22], vol. 1, p. 195. See also the already noted statements by Tauler; see note 3 above.

30. His final position is well expressed in some parts of his exegesis of Genesis [*Genesis-exegetica opera Latina*, see note 10] (vol. iv, p. 109): "Neque haec fuit levis tentatio, intentum esse suae vocationi et de aliis non esse curiosum. . . . Paucissimi sunt, qui sua sorte vivunt contenti. . . . (P. 111): Nostrum autem est, ut vocanti Deo pareamus . . . (P. 112). Regula igitur haec servanda est, ut unusquisque maneat in sua vocatione, et suo dono contentus vivat, de aliis autem non sit curious." [Even this was not an easy testing, namely, to remain oriented to one's calling while also having to attend to everything else. . . . Only a very few, live content with their destiny (p. 109). Our duty, however, is to obey God's call. . . . (p. 111). Hence, the following rule is to be upheld: every one stays in his calling and lives content with his talents; he should not be concerned with other mat-

ters (p. 112).] This conforms thoroughly, in regard to its *conclusion*, to the definition of traditionalism in the works of Thomas Aquinas *(Secunda secundae,* Quest. 118, Art. i):

> Unde necesse est, quod bonum hominis circa ea consistat in quadam mensura, dum scilicet homo . . . quaerit habere exteriores divitias, prout sunt necessariae ad vitam ejus secundum suam conditionem. Et ideo in excessu hujus mensurae consistit peccatum, dum scilicet aliquis supra debitum modum vult eas vel acquirere vel retinere, quod pertinet ad avaritiam.

[("Bona autem exteriora habent rationem utilium ad finem, sicut dictum est.") As already noted, external goods are justified when used for the purpose of fulfilling a utilitarian end. For this reason it is necessary that the wealth of a person stand in a certain proportion to usefulness. . .—that is, a person can aspire to possess external riches to the extent that goods are necessary to live according to his status *(Stand)*. Therefore, sinfulness occurs when wealth exceeds this standard; that is, when someone acquires or retains wealth beyond this proper extent. (". . . avaritiam quae definitur esse immoderatus amor habend, Unde patet quod est peccatum.") And at this point we move easily to the concept greed, which is defined as an excessive desire for possessions; hence, for this reason, greed is sinful. (The Latin sentences here precede and conclude the original passage Weber selected; they have been added on behalf of claritiy.)]

Thomas grounds the sinfulness of pursuing goods beyond the level of consumption in one's status in *lex naturae;* this natural law becomes manifest [according to Thomas] through [questions regarding] the *rationality* of the consumer goods. In contrast, Luther grounds this sinfulness in God's judgment. On the relation between faith and the calling in Luther, see also vol. 7, p. 222:

> . . . quando es fidelis, tum placent Deo etiam physica, carnalia, animalia, officia, sive edas, sive bibas, sive vigiles, sive dormias, quae mere corporalia et animalia sunt. *Tanta res est fides* . . . Verum est quidem, placere *Deo etiam in impiis sedulitatem et industriam in officio* (This *activity* in the vocational calling is a virtue *lege naturae.)* Sed obstat incredulitas et vana gloria, ne possint opera sua referre ad gloriam Dei (echoing Calvinist ways of speaking). . . . *Merentur* igitur etiam impiorum bona opera in hac quidem vita praemia sua (as distinct from Augustine's 'vitia specie virtutum palliata') sed non numerantur, non colliguntur in altero.

[If you are a believer, then God is pleased even by the physical, sensual, and sexual functions, and whether one is eating or drinking, awake or asleep. Even these purely bodily and physical functions are pleasing to him. *Belief, great as it is,* is capable of even this!. . . It is indeed true that *God is pleased even by the diligence and industriousness in business* of unbelievers. (This *activity* in the vocational calling is a natural-law virtue). However, their lack of faith and empty extolling of self prevent them from attributing their achievements to God's glory (echoing Calvinist ways of speaking). . . Hence, *although* the good works of unbelievers in this earthly life deserve their rewards (in contrast to St. Augustine, who sees this as simply "an embroidering of wickedness to render it a virtue"), they appear not to be counted and collected in the next life.]

31.　This idea is expressed in the *Kirchenpostille* [*Church Devotions*] (Erlangen edition, vol. 10, pp. 233, 235–36) in the following manner: "*Everyone* is called into some calling." *This* calling (on p. 236 it is directly a "command") should be heeded, and doing so serves God. The achievement [within the calling] does not please God; rather, the *obedience* to the duties in the given calling pleases God.

32.　This statement corresponds to the occasional assertion by modern businesspersons to the effect that (*in contrast to* the statements above on the effect of Pietism on the work habits of female employees) female textile workers, for example, from fundamentalist Lutheran [Pietist], church-going backgrounds commonly *today* (for example, in Westphalia), [continue to] think in the manner of the traditional economic ethic, indeed to an especially high degree. [These businesspersons report that these women] are disinclined to alter their modes of work (even when a transition to the factory system is not involved), despite the temptation of higher earnings. As an explanation, these women then refer to the next world—where all will be, in any case, balanced out in a fair manner. This example indicates that the simple facts of *church membership* and faith are not of any essential significance for the organizing of the believer's entire life. Rather, more important are the more practical *values and ideals* of religious life, for these values and ideals have a direct impact upon the believer. Indeed, their impact played a role in the epoch of capitalism's development. To a lesser degree, they still do.

33. See Tauler, Basel edition [see note 3], pp. 161 f.

34. See the peculiarly emotional sermon of Tauler referred to above [note 3], and chapters 17 and 18 (verse 20) of this work.

35. Because this constitutes, at this point, the single purpose of these comments on Luther, we must be satisfied with this thin, preliminary sketch. If viewed from the standpoint of an evaluation of Luther's achievements, this sketch is not in the least satisfactory. [1920]

36. Although highly influenced by Luther, Zwingli also frequently disagreed with him (especially over the symbolic meaning of communion) [sk].

37. Verses 1532–1540 (bk. 10). See Milton, *Paradise Lost* (London: Folcroft Library Editions, 1972). The two-line emphasis is Weber's [sk].

38. *Ibid.*, verses 1473–1478. The emphasis is Weber's [sk].

39. This subheading appears in the original table of contents but nowhere in the text. I have inserted it at this point. Weber here turns away from Lutheranism and to more general questions related to the overall "task" of this study [sk].

40. Whoever, of course, shared the Levellers' construction of history would have been in the fortunate circumstance of being able to reduce also [this distinction between Cavaliers and Roundheads] to racial differences. As representatives of the Anglo-Saxons, the Levellers believed it their "birthright" to be able to defend themselves against the descendants of William the Conqueror and the Normans. Until now—and this is quite astonishing—no one has asserted that the plebeian "Roundheads" had "round heads" in the anthropometric sense!

41. English national pride, in particular [cannot be explained by reference to "national character"]. Rather, it results from Magna Carta and the great wars [of the seventeenth century]. The saying so typical today [in Germany] at the sight of a pretty foreign girl—"she looks like an English girl"—is reported as early as the fifteenth century. [1920]

42. These distinctions have, of course, also remained viable in England. Namely, the "squirearchy," to the present, has remained the social carrier of "merry old England," and the entire era since the Reformation can be understood as a struggle between these two aspects of "the English." I agree on this point with the observations by M. J. Bonn (in the *Frankfurter Zeitung*) on the excellent study by Gerhart von Schulze-Gaevernitz on British imperialism. [See *Britischer Imperialismus und englischer Freihandel zu Beginn des 20. Jahrhunderts* (Leipzig: Duncker & Humblot, 1906).] See also Hermann Levy [*Soziologische Studien über das englische Volk* (Jena, 1920)]. [1920]

43. Precisely these positions—despite this remark and the remarks that follow, which have never been changed and are sufficiently clear, in my opinion—have been, strangely, repeatedly attributed to me. [1920]

44. See Weber's dissertation, *The History of Commercial Partnerships in the Middle Ages.* Translated by Lutz Kaelber. (Lanham, MD: Rowman and Littlefield, 2003). See also Weber, *General Economic History* [sk].

Chapter IV

1.   After a short period of expansive domination, Zwinglianism quickly lost its significance. For this reason it will not be treated separately. "Arminianism," whose *dogmatic* uniqueness consisted of the rejection of the predestination dogma in its strict formulation as well as that of "this-worldly asceticism," became established as a sect only in Holland (and the United States). Hence, it is of little interest to us in this chapter. Or, more clearly stated, Arminianism is of interest to us only as a negative case: it was the religion of the merchant elite in Holland (see below). Its dogma was viewed as legitimate in the Anglican Church and in the Methodist denominations. Finally, Arminianism's "Erastian" position (that is, its acknowledgment of the state's sovereignty even in matters regarding the church) was held in common with *all* established authorities with purely political interests: the Long Parliament in England, as well as the Elizabethan monarchy, and the Dutch parliament. Above all, Oldenbarneveldt [see note 12 below] upheld Erastianism.

2.   Phillipp Jacob Spener wrote an essay of decisive significance for the expansion of Pietism: *Pia desideria* [*Pious Desire*] (Frankfurt: Friedgen, 1676). He proved a skilled organizer, owing in part to his connections to the court of Brandenburg-Prussia, on behalf of ecclesiastical and educational reform [sk].

3.   A distinguished Pietist, Zinzendorf was a founder of the Herrnhuter Brotherhood (1722) [sk].

4.   The Moravian Brethren were founded in 1622 in Bohemia (now in the Czech Republic). They opposed military service, the swearing of oaths, and the owning of private property. Persecuted, in 1722 the Brethren settled in Saxony in the territory of Count Zinzendorf in the village of Herrnhut (north of Zittau in far eastern Germany). One branch emigrated to Pennsylvania and became known as the Church of the Brethren. In the colony, smaller groups split off. In 1946 the major Brethren church merged with the Evangelical Church to form the Evangelical United Brethren Church. This church merged in 1968 with the Methodist Church. Other Brethren churches in Pennsylvania remain independent to this day [sk].

5.   See, on the development of the concept of Puritanism, instead of others, John L. Sanford, *Studies and Reflections of the Great Rebellion* (London: J.W. Parker & Son, 1858), pp. 65 f. At all times we are using this term in the way that it was used in the everyday language of the seventeenth century, namely, to refer to the religious movements oriented toward asceticism in Holland and England, and without distinctions regarding a church's organizational agenda and dogma. Hence, the term encompasses the "Independents," Congregationalists, Baptists, Mennonites, and Quakers.

6.   Casuistic manuals provided believers with exact instruction in regard to all the major activities of life [sk].

7.   This distinction has been the subject of hopeless confusion in the literature. Sombart, though also Brentano, continuously cites writers on ethics (generally ones he has become acquainted with through my writings) and their codifications of rules for appropriate conduct. They offer these citations without *ever* asking which of these rules were penetrated by *salvation* rewards. A rule became psychologically effective only if subject to such rewards. [1920]

8.   I hardly need to emphasize that this sketch, at those points where it addresses questions of pure dogma, relies at all times on statements from the literature on church history and the literature that traces the historical development of dogma. Thus, it relies on the secondary literature and, consequently, can hardly claim any *originality*. Of course, to the extent possible, I have sought to become immersed in the primary sources in Reformation history. However, any desire to ignore the in-depth and subtle theological secondary studies of many decades would be extremely presumptuous. Rather, one

should (as is entirely unavoidable) allow this research to *guide* one's understanding of the sources.

I can only hope that the necessary brevity of this sketch has not led to incorrect statements, and that I have at least avoided objectively significant misunderstandings. For those familiar with the most important theological literature, this presentation contains something "new" only to the extent that everything here is oriented to the vantage point important for *us*. Many of the highly significant theological investigations are, quite naturally, distant from this vantage point—for example, our concern with the *rational character of asceticism* and its significance for the modern "style of life."

Since this essay originally appeared [1904–05], Ernst Troeltsch's *Social Teachings of the Christian Churches* [New York: Harper & Row, 1960 (1911)] has systematically addressed this theme and in general examined the *sociological* side of the issue. (Troeltsch's *Gerhard und Melanchthon* [1891], as well as numerous reviews in the *Göttingische Gelehrte Anzeigen* [*Scholar's Review*], contained many preliminary studies for this great book.) I have not cited Troeltsch's work below every time I have made use of it (purely for reasons of space); instead, I have made reference *only* to his studies that follow relevant passages in my text or when his works connect directly to it. Not infrequently, I have cited the works of earlier authors, as the vantage points of interest in my study have stood closer to them. The completely inadequate financing of the German libraries has led to a situation in which people in the "provinces" can acquire the most important primary sources and studies only through interlibrary loan from Berlin, or other great libraries, and then only for less than a week [Weber resides in Heidelberg]. This is, for example, the case for Voët, Baxter, Tyerman, Wesley, and all Methodist, Baptist, and Quaker writers. It is also true for many of the nonmainstream Reformation writers of the early period.

Indispensable for every *thorough* investigation are regular visits to the English and, especially, American libraries. What was available in Germany had, in general of course, to suffice for the following sketch. In America, in recent years, a characteristic and intentional denial of the indigenous *sectarian* past has led to a situation in which the libraries acquire little or nothing of this literature. This very tendency can be seen as a particular manifestation of that general tendency toward *secularization* in American life. In a not-too-distant future, as a result of this tendency, all historical legacies of the general American character will have been dissipated. As this takes place, the meaning of many of that country's foundational institutions will be completely and definitively altered. One must travel to the orthodox, small sectarian colleges in the countryside [to document America's sectarian past].

9.   In the following sections we are not interested *mainly* in the ancestry, antecedents, and developmental history of the ascetic movements. Rather, we are taking their ideas as given, namely, as completely developed and as they actually were.

10.   On Calvin and Calvinism, in addition to the fundamental work of F. W. Kampschulte [*Johann Calvin, seine Kirche und sein Staat in Genf* (Leipzig: Duncker & Humblot, 1869–99)], the exposition by Erich Marcks is in general among the best. [See his *Gaspard von Coligny: Sein Leben und das Frankreich seiner Zeit* (Stuttgart: Cotta, 1892).] D. Campbell's *The Puritans in Holland, England, and America* (2 vols.) is not always reliable and without bias. A. Pierson's *Studiën over Johannes Kalvijn* [Amsterdam: P.N. van Kemper, 1881–91] is a strongly anti-Calvinistic study.

For the development in Holland see (in addition to J. L. Motley) the classical Dutch studies, especially G. Groen van Prinsterer, *Handboek der Geschiedenis van het Vaderland* [Leiden: Luchtmans, 1841–46]; and *La Hollande et l'influence de Calvin* (Amsterdam: H. Hoveker, 1864). For *modern* Holland see *Le parti anti-révolutionnaire et confessionnel dans l'église des Pays-Bas* (Amsterdam: H. Hoveker, 1860). See further, above all, R. J. Fruin's *Tien jaren uit de tachtig jarigen oorlog* [Gravenhage: M. Nijhoff, 1857], and especially, in order to compare, J. Naber, *Calvinist of Libertijntsch* (Utrecht: Beijers, 1884). See also W. J. F. Nuyens, *Geschiedenis der kerkelijke en politieke geschillen in de Republic der zeven Vereenigde*

Provinciën voonamelijk gedurende het Twaalfjarig Bestand (1598–1625) (Amsterdam, 1886). For the nineteenth century, see A. Köhler, *Die niederländische reformierte Kirche* (Erlangen: A. Deichert, 1856).

For France, in addition to G. von Polenz, *Geschiedenis des französischen Calvinismus* (Gotha: F.A. Perthes, 1857–69), see Henry M. Baird, *History of the Rise of the Huguenots in France* (New York: Scribner's Sons, 1879).

For England, in addition to Thomas Carlyle, Thomas B. Macaulay, David Masson, and (last but not least) Leopold von Ranke, see now, above all, the various works of Gardiner and Firth (to be cited later). See also, for example, John James Tayler, *A Retrospect of the Religious Life in England* (London: J. Chapman, 1845; 2nd ed. 1853), and the excellent book by Hermann Weingarten, *Die Revolutionskirchen Englands* (Leipzig: Breitkopf & Hartel, 1868). Further, see the essay on the English *moralists* by Ernst Troeltsch in the *Realencyklopädie für protestantische Theologie und Kirche* (3rd ed., 1903), and of course his *Social Teachings of the Christian Churches* (*op. cit.*). Also note Eduard Bernstein's excellent [see notes 210, 220] essay, "Kommunistische und demokratisch-sozialistische Strömungen während der englischen Revolution des 17. Jahrhunderts" in *Geschichte des Sozialismus* (Stuttgart, 1895, vol. 1, sect. 2, pp. 507 ff.). The best bibliography (more than 7,000 titles) is in H. M. Dexter, *The Congregationalism of the Last Three Hundred Years* (New York: B. Franklin, 1920 [1876–79], 1880). Admittedly, this volume concerns mainly, although not exclusively, questions of church *governance*. It is quite superior to Theodore Price, *The History of Protestant Nonconformity in England* (London, 1836–38), to H. S. Skeats, *History of the Free Churches of England, 1688–91* (London: Shepheard Pub., 1891), and to other studies.

For Scotland see, for example, Karl H. Sack, *Die Kirche von Schottland* (Heidelberg: Carl Winter Verlag, 1844) and the literature on John Knox.

For the American colonies, a large step above numerous other studies is John Doyle, *The English in America* (London: Longmans, Green, 1887). See further Daniel Wait Howe, *The Puritan Republic of the Massachusetts Bay in New England* (Indianapolis: Bowen-Merrill, 1899); John Brown, *The Pilgrim Fathers of New England and Their Puritan Successors* (New York: Revell, 1895). Further references will be given at the appropriate places throughout this chapter.

For differences in respect to *doctrine* the following exposition is indebted especially to Matthias Schneckenburger's lecture series, *Vergleichende Darstellung des lutherischen und reformierten Lehrbegriffs* (Stuttgart: J.B. Metzler, 1855). Albrecht Ritschl's fundamental work, *Die christliche Lehre von der Rechtfertigung und Versöhnung* (3rd ed., Bonn: A. Marcus, 1870–74), demonstrates, in closely interweaving historical exposition and value judgments, the unique qualities of its author; despite the author's exceptional conceptual acuity, the reader is not always given complete certainty about Ritschl's *objectivity*. For example, wherever he rejects Schneckenburger's interpretation, I often doubt Ritschl's correctness, even though I do not presume in general to be able to formulate an independent judgment. Moreover, for example, what he establishes out of the great diversity of religious ideas and moods (even in the case of Luther himself) to be *Lutheran* appears often to be defined by his own value judgments. This is so because Ritschl attends to what, for him, is the *eternally valued* in Lutheranism. His Lutheranism is a Lutheranism of what this religion *ought* to be and not what it always *was*. That the studies of Karl Müller, Reinhold Seeberg, and others have *everywhere* been used does not require special mention here.

If I have in the following pages imposed upon the reader (as well as *myself*) a malignant growth of evil endnotes, I had a single decisive hope in doing so: to provide the reader—especially the *non*theologian—with at least the preliminary possibility of independently evaluating the ideas in this essay. The literature noted here can also assist the evaluation of my argument through an investigation of related vantage points.

11.   It should be emphasized from the beginning that we are here *not* considering the personal views of Calvin. Rather, our concern is with *Calvinism*. We are concerned, moreover, with Calvinism in *the form* it had developed at the end of the sixteenth century and in the seventeenth century. Finally, we wish to investigate its form in this era in the large territories of its dominant influence that were, simultaneously, carriers of a capitalist culture. Germany must remain for now *completely aside* for the simple reason that pure Calvinism nowhere in Germany *dominated* large territories. "Reformed" is of course by no means identical with "Calvinist." [See Glossary]

12.   Oldenbarneveldt was a Dutch diplomat. He negotiated the 1609 armistice with Spain and was executed after conflicts with state authorities [sk].

13.   Even though the declaration of the 17th article of the Anglican Confession (the so-called Lambeth Article of 1595, which expressly taught, contrary to the official version, that predestination to eternal death existed) was agreed to by the University of Cambridge and the archbishop of Canterbury, it was not ratified by the queen. The radicals in particular emphasized strongly explicit predestination to death (and not only the *admission* of the condemned, as upheld by the milder doctrine). This was clear from Hanserd Knollys' confessions. [1920] [Weber is most likely referring to Knollys, William Kiffin, and H. Keach, *London Baptist Confessions* (London: 1689).]

14.   *Westminster Confession* (5th official ed., London, 1717). See the Savoy Declaration and the (American [edition of]) Knollys (*ibid.*). On the Huguenots' view of predestination, see, among others, Polenz, *op. cit.*, vol. 1, pp. 545 ff.

15.   On Milton's theology see the essay of R. Eibach ("John Milton als Theologe") in the *Theologische Studien und Kritiken,* vol. 52 (1879). See also Thomas Macaulay's essay on it (in *Critical and Miscellaneous Essays* [New York: D. Appleton], vol. 1, 1843), on the occasion of Sumner's translation of the *Doctrina Christiana,* rediscovered in 1823 (Tauchnitz edition, vol. 185, pp. 1 ff.), is superficial. For more detail see the (somewhat too schematic) six-volume English work of David Masson, *The Life of John Milton* (London, 1859–94). See also the German biography of Milton, based on Masson, by Alfred Stern, *Milton und seine Zeit* (Leipzig: Duncker & Humblot, 1877–99).

At an early point, Milton began to grow away from the doctrine of predestination in the form of a double decree. He moved eventually in his advanced years to an entirely unbounded Christianity. He can be compared, in respect to his distance from his own epoch, in a certain sense to Sebastian Franck. Yet Milton's nature was more oriented to the practical, while Franck's was substantially more critical. Milton can be said to be a *Puritan* only in the broader sense of *rationally* orienting his practical life to God's will. This orientation represented Calvinism's lasting legacy to the world. One could call Franck a *Puritan* in an entirely similar manner. As "lonely and isolated figures," both must remain outside our concern.

16.   Through his *Confessions* and other works, St. Augustine significantly influenced Christian theology until the mid-thirteenth century [sk].

17.   *Hic est fidei summus gradus: credere Deum esse clementem, qui tam paucos salvat, justum, qui sua voluntate nos damnabiles facit* [This is the highest level of faith: The belief that God is mild is justified; through His will He made us deserving of condemnation, yet He saves the poor.] is the text of the famous passage in *De servo arbitrio* [Of observant witnessing].

18.   Melanchthon was closely associated with Luther and author of the first major Lutheran doctrinal statement, the Augsburg Confession (1530) [sk].

19.   Both Luther and Calvin basically knew a double God: the revealed, forgiving, and benevolent Father of the New Testament (who ruled the first books of Calvin's *Institutio christianae religionis* [1536; Engl. transl. 1561; London: Wolfe & Harison), and the distant *Deus absconditus* [hidden God], who was a thundering and arbitrary despot. See Ritschl's remarks in *Geschichte des Pietismus* (Bonn: Marcus, 1880–86) and Köstlin's article "Gott" in *Realencyklopädie für protestantische Theologie und Kirche* (3rd ed.). The God of the

New Testament completely retained the dominant position for Luther. This resulted from his increasing avoidance of *reflection* on the metaphysical realm, which he saw as useless and dangerous. In contrast, the idea of a transcendent Divine power over and above life acquired an increasingly prominent position in Calvin's thinking. Of course, this idea could not be defended and endure with the development of a more popular Calvinism. Nevertheless, the [benevolent] heavenly father of the New Testament did not replace this idea; rather, the [distant and arbitrary] Yahweh of the Old Testament came to the fore as Calvinism developed.

20. Regarding that which follows, see Max Scheibe, *Calvins Prädestinationslehre* (Halle a. S., 1897). On Calvinist theology in general, see Johann Heinrich Heppe, *Dogmatik der evangelisch-reformierten Kirche* (Elberfeld: R.L. Friderichs, 1861).

21. *Corpus Reformatorum* (vol. 77, pp. 186 ff.).

22. The preceding exposition of Calvinist doctrinal concepts can be reviewed in, for example, Hoornbeek's *Theologiae practicae* (Utrecht: Ex officina Henrici Versteeg, 1663.89). See the section on predestination (vol. 50, sect. 2, ch. 1). Characteristically, this discussion comes *directly* after the title: "De Deo" [Of God]. My presentation of these concepts has closely followed Hoornbeek. The first chapter of the Epistle to the Ephesians constitutes the major biblical foundation for his analysis. It is not necessary for us to analyze here the various inconsistent attempts to combine God's predestination and providence with the responsibility of the individual and [thereby] to save the empirical "freedom" of the will (as has been attempted even as early as the first developments of doctrine by Augustine).

23. "The deepest community (with God) is found not in institutions or corporations or churches, but in the secrets of a solitary heart," as Edward Dowden states the pivotal point in his fine book *Puritan and Anglican Studies in Literature* (London: Holt, 1901), p. 234. This deep spiritual loneliness of each believer makes its appearance in the same manner with the Jansenists from Port Royal. They also believed in predestination. [Close to Paris, Port Royal was a convent of Cistercian nuns (founded in 1204). It became a center of Jansenism. Cornelius Otto Jansen (1585–1638), a Dutch and French theologian, founded Jansenism. This movement inside the Catholic Church in Holland and France opposed the Jesuits. It advocated a great moral rigorism and a return to the teachings of St. Augustine's ancient Christianity, especially its indifference to the world. Jansenists were persecuted in eighteenth-century France by the church as unorthodox. See note 53.]

24. "Contra qui hujusmodi coetus tum contemnunt . . . salutis suae certi esse non possunt; et qui in illo contemtu perseverat electus non est." Olevian, *De substantia foederis gratuiti inter Deum et electos* [1558], p. 222. [Those who scorn a church that upholds pure doctrine, the sacraments, and discipline cannot be certain of their salvation; and the person who stubbornly remains disrespectful is not among the saved.]

25. "One says readily that God sent His Son to save the human species. However, that was not his aim. Rather, he wanted to help only a few out of their sinfulness. . . . And I say to you that God died only for the predestined" (sermon preached in 1609 at Broek; found in H. C. Rogge, *Johannes Uytenbogaert*; 1874–76, vol. 2, p. 9; see also Nuyens, *op. cit.*, vol. 2, p. 232). The legitimating foundation for the intermediating role of Christ is also confusing in Hanserd Knollys' confessions [*op. cit.*, note 13]. It is actually universally assumed that God in fact would not have needed this mediation at all. [1920]

26. [This expression is widely believed to be from the German dramatist, historian, and philosopher of aesthetics Friedrich Schiller (1759–1805).] On this process see my Economic Ethics of the World Religions series. [See pp. 183–84, 223–37, 313–19.] Even the unusual nature of the ancient Israelite ethic (in contrast to Egyptian and Babylonian ethics, despite their close substantive relationship), and its development since the epoch of the prophets [800–500 BCE], was founded completely upon this fundamental point: this ethic rejected the practice of sacramental magic as a means to acquire salvation. [1920] [As implied in the text, Weber will view this rejection of magic as pivotal for the develop-

ment of the Western religious tradition. This will become apparent in this volume; see also, for example, *E&S*, pp. 399–634; *The Religion of China*, pp. 226–49; "Social Psychology," in H. H. Gerth and C. W. Mills, eds., *From Max Weber*.]

27.   [Because not only Calvinism but *all* the churches and sects of ascetic Protestantism—Puritanism—broadly upheld the predestination doctrine, Weber is expanding upon his comments in the next few pages on the influence of this doctrine upon Puritanism as a whole.] Similarly, according to the most consistent views, baptism was obligatory (owing to clear regulations) yet not necessary for salvation. *For this reason*, the strict Scottish Puritans and the English Independents sought to put into practice a basic principle: the children of obvious *reprobates* should not be baptized (children of drunkards, for example). The Synod of Edam (1586, Article 32, 1) recommended that adults who desired to be baptized but were not yet *ready* to take communion, should be baptized only if their conduct was blameless and if they had placed their desire *sonder superstitie*. [Their wish to be baptized must not be influenced by superstition, cult beliefs, or beliefs in miracles or magic.] [1920]

28.   This negative relationship to *all culture that appeals to the senses* is a central constitutive element of Puritanism (as Edward Dowden has explained in elegant fashion; see *op. cit.* [note 23]). [1920]

29.   The expression *individualism* encompasses the most heterogeneous phenomena to be imagined. It is to be hoped that what is understood *here* by this term will become clear in the following clarifications. Some (using the term differently) have called Lutheranism "individualistic" because it does *not* involve an ascetic regimentation of life. The term is used in a very different manner by Dietrich Schäfer, for example, when he, in "Zur Beurteilung des Wormser Konkordats" (in *Abhandlung der Berliner Akademie*, 1905), calls the *Middle Ages* the era of "marked individuality." He does so because, for the occurrences *relevant* for the historian, "irrational aspects" [indicating "individuality"] assumed a significance in the Middle Ages that they no longer possess today. He is correct, but perhaps those who oppose his observations are also correct; varying understandings are apparent here when all concerned speak of "individuality" and "individualism." The ingenious formulations by Jacob Burckhardt, [the cultural historian of the Italian Renaissance, 1818–97], are today in part outmoded, and a thorough, historically oriented analysis of individualism would be, especially now, again a highly valuable scientific contribution. The results would be, of course, just the opposite if the playful instincts of certain historians push them, in order simply to be able to stick a label on an historical epoch, to "define" the concept as if it were an advertisement.

30.   Similar, although of course less pointed, is the contrast between this pessimistic Puritan individualism and later Catholic doctrine. Pascal's deep pessimism, which likewise rests upon the doctrine of predestination, locates its origin, on the other hand, in Jansenism [see notes 23 and 57]. The flight-from-the-world individualism of Pascal, which arose out of his pessimism, does not at all accord with the official Catholic position. See Paul Honigsheim, *Die Staats- und Soziallehren der französischen Jansenisten im 17 Jahrhundert* [Darmstadt: Wissenschaftliche Buchgesellschaft, 1969 (1914)]. [1920]

31.   Just like the Jansenists. [See notes 23 and 57.]

32.   Lewis Bayly, *Praxis pietatis*, German edition (Leipzig, 1724 [orig.: Basel: Johann Brandmuller, 1708]), p. 187. [As is clear from its title in English, *The Practice of Piety: Directing a Christian How to Walk That He May Please God* (London: Algonquin Press, 1642), this very popular book in Puritan circles offered the devout practical advice on correct conduct.] Also Spener takes a similar point of view in his *Theologische Bedenken*, 3rd ed. (Halle, 1712): One's friend rarely gives advice grounded in reference to God's honor; rather, his advice usually derives from intentions rooted in physical desires (although not necessarily egoistic motives).

> He—the 'knowing man'—is blind in no man's cause, but best sighted in his own. He confines himself to the circle of his own affairs, and thrusts not his fingers in needless fires. . . . He sees the falseness of it (the world) and therefore learns to trust himself ever, others so far, as not to be damaged by their disappointment.

Thomas Adams philosophizes in this manner (see *Works of the Puritan Divines*, p. 51). [This, and the studies cited below as *Works of the Puritan Divines*, were published in 10 volumes as *Works of the English Puritan Divines* (London: Nelson Publishers, 1845–47).] Bayly (*op. cit.*, p. 176) further recommends that one should imagine, every morning before going out among people, that one is walking into a wild forest full of dangers. Hence, one should pray to God for the "cloak of *caution and justice.*"

This sensibility penetrates, without exception, all the ascetic denominations and leads directly, for many Pietists amidst the world's activities, to a type of solitary life. Even Spangenberg [see note 162 below], in the (Herrnhuter) *Idea fidei fratrum* (Leipzig: Weidmanns, 1779, p. 328), emphatically calls attention to Jeremiah 17:5: "Cursed is the man who trusteth in man." One should note also, in order to assess the strange misanthropy of this view of life, Hoornbeek's remarks (*Theologia practica*, vol. 1, p. 882) on the duty to love one's enemy: "Denique hoc magis nos ulciscimur, quo proximum, inultum nobis, *tradimus ultori Deo* . . . Quo quis plus se ulciscituur, eo minus id pro ipso agit Deus." [In the end, we more likely invite revenge upon us as a result of what we see in a vindictive God and qualities we attribute to Him. Wherever a person takes revenge, however, it is not God who is acting but the person himself.] The same "displacement of revenge" is found here as is found in the post-Exile sections of the Old Testament: a refined intensification and internalization of the feeling of revenge is apparent, in contrast to the ancient maxim "an eye for an eye." On "brotherly love" see also note 43 below.

33. Of course, confession surely not *only* had such an effect. The discussions, for example, by A. Muthmann are all too simple for a psychological problem as highly complicated as confession. See his "Psychiatrisch-theologische Grenzfragen," in *Zeitschrift für Religionspsychologie* (vol. 1, no. 2, 1907), p. 65. [1920]

34. Precisely *this* combination is very important for the ascertainment of the psychological foundation of Calvinist social *organizations*. *All* rest internally upon "individualistic," "means-end rational," or "value-rational" motives. [On these "types of social action," see 1968, pp. 24–26.] The individual never moves into social organizations on the basis of *feelings*. Such movement is prevented by the orientation to "God's glory" and one's *own* salvation, which continuously hovers *above* one's consciousness. Among those peoples with a Puritan past, this psychological foundation even today imprints the uniqueness of their social organization with certain characteristic traits. [See pp. 200–04.]

35. The *anti-authoritarian* grounding of the doctrine, which basically devalued, as meaningless, all church and state caretaking responsibility for ethical action and the believer's salvation, led perpetually anew to the prohibition of caretaking initiatives. Such was the situation, for example, in the Dutch parliament. The consequence was clear: the continuous formation of conventicles (as occurred after 1614).

36. On John Bunyan see the biography by James A. Froude, *Bunyan* (London: Macmillan, 1880), in the English Men of Letters series. See also Thomas B. Macaulay's (superficial) sketch on Bunyan in his *Critical and Miscellaneous Essays*, *op. cit.* [note 15], vol. 2 (New York: D. Appleton, 1860), p. 227. Although a strict Calvinist Baptist, Bunyan is indifferent to the denominational differences within Calvinism.

37. In Italy, Alphonsus of Liguori founded a religious order, the Redemptorists, in 1732. A Catholic reform theologian as well as a church historian, Döllinger was excommunicated because of his challenges to doctrines on the virgin birth and the infallibility of the pope [sk].

38. In citing this passage from Richard Wagner's opera, Weber wishes to convey the warrior's ethos of honor and stoic resignation before death, and to note its clear contrast to the ethos of Christians on the one hand and to the ethos of the citizens of Florence on the other. See Wagner, *Ring of the Nibelung* (New York: Thames & Hudson, 1993), pp. 161, 163 [sk].

39. One might be inclined to explain the *social* character of ascetic Christianity by noting the undoubtedly large importance of the Calvinist idea of an "incorporation into the body of Christ" (Calvin, *Instituto christianae religionis,* vol. 3, sects. 11, 10). In other words, because it is necessary for salvation, there must be admission into a *community* governed by God's prescriptions. For *our* particular vantage point, however, the major issue lies elsewhere.

This dogmatic idea [the importance of an incorporation into the body of Christ] could have been formulated if the church had assumed the character of an institution with membership granted to all; indeed, this type of institution did develop [Catholicism], as is well-known. Yet such a church did not have the psychological power to awaken community-building *initiatives* and to endow them with the sheer strength that Calvinism possessed to do so. In particular, the effects of Calvinism's community-building tendencies played themselves out *beyond* the divinely prescribed church congregation and in the "world." At this point the belief becomes central that the Christian, through activities *in majorem Dei gloriam* [in service to the greater glory of God], testifies to his state of grace (see below).

The sharp condemnation of the deification of human wants and desires and of all clinging to *personal* relationships with others must have directed this energy, imperceptibly, into this pathway of impersonal activity. The Christian, whose entire existence was burdened by the necessity of testifying to his own state of grace, now acted on behalf of *God's* aims. And these could only be *impersonal* aims. Every purely feeling-based *personal* relationship of individuals to one another—that is, relationships not determined by rational aims—now easily fell under suspicion, for Puritanism as well as for every other ascetic ethic, as involving a deification of human wants and desires. The following warning (in addition to what has already been noted) indicates just this tendency clearly enough: "It is an irrational act and not fit for a rational creature to love any one farther than *reason* will allow us. . . . It very often taketh up men's minds so as to *hinder* their *love of God*" (Baxter, *Christian Directory* [London: G. Bell & Sons, 1925 (1673)], vol. 4, p. 253) [emph. in orig.]. We will confront such arguments repeatedly.

The Calvinists greeted with enthusiasm the idea that God, in creating the world and also the social order, must have wanted *impersonal and purposive activity* to constitute a means for the glorification of His reputation. He did not create, the Calvinists realized, human beings for their own sake, simply for the fulfillment of the physical needs of the body. Rather, He created a world in which the physical being would be *ordered* under His will. Liberated by the doctrine of predestination, the fervid activity of the chosen could now flow entirely into a striving to make the world rational (*Rationalisierung der Welt*). More precisely, the idea that the "public" good (or, as Baxter says, *"the good of the many"*; see, with its rather strained citation to Romans 9:3, p. 262 of his *Christian Directory*, vol. 4, p. 262), which was formulated in the same manner entirely as the later liberal rationalism [classical economics], is to be given preference over the "personal" or "private" prosperity of each person, followed for Puritanism (even though not a new idea as such) from the rejection of all glorification of human wants and desires. The long-standing American deprecation of those who *carry out* the personal commands of others, although it must be viewed in combination with many other causes that derive from "democratic" sentiments, nonetheless goes together (in an indirect manner) with this opposition to the deification of wants and desires.

This rejection of all human glorification is likewise related to the *relatively* high degree of immunity to authoritarianism possessed by peoples influenced by Puritanism. Furthermore, this rejection is related, in general, to the internally less inhibited posture of the English vis-à-vis their great statesmen (and their greater capacity to criticize them). This posture contrasts to some of our experiences in Germany from 1878 to the present (both positively and negatively) in respect to our statesmen. The posture of the English is characterized by a tendency, on the one hand, to acknowledge leadership in distinguished persons. It is marked, on the other hand, despite this acknowledgment, by a further proclivity to reject all hysterical idolization of leaders.

Finally, the tendency to oppose a naive idea is also apparent in Puritanism; namely, that one can render a person duty-bound, out of a sense of "thankfulness," to obey political authorities [as in Germany]. On the sinfulness of the belief in authority, see Baxter, *Christian Directory*, 2nd ed. (London: Robert White, 1678, vol. 1, p. 56). He makes it clear that a belief in authority is permissible only if the authority is *impersonal*; that is, the belief is oriented to the content of a written [statute or regulation in a] document. Likewise, an exaggerated respect for even the most holy and wonderful person is sinful. The great danger exists, in attributing both authority and respect, that eventually the obedience to *God* will thereby be endangered.

A discussion of what the rejection of the "deification of human wants and desires" meant *politically*, as well as the principle that (first in the church and then in the end also in life as a whole) only God should "rule," does not belong in this context.

40.   The relationship between dogmatic and practical-psychological "consequences" will be often discussed. It scarcely needs to be remarked that these two types of consequences are not identical. [1920]

41.   "Social," of course, without any echo of the modern sense of the word. [Weber wants to steer his German audience away from the (modern) nineteenth and early twentieth century use of "social" in Germany in certain religious groupings and political parties; it referred to the obligations of major societal institutions (the state, churches, etc.) to the welfare of all.] [For the Calvinist,] the term merely implies being active in political or church groups, or other organizations that build community.

42.   Good works for *any* purpose other than to serve the honor *of God* are *sinful*. See Hanserd Knollys' confession, *op. cit.* [note 13], ch. 16. [1920]

43.   What such a rendering of the "love thy neighbor" commandment as "impersonal," resulting from the exclusive relating of one's life to God, meant for the believer's own realm—the life of the religious community—can be very well depicted by a glance at the conduct of the "China Inland Mission" and the "International Missionaries' Alliance." See Warneck, *Abriß einer Geschichte der protestantischen Missionen* (Berlin: M. Warnerk, 1898, 5th edition, pp. 99, 111). At enormous cost, a huge squad of missionaries (for example, approximately 1,000 for China alone) was equipped in order "to offer" the gospel in a strictly literal sense, through itinerant preachers, to all heathens. It was necessary to do so because Christ had commanded this activity and had made his second coming dependent upon it. Whether those preached to in this manner were converted to Christianity, and hence became among the saved, and whether they *understood* the language of the missionary, even grammatically—all this is in principle a thoroughly secondary matter and a concern of God alone (who of course exclusively decides such issues). According to Hudson Taylor (see Warneck), China has approximately 50 million families. A thousand missionaries [each] could "reach" 50 families per day (!). Thus, in 1,000 days, or less than three years, the gospel could be "offered" to all Chinese.

As is apparent from Calvinist church discipline, for example, Calvinism operated exactly according to this model. The goal was *not* the salvation of those subject to church discipline. That remained true for the simple reason that the believer's salvation fate was to be decided in the end by God (and, in actual practice, by believers themselves). This fate could not be influenced in any way by the disciplinary measures available to the church. The aim of such measures was instead to increase the glory of God.

Calvinism as such is not responsible for the achievements of the modern missions, for the simple reason that the mission is based upon an interdenominational foundation. (Calvin himself rejected the duty of missionizing to the heathens; to him, the further expansion of the church was *unius Dei opus* [the work of the single Christian God].) Nevertheless, the missions originate apparently out of the circle of ideas (extending throughout the Puritan ethic) that argue in favor of viewing the commandment to love one's neighbor as one loves oneself as adequately practiced if believers fulfill it for the sake of God's glory. In this way one's neighbor is given his due, and everything else is God's concern alone. The "humanity" of the relations to "one's neighbor" has, so to speak, died out. This is apparent in the most diverse situations.

For example, if we wish to note a further basic aspect of the Calvinist milieu, giving to charity by ascetic Protestants could be discussed. In a certain sense such giving is justifiably famous. Even in the twentieth century, the orphans of Amsterdam, with their skirts and pants vertically divided into black and red or red and green halves, are led in parades to church. Dressed in this sort of fool's costume, the orphans were, for the sensibilities of the past, surely a highly delightful show. Moreover, and precisely to the extent that a show took place, the children served the glory of God: as the entertainment proceeded, all personal "human" sensibilities had to feel insulted. And, as we shall see, the effects of this dulling of human sensibilities then extended into personal relationships in all aspects of one's private occupational activities.

Of course, this example depicts only a *tendency*. We will later have to define certain qualifications. However, this tendency, *as* one element (and indeed a very important one) of ascetic devoutness, must be pointed out here.

44. The problem of theodicy refers to the enduring existence of evil despite the existence of an all-knowing, all-powerful, and fundamentally benevolent God [sk].

45. In all these ways the ethic of Port Royal [see note 23, above] which was determined by predestination, diverged. As a result of its mystical and *other*-worldly (and hence, to the same degree, Catholic) orientation, this ethic was entirely different. See Paul Honigsheim, *op. cit.* [note 30]. [1920]

46. Karl Bernhard Hundeshagen (see *Beiträge zur Kirchenverfassungsgeschichte und Kirchenpolitik, insbesonders des Protestantismus* [Wiesbaden: J. Neidner, 1864], vol. 1, p. 37) defends the position (which has been often repeated) that the doctrine of predestination came from the teachings of theologians rather than from the people. This view is correct, however, only if one identifies the concept "people" (*Volk*) with the uneducated *masses* of the lower strata. And even then this argument holds only to a highly limited extent. In the 1840s, Köhler (*op. cit.*) found that just these "masses" (he refers to the lower middle-class in Holland) were strict followers of the idea of predestination. To them, any person who denied the double decree was a heretic and among the condemned. Even Köhler was asked about the *particular time* of his rebirth (in the sense of its predestined determination).

Moreover, the [seventeenth-century] da Costa and de Kock independence revolts were highly influenced by the idea of predestination. Not only Cromwell, whom Zeller has already viewed as exemplifying the effect of the doctrine (see *Das Theologische System Zwinglis* [Tübingen: L.F. Fues, 1853], p. 17), but also his troops, knew full well what was involved. The canons on predestination issued by the Dordrecht and Westminster synods were major national events. Cromwell's tryers and ejectors [who examined candidates for the ministry] admitted only those who believed in predestination, and Baxter (*Life,* vol. 1, p. 72), although otherwise its opponent, judged the effect of predestination upon the quality of the clergy as significant. It is quite impossible that the doctrine was unclear to the Reformed Pietists (the participants in the English and Dutch conventicles). On the contrary, it was precisely *predestination* that drew this group together to search for the *certitudo salutis*. Wherever predestination was a teaching *of theologians*, its significance (or lack thereof) can be indicated by a glance at orthodox Catholicism, where it was

by no means unknown (in precarious forms) as an esoteric teaching. (What was decisive—the view that the *person* must *consider* himself as among the predestined and testify
to this elect status through conduct—was continuously omitted.) On Catholic doctrine
see, for example, Adolf Van Wyck, *Tractatus de praedestinatione* [Cologne, 1708]. The extent to which [the Catholic Blaise] Pascal's [1623–1662] belief in predestination was correct cannot be investigated here.

Hundeshagen, to whom the doctrine is unappealing, acquired his impressions of it apparently predominantly from the German circumstances. All of his hostility is rooted in
an opinion, acquired through pure deduction, that predestination must necessarily lead
to moral fatalism and antinomianism [The moral law is not binding upon believers.].
Zeller has already refuted this opinion (see *op. cit.*). Nevertheless, the *possibility* of such
an interpretation cannot be denied. Both Melanchthon and Wesley discuss it. It is characteristic for both, however, that the doctrine is combined with a *feeling*-based "faith."
Hence, in this context, given the absence of the rational idea of *testifying to belief through
conduct*, this result—moral fatalism and antinomianism—in fact lies at the essence of the
matter.

These fatalistic results appear in *Islam.* But for what reason? Because the prior decision
making in Islam referred to a *predetermination* (not a predestination) of the believer's religious destiny in *this* world, and not to an *other-worldly* salvation. Consequently, that
which is ethically decisive—a testifying by the believer, through conduct, that he belongs
among the predestined elect—plays no role in Islam. Hence, only the warrior's fearless-
ness (as with *moira* [the idea that death in battle was in God's hands]), rather than a *methodical ordering* of the believer's life (because the religious "reward" was absent), could
follow from Islam's ideas of predestination. See the study by F. Ullrich, *Die
Vorherbestimmungslehre im Islam und Christenheit* (Heidelberg University, School of Theology [diss.], 1912). [1920]

The doctrine of predestination was not substantially weakened as long as the idea remained uncontested that God's decision took place in respect to a *particular* individual
and his *testing*. (The later alterations by Baxter, for example, addressed difficulties encountered by ministers when they sought, on the basis of the *doctrine's* tenets, to provide
pastoral care to believers.) Above all, all the great figures of Puritanism (in the broadest
sense of the term) ultimately located their journey's point of departure in the doctrine of
predestination. Its melancholy seriousness influenced the development of their youth.
This was true for Milton, just as for Baxter (although, admittedly, less effectively) and
even later for the very freethinking Franklin. Their later emancipation from a strict interpretation of the doctrine corresponded entirely to the development, even in its details
and direction, of the religious movement as a whole. Nevertheless, *all* great church reviv-
als—at least in Holland and usually also in England—connected directly and continuously to the doctrine of predestination.

47.   This question repeatedly, and in so powerful a manner, formulates the basic
mood in John Bunyan's *Pilgrim's Progress* [London: Penguin, 1965 (1676–84)].

48.   This *question,* and without regard to the predestination doctrine, was even as
early as the Lutheran epigone more distant than to the Calvinists. A putatively lesser interest on the part of Lutherans in the salvation of their souls was not the issue here.
Rather, this question was more distant because the development taken by the Lutheran
Church placed the character of the church—as an institution that *offers salvation*—in the
forefront. Hence, the single believer became an object of the church's activity and felt
cared for by the church. Characteristically, this problem of how the faithful could become
certain of their salvation in Lutheranism was first awakened by Pietism. However, the
question of the *certitudo salutis itself* was absolutely central for every religion based in
non-sacramental salvation, whether Buddhism, Jainism, or any other. This point should
not be mistaken. From *this* question arose all psychological motivations of a purely *religious* character. [The last three sentences were added in 1920.]

49.   As directly stated in the letter to Bucer, *Corp. Ref.* (29, pp. 883 f.). See, in this regard, again Scheibe (*op. cit.*, p. 30 [see note 20]).

50.   The Westminster Confession (vol. xviii, pt. 2) holds out to the chosen the prospect of an *undeceiving certainty* of grace, even though we remain, despite our constant activity, "useless servants" (vol. xvi, pt. 2). Moreover, the struggle against evil lasts our entire life long (vol. xviii, pt. 3). Even the chosen often must struggle for a very long time in order to acquire the *certitudo salutis* that provides their consciousness with a sense of having done their duty. The believer is never completely robbed of this consciousness. [1920]

51.   For example, see [Caspar] Olevian, *De substantia foederis gratuiti inter Deum et electos* (Geneuae: Apud Eustathium Virgnon, 1585, p. 257); [Johann Heinrich] Heidegger, *Corpus theologiae Christianae*, vol. xxiv (Tiguri: Ex officina Heideggaeriana, 1732), pp. 87f; see also further passages in Heppe, *op cit.* [note 20], p. 425.

52.   Genuine Calvinist doctrine referred to both *faith* and a consciousness of a community with God as acquired through the sacraments. This doctrine viewed the "other fruits of the spirit" as secondary. See the passages in Heppe (*op. cit.*, p. 425). Calvin himself strongly emphasized good works, even though they were for him, as for the Lutherans, outgrowths of belief rather than *signs*, to those who performed them, of God's favor (Calvin, *Institutio christianae religionis*, vol. 3, pts. 2, 37, 38). The practical turn to the notion of good works as themselves testifying to the believer's faith, which is characteristic of *asceticism*, develops parallel with a gradual transformation of Calvin's teachings. As with Luther, according to Calvin, the true church was *primarily*, at its origin, designated by pure doctrine and sacraments, and later by the elevation of *disciplina* [church discipline] to a position of equal importance. This development can be traced, for example, in passages in Heppe (*op. cit.*, pp. 194–95). It is also apparent in the manner in which, even at the end of the sixteenth century, membership in a religious congregation was acquired in Holland. (An explicit, contract-based submission to church *discipline* constituted a central condition.)

53.   See the remarks by Schneckenburger (note 10, p. 488) on this point.

54.   For example, the distinction between a "mortal" and a "venial" sin appears again (entirely in the manner of Catholicism) in Baxter's works. A mortal sin constitutes a sign that the state of grace is absent (or, at any rate, not felt by the believer). In this case, only a "conversion" of the entire person can testify to the possession of this state of grace. It is not to be acquired in the case of a venial sin.

55.   In various shadings, this idea can be found in Baxter, Bayly, Sedgwick, and Hoornbeek. See also the examples given by Schneckenburger (note 10, p. 262).

56.   The view of the "state of grace" as a sort of social *status* (similar, for example, to that of the state of asceticism in the old church) is to be found often, among others, in Wilhelmus Schortinghuis. See his *Het innige Christendom* [Groningen: Jurjen Spandaur, 1752]. (This volume was *banned* by the Dutch parliament!) [1920]

57.   As will be discussed later, this is apparent in innumerable places in Baxter's *Christian Directory* [note 39], as well as in its concluding passage. This recommendation to work in a calling, as a mechanism of distracting oneself from the anxiety that results from perceived moral inferiority, reminds one of Pascal's psychological interpretations of the drive to pursue money and of vocational asceticism. Both represented to him self-invented mechanisms believers used to delude themselves regarding their own moral worthlessness. Moreover, for Pascal, precisely the belief in predestination, together with the conviction (owing to original sin) that everything having to do with the body is worthless, is placed completely in the service of a renunciation of the world and a recommendation to practice contemplation. Renunciation and contemplation are the single means both for the believer's relief from the oppression of a sense of sinfulness and for the acquisition of the certainty of salvation.

In his fine dissertation, Paul Honigsheim has offered cogent remarks on the correct Catholic and Jansenist formulation of the concept of vocation. The Jansenists omit every trace of a linkage between the quest for a certainty of salvation and this-worldly *activity*. Their conception of a "calling," far more than in Lutheranism and even more than in orthodox Catholicism, clearly possesses the sense of an *acceptance* of one's situation in life as given. This Jansenist conception was ordained not only (as in Catholicism) by the social order, but also by the voice of one's own conscience. (Honigsheim, *op. cit.* [note 30], pp. 139 ff.; this is part of a larger work that will be, one hopes, pursued.) [1920]

58.   Schneckenburger's point of view is also pursued by P. Lobstein in his very lucidly written sketch. See "Zum evangelischen Lebensideal in seiner lutherischen und reformierten Ausprägung," in *Theologische Abhandlungen für H. J. Holtzmann* (Tübingen: Mohr, 1902). Lobstein's work can be compared with the following paragraphs. Others have criticized his work for placing too strong an emphasis on the guiding idea of *certitudo salutis*.

Just at this point a distinction must be made between the theology of Calvin and *Calvinism*, and between the theological system and the necessities of pastoral care. *All* religious movements that encompass broad strata depart from the question: How can I become *certain* of my salvation? As noted, this question plays a central role not only in Calvinism but also in the history of religion generally (for example, also in India). How could it actually be otherwise? [The last two sentences were inserted in 1920.]

59.   Nevertheless, it is not to be denied that the *full* development of this *concept* came to the fore first in the *late* Lutheran epoch (Praetorius, Nicolai, Meisner). (The *unio mystica* exists also in the works of [the hymnist] Johann Gerhard, indeed in a manner in complete conformity with its usage here.) For this reason Ritschl, in book 4 of his *Geschichte des Pietismus* ([note 10], vol. 2, pp. 3 f.), claims that the introduction of the concept of *unio mystica* into Lutheranism constituted a renaissance, or borrowing, from Catholic piety. He agrees (p. 10) that the problem of the individual's sense of certainty of his salvation was the same for Luther and the Catholic mystics. Nevertheless, he believes they offer polar opposite solutions.

I should certainly not trust myself to offer an independent judgment on this point. However, every person perceives of course that the mood penetrating Luther's *On the Freedom of a Christian* is different from the contrived sweet flirtation with the "childlike and loving Jesus" of the later Lutheran writers on the one hand, and [the mystic] Tauler's religious mood on the other hand. Moreover, similarly, the maintenance of a mystical-magical component in the Lutheran teachings on communion certainly has different religious motives from that "Bernardian" piety (as in the mood of the Song of Solomon) which Ritschl repeatedly sees as cultivating [mystical] interactions with a Christ figure. [Bernard of Clairvaux (1090–1153) was a mystic and founder of the Cistercian Order.] Nevertheless, should not the teachings of Luther himself on communion have, among other things, also *co-favored* the rejuvenation of a religion of mystical devotion?

Moreover, it is by no means adequate (see Ritschl, *ibid.*, p. 11) to argue that the freedom of the mystic existed simply in his *withdrawal* from the world. Tauler, in particular, in analyses of great interest to the psychology of religion, has understood *order* as a *practical* effect of nighttime contemplation (which he recommends for insomnia). Order is then, he argues, through contemplation, brought into this-worldly work in a calling (which shares with contemplation a related way of thinking):

> Only in this way—through the mystical unifying with God in the evening before sleeping—is *reason purified and, thereby, the mind strengthened*. This spiritual exercise allows persons to live their days in a more peaceful and providential manner, and truly to unify themselves with God. At this point all of the believer's activities will be *ordered*. Hence, if persons have admonished themselves (that is, prepared themselves) and decided beforehand to stand on the side of *virtue*, and only then com-

mence their everyday activities, these activities will be carried out in a *virtuous* and divine manner. (*Predigten* [sermons], brochure 318)

At any rate, we can see (and we will return to this point) that mystical contemplation and a rational view of the calling *do not exclude each other*. They do so only at that point where religious belief acquires a clearly hysterical character. Neither for all mystics nor, especially, for all Pietists was this the case.

60.   On this point see my essay, "The Social Psychology of the World Religions." [1946e; see below, pp. 341–43, 247–52.]. This essay is the introduction to my Economic Ethics of the World Religions series. [1920]

61.   In respect to this position, Calvinism comes into contact with orthodox Catholicism. However, while the necessity of confession resulted from this position for Catholicism, the result for Calvinism was the necessity for a practical *testifying* to belief through activities in the everyday world.

62.   See, for example, as early as Theodor Beza, *De praedestinationis doctrina et vero usu tractatio (. . .) ex (. . .) praelectionibus in nonum Epistolae ad Romanos caput, a Raphaele Eglino (. . .) excerpta* (Genevae: Apvd Evstastivm Vignon, 1582), p. 133:

> . . . sicut ex operibus vere bonis ad sanctificationis donum, a sanctificatione ad fidem . . . ascendimus: ita ex certis illis effectis non quamvis vocationen, sed efficacem illam, et ex hac vocatione electionem et ex electione donum praedestinationis in Christo tam firmam quam immotus est Dei thronus certissima connexione effectorum et causarum colligimis. . ."[Just as we are offered the gift of salvation from the performance of good works and then, from salvation, ascend to faith, so do we acquire from actions, if ones of continuity, not merely a random calling but an effective calling. From this calling we then attain, through Christ, the gift of predestination. It has come to us from the effective connection, which is as unmovable as the throne of God, between activity and principles.]

One had to be cautious only about the signs of one's *damnation*, for on these depended one's *final* condition. (The first group to think otherwise on this point were Puritans.) See, further, the detailed discussions by Schneckenburger (*op. cit.*), who admittedly cites only a demarcated category of studies.

This feature—the signs of one's salvation—comes to the fore repeatedly throughout the entire Puritan literature. Bunyan states: "It will not be said: did you believe?—but: were you Doers, or Talkers only?" Faith is, according to Baxter (*The Saints' Everlasting Rest* [Welwyn, UK: Evangelical Press, 1651/1978], ch. 12), who teaches the mildest form of predestination, the submission in heart and *in deeds* to Christ. "Do what you are able first, and then complain of God for denying you grace if *you have cause.*" This was his answer to the objection that the human will is not free and it is God alone who possesses the capacity to bestow salvation. See *Works of the Puritan Divines* (vol. 4, p. 155). Fuller, the church historian, limited his investigation to the specific question of the practical testifying believers could give and the believer's self-demonstration of his state of grace through conduct. Howe makes the same point (*op. cit.* [note 10]). Every scrutiny of the *Works of the Puritan Divines* also provides regular evidence on this point. Not infrequently, it was the *Catholic* writings on asceticism that had the effect of "converting" believers to *Puritanism*, as a Jesuit tract did in the case of Baxter.

If compared to Calvin's own teachings, these conceptions were not completely new. See *Institutio christianae religionis* (original edition of 1536; ch. 1, pp. 97, 113). For Calvin himself, however, the certainty of salvation could not be acquired in this manner (see p. 147). Normally, one referred to 1 John 3:5 and similar passages. The demand for a *fides efficax* was (to note at the outset) not an exclusive demand of the Calvinists. *Baptist* confessions of faith addressed this demand in their statutes on predestination, and they discussed also the fruits of faith: "Proper evidence of its regeneration appears in the holy fruits of

500 / NOTES: CHAPTER IV

repentance and faith and *newness of life."* See Article 7 of J. N. Brown, D.D., *The Baptist Church Manual* (Philadelphia: American Baptist Publications Society, 1876–99). (This document concerns printed confessions.) A *Mennonite*-influenced tract begins in the same way. See *Olijf-Tacxken,* which the Harlem Synod adopted in 1649. It begins (p. 1) with the question of how the children of God are to be *recognized,* and answers (p. 10): "Nu al is't dat dasdanigh *vruchtbare* ghelove alleene zii het seker fondamentale kennteeken . . . om de conscientien der gelovigen in het nieuwe verbondt der genade Gods te versekeren." [Only such *visible fruits* of belief offer the certain and absolutely reliable sign that *certifies* to the consciousness of believers their belonging among the saved.] [1920]

63.   A few observations on the significance of *this* for the substantive content of the social ethic were noted above. Our concern now is not the *content* but the *motivation* toward ethical *action.*

64.   How this idea must have promoted the penetration of Puritanism by the Jewish spirit of the Old Testament is apparent.

65.   This is stated in the Savoy Declaration about the members of the *ecclesia pura* [true church]: they are "saints by *effectual* calling, *visibly manifested* by their vocation *and walking."* [1920]

66.   Stephen Charnock [1628–80], "A Principle of Goodness," in *Works of the Puritan Divines* (p. 175).

67.   As Sedgwick occasionally expresses it, a conversion has "the exact same sound as the decree of predestination." And, as Bayly [*op. cit.*] teaches, those who are chosen are also called to obey *and rendered capable of obeying. Only* those *God* has called to believe (as becomes manifest in their conduct) are actually believers, not simply "temporary believers." This doctrine is taught by the (Baptist) Hanserd Knollys [see note 13].

68.   One could compare the conclusion to Baxter's *Christian Directory* [see note 39].

69.   See, for example, Stephen Charnock, "Self-Examination," in *Works of the Puritan Divines* (p. 183), on the refutation of the Catholic doctrine of *dubitatio* [doubt].

70.   This argument recurs again and again, for example, in John Hoornbeek, *Theologia practica (op. cit.).* See, for example, vol. 2, pp. 70, 72, 182; vol. 1, p. 160.

71.   For example, as stated in the *Confessio Helvetica,* vol. 16: "et improprie his (the works) *salus adtribuitur"* [works bestow health].

72.   On all the above, see Schneckenburger (*op. cit.,* pp. 80 f.).

73.   Allegedly, as early as Augustine, this was already noted: "Si non es praedestinatus, fac ut praedestineris." [If you have not determined the matter beforehand, make sure that you are able the next time to determine the matter beforehand.]

74.   One is reminded of the maxim from Goethe that carries, in essence, the same meaning: "How can a person know himself or herself? Never through pondering, but surely through activity. Attempt to fulfill your obligations, and then you will immediately know yourself. But what are your obligations? The demands of the day." [See *Maximen und Reflexionen,* ed. by Max Hecker (Weimar: Goethe-Gesellcraft, 1907), nos. 442, 443; see also The passage in, "Science as a Vocation"; 2005; pp. 339–40.]

75.   Even though Calvin himself argued that *saintliness* must be apparent in one's *outward appearance* (see *Institutio christianae religionis,* vol. 4, p. 1, pars. 2, 7, 9), human knowledge could not grasp the boundary between the elect and the nonelect. We have to believe that in those places where the word of God is announced in pure form—in churches organized and administered according to His law—the elect are present also (even if unrecognizable to us).

76.   Calvinist piety offers one of the many examples in the history of religion in which *logical* and *psychological* consequences for practical religious *behavior* have been mediated from certain religious ideas. Viewed *logically,* fatalism would naturally follow [see note 46 above], as a deduction, from the idea of predestination. However, as a consequence of the insertion of the idea of "conduct as testifying to one's belief," the *psychologi-*

cal effect was exactly the opposite. (For reasons in principle the same, the followers of Nietzsche, as is well-known, have claimed that actual ethical significance must be bestowed upon the idea of eternal rebirth. In this case, however, the responsibility for the future life is in no way connected, through a continuity of consciousness, to the acting person. For the Puritan, on the contrary, this connection was *tua res agitur* [your situation will be negotiated].)

Hoornbeek (see *Theol. pract.* [see note 22], vol. 1, p. 159) offers a fine analysis of the relationship between predestination and action. He does so in the language of the period. To him, the chosen are simply, on the basis of their selection, inoculated against fatalism. Indeed, they testify to their chosen status precisely in the act of turning away from the fatalistic consequences of the idea of predestination; *Quos ipsa electio sollicitos reddit et diligentes officiorum* [The predestination choice itself awakens persons and makes them conscientious about their duties]. The entanglement of *practical* interests cuts off the conclusion—fatalism—that can be *logically* drawn (which, by the way, in spite of all, occasionally actually appeared).

On the other hand, the content of the *ideas* of a religion (as Calvinism is demonstrating to us) are of *far* greater significance than, for example, William James is inclined to concede. See *The Varieties of Religious Experience* [New York: Penguin American Classics, 1985 (1902)], pp. 444 f. The very significance of the rational element in religious metaphysics is demonstrated, in a classical manner, in the grandiose effects that precisely the structure of *thought* comprising the Calvinist concept of God exercised on life. If the God of the Puritans has influenced history unlike any other God before or after Him, this influence resulted mainly from those attributes that the power of *thinking* bestowed upon Him. (By the way, the "pragmatic" evaluation by James of the significance of religious ideas—namely, according to the extent to which the believer's life testifies to them—is itself a true legacy of that world of ideas in the Puritan homeland of this excellent scholar.)

As is true of *every* experience, the religious experience as such is obviously irrational. In its highest mystical form it is exactly *that* inner experience [that is singular and extraordinary]. As so beautifully analyzed by James, it is distinguished by its absolute incommunicability. This inner experience possesses a *specific* character and appears to us as if it were *knowledge*, even though the tools given to us by language and concepts do not allow us to capture it adequately. Moreover, it is also correct that *every* religious experience, whenever one attempts to formulate it *rationally*, immediately loses part of its content—and loses all the more the greater the development of the conceptual formulation. Here lies the reason for the tragic conflicts in all rational theology, as the baptizing sects knew even in the seventeenth century.

This irrationality, however (which, by the way, does *not at all* hold *exclusively* for the *religious* "experience," but—although with varying meanings and to varying degrees—for *every* experience), does not call into question one important matter: the particular *type of idea* system, which takes for itself what is directly "experienced" as religious and (so-to-speak) confiscates it, directing it into its pathways, is of the highest importance for practical activity. For, *according to this directing* (in those eras of intense influence of the church on life and of a stronger development, within it, of dogmatic interests), most of the differences among the world's various religions with respect to ethical consequences have unfolded. These differences have been very important for practical action.

Everyone who knows the historical sources is aware how unbelievably intense (when measured by today's standards) was the interest in dogma in the era of the great religious struggles [the sixteenth and seventeenth centuries]. One can see a parallel between that interest and the (basically even superstitious) idea among the proletariat today regarding that which "science" can accomplish and prove. [This paragraph is from 1920, as are several earlier sentences in this note.]

77. In *The Saints' Everlasting Rest* (vol. 1, p. 6), Baxter answers the question: "Whether to make salvation our end be not mercenary or legal? It is properly mercenary

when we expect it as *wages* for work done. . . . Otherwise it is only such a mercenarism as Christ commandeth . . . and if seeking Christ be mercenary, I desire to be so mercenary." Actually, a collapse back to the practice of an entirely crass "salvation through good works" was not lacking among many who were viewed as orthodox Calvinists. According to Bayly, the giving of alms constituted a means of preventing *a temporal* punishment (see *Praxis pietatis, op. cit.* [note 32], p. 262). Other theologians recommended the performance of good works to the *damned.* They argued that damnation would then become, perhaps, more bearable. To the elect, however, the performance of good works was recommended for a different reason: God would then love them not only without reasons but *ob causam* [for a cause]. And surely this love would somehow lead to benefits. The apologists also made certain silent concessions about the significance of good works for the extent of one's salvation. See Schneckenburger ([note 10], p. 101).

78.   It is indispensable also here, in order to isolate the characteristic differences, to discuss these matters in the language of "ideal-type" concepts. Doing so implies, in a certain sense, doing violence to historical reality. If this procedure were abandoned, however, qualifying clauses would have to be inserted incessantly, and thus a clear formulation would be fully impossible. The contrasts noted here have been drawn as sharply as possible. Yet the extent to which, on the one hand, they actually hold in empirical reality, or, on the other hand, the degree to which the contrasts are only relative, will have to be discussed separately. [See Weber, "'Objectivity' in Social Science and Social Policy," in 1949, pp. 89–111; 1968, pp. 19–22. See also John Drysdale, "How Are Social-Scientific Concepts Formed?" *Sociological Theory* 14 (March, 1996): 71–88.]

It is self-evident that official Catholic *doctrine,* as early as the Middle Ages, for its part also formulated an ideal of a systematic striving for salvation that engaged the believer's *entire life.* Nevertheless, it remains just as doubtless that (a) the everyday practices of the church, owing precisely to its most effective disciplinary mechanism (confession), facilitated the learning of an "unsystematic" organization of life. Moreover, (b) it is likewise doubtless that the Calvinists' underlying mood of strictness and cold distance, and their complete, self-reliant isolation, had to be perpetually lacking in medieval lay Catholicism.

79.   As already noted, the absolutely central significance of *this* theme will gradually come to the fore only in the Economic Ethics of the World Religions essays. [1920]

80.   And, to a certain extent, *also* to the Lutheran. Luther did not *want* to strike down this last residual of sacramental magic. [1920]

81.   [This term is in English in the original.] See, for example, Sedgwick, *Buss- und Gnadenlehre* (German translation by Röscher, 1689). The penitent person has "a firm rule," which he strictly holds to. He orients and transforms his entire life according to it (p. 591). He lives, according to the rule, in an intelligent, awake, and cautious manner (p. 596). *Only* a lasting alteration of the *entire* person can, because a consequence of predestination, bring about this way of living (p. 852). Actual repentance is expressed continuously in conduct (p. 361). The difference between good works, which are only "moral," and the *opera spiritualia* [spiritual tasks], is apparent (a) in that the latter is the consequence of life's rebirth (as Hoornbeek explains; see *op. cit.,* vol. 1, pt. 9, ch. 2), and (b) in that a perpetual progress in regard to the *opera spiritualia* is perceptible (see vol. 1, p. 160). As concerns a transformation of conduct, this progress can be attained only as a result of the supernatural influence of God's grace (p. 150). Salvation implies a metamorphosis of the *entire* person, and this results from God's grace (pp. 190 f.).

These are ideas common to all Protestantism. They are found also, of course, in the highest ideals of Catholicism. *However,* they could first demonstrate consequences for the world when manifest in the *this*-worldly asceticism of the Puritan denominations. Above all, these ideas became endowed with a sufficiently strong psychological *reward* only in these denominations.

82.   Although, in Holland, "Precisians" stem from the "fine" among the devout who led their lives precisely according to the *Bible*'s statutes (as Voët notes) [See Troeltsch, *Social Teachings*, pp. 682–84]. Occasionally, by the way, "Methodists" is used in the seventeenth century to refer to the Puritans.

83.   For, as the Puritan preachers emphasize (Bunyan, for example, in "The Pharisee and the Publican," *Works of the Puritan Divines*, p. 126), *every* single sin destroys *all* that could be accumulated as *service*, through good works, in the course of an entire lifetime. Yet they also emphasized how fully inconceivable it is that human beings could be at all capable of achieving anything God would then be compelled to *attribute* to them as service. Similarly, it remains inconceivable to these preachers that anyone could live permanently without sin. For them, there simply does not exist, unlike in Catholicism, a sort of bank account book and then balancing-out procedures [for sins and confessions]. (This image was common even in antiquity.) Rather, for the Puritans, a harsh either-or prevailed; damnation or grace. On this bank account image, see note 115 below.

84.   This is the difference compared to simple *Legality* and *Civility*, which Bunyan depicts as fellow travelers who live with Mr. "Worldly wiseman" (who is depicted as "Morality") in the city. [See *Pilgrim's Progress* (note 47).]

85.   Stephen Charnock, "Self-examination" (*Works of the Puritan Divines*): "*Reflection* and knowledge of self is a prerogative of a *rational* nature" (p. 172). See the accompanying footnote: "*Cogito, ergo sum* is the first principle of the new philosophy."

86.   This is not the appropriate occasion to discuss the relationship of certain streams of ideas in ascetic Protestantism to the [Scholastic] theology of [the Franciscan] Duns Scotus [1266–1308]. (This theology never became dominant; generally only tolerated, it was occasionally considered heresy.) The later animosity of the Pietists to Aristotelian philosophy was shared by Calvin (and, although in a somewhat different manner, by Luther), who stood consciously opposed, on this point, to Catholicism (see *Institutio christianae religionis*, vol. 2, ch. 12, par. 4; vol. 4, ch. 17, par. 24). In the words of Wilhelm Kahl, the "primacy of the will" is common to all these denominations. [See *Die Lehre vom Primat des Willens* (Strasbourg: Trubner, 1886).] [1920]

87.   St. Benedict founded a monastic order in Italy in 529. The Benedictine abbey at Cluny in France, founded in 910, became a center of monastic reform in the tenth and eleventh centuries. The Cistercian Order was founded in France in 1098 by Benedictine reformers. St. Ignatius of Loyola founded the Society of Jesus (Jesuits) in 1534 [sk].

88.   For example, the article "asceticism" in the Catholic *Church Lexicon* [*Kirchen-Lexikon oder Encyklopädie der katholischen Theologie und ihrer Hilfswissenschaften* (Freiburg: Herder, 1847)] defines the word in just this way. This definition accords completely with the highest form of its historical manifestation. Likewise, Seeberg; see *Realencyklopädie für protestantische Theologie und Kirche*. For the purposes of this discussion, the use of *asceticism* in this manner must be permitted. It is well-known to me that the term can be defined differently, both more broadly and more narrowly (and usually the attempt is made to do so).

89.   The Puritans, in Samuel Butler's *Hudibras* [London: Oxford/Clarendon Press, 1967 (1664–78)], are compared to barefoot monks. A report of the ambassador from Geneva, Fieschi, calls Cromwell's army an assembly of "monks." [1920]

90.   In light of this entirely direct assertion of mine regarding the internal continuity between the other-worldly asceticism of monks and the this-worldly asceticism of the vocational calling, I am surprised to discover Brentano's recommendation to me that I note the asceticism oriented toward work in *monks* (see *op. cit.* [ch. 1, note 15], p. 134 and *passim*)! His entire *excursus* against me culminates in this point. However, just such a continuity (as everyone can see) is a foundational assumption of my entire discussion: the Reformation carried rational Christian asceticism and the methodicalness of life out of the monastery and into the life of work in a calling. See the following, unrevised analyses. [1920]

91.   As apparent in the many, and often repeated, reports on the trials of Puritan heretics. See Daniel Neal, *The History of the Puritans* [London: D.R. Hett, 1732–38] and Thomas Crosby, *The History of the English Baptists* [London: The editor, 1738–40].

92.   Sanford already (*op. cit.* [note 5]; and before and after him many others) has traced the origin of the ideal of "[social] distance" back to Puritanism. On this ideal, see, for example, also the observations by James Bryce on the American college (*American Commonwealth* [New York: Macmillan, 1888], vol. 2). The ascetic principle of "self-control" also renders Puritanism one of the fathers of modern *military discipline*. On Maurice of Orange, as the founder of the modern army, see G. Roloff, *Preußische Jahrbücher,* vol. III (Jan.–March, 1903): 255. Cromwell's "Ironsides" [soldiers], striding forth toward the enemy at a brisk pace with cocked pistols in their hands, yet without shooting, were not superior to the "Cavaliers" because of a fanatic passion; rather, the dispassionate self-control of Cromwell's men (which remained perpetually in the hands of their leader) proved decisive. The knightly, boisterous, and impetuous style of attack of the Cavaliers dissolved their troops every time into single fighters. On this theme see Charles Firth, *Cromwell's Army* [London: Greenhill Books, 1992 (1902)].

93.   See Wilhelm Windelband, *Über Willensfreiheit* (Tübingen: Mohr, 1904), pp. 77f.

94.   Yet not in such a straightforward manner in Catholic monasticism. The procedures of contemplation, occasionally bound together with a foundation based on feeling, are intertwined in monasticism with these rational elements in multiple ways. Just for this reason, contemplation is further *methodically* regulated.

95.   According to Richard Baxter, *sinful* is *everything* that stands against "reason." Reason is created in us by God and given by Him as a norm for our action. In other words, not simply passions, because of their content as such, are sinful. Rather, all meaningless or unrestrained affects *as such* are sinful—because they destroy the "countenance." [Weber has here used the English word.] Moreover, as processes purely of the realm of physical desires, they turn us away from the rational relationship with God that all of our activity and sensibility should cultivate. As such, these emotions insult God. See, for example, what is said about the sinfulness of moodiness (Baxter, *Christian Directory,* 2nd ed. [London: Robert White, 1678, vol. 1, p. 285]; Tauler is cited on this subject on p. 287). On the sinfulness of *anxiety,* see p. 287. If our *appetite* becomes "the rule or measure of eating," then idolatry, it is emphasized, is apparent (pp. 310, 316, and *passim*). Baxter frequently cites mainly, as the opportunity presents itself, Proverbs; however, he also cites other treatises, such as Plutarch's *De tranquillitate animi* [*On Tranquillity of Mind*]. Not infrequently, he also calls attention to the writings of the Middle Ages on asceticism (St. Bernhard, St. Bonaventure, and others).

.The contrast to the way of life represented by "who does not love wine, women, and song. . ." could scarcely be more sharply formulated than through the expansion of the concept of idolatry to encompass *all* pleasures of the senses—*as long as* they are not justified for *hygienic* reasons. If they are, these pleasures are allowed (as are, within these boundaries, sports, and also other "recreations"). This theme will be addressed further below [see ch. 5].

We wish here only to note that the sources cited here and elsewhere are neither dogmatic nor edifying works; rather, they grew out of the daily practice of pastoral care. Hence, these sources offer a good picture of the direction in which they had an *effect*.

96.   In passing, I would find it regrettable if an *evaluation* of any sort would be read out of this presentation, whether regarding one or the other form of religious devotion. Such an evaluation lies distant from our concern here. The *effect* of specific important features of this devotion on practical *behavior* is the only concern here (however comparatively peripheral such a concern may be for those looking for a pure evaluation, according to religious standards, of this behavior). [1920]

97.   Although this title may refer to a compilation of writings of diverse authorship, it more likely refers to a volume written by Thomas à Kempis (1380–1471; from Kempen,

Holland). Kempis possessed an enormous knowledge of the Bible and wrote many inspirational works, ranging from treatises on the practical piety of daily life to the mystical experience [sk].

98. On this point in particular see the article "Moralisten, englische" by Ernst Troeltsch, in the *Realencyklopädie* [see note 10], vol. 13.

99. The great extent to which *entirely matter-of-fact* religious ideas and situations, which appear to be "historical accidents," have had an effect is revealed with unusual clarity in [two examples]: (a) those circles of Pietism arising out of a Reformed foundation occasionally directly *regretted,* for example, the absence of a monastery; and (b) the "communist" experiments of Labadie, among others, were in the end a surrogate (*Surrogat*) for the monastic life. [Jean de Labadie (1610–74), originally a Jesuit, was a major representative of mysticism-oriented French Spiritualism. He later became a Calvinist and then a Mennonite. His writings influenced Spener.]

100. Because of his unorthodox views of Christianity, Franck became defined as an opponent of the Reformation [sk].

101. Indeed, this idea was in some denominations of the Reformation period itself. Even Ritschl (see *Pietismus, op. cit.* [note 19]; vol. 1, pp. 258 f.), although he sees the later development as a degeneration of Reformation ideas, does not contest that "the Reformed Church was characterized by completely empirical features and that believers could not be counted as members of this true church *without the sign of ethical activity*" (see, for example, *Confessio Gallicana* [1559] 25, 26; *Confessio Belgica* [1562] 29; and *Confessio Helvetica posterior* [1568] 17).

102. "Bless God that we are not of the many" (Thomas Adams, *Works of the Puritan Divines,* p. 138).

103. The historically so important idea of "birthright" thus received in England a significant bolstering: "The first born which are written in heaven.... As the first born is not to be defeated in his inheritance and the enrolled names are never to be obliterated, so certainly shall they inherit eternal life" (Thomas Adams, *Works of the Puritan Divines,* p. 14).

104. The Lutheran feeling of penitent *contrition* is not internally foreign to developed Calvinist asceticism in theory. In practice, however, it surely is. To this Calvinism, such contrition is ethically worthless and of no use to the damned. To the person who is more certain of his election, his own sins (which are acknowledged to some extent) constitute a symptom of backward development and incomplete striving toward elect status. Instead of showing contrition for the sin, the Calvinist *hates* it and endeavors to overcome it through activity on behalf of God's glory. See the analysis by Howe (who was Cromwell's chaplain from 1656 to 1658) in "Of Men's Enmity Against God" and "Of Reconciliation Between God and Man" (*Works of the Puritan Divines*): "The carnal mind is *enmity* against God. It is the mind, therefore, not as speculative merely, but as practical and active, that must be renewed" (p. 237). Moreover, "Reconciliation . . . must begin in (a) a deep conviction . . . of your former *enmity* . . . [and awareness that you] have been *alienated* from God . . ." (p. 246), [and] (b) "A clear and lively apprehension . . . of the monstrous iniquity and wickedness thereof [must occur]" (p. 251).

A hatred of sin alone is spoken of here, rather than a hatred of the sinner. Yet the famous letter of the Duchess Renata d'Este (Leonore's mother) to Calvin already indicates that sins are being transferred to persons. Here, among other subjects, she writes of the *hatred* she would carry for her father and husband *if* she became convinced they belonged among the damned. Above I spoke about the separation of the individual internally, as a result of the doctrine of predestination, from the ties to communities established through a "natural" feeling (see p. 61, 108). This letter offers an example of this separation and, simultaneously, of its transference to relationships with specific persons.

105. The "Independents" (founded 1581 in England) wanted the full independence of each congregation from the Anglican Church. American branches were instrumental in the founding of Harvard and Yale universities [sk].

106. Owen, the Independent-Calvinist vice-chancellor of Oxford University under Cromwell, formulated the principle thus: "None but those who give evidence of being *regenerated or holy* persons, ought to be received or counted fit members of visible churches. Where this is wanting, *the very essence of a church is lost*" (*Investigation into the Origin of Evangelical Christianity*). On this theme, see further "The Protestant Sects" essay below.

107. Founded by Donatus, a bishop from Carthage, the Donatist Church existed in northern Africa in the fourth to seventh centuries. Donatus advocated that churches impose extreme disciplinary measures upon members [sk].

108. See pp. 185–99 essay below.

109. *Catéchisme genevois*, p. 149. Bayly, *Praxis pietatis* [see note 32], p. 125: "In life we should act as though no one but Moses had authority over us."

110. "The law is a favorable presence in the minds of the Reformed Christians, constituting an ideal norm. On the other hand, to the Lutherans, because an unreachable norm, the Law disheartens and crushes them." In Lutheranism, in order to awaken the necessary *humility*, the law stands *at the beginning* of the catechism and before the gospel, whereas, in the Reformed catechism, the law stands commonly *behind* the gospel. The Reformed churches reproached the Lutherans for having a "true fear of becoming holy" (Möhler), while the Lutherans criticized the Reformists for their "slavish servitude to the Law" and their arrogance.

111. *Studies and Reflections of the Great Rebellion, op. cit.* [note 5], pp. 79 f.

112. The Song of Solomon, in particular, should not be forgotten. Entirely ignored by the Puritans, its Oriental eroticism influenced, for example, the development of the notion of piety in St. Bernard's writings.

113. On the necessity for this self-discipline, see, for example, the sermon already noted [see note 85] by Charnock on 2 Cor. 13:5, *Works of the Puritan Divines*, pp. 161 f.

114. Most moral theologians advised in favor of such procedures. Also Baxter; see *Christian Directory, op. cit.*, vol. 2, pp. 77 ff. He does not, however, conceal its "dangers."

115. Bookkeeping, as concerns one's ethical conduct, has of course also been widespread elsewhere. The *accent* placed upon it, however, was heretofore missing. Bookkeeping now becomes the single means of *knowing* the decision made for eternity regarding one's elect or condemned status. Hence, also missing earlier was a psychological *reward*. When placed upon the diligence and attentiveness of this "calculation," this reward became decisive. [1920]

116. *This* was the decisive distinction vis-à-vis other, externally similar, types of behavior. [1920]

117. Baxter also (*Saints' Everlasting Rest*, ch. 12) explains God's *invisibility*: just as it is possible to carry out a profitable trade with an unseen foreigner through written correspondence, it is also possible, through "holy commerce" with an invisible God, to acquire the "one expensive pearl." These commercial similes, instead of the forensic similes common in the writings of the earlier moralists and in Lutheranism, are highly characteristic of Puritanism. In effect, Puritanism allowed people "to acquire through bargaining" their own salvation. See also, for example, the following passage from a sermon: "We reckon the value of a thing by that which a wise man will give for it, who is not ignorant of it nor under necessity. Christ, the Wisdom of God, gave himself, his own precious blood, to redeem souls, and He knew what they were and had no need of them" (Matthew Henry, "The Worth of the Soul," in *Works of the Puritan Divines*, p. 313).

118. On Knollys, see note 13 [sk].

119. In contrast, Luther himself said, "Crying goes before all the tasks that we undertake, and suffering is more noble than all of our initiative-taking."

120. "Complete transcendence" refers to the Puritan's Old Testament God. Because He is distant from believers, all-mighty and omniscient, His motives remain completely unknowable by mere earthly mortals. One might easily conclude that such an unfathomable Deity would be dismissed and ignored. Weber argues just the opposite here, however, namely, because the doctrine of predestination linked even this God to His children, and even in an intense manner ("with absolute determinism"). Once this linkage had been established, His norms—owing to His omnipotence and omniscience—became "unconditionally valid" [sk].

121. Weber has succinctly summarized his "yardstick" usage of the "ideal type" in the above few lines. Once formulated, a model (ideal type) is used as a point of orientation for empirical investigations. Particular cases are then "measured" against the model. Once their "deviation" from the model becomes demarcated, empirical cases are then clearly defined. See Weber, "Objectivity" and E&S (see note 78 above). See also 1994), pp. 81–142 [sk].

122. This is also demonstrated most clearly in the development of Lutheran ethical theory. On this subject see G. Hoennicke, *Studien zur altprotestantischen Ethik* (Berlin, 1902). See also Ernst Troeltsch's informative review in *Göttingische Gelehrte Anzeigen* (1902, no. 8). The movement of Lutheran doctrine in the direction of the older *orthodox*-Calvinist doctrine in particular was often, in form, quite significant. The different religious orientation, however, again and again became manifest.

[Luther's advisor] Melanchthon placed the concept of *penitence* in the forefront in order to provide a firm base for the connection of morality to faith. Penitence, which arose out of the believer's relationship to the commandments, must precede faith, but good works must follow faith. Otherwise, the believer's faith (formulated almost in a Puritan manner) could not be the true faith—namely, the faith on the basis of which salvation is justified.

To Melanchthon, a certain degree of (relative) perfection could be attained also on earth. Indeed, he even taught originally that a sense of justification that one is saved was awarded to persons in order to render them capable of good works. Moreover, the increasing perfection of the faithful itself implies at least that degree of this-worldly salvation that faith is capable of providing. And the later Lutheran dogmatists also developed the idea that good works were the necessary *fruits* of faith, and that faith could call forth a new life. This idea was externally entirely similar to ideas developed by the Reformed churches.

The question of what "good works" are was answered as early as Melanchthon (and even more so among the later Lutherans) increasingly by reference to the commandments. There remained, as a legacy of Luther's original ideas, only the lesser seriousness accorded to Bible learning and, in particular, to an orientation toward the particular norms of the Old Testament. Essentially, only the Decalogue remained. It codified the most important principles of the *natural* moral law and hence was viewed as offering norms for action. *However,* no secure linkage led from the statutory validity of the Decalogue to justification through *faith*, which was more and more emphasized by Lutherans as of exclusive significance for salvation. This linkage was absent simply because Lutheran faith had a completely different psychological character—see above—from that of faith in Calvinism.

The orthodox Lutheran standpoint of the first period was abandoned. This had to occur because Lutheranism now took the form of a church that considered itself an institution for the saving of souls (*Heilsanstalt*) [see 1968, pp. 557–63]. Lutheranism, however, abandoned the old without having formulated a new standpoint. In particular, one could not introduce (for fear of losing the dogmatic *sola fide* foundation) the notion of an ascetic rationalization of the entire life as the ethical task of each believer. Missing was just the motivation that would allow the idea of a *testifying* by believers to grow to the significance it attained, through the effect of the doctrine of predestination, in Calvinism. In addition, and taking place in harmony with the absence of this doctrine, the interpretation of the sacraments in Lutheranism as being based on magic (which occurred once the notion of a *regeneratio* [regeneration of one's hopes for salvation], at least in its early forms, became transferred into the practice of *baptism*) must have had the effect, assuming the *universalism* of grace, of working against the development of a methodical morality [as in Calvinism]. This followed as well because the magical interpretation of the sacraments in Lutheranism must also have weakened the contrast between the *status naturalis* and the state of grace—all the more owing to the strong Lutheran emphasis on original sin.

Yet any development in the direction of a methodical morality was weakened even more in Lutheranism by a factor of no less significance: Lutheranism's *exclusively juridical* interpretation of the act of justification. This interpretation assumed the changeability of God's decisions as a consequence of the converted sinner's *specific* act of penitence. Just this effect was increasingly emphasized by Melanchthon. This entire alteration of his teaching, which comes to the fore in the increasing weight he gives to *penitence*, in fact internally develops together with his professions on the *freedom of the will*.

All this determined the *un*methodical character of the Lutheran organization of life. Simply as a consequence of the continuation of the confessional, *specific* acts of grace in exchange for specific sins must have constituted the content of salvation for the average Lutheran. The development of an aristocracy of elect saints, who themselves created the certainty of their own salvation, did not characterize Lutheranism. Neither a development in the direction of a morality *without* God's law, nor a movement toward a rational *asceticism* oriented toward this law, could occur. Instead, God's law remained in Lutheranism, as a statute and an ideal claim, side-by-side with *faith*, yet organically unconnected to it. Furthermore, because a rigorous study of the Bible was rejected (for it implied salvation through good works), the law remained quite uncertain, imprecise, and, above all, unsystematic in terms of its exact content.

As Troeltsch has written (*op. cit.*), the life of the Lutheran, from the perspective of ethical theory, remained a "sum of mere beginnings, never entirely successful," and a piecing together of fragmented and uncertain maxims. None had the effect of directing life "toward a coherently organized unity." Rather, and fully in accord with the route that Luther himself had already taken, life became oriented toward a resignation to the existing situation, large or small.

The "resignation" of the Germans to the influence of foreign cultures and their more rapid change of nationality than other peoples (which is so often complained about in Germany) is *also*, essentially, to be explained by this development (*together* with certain political destinies of the nation). Even today this general posture of resignation has an impact on all of our relationships. The individual's absorption of culture in Germany, *because* it occurred essentially along the pathway of passive reception of what was offered in an "authoritarian" manner, remained weak.

123. On these matters, see, for example, the rumor-mill book by [August] Tholucks' *Vorgeschichte des Rationalismus* [Halle: Eduard Anton, 1853–1862].

124. Largely owing to Prussian-based stereotypes formed in the aftermath of World Wars I and II, Germans today are often viewed differently [sk].

125. On the entirely different effect of the *Islamic* doctrine of predestination (or better: *predetermination* [see note 46]) and its causes, see F. Ullrich, *op. cit.* [note 46]. On the predestination doctrine of the Jansenists, see P. Honigsheim, *op. cit.* [note 30]. [1920]

126. See "The Protestant Sects" essay [below, pp. 185–99]. [1920]

127. In his *Geschichte des Pietismus* (*op. cit.* [note 19], vol. 1, p. 152), Ritschl seeks, for the period before Labadie (and, by the way, only on the basis of examples from the Netherlands), to define these boundaries in the following ways: (a) the Pietists formed conventicles; (b) they cultivated the idea of the "worthlessness of physical and bodily existence" in a "manner that opposed the Protestant interest in salvation"; and (c) they

sought, "in a tender relationship with the Lord Jesus, the certainty of grace" in a manner opposed to the Reformist tradition.

[Yet there are many problems with Ritschl's criteria.] For this earlier period, the last criterion is correct only for *one* of the representatives of Pietism he discusses. Moreover, the notion of a "worthlessness of physical and bodily existence" was an indigenous, true product of the Calvinist spirit, and this notion directed Calvinism out of Protestantism's normal line of development only in those instances where the "worthlessness of the human desires" led to an actual flight from the world. Finally, the conventicles (to a certain degree and, in particular, for reasons concerning the catechism) had been established by the synods of Dordrecht themselves [and hence related not only to Pietism].

Only some of the features of Pietist piety analyzed by Ritschl's study are relevant to us here: (a) the greater "precision" with which, in all "external aspects" of life, chapter and verse of the Bible were followed, even in a servile manner (as occasionally with Gisbert Voët); (b) the treatment of the justification before God and reconciliation with Him not as ends in themselves but simply as *means* toward the holy, ascetic life (as is perhaps to be found in Lodensteyn but as also suggested by Melanchthon; see note 122 above); (c) the high evaluation of the "penitence struggle" as a sign of genuine rebirth (as was first taught by W. Teellinck); (d) the abstinence from participation in communion by persons who have not been reborn (as will be discussed later in a different context) and the related formation of conventicles once "prophecy" had been revived—that is, the exegesis of texts also by nontheologians, even women (Anna Maria Schürmann), became permitted (although this transgressed the boundaries of the Dordrecht canons).

All of the above points involve Pietist deviations—at times to a significant extent—from the doctrine and practice of the Reformed churches. Nevertheless, and in contrast to the denominations Ritschl has not included in his study (especially the English Puritans), all of the putatively distinguishing features he notes (except for point "c" [the Pietists sought, "in a tender relationship with the Lord Jesus, the certainty of grace"]) represent actually only an intensification of tendencies within the entire line of development of Reformist piety.

The even-handedness of Ritschl's analysis is weakened in a specific manner: this great scholar brings into his study his own value judgments in respect to church-political or (perhaps, better stated) religious policy debates. In particular, his hostility to all ascetic devoutness leads him to interpret all developments toward asceticism as reversions to "Catholicism." The old Protestantism, however, just as is true of Catholicism, refers to "all sorts and conditions of men" [Sir Walter Besant]. *Certainly* the Catholic *Church*, in its Jansenist [reform] manifestation, [still] rejected the rigor of this-worldly asceticism, just as Pietism [which inclined toward contemplation] opposed the Catholic Quietism of the seventeenth century.

At any rate, for our particular investigation, Pietism began to diverge qualitatively (not simply in degree) from Calvinism when the intensified anxiety of Pietist believers, in the face of "worldly" tasks, led to a flight away from one's vocational life in the private economy. Namely, this flight led Pietists to form conventicles anchored in a monastic-communistic foundation (as Labadie advocated). It also led, as contemporaries reported regarding some extreme Pietists, to the intentional *neglect*, in favor of contemplation, of this-worldly work in a vocational calling.

This turn naturally appeared with particular frequency wherever contemplation began to acquire that feature referred to by Ritschl as "Bernardianism" (because echoes of it first appeared in Bernard's exegesis of the Song of Solomon): a mystical religion of devotional mood that strives for the *unio mystica*, which is secretly tinged with sexuality. Even from the point of view of a psychology of religion, the *unio mystica* undoubtedly presents an *aliud* [different vantage point] antagonistic to Reformist piety, yet one "also" opposed to Calvinism's *ascetic* form as exemplified by Voët. Ritschl, however, seeks continuously to couple this [mystic] Quietism with Pietist *asceticism*, and thus to render the latter asceticism subject to [his usual] criticisms. He attempts to do this by putting his finger on every citation to be found in the Pietist literature that comes from Catholic mysticism or asceticism. Yet even English and Dutch moral theologians entirely "above suspicion" cite [the mystics] Bernard, Bonaventure, and Thomas à Kempis [as antagonistic to asceticism].

For all Reformed churches, the relationship to the Catholic past was a very complex one. According to the vantage point that one places in the forefront, first one feature of Calvinism, then the other appears as standing more closely to Catholicism (or certain features of it).

128. The highly informative article "Pietism" by K. M. Mirbt (*Realencyklopädie für protestantische Theologie und Kirche*, 3rd ed.) addresses the origin of Pietism. His omission of its Reformist antecedents and his concern exclusively with the personal religious experience of Spener strike one as rather strange. The description by Gustav Freytag in the *Bilder aus der deutschen Vergangenheit* series offers even today an introduction to Pietism that is well worth reading. For the beginnings of English Pietism as it was viewed at the time, see W. Whitaker, *Prima Institutio disciplinaque pietatis* (1570).

129. As is well-known, this view had enabled Pietism to become one of the major social carriers of the idea of *tolerance*. This opportunity should be taken to insert a few points on this theme. If we leave aside for the moment the Humanist-Enlightenment idea of *indifference*, the idea of tolerance in the West had the following major sources: (a) purely political *Staatsraison* [reasons of state] (as represented by William of Orange [1650–1702]); (b) mercantilism (for example, as particularly apparent in the city of Amsterdam and the numerous cities, lords of manors, and monarchs who supported sect members as important social carriers of economic progress); and (c) Calvinist piety in its radical manifestation. [Before turning to a further source of the idea of tolerance in the West, several remarks must be offered regarding the manner in which Calvinist piety constituted an important source for this idea.]

The idea of predestination basically prevented the state, through its intolerance, from actually promoting religion. In light of this idea, the state's intolerance did not enable it to save a single soul; only the idea of *God's honor* induced the church to request the state's assistance in suppressing heresy. However, the more the emphasis was placed on the necessity for the minister and all participants in communion to be members of the elect, all the more unacceptable was (a) every instance of the state's intervention in processes to appoint new clergy, (b) every appointment to the ministry of students from the university made simply on the basis of completed theological training (which might include someone who perhaps did not belong among the elect), and in general (c) every intervention in the congregation's concerns by the political powers (whose conduct was often not above reproach).

Reformed Pietism strengthened this opposition to external intervention by devaluing dogmatic correctness and by gradually loosening the axiom *extra ecclesiam nulla salus* [no salvation outside the church]. To Calvin, the *subjection* of all, including the damned, under the church's divine guidance was alone consistent with God's glory. Nonetheless, in New England the attempt was made to establish the church as an aristocracy of the chosen. As early as the radical Independents, however, every intervention of civic groups, as well as any hierarchical powers, in the process of monitoring the devout's testifying to belief (which was possible only inside the *particular* congregation) was rejected. The idea that God's glory required a bringing of even the damned under the church's discipline became subjugated to a different idea (present from the beginning, but then gradually more and more passionately emphasized): if one whom God had condemned were allowed to participate in communion, God's glory would be violated. This idea had to lead to voluntarism, it was argued, for it would lead to a "believer's church," namely, to a religious community that encompassed only the elect.

Calvinist Baptism (to which, for example, Praisegod Barebone, the leader of the "parliament of the saints" belonged) drew the consequences from this line of thought with greater consistency than did other congregations. Cromwell's army upheld freedom of conscience, and the "parliament of saints" supported even the separation of church and state, *because* its members were devout Pietists. That is, religious reasons *were effective* in providing their motivation to uphold the freedom of conscience and, hence, the idea of tolerance.

[Now let us turn to a fourth major source of the idea of tolerance in the West.] (d) From the beginning of their existence, the *baptizing sects* (which will be discussed later) have continuously upheld the basic principle that only the elect can be taken into the community of the church. (They have done so more forcefully and with greater internal consistency than the other ascetic Protestant congregations.) For this reason, they (a) repudiated the idea of the church as an institution (*Anstalt*) offering salvation to all [see pp. 306–09; 1968, pp. 557–60], and (b) opposed every intervention by secular powers. Hence, it was an *effective religious* reason also in this case that produced the demand for unconditional tolerance.

The first who for these reasons upheld an unconditional tolerance *and* the separation of church and state was surely [the English theologian and opponent of the Anglican Church] Robert Browne [1550–1633]. He was almost a generation before the Baptists and two generations before Roger Williams [1628–80], the Puritan founder of the colony of Rhode Island and pioneer of religious liberty. The first declaration of a church community in this regard appears to have been the resolution of the English Baptists in Amsterdam in 1612 or 1613: "The magistrate is not to meddle with religion or matters of conscience . . . because Christ is the King and lawgiver of the Church and conscience." The first official document of a church community that demanded the *effective* protection of freedom of conscience from the state as *a right* was surely Article 44 of the Confession of the (Particular) Baptists of 1644.

It should once again be emphasized that the view occasionally found—that tolerance *as such* favored capitalism—is of course completely wrong. Religious tolerance is not specifically modern, nor is it unique to the West. It dominated in China, in India, in the great empires of the Near East in the Hellenic era, in the Roman Empire, and the Islamic empires. It ruled for longer epochs, circumscribed only for reasons connected to the state itself (*Staatsraison*) (and these reasons even today define the limits of its expanse). This degree of tolerance, however, was nowhere in the world to be found in the sixteenth and seventeenth centuries. It was least to be found in those regions where Puritanism *dominated*, as, for example, in Holland and Zeeland [the Dutch island province off the coast of Denmark] in the era of political-economic expansion, or in Puritan England or New England. Clearly characteristic of the West (after the Reformation, as well as prior to it, and similar to, for example, the Sassanian dynasty [of Persia, 226–651], was *religious intolerance*, as had reigned also in China, Japan, and India during particular epochs (although mostly for political reasons). It follows that tolerance as such certainly has not the slightest thing to do with capitalism. It depended on *who was favored by it*. The consequences of the requirement for religious tolerance in the "believer's church" will be discussed further [in "The Protestant Sects" essay] below. [The last two paragraphs were added in 1920.]

130. The practical application of this idea appeared, for example, among the Cromwellian "tryers," who were the examiners of candidates for the ministry. They attempted to ascertain the individual state of grace of candidates more than they sought to assess their theological knowledge. See also the ["Protestant Sects"] essay below.

131. Pietism's characteristic mistrust of Aristotle, and of classical philosophy in general, is already stated in an early form in Calvin (see *Institutio christianae religionis*, vol. 2, ch. 2, sect. 4; vol. 3, ch. 23, sect. 5; vol. 4, ch. 17, sect. 24). In Luther's writings, as is well-known, this mistrust was no less intense. The antagonism in Luther, however, is pushed to the side by the influence of humanism (mainly through Melanchthon) and compelling circumstances related to apologetics and the educational training of minis-

ters. What is *necessary* for salvation, also for the uneducated, is contained in the scriptures in a clear manner. Of course, the Westminster Confession also taught this and did so in a manner in conformity with Protestant traditions (see ch. 1, pt. 7). [1920]

132. The official churches protested against this development in Pietism. See, for example, even the (shorter) catechism of the Scottish Presbyterian Church of 1648 (sect. 7). Participation of *non*family members in family prayers is viewed, by the official churches, as an infringement upon the authority of the church *office* and prohibited. Pietism also, as occurred with the formation of every ascetic congregation, loosened the ties of the individual to all family patriarchalism (which always had an interest in the prestige of established offices). [1920]

133. For good reasons, we are here intentionally omitting a discussion of the "psychological" relationships (in the sense of the scientific and *technical* usage of the term) between the substantive elements in this religious consciousness. Even the use of the corresponding terminology is avoided where possible. The accepted and reliable conceptual armament of psychology, and also of *psychiatry*, does not extend far enough at present to be used directly for the purposes of historical research in the area of our themes—at least not without casting doubt on whether historical judgments have been formed in an unprejudiced manner. The use of the terminology of psychology would in the end create the temptation to drape a veil, comprised of the scholarly obfuscation that follows from the dilettante's fondness for obscure and strange words, around the easily understandable and often quite trivial facts of the given case. The result would be to produce an illusion of increased conceptual precision.

Unfortunately, the writings, for example, of Karl Lamprecht [1856–1913, the cultural and economic historian, and founder of the Department of Culture and Universal History at the University of Leipzig] are typical in this regard. Some approaches to the application of psychopathological concepts for the understanding of certain historical collective action can be taken more seriously. See chapter 12 of W. Hellpach's *Grundlinien einer Psychologie der Hysterie* [Leipzig: W. Engelmann, 1904] and his *Nervosität und Kultur* [Berlin: J. Rade, 1902]. In my view, even this versatile author has been adversely influenced by certain theories of Lamprecht (although I cannot here attempt to confront this issue). Even those acquainted only with the introductory literature on Pietism know full well how completely worthless Lamprecht's schematic remarks on Pietism are compared to the older studies (see vol. 7 of his *Deutsche Geschichte* [Berlin: Weidman, 1909–20, 12 vols.]).

134. As, for example, occurred with the adherents of "Spiritual Christianity" led by Schortinghuis [see note 56]. In the history of religion, this idea can be traced back to the verse about the servant of God in Isaiah [53] and the 22nd Psalm.

135. As appeared occasionally in Dutch Pietism and then later under influences stemming from *Spinoza*.

136. See Labadie [the hymnist, mystic, and psychologist Gerhard], Teersteegen, etc.

137. Francke founded schools for orphans and homeless children that practiced a severe discipline designed to strengthen independence and religious devotion [1697–1769]. See note 2 above on Spener and notes 3 and 4 on Zinzendorf [sk].

138. Perhaps this train of thought appears most clearly when Spener (one thinks: Spener!) protests against the competence of the ruling power to control the conventicles (except in cases of disorder and abuse). To him, the issue here concerns the *basic rights* of Christians, which are guaranteed by apostolic decree (see *Theologische Bedenken*, vol. 2, pp. 81 f.). In principle, this is exactly the Puritan standpoint in respect to the extent and validity of the rights of each person, namely, they follow *ex jure divino* [from divine law] and are therefore inalienable.

Neither this heresy [from the point of view of Lutheranism] nor the one mentioned later in Bayly's text has eluded Ritschl (see his *Pietismus, op. cit.* [note 19], pp. 115, 157). Ritschl's positivistic criticism of the idea of "basic human rights" is highly unhistorical (not to mention philistine). We owe not much less than *everything* to the idea of basic human rights, and today even the most "reactionary" person values it as basic to his sphere of individual freedom. Nonetheless, we must of course completely agree with Ritschl that, regarding both the extent and validity of the rights of each person, an organic connection to this idea is missing from Spener's thinking, which remains at this point Lutheran. [On Weber on "basic human rights," see, e.g., 1968, p. 1403; "Prospects for Democracy in Tsarist Russia," in Weber 1978, pp. 282–83.]

The conventicles (*collegia pietatis*) themselves, which became theoretically grounded in Spener's famous *Pia desideria* [see note 2] and which were in practice founded by him, basically corresponded to the English "prophesyings." The latter appeared first in Johannes of Lasco's Bible study groups in London (1547). Since then, they have belonged among the permanent inventory of forms of Puritan piety utilized against church authority. Finally, as is well-known, Spener legitimized his rejection of church discipline (as defined in Geneva) by arguing that its designated social carrier, the "third estate" (namely, the *status oeconomicus:* the lay Christians) is *not*, in the Lutheran Church, integrated into the church's organization. On the other hand, a typical instance of Lutheranism's weakness is apparent in the discussion of excommunication: the landed gentry, who were appointed as secular members of the governing court body, were recognized as representatives of the "third estate."

139. What was characteristic, according to the views of contemporaries, is visible even in the *name* "Pietism" (which appeared first in Lutheran regions); namely, that a methodical business *company* was produced out of *pietas.*

140. Admittedly, while this motivation fit extremely well with Calvinism, it did not *only* fit with this denomination. It can be found with particular frequency in the *oldest* Lutheran church statutes.

141. In the sense of Hebrews 5:13, 14. See Spener, *Theologische Bedenken,* vol. 1, p. 306.

142. Alongside Bayly and Baxter (see Spener, *Consilia et judicia theologica latina* [Frankfurt: Jungi, 1709], vol. 3, ch. 6, pt. 1, pars. 1, 47; ch. 6, pt. 1, pars. 3, 6), Spener was especially fond of Thomas à Kempis, and, above all, Tauler (whose writings he did not entirely understand; *ibid.,* vol. 3, ch. 1, pt. 1, par. 1). For detailed discussion of Tauler, see *op. cit.* [note 19], vol. 1, ch. 1, par. 1, no. 7. According to Spener, Luther's thinking is derived directly from Tauler.

143. See Ritschl, *op. cit.,* vol. 2, p. 113. Spener rejected the "penitence struggle" of the later Pietists (and of Luther) as the *single* decisive indication of a true conversion (Spener, *Theologische Bedenken,* vol. 3, p. 476). On the striving toward salvation as the result of thankfulness that stems from faith in reconciliation (a specifically Lutheran formulation; see ch. 3, note 7 above), see passages cited in Ritschl, *op. cit.,* p. 115, note 2. On the *certitudo salutis* see, on the one hand, *Theologische Bedenken* (vol. 1, p. 324): the true faith will not so much be *perceived as based on feeling* as it will be *recognized* by its *fruits* (love and obedience to God). On the other hand (see *Theologische Bedenken,* vol. 1, pp. 335 f.): "As concerns your anxiety regarding how you should become certain of your state of grace, it is more secure if you are guided by our"—that is, the Lutheran—"books rather than by the English writings." Spener agrees, however, with the English on the nature of the striving toward salvation.

144. The religious diaries, as recommended by A. H. Francke, were also here the external signs of one's state of grace. The methodical practice and *habit* of striving toward salvation should produce growth in this direction and the *separation* of good persons from evil persons. This is, approximately, the basic theme of Francke's book, *Von des Christen Vollkommenheit.*

145. Characteristically, the deviation of this rational, Pietist belief in predestination from its orthodox meaning came to the fore in the famous debate between the Pietists in Halle and Löscher, the representative of Lutheran orthodoxy. In his *Timotheus Verinus,* Löscher goes so far as to argue that everything attained through *human* activity can be set

against the decrees of predestination. Francke's position, which became increasingly firm, stood against Löscher: every lightning flash of clarity regarding what should occur—and these insights resulted only from patient *waiting* for God's decision—must be considered as "God's hint." All this takes place in a manner fully analogous to Quaker psychology and corresponds to a general notion in asceticism: the believer becomes closer to God through the pathway of rational *methodicalness*. Of course, Zinzendorf, who in one of his most important decisions, submitted the destiny of his community to a lottery, stands far removed from Francke's belief in predestination. In *Theologische Bedenken* (vol. 1, p. 314), Spener, in examining the Christian "calm tranquility and resignation," and then concluding that believers should be left to God's acts and, thus, that they should not undertake hasty, self-reliant activity, referred back to [the mystic] Tauler. This was, in essence, also Francke's position.

Compared to Puritanism, the essentially weakened activity of Pietist devotion, which sought (this-worldly) peace, appeared everywhere clear enough to see. A leading Baptist (G. White, in a lecture that will be cited later) formulated the ethical agenda for his denomination in 1904 in opposition to this Pietist devotion: "First righteousness, then peace." See *Baptist Handbook* (1904, p. 107).

146. *Lectiones paraeneticae*, vol. 4, p. 271.

147. Ritschl's criticism is oriented primarily against this recurring idea. Francke's *Von des Christen Vollkommenheit* contains this teaching.

148. It is found also among the English Pietists who did *not* uphold predestination; Goodwin, for example. On him and others, see Heppe, *Geschichte des Pietismus und der Mystik in der reformierten Kirche* [in Holland] (Leiden: E.J. Brill, 1879). Despite Ritschl's standard work, Heppe's book is not yet out of date for England or (occasionally) Holland. Köhler was often asked, even in the nineteenth century, in Holland about the *exact time* of his rebirth. See his *Die niederländische reformierte Kirche, op. cit.* [note 10].

149. In this way one sought to confront the lax consequences of the Lutheran teaching regarding the reacquisition of grace (and especially to counteract the common "conversion" *in extremis* [in extreme circumstances, such as immediately prior to death]).

150. In opposition to the necessity of knowing the day and hour of the "conversion" (which was connected to this penitence and breakthrough), as an *unconditional* sign of its authenticity, see Spener, *Theologische Bedenken*, vol. 2, pt. 6, par. 1, p. 197. A "penitence struggle" was as unknown to him as Luther's *terrores conscientiae* [terrors of conscience] was to Melanchthon.

151. Of course, the anti-authoritarian interpretation of the "universal priesthood," specific to all asceticism, also played a related part. It was occasionally recommended to the minister to postpone absolution until a "testifying" to genuine contrition was forthcoming. Ritschl characterizes this practice correctly as Calvinist in principle.

152. The points essential for us are most accessible in H. Plitt, *Zinzendorfs Theologie* (3 vols., Gotha: F. A. Perthes, 1869–1874), vol. 1, pp. 325, 345, 381, 412, 429, 433 f., 444, 448; vol. 2, pp. 372, 381, 385, 409 f.; vol. 3, pp. 131, 167, 176. See also Bernhard Becker, *Zinzendorf und sein Christentum* (Leipzig: F. Jansa, 1900), bk. 3, ch. 3.

153. Weber is here referring to The Book of James (central to The Pietists) [sk]

154. Admittedly, Zinzendorf held the Augsburg Confession to be a suitable document of the Lutheran-Christian faith only if a "scalding sore" were poured over it (as he expressed it in his repulsive terminology). Because his language, which dissolves ideas in a sloppy brew, has an even worse effect than the "christo-turpentine" so wretched in the writing of F. [Friedrich] Theodor Vischer (see his polemics on the Munich "Christoterpe"), to read him is an act of penitence. [Vischer was polemicizing against the yearbook *Christoterpe*.]

155. See note 4 above [sk].

156. "No religion recognizes as brothers those who have not been, through the sprinkling with holy water, bathed in the blood of Christ. These believers are *thoroughly changed*, and this becomes manifest in the manner in which their striving for the salvation

of the spirit *is continued.* We recognize no evident (visible) congregation of Christ. This congregation comes into being only where the word of God is taught in an authentic and candid manner, and only where members of the congregation, as the children of God, *also live* the *holy life according to* God's word." Admittedly, the last sentence is taken from Luther's "small" catechism [which was addressed to ministers for instruction of lay believers rather than to theologians (the "large" catechism)]. Yet, as Ritschl has already emphasized, it serves *there* as an answer to the query of how the name of *God* can be made holy. *Here* it serves, in contrast, to demarcate the church of the *elect saints.*

157. See Plitt, *op. cit.* (vol. 1, p. 346). Even more decisive is the answer, quoted in Plitt (p. 381), to the question of whether "good works are necessary for salvation." "They are," Zinzendorf answers, "unnecessary and harmful for the acquisition of holiness. However, after salvation has been attained, they are so necessary that those who fail to perform them must be said not actually to be saved." Hence, it is also clear here that, for Zinzendorf, good works are not the cause of salvation; rather, they are the means—and the *single* means!—of recognizing it.

158. See note 4 [sk].

159. For example, in those caricatures of "Christian freedom" (which Ritschl lashes out against; see *op. cit.,* vol. 3, p. 381).

160. They did so primarily through an intensified emphasis on the idea of retributive punishment in the doctrine of salvation. After the rejection of his missionary attempts by the American sects, Zinzendorf made this idea the foundation of his salvation-striving methodology. From this point onward, he places the maintenance of *childlikeness* and the virtues of a humble modesty in the foreground as the aim of Herrnhuter asceticism. Doing so places Zinzendorf in sharp opposition to tendencies in his community clearly analogous to Puritan asceticism.

161. His impact, however, had its limits. For this reason alone it is incorrect to attempt to incorporate Zinzendorf's teachings in a *social*-psychological developmental stage model [along with the other Protestant sects and churches], as Lambrecht does. Moreover, Zinzendorf's entire religious outlook is influenced by nothing more strongly than one circumstance: he was a *count* with fundamentally feudal instincts. Precisely the *element* of *feeling* in these instincts would fit, from the point of view of "social psychology," just as well into the epoch of chivalry's sentimental decadence as into the epoch of religious "experience." The opposition of the element of feeling in this experience to Western European rationalism, if at all to be understood "social-psychologically," can be best comprehended by reference [to the forms of organization and rulership] in the German eastern territories [such as Prussia and Bohemia] that have remained entirely unsevered from patriarchalism.

162. The controversies of Zinzendorf with Dippel lead to the same conclusion, as do statements from the Synod of 1764 (after Zinzendorf's death). These indicate clearly that Herrnhuter congregations had the character of salvation *institutions* [of open membership rather than as sects with exclusive membership; see pp. 306–09]. See Ritschl's criticism (*op. cit.* [n. 19], vol. 3, pp. 443 f.).

163. Spangenberg was a bishop in the German Brethren Congregation and Zinzendorf's successor. He was sent by Zinzendorf to found a church in Pennsylvania (the United Brethren) [sk].

164. See, for example, paragraphs 151, 153, 160. That it is possible to exclude striving for salvation, *in spite of* true contrition and the forgiveness of sins, derives in particular from statements on p. 311. This view corresponds to the Lutheran doctrine on salvation and contradicts Calvinism (and Methodism also).

165. See Zinzendorf's statements (cited in Plitt, *op. cit.,* vol. 2, p. 345). Similarly, see Spangenberg, *Idea fidei fratrum,* p. 325.

166. See, for example, Zinzendorf's remark on Matthew 20:28 as cited by Plitt, *op. cit.* [n. 152], vol. 3, p. 131:

> When I see a person to whom God has given a fine talent, I am delighted and share in the talent with pleasure. However, if I note that this person is not content with his talent, and instead wants to render it manifest in something more beautiful, then I see here the beginning of the ruin of this person.

Hence, and especially in his discussion with John Wesley (1743), Zinzendorf denied *progress* in striving for salvation. He does so because on the one hand he identifies such striving with [Luther's emphasis upon] justification of salvation through faith; he does so because on the other hand he remains in a relationship to Christ that has been acquired *exclusively* through the *feelings* (Plitt, *op. cit.* [n. 152], vol. 1, p. 413). In place of the feeling of being an *instrument of God* there appears a feeling of a *possession* by the Divine. In other words, mysticism replaces asceticism (as discussed in my "Social Psychology of the World Religions" essay See below, pp. 248–50; 1946e, p. 285; see also below, pp. 247–50; 1946c, pp. 324–28]). As examined in the "Social Psychology" essay, the Puritan is also of course *really* striving for a present, *this-worldly* disposition (*habitus*). Yet this disposition, which he interprets to be the *certitudo salutis*, involves a *feeling* of being an active *instrument* of God's Will. [The last four sentences were added in 1920.]

167. On account of this derivation, however, work in a calling here was not consistently grounded in ethics. Zinzendorf rejects Luther's idea of the calling as a "service to God" and this service as the *decisive* aspect for loyalty to a calling. Rather, for Zinzendorf, loyalty to a calling is more *a payback* to Christ for "Christ's loyalty to his trade" (Plitt [n. 152], vol. 2, p. 411). [Zinzendorf's meaning is also metaphorical, as Weber knows the German will imply to readers: our loyalty to our calling is a form of thankfulness to Christ for having sacrificed himself for our sins.]

168. His maxim from his essay on Socrates is well-known: "A reasonable person should not be without belief and a believer should not be unreasonable." In other words, as he notes also in this essay: "The reasonable person should be able to reveal with candor not only various unknown basic truths, but also contested basic truths" (1725). Well-known also is his partiality for writers such as [the French opponent of systematic philosophy, Pierre] Bayle [1647–1707].

169. The distinct predilection of Protestant asceticism for an empiricism that is rationalized through the application of mathematics is familiar to us and need not be discussed here. On the turn of the sciences toward a mathematical-rationalized, "exact" form of research, see Wilhelm Windelband, *Lehrbuch der Geschichte der Philosophie* [Tübingen: Mohr, 1980 (1892)], pp. 305–7 [*A History of Philosophy* (New York: Harper, 1958)]. Windelband [1848–1915] examines the philosophical motivations behind this turn and the contrasting position held by Bacon. See in particular the comments appropriately rejecting the idea that the modern natural sciences can be comprehended as a *product* of material-technological interests (p. 305). Highly important relationships of this sort are naturally present, but the issue is far more complex. See also Windelband, *Geschichte der neueren Philosophie* ([Leipzig: Breitkopf and Hertel, 1878–1880], vol. 1, pp. 40 ff.).

The *point of view* decisive for the position of ascetic Protestantism, as surely appears in its clearest form in Spener's *Theologische Bedenken* (vol. 1, p. 232; vol. 3, p. 260), was certainly that, just as one could know the Christian by the *fruits* of his beliefs, so one could know God and His intentions only out of knowledge of His *deeds*. Accordingly, the favorite scientific field of all Puritan, baptizing, and Pietist Christianity was physics. Other disciplines that utilized the methodologies of similar mathematical and natural sciences were the next choices. Quite simply, one believed, starting from the *empirical* comprehension of the divine laws of nature, that one was able to ascend to knowledge of the "meaning" of the world. As a result of the fragmentary character of divine revelation (a Calvinist idea), this meaning could surely never be known through the avenue of conceptual speculation.

The empiricism of the seventeenth century was the mechanism for asceticism to seek "God in nature." [See "Science as a Vocation" in Weber, 2005, p. 325.] *Empiricism* appeared to lead *toward* God, and philosophical speculation appeared to lead away from God. Aristotelian philosophy in particular has been a fundamental detriment to Christianity, according to Spener. *Every* other philosophy would be better, especially "Plato's." See Spener's *Consilia et judicia theologica latina* [Frankfurt, 1709] (vol. 3, ch. 6, pt. 1, par. 2, no. 13). Further, see the following passage, which is characteristic:

> Unde pro Cartesio quid dicam non habeo (he had not read him), semper tamen optavi et opto, ut Deus viros excitet, qui veram philosophiam vel tandem oculis sisterent in qua nullius hominis attenderetur auctoritas, sed sana tantum magistri nescia ratio [I have always very much wished for Descartes (he had not read him), and continue to do so, that God would be able to frighten men into recognizing the true philosophy as one comprehended with the eyes and not with human cognition. A healthy power of understanding should be oriented in this direction, which is so unknown to teachers]. (Spener, vol. 2, ch. 5, no. 2)

The significance of these views of ascetic Protestantism for the development of education (especially for those courses of studies oriented more toward the acquisition of practical skills and technical knowledge) is known. The educational agenda of ascetic Protestantism became formulated once these views had combined with its position [versus Catholicism] on *fides implicita*. [Namely, while recognizing that the devout believe (even as individuals) in the revelation of God, the Catholic Church reserved the right to give instructions to the faithful regarding correct belief and to require that believers support the authority of the church. This position was denounced strongly by both Lutheranism and Calvinism.]

170. "That type of person seeks his happiness in roughly four ways. . . : (1) to be lowly, despised, and ill-spoken of; (2) to neglect . . . all senses not needed in order to serve his God. . . ; (3) to either have nothing or to give away all that he receives. . . ; and (4) to work on the basis of a *daily wage*, and to do so not in order to earn the wage, *but on behalf of a calling* and a service to God and his neighbors" (Zinzendorf, *Religiöse-Reden*, vol. 2, p. 180; see Plitt, *op. cit.*, vol. 1, p. 449). *Not all* could or should become "disciples"; rather, only those called by God. However, according to Zinzendorf's own confession, difficulties still remain because the Sermon on the Mount is addressed formally to *all* (see Plitt, *op. cit.*, vol. 1, p. 449). The affinity of this "free, acosmic love" with the old Anabaptist ideals is obvious. [On the Reformation's "radicals," the Anabaptists, from which the Baptists, Quakers, and Mennonites (see pp. 193 ff. below) trace their roots, see notes 194 and 214 below.]

171. For the internalization (*Verinnerlichung*) of piety on the basis of feelings was actually by no means foreign to Lutheranism. This holds even for its later period of weak leadership. Rather, the fundamental difference *here* involved the *ascetic* dimension. Lutherans viewed asceticism with suspicion as a regimentation of life with overtones of "good works."

172. For Spener, a "strong dose of anxiety" constituted a better sign of one's salvation than did "security." See his *Theologische Bedenken* (*op. cit.*, vol. 1, p. 324). We find, of course, strong warnings against a "false certainty" also in Puritan writers. Nonetheless, at least the doctrine of predestination had the opposite effect, to the extent that its influence determined the nature of the pastoral care believers received.

173. For the *psychological* effect of confession was everywhere to *unburden* individuals of their own responsibility for their conduct. Indeed, this effect is why confession was sought. It relieves the rigorous consequences of asceticism's demands. [Lutheranism offers in principle to each the possibility of confession. In practice, however, believers stated their sins to God in silence before taking communion.]

174. The strong role played, in the process, by purely *political* forces—even for the *type* of Pietist piety—has already been suggested by Ritschl in his presentation of Pietism in Württemberg. See his volume 3 (*op. cit.* [note 19]).

175. See Zinzendorf's statement (quoted at note 170 above).

176. Of course Calvinism (at least the genuine version) is also "patriarchal." And the connection to success is clearly visible in Baxter's autobiography (for example, in his activity in Kidderminster, which had a cottage industry). See the passage quoted in *Works of the Puritan Divines:* "The town liveth upon the weaving of Kidderminster stuffs, and as they stand in their loom, they can set a book before them, or edify each other" (p. 38). Nevertheless, patriarchalism rooted in the Calvinist ethic, and especially when anchored in the ethic of the baptizing congregations, is constituted differently from what is found on the soil of Pietism. This problem can be addressed only in a different context.

177. See his *Lehre von der Rechtfertigung und Versöhnung* ([see note 10], vol. 1, p. 598). The description of Pietism by Frederich William I [1648–1740]—a religion that offers beliefs suitable to persons of independent means—clearly tells us more about this king than about the Pietism of Spener and Francke. Moreover, the king knew well why he opened, through his edict on tolerance, his territories to Pietism. [Weber here alludes to Frederick William's knowledge of the Pietists as conscientious and obedient workers, and his need for such a population.]

178. The article by [Friedrich] Loofs offers an excellent introductory overview to Methodism. See "Methodismus," in the *Realencyklopädie für protestantische Theologie und Kirche* (3rd ed.). The studies by L. Jacoby (especially the *Handbuch des Methodismus*), Kolde, Jüngst, and Southey are useful [Robert Southey, *The Life of Wesley* (New York: Harper & Brothers, 1847)]. On Wesley: Luke Tyerman's *Life and Times of the Rev. John Wesley* [New York: Harper, 1872]. The book by [Richard] Watson (*The Life of Rev. John Wesley* [London: Mason, 1831]) is popular Northwestern University in Evanston (near Chicago) has one of the best libraries on the history of Methodism. The religious [psalmist and hymnist] Isaac Watts [1674–1748] has built a chain of sorts from classical Puritanism to Methodism. He was a friend of Oliver Cromwell's chaplain (Howe), and then of Richard Cromwell. Presumably, Whitefield sought his advice (see Skeats, *History of the Free Churches of England, 1688–1891* [op. cit. (see note 10)], pp. 254 f.).

179. This affinity (if the personal influences of the Wesleys are left aside) results historically from, on the one hand, the dying out of the dogma of predestination and, on the other hand, the powerful reawakening among the founders of the idea of *sola fide*. This affinity, however, was primarily motivated by Methodism's specifically *missionary* character. This missionary component introduced a (transforming) rejuvenation of certain medieval methods stemming from "awakening" preaching, and these methods then combined with Pietist forms.

Methodism's systematic organization of life, with the aim of attaining the *certitudo salutis*, certainly does not belong in a *general* line of development toward "individualism." On the contrary, in this respect, this systematic organization of life can be seen to be not only prior to Pietism but also prior to the Bernhardian piety of the Middle Ages.

180. A bench in the Methodist church set aside for those suffering particular internal turmoil as a result of uncertainty regarding their state of salvation. The open expression of fear and anxiety is here permitted [sk].

181. Wesley himself occasionally characterized the effect of Methodist belief in this way. The affinity with the "blessedness" (*Glückseligkeit*) of Zinzendorf is apparent.

182. The same point is made, for example, in Watson's [book; see n. 178] *Life of Wesley* (German edition [Frankfurt: Sehmerber, 1839]), p. 331.

183. Matthias Schneckenburger, *Vorlesungen über die Lehrbegriffe der kleinen protestantischen Kirchenparteien*, ed. by K. B. Hundeshagen (Frankfurt: H.L. Bonner, 1863), p. 147.

184. Whitefield, the leader of the group upholding predestination (which disbanded, owing to disorganization, after his death), essentially rejected Wesley's doctrine of "perfection." Actually, this doctrine is only a *surrogate* for Calvinism's idea of conduct as testifying to belief.

185. Schneckenburger (*ibid.,* p. 145). Loofs takes a slightly different position. See *op. cit.* Both outcomes are typical of all similar devoutness.

186. As in the case of the conference of 1770. The first conference of 1744 had already recognized that the words of the Bible skirted "within a hair" of Calvinism on the one hand and Antinomianism on the other. Given this unclarity, and as long as the Bible's validity as a *practical* norm remained firm, doctrinal differences [it was believed] should not lead to a separation. [Followers of Antinomianism argued that Christians, through God's grace, are not obligated to adhere to the commandments. Obedience as such was rejected as legalistic, for life must be guided by the Holy Spirit within.]

187. On the one hand, the Methodists were separated from the Herrnhuter by the former's doctrine on the possibility of sinless perfection. Zinzendorf [a Herrnhuter founder], in particular, also rejected this teaching. On the other hand, Wesley perceived the element of *feeling* in Herrnhuter devoutness to be "mysticism." Furthermore, he characterized Luther's position on "God's law" as "blasphemy." One can see here the barrier that unavoidably remained between every type of *rational* organization of life and Lutheranism.

188. John Wesley occasionally points out that everywhere—for the Quakers, the Presbyterians, and the Anglican Church—dogma must be believed. This did not hold only in the case of the Methodists, he contends. Compare also the (admittedly rather summary) discussion in Skeats, *op. cit.,* to the above paragraphs.

189. See, for example, Dexter, *The Congregationalism of the Last Three Hundred Years* (*op. cit.* [note 10]), pp. 455 ff.

190. Of course, however, it *can* detract from the rational character of the organization of life, as occurs today with the American Negroes. The frequently pathological character, by the way, of Methodist emotionalism, in contrast to the relatively mild orientation to the feelings characteristic of Pietism, *perhaps* also (in addition to purely historical reasons and the publicity of the procedure) goes closely together with a stronger *ascetic* penetration of life in the regions where Methodism is widespread. A decision on this point, however, belongs to the domain of the neurologist.

191. See chapter 5, below [sk].

192. Loofs (*op. cit.* [note 178], p. 750) emphasizes strongly that Methodism distinguishes itself from other ascetic movements in that it appeared *after* the period of the English Enlightenment [in the seventeenth century]. He then places Methodism in a parallel relationship to the renaissance of Pietism in the first third [of the nineteenth century] in Germany. Although, as Loofs admits, Pietism was a much weaker movement, the parallel can stand. (Loofs is following Ritschl's *Lehre von der Rechtfertigung* [see note 10], vol. 1, pp. 568 f.) It holds even for Zinzendorf's version of Pietism, which, in contrast to the Pietism of Spener and Francke, *also,* like Methodism, reacted against the English Enlightenment. Nevertheless, this reaction in Methodism (as we saw) indeed took a very different direction from that of the Herrnhuter, at least to the degree that the latter were influenced by Zinzendorf.

193. Methodism, however, developed this idea of a calling (as the passage above from John Wesley indicates) in the same manner, and with the exact same effect, as the other ascetic denominations. [1920]

194. This section concerns *das Täufertum,* namely, "the baptizing sects" (Mennonites, Baptists, and Quakers; see next para. in the text) rather than "the Baptist sect," as the translation by Parsons implies. Central to all was the baptism of adult believers (even if they had been baptized as children), namely, when the "age of reason" had been attained. This maturity, it was argued, enabled believers to reach a conscious decision regarding their beliefs. Baptism (by full immersion) then constituted the external sign of an inner experience of adulthood: the spirit's rebirth. (See "The Protestant Sects" essay below for Weber's observations on the social significance of baptism in 1904 in the United States.)

Following Weber, the terms *baptizers, baptizing sects, baptizing communities, baptizing congregations, baptizing denominations,* and *the baptist movement* are used synonymously [sk].

195. And, as shown, *weakened forms* of the consistent ascetic ethic of Puritanism. If one wanted, following the more preferred [Marxist] manner, to interpret these religious conceptions only as "manifestations" or "reflections" of the development of capitalism, then *precisely the opposite* of such a weakening would have occurred. [1920]

196. Among the Baptists, only the "General Baptists" [Christ died for all and not only for an elect] can be traced back to the old Anabaptists [of the early-to-mid sixteenth century, the Reformation's left-wing radicals]. As already noted, the "Particular Baptists" were Calvinists who, in principle, restricted church membership to the elect (or at least to those who had made a "personal" confession of belief). Hence, this group stayed, in principle, voluntaristic and remained an opponent of all state churches. Admittedly, in practice, under Cromwell they did not always hold consistently to this position. Nonetheless, the Particular Baptists, although also the General Baptists, however important historically they were as the carriers of the baptizing tradition, fail to offer to us adequate reason to undertake here a special analysis of their dogma. Formally, the Quakers were a new creation by George Fox and his compatriots. However, when scrutinized in terms of their basic ideas, they must unquestionably be seen in the end as a group that continued the Anabaptist tradition. [A few bibliographical sources should be noted.]

The best introduction to the history of the Quakers, and simultaneously to their relationship to the Baptists and Mennonites, is by Robert Barclay. See his *The Inner Life of the Religious Societies of the Commonwealth* [London: Hodder & Stoughton, 1876].

On the history of the Baptists, see, among others, H. M. Dexter, *The True Story of John Smyth, as Told by Himself and His Contemporaries* (Boston: Lee & Shepard, 1881); on this volume, see J. C. Lang in *The Baptist Quarterly Review* (1883, p. 1). See also J. Murch, *A History of the Presbyterian and General Baptist Church in the West of England* (London: Hunter Pub., 1835); A. H. Newman, *A History of the Baptist Church in the United States* (New York: Christian Literature, 1894) (American Church History Series, vol. 2); Henry Clay Vedder, *A Short History of the Baptists* (London, 1897 [Philadelphia: American Baptist Publication Society, 1952 (1907)]); Ernest Belfort Bax, *Rise and Fall of the Anabaptists* (New York: American Scholar Publications, 1966 [1903]); George Lorimer, *The Baptists in History* [Boston: Silver, Burdett, 1893]; Joseph Augustus Seiss, *The Baptist System Examined* (Lutheran Publication Society, 1902).

See also the material in the *Baptist Handbook* (London, 1896 ff.); *Baptist Manuals* (Paris, 1891–93); *The Baptist Quarterly Review;* and the *Bibliotheca Sacra* (Oberlin, 1900). The best Baptist library seems to be found at Colgate College in the state of New York.

The collection in Devonshire House in London (which I have not used) is considered the best for the history of the Quakers. The official, modern volume on Quaker orthodoxy is the *American Friend,* edited by Professor Rufus Jones [1894 ff.]. The best Quaker history is that of Rowntree. In addition, see: Rufus B. Jones, *George Fox, an Autobiography* [New York: Harper & Brothers, 1930 (1903)]; Alton C. Thomas, *A History of the Society of Friends in America* (Philadelphia, 1895); Edward Grubb, *Social Aspects of the Quaker Faith,* (London: Headley Brothers, 1899). See also the large and very good *biographical* literature. [1920]

197. Karl Müller's *Kirchengeschichte* (Tübingen: Mohr, 1892–1919 [3 vols.]) makes many contributions. Among them is his awarding to the Anabaptists (a movement great in its own way, although outwardly barely visible) the position they deserve. Like no other religious grouping, the Anabaptists suffered from relentless persecution by *all* churches—simply because they *wanted* to be, in the specific sense of the term, a *sect.* As a result of the catastrophe suffered in Münster by the branch that unfolded in an eschatological direction, the sects still remain, after five generations, discredited throughout the entire world (in England, for example). [See notes 213 and 214 below.] Above all, op-

pressed repeatedly and chased underground, the Anabaptists achieved a coherent formulation of their religious *ideas* only long after their period of origin.

Hence, they produced *even* less "theology" than would have been consistent with their
principles, which were at any rate antagonistic to the technical managing of the belief in
God as if it were a "science." [Weber is saying that theology often does just this.] This situation induced the older specialist theology (even in its own period) to show little sympathy for the Anabaptists and to remain unimpressed by them. Yet even many later
theological schools were equally unimpressed. Ritschl (see *Pietismus* [note 19], vol. 1, pp.
22 f.) treats the "Re-Baptizers" with many preconceptions; indeed, he addresses them
with scorn and in a condescending manner. In reading him, the reader feels as if spoken
to from the point of view of a theological "bourgeoisie." This remains the case even
though the excellent study by [Carl Adolph] Cornelius was published several decades
before Ritschl's volumes. See *Geschichte des Münsterischen Aufruhrs* (Leipzig: T. O.
Weigel, 1855–1860, 2 vols.).

In this analysis, Ritschl constructs the notion of Anabaptism's general collapse (viewed
from his vantage point) into "the Catholic." He suspects here the direct influence of the
Franciscans (including their more strict wing, the Spiritualist Franciscans). However,
even if demonstrable in regard to particulars, the evidence would still be very thin.
Moreover, and above all, the historical circumstances were different. On the one hand,
the orthodox Catholic Church treated the *this*-worldly asceticism of the laity with great
mistrust as soon as it began to form conventicles. The church then sought to direct this asceticism toward the formation of a religious order—hence, to push it *out* of the world. On
the other hand, the church also deliberately attempted to integrate lay asceticism into the
existing monasteries, but only with second-class status. In this manner the church
sought to bring this new asceticism under its control. Wherever this attempt failed, it saw
again the danger that the cultivation of an individualistic, ascetic morality would lead to
a denial of authority and to heresy. The Anglican Church under Elizabeth I [1558–1603]
took just such a posture of antagonism—with the same line of justification—against the
"prophesyings," namely, against the half-Pietist Bible conventicles (even in those cases
where this group assumed an entirely correct position in respect to "conformism"). Under the Stuarts [1603–1714] this conflict became expressed in their *Book of Sports* (see below, p. 148).

The history of numerous heretical movements offers evidence for this argument,
though the history of, for example, the Humiliati [northern Italian wool workers who,
amidst poverty, became a monastic brotherhood in 1170] and the Beguins [f. 1200, pious
women who lived in voluntary poverty and chastity, mainly in Holland and Germany]
does so as well, as does the fate of St. Francis. The preachings of mendicant friars, especially the Franciscans, helped in many ways to prepare the path for the ascetic lay morality of the Reformist-Anabaptist Protestantism. However, the massive elements of
affinity between asceticism inside religious orders in the West and the ascetic organization of life in Protestantism—which will be repeatedly emphasized as highly instructive
precisely for the themes addressed here—derive their ultimate legitimation not so much
from the preachings of friars. Rather, they are rooted otherwise, namely, in the circumstance that, of course, *every* asceticism standing on the foundation of biblical Christianity
must necessarily have certain important common features. To be more specific, *every*
such asceticism, regardless of its denominational heritage, requires specific tried and
proven mechanisms that *subdue* the desires of the body.

Still to note is the brevity of the following sketch. Its shorter length must be ascribed to
the circumstance that the ethic of the baptizing communities is of only very limited significance for the particular problem to be discussed in *this* study: the development of the
religious foundation of the idea of a *calling* shared by a "middle class." This ethic did not
add anything qualitatively new to this idea. The far more important social side of the
baptizing movement will be left aside for the moment. [See "The Protestant Sects" essay
pp. 185–200.] Of the substantive historical issues surrounding the *older* Anabaptist

movement, we can discuss, as a result of our definition of the particular problem, *only* those issues that influenced the uniqueness of the baptizing sects in the foreground here: the Baptists, the Quakers, and (less directly) the Mennonites.

198. See above [note 106].

199. On their origin and changes, see A. Ritschl in his *Gesammelte Aufsätze*, vol. 1 (Tübingen: J.C.B. Mohr, 1893), pp. 68 ff.

200. Of course, the baptizers continually rejected other Christians' characterization of them as "sects." They were, in the sense of the Epistle to the Ephesians (5:27), *the* church. For *our* terminology, however, they were sects *not only* because they renounced every relationship to the state. Admittedly, the relationship between church and state in ancient Christianity was their ideal, even for the Quakers (see Barclay, *op. cit.* [n. 196]), because to them (as for some Pietists; see Teersteegen [note 136]) *only* the purity of the early churches was without suspicion. Yet, if oppressed under a *secular* state, or even under a theocracy, then [not only the baptizing movement] but also the Calvinists had to be in favor (for want of something better) of a separation of state and church (similar to, in the same situation, even the Catholic Church). [Therefore, this reason—their renunciation of every relationship to the state—cannot be decisive in defining the baptizing congregations as sects.] Moreover, the baptizers are defined as a sect not *because* the entry into church membership *de facto* followed from an induction contract between the congregation and the candidate. This was true *formally*, for example, also in the Dutch Calvinist congregations (as a result of the original political situation), according to the old church constitution (see H. von Hoffmann, *Kirchenverfassungsrecht der niederländischen Reformierten* [Leipzig, 1902].

Rather, the baptizing congregations are defined as a sect because, to them, the religious community *can only* be organized voluntaristically, namely, as a sect (and not as a church, in the way that a large institution is organized) if it wants to exclude the unsaved from membership and, thereby, to follow the ideal of the earliest Christian community [which was a community of the elect]. To the baptizing communities, the *concept* "church" included this voluntaristic organization. For the Reformists, on the other hand, the church, as a large institution that allowed membership to [include] the unsaved, already existed as an actual condition. Admittedly, very definite religious motives pushed even the Calvinists toward a "believers' church," as has been already suggested.

See "The Protestant Sects" essay below for more detail on "church" and "sect" [pp. 187–88, 194–9; see pp. 201–04]. As used here, the concept "sect" overlaps in part with and (I assume) deviates from Kattenbusch's usage. See the article "Sects" in the *Realencyklopädie für protestantische Theologie und Kirche* [1906, vol. 18, pp. 157–166]. Troeltsch accepts my definition, and discusses it in more detail, in his *Social Teachings* (*op. cit.* [note 8]). See also the introduction to my essays in the Economic Ethics of the World Religions series [1946e; see also below, pp. 412–15; 1968, pp. 1204–07; *Gesammelte Aufsätze zur Soziologie und Sozialpolitik* (Tübingen: Mohr: 1924), pp. 442–46.]

201. How important this symbol was historically, for the preservation of the community of churches (because it created for them an unambiguous and unmistakable identifying characteristic), has been examined by Cornelius in a very clear manner (see *op. cit.* [note 197]).

202. Certain approximations to this orthodox dogma in the Mennonite doctrine of justification can be omitted here.

203. The fourth-century Pneumatics believed that God's will could be understood through natural reason, angels and demons, and the human soul. This sect was viewed as a predecessor to the "awakening" movements of ascetic Protestantism [sk].

204. On this idea rests perhaps the religious interest in the questions of how the incarnation of Christ and his relationship to the Virgin Mary are to be understood. Often as the *single* purely dogmatic component, they appear quite peculiar, even in the oldest documents of the Anabaptists (for example, in the "confessions" printed in Cornelius, *op. cit.*

[note 197], appendix to vol. 2; see also, among others, Karl Müller, *Kirchengeschichte* [note 197], vol. 2, pt. 1, p. 330). Similar religious interests lay at the foundation of the difference in the christologies of the Reformists and the Lutherans (as concerns the doctrine of the so-called *communicatio idiomatum*). [Weber refers here to Calvin's view that the unity between God and human beings did not result from Christ's divinity, but owing to his possession of both divine and human features.]

205. It became expressed in particular in the (originally) strict avoidance of the excommunicated, even in interaction in middle-class economic activities. In this regard, even the Calvinists, who held the view that religious censors in principle should not interfere with middle-class economic activity, made strong concessions. See "The Protestant Sects" essay [pp. 185–99].

206. We know how this principle was expressed among the Quakers in the apparently unimportant external aspects of life (the refusal to remove the hat, to kneel down, to bow, to use the formal form of speech ["vous" in French]). However, the *basic* idea is indigenous to *every* asceticism to a certain degree. For this reason, in its *authentic* form, asceticism is always "hostile to authority." This hostility became manifest in Calvinism in the principle that only *Christ* should rule in the *church*. As concerns Pietism, on the other hand, one thinks of Spener's efforts to justify, by reference to the Bible, the *use of titles*. *Catholic* asceticism, in regard to matters concerning rulership in the *church*, did not share this hostility to authority. Instead, through the oath of obedience, it interpreted *obedience* itself as ascetic.

The "inverting" of this principle by Protestant asceticism is the historical foundation for the uniqueness, even today, of the *democracy* among peoples influenced by Puritanism. It is also the foundation for the differences between this democracy and the democracies that flowed out of the "Latin spirit." This hostility to authority among Protestants is also constitutive for that "lack of respect" at the foundation of American behavior. Some view this feature of American life as offensive, while others view it as refreshing. [Weber is here referring to widespread prejudices (hence the quotation marks) among many Germans who viewed Americans as rude, boisterous, and unruly, and as not showing adequate respect for high status and authority. Other Germans experienced the American "lack of respect" for authority as relief from a German climate of widespread and unquestioned respect for authority, which they perceived as oppressive. For a discussion of this point, see S. Kalberg, "West German and American Interaction Forms: One Level of Structured Misunderstanding" (*Theory, Culture and Society* 4 [Oct. 1987]: 602–18).]

207. Admittedly, this holds for the baptizing sects, from their beginnings in Anabaptism, essentially only for the *New* Testament. It cannot be said for the Old Testament in the same way. As a social-ethical program, the Sermon on the Mount in particular enjoyed, in all denominations, a clear prestige.

208. Condemned by Luther (1540) for his opposition to the doctrine of consubstantiation, Schwenckfeld had sought to mediate between conflicting parties during the early Reformation. Some of his followers emigrated to Pennsylvania in the eighteenth century [sk].

209. Even Schwenckfeld saw the external performance of the sacraments as an *Adiaphoron* [a matter of indifference in the eyes of the church]. The "General Baptists" [see note 195] and the Mennonites, however, continued to uphold strictly infant christening and communion. The Mennonites also practiced the bathing of feet. Among all denominations that upheld predestination, however, the downplaying of the sacraments was very apparent (one could even, with the exception of communion, speak of *suspicion*). See "The Protestant Sects" essay below.

210. At this point the baptizing denominations, especially the Quakers, referred to Calvin's statement (see [the distinguished and prolific Quaker] Robert Barclay's *Apology for the True Christian Divinity* (London: T. Sowle, 4th ed., [1678], 1701; made available to

me through the gracious assistance of [the prominent German socialist and member of the Reichstag] Eduard Bernstein); see also Calvin's *Institutio christianae religionis* [note 19], vol. 3, p. 2. Indeed, quite unmistakable approximations to the doctrine of the baptizing communities are found here. Even the older *distinction* regarding the dignity of "God's word" (as words that God had revealed to the patriarchs, prophets, and apostles) and the "holy scriptures" (as what of God's word had been *written down* by the patriarchs, prophets, and apostles) related internally, although a historical context was lacking, to the view of the baptizers on the essence of the revelation.

The mechanical doctrine of inspiration [according to which God had decreed that the Bible is to be understood literally as the Word of God], and hence the strict Bible learning of the Calvinists, likewise arose only as a product of a development (which had begun in the course of the sixteenth century) that unfolded in a particular direction. Similarly, the Quaker doctrine regarding an "inner light" (which rested upon an Anabaptist foundation) was the result of a development in the exactly opposite direction. The sharp separation was actually here also in part a consequence of a continuous confrontation.

211. This was emphasized sharply against certain tendencies of the Socinians [a northern Italian brotherhood of the sixteenth century, a precursor to English and American Unitarianism]. "Natural" reason knows *nothing at all* of God (Barclay, *op. cit.*, p. 102). Thus, the position that *lex naturae* [natural law] otherwise held in Protestantism was once again altered. "General rules" and a moral *code*, in principle, could not exist, for now the "calling," which every person has and which is *particular* to every person, reveals God to each—through the *conscience*. We should *not* do "the good" (as known to us in the form of a generalizing concept called natural reason); rather, we should do *God's Will*, as it is now—in a new contract with God—written in our hearts and expressed in our conscience (Barclay, *op. cit.*, pp. 73 f., 76).

This *irrationality* of morality [in the sense of being now particular to each person rather than a general code], which follows out of the accentuated contrast [in ascetic Protestantism] between the Divine and the mortal human being, becomes manifest in tenets foundational to the Quaker ethic: "What a man does contrary to his faith, *though his faith may be wrong*, is no ways acceptable to God . . . though *the thing might have been lawful to another*" (Barclay, *op. cit.*, p. 487). Of course, in daily life this standard could not be upheld. The "moral and perpetual statutes acknowledged by all Christians" are, for example for Barclay, actually the demarcation lines for *tolerance* [rather than the individual conscience]. In practice, the contemporaries understood their ethic (with a few exceptions) to be the same as that of the Reformist Pietists. Spener repeatedly emphasizes that "everything that is good in the church is suspected of being Quakerism." Hence, he would like the Quakers, on account of their reputations, to be envied (see *Cons. Theol.* [note 142], vol. 3, pt. 6, sect. 1, par. 2, no. 64). The rejection of taking an oath on account of a passage from the Bible demonstrates that an actual emancipation from the Bible had scarcely occurred. We cannot here address the *social*-ethical meaning of that principle viewed by some Quakers as the essence of the *entire* Christian ethic: "Do unto others as you would have them do unto you."

212. Barclay legitimizes the necessity for the acceptance of this *possibility* by arguing that, without it, "there should never be a place known by the Saints wherein they might be free of doubting and despair, which . . . is most absurd." One can see that the *certitudo salutis* connects to this passage. This is clear in Barclay (*op. cit.*, p. 20).

213. Eschatology is concerned with religious beliefs about the end of the world and events associated with it. Chiliasm is the belief that a new society, in which only the just and good live, will exist at the end of time [sk].

214. Weber is referring to the victory of the radical Anabaptist sect in the city of Münster in northwestern Germany in 1534 and the religious fanaticism, chiliasm, polygamy, collective ownership of property, and terror that followed. The brutal defeat they suffered in 1535 marked the end of Anabaptist radicalism [sk].

215. Hence, a difference in accent between the Calvinist and the Quaker rationalization of life continues to exist. However, Baxter's formulation—for the Quakers, "reason" should have an effect on the soul as it has on a corpse, whereas for Reformists (characteristically formulated) "reason and spirit are conjunct principles" (*Christian Directory* [see note 39], vol. 2, p. 76)—fails to recognize that this difference, for all practical purposes, ceases to exist in *this* form for Baxter's own time.

216. See the selection below on ancient Christianity (pp. 304–06 [sk].

217. See the very careful articles "Menno" and "Mennoniten" by S. Cramer in the *Realencyklopädie für Protestantische Theologie und Kirche* (esp. p. 604). Although these articles are very good, the article "Baptisten" in the same encyclopedia is not very compelling and is, in some respects, completely imprecise. Its author is not familiar with, for example, the Publications of the Hanserd Knollys Society series. These articles remain indispensable for the history of the Baptists.

218. The Dunkers were founded in Germany (in Hesse) by Alexander Mack and soon thereafter emigrated to Pennsylvania. Today they are allied with the Church of the Brethren [sk].

219. Hence, Barclay (*op. cit.* [n. 210], p. 404) explains that eating, drinking, and the *acquisition of goods* are *natural*, rather than spiritual, acts that can be pursued without a special call from God. His explanation is an answer to the (characteristic) criticism: if (as the Quakers teach) one is not allowed to pray without a special "motion of the spirit," then one would not even be allowed, without such a special motivation bestowed by God, to plow the fields.

It is also characteristic (even if such ideas are also occasionally found in the other denominations, even among the Calvinists) that Quakers advise, even in modern resolutions of the Quaker synods, one to withdraw from making a living after one has earned a sufficient fortune. One should withdraw in order, in the peacefulness outside the world's hustle and bustle, to be able to live fully in the kingdom of God. It becomes apparent, in this advice, that the adoption of a middle-class vocational ethic by its social carriers constituted the this-worldly turn of an originally world-*fleeing* asceticism. [Weber refers to the asceticism of medieval Catholicism within monasteries (see the end of this chapter); he sees the Quaker advice as a manifestation of asceticism because it assumes the believer had remained focused upon God's will despite the acquisition of (corrupting) material goods.]

220. The excellent studies by Eduard Bernstein should here again be emphasized (*op. cit.* [see note 10]). An opportunity will be available at another time to address Kautsky's extremely schematic presentation of the Anabaptist movement and his theory of "heretical communism" in general.

221. In his stimulating book, *The Theory of Business Enterprise* [New York: Scribner, 1904], Thorstein Veblen is of the opinion that this maxim belongs exclusively to the epoch of "early capitalism." Yet economic "supermen," who have stood beyond good and evil, have always existed [and did not follow this policy of honesty]. Indeed, the "captains of industry" [original in English] today are no different from these supermen. This maxim—"honesty is the best policy" [in text in English]—is valid even today for the broad stratum, exhibiting capitalist conduct, just below these heroic figures.

222. [From *Maximen und Reflexionen,* edited by Max Hecker (Weimar, 1907, no. 241).] "In civil actions it is good to be *as the many,* in religious, to be as the best," as, for example, Thomas Adams notes (*Works of the Puritan Divines,* p. 138). Admittedly, this advice sounds somewhat more far-reaching than is actually meant. It implies that the Puritan candor constitutes a sort of *formalistic legality,* as does the claim gladly made by peoples with a Puritan heritage that "truthfulness" or "uprightness" is a national virtue. It is entirely *different,* re-fashioned in a formalistic and cognitive manner, from the German "honesty." Some good remarks on this theme, from the point of view of an educator, can be found in the *Preußischer Jahrbücher,* vol. 112 (1903): 226. [See also Henry James, *The Eu-*

ropeans (New York: Penguin Books, 1974 (1878).] For its part, the *formalism* of the Puritan ethic is the entirely expected consequence of its tie to *God's law.*

223. Which will be somewhat examined in "The Protestant Sects" essay [see pp. 197–99; 1968, pp. 455–56, 460–63].

224. *Here* is to be found the reason for the acute effect upon economic action of (ascetic) Protestant (but not Catholic) *minority status.* [1920] [See chapter 1.]

225. The grounding of dogma, which varied widely, could be unified through a decisive interest in "testifying" to belief. The *ultimate* reason why this could occur is to be located in Christianity's religious-historical particular features in general. This reason is still to be discussed. [1920]

226. "Since God hath gathered us to be a people," as, for example, Barclay also states (*op. cit.* [note 210], p. 357). The Quaker sermon that I myself heard at Haverford College placed the emphasis entirely upon the "saints" as separate from other believers.

Chapter V

1.   For later examples, see the "Protestant Sects" essay below [sk].

2.   These terms refer to Catholic Church documents that recorded the multiple ways in which guidance was offered by the church [sk].

3.   Throughout this chapter, as well as earlier, Weber generally places this term in quotation marks in order to signify that national character must be understood as constructed from social forces (and religious forces in particular) rather than as a genetic predisposition. Weber's position stood in opposition to views in his time widespread in the political arena, as well as to major schools of scholarship. See the concluding pages of the "Prefatory Remarks" essay below (pp. 219–20; see also Weber, 2005, pp. 291–314) [sk].

4.   See the fine characterization of Baxter in Edward Dowden [*Puritan and Anglican* (ch. 4, note 23). His various works are reprinted in the Works of the Puritan Divines series [see note 6]. The introduction to them examines Baxter's theology in a reasonably satisfactory manner. Written by Jenkyn, it is oriented to his thinking after his gradual movement away from a strict belief in the "double decree" [predestination].

Baxter's attempt to combine "universal redemption" and "personal election" had not pleased anyone. For our purposes it is only important *that* he nonetheless retained a belief in *personal* election. In other words, he held to the ethically crucial point in the predestination doctrine. On the other hand, because it indicates a certain convergence with the baptizing groups, his downplaying of the *juridical* conception of exculpation is important [as opposed to Lutheranism; see p. 134]. .

5.   On St. Bartholomew's Day (August 24, 1572), which followed the marriage of the Protestant Henry of Navarre (later Henry IV) to a Catholic princess, thousands of French Protestants (Huguenots) were persecuted and murdered [sk].

6.   Tracts and sermons by Thomas Adams, John Howe, Matthew Henry, J. Janeway, Stephen Charnock, Baxter, and Bunyan have been collected in the 10 volumes of the *Works of the Puritan Divines* (London: Nelson Publ., 1845–47). The selection is often somewhat arbitrary. Editions used of the works by Bayly, Sedgwick, and Hoornbeek have been noted above.

7.   Works by Voët or other continental representatives of this-worldly asceticism could have just as well been utilized. Brentano's view [*op. cit.*, ch. 1, note 15]—this development occurred "only among the Anglo-Saxons"—is completely erroneous. [1920]

The selection rests upon the wish to give expression, not exclusively but as much as possible, to the ascetic movement of the second half of the seventeenth century directly *before its turn into utilitarianism.* In light of the focus of this sketch, the stimulating task of illuminating the ascetic Protestant style of life in a further manner, namely through biographies, unfortunately must be abandoned. Exploring the case of the Quakers in particular, because relatively unknown in Germany, would be particularly worthwhile.

8.   One could just as well take the writings of Gisbert Voët or the proceedings of the Huguenot synods or the literature from the Baptist movement in Holland. In a very unfortunate manner, Sombart and Brentano have emphasized precisely that "ebionitic" component [see note 10] in Baxter's writings (which I stressed myself) in order to confront my thesis with the undoubtedly (capitalist) "backwardness" of his *doctrines*. However, one must *know* this entire literature very thoroughly in order to use it correctly. Furthermore, one should not overlook that I sought to demonstrate how, *despite doctrines* opposed to mammonism, the spirit of this ascetic *religious devotion* gave birth, just as in the businesses run by cloisters, to *economic rationalism*. This religious devotion did so because it *placed a psychological reward* upon what was crucial: rational *motivations* conditioned by asceticism. This alone mattered, and this is precisely the point of my entire essay. [1920]

9.   This held in the same way for Calvin, who was certainly no enthusiast of middle class wealth. (See his sharp attacks on Venice and Antwerp in [Commentary on] *Jesaia Opera*, vol. 3, 140a, 308a.) [1920]

10.   The Ebionite sect was founded in the first century in Jerusalem, with lineage tracing back to the apostles. Members rejected St. Paul and believed that Judaic law was binding on Christians. As in the original Christian community, they attributed moral worth to poverty and scorned wealth [sk].

11.   *Saints' Everlasting Rest* [see ch. 4, note 62], chs. 10, 12. See Bayly (*Praxis pietatis, op. cit.* [ch. 4, note 32], p. 182) or Matthew Henry: "Those that are eager in pursuit of worldly wealth despise their soul, not only because the soul is neglected and the body preferred before it, but because it is employed in these pursuits"; see Ps. 127:2 ("The Worth of the Soul," in *Works of the Puritan Divines*, p. 319). (However, the remark on the sinfulness of the squandering of time, especially on recreations, is found on the *same page*; this remark will be cited later.) Similar commentaries are found throughout this literature, especially in English-Dutch Puritanism. See, for example, Hoornbeek's tirade against *avarice (op. cit.* [ch. 4, note 22], vol. 50, no. 10, chs. 18 and 19). (It should be noted that, in Hoornbeek's works, sentimental-Pietistic influences enter into his analysis; see his praise of the *tranquillitas animi* [tranquil mind] as more pleasing to God than the *sollicitudo* [activities] of the mundane world.) The same idea is apparent in Bayly when he remarks, paraphrasing the familiar passage from the Bible, "it is not easy for a rich man to become saved" (*op. cit.*, p. 182). The *Methodist* catechism also warns against "gathering treasures in this life." This idea is completely self-evident to Pietism, as it is for the Quakers. As Barclay states, ". . . and therefore beware of such temptation as to use their callings and engine *to be richer*" (*op. cit.* [ch. 4, note 210], p. 517).

12.   Not only riches, but also the *obsessive pursuit of profit* (or what passes for it) was similarly severely condemned. This position became clear in the response to a question posed at the South Holland Synod of 1574: although the charging of interest for loans was legally permitted, its practitioners, the bankers from Lombardy, should not be allowed to attend communion. The Deventer Provincial Synod of 1598 (Article 24) expanded the decision to include the employees of the Lombard bankers, and the Synod of Gorichem in 1606 passed statutes according to which severe and humiliating conditions accompanied the admission of the wives of "usurers" to communion. Whether the Lombard bankers should be allowed to participate in communion was still discussed in 1644 and 1657. (This latter point contradicts Brentano, who offers the case of his Catholic ancestors as evidence for his argument, even though foreign-born traders and bankers have existed in the entire European-Asian world for millennia.) Even Gisbert Voët wanted to exclude the "Trapezites" [the bankers from Lombardy and Piedmont] from communion (see "De usuris," in *Selectae disputationes theologicae* [1667], p. 665). The Huguenot Synods took the same position. *These* types of capitalist strata were not at all the typical carriers of the

frame of mind and organization of life of concern to this investigation. Moreover, these strata were, compared to the ancient and medieval worlds, not at all *new*. [1920]

13.   This point is developed in the *Saints' Everlasting Rest* (ch. 10):

> He who should seek to rest in the "shelter" of possessions which God gives, God strikes even in this life. A self-satisfied enjoyment of wealth already gained is almost always a symptom of moral degradation. If we had everything which we *could* have in this world, would that be all we hoped for? *Complete satisfaction of desires* is not attainable on earth because God's will has decreed it *should* not be so.

14.   *Christian Directory, op. cit.* [ch. 4, note 39], vol. 1, pp. 375–76:

> It is for *action* that God maintaineth us and our activities: work is the moral as well as the natural *end of power.* . . . It is *action* that God is most served and honoured by. . . . *The public welfare or the good of many* is to be valued above our own.

Just at this point the point of departure for the transformation from the will of God to the purely utilitarian perspectives (see note 7) of classical [early nineteenth-century English] Liberalism becomes apparent. On the religious sources of Utilitarianism see below in the text and above (ch. 4, note 169).

15.   The commandment of silence has been, beginning with the biblical threat of punishment for "every unnecessary word," namely, since the [Benedictine] monks of Cluny [981], a proven ascetic means of socialization toward self-control. Even Baxter goes into detail on the sinfulness of unnecessary speech. The significance of this development for the development of character has already been noted by Sanford (*op. cit.* [see ch. 4, note 5], pp. 90 ff.).

The "melancholy" and "moroseness" of the Puritans, so clearly perceived by contemporaries, was actually a consequence of the displacement of the *spontaneity* inherent to the *status naturalis*. The prohibition upon thoughtless speech served this purpose. Washington Irving in *Bracebridge Hall* (New York: Putnam, 1865) discovers the reason for this melancholy and moroseness in part in capitalism's "calculating spirit" and in part in the effect of political freedom, which leads to self-responsibility (ch. 30). It must be noted, however, that this melancholy and moroseness did not appear among the peoples of the Mediterranean [where a calculating, "practical rationalism" is widespread; see pp. 87–88]. The situation for the English was clearly different: (1) Puritanism enabled its adherents to develop free institutions and, nonetheless, to become a world power, and (2) Puritanism transformed that "calculatedness") (called by Sombart a "spirit"), which indeed is definitive for capitalism, from an instrument utilized in economic transactions into a *principle* for the entire organization of life.

16.   Baxter, *op. cit.*, vol. 1, p. 111.

17.   Baxter, *op. cit.* [ch. 4, note 10], vol. 1, pp. 383 f.

18.   Similarly on the preciousness of time, see Barclay, *op. cit.* [ch. 4, note 10], p. 14.

19.   Baxter, *op. cit.*, vol. 1, p. 79:

> Keep up a high esteem of time and be every day more careful that you lose none of your time, than you are that you lose none of your gold and silver. And if vain recreation, dressings, feastings, idle talk, unprofitable company, or sleep, be any of them temptations to rob you of any of your time, accordingly heighten your watchfulness.

"Those that are prodigal of their time despise their own souls" says Matthew Henry ("Worth of the Soul," *Works of the Puritan Divines*, p. 315). Protestant asceticism is moving also here in its old tried and proven pathway. Today we are accustomed to observe that the modern professional "has no time" and to measure (as did even Goethe in his *Wilhelm Meister's Years of Travel*) the degree of capitalist development according to whether the *clocks* strike every quarter hour (as Sombart notes in his *Der moderne Kapitalismus*). We should not forget, however, that the first person who (in the Middle Ages) lived according to a *differentiated notion of time* was the *monk*. The church bells originally had to serve *his* need to measure time.

20. See Baxter's discussion of the calling (*Christian Directory, op. cit.* [ch. 4, note 39], vol. 1, pp. 108 ff.). These pages include the following passage:

> Question: But may I not cast off the world that I may only think of my salvation? Answer: You may cast off all such excess of worldly cares or business as unnecessarily hinder you in spiritual things. But you may not cast off all bodily employment and mental labour in which *you may serve the common good*. Every one as a member of Church or Commonwealth must employ their parts to the utmost for the good of the Church and the Commonwealth. To neglect this and say: I will pray and meditate, is as if your servant should refuse your *greatest* work and tye himself to some lesser easier part. And *God hath commandeth* you some way or other to *labour for your daily bread and not to live as drones of the sweat of others only.*

God's commandment to Adam—"in the sweat of your face you shall eat bread" [Gen. 3:19]—and the admonition of St. Paul ("If anyone will not work, let him not eat" [2 Thess. 3:10]) were also quoted. It has always been known that the Quakers always sent sons, and even those from the most wealthy families, to learn a vocation. (They did so for ethical reasons rather than, as Alberti recommends, for utilitarian reasons.) [1920; last par. only]

21. Pietism, on account of its *feeling* character, deviates from these points. Although Spener emphasizes, fully in keeping with the Lutheran meaning, that work in a calling is a *service to God*, he nonetheless contends (and even this is Lutheran) that the *commotion* in places of business has the effect of distracting the faithful from their orientation to God (see *Theologische Bedenken,* vol. 3, *op. cit.* [ch. 4, note 32], p. 445). This idea constitutes a highly characteristic contrast to Puritanism.

22. Baxter, *Christian Directory* [see ch. 4, note 39], p. 242. "It's they that are lazy in their callings that can find no time for holy duties." This is the origin of the opinion that primarily the *cities*—the location of a middle class oriented to rational acquisition—are the location of the ascetic virtues. Accordingly, in his autobiography, Baxter says of his hand-loom weavers in Kidderminster: "And their constant *converse and traffic with London* doth much to promote civility and piety among tradesmen . . ." (selections in *Works of the Puritan Divines,* p. 38). The notion that proximity to a large city ought to have a positive influence upon virtue will be a great surprise to the clergy today, at least to the German clergy. Yet similar views are apparent even in Pietism, as is clear in Spener's occasional letters to a young colleague:

> At any rate, it is apparent that, although most inhabitants in cities of large populations are completely wicked, persons of good spiritual natures can occasionally be found. These persons can be depended upon to do good. In villages, in contrast, it is frequently the case that scarcely anything involving good spiritual activity can be found. (*Theologische Bedenken,* vol. I, sect. 66, *op. cit.,* p. 303)

The peasant is actually poorly suited for the ascetic and rationally organized life; *ethical* glorification is quite modern. We cannot here examine the significance of this comment, as well as similar statements, in respect to the question of the extent to which asceticism is conditioned by *class*.

23. One could take, for example, the following passages:

> Be wholly taken up in diligent business of your lawful callings when you are not exercised in the more immediate service of God. Labor hard in your callings.

> See that you have a calling which will find you employment for all the time which God's immediate service spareth. (Baxter, *op. cit.,* pp. 336 f.)

24.   That the specifically ethical valuation of work and its "dignity" was not one of the ideas that *originally* belonged to Christianity, or was even specific to Christianity, has been again recently emphasized sharply by [the theologian Adolf von] Harnack. See *Mitteilungen des Evangelischen-sozialen Kongresses*, vol. 14 (1905), no. 3/4, pp. 48 f.

25.   It is the same also in Pietism (see Spener, *op. cit.* [see ch. 4, n.32], vol. 3, pp. 429–30). For Pietism, characteristically, loyalty to a vocational calling, which has been imposed upon us on account of original sin, serves to *kill* the believer's own *will*. Work in a vocation is, as a service that expresses love of one's neighbor, a duty performed out of gratitude to God for his grace (a Lutheran idea!). For this reason God is not pleased when it is offered unwillingly and reluctantly (*op. cit.*, vol. 3, p. 272). Thus, the Christian should show himself "to be industrious in his work as any person engaged actively in the world" (*op. cit.*, vol. 3, p. 278). This Pietist motivation to work is clearly less developed than the Puritan outlook.

26.   Only a far more comprehensive investigation would be able to explore the foundation upon which *this* important contrast rests. It exists apparently since the Benedictine dictum [*Ora et labora* (prayer and work)]. [1920]

27.   According to Baxter, its purpose is "a *sober procreation* of children" (Gen. 9:1). [The Pietist] Spener is similar, although he makes concessions to the coarse Lutheran view according to which the avoidance of immorality is a secondary matter (and, in any case, for Luther immorality cannot be suppressed). Concupiscence, which is inherent to impregnation, even in marriage, is sinful. According to the view, for example, of Spener, concupiscence is a *consequence* of original sin, which transformed a natural and God-ordained process into something unavoidably interwoven with sinful sensations and hence into shamefulness. The highest form of Christian marriage, according to the view of some Pietist groups, preserves virginity. Ranking second is the type of marriage in which sexual intercourse serves exclusively to produce children. On the other end of the spectrum stands the marriage that occurs for purely erotic or purely external reasons—which, viewed ethically, constitutes concubinage. At these lower levels the marriage that exists for purely external reasons (because, at any rate, such marriages arise out of *rational* considerations) is preferred over the marriage entered into for erotic considerations.

The theory and practice of the Herrnhuter should not be considered here. The rationalist philosophy [[of the philosopher and legal scholar] Christian Wolff [1679–1754]) adopted the ascetic theory, according to which what is ordained as *means* to an end—concupiscence and its satisfaction—should not be turned into an end *in itself*. The turn into a purely hygienic [health-oriented] utilitarianism has occurred already with Franklin, who took approximately the same ethical standpoint as the modern physician. Franklin defines "virtue" as the limitation of sexual intercourse to that which is desired *for health*. As is well-known, he even offered theoretical advice on the question of "how?" As soon as these matters are in general made the object of purely "rational" considerations, this turn into a hygienic utilitarianism everywhere began. The Puritan and the hygienic sexual-rationalist, who move along very different pathways, "comprehend each other immediately" on this particular point. [For example], in a lecture on the regulation of houses of prostitution, a zealous representative of "hygienic prostitution" defended the moral permissibility of "extra-marital sexual intercourse" (which was interpreted as *hygienically* useful) by noting its literary glorification in [Goethe's characters] *Faust and Margaret*. The treatment of Margaret as a prostitute and the equating of the powerful rule over one's human passions with sexual intercourse undertaker on behalf of one's health—all this corresponds *thoroughly* to the Puritan position.

This connection to the Puritan point of view is also evident, for example, in the genuinely specialist viewpoint occasionally upheld by very prominent physicians. They argue, namely, that the question of the significance of sexual abstinence, which penetrates into the most subtle problems of the personality and cultural milieu, belongs "exclusively" in a forum of physicians (as the *specialists* on this subject). While the moral person was the "specialist" for the Puritans [those who work in vocational callings], he has now become the hygienic [medical] theorist. However, it should be noted that the resolution of questions and issues by reference to the principle of specialized "competence," which appears to us today rather provincial, is common to both cases (although the direction has been reversed [in the one case toward the moral, in the other toward the utilitarian]).

Yet, and despite its developed prudery, the powerful idealism of the Puritan view could demonstrate favorable results. This is the case if Puritanism is viewed from the perspective of the preservation of the boundaries of races and if examined purely in terms of the "hygiene" it introduced. On the other hand, the modern sexual hygiene movement, on account of the call for a "lack of prejudice" which it must make, runs the risk of destroying the very foundation [the moral] on which it rests.

How, in the end, a refinement of the marital relationship, its penetration by a spiritual-ethical dimension, and a blossoming of matrimonial chivalry indeed arose out of this rational understanding of sexual relations among those peoples influenced by Puritanism must be omitted here. This development stands in contrast to the patriarchal bluster in Germany that has expanded, even in the form of frequently perceptible residues, into circles of the intellectual elite. This theme likewise cannot be considered here. (Influences from the baptizing groups have played a role in the "emancipation" of women. The protection of women's *freedom of conscience* and the extension of the "universal priesthood" idea to include women were in these groups the first breakthroughs against patriarchalism.)

28.   This idea appears repeatedly in Baxter. Support in the Bible is regularly found either in those passages well-known to us from Franklin (Prov. 22:29) or the praise of work in Proverbs (31:16). See Baxter, *op. cit.* [ch. 4, note 39], vol. 1, pp. 377, 382, *et passim*.

29.   Even Zinzendorf says occasionally: "One doesn't work alone in order to live; rather, one lives owing to the wish to work. If one must work no longer, then one suffers or dies." (Plitt, vol. 1, *op. cit.* [ch. 4, note 152], p. 428).

30.   [2 Thess. 3:10] Even a symbol of the Mormons closes (according to quotations) with the words: "But a lazy or indolent man cannot be a Christian and be saved. He is destined to be struck down and cast from the hive." Nevertheless, it was in this case primarily the grandiose discipline, which held a middle position between the cloister and the factory, that presented the person with the choice to either work or perish. It was this discipline, *bound up* of course with religious enthusiasm and made possible *only through it*, that brought forth the amazing economic achievements of these sects.

31.   Hence, its manifestations are carefully analyzed by Baxter (*Chr. Dir.*, vol. 1, *op. cit.*, p. 380). "Sloth" and "idleness" are *therefore* such burdensome sins because they have the character of being continuous. Baxter sees them as the "destroyers of one's state of grace" (vol. 1, *op. cit.*, pp. 279–80). They are the diametrical opposite of the *methodical* life.

32.   See above, ch. 3, note 6.

33.   Baxter, *Chr. Dir.*, vol. 1, *op. cit.*, pp. 108 ff. The following passage strikes one immediately. "Question: But will not wealth excuse us? Answer: It may excuse you from some sordid sort of work, by making you more serviceable to another, but you are no more excused from service of work . . . than the poorest man." Also: "Though they [the rich] have no outward want to urge them, they have as great a necessity to obey God. . . . God had strictly commandeth it (labor) to all" (vol. 1, *op. cit.*, p. 376). See ch. 4, note 57.

34.   Similarly, Spener (vol. 3, *op. cit.* [ch. 4, n. 32]), pp. 338, 425. For this reason, he opposes as morally troubling the tendency of persons to retire early. Moreover, he emphasizes (in rejecting an objection to the legality of taking interest, namely, that living off interest leads to laziness) that even those able to live off interest are nonetheless, according to God's commandment, *obligated* to work.

35.   Including Pietism. Spener takes the position, as concerns the question of a *change* of vocation, that, once work in a particular vocation has commenced, a continuation of and devotion to it is a duty of obedience vis-à-vis God's predestination.

36.   On Scholasticism, see ch. 3, note 9 [sk].

37.   With what high pathos, which dominates the entire organization of life, the salvation doctrine of India [Hinduism] connects vocational traditionalism with prospects for a favorable rebirth, is explored in the essays in the Economic Ethics of the World Religions series [see Weber, 1958; see below, pp. 183–84, 229–37, 257–67]; see below. Precisely through such an example one can become acquainted with the difference between merely an ethical, *doctrinal* concept and the creation, through religion, of psychological *motivations* of a specific type. The pious Hindu could acquire favorable rebirth prospects *only* through a strict, *traditional* fulfillment of the duties associated with the caste into which he was born. This constituted the most rigid religious anchoring of economic traditionalism that can be conceived. In fact, in this respect the ethic of India is actually the most consistent antithesis to the Puritan ethic, just as it is, in a different respect (status traditionalism) the most consistent antithesis to Judaism. [1920]

38.   Baxter, *Chr. Dir.*, vol. 1, *op. cit.*, p. 377.

39.   But this does not imply that the utilitarian motivation can be historically derived out of these points of view. On the contrary, moreso manifest is an entirely central Calvinist idea: the cosmos of the "world" serves the majesty of God and his self-glorification. The utilitarian turn, namely, that the economic cosmos should serve the common good (good of the many, etc.), was a result of the idea that every other interpretation would lead to the deification of human wants and desires (an idea closely associated with the aristocracy) or, at any rate, to a serving of human "cultural ends" [everything is created by and for human beings] rather than God's glory. However, God's will, as expressed in the purposeful formation of the economic cosmos (see ch. 4, note 43), can only be, at least to the extent that *this*-worldly ends at all come into consideration, the well-being of the "whole community"; that is, *im*personal "usefulness." Hence, as noted earlier, [classical] utilitarianism is a result of the *im*personal formulation of the "love thy neighbor" commandment and the rejection of all glorification of this world that followed from the Puritan's exclusive earthly purpose: *in majorem Dei gloriam* [to serve the greater glory of God].

That every glorification of human nature violates God's glory and is therefore unconditionally reprehensible is an idea that dominates all of ascetic Protestantism. Just how intensively it does so is revealed overtly in the hesitation and pain experienced even by Spener, a man surely without "democratic" proclivities, as he maintained usage of *titles* ἀδιάφορον [because he saw this issue as a matter of indifference to the church] in the face of numerous objections. In the end he comforted himself with the knowledge that even in the Bible [Porcius] Festus [the procurator of Judea, 60–62], was given the title κράτιστος [Excellency] by the apostles. [The use of titles, Weber is noting, in calling attention to persons, involves to ascetic Protestants self-glorification (see above para.) and hence in sublimated form a deification of the human species.] The *political* side of this issue does not belong in this context.

40.   "The *inconstant* man is a stranger in his own house," is said also by Thomas Adams (*Works of the Puritan Divines*, p. 77).

41.   Weber's emphasis and parenthetic comment [sk].

42.   On this theme see, in particular, George Fox's remarks in the *Friends' Library*, edited by W. & Thomas Evans, vol. 1 (Philadelphia: Joseph Rakestraw, 1837), p. 130.

43.   Clearly, this turn of the religious ethic of course cannot be seen as a reflection of the actual economic conditions. Vocational specialization was far further developed in Italy than in England in the Middle Ages. [1920]

44.   For God, as is frequently emphasized in the Puritan literature, nowhere ordered that one's neighbor should be loved *more* than oneself. Rather, he commanded the love of one's neighbor *as* one loves oneself. Hence, the *duty* to love oneself is apparent. Whoever knows, for example, how to utilize his property in a more efficient manner than his neighbor, and thus in a way that better serves God's honor, is not duty-bound, owing to his love of his neighbor, to convey this useful knowledge to him.

45.   Spener's thinking also comes close to this position. Nonetheless, he remains, even in the example of a change from the vocation of businessman (which is morally especially dangerous) to the vocation of theologian, quite hesitant and generally opposed (see vol. 3, *op. cit.* [see ch. 4, note 32], pp. 435, 443; vol. 1, p. 524). The frequent appearance of the answer to precisely *this* question (regarding the permissibility of changing one's vocation) in Spener's unsurprisingly tendentious writing on this theme shows, by the way, how the various interpretations of 1 Corinthians 7 [on the obligations of the married and unmarried] were eminently *practical*, relating directly to everyday circumstances.

46.   These ideas, at least in their writings, are *not* found in the leading continental Pietists. The position of Spener in regard to "profit" vacillates between Lutheran (the "livelihood" standpoint) and mercantilist arguments on the usefulness of, for example, the *Flor der Commerzien* [prosperity of commerce] (see vol. 3, *op. cit.*, pp. 330, 332; vol. 1, p. 418). The *cultivation of tobacco* brings money into the country and is *therefore* useful; that is, *hence*, not sinful (see vol. 3, pp. 426–27, 429, 434)! However, his writings do not fail to note that, as is apparent from the example of the Quakers and Mennonites, one can make profits and still remain pious—and that especially large profits (as we will have occasion later to note) can be a direct *consequence* of pious uprightness (*op. cit.*, p. 435).

47.   These views of Baxter are *not* merely a reflection of the economic milieu in which he lived. His autobiography stresses the *opposite*: the success of his domestic missionary work was in part owing to the fact that the merchants who lived in [his home town] Kidderminster were *not* wealthy (rather, they earned only "food and raiment") and that the master craftsmen had to live, in a manner no better than their workers, "from hand to mouth." "It is *the poor* that receive the glad tidings of the Gospel."

Thomas Adams remarks on the striving for profit: "He (the knowing man) knows . . . that money may make a man richer, not better, and thereupon chooseth rather to sleep with a good conscience than a full purse . . . therefore desires no more wealth *than an honest man may bear away.*" Yet *he does want this amount* (Adams, *Works of the Puritan Divines*, vol. 51). And this means that every formally *honest* earning is also *legitimate*.

48.   Thus Baxter (*Chr. Dir.*, vol. 1, *op. cit.*, ch. 10, pt. 1, ch. 9, par. 24): "Weary thyself not to be rich" (vol. 1, p. 378, column 2; see Prov. 23:4) means only "riches for our fleshly ends must not ultimately be intended." Possession, in the feudal-seigneurial form of *use*, is actually what is odious (see the remark on the "debauched part of the gentry"; vol. 1, *op. cit.*, p. 380), not possession *as such*. Milton, in his first *Defensio pro populo Anglicano* [Defense of the Anglican Peoples], upheld the well-known theory that only the "middle stratum" (*Mittelstand*) can be a social carrier of *virtue*. It must be noted that he here means a middle stratum in the sense of a "class oriented to work and business" (*bürgerliche Klasse*), and he is contrasting this group to the "aristocracy." His explanation clarifies that he is referring to just this distinction, namely, when he notes that both "luxury" [the aristocracy] and "necessity" [the destitute] hinder the exercise of virtue.

49.   *This* is what is pivotal. To this statement should be added, once again, the general comment: whatever theology-oriented ethical theory developed conceptually is naturally for us not the important matter. Rather, central here is the question of what morality was *valid* in the *practical* life of believers. In other words, our concern involves the question of *how* believers' religious orientation exercised a practical *effect* upon their vocational ethic. One can read, at least occasionally, discussions in Catholicism's casuistic literature (namely, the Jesuit) that sound similar to the many casuistic discussions in the Protestant literature (for example, on the question of the permissibility of usury, which we cannot address here). Indeed, in respect to that which is understood as "allowed" or "probable," the Protestants appear to have moved beyond the Catholic positions. (The Puritan position was frequently criticized later on as basically the same as the Jesuit ethic.) Just as Calvinists were concerned to cite Catholic moral theologians, and not only Thomas of Aquinas, Bernhard von Clairvaux [*ca.* 1090–1153], and Bonaventure [1221–74], but also their contemporaries, so also Catholic casuistic thinkers regularly at-

tended to the heretical ethic's development (though this as well cannot be further examined here).

Nonetheless, leaving aside the central placing of religious *rewards*, by ascetic Protestants, upon an ascetic life for the *laity*, a massive distinction is apparent even in theory: in Catholicism these latitudinal [broad and liberal] views were a product of especially *lax* ethical theories not approved by church authorities and from which the most sincere and strict adherents of the church distanced themselves. The Protestant idea of a vocational calling, on the other hand, placed the striving for success of precisely the *most sincere* adherents of the ascetic life in the service of a capitalist earning of one's livelihood. That which in the one case could be conditionally *allowed*, appeared in the other case as a positive moral *good*. These foundational differences in the two ethics, which were very important for the *practical* life of believers, have been conclusively defined, even for the modern period, since the controversy over Jansenism [1641–1705; ch. 4, note 23] and the Bull *Unigenitus* [of 1713 against Jansenism].

50. "You may labour in that manner as tendeth most to your success and lawful gain. You are *bound* to improve all your talents." This passage [from Baxter] follows the passage cited in the text above [see note 47]. For a discussion that draws a direct parallel between the striving for riches in God's kingdom and the striving after success in an earthly vocation, see, for example, James Janeway, *Heaven upon Earth* (in *Works of the Puritan Divines*, p. 275).

51. A protest against the *oath* of poverty is rendered already in the (Lutheran) confession of Duke Christoph of Württemberg [1515–1568], which was submitted to the Council of Trent [1545–1563]: those who are poor according to their stratum should tolerate their situation; however, for the poor to vow to *remain* poor is the same as vowing to be continuously sick or to have a *bad reputation*.

52. This is clear in Baxter and also in Duke Christoph's confession. Further, see passages such as: ". . . the vagrant rogues whose lives are nothing but an exorbitant course: the main begging," etc. (Thomas Adams, *Works of the Puritan Divines*, p. 259).

Already Calvin strictly prohibited begging, and the Dutch Synods declaimed against begging letters and certificates for begging purposes. [These letters allowed itinerant preachers to offer sermons in the churches of a specific region. Afterwards, donations would be requested. The preacher was permitted to retain these funds for his organization (perhaps a monastery). Because those who donated were in turn offered salvation, the begging-letter system worked quite well. However, the work ethic of the Puritans diametrically opposed this mode of raising funds.] During the reign of the Stuarts, and especially the regime of [William] Laud under Charles I [1635–44; see note 125], when the principle of public support for the poor and of governmental allocation of work to the unemployed was systematically formulated, the battle-cry of the Puritans was: "Giving alms is no charity." (This became the title of a later well-known work by Daniel Defoe.) The deterrent system, the "workhouses" for the unemployed, developed out of this precedent near the end of the seventeenth century. See E. M. Leonard, *Early History of English Poor Relief* (Cambridge, 1900 [London: Frank Cass, 1965]), and Hermann Levy, *Die Grundlagen des ökonomischen Liberalismus in der Geschichte der englischen Volkswirtschaft* (Jena: G. Fischer, 1912), pp. 69 ff., *op. cit.* [ch. 3, note 17]. [1920]

53. In his inaugural address before the assembly in London in 1903, the President of the Baptist Union of Great Britain and Ireland, G. White, emphasized: "The best men on the roll of our Puritan Churches were *men of affairs*, who believed that religion should permeate the whole of life" (*Baptist Handbook*, 1904, p. 104).

54. Just *at this point* the characteristic contrast to all outlooks rooted in feudalism becomes apparent. According to the feudal conception of things, the benefits of the parvenu's (political or social) success and sacred blood can be reaped only by the descendants. (This is characteristically expressed in the Spanish *Hidalgo [parvenu]* = *hijo d'algo* = *filius de aliquo*; the *aliquid* refers directly to *wealth* that is inherited from ancestors.)

In the United States today, in view of the rapid transformation and Europeanization of the American "national character," these distinctions are rapidly fading. Nonetheless, the specifically middle-class outlook *diametrically opposed* to feudalism is still today occasionally apparent. This outlook glorifies business *success* and *acquisition* as a symptom of spiritual *achievement* and cannot muster respect for mere (inherited) *wealth* as such. In contrast, in Europe money can in effect purchase almost every social honor (as James Bryce [the author of *The American Commonwealth*, 1888], already once remarked)—if only its owner has not *himself* stood behind the counter and the necessary metamorphosis of his wealth is executed (through the formation of trusts, etc.). *Against* the feudal view that the *blood* bond is an honorable one, see, for example, Thomas Adams, *Works of the Puritan Divines* (*op. cit.*), p. 216.

55.   This phrase, and "self-made man," appear in English in the original [sk]

56.   This held, for example, already for the founder of the Familist sect, Hendrik Nicklaes [*ca.* 1501–1580], who was a merchant. See Barclay, *Inner Life of the Religious Societies of the Commonwealth, op. cit.* [ch. 4, note 22], p. 34. [Members of the Familist sect (f. in 1530 in Amsterdam) believed themselves to be the true children of God who have overcome sin; they were direct predecessors of the Quakers.]

57.   Weber is here alluding to a wrathful, vengeful, distant God, all-knowing and omnipotent [sk].

58.   Hoornbeek, for example, firmly draws this conclusion because also Matt. 5:5 and 1 Tim. 4:8 made promises for the saints that concerned purely earthly matters (see vol. 1, *op. cit.* [ch. 4, note 22], p. 193). Everything is a product of God's providence. Yet he especially cares for His saints: "Super alios autem summa cura et modis singularissimis versatur Dei providentia circa fideles" [Above and beyond the others is to be found God's providence, offering the greatest care, and in an unusual manner, to believers] (*ibid.*, p. 192).

There then follows the explanation of how one can recognize that a fortunate occurrence derives from this special care *and not* from a *communis providentia* [common ordering of the world]. Bayly also refers to God's predestation to explain success in one's vocational work (*op. cit.* [ch. 4, note 32], p. 191). And the notion that prosperity "often" is the reward for a godly life is perpetually found in the writings of the *Quakers*. See, for example, such passages even as late as 1848 in *Selection from the Christian Advices*, issued by the yearly meeting of the Society of Friends in London, 6th ed. (London, 1851), p. 209. The connection to Quaker ethics will be returned to later.

59.   Thomas Adams's analysis of the conflict between Jacob and Esau can serve as an example of this orientation to the Old Testament patriarchs. It is equally characteristic of the Puritan view of life: "His (Esau's) folly may be argued from the base estimation of the birthright that he would so lightly pass from it and on *so easy condition* as a pottage [thick soup]."(*Works of the Puritan Divines*, p. 235; the passage is also important for the development of the idea of birthright, which will be noted later). However, that Esau then wished to call the sale invalid, on account of fraud, was perfidious. Rather, he is "a cunning hunter, a man of the fields," and a person living irrationally and without civility. Jacob, on the other hand, represents "a plain man, dwelling in tents" and the "man of grace."

The sense of an inner relationship between Puritanism and Judaism, as expressed as late as the well-known letter of Theodore Roosevelt [see Guenther Roth, "Max Weber's Views on Jewish Integration and Zionism: Some American, English, and German Contexts" (*Max Weber Studies* 3, 1 [Nov. 2002]: 56–73; see p. 61)], was discovered by Köhler to be widespread in Holland even among peasants (*op. cit.* [ch. 4, note 10]). On the other hand Puritanism, in regard to its practical dogma, was well aware of its *opposition* to Jewish ethics [see pp. 290–99]. This is clearly demonstrated in the essay by Prynne against the Jews (on the occasion of the Cromwellian proposals for tolerance). See note 127 below. [1920]

60.   Those books in the Greek and Latin versions of the Old Testament that were not originally written in Hebrew. Not considered genuine by the Jews, they were also denigrated by early Reformation theologians as uninspired by God (the Vulgate). Translations of the Bible influenced by ascetic Protestantism (the King James Version of 1611, the American Standard Version of 1901, and the Revised Standard Version of 1952) omitted these books (unlike the translation by Luther and the Bibles of Catholocism and Greek orthodox Christianity) [sk].

61.   A rural Thuringian pastor [Hermann Gebhardt] published *Zur bäuerlichen Glaubens- und Sittenlehre* [On Peasant Beliefs and Moral Teachings], 2nd ed. (Gotha: G. Schlossmann, 1895), p. 16. The peasants depicted in this volume are, in a characteristic manner, products of the *Lutheran* Church. I have repeatedly written "Lutheran" in its margins where the excellent author assumed a general "peasant" devoutness.

62.   Compare, for example, the passage cited in Ritschl, *Pietismus*, vol. 2 (*op. cit.* [ch. 4, note 19]), p. 158. Spener likewise bases his objections to a change of vocational calling and to the pursuit of profit *partly* on passages from Jesus Sirach. *Theologische Bedenken*, vol. 3 (*op. cit.* [ch. 4, note 32]), p. 426.

63.   Of course, nonetheless, Bayly, for example, recommends its reading. He does quote from the Apocrypha, at least here and there, although rarely of course. I cannot (perhaps not accidentally) recall any such quotation from Jesus Sirach.

64.   When the obviously condemned are then allotted external success, the Calvinist comforts himself (according to Hoornbeek, for example), in accordance with the "theory of hardening," with the certainty that God allows this success to come to them in order to harden them and hence to condemn them with all the more certainty.

65.   In this context we cannot examine this point in more detail. Of interest here is only the formalistic character of Puritan "legal correctness." There is a great deal in [Ernst] Troeltsch's "social teachings" on the significance of the Old Testament ethics for *lex naturae* [see Troelfsch, 1960/1911)].

66.   The obligatory character of the Bible's ethical norms is so encompassing in nature that, according to Baxter, they must be seen (1) as a "transcript" of the law of nature or (2) as actually carrying the "express character of universality and perpetuity." See *Christian Directory*, vol. 3, *op. cit.* [ch. 4, note 39], pp. 173 f.)

67.   Dowden, for example (with reference to Bunyan). [See the later edition, *op. cit.* (ch. 4, note 23), pp. 26–34.]

68.   On the economic ethic of Judaism, see pp. 290–99; and *Ancient Judaism* (1952). Weber is here opposing in particular Sombart's argument that the Jews were the driving force behind the development of modern capitalism. See p. xviii above and Sombart, 1969) [sk].

69.   More details are offered on this point in my Economic Ethics of the World Religions series [see pp. 183–84, 229–37]. The vast influence of these norms, and of the *second commandment* in particular ("thou shalt not make unto thee a graven image") on, for example, the characterological development of Judaism—its rational character foreign to all culture oriented to the senses—cannot be analyzed here. Nonetheless, perhaps as characteristic, it may be noted that one of the leaders of the "Educational Alliance" in the United States—an organization that furthers the Americanization of Jewish immigrants with amazing success and munificent resources—described the primary purpose of its cultural acquisition program (*Kulturmenschwerdung*) to me, which is pursued through all manner of artistic and social instruction, as the "emancipation from the second commandment." The tabooing of all anthropomorphic rendering of God in human form among the Israelites corresponds to Puritanism's prohibition upon all deification of human wants and desires; although somewhat different, the effect is nonetheless in a related direction.

As concerns Talmudic Judaism, even principal features of Puritan morality are certainly related. The Talmud emphasizes, for example (as noted by August Wünsche,

Babylonische Talmud [Leipzig: Schulze], 1886–89, vol. 2, p. 34), that it is better, and more rewarded by God, if one does something good because of a *duty* to God's law than if one performs a good deed *not* obligated by God's law. In other words, loveless fulfillment of duty stands ethically higher than emotion-infused philanthropy. And, in essence, Puritan ethics would accept this. Kant, as well, who descended from Scots and whose socialization was strongly influenced by Pietism, would in the end come close to these passages. (Many of his formulations tie in directly to ideas of ascetic Protestantism—but this cannot be discussed here.) Talmudic ethics were, however, also once deeply immersed in the traditionalism of the Middle East. As R. Tanchum ben Chanilai said: "A person never changes a custom" (Gemara to Mischna; vol. 7, pt. i, sect. 86b, no. 93; cited in Wünsche; the context concerns the boarding costs of day laborers). This maxim was not valid in relationships with persons outside one's own blood group. However, the Puritan conception of "legal correctness" as a means of *testifying* to sincere belief provided, when compared to the Jewish obligation simply to fulfill the commandment, visibly stronger motives for *activity*.

Of course, the idea that one's success revealed God's blessing is not totally foreign to Judaism. Yet the variation in fundamental religious-ethical meaning that success assumed in Judaism as a consequence of its ethical dualism (according to which relations with non-Jews were not bound to the same ethical standards as relations with Jews) prevented, in regard to this decisive point, a similarity of effects. What was *permitted* in regard to the "outsider" was *prohibited* in regard to one's "brother." It was impossible (for this reason alone) for success in the arena of the "not commanded" but "permitted" to become a sign that testified to *religious* belief. Hence, a motivation for the methodical formation of life in every respect, as occurred with the Puritans, could not arise. On this entire problem, which Sombart has in many ways incorrectly addressed in his *The Jews and Modern Capitalism* [1969], see [the Economic Ethics of the World Religions series]. As strange as it first sounds, Judaism's economic ethic remained very strongly traditionalistic. [1920]

Christianity implied a massive alteration of the believer's inner posture toward the world. This change occurred through the Christian version of the ideas of "grace" and "salvation." In peculiar ways, the seed for *new* possibilities of development was continuously borne within these ideas. Likewise, this theme cannot yet be explored. See also, for example, Albrecht Ritschl on Old Testament "legal correctness," *Die christliche Lehre von der Rechtfertigung und Versöhnung*, vol. 2 [Bonn: A. Marcus, 1870–74], p. 265.

The Jews, to the English Puritans, represented that type of capitalism oriented to war, government subsidy programs, state monopolies, the speculative promotion of companies, and the construction and finance projects of princes. Just these sorts of business activities were roundly condemned by the Puritans. Indeed, if we keep constantly in mind the unavoidable qualifications, the general difference can be formulated in this manner: Jewish capitalism was a speculative, *pariah*-capitalism, while Puritan capitalism involved the organization of work by a middle class. [1920] [See *Economy and Society*, pp. 615–23.]

70.   For Baxter, the *truth* of Holy Scripture follows ultimately from the "wonderful difference of the godly and ungodly," the absolute difference of the "renewed man" from others, and the evident, entirely unusual care of God for the salvation of the soul of His people (which naturally *can* be expressed in *testing*). See *Christian Directory*, vol. 1 (*op. cit.*) [ch. 4, note 39], p. 165, col. 2.

71.   What characterizes this mood of life can be seen if only we read Bunyan's account of his inner torture when reconciling himself to the parable of the Pharisee and the publican [collector of customs] (see the sermon *The Pharisee and the Publican, op. cit.* [ch. 4, note 83], pp. 100 f.). Even with Bunyan there can occasionally be found an approximation to Luther's mood in Luther's *Freiheit eines Christenmenschenc*; see, for example, Bunyan's "Of the Law and a Christian" in *Works of the Puritan Divines*, p. 254).

Why is the Pharisee condemned? He does not truly uphold God's commandments; rather, as clearly a *sectarian*, he is concerned only with ceremonies and external matters of little significance (p. 107). Most importantly, he is condemned because he attributes merit to himself but still thanks God for his virtue. He does so "as the Quakers do," by misusing God's name. In sinful ways, he relies on the value of his virtue (p. 126) and thus implicitly rejects *God's predestination* (p. 139). His prayer, therefore, involves a deification of human nature, and this constitutes its sinfulness.

On the other hand, as the sincerity of his confession demonstrates, the publican is spiritually reborn, for—as expressed in a manner that reveals the characteristic Puritan weakening of the Lutheran feeling of sin—"to a right and sincere conviction of sin there must be a conviction of the *probability* of mercy" (p. 209).

72.   Printed, for example, in S. R. Gardiner's *Constitutional Documents*. One may draw parallels between this struggle against (anti-authoritarian) asceticism to, for example, Louis XIV's persecution of the Port Royal settlement and the Jansenists [see ch. 4, note 23]. [On this controversy, see Sharpe, 1992, pp. 351–59.]

73.   In this respect the standpoint of *Calvin* was significantly milder, at least to the extent that the finer aristocratic forms of enjoying life were considered. The only limitation is the Bible. The person who stays oriented to it and maintains a good conscience is not required to be suspicious, amidst anxiety, of every stirring in himself to enjoy life. The discussions, which belong here, in chapter 10 of Calvin's *Institutio christianae religionis* (for example, "nec fugere ea quoque possumus quae videntur oblectatione; magis quam necessitat; inservire" [we cannot flee from those things that clearly serve pleasure more than necessity]), might have alone been able to open the floodgates to a very lax praxis. Nonetheless, the distinction between Calvin and Puritanism at this point becomes clear. In addition to an increasing anxiety among the Puritans in regard to the *certitudo salutis* question, it is also the case that, as we will appreciate fully elsewhere, members of the lower *middle-class* became the social carriers of the ethical development of Calvinism in the *ecclesia militans* [militant church] regions.

74.   As was common in the German scholarship of his day, Weber here (in contrast to the Anglo-Saxon division between the humanities and the natural sciences) includes in "science," in addition to the natural sciences, literature, history, and languages (the "humanities") [sk].

75.   Thomas Adams (*Works of the Puritan Divines*, p. 3) begins a sermon on the three divine sisters ("but love is the greatest of these") with the remark that even Paris gave the golden apple to Aphrodite!

76.   Novels and the like, considered as "wastetimes," should not be read (Baxter, *Christian Directory*, vol. 1, p. 51). The decline of lyric poetry and folk music, and not only drama, after the Elizabethan Age in England is well-known. Puritanism did not discover all that much to oppress in the realm of the visual arts. Striking, however, is the decline, from a very good level of musical talent (the role of England in the history of music was not insignificant), to that absolute nothingness in respect to musical giftedness that we later observe among the Anglo-Saxon peoples, and even today. In America, except for the singing in the Negro churches and for the professional singers, who the churches now hire as "attractions" (for $8,000 annually in 1904 in Trinity Church in Boston), one hears mostly "congregational singing"—a noise that is intolerable to German ears. (*Partly* analogous developments appeared also in Holland.)

77.   As the proceedings of the synods make clear, the same occurred in Holland. See the resolutions on the may pole in the Reitsma'schen Collection, vol. 6, pt. 78, ch. 139. [J. Reitsma and S. D. van Veen, *Acta der Provinciale en Particuliere Synoden, 1572–1620*, 8 vols. (Groningen: J. B. Walters, 1892–99). The may pole celebration involved a tall, fixed pole. Dancers on May Day, each holding a ribbon attached to the top of the pole, danced around the pole, weaving the ribbons.]

78.   It is apparent that the "Renaissance of the Old Testament" and the Pietist orientation to certain Christian sensibilities in art antagonistic to beauty, which in the last analysis refer back to Isaiah [verse 53] and the 22nd Psalm, must have contributed to making *ugliness* more of a possible object of art. It is also evident that, in regard to this development, the Puritan rejection of the deification of human wants and desires played a part. All details, however, appear uncertain. Entirely different motives (demagogical) in the Catholic church brought about developments that, although externally related, led artistically to an entirely different conclusion. Whoever stands in front of Rembrandt's "Saul and David" (in the Mauritshuis museum) believes he directly experiences the powerful effect of the Puritan sensibility. The inspired analysis of Dutch cultural influences in Karl Neumann's *Rembrandt* (Berlin: Spemann, 1902) probably demarcates the extent to which one *can*, as of today, know the extent to which creative effects in the realm of art can be attributed to ascetic Protestantism.

79.   In Holland, a diverse number of pivotal causes (which are impossible to delve into here) were decisive for a comparatively lesser penetration of the Calvinist ethic into everyday life and for a weakening of the ascetic spirit. This situation was visible as early as the beginning of the seventeenth century (the English Congregationalists who fled to Holland in 1608 believed the Dutch sabbath to inadequately uphold the "day of rest" decree); however, it became widely apparent under the [provincial military governor] Friedrich Heinrich [1584–1640]. This decline of the ascetic spirit weakened the expansionary thrust of Dutch Puritanism generally.

The causes for this decline must be located in part in the political constitution (a decentralized federalism of cities and states) and in part in Holland's far lesser development of military forces. (The War of Independence [against Spain, 1568–1648] was early on, for the most part, fought with *money* from Amsterdam and by mercenary soldiers; English preachers illustrated the confusion of tongues among the Babylonians by reference to the Dutch army.) The result was clear: the fervor surrounding the conflict over religious belief was, to a great degree, shifted onto others. As a consequence, however, the chance for participation in political power was flittered away. In contrast, Cromwell's army, although in part conscripted, felt itself to be an army of *citizens*. (To be sure, even more characteristic is that *precisely this* army abolished conscription—because one should fight only for the glory of God and for a cause recognized by the conscience, and not to satisfy the moods of princes. Hence, that English military referred to, according to traditional German views, as possessing an "unethical" constitution, had *historically* very ethical motives at its beginning. Their implementation was demanded by soldiers who had never lost a battle. The ethical values of these soldiers were placed into service in the interest of the Crown only after the Restoration [after 1665].)

As visible in the paintings of [Frans] Hals [1580–1666], the Dutch *schutterijen* [militia], the social carriers of Calvinism in the period of the Great War [1568–1648], appear scarcely "ascetic" as early as one-half generation after the Dordrecht Synod [1574]. Protests in the synods against the organized lives of the *schutterijen* are found repeatedly. The Dutch notion of stiff, haughty formality [*deftigheid*—Weber used a German amalgam: *Deftigkeit*] is a mixture of middle class, rational "respectability" and patrician consciousness of status. This aristocratic character of the Dutch church is evident even today in the allocation of church pews according to class.

The endurance of the city economy in Holland inhibited the development of industry, which expanded only when a new wave of refugees appeared—and therefore only sporadically. Nevertheless, the this-worldly asceticism of Calvinism and Pietism proved effective also in Holland, and in entirely the same direction as elsewhere (even in the sense of an "ascetic compulsion to save," as will be discussed immediately and as G. Groen van Prinsterer demonstrated; see the passage referred to in note 97). The almost entire absence of a belletristic literature in Calvinist Holland is naturally not accidental. [1920]

On Holland see, for example, C. Busken-Huet, *Het Land van Rembrandt*; see also von der Ropp, *Rembrandts Heimat* (Leipzig, 1886–1887).

The understanding of Dutch religious devoutness as involving an "ascetic compulsion to save" is quite apparent even in the eighteenth century; see, for example, the drawings of Albertus Haller. On the characteristic features of Dutch evaluations of art and the motives behind its production, see, for example, the autobiographical remarks of Constantine Huyghens (written 1629–31) in *Oud Holland* (1891). (The work of Groen van Prinsterer, *La Hollande et l'influence de Calvin* [1864], offers for *our* problem nothing pivotal.) The New-Netherlands colony in [New York] involved, viewed in terms of its social composition, a quasi-feudal rulership by "patrons," namely, businessmen who were money-lenders. In contrast to New England, it proved difficult to persuade those near the bottom to emigrate to this region. [1920]

80.   It should be remembered that the Puritan city officials closed the Stratford-on-Avon theater even during Shakespeare's time and even when he was, in his later years, still living in Stratford. (His hatred and contempt for the Puritans comes to the surface at every opportunity.) Even in 1777 the city of Birmingham refused to license a theater, arguing that it would promote "slothfulness" and thus adversely influence commerce. See W. J. Ashley, *Birmingham Industry and Commerce* (London, 1913), pp. 7–8. [1920]

81.   It is decisive that, for the Puritans, also in this case only an either–or alternative existed: either God's will or the vanity of the flesh. Thus, there could not be, for them, an "Adiaphora" situation [of indifference]. Calvin, as mentioned, in this regard took a different position: as long as an enslavement of the soul under the power of the desires does not take place, what one eats, wears, etc., is a matter of indifference. Freedom from the "world" should be expressed, as for the Jesuits, in indifference; that is, for Calvin, in an undiscriminating, uncovetous usage of whatever goods earthly life offered (see Calvin, *Institutio christianae religionis*, 1st ed. (*op. cit.* [ch. 4, note 19]), p. 409. This position evidently stood closer to Lutheranism than to the precisionism of Calvin's epigones.

82.   The behavior of the Quakers is well-known in this regard. Even as early as the beginning of the seventeenth century, tumultuous crowds of pious believers thronged the streets in Amsterdam for a decade in protest against the fashionable hats and apparel of a preacher's wife. (See Dexter's *op. cit.* [ch. 4, note 10], for a charming description). Sanford (*op. cit.* [ch. 4, note 5]) already noted that the male haircut of today is that of the often-mocked "Roundheads." He also observes that the similarly mocked male *apparel* of the Puritans is essentially the same as apparel today, at least in terms of the *principle* at its foundation.

83.   [This term, as well as the above three in quotation marks, are in English in the original.] See again on this point Veblen's *Theory of Business Enterprise, op. cit.* [ch. 4, note 221].

84.   We will return continuously to this vantage point. Statements such as the following are explained by reference to it: "Every penny which is paid upon yourselves and children and friends must be done as by God's own appointment and to serve and please Him. Watch narrowly, or else that thievish carnal self will leave God nothing" (Baxter, *Chr. Dir., op. cit.,* vol. 1, p. 108). This is decisive: Whatever is turned toward one's *personal* purposes is *withdrawn* from service to God's glory.

85.   One is correctly in the habit of remembering (as does Dowden, *op. cit.* [note 4]), for example, that Cromwell saved Raphael's drawings and [Andrea] Mantegna's [1431–1506] *Triumph of Caesar* from extinction while Charles II attempted to sell them. Restoration society, as is well-known, likewise remained thoroughly cool toward, or directly opposed to, England's national literature. The influence of Versailles among the aristocracy was simply everywhere dominant.

Puritanism uprooted believers from an unreflected enjoyment of everyday life. To analyze in detail the impact of this uprooting on the intellect of the highest types of Puritanism and on those persons influenced by it is a task that cannot be undertaken in the context of this sketch. Washington Irving formulates this influence in the familiar English terms: "It (he means political freedom where we would say Puritanism) evinces less play of the fancy, but more power of the imagination" (*Bracebridge Hall, op. cit.*). One needs only to think of the position of the *Scots* in England in science, literature, technical innovation, and business life in order to sense that this observation strikes the right chord, even though somewhat too narrowly formulated.

We cannot here address the significance of Puritanism for the development of technology and the empirical sciences. The relationship itself between Puritanism and science appears overtly and comprehensively even in daily life [see Robert K. Merton, "Puritanism, Pietism, and Science," in *Social Theory and Social Structure* (New York: Free Press, 1968); F. H. Tenbruck, "Max Weber and the Sociology of Science: A Case Reopened," *Zeitschrift für Soziologie* 3 (1974): 312–20; "'Science as a Vocation'—Revisited," *Standorte im Zeitstrom*, ed. by Ernst Forsthoff and Reinhard Hörstel (Frankfurt: Athenäum Verlag, 1974)]. Permitted "recreations" for the Quakers, according to Barclay, are, for example: the visiting of friends, the reading of history, carrying out of experiments in *mathematics and physics*, gardening, the discussion of business and other practical proceedings, etc. The cause of this relationship is that which has been explained earlier.

86. Excellently and beautifully already analyzed in Karl Neumann's *Rembrandt* (*op. cit.*). His analysis should be compared in general with the above remarks.

87. According to Baxter. See the passages cited above [p. 146 and note 49] and *Chr. Dir., op. cit.*, vol. 1, p. 108.

88. See, for example, the well-known description of Colonel Hutchinson (which is often quoted, for example, in Sanford, *op. cit.*, [ch. 4, note 5], p. 57) in the biography written by his widow. After a presentation of all of his chivalrous virtues and his nature inclined toward cheerfulness and an enjoyment of life, she continues: "He was wonderfully neat, cleanly and genteel in his habit, and had a very good fancy in it; but he left off very early the wearing of anything that was costly." According to the description in Baxter's funeral oration for Mary Hammer, the ideal of this cosmopolitan and well-educated Puritan woman is quite similar. However, she is thrifty in regard to time and expenditures for "pomp" and pleasure. See Baxter, *Works of the Puritan Divines* (*op. cit.* [note 6]), p. 533.

89. In addition to *many* other examples, I remember one in particular. A manufacturer, who had been unusually successful in business and had become very wealthy in his later years, suffered from a stubborn digestive disorder. His physician advised him to enjoy daily a few oysters—yet he complied only after great resistance. That here the issue involved a residual of an "ascetic" disposition (and not simply something related to "stinginess") suspicious of all personal *enjoyment* of wealth becomes apparent *in the end* when one notes that this same manufacturer had made very significant philanthropic contributions throughout his lifetime and had always shown an "open hand" to those in need.

90. The *separation* of workshop, office, and "business" in general from the private residence, of business firm and one's own name, of business capital and private wealth, and the tendency to define the "business" as a *corpus mysticum* [mystical organization] (at least in the case of corporate assets)—all of these developments go back to the Middle Ages. See my *Handelsgesellschaften im Mittelalter* [in *Gesammelte Aufsätze zur Sozial- und Wirtschaftsgeschichte* (Tübingen: Mohr, 1924/1889), pp. 312–443].

91. In his *Der moderne Kapitalismus*, 1st ed. (Leipzig: Duncker & Humblot, 1902), Sombart has cogently referred occasionally to this characteristic phenomenon. It should be noted, however, that the accumulation of wealth derives psychologically from two very different sources.

One such source extends far back into the nebulous periods of antiquity and becomes manifest in foundations, family fortunes, trusts, etc. It is just as apparent in these ways, or even in a far more pure and clear form than in the same kind of pursuit, namely, at once to die weighted down with one's own massive accumulation of material possessions and, above all, to insure the continued viability of one's "business," even when doing so violates the personal interests of the majority of the inheriting children. In *these* cases the issue involves, in addition to the wish to lead an ideal life beyond death on the basis of personal achievements that maintain the "splendor familiae," a vanity that takes, so to speak, the expanded personality of the founder as its point of reference. Hence, fundamentally egocentric goals are here apparent.

It is different when one considers the "middle class" motives with which *we* are here concerned. The maxim of asceticism—"renounce, you should renounce"—holds here and becomes turned toward capitalist activity: "earn, you should earn." And this maxim, with its irrationality, now stands before us plain and pure as a sort of categorical imperative. Only God's glory and one's own duty, not the vanity of human beings, was the motivating force for the Puritans—and *today only* the duty to one's "vocational calling" constitutes one's motivation.

Whoever derives pleasure from illustrating an idea by looking at its extreme consequences will remember, for example, that theory of certain American millionaires: their earned millions should *not* be left to the children. Doing so would only deny to them the moral task of having to work and earn for themselves. Of course *today* this idea is only "theoretical" bubble-blowing.

92.   As must be emphasized repeatedly, *this* is the final, decisive religious motive (in addition to the purely ascetic points of view on the mortification of the flesh). It comes to the forefront especially clearly with the Quakers.

93.   Baxter (see *Saints' Everlasting Rest, op. cit.* [ch. 4, note 62], p. 12) completely repudiates this position by reference to the common motive, which is also found normally among the Jesuits: the body must be able to acquire what it needs. Otherwise, one becomes its slave.

94.   This ideal, particularly in Quakerism, already clearly existed even in the first period of its development, as has been demonstrated in respect to important points by Hermann Weingarten. See his *Englische Revolutionskirchen* (*op. cit.* [ch. 4, note 10]). Barclay's detailed discussions also illustrate this point very clearly (*op. cit.* [ch. 4, note 10], pp. 519 ff., 533). To be avoided is bodily vanity thus all ostentation, and sparkling trinkets. This includes the use of things that have no *practical* purpose or that are valued only on account of their rarity (hence, for vanity's sake). Also to be avoided is all unconscientious use of possessions. This takes place when spending occurs, to a *disproportionate degree*, for less necessary needs instead of for the indispensable needs of life and the provision for the future.

The Quaker life, which was organized according to a living "law of marginal utility," so to speak, exemplified these maxims. "Moderate use of the creature" is completely permitted; *namely*, an emphasis may be placed upon the quality and solidity, etc., of the material used only as long as doing so does not lead to "vanity." On all these matters, see *Morgenblatt für gebildete Leser* (1846), no. 216 ff. (In particular, on the comfort and solidity of materials among the Quakers, see Matthias Schneckenburger, *Vorlesungen, op. cit.* [ch. 4, note 183] (1863), pp. 96 f.)

95.   Weber is here playing on the words of Goethe's Mephistopheles, who characterizes himself as "that power which always intends evil, and always creates good" (see *Faust*, Act 1, lines 1336–37) [sk].

96.   As already mentioned, the question of the determination of the religious movements' social class cannot be addressed *here* (on this theme see the EEWR essays). However, in order to see that Baxter, for example, who is referred to more than others in this investigation, does not view matters through the eyes of the "bourgeoisie" of his period, it suffices only to note his rank ordering of the vocations pleasing to God: after the teaching vocations, there follows husbandman, and only *then*, in a colorful mix, mariners,

clothiers, booksellers, tailors, etc. Even the (characteristically enough) "mariners" are probably at least just as likely thought of as fishermen as ship owners.

In this regard, many statements in the *Talmud* express a different notion. For example, see the, admittedly, not unchallenged sayings of Rabbi Eleasor. All imply that business is better than agriculture. See A. Wünsche, *Der babylonische Talmud*, vol. 2, *op. cit.* [note 67], pp. 20–21. Several later sayings are milder. Here he offers advice for the investing of capital: one-third in land, one-third in merchandise, and one-third in cash (see Wünsche, vol. 2, p. 68).

For those whose conscience remains troubled whenever an economic (or "materialistic" as one, unfortunately, says even today) interpretation is omitted from discussions on causality, let it be noted here that I find the influence of economic development on the destiny of the formation of religious ideas very significant. I will later seek to demonstrate how, in our cases, mutually interacting adaptive processes and relationships produced both economic development on the one hand and religious ideas on the other. [See the Economic Ethics of the World Religions series.] Nonetheless, by no means can the content of religious ideas be *deduced* from "economic" forces. These ideas are, and nothing can change this, actually, *for their part*, the most powerful elements shaping "national character"; they carry purely within themselves an autonomous momentum, lawful capacity (*Eigengesetzlichkeit*), and coercive power. Moreover, the *most important* differences—those between Lutheranism and Calvinism—are predominantly, to the extent that non-religious forces play a part, conditioned by *political* forces.

97. Eduard Bernstein is thinking of this compulsive saving when he says: "Asceticism is a middle-class virtue" (*op. cit.* [ch. 4, note 10], p. 681; see also p. 625). His discussions *are the first* to have suggested these important connections. However, the association is a far more comprehensive one than he suspects. Decisive was not merely capital accumulation; rather, central was the ascetic rationalization of the entire vocational life.

In the case of the American colonies, the contrast between the American North and South was emphasized as early as John Doyle (*The English in America, op. cit.* [ch. 4, note 10]. As a consequence of the "ascetic compulsion to save," capital continuously existed in the Puritan north that needed to be invested. Conditions were quite different in the South. [1920]

98. See Doyle (*ibid.*, vol. 2, ch. 1). The existence of iron works companies (1643) and weaving (1659) for the market (and, by the way, the great prospering of handicrafts) in [northern] New England in the first generation after the founding of the colonies are anachronisms if examined from an economic point of view. These developments stand in striking contrast both to conditions in the South and in Rhode Island. In this non-Calvinist state, which enjoyed full freedom of conscience and despite an excellent harbor, a shortage of merchants existed. According to a 1686 report by the "governor and council": "The great obstruction concerning trade is the want of merchants and men of considerable estates amongst us" (S. G. Arnold, *History of the State of Rhode Island*, [Newport, RI: John P. Sanborn & Co., 1876], p. 490.) It can scarcely be doubted that the compulsion repeatedly to invest savings, which resulted from the Puritanical limitation placed upon consumption, played a role here. Church discipline was also important. The role of this factor cannot yet be discussed.

99. The discussion by Busken-Huët indicates that these circles, however, quickly declined in numbers (*op. cit.* [note 77], vol. 2, chs. 3, 4).

Nevertheless, Groen van Prinsterer notes: "De Nederlanders verkoopen veel en verbruiken wenig" [The Dutch sell much and use little], even in the period *after* the Peace of Westphalia [1648]. See his *Handboek der Geschiedenis* [History] *van het Vaderland*, 3rd ed. (p. 254n.). [1920]

100. The petition, for example, of a Royalist aristocrat presented after the entry of Charles II into London [1660] advocated a legal prohibition upon the acquisition of

landed estates using business capital. The aim was to force the owners of this capital to invest it in trade (quoted in Leopold von Ranke, *Englische Geschichte,* vol. 4 [Leipzig: Duncker & Humblot, 1861], p. 197).

The stratum of Dutch "regents" [governors] separated itself as a "status group" from the wealthy, old-family patrician merchants in the cities *through* the purchase of old feudal manors. (In 1652 many complaints were heard that the regents had become landlords and were no longer merchants; cited by Robert Fruin, *Tien jaren uit den tachtigjarigen oorlog* [Ten Years after the Eighty Years' War].) Admittedly, these circles were never spiritually sincerely Calvinist. And the notorious pursuit of titles and entry into the nobility across broad circles of the Dutch middle class in the second half of the seventeenth century itself indicates that for *this* epoch, at any rate, such a contrast [as indicated in the text] between English and Dutch conditions can be accepted only with caution. In this case the superior power of inherited wealth broke the ascetic spirit.

101. The great epoch of English agricultural prosperity [in the eighteenth century] followed upon the period of widespread purchase of English landed estates by middle-class persons with business capital.

102. Even into [the twentieth] century Anglican landlords have not infrequently refused to rent land to the Nonconformists. (At present, both religious parties are of approximately equal numerical strength, whereas earlier the Nonconformists were perpetually in the minority.) [1920]

103. Hermann Levy correctly observes that the "character disposition" of the English, which can be compiled from their numerous features, is one *less* disposed than that of other peoples to adopt an ascetic ethos and middle-class, business-oriented virtues (see "Studien über das englische Volk," in *Archiv für Sozialwissenschaft und Sozialpolitik* 46 [1918–19]: 636–90). A basic feature of the English was (and is) a robust and raw enjoyment of life. The power of Puritan asceticism in the era of its dominance is demonstrated overtly in the amazing extent to which this character trait was *tempered* among Puritanism's adherents. [1920]

104. This polarity appears time and again in the exposition by John Doyle [*op. cit.*, ch. 4, note 10]. In the positions taken by the Puritans, religious motivations were continuously a decisive influence (of course not always *exclusively* decisive). The New England colony (under the leadership of [Governor John] Winthrop) was inclined to permit the settlement of [English] Gentlemen in Massachusetts, and even an upper house in which nobles would pass on their seats to their descendants, *if only* the Gentlemen would agree to join the *church*. On account of *church* discipline it was decided to retain a *closed* settlement. (Anglican merchants of great wealth, who created large stock-raising plantations, colonized New Hampshire and Maine; only a much smaller social connection to Puritanism existed in these colonies.) Complaints about the strong "greed for profit" of the New Englanders were heard as early as 1632; see, for example, W. Weeden, *Economic and Social History of New England, 1620–1789*, vol. 1 [Boston: Houghton Mifflin, 1890], p. 125. [1920]

105. The literal translation of Weber's term here, *Wirtschaftsmenschen*—"persons oriented to economic activity"—better conveys his thought. He is seeing, with modernity, an "elevation" of economic activity in people's lives to a position of heretofore unknown salience [sk].

106. This point is emphasized by Sir William Petty. See *Political Arithmetick, op. cit.* [ch. 1, note 13], vol. 1, p. 262. Without exception, all contemporary sources speak especially of the Puritan *sectarians*; the Baptists, Quakers, and Mennonites are noted as belonging partly to a group without means and partly to a stratum of *small*-scale capitalists (*kleinkapitalistische Schicht*). They are then portrayed as standing in opposition to both the aristocracy of large-scale merchants and financiers engaged in adventurous and speculative enterprises. That which was *characteristic* of Western capitalism—a middle-class, private-ownership organization of industrial work—originated, however, out of just this stratum of *small*-scale capitalists and *not* out of the hands of the great financial mag-

nates: monopolists, government contractors, those who financed the state, colonial entrepreneurs, promoters, and the like (see G. Unwin, *Industrial Organization in the Sixteenth and Seventeenth Centuries* [Oxford: Clarendon Press, 1904], pp. 196 ff.). This opposition was familiar already to contemporaries themselves; see [William] Parker's *Discourse Concerning Puritans* [London: Robert Bostock, 1641]. Here, similarly, the contrast between those engaged in projects and those engaged in court society is also stressed. [1920]

107. On the way in which this became expressed in Pennsylvania's politics in the eighteenth century, and especially in the American Revolution, see I. Sharpless, *A Quaker Experiment in Government* [Philadelphia: Ferris, 1902].

108. Quoted in Robert Southey, *Life of Wesley* , 2nd ed., vol. 2 [New York: Harper & Brothers, 1847], ch. 29. I received this reference, which I did not know, in a letter from Professor W. J. Ashley (1913). Ernst Troeltsch (to whom I communicated it for the purpose) has already occasionally cited it [see Troeltsch, 1960)]. [1920]

109. This passage should be recommended to be read by all those today who wish to be better informed and more intelligent in regard to these matters than the leaders and contemporaries of this religious movement *themselves*. As one can see, these leaders knew very precisely what they were doing and what presented a risk to their activities. It is really not acceptable, as some of my critics unfortunately have done, to call into question so lightly matters that have been entirely uncontested and have remained until now unchallenged by anyone. I simply investigated these matters in the end more in terms of their internal driving forces than have others. Not a single person in the seventeenth century doubted these interrelationships. See further Thomas Manley, *Usury of 6% Examined* [London: Thomas Ratcliffe, 1669], p. 137. They have been treated as obvious by, in addition to the modern writers earlier cited, poets such as Heinrich Heine and John Keats, representatives of science such as Macaulay, Cunningham, and Rogers, or writers such as Matthew Arnold. From the most recent literature, see W. J. Ashley, *Birmingham Industry and Commerce, op. cit.* [note 80]. Ashley has just now expressed to me his complete agreement, also by letter. On this entire problem see the essay by Hermann Levy (*op. cit.* [note 103]). [1920]

110. Exactly the same connections were obvious even to the Puritans of the classical period. Perhaps this cannot be more clearly demonstrated than by reference to Bunyan. His Mr. Money-Love argues: "By becoming religious he may mend his market. . . . To become religious is a virtue, by what means soever a man becomes so. . . . Nor is it unlawful to get a rich wife or more custom[ers] to my shop . . . or a good gain . . . to become religious to get all these is a good and profitable design" (*Pilgrim's Progress* [Middlesex, UK: Penguin, 1965], pp. 141–42). [1920]

111. [The author of *Robinson Crusoe*, Daniel] Defoe was a zealous Nonconformist opponent of Puritanism.

112. This phrase appears in English in the original [sk].

113. According to this adage, the good conscience, like a soft pillow, is soothing and allows deep sleep [sk].

114. Weber is here referring to the legalistic and ritualistic posture of the Pharisees, as criticizes by Jesus. He seems to imply that this "startling clear conscience" bequeathed by the seventeenth centeury, although just as inflexible as the strict ritualism of the Pharisees, will become weakend and even corrupted. See the following pages and the previous passage on Wesley [sk].

115. Although Spener also considers the businessman's vocation to be one of temptations and pitfalls, he nonetheless, in response to a query, explains:

> It is pleasing to me that my dear friend does not hesitate to become engaged in business and instead recognizes this commercial activity as a legitimate way of life, as it is. A great deal is offered by business that is useful to the human species; hence, *love*

is exercised through such activity and this accords with God's will. (See *Theologische Bedenken, op. cit.* [ch. 4, note 32], pp. 426, 429, 432 ff.)

This idea is more fully defended by arguments in favor of mercantilism in various other passages. Spener occasionally, in a fully Lutheran manner, depicts the lust to become rich as the main pitfall and as to be unconditionally rejected (in keeping with 1 Tim. 6:8–9 and by reference to Jesus Sirach [see note 60]; see above!); he then upholds the [Lutheran] "basic sustenance" position (*ibid.,* vol. 3, p. 435). However, he then reverses himself by referring to the sectarians—who are prosperous and at the same time live with God's blessing (see note 46 above). Moreover, as an *effect* of industrious work in a vocation, wealth is to him without suspicion. As a consequence of Lutheran influences on his thinking, his position is less consistent than Baxter's.

116. Baxter warns against the hiring of "heavy, flegmatik, sluggish, fleshly, slothful persons" as "servants" and recommends that preference be given to "godly" servants. He does so not only because "ungodly" servants would be merely "eye-servants," but above all because "a truly godly servant will do all your service in obedience *to God, as if God Himself had bid him do it.*" In contrast, ungodly servants are inclined "to make no great *matter of conscience* of it." Moreover, it is not the external allegiance to a religion that constitutes a sign of holiness among workers, but the "conscience to do their duty" (*Chr. Dir.,* vol. 2, p. 16). One sees that the interests of God and the interests of employers here suspiciously interweave one with another. Even Spener, who otherwise urgently warns the faithful to allow *time* for meditation on God, assumes as self-evident that workers must be satisfied with a bare minimum of free time (even on Sundays) (*Theologische Bedenken,* vol. 3, *op. cit.* [ch. 4, note 32], p. 272).

English writers have correctly called the Protestant immigrants the "pioneers of skilled labor." See also the convincing demonstration of this in a discussion by H. Levy, *Die Grundlagen des ökonomischen Liberalismus in der Geschichte der englischen Volkswirtschaft, op. cit.* [ch. 3, note 17], p. 53. [1920]

117. The analogy between the "unjust," according to human standards, predestination of only a few and the similarly unjust distribution of goods (ordained by God as much as is the predestination of the few)—this is an infinitely tight connection. It is noted, for example, in Hoornbeek, vol. 1, *op. cit.* [ch. 4, note 22], p. 153. Furthermore, according to Baxter, poverty is very often a symptom of sinful laziness (*Chr. Dir, op. cit.* [ch. 4, note 39], vol. 1, p. 380).

118. According to Thomas Adams, God presumably allows so many to remain poor because He knows that many will not be able to withstand the temptations that come from wealth—for riches all too frequently drive religion out of persons (*Works of the Puritan Divines*, p. 158).

119. See above note 52 and H. Levy, *English Liberalism, op. cit.*[note 52]; all descriptions emphasize this same point; see for example Manley on the Huguenots, *op. cit.* [note 109]).

120. Similar developments were not missing in England. Belonging together with them are, for example, also that Pietism which, tied to W. Law's *Serious Call* (1728), preached *poverty*, chastity, and, originally, even isolation from the world.

121. Baxter's great success in his Kidderminster community, which had declined into absolute rack and ruin by the time of his arrival, is almost without precedent in the history of pastoral care. His accomplishments can serve as a typical example of *how* asceticism socialized the masses to work, or in Marxist terms, to produce "surplus value." In doing so, asceticism *first made possible* the utilization of the masses in the capitalist workplace (such as in cottage industries, textile factories, etc.). The causal relationship lies largely in this direction.

Viewed from Baxter's perspective, he understood the adaptation of his flock to the machinery of capitalism as occurring in the service of his religious-ethical interests. Viewed from the perspective of the development of capitalism, his religious-ethical interests entered into the service of the development of the capitalist spirit.

122. And one more point: a notion that one so often works with today may well be questioned, namely, the assumption that the medieval craftsman's "enjoyment" of "that which he produced himself" was quite strong. One must ask to what extent this enjoyment played a substantial role as a psychological motivating force. Undoubtedly, something important is touched upon here. At any rate, [with the arrival of Puritanism] asceticism *stripped away* from work all this-worldly appeal—which today has been destroyed by capitalism for eternity—and oriented work toward the next world. Work in a vocational calling *as such* was desired by God. In other words, the impersonal character of work today, which offers little enjoyment and is meaningless when considered from the point of view of each person, was at that time, because desired by God, still transfigured and glorified by religion. In the period of its origin capitalism required workers who stood available, for the sake of the *conscience*, to be economically exploited. Capitalism today sits in the saddle and is capable, without any other-worldly reward, of coercing a willingness to work. [The last sentence was added in 1920.]

123. Weber here implies that the greater quantitative productivity of work under capitalism should not be viewed as an unequivocal blessing. Viewed from particular vantage points, it may have unintended, negative consequences. In this respect, see the next paragraphs.] [sk].

124. See *Political Arithmetick, op. cit.* [ch. 1, note 13]. [The last two sentences were added in 1920 [sk].

125. Laud was a central figure in the seventeenth-century Anglican Church. He used his power effectively to suppress the Puritans [sk].

126. On these oppositions and developments, see H. Levy, *op. cit.* [note 52]. The very powerful posture opposed to monopolies, which is characteristic for public opinion in England, originated historically in the seventeenth century from a linking of *political* power struggles against the Crown (the Long Parliament [1640–53] excluded the monopolists as Members) with the ethical motives of Puritanism and the economic interests of small- and middle-scale capitalists against the financial magnates. The declaration of the Army on August 2, 1652 and, similarly, the petition of the Levellers on January 28, 1653 demanded, in addition to the removal of excise, customs, and indirect taxes, the introduction of a single tax on all estates and, above all, "free trade." This latter demand involved the removal of all monopolistic barriers to trade, both internally and externally, for such obstacles were viewed as violating human rights. The "Great Remonstrance" [presented as a statement of grievances by the House of Commons to the Crown in 1641] placed similar demands. [1920]

127. A controversial Puritan, Prynne's writings, especially on the theater, brought him into conflict with the Anglican Church and the English monarchy. He attacked the *Book of Sports*. Nevertheless, he later defended the monarchy, criticized Cromwell, and advocated a subjection of the clergy to the Crown. A moderate reformer, Parker became an archbishop in the Anglican Church and the subject of considerable criticism by the Puritans [sk].

128. See Levy, *op. cit.* [note 52] [1920]

129. That even the components here (which have not yet been traced back to their religious roots)—namely, the maxim honesty is the best policy (Franklin's discussion of *credit*)—are also of Puritan origins is a theme that belongs in a somewhat different context (see the "Protestant Sects" essay below). Only the following observation of J. S. Rowntree (*Quakerism, Past and Present* [London: Smith, Elder and Co., 1859], pp. 95–96), to which Eduard Bernstein called my attention, needs to be repeated:

> Is it merely a *coincidence*, or is it a *consequence*, that the lofty profession of spirituality made by the Friends has gone hand in hand with shrewdness

and tact in the transaction of mundane affairs? Real piety favours the success of a trader by insuring his integrity and fostering habits of prudence and forethought. [These are] important items in obtaining that standing and credit in the commercial world, which are requisite for the steady accumulation of wealth (see the "Protestant Sects" essay).

"Honest as a Huguenot" was as proverbial in the seventeenth century as the respect for law of the Dutch (which Sir W. Temple admired) and, a century later, that of the English. The peoples of the European continent, in contrast, had not moved through this ethical schooling. [1920]

130. This theme is analyzed well in Albert Bielschowsky's *Goethe: sein Leben und seine Werke*, 3rd ed., vol. 2 (Munich: C. H. Beck, 1902–04), ch. 18. A related idea is articulated in regard to the development of the *scientific* "cosmos" by [Wilhelm] Windelband at the end of his *Blütezeit der deutschen Philosophie* (vol. 2 of his *Geschichte der neueren Philosophie* [Leipzig: Breitkopf und Hartel, 1899], pp. 428 ff.).

131. See Weber, "The Meaning of 'Ethical Neutrality'," p. 18 (Weber 1949).

132. *Saints' Everlasting Rest, op. cit.* [ch. 4, note 62], p. 310. [The text varies slightly from Weber's quote. It reads: "Keep these things loose about thee like thy upper garments, that thou mayest lay them by whenever there is need."]

133. Translated by Parsons as "iron cage," this phrase has acquired near-mythical status in sociology. Weber elaborates upon its meaning in several passages in his "Parliament and Government in Germany" essay, which was taken by the editors of *Economy and Society* from the corpus of his political writings and incorporated into this analytic treatise (see pp. 1400-03), and in "Prospects for Liberal Democracy in Tsarist Russia" (see *Weber: Selections in Translation*, ed. by W. G. Runciman [Cambridge, UK: Cambridge University Press, 1978], pp. 281–83). Parallel German expressions are translated in these passages as "housing," "shell of bondage," and "casing."

There are many reasons that speak in favor of "steel-hard casing." Not least, it is a literal rendering of the German. Had Weber wished to convey an "iron cage" to his German readership he could easily have done so by employing a commonly used phrase, *eisener Käfig* (or even *eisenes Gefängnis* [iron prison]; see Stephen Kent, "Weber, Goethe, and the Nietzschean Allusion," *Sociological Analysis* 44 (1983): pp. 297–320 (esp. at pp. 299–300). Let us turn first to the adjective.

Weber's choice of *stahlhart* appropriately conveys (even more than *eisen*) the "hardness" of the constraining casing, as emphasized in the mechanistic images utilized in this passage to describe this new "powerful cosmos." This same image of hardness, however, is visible also in the "lightweight coat" metaphor above: once supple, it has now hardened itself into something (the power of material goods over the individual) that encases persons and cannot be thrown off. Appropriately, because ascetic Protestantism constitutes to Weber a direct precursor to this cosmos, the same adjective is used to describe the Puritan merchant (see p. 111). This lineage is apparent, he argues, even though the dimension foremost for this "merchant saint"—the ethical—has today vanished and left, unforeseeably, in its wake instrumental (or "mechanical") modes of action devoid of genuine brotherhood and resistant to ethical regulation (see, again, the images above and below; see also pp. 426–30). Finally, although not directly apparent in this passage, "steel-hard" conveys a related theme crucial to Weber (as well as Marx and Simmel): the massively impersonal, coldly formal, harsh, and machine-like character of modern public sphere relationships whenever they remain uninfluenced by either traditions or values (see, e.g., the last page of "Science as a Vocation" [Weber, 2005, p. 339].

Now let us turn to the noun. There are substantive reasons also to prefer "casing" over "cage." Almost without exception, the secondary literature has argued that *stahlhartes Gehäuse* is a phrase intended to call attention to a bleak future inevitably on the horizon. Once in place, this commentary asserts, according to Weber, a nightmare society is putatively permanent. He is then characterized as a dour prophet of doom who, heroically, performs the worthy service of analyzing in a realistic manner a civilization on its death-bed. However, through conditional terms such as "if," "perhaps," "might," "would," "potentially," and "possibly," the usages of this and similar expressions in Weber's other works (as noted above) stress that such a cosmos arises from a series of identifiable eco-nomic, religious, political, historical, etc., forces that have become juxtaposed in a unique manner rather than from an unstoppable unfolding of "bureaucratization and rational-ization." In other words, if a *stahlhartes Gehäuse* does appear, it must be seen, Weber in-sists, as a contingent occurrence with, as other occurrences, a period of development and a period of decline.

In my view, this interpretation conforms to the overall tenor of Weber's sociology—a body of work that attends on the one hand to configurations of forces and their contexts rather than to linear historical change and, on the other hand, sees change, conflict, dyna-mism, and upheaval nearly universally (see 1968 and Kalberg, 1994b, pp. 71–78, 98–117, 168–77, 189–92). Of course, Weber notes that a few civilizations have been quite ossified, such as China for 1500 years and ancient Egypt. Yet their closed character did not result from an "inevitable development" or "evolutionary historical laws" (see above, pp. 87–88, 96–97). Rather, their rigidity must be understood as a consequence of an identifi-able constellation of historical, political, etc., forces. (See also the paragraph below on "new prophets . . . ideas and ideals.") "Cage" implies great inflexibility and hence does not convey this contingency aspect as effectively as "casing" (which, under certain cir-cumstances, can become less restrictive and even peeled off).

In general, in regard to *stahlhartes Gehäuse*, the commentary has vastly exaggerated the importance of this metaphorical image in Weber's works, in the process transforming him from a rigorous comparative-historical sociologist into a social philosopher of mo-dernity (see Lawrence A. Scaff, *Fleeing the Iron Cage* [Berkeley: The University of Califor-nia Press, 1989]). Notably, *stahlhartes Gehäuse*, and its equivalents, appear in Weber's works either at the end of an empirical study, where he cannot resist the temptation to of-fer more general speculations (this volume and this volume only), or in his political writ-ings ("Prospects" and "Parliament and Government"), but only once in the body of his sociology; see above (p. 73). Not a single entry can be found in the detailed index to *E&S*, for example, nor in the comprehensive index to the German edition. On the "steel-hard cage" theme generally, see Kalberg, "The Modern World as a Monolithic Iron Cage? Uti-lizing Max Weber to Define the Internal Dynamics of the American Political Culture To-day," in *Max Weber Studies* 1, 2 (2001): 178–97 [sk].

134. "Couldn't the old man be satisfied with his $75,000 a year and retire? No! The frontage of the store must be widened to 400 feet. Why? That beats everything, he says. Evenings, when his wife and daughter read together, he longs for bed. Sundays, in order to know when the day will be over, he checks his watch every five minutes. What a miser-able existence!" In this manner the son-in-law (who had emigrated from Germany) of this prosperous dry-goods-man from a city on the Ohio River offered his judgment. Such a judgment would surely appear to the "old man" as completely incomprehensible. It could be easily dismissed as a symptom of the lack of energy of the Germans.

135. This phrase (*letzte Menschen*) is from Friedrich Nietzsche. It could as well be translated as "last people." It is normally rendered as "last men." See *Ecce Homo* (New York: Vintage Books; transl. by Walter Kaufmann, 1967), p. 330; see also *Thus Spoke Zarathustra* (New York: Penguin; transl. by R. J. Hollingdale, 1961), pp. 275–79, 296–311. The "last humans," to Nietzsche, are repulsive figures without emotion. Through their "little pleasures" they render everything small—yet they claim to have "invented happi-ness." Weber uses this phrase also in "Science as a Vocation." See *Weber*, 2005, p. 325 [sk].

136. Despite thorough investigations by several generations of Weber scholars, the source of this quotation has remained unidentified. Although it appears not to be di-rectly from Nietzsche, as often believed, it is clearly formulated from the tenor of *Thus Spoke Zarathustra*. In full accord with the common usage in academic circles in his time,

Weber is using the term *Geist* here to denote a thinker's "multidimensional" capacity to unify and integrate diverse ideas and concepts. This vital capacity was lamented as lacking among specialists (*Fachmenschen*). This passage links back to the above paragraph on Goethe [sk].

137. This term is a synonym for "ascetic Protestantism" and "spirit of asceticism" [sk].

138. This remark (which remains here unchanged) might have indicated to Brentano [*Die Anfänge des modernen Kapitalismus, op. cit.* (ch. 1, note 15)] that I never doubted the *independent* significance of humanistic rationalism. That even Humanism was not *pure* "rationalism" has been strongly emphasized recently again. See Karl Borinski, "Die Wiedergeburtsidee in den neueren Zeiten," in *Abhandlungen der Münchener Akademie der Wissenschaft* (1919). [1920] [Humanistic rationalism, which Weber is here contrasting to his subject, ascetic rationalism, refers to Humanism generally as it arose out of the Renaissance.]

139. This phrase (*geistige Kulturgüter*) refers to the entire spectrum of "products of the mind," ranging from mathematical ideas and philosophical theories to interpretations of art and history. In Weber's time, they were more frequently referred to as "cultural ideas" (*Kulturideen*) or, simply, "ideas" (*Ideen*) [sk].

140. Namely, the relationship between religious belief and economic activity [sk].

141. The university lecture by Georg von Below, *Die Ursachen der Reformation* [Munich: Oldenbourg, 1917], is not concerned with this problem, but with the Reformation in general, especially with Luther. For the theme addressed *here*, and in particular the controversies that have tied into this study, the book from Heinrich Hermelink should be noted finally. See *Reformation und Gegenreformation* (Tübingen: Mohr, 1911). Nonetheless this investigation primarily addresses other problems. [1920]

142. The sketch above has intentionally taken up only the relationships in which an influence of religious ideas on "material" life is actually beyond doubt. It would have been a simple matter to move beyond this theme to a conventional "construction," according to which *all* that is "characteristic" of modern civilization is logically *deduced* out of Protestant rationalism. However, this sort of construction is better left to that type of dilettante who believes in the "unity" (*Einheitlichkeit*) of the "social psyche" and its reducibility to *one* formula. It should only further be noted that naturally the period of capitalist development *before* the development we have considered was *comprehensively co*-determined by Christian influences, both inhibiting and promoting. What type of influences these were belongs in a later chapter.

Whether, by the way, of those further problems outlined above, one or another can be discussed in the pages of *this* journal remains, in light of its particular tasks, uncertain. [Weber was an editor of *Archiv für* Sozialwissenschaft und Sozialpolitik where *PE* was originally published.] I for one am not at all inclined to write large treatises that rest upon, as would occur if these "further problems" were to be pursued, unfamiliar (theological and historical) investigations. (I am allowing [1920] these sentences to stand unchanged [despite Weber's authorship over a decade-long period of a three-volume treatise, *E&S* and the three-volume EEWR series].)

On the *tension* between life-ideals and reality in the "early capitalist" period before the Reformation, see now Jakob Strieder, *Studien zur Geschichte kapitalistischer Organisationformen*, vol. 2 (Munich: Duncker & Humblot, 1914). (This study stands against the earlier cited work of Franz Keller, which Sombart used [see ch. 1, note 24; ch. 2, note 31].) [1920]

143. I would have believed that this sentence and the directly preceding observations [in the text] and endnotes might well have sufficed to exclude every misunderstanding regarding what this investigation *wanted* to achieve—and I find *no occasion for any sort of supplement*. Instead of pursuing the originally intended, direct continuation of this study, in the sense of the *agenda* outlined above, I have decided to follow a different

course. This conclusion was arrived at in part owing to accident (especially the publication of Ernst Troeltsch's *The Social Teachings of the Christian Churches*, which comes to conclusions on subjects I would have taken up; yet, as a non-theologian, I could not have addressed them adequately), and in part as a consequence of a decision to strip this study on the Protestant ethic of its isolation and to place it in relation to the entirety of civilizational development. In order to do so I decided at the time to write down first of all the results of several comparative studies on the *universal*-historical relationships between religion and society. [See The EEWR series and pp. 182–84.]

There follows now only a short, informal essay (*Gelegenheitsaufsatz*) that seeks to clarify the concept of "sect," as it was used above. This essay [pp. 127–48] simultaneously attempts to offer an explanation for the significance of the Puritan conception of *churches* for the capitalist spirit of the modern period. [from 1920]

LITERATURE CITED

A. WRITINGS OF MAX WEBER[*]

Weber, Max. 1927 (1923). *General Economic History*. Translated by Frank H. Knight. Glencoe, Il.: Free Press.

——. 1930 (1920). *The Protestant Ethic and the Spirit of Capitalism*. Translated by Talcott Parsons. New York: Scribner's.

——. 1936. *Jugendbriefe*. Edited by Marianne Weber. Tübingen: Mohr

——. 1946a. "Capitalism and Rural Society in Germany." Pp. 363–85 in *From Max Weber: Essays in Sociology (FMW)*, edited and translated by H. H. Gerth and C. Wright Mills. New York: Oxford.

——. 1946b (1919). "Politics as a Vocation." Pp. 77–128 in *FMW*.

——. 1946c (1920). "Religious Rejections of the World." Pp. 323–59 in *FMW*.

——. 1946d (1920). "Science as a Vocation." Pp. 129–56 in *FMW*.

——. 1946e (1920). "The Social Psychology of the World Religions." Pp. 267–301 in *FMW*.

——. 1949 (1922). *The Methodology of the Social Sciences*. Edited and translated by Edward A. Shils and Henry A. Finch. New York: Free Press.

——. 1951 (1920). *The Religion of China*. Edited and translated by Hans H. Gerth. New York: The Free Press.

——. 1952 (1920). *Ancient Judaism*. Edited and translated by Hans H. Gerth and Don Martindale. New York: Free Press.

——. 1958 (1920). *The Religion of India*. Edited and translated by Hans H. Gerth and Don Martindale. New York: The Free Press.

——. 1968 (1921). *Economy and Society*. Edited by Guenther Roth and Claus Wittich. New York: Bedminster Press. [Reprinted 1978; The University of California Press.]

——. 1971a (1910). "Max Weber on Race and Society." Introduction by Benjamin Nelson and translated by Jerome Gittleman. *Social Research*, 38, 1 (Spring): 30–41.

——. 1971b (1924). "Socialism." Pp. 101–219 in *Max Weber*, edited by J. E. T. Eldridge. London: Nelson and Sons.

——. 1973 (1910). "Max Weber, Dr. Alfred Ploetz, and W. E. B. DuBois." Edited and translated by Benjamin Nelson and Jerome Gittleman. *Sociological Analysis*, 34, 4: 308-12.

——. 1976 (1909). *The Agrarian Sociology of Ancient Civilizations*. Translated by R. I. Frank. London: New Left Books.

——. 1978a. "Freudianism." Pp. 383–88 in *Weber: Selections in Translation*, edited by W. G. Runciman. Cambridge: Cambridge University Press.

——. 1978b. (1906). "The Prospects for Liberal Democracy in Tsarist Russia." Pp. 269–84 in *Weber: Selections in Translation*, edited by W. G. Runciman. Cambridge: Cambridge University Press.

——. 1988 (1924). "Diskussionsrede zu W. Sombarts Vortrag über Technik und Kultur. Erste Soziologentagung Frankfurt 1910." Pp. 449–56 in *Gesammelte Aufsätze zur*

---

[*]   Original source material can be found at p. 58.

Soziologie und Sozialpolitik, edited by Marianne Weber. Tübingen: J.C.B. Mohr (Paul Siebeck).

——. 1993 (1904—05/1920). *Die protestantische Ethik und der "Geist" des Kapitalismus*. Edited by Klaus Lichtblau and Johannes Weiß. Bodenheim: Athenäum-Hain-Hanstein.

——. 2001 (1907-10). *The Protestant Ethic Debate: Max Weber's Replies to his Critics, 1907–1910*. Edited by David Chalcraft and Austin Harrington and translated by Harrington and Mary Shields. Liverpool: Liverpool University Press.

——. 2002a (1904–1905 and 1907–10). *The Protestant Ethic and the "Spirit" of Capitalism and Other Writings*. Edited, translated, and with an introduction by Peter Baehr and Gordon C. Wells. London: Penguin Books.

——. 2002b (1920). "The Protestant Sects and the Spirit of Capitalism." Translated by H. H. Gerth and C. Wright Mills. Pp. 127–47 in Weber, *The Protestant Ethic and the Spirit of Capitalism*. Translated by Stephen Kalberg. Los Angeles: Roxbury Publ.

——. 2005. *Max Weber: Readings and Commentary on Modernity*. Edited by Stephen Kalberg. Oxford, UK: Blackwell Publishers.

B. SECONDARY LITERATURE CITED[*]

Aptheker, Herbert, ed. 1973. *The Correspondence of W. E. B. Du Bois* (vol. 1, 1877–1934). Amherst, MA: The University of Massachusetts Press.

Becker, George. 1997. "Replication and Reanalysis of Offenbacher's School Enrollment Study: Implications for the Weber and Merton Theses." *Journal for the Scientific Study of Religion*, 36, 4: 483–96.

Collins, Randall. 1980. "Weber's Last Theory of Capitalism." *American Sociological Review*, 45, 6: 925–42.

Groot, Johann Jakob Maria de. 1910. *Religion in China*. New York: Putnam's Sons.

Kaelber, Lutz. 2005. "Rational Capitalism, Traditionalism, and Adventure Capitalism: New Research on the Weber Thesis." Pp. 139–64 in *The Protestant Ethic Turns 100*, edited by William H. Swatos and Kaelber. Boulder, CO: Paradigm Publishers.

Kalberg, Stephen. 1990. "The Rationalization of Action in Max Weber's Sociology of Religion." *Sociological Theory*, 8 (Spring): 58–84.

——. 2001a. "Should the 'Dynamic Autonomy' of Ideas Matter to Sociologists? Max Weber on the Origin of Other-Worldly Salvation Religions and the Constitution of Groups in American Society Today." *Journal of Classical Sociology*, 1, 3 (Dec.): 291–327.

——. 2001b. "The Modern World as a Monolithic Iron Cage?" *Max Weber Studies*, 1 (May): 178–95.

——. 2001c. "The 'Spirit' of Capitalism Revisited: On the New Translation of Weber's *Protestant Ethic* (1920)." *Max Weber Studies*, 2, 1 (Dec.): 41–57.

——. 2003a. "Max Weber." Pp. 132-92 in *The Blackwell Companion to Major Social Theorists*, edited by George Ritzer. Oxford: Blackwell Publishers, 2003.

——. 2003b. "The Influence of Political Culture Upon Cross-Cultural Misperceptions and Foreign Policy: The United States and Germany." *German Politics and Society*, 21, 3 (Fall): 1–23.

——. 2004. "The Past and Present Influence of World Views: Max Weber on a Neglected Sociological Concept." *Journal of Classical Sociology*, 4, 2 (July): 139–64.

---

[*] This list supplements the lists above. See pp. 54–58, 455–57.

——. 2005. "Utilizing Max Weber's 'Iron Cage' to Define the Past, Present, and Future of the American Political Culture." Pp. 191–208 in *The Protestant Ethic Turns 100*, edited by William H. Swatos and Lutz Kaelber. Boulder, CO: Paradigm Publishers.

——. 2008. "The Perpetual and Tight Interweaving of Past and Present in Max Weber's Sociology." Pp. 30–54 in *History Matters*, edited by David Chalcraft, Fanon John Howell, Marisol Lopez Menendez, and Hector Vera Martinez. Aldershot, UK: Ashgate Publishers.

——. Forthcoming. *Max Weber's Sociology of Civilizations.*

Keeter, Larry G. 1981. "Max Weber's Visit to North Carolina." *Journal of the History of Sociology*, 3, 2 (Spring): 108–14.

Klages, Ludwig. 1910. *Prinzipien der Charakterologie*. Leipzig: J.A. Barth.

Legge, James. 1861–1872. *The Chinese Classics*. Oxford: Oxford University Press.

Lenger, Friedrich. 1994. *Werner Sombart, 1863–1914: Eine Biographie.* Munich: Beck Verlag.

Lenski, Gerhard. 1974. *The Religious Factor*. New York: Doubleday.

Manasse, Ernst Moritz. 1947. "Max Weber on Race." *Social Research*, 14: 191–221.

Merton, Robert K. 2001 (1938). *Science, Technology and Society in Seventeenth Century England*. New York: Howard Fertig.

Mommsen, Wolfgang. 1974. "Die Vereinigten Staaten von Amerika." Pp. 72–96 in Mommsen, *Max Weber. Gesellschaft, Politik und Geschichte*. Frankfurt: Suhrkamp.

——. 2000. "Max Weber in America." *American Scholar*, 69, 3 (Summer): 103–12.

Nielsen, Donald A. 2005. "*The Protestant Ethic and the "Spirit" of Capitalism* as Grand Narrative: Max Weber's Philosophy of History." Pp. 53–76 in *The Protestant Ethic Turns 100*, edited by William H. Swatos and Lutz Kaelber. Boulder, CO: Paradigm Publishers.

Peukert, Detlev J. K. 1989. *Max Webers Diagnose der Moderne*. Göttingen: Vandenhoeck u. Ruprecht.

Rachfahl, Felix. 1978. "Anti-Critical Last Word on *The Spirit of Capitalism*." Translated by Wallace Davis. *American Journal of Sociology*, 83, 5: 1110–32.

Ringer, Fritz. 1969. *The Decline of the German Mandarins*. Cambridge: Harvard University Press.

——. 2004. *Max Weber*. Chicago: The University of Chicago Press.

Roth, Guenther. 2005. "Transatlantic Connections: A Cosmopolitan Context for Max and Mariannne Weber's New York Visit 1904." *Max Weber Studies*, 5, 1 (January): 81–112.

Salomon, Albert. 1962. *In Praise of Enlightenment*. Cleveland, OH: World Publ. Co.

Scaff, Lawrence. 2005. "Remnants of Romanticism: Max Weber in Oklahoma and Indian Territory." Pp. 77–110 in *The Protestant Ethic Turns 100*, edited by William H. Swatos and Lutz Kaelber. Boulder, CO: Paradigm Publishers.

Schluchter, Wolfgang. 1981. *The Rise of Western Rationalism*. Translated by Guenther Roth. Berkeley: The University of California Press.

Sharpe, Kevin. 1992. *The Personal Rule of Charles I*. New Haven: Yale University Press.

Tawney, R. H. "Foreword." 1958 (1930). Pp. 1–11 in *Max Weber: The Protestant Ethic and the Spirit of Capitalism*. Translated by Talcott Parsons. New York: Charles Scribner's Sons.

Tocqueville, Alexis de. 1945. *Democracy in America*, Vol. 2. New York: Vintage.

Tönnies, Ferdinand. 1957 (1887). *Community and Society*. New York: Harper Torchbooks.

Winter, Elke. 2004. *Max Weber et les relations ethniques. Du refus du biologisme racial a l'Etat multinational*. Quebec: Presses de l'Universite Laval.

ACKNOWLEDGMENTS

Pages 243, 252, 409, 410, 427: Selections from *Wirtschaft und Gesellschaft* used by permission of Mohr Siebeck.

Pages 257, 417: Selections from *Die Wirtschaftsethik der Weltreligionen* used by permission of Mohr Siebeck.

Pages 268, 272, 352, 275, 360: Selections from *The Religion of China* © 1951 by The Free Press. Copyright © renewed 1979 by The Free Press. All rights reserved.

Pages 361, 259: Selections from *The Religion of India* © 1952, 1958 by The Free Press. Copyright © renewed 1980 by The Free Press. All rights reserved.

Page 200: Selection from *Sociological Theory* reprinted by permission of the American Sociological Association and Colin Loader.

Pages 202, 400, 402, 416, 422, 424, 426, 429: Selections from *Max Weber: Readings and Commentary on Modernity* used by permission of Wiley-Blackwell Publishing Ltd.

Pages 263, 290, 300, 304, 306, 397, 349, 359, 374, 393, 399, 404, 406, 412, 417, 418, 419: Selections from *Economy and Society* used by permission of The University of California Press.

Page 370: Selection from *The Agrarian Sociology of Ancient Civilizations* used by permission of Verso.

A CHRONOLOGY OF MAX WEBER'S LIFE

April 21, 1864 Born in Erfurt, Thuringia: eldest of six children.

1866 The child becomes ill with meningitis; sister Anna dies in infancy.

1868 Brother Alfred, who will become a prominent economist and sociologist, is born.

1869 The family moves to Berlin.

1872–82 Attends the Königliche Kaiserin-Augusta-Gymnasium (elite German high school) in the Berlin suburb of Charlottenburg.

1876 Four-year-old sister Helene dies.

1877–81 School papers on ancient history and letters on Homer, Herodotus, Virgil, Cicero, Goethe, Kant, Hegel, and Schopenhauer.

1882 Attends the University of Heidelberg; joins the Allemannia dueling fraternity; studies law, economic history, philosophy, and history of late Antiquity.

1883–84 One year of military service at Strasbourg; occasional attendance at the University of Strasbourg.

1884–85 Continuation of studies, now at the University of Berlin.

1885 Officer training in Strasburg; studies in Berlin for the bar exam.

1885–86 Completion of law studies at the University of Göttingen.

1886 Passes the bar exam in Berlin; returns to parental home and remains there (except for military duty) until 1893; studies commercial law and ancient rural history.

1887–88 Military service in Strasbourg and Posen.

1889 Doctoral dissertation on the development of joint liability in medieval trading companies.

1890 Participates with mother in the first Evangelical Social Congress.

1891 Finishes his second academic dissertation (on the agrarian history of Rome), thus becoming qualified to teach at a German university (*Habilitation*).

1891–92 Study of farmworkers in East Elbia region (East and West Prussia); publication in 1892.

1893 Engagement to Marianne Schnitger in March; marriage in September; wedding trip to London; moves out of parental home; substitutes for his teacher Levin Goldschmidt at the University of Berlin; Associate Professor of Commercial and German Law.

1894 Military exercises in Posen (spring); appointed Professor of Economics, University of Freiburg; moves to Freiburg (fall); participates in the Evangelical Social Congress in Frankfurt (report on farmworkers); publishes study on the stock exchange.

1895 Second trip to England, Scotland, and Ireland (August–October); inaugural academic lecture, University of Freiburg.

1896 Participates in Evangelical Social Congress; appointed Professor of Economics at the University of Heidelberg.

1897 Declines to run for election to the Reichstag; father dies in summer; trip to Spain in fall.

1897–1903 Prolonged incapacity.

1898 Travel to Geneva; first sanatorium visit (Lake Constance); further breakdown at Christmas.

1899 Excused from teaching in the spring semester; resumes teaching in the fall but suffers another breakdown; offers his resignation to University of Heidelberg (declined); trip to Venice.

1900 Leaves Heidelberg in July; sanatorium residence until November (Urach); fall and winter in Corsica.

1901 Resides in Rome and southern Italy in spring; summer in Switzerland; fall and winter in Rome.

1902 Lives in Florence; again submits his resignation; returns in April to Heidelberg and begins to write on social science methodology questions; travels in winter to the French Riviera; reads Georg Simmel's *Philosophy of Money*.

1903 Trips to Rome, Holland, Belgium and northern Germany; resigns his position at the University of Heidelberg and becomes *Honorarprofessor*; publishes "Roscher and Knies" and begins intense work on *The Protestant Ethic and the Spirit of Capitalism*.

1904 August–December travels widely in the United States; publication of half of *PE* in November and " 'Objectivity' in Social Science and Social Policy" (1949), both in a journal Weber begins to co-edit, *Archive for Social Sciences and Social Policy*.

1905 Publication of second half of *PE* in *Archive* in spring; debates with the economist Schmoller on value-judgments; studies Russian before breakfast.

1906 Attends the Social Democracy Party Convention; travels to southern Italy in the fall; publication of " 'Churches' and 'Sects' in North America" (1985) and "Prospects for Liberal Democracy in Tsarist Russia" (1978b).

1907 Relapse of illness; travels to Italy, Holland, and western Germany; publishes a further essay on methodology questions.

1908 Trip to Provence and Florence in spring; travel to Westphalia in the fall to study the psycho-physics of work in his relatives' textile factory; publication of *The Agrarian Sociology of Ancient Civilizations* (1976); attacks in a newspaper article the practice in German universities of refusing to promote Social Democrats.

1909 Travel in southern Germany in spring; summer in the Black Forest after a relapse; attends meeting of the Association for Welfare Politics in Vienna; attacks bureaucratization together with brother Alfred; co-founds the German Sociological Association; assumes editorial leadership of the multi-volume *Outline of Social Economics*, a task that eventually leads to *Economy and Society*.

1910 Trips to Berlin, Italy, and England; Georg Lukács and Ernest Bloch begin regular visits to Weber's home; the poet Stefan George attends the *jour fixe* twice; speaks against "race biology" at the first German Sociological Association Convention.

1911 Travels to Italy in the spring and Munich and Paris in the summer; criticisms of higher education policies in Germany and fraternity practices in schools of business lead to intense newspaper controversies; begins his Economic Ethics of the World Religions (EEWR) series and continues work on *E&S*.

1912 Spring in Provence; trips to Bayreuth for the Richard Wagner Festival with Marianne and the pianist Mina Tobler, and to further regions in Bavaria in summer; defends a value-free definition of the nation at the German Sociological Association conference in Berlin; resigns from the Association.

1913 Italy in spring and fall (Ascona, Assisi, Siena, Perugia, Rome); residence for several months in the counter-culture community in Ascona; publishes an early version of *E&S*'s "Basic Concepts" (Chapter 1); continues to work on *E&S*.

1914 Travels in spring to Ascona and Zurich to defend Frieda Gross in a child custody case; after outbreak of war in August commissioned as reserve officer to establish and manage nine military hospitals around Heidelberg; participation in further debates on value-judgments.

1915 Youngest brother Karl dies on the Russian Front; returns to research on EEWR; political activity in Berlin against German annexation policy; honorably retired in fall as hospital administrator.

1916 Trip to East Prussia with sister Lili in spring to visit Karl's grave; further trips to Vienna and Budapest; summer travel to Lake Constance; first public lecture in Germany given in nineteen years; newspaper articles opposing intensified German submarine warfare against English and American ships; participates in a study group focussing on the Polish problem and the creation of a European-wide free trade zone and economic community; publishes *The Religion of China* and *The Religion of India* in the *Archive*.

1917 *Ancient Judaism* published in the *Archive*; lectures in Munich on science as a vocation; extensive advocacy in newspapers for electoral and parliamentary reform, and argues against censorship; alienates, despite adulation, younger generation at conferences in May and October at Lauenstein Castle in Thuringia; professorship (Economics) offered by the University of Vienna; reads Stefan George's poetry while vacationing in summer in western Germany; publishes essay on value-judgments.

1918 Begins teaching after a nineteen-year hiatus; two courses in Vienna offered in the university's largest lecture hall: "A Positive Critique of the Materialist View of History" and "Sociology of the State"; twenty-fifth wedding anniversary; supports a British-style constitutional monarchy for Germany; member of the founding committee of a new liberal party (the German Democratic Party); gives several election campaign speeches; encourages the Kaiser to abdicate; fails to gain a seat at the Constitutional Convention.

1919 Continues speeches on behalf of the German Democratic Party and is elected to its executive committee; lectures in Munich on "politics as a vocation"; member of the German peace delegation to Versailles charged with drafting a reply to the Allies' war guilt memorandum; in May tried to persuade General Luddendorff in Berlin to voluntarily surrender to the Allies; appointed Professor of Economics at the University of Munich; lecture courses on "General Categories in Sociology" spring/summer and "Outline of a Universal Social and Economic History" in fall/winter; moves to Munich; farewell party in Heidelberg; mother dies in October.

1920 Writes "Prefatory Remarks" to *Collected Essays on the Sociology of Religion*; revises first volume (*PE*, "Sects," 1946c, 1946e, *Religion of China*) of this three-volume project; Part I of *E&S* goes to press; "Political Science" and "Socialism" lecture courses offered in Munich; suicide of youngest sister in April; marriage crisis leads to practical separation; flu develops into pneumonia at the beginning of June; dies on June 14 in Munich.

GLOSSARY

This listing includes (a) historical terms that are often forgotten today and (b) terms that are key to Weber's analysis. When first used in Sections 1 and 2, all Glossary terms have been set in bold type. Italics here indicate a cross-reference to another entry in this Glossary.

Adventure capitalism (promoter, colonial). This type of capitalism has appeared universally. Since the dawn of history, entrepreneurs and speculators have financed wars, piracy, construction projects, shipping, plantations using forced labor, political parties, and mercenaries. These money-making enterprises are of a purely speculative nature and often involve wars and violent activities. Loans of every sort are offered. To be distinguished from *modern capitalism*.

Affinity (elective, inner) (*Wahlverwandtschaft, innere Verwandtschaft*). A notion taken from Goethe that implies an "internal" connection between two different phenomena rooted in a shared feature and/or a clear historical linkage (for example, between certain religious beliefs and a vocational ethic). The causal relationship is not strong enough to be designated "determining."

Ascetic Protestantism. This generic term refers to the Calvinist, Pietist, Methodist, Quaker, Baptist, and Mennonite churches and sects. Weber compares and contrasts the vocational ethics of these faiths to each other and to those of Lutheran Protestantism and Catholicism.

Asceticism. An extreme taming, channeling, sublimating, and organizing of the believer's spontaneous human drives and wants (the *status naturae*) by a set of values. Western asceticism grounded a "methodical-rational organization of life" in values in two "directions": ascetic Protestantism did so *in* the world ("this-worldly asceticism") and medieval Catholic monks, living sequestered in monasteries, did so *outside* the world ("other-worldly asceticism").

Authority (domination, rulership; *Herrschaft*). Why do people obey commands? To Weber, in contrast to sheer *power*, authority implies that persons attribute, for a variety of reasons, legitimacy to the commands. Hence, a voluntary element is characteristic; that is, a belief, in the end, that the authority is justified. Weber identifies three types of authority: *traditional* (patriarchalism, feudalism, patrimonialism), *charismatic*, and *rational-legal* (bureaucratic).

Autocephalous. Possessing an independent authority. In contrast to entities under the power of an external authority (heterocephalous).

Bureaucratic authority (rational-legal). Authority resides in a position in an organization, and the rights it grants to incumbents, rather than in persons or traditions. Hence, obedience to authority rests upon belief in the appropriate enactment of impersonal statutes and regulations. Attached to "the office," authority remains even though people come and go. Historically unusual, this type of authority has largely been found in the West in the past 100 years.

Caesaropapism. A secular ruler dominates the realm of religion and constitutes its highest authority. The extreme opposite of *hierocratic* rulership.

Calling (*Beruf*). See *vocational calling*.

Capitalism. Capitalism has existed in all the world's civilizations. It involves the expectation of profit and peaceful opportunities for acquisition. A calculation of earnings in money terms occurs—at the beginning (starting balance) and end of the project (concluding balance), and in respect to the utility of all potential transactions. The origins of profits and losses are ascertained.

Carriers. See *social carriers*.

Charismatic authority. See *authority*. Obedience results from a belief in and devotion to the extraordinary sanctity and heroism of an individual person who is viewed as exceptional. This type of authority opposes all existing values, customs, laws, rules, and traditions.

Clan charisma. Exceptional, even supernatural qualities are attributed not to a single person (such as a prophet), but to a group of persons. This group shares a blood bond.

Confraternization (fraternization). Association of persons across groups with firm boundaries (whether familial, tribal, ethnic, or religious). The cities of the Western Middle Ages practiced a greater confraternization than elsewhere.

Conventicles. Small group Bible and prayer gatherings ("house churches") of the faithful that aimed to counteract any weakening of belief. The Scriptures and devotional literature were studied and spiritual exercises performed.

Deification of human wants and desires. The Puritan's loyalty must be exclusively to God. For him, human wants and desires (personal vanity, sexual fulfillment, the enjoyment of love, friendship, luxury, etc.) must be tamed and remain subordinate to this noble and prior allegiance.

Disenchantment of the world (*Entzauberung*). This famous phrase refers, on the one hand, to a development within the domain of religion from ritual and magic to "other-worldly salvation religions" in which paths to salvation completely devoid of magic (*Puritanism*) are formulated (see The *Protestant Ethic*), and, on the other, to a broad historical development in the West according to which knowledge of the universe is less and less understood by reference to supernatural forces and salvation doctrines, and more and more by reference to empirical observation and the experimental method of the natural sciences (see "Science as a Vocation," 1946d).

Dispassionate (*nüchtern*). A term Weber uses repeatedly to characterize the temperate and restrained frame of mind of Puritans. This disposition implies rigorous self-control and a capacity to organize life systematically around defined goals.

Dordrecht Synod. An Assembly of the Reformed Churches of the Netherlands in Dordrecht in 1618–1619. It sought to confront Arminianism by rejecting its denial of the doctrine of predestination and reinvigorating Reformed orthodoxy.

Earning a living (making a living; orientation toward acquisition; *Erwerbsleben*). Carried by Puritanism, a middle-class activity that is necessary in profit-oriented economies; contrasted in *PE* mainly to persons who live off rents ("rentier wealth") and to the life-style of feudal nobles .

Economic ethic (work ethic). See *economic traditionalism* and *modern economic ethic*.

Economic ethics of the world religions. This is the title Weber gave to a series of studies on the world's great religions.

Economic form. An economic form refers to the way in which a company is organized and managed, the relationship of employers to workers, the type of accounting, the movement of capital, etc. Contrasted by Weber to an "economic spirit" or "economic ethic."

Economic rationalism. This term refers to the modern capitalism that developed in the sixteenth and seventeenth centuries in the West. It implies the utilization of science on behalf of a systematic organization of labor and the entire production process, and hence qualitative increases in productive capacity.

Economic traditionalism (traditional economic ethic). A frame of mind in respect to work. Work is viewed as a necessary evil and only one arena of life, no more important than the arenas of leisure, family, and friends. "Traditional needs" are implied: when fulfilled, then work ceases. This frame of mind stands in opposition to the development of modern capitalism. ("Traditionalism," in Weber's time, referred to the conduct of activities in an accustomed, habitual fashion.)

Elective affinity. See *affinity*.

Ethic of conviction (*Gesinnungsethik*). Adherence to an ethical position in an absolute manner; that is, regardless of the possible negative consequences that might result from doing so. (Luther: "Here I stand, for I can do no other.") Good intent alone is central. Opposed to the *ethic of responsibility*.

Ethic of responsibility (*Verantwortungsethik*). An account is given to oneself of the foreseeable results of an action, and responsibility for them is accepted. Conceivably, the action might be abandoned if assessment of its outcome reveals negative consequences. Opposed to the *ethic of conviction*.

Ethical action. Rooted in values and a strong "obligatory" element, Weber sees ethical action as weakened and circumscribed in the modern era to the extent that *practical, theoretical,* and *formal rationality* expand.

Ethnic group. Weber contends that this concept is of little utility to a social science that seeks to explain how social action arises and becomes patterned so that groups are formed. Many other social factors are generally more important. Weber counsels caution and circumspection. See *race*.

Feeling (feeling-based; *Gefühl*). The "strangely warmed heart" (Wesley) sought especially by Pietists and early Methodists that indicated the presence within of God and strengthened commitment and ethical responsibility toward Him. At the vital core of these denominations because tantamount to the subjective experiencing of salvation (and out of which emotions—exhilaration, joy, relief—flowed), feeling remained suspect to Calvinists, who viewed salvation in terms of a *striving to render one's life holy* (see below). In Weber's analysis, feeling provided a less firm foundation for the vocational calling than the Calvinist's striving.

Formal rationality. Central to *"modern Western rationalism"* and *bureaucratic authority*. Omnipresent in *modern capitalism, modern law,* and the modern state, this type of rationality implies decision-making "without regard to persons"; that is, by reference to sets of universally applied rules, laws, statutes, and regulations.

Frame of mind (*Gesinnung*). The temperament or disposition that Weber sees as specific to a group of people. He uses the term to refer to characteristic features (in the sense of an ideal type) of Calvinists, Catholics, Lutherans, adventure capitalists, feudal aristocrats, old commerce-oriented (patrician) families, persons in the middle class, etc. Each group has its own temper or outlook. The frame of mind in some groups may be more weighted toward values, even ethical values (the religious groups); in others it tends more toward endowing interests (adventure capitalists) or traditions (peasants) with greater meaning.

Glorification of desires. See *deification of human wants and desires*.

Heterocephalous. See *autocephalous*.

Hierocracy (hierocratic rulership). The ecclesiastical power here penetrates into a bureaucratic organization. If a developed dogma and educational system rooted in religious doctrine are typical, this type of organization cannot be altered. Its power rests on the principle that "God must be obeyed more than men." The hierocracy proves effective as a check against political power; indeed, secular rulers must be legitimated by priests. *Caesaropapism* contrasts directly.

Honoratiores (notables). With the development of the economy, only the wealthy (landowners, patrician merchants) will possess the time and resources to fulfill administrative tasks. Hence, direct democracy will likely turn into rule by notables. The bureaucratic function generally carries out tasks in a manner *technically* superior (speed, precision, knowledge of the files, etc.) to the avocational and honorific service of honoratiores.

Ideal type. Weber's major methodological tool. He creates in *PE* "ideal types" for an array of groups (Catholics, Lutherans, Calvinists, adventure capitalists, etc.). Each ideal type, by accentuating that which is *characteristic* from the point of view of *Weber's* theme, seeks to capture that which is essential to a group.

Ideas and Interests. See *world and religion*.

Individual autonomy. Weber is worried that, in a modern world in which impersonal political, economic, and legal orders dominate, and large-scale bureaucracies characterized by rigid hierarchies, specialized tasks, conformist pressures, and routine work are ubiquitous, individual autonomy and ethical responsibility will be eroded.

Interpretive understanding (*Verstehen*). This is the term Weber uses to describe his own methodology. He wishes to understand the actions of people in demarcated groups by reconstructing the milieu of values, traditions, interests, and emotions within which they live, and thereby to understand how *subjective meaning* is formulated.

Life-sphere. See *societal domains*.

Location (*Ort*). Integral to his methodology of interpretive understanding, Weber perpetually "locates" particular ideas, economies, values, interests, salvation-striving, types of authority and law, power, social honor, etc., within complex social contexts.

Middle class (*bürgerlich, das Bürgertum*). *PE* offers an analysis of the religious origins of the ethos and frame of mind of a new class that elevated steady and constant work to the center of life. Composed of both employers and workers, this middle class was the *social carrier* (see below) of a set of values oriented to economic activity and *earning a living* that distinguished it significantly from the destitute urban poor, feudal nobles, patrician old-family capitalists, and adventure capitalists. Weber seeks to offer an explanation for the origin of this set of values and to argue that they played a role in calling forth the spirit of capitalism.

Modern capitalism (middle-class industrial capitalism). Weber sees *capitalism* as universal. He is interested in the origins of *modern* capitalism as it appeared in the West in the sixteenth and seventeenth centuries. This capitalism involved the rational organization of free labor, the systematic pursuit of profit, and a *modern economic ethos* or "spirit." He concludes that a *Protestant ethic* played a role in giving rise to modern capitalism.

Modern capitalism's substantive conditions. To Weber, modern markets do not develop out of the "natural propensity" discovered by Adam Smith to "truck, barter, and exchange." Nor do they arise from the rational choices of individuals. Rather, many "substantive conditions" must have developed beforehand, such as rational modes of accounting and administration, enacted formal law "rationally interpreted and applied" by jurists, the concept of the citizen, advanced science and technology, *a modern economic ethic*, the separation of the household from the industrial company, and the absence of strict market monopolies.

Modern (rational) economic ethic. See *spirit of capitalism.*

Modern law. Characterized by formal legal equality and a rootedness in documents (such as a constitution) and judicial precedent rather than sacred traditions or charismatic persons, modern law is enacted and implemented by specialists (legislators, judges). The impersonal execution of laws, by reference to systematic and universally applied procedures, is taken as an ideal.

Modern science. Although highly technologically advanced, modern science, unlike science in Antiquity, the Middle Ages, and the seventeenth century in the West, is characterized by an incapacity to offer a justification for its own foundations. Hence, it fails to assist us to find an answer to Tolstoi's question: "How should we live?" Fearing yet another "caste of specialists" that would intrude upon the individual's autonomy, now in the name of science, Weber wishes to limit its legitimate goals to insight, clarity, and knowledge.

Modern Western rationalism. Weber's term for the modern West. Through wide-ranging comparisons to the ancient and medieval civilizations of China, India, and the West, he wishes to identify the modern West's unique features and causes behind its development. Prominent are the *formal, practical* and *theoretical types of rationality.*

Mysticism. The mystic devout seek, through meditation techniques that "silence the self," to merge into an eminent and impersonal supernatural Being. Hence, action in the world possesses no salvation meaning; rather, a "flight from the world"—through withdrawal and meditation—is required of this believer. Mainly Buddhist. Contrasts in Weber's sociology with *asceticism.*

Nation. An "entirely ambiguous" concept, according to Weber. Rejecting common language, religious creed, and "common blood" as definitive features of nations, he instead emphasizes a "sentiment of solidarity," rooted in values.

National character. Explanation of differences between groups by reference to national character was widespread in Weber's time. Because it failed to acknowledge the influence of religious, historical, economic, political, social, etc. forces, Weber thoroughly rejected this mode of explanation.

Notables. See *honoratiores.*

Objectivity. Social scientists never approach empirical reality in an "objective" manner, Weber argues; rather, they bring to it sets of questions and interests related to their *values* ("value-relevant"). Hence, every approach to "the data" is "perspectival"—all the more as every epoch defines in its own way, in accord with its predominant concerns and currents of thought, certain aspects of empirical reality as "culturally significant." And even though new fashions, themes, and concerns render heretofore occluded aspects of social reality visible, other aspects, by the same token, always remain in the shadows. See *value-freedom.*

Office charisma. An exceptional, even supernatural quality is attributed to an organization's office (bishop, cardinal). This occurs to such a degree that all office incumbents are perceived as possessing charisma.

Organization of Life, Organized Life. Weber's term *Lebensführung* implies a conscious directing, or leading, of life. Although for him the organized life is generally "internally" rooted in a set of values (even ethical values), this is not always the case (interests anchor the "practical rational" *Lebensführung*). This term stands as a contrast in Weber's writings generally to the undirected life that simply, like a natural event, flows on in time without guidance. Because Weber emphasizes in *PE* that the Puritans must organize and direct their lives in a *methodical-rational* according to their beliefs, the phrase "organization of life" appears best to capture his meaning here.

Ossification. Dominated by extreme bureaucratization, ossified—or closed and stagnant—societies are ones in which social and political hierarchies become massive and rigid. Opposite of societal dynamism. Weber argues that ossified societies will not allow conflicts to surface over interests and ideals—and these are indispensable if political leadership and a sense of ethical responsibility are to develop and be sustained. He fears that such stagnant societies *may* be on the horizon in the West.

Patrimonialism. One of Weber's "traditional" types of rulership. Rulers (monarchs) acquire hegemony over large territories and seek to administer them. They do so through the creation of a staff organized in a quasi-bureaucratic manner.

Power. In direct contrast to *authority*, power, in Weber's classic definition, implies sheer coercion, or "the likelihood that one person in a social relationship will be able, even despite resistance, to carry out his own will."

Practical rationality. The random flow of daily interests is here central, and the individual's adaptation—through means-end rational calculation—to them. Contrasts directly with substantive rationality, according to which the random flow of interests is confronted and ordered by an orientation of action to values.

Predestination (doctrine of). Prominent especially among Calvinists. God has willed a few to be saved; most people are condemned. His reasons are unknowable and no human activity can change one's "predestination status." The logical consequence of belief in this doctrine was fatalism and despair among the devout. Revisions by theologians and ministers led to *the Protestant ethic*.

Protestant ethic. The source of the *spirit of capitalism*. Sixteenth- and seventeenth-century interpretations of the Calvinist doctrine of *predestination* eventually led to a situation in which believers could experience "psychological rewards" vis-à-vis their salvation status once they oriented their activities to methodical work, economic competition, profit, and the attainment of wealth.

Providential (sanctifying). Rendering with religious (salvation) significance an activity heretofore purely utilitarian (work, wealth, and profit, for example).

Psychological motivations (*Antriebe*). Weber is concerned throughout *PE* with the motivation behind action, particularly action directed toward work, making a living, and profit as it originates from religious beliefs. The important psychological motivations for religion-oriented action derive, he argues, not from the ethical theory implied by doctrines or what is officially taught in ethical manuals, but from the motivations that arise out of a combination of belief and the regular *practice* of the religious life as transmitted by the clergy to believers through pastoral care, church discipline, and preaching (see *psychological reward*).

Psychological rewards *or* premiums (*psychologische Prämien*). Through belief and the practice of religion, "salvation premiums" are awarded to particular activities (such as the accumulation of wealth or the organization of life in accord with God's laws), thereby assisting the devout, as long as they can perform this activity, to more easily convince themselves of their membership among the saved.

Puritans. Weber's general term for the ascetic Protestant churches and sects of England and North America: the Calvinists (later Presbyterians), Methodists, Baptists, Quakers, and Mennonites. All Puritans organized their lives around work and a this-worldly, morally rigorous asceticism. Hence, Puritanism, Weber argues, provides a consistent foundation for the idea of a vocational calling found in *the Protestant ethic*. Remarkably, because oriented to salvation in the next life rather than worldly goods or interests, the intense activity of Puritans was *in* the world but not *of* the world.

Race. Weber opposes the notion that reference to innate and inheritable qualities can be helpful in sociological analysis. "Racial theories" anchored in notions of inherited instincts, he argues, are hypothetical and methodologically weak. *Social action* that appears to be oriented to race is, on closer inspection, Weber holds, actually a consequence of the juxtaposition of other (e.g., economic, political, social) forces. See *ethnic group*.

Rational. A systematic, rigorous, disciplined element to action.

Rationalization. Weber is using this term in accord with the usage of his time. It implies a systematizing of one's actions (usually to accord with religious values) in the sense of an increased rigor and methodicalness and a taming of the *status naturae*.

Rationalization of Western civilization (Rationalism). This term implies the predominance, in a civilization, of systematic work, a modern economic ethic, cities characterized by the presence of autonomous governing units, modern law, bureaucratic authority, impersonal judiciary codes and civil servants to implement them, a modern bureaucratic state, modern science, advanced technology, etc. It does not imply the "superiority" of the West.

Reformed (*reformierte*) Church. Although "by no means identical with Calvinism," Calvinism constituted to Weber the major theological force behind the broader Reform movement of ascetic Protestant churches and sects in Holland, England, and America (except for the Methodists). He tends in *PEs* chapter 4 to use "Calvinism" when referring to ideas, doctrines, and values stemming from John Calvin, and "Reformed" when referring to the several organized churches he founded. All Reformed churches stood in stark contrast to the Lutheran "state church" in Germany as well as to Catholicism.

Religious reward. See *psychological rewards*.

Routinization. The patterned action of persons in groups moves across the four types of *social action*. If action originally oriented toward values later becomes calculating and exclusively means-end rational, it has become "routinized."

Savoy Declaration (1658). A statement of faith by English Congregationalists. Advocated (unlike the Westminster Confession) the autonomy of local churches.

Sect. As opposed to a church, an exclusive, voluntary, and tightly knit group that admits new members only once specific criteria have been fulfilled. Membership implies both "good character" and a monitoring of behavior by other sect members to ensure compliance.

Social action (meaningful action). Weber's sociology seeks "to offer an interpretive understanding of social action." Unlike "reactive" or "imitative" action, social action implies a subjectively meaningful component "that takes account of the behavior of other.s" This aspect can be understood by the researcher. Weber identifies (as *ideal types*) four "types of social action": affectual, traditional, means-end rational, and value-rational. Among other major goals, *Economy and Society* seeks to chart out the social contexts that call forth meaningful action in a variety of *societal domains*.

Social carrier (*Träger*). Ideas are important causal forces of historical change, for Weber, but only if they are "carried" by demarcated and influential groupings, strata, and organizations (a Calvinist church or a middle class, for example). Weber wishes to know in *PE* what groups carried specific types of vocational ethics. A central concept in Weber's sociology.

Societal domains (orders, arenas, realms, spheres; *gesellschaftliche Ordnungen*). S *o-cial action* arises, to Weber, mainly within the law, the economy, authority, religion, status groups, and "universal organizations" (family, clan, and traditional neighborhood) domains. Each constitutes a demarcated realm characterized by definable constellations of subjective meaning. His comparative-historical analyses are organized around these spheres (and their various manifestation in different civilizational settings), and the different themes, dilemmas, and problematics typical of each, rather than "society," institutions, or the individual's "rational choices." In certain epochs, such as our own, some domains may fall into relationships of irreconcilable antagonism (e.g. the rational economy and the religious ethos of brotherhood and compassion).

Specialists People who develop only one talent or ability. This occurs, Weber emphasized following Goethe, to the detriment of other talents or abilities. In contrast to the "cultivated" person who possesses *Bildung*—a broad and deep education and a wide range of experience—that integrates and unifies the personality.

Spirit of capitalism Represented by Benjamin Franklin, the spirit of capitalism constitutes a secularized legacy of the *Protestant ethic*. It refers to a methodical orientation toward profit, competition, work "as an absolute end in itself," and a perceived duty to increase one's wealth (yet the avoidance of its enjoyment). Weber insists that its origin cannot be located in economic interests; rather, a set of religious values and the quest for certainty of salvation constitute the source of this *frame of mind:* the *Protestant ethic.* As an important causal factor, among many others, this "spirit" played a part in giving birth to *modern capitalism.*

The state. An organization that monopolizes the legitimate use of force within specified territorial boundaries. Its laws, statutes, and legal procedures must be conceptualized as possessing autonomy, even *vis-à-vis* a modern capitalist economy.

Status (status groups). Status groups appear where social action is patterned and oriented to social honor, social esteem, and a shared style of life and consumption patterns. Inequality arises not only from property ownership, Weber holds, but also from status differences.

Status naturae. The "natural status" of the human species. The spontaneous aspects of human nature are not tamed, channeled, sublimated, or organized. Puritanism, Weber argues, by systematically *organizing the lives* of believers according to a set of values, accomplished just this—indeed in an extremely rigorous manner.

Stereotypization. A custom, convention, or law may become viewed as permeated by magical forces. It becomes then "stereotyped" and, as a consequence, rigid and unchangeable.

Striving to make life holy (sanctified; *Heiligung*). Puritans organized their entire lives around a search for psychological certainty of their salvation status. Despite the doctrine of predestination, they came to believe (especially owing to Baxter's revisions) that their capacity to adhere to specific modes of conduct approved by God *testified* to their membership among the saved. Hence, through their righteous conduct, they could "strive" for salvation. Pietists and Methodists believed that certainty of salvation came also through a *feeling* (see above) of being possessed by God.

Subjective meaning. Weber seeks, throughout his sociology, to understand how persons view their own behavior and how they justify it to themselves, or lend it "meaning" (no matter how odd it may appear to the observer). He wishes in *PE* to understand, for example, why continuous hard work and a systematic search for profit and wealth constitutes a subjectively meaningful endeavor for Puritans.

Substantive rationality. A constellation of values. If regular social action is oriented to it, people are uprooted from the random flow of interests typical of everyday life. Weber fears that the dominance under *modern Western rationalism* of *formal, theoretical,* and *practical rationality* will weaken all substantive rationalities.

Surpassing (*Überbietung*). The Puritans, in organizing their lives according to God's laws, surpassed "this-worldly" (utilitarian) morality.

Testify (*Bewährung*). This central notion for Calvinists (and for all ascetic Protestants' *striving* for salvation) implies both an outward demonstration visible to others (one's conduct, demeanor, and bearing) and a psychological element: the devout understand their strength to testify to their belief through perpetual righteous conduct as emanating from God—and hence, they feel an inner confidence regarding their salvation status.

Theocracy. A society in which the influence of sincere belief and religious figures are dominant.

Theoretical rationality. The mastering of reality, which is undertaken alike by theologians in search of greater doctrinal consistency and modern-day scientists, here occurs through systematic thought and conceptual schemes. Reality is confronted cognitively rather than through values, interests, or traditions, although the confrontation for theologians, unlike for modern scientists, ultimately aims to introduce new values.

This-worldly (*innerweltlich, diesseitig*). This term implies activity "in" the world in contrast to the monks', activity "outside" the world (in the cloister). With Puritanism, Weber argues, asceticism moved out of the monastery and "into" the world. Remarkably, the intense activity of Puritans was *in* the world but not *of* the world (since its major orientation was not to this-worldly goods or interests but to salvation in the next life).

Traditional authority. See *authority*. Obedience results from an established belief in the sanctity of immemorial traditions and the legitimacy of those exercising rulership under them (for example, clan patriarchs). This type of authority has been far more widespread throughout history than either *charismatic* or *bureaucratic authority*. Unlike the latter, under traditional authority a personal bond between ruler and ruled exists, which implies that an ethical appeal can be made directly to the ruler in the event of abuse.

Traditional economic ethic. See *economic traditionalism*.

Types of rationality. See *formal rationality, practical rationality, substantive rationality,* and *theoretical rationality*.

Utilitarian adaptation to the world. The orientation of life to the pragmatic morality of the everyday world rather than a *surpassing* (see above) of this morality on the basis of a rigorous orientation to God's laws and a striving for salvation.

Value-freedom, freedom from values (*Wertfreiheit*). Weber insisted that all social science research must be "value-free." Once investigators have selected their theme of inquiry (see *objectivity*), personal values, preferences, and prejudices must not be allowed to interfere with the collection of empirical data and its evaluation. An intermixing of the researcher's values with those of the actors being studied must be avoided. This axiom also implied a strict division between that which *exists* (the question for scientific analysis) and that which *should be* (the realm of personal values and preferences). Social scientists must attempt, also in the classroom, to uphold this ideal.

Value-judgment. An insertion of one's personal values (whether rooted in political, religious, or philosophical positions) into the lecture hall or the collection and evaluation of empirical data. See *value-freedom* and *objectivity.*

Value-rational action (motives). One of Weber's "four types of social action," this term implies that a person's action is oriented to values to a significant extent, indeed even to the degree that values become obligatory, or "binding," upon action. It contrasts, in particular, to "means-end rational action" in Weber's sociology.

Virtuoso believers. These persons possess "religious qualifications" and are focused strongly on religious questions generally and salvation in particular (in contrast to lay believers).

Vocational calling (*Beruf*). Denotes a task given by God and the incorporation of a demarcated realm of work into the Protestant believer's life in the sixteenth and seventeenth centuries in the West. Despite a vast comparative-historical search, Weber found this definition of a "calling" only in Protestantism.

Westminster Confession [Synod]. A confession of faith by Calvinists that, in thirty-three chapters, reaffirmed predestination and the central role of scripture. Approved by the Long Parliament in 1648, but denied official status after the restoration of the monarchy in 1660. Adopted later by several American and English ascetic Protestant churches.

World and religion. Weber's shorthand phrase to indicate his mode of causal analyses. It does not focus narrowly on "one side of the equation"; rather, it seeks to undertake *multi*causal investigations. It assumes that motivations for action range across a broad spectrum. Synonymous with *ideas and interests.*

World mastery. The posture of Puritan believers. They seek to "master" worldly obstacles, randomness, and injustice in order to create an orderly earthly kingdom in accord with their God's commandments.

NAME INDEX

SUBJECT INDEX

Items in bold type are defined in the Glossary.